# Data-Centric Engineering: From Sensors to Decisions

by

ant

The landscape of engineering is undergoing a profound transformation, driven by the unprecedented explosion of data and the ever-increasing capabilities of machine learning. From the intricate design of aerospace components to the colossal scale of civil infrastructure, and the complex dynamics of manufacturing processes, data is no longer just a byproduct; it is the lifeblood of innovation, efficiency, and safety. This book is born from the recognition that traditional engineering disciplines, while foundational, now require a sophisticated understanding of data science and machine learning to unlock their full potential. We aim to bridge the gap between established engineering principles and the cutting-edge tools that are revolutionizing how we design, operate, and maintain systems.

Our primary audience comprises undergraduate and graduate engineering students seeking to equip themselves with the essential skills for the modern engineering workforce, as well as practicing data engineers and machine learning engineers looking to specialize in applying their expertise to real-world engineering challenges. We understand that you possess a strong foundation in engineering and a grasp of basic data manipulation, but you are eager to delve deeper into building practical, production-ready systems that can automate complex decision-making, detect subtle anomalies, and extract invaluable insights from the rich datasets generated by engineering applications.

This book adopts a practical, hands-on, and example-driven approach. We believe that the most effective way to learn is by doing. Therefore, we have meticulously crafted detailed explanations, step-by-step tutorials, and compelling case studies drawn directly from authentic engineering scenarios. Whether we are analyzing vibration data from bridges for early structural degradation detection, processing sensor readings from industrial machinery for predictive maintenance, or deriving features from time-series automotive data to understand driving behavior, our examples are designed to be both illustrative and immediately applicable. Our goal is to empower you with the knowledge and practical skills to tackle complex data-driven projects, moving beyond theoretical concepts to tangible, deployable engineering solutions that drive tangible improvements in performance, safety, and efficiency.

The modern engineering world is awash in data. Sensors embedded in bridges, aircraft, vehicles, and manufacturing plants generate continuous streams of information, capturing the intricate behaviors and conditions of complex systems. This data-rich environment presents an unparalleled opportunity to move beyond traditional, reactive engineering approaches towards predictive, proactive, and highly optimized systems. The evolution from manual inspection and scheduled maintenance to intelligent systems capable of anticipating failures, optimizing performance in real-time, and enhancing design through data-driven insights is not a distant future; it is happening now. This book serves as your guide to navigating this exciting frontier, focusing on the practical application of machine learning to solve real-world engineering problems.

We will begin by establishing a clear understanding of the evolving landscape of engineering data and the critical need for robust decision-making pipelines. These pipelines are the automated workflows that ingest, process, analyze, and act upon data, forming the backbone of intelligent engineering systems. You will learn how to define these pipelines, understand their essential components from data ingestion and preprocessing to model deployment and continuous monitoring, and appreciate the fundamental principles that ensure their reliability, scalability, and maintainability in operational environments. The journey from raw, often noisy, engineering data to actionable insights is complex, and this book is dedicated to demystifying this process. We will emphasize the crucial interplay between domain expertise and data science, highlighting how to bridge the gap and leverage data not merely as a source of information, but as a powerful tool for problem-solving and system improvement.

The role of machine learning in this transformation cannot be overstated. ML algorithms are becoming indispensable for tackling sophisticated engineering tasks such as predictive maintenance, anomaly detection, design optimization, and sophisticated control systems. This book will provide a comprehensive overview of how ML techniques are synergistically integrated with engineering principles to revolutionize traditional practices and unlock new levels of efficiency and innovation. Throughout this text, you will find a consistent emphasis on a practical, hands-on, and example-driven approach. We will walk through detailed explanations, provide step-by-step tutorials, and present case studies drawn from authentic engineering applications. Our aim is to equip you with the tangible skills and conceptual framework necessary to build production-ready machine learning pipelines that address the unique challenges and opportunities within the engineering domain. By the end of this book, you will be empowered to design, implement, and deploy data-driven solutions that enhance system performance, ensure safety, and drive forward the future of engineering.

**Table of Contents**

**Part I: Foundations of Data-Centric Engineering**

# Chapter 1: Introduction to Engineering Data and Decision Pipelines

The world of engineering is undergoing a profound transformation, driven by an unprecedented surge in data. What was once a domain primarily reliant on physical experiments, manual calculations, and expert intuition is rapidly evolving into a data-centric discipline. This seismic shift is not confined to a single engineering branch; it is a pervasive phenomenon impacting civil, mechanical, aerospace, electrical, chemical, and virtually every other engineering field. The very fabric of how engineers design, operate, maintain, and innovate is being rewoven with threads of data. This burgeoning field of engineering data is unlocking possibilities that were previously unimaginable, paving the way for enhanced efficiency, predictive capabilities, and sophisticated automation across a vast spectrum of applications.

At the heart of this revolution lies the exponential growth in data generation. The ubiquitous deployment of sensors across all engineering domains has become a primary catalyst. From the strain gauges monitoring the health of a suspension bridge to the myriad sensors within an aircraft's propulsion system, or the delicate instruments measuring atmospheric conditions for satellite trajectory calculations, these digital observers are constantly streaming information. Modern machinery in manufacturing plants is equipped with sensors monitoring temperature, vibration, pressure, and current, creating a rich tapestry of operational data. In civil engineering, smart cities are being built with sensors embedded in infrastructure, monitoring traffic flow, energy consumption, and environmental quality. The automotive industry generates vast amounts of data from vehicle sensors, enabling sophisticated diagnostics, adaptive cruise control, and autonomous driving capabilities. Electrical engineering benefits from data generated by power grids, communication networks, and integrated circuits, facilitating optimization and fault detection. Even fields like chemical engineering are seeing increased data generation from advanced process monitoring and control systems, optimizing reactions and yields. This proliferation of sensors, coupled with the decreasing cost and increasing capability of data acquisition hardware, means that more data is being collected than ever before.

This explosion in data is inextricably linked to advancements in computational power. The processing capabilities of modern computing systems, from powerful servers in data centers to microcontrollers embedded in devices, have dramatically increased. This allows for the storage, processing, and analysis of the massive datasets generated by these sensors in ways that were not feasible just a decade or two ago. Cloud computing platforms offer scalable and on-demand computational resources, further democratizing the ability to handle large-scale data analysis. The development of specialized hardware, such as Graphics Processing Units (GPUs), which are highly effective at parallel processing, has also accelerated the training of complex machine learning models, a key component of many modern data-driven engineering solutions. This synergy between data generation and processing power creates a virtuous cycle: more data allows for the development of more sophisticated analytical tools and models, which in turn can drive the need for even more data to refine and validate them.

This confluence of abundant sensor data and powerful computation has created a fertile ground for new opportunities. One of the most significant is

**optimization**. In manufacturing, for instance, data from production lines can be analyzed to identify bottlenecks, inefficiencies, and areas where material or energy usage can be reduced. This might involve optimizing machine parameters in real-time based on sensor feedback, or reconfiguring assembly line layouts based on historical performance data. In aerospace, flight data can be analyzed to optimize fuel consumption and flight paths, leading to significant cost savings and reduced environmental impact. Civil engineers can use sensor data from bridges and buildings to optimize maintenance schedules, ensuring that resources are allocated to the most critical areas before minor issues escalate into major problems. Electrical engineers can optimize the performance of power grids by analyzing load data and predicting demand, ensuring stable and efficient energy distribution.

Beyond optimization, the ability to analyze historical and real-time data opens up immense possibilities for
**prediction**. Predictive maintenance is a prime example. Instead of performing maintenance on a fixed schedule or waiting for a component to fail, engineers can use sensor data to predict when a piece of equipment is likely to fail. Vibration patterns in a motor, temperature fluctuations, or subtle changes in current draw can all be indicators of impending failure. By analyzing these patterns, engineers can schedule maintenance proactively, avoiding costly downtime, preventing catastrophic failures, and extending the lifespan of valuable assets. This is critical in industries where downtime can cost millions of dollars per hour, such as oil and gas, heavy manufacturing, and aviation. In civil engineering, sensors on structures can predict potential failures due to fatigue, corrosion, or seismic activity, allowing for timely interventions and preventing disaster. In the automotive sector, predictive analytics can forecast component failures, enabling proactive repairs and improving vehicle safety.

**Automation** is another transformative outcome. As engineers gain a deeper understanding of system behavior through data analysis, complex decision-making processes can be automated. This can range from simple automated adjustments to operational parameters to highly sophisticated autonomous systems. For example, in chemical plants, process control systems can use sensor data and predictive models to automatically adjust reaction conditions to maintain optimal output and safety. In robotics, machine learning models trained on sensor data can enable robots to perform complex tasks with greater precision and adaptability. Autonomous vehicles rely heavily on data from a multitude of sensors and sophisticated algorithms to navigate and make real-time driving decisions. Smart grids can use AI to automatically balance supply and demand, reroute power in case of outages, and optimize energy distribution.

However, the data encountered in engineering contexts often possesses unique characteristics that distinguish it from data found in other domains, such as social media or retail. Understanding these characteristics is crucial for aspiring data engineers and students aiming to build effective decision-making pipelines. One of the most pervasive features is the
**temporal nature** of engineering data. Much of the data collected comes from sensors that record measurements over time, creating time-series datasets. This could be the continuous stream of temperature readings from a jet engine, the periodic vibration measurements from a bridge, or the sequential sensor readings from a robot arm performing a task. The time stamps associated with these data points are not mere metadata; they are fundamental to understanding the behavior of the system. Temporal dependencies are critical – what happens at one point in time is often influenced by what happened previously, and can influence what happens in the future. Analyzing these time-series requires specialized techniques that account for sequential dependencies, trends, seasonality, and autocorrelation.

Beyond its temporal dimension, engineering data frequently exhibits **spatial characteristics**. This is particularly evident in civil engineering, where data might represent the physical layout of a structure, geological formations, or environmental conditions across a geographical area. In aerospace, data related to fluid dynamics or structural integrity often has inherent spatial relationships. Even in seemingly non-spatial domains, there can be spatial correlations. For example, in a manufacturing plant, sensors placed on adjacent machines might exhibit correlated behavior due to shared environmental factors like temperature or vibration. Understanding these spatial relationships is vital for tasks such as identifying the location of a fault, interpolating measurements across a surface, or modeling phenomena that vary across space.

Another defining characteristic is **heterogeneity**. Engineering systems are often complex and comprised of many different types of components, each with its own sensors and data outputs. This leads to data that is heterogeneous in nature, meaning it comes from various sources and in different formats. A single industrial machine might have pressure sensors (analog output), temperature sensors (digital), vibration sensors (high-frequency time series), and cameras for visual inspection (image data). Each of these data types has different properties, scales, and requires different methods of processing and analysis. Furthermore, even data from the same type of sensor can be heterogeneous due to differences in calibration, manufacturing variations, or the specific operating conditions of each individual component. Integrating and making sense of these diverse data streams is a significant challenge that requires careful data engineering.

Closely related to heterogeneity is **multimodality**. This refers to data coming from multiple different types of sources or modalities, which can be thought of as different "senses" through which we perceive the system. For example, in a manufacturing process, we might have numerical sensor readings (temperature, pressure), visual data (images from cameras for quality control), acoustic data (sound from machinery for anomaly detection), and even textual data (maintenance logs, operator notes). Each modality captures a different aspect of the system's state. The real power often lies in fusing information from these multiple modalities to gain a more complete and robust understanding. A crack in a manufactured part might be detectable visually (image data), but its presence might also manifest as a change in acoustic signature or a shift in vibration patterns. Combining these different data streams can lead to more accurate and reliable detection and diagnosis than relying on a single modality alone.

The practical reality of engineering data is that it is rarely perfect. **Noise** is an inherent part of any measurement process. Sensors are subject to electrical interference, environmental fluctuations, and manufacturing imperfections that can introduce random errors into the readings. This noise can obscure the underlying signals and make it difficult to extract meaningful information. In vibration analysis, for instance, ambient noise from other machinery or wind can contaminate the signal from the structure being monitored. In electrical systems, electromagnetic interference can corrupt sensor readings. Engineers must develop strategies to filter out or mitigate the effects of this noise to reveal the true behavior of the system.

**Uncertainty** is also a fundamental aspect. Measurements are never perfectly precise; there is always a degree of uncertainty associated with any reading. This uncertainty can stem from the sensor's accuracy limitations, the resolution of the measurement, or inherent stochasticity in the physical process being measured. Understanding and quantifying this uncertainty is critical, especially in safety-critical applications where the consequences of a wrong decision can be severe. For example, in assessing the structural integrity of a bridge, the uncertainty associated with the strain gauge readings must be factored into the decision-making process regarding load limits or repair needs.

Furthermore,
**missing values** are an almost unavoidable aspect of real-world data collection. Sensors may fail intermittently, data transmission can be disrupted, or data logging systems may encounter errors. This can result in gaps in the data, where a value is expected but is not present. These missing values can disrupt analysis and machine learning algorithms, which often require complete datasets. Developing strategies to handle missing data, such as imputation (filling in the gaps) or designing algorithms that can cope with missing information, is a crucial part of

data engineering in practice. The context of the missing data is also important; a missing reading from a critical safety sensor might require a different approach than a missing reading from a non-essential environmental sensor.

The sheer **scale and volume** of engineering data can also present significant challenges. In applications like monitoring large-scale infrastructure (e.g., a national power grid, a network of oil pipelines, or vast agricultural fields), the number of sensors can be enormous, and the data is generated at high frequencies. This can lead to datasets that are measured in terabytes or even petabytes. Storing, processing, and analyzing such massive datasets requires scalable infrastructure and efficient algorithms. Traditional data processing techniques that might work well for smaller datasets can quickly become inadequate. Distributed computing frameworks, efficient data storage solutions (like data lakes), and optimized processing pipelines are essential for handling this scale. Even in smaller-scale applications, the continuous generation of high-frequency data can lead to substantial volumes over time, requiring careful data management strategies.

Finally, engineering data often contains **domain-specific anomalies and outliers** that are not simply random noise but carry significant meaning. These can be indicators of critical events, equipment malfunctions, or deviations from normal operating conditions. For instance, a sudden spike in temperature in a nuclear reactor, an unusual vibration pattern in a wind turbine blade, or a sudden drop in pressure in a fluid system are not random occurrences but signals that something is wrong. Detecting and correctly interpreting these domain-specific anomalies is often the primary goal of data analysis in engineering. These anomalies might represent incipient failures, safety hazards, or opportunities for process improvement. Understanding the physics and engineering principles behind these events is crucial for distinguishing meaningful anomalies from mere noise and for building effective detection systems.

This evolving landscape of engineering data presents both immense opportunities and significant challenges. The potential for optimizing designs, predicting failures, automating complex tasks, and ultimately improving the safety, efficiency, and sustainability of engineering systems is vast. However, realizing this potential requires a new set of skills and a disciplined approach to data management, analysis, and the development of robust decision-making pipelines. Aspiring engineers and data scientists must equip themselves with the knowledge to navigate the complexities of engineering data, from understanding its unique characteristics to developing the tools and methodologies needed to harness its power effectively. This book aims to provide that foundation, guiding readers through the essential concepts and practical techniques required to excel in this exciting and rapidly expanding field.

A robust decision-making pipeline in the engineering domain transcends mere data processing and model execution. It represents a meticulously orchestrated sequence of operations designed to transform raw, often noisy, engineering data into actionable insights that drive critical decisions. At its core, such a pipeline is a testament to the engineering principle of reliability, ensuring that the outputs are consistently accurate, dependable, and trustworthy, even under varying operational conditions and within dynamic environments. It is a framework that acknowledges the inherent complexities and uncertainties of engineering systems and data, building in mechanisms to address them proactively.

The foundational components of a robust decision-making pipeline can be broadly categorized into several interconnected stages. The journey begins with

**Data Ingestion**, the critical first step where data is collected from its myriad sources. In engineering, these sources are incredibly diverse: sensor networks embedded in infrastructure, diagnostic systems within machinery, simulations generating synthetic data, historical operational logs, and external data streams like weather patterns or market prices. The robustness of this stage hinges on the ability to reliably connect to these sources, handle different data formats (e.g., time-series, images, logs, structured tables), and establish a consistent flow of information into the pipeline. This involves implementing resilient data connectors that can manage network interruptions, authentication protocols, and data integrity checks to ensure that what enters the pipeline is a faithful representation of what was generated. For example, a pipeline designed to monitor the structural health of a bridge might ingest data from strain gauges, accelerometers, anemometers, and even visual inspection cameras. The ingestion mechanism must be capable of handling the high volume and varying frequencies of data from these disparate sensors without loss or corruption.

Following ingestion, the data must undergo
**Data Preprocessing and Feature Engineering**. Raw data, as discussed, is rarely in a state suitable for direct analysis. This stage is where the raw data is cleaned, transformed, and enriched to extract meaningful features that will drive the decision-making process. Cleaning involves handling missing values (imputation, removal, or flagging), correcting erroneous readings (e.g., outliers that are clearly sensor malfunctions), and dealing with inconsistencies in data formats or units. Transformation might include scaling numerical features to a common range, encoding categorical variables, or applying mathematical operations to derive new metrics. Feature engineering is arguably the most crucial and often the most creative part of this stage. It involves leveraging domain knowledge to create new variables that better represent the underlying phenomena and improve model performance. For instance, in predictive maintenance for an industrial pump, raw vibration data might be transformed into frequency domain features (e.g., power spectral density components) or statistical features (e.g., root mean square, kurtosis) that are more indicative of specific failure modes. A robust preprocessing stage will incorporate automated checks and balances to ensure that these

operations are applied consistently and that the resulting features are interpretable and relevant. Version control for preprocessing logic is also essential, allowing for reproducibility and auditing.

Once the data is prepared, it moves to the **Model Development and Training** phase. This is where algorithms are selected, trained, and validated to perform the desired task, whether it be classification, regression, anomaly detection, or forecasting. The choice of model will depend on the problem at hand, the nature of the data, and the desired interpretability. However, for a pipeline to be robust, model development cannot be a one-off event. It requires a systematic approach to experimentation, hyperparameter tuning, and rigorous validation. Cross-validation techniques are essential to assess how well a model generalizes to unseen data. For engineering applications, interpretability is often paramount. Models that provide insights into *why* a certain decision is made are far more valuable than black-box solutions, especially when safety or compliance is a concern. Techniques like SHAP (SHapley Additive exPlanations) or LIME (Local Interpretable Model-agnostic Explanations) can be integrated into the development process to explain model predictions. Furthermore, robust pipelines will have versioning for models and their associated training data, ensuring that the exact configuration that produced a specific outcome can be re-created.

The trained model is then integrated into the **Inference and Decision Engine** component. This is where the processed data is fed into the deployed model to generate predictions or classifications in real-time or in batches. The decision engine then translates these model outputs into actionable decisions. This might involve setting thresholds, triggering alerts, initiating automated control actions, or recommending specific interventions to human operators. The robustness here lies in the efficiency and reliability of the inference process. Latency requirements are often critical in engineering; a delayed prediction can render it useless or even dangerous. The decision engine must be designed to handle high throughput and provide timely results.

Furthermore, it needs to incorporate logic for handling edge cases or situations where the model might be uncertain. For instance, if a predictive maintenance model has low confidence in its prediction, the decision engine might escalate the alert to a human expert rather than automatically scheduling maintenance, thereby adding an extra layer of safety.

Crucially, a robust decision-making pipeline does not end with a decision. **Monitoring and Feedback** form an indispensable part of the system. This stage involves continuously tracking the performance of the deployed model and the pipeline itself. Key metrics to monitor include model accuracy, precision, recall, F1-score, and any domain-specific performance indicators. Equally important is monitoring for data drift (changes in the statistical properties of incoming data that can degrade model performance) and concept drift (changes in the underlying relationship between features and the target variable). The pipeline should be equipped with automated alerting systems that notify stakeholders when performance degrades below acceptable thresholds or when anomalies are detected in the data or model behavior. This feedback loop is vital for triggering retraining, model updates, or even a complete re-evaluation of the pipeline's design. For example, if a model predicting the efficiency of a solar farm starts to underperform, the monitoring system should detect this, identify the potential cause (e.g., significant changes in weather patterns not accounted for), and trigger a retraining process with updated data.

Finally,
**Scalability and Maintainability** are overarching design principles that must be embedded throughout the pipeline. Engineering systems can grow in complexity and data volume over time. A robust pipeline must be architected to scale horizontally and vertically to accommodate increasing workloads without sacrificing performance. This often involves leveraging cloud-native technologies, microservices architectures, and distributed computing frameworks. Maintainability

refers to the ease with which the pipeline can be updated, debugged, and managed over its lifecycle. This includes aspects like modular design, clear documentation, standardized coding practices, and robust testing strategies. A pipeline that is difficult to maintain will inevitably become a liability, leading to increased operational costs and a higher risk of errors. This implies that the choice of technologies, the overall architecture, and the operational processes must all prioritize long-term manageability.

The interconnectedness of these components is key. A failure in data ingestion can propagate through the entire pipeline, leading to incorrect decisions. A poorly engineered feature can render even the most sophisticated model ineffective. Similarly, a robust monitoring system can catch subtle issues that might otherwise go unnoticed until a critical failure occurs. Therefore, building a robust decision-making pipeline requires a holistic approach, where each component is designed with the overall system's reliability, performance, and longevity in mind. It's a continuous cycle of design, implementation, operation, and refinement, driven by data and guided by engineering principles.

Consider, for instance, the deployment of a pipeline for autonomous navigation in a fleet of industrial robots within a large manufacturing facility. The

**Data Ingestion** would involve real-time streams from LiDAR sensors, cameras, odometry systems, and proximity sensors on each robot, as well as potentially static maps of the facility. Robustness here means ensuring that even if a Wi-Fi connection is temporarily lost, data is buffered and transmitted once connectivity is restored, and that sensor readings are time-synchronized accurately across all robots.

Moving to

**Data Preprocessing and Feature Engineering**, the raw point cloud data from LiDAR might be processed to extract features like obstacle boundaries, traversable path estimates, and the relative positions of other robots. Camera data could be processed for object recognition (e.g., identifying human operators, specific equipment) and lane detection. Odometry data might be filtered to correct for wheel slippage. The engineering here would involve creating features that are invariant to the robot's own motion and robust to varying lighting conditions or the presence of reflective surfaces. For example, a feature indicating the distance to the nearest static obstacle would be critical for collision avoidance, and its calculation must be reliable.

In
**Model Development and Training**, deep learning models might be trained for semantic segmentation of camera feeds to identify safe zones, or reinforcement learning algorithms could be employed to learn optimal navigation policies that balance speed with safety. Model robustness would be assessed by testing on diverse simulated environments and real-world scenarios that include unexpected events, such as a sudden obstacle appearing in the robot's path or another robot deviating from its planned route. Ensuring the models are well-generalized and can handle novel situations is paramount.

The
**Inference and Decision Engine** would then take these processed features and model outputs to generate steering commands, speed adjustments, and path planning decisions. For example, if the perception model identifies a human entering the robot's designated path, the decision engine must immediately trigger a braking maneuver. This requires low-latency inference and a highly reliable decision logic that prioritizes safety above all else. The decision engine might also incorporate a "safety override" mechanism, a hard-coded rule that intervenes if the AI-driven decision falls outside of predefined safe operating parameters.

The

**Monitoring and Feedback** stage is where the performance of the navigation system is continuously evaluated. Metrics like the number of near-misses, the time taken to complete tasks, and the rate of successful obstacle avoidance would be tracked. Anomaly detection algorithms could identify unusual patterns in sensor readings or unexpected robot behaviors. If the robots start exhibiting a pattern of repeatedly getting stuck in certain areas, this would trigger an alert, leading to an investigation and potential retraining of the navigation models or refinement of the facility map. Feedback from human supervisors observing the robots' operation would also be crucial for identifying subtle issues that automated metrics might miss.

Finally,
**Scalability and Maintainability** are critical. As the number of robots in the fleet increases, or as the facility layout changes, the pipeline must adapt. This means that the software architecture should support adding new robots seamlessly, and the data infrastructure should be able to handle the aggregated data from hundreds or thousands of robots. Maintainability would involve having well-documented code, standardized APIs between components, and automated deployment processes, making it easier for engineers to update models, fix bugs, or reconfigure the system as needed.

This intricate interplay of components, principles, and practical considerations underscores that a robust decision-making pipeline in engineering is not just about deploying a machine learning model. It is about building an end-to-end system that is resilient to the inherent complexities of the physical world, reliable in its operation, and adaptable to evolving conditions, ultimately enabling confident and effective decision-making in mission-critical engineering applications. The subsequent chapters will delve deeper into the specific techniques and technologies that enable the construction of such pipelines, providing the foundational knowledge for building sophisticated, data-driven engineering solutions. The emphasis throughout will remain on the practical aspects, ensuring that readers are equipped not just with theoretical understanding but with the practical skills to implement these systems in real-world engineering contexts. This includes understanding the trade-offs involved in different architectural choices, the importance of rigorous testing at every stage, and the ongoing effort required to maintain and evolve these pipelines as systems and data change.

The notion of "robustness" in this context can be further elaborated by considering the various dimensions of system resilience. A pipeline must be robust against
**data quality issues**. This means it should not collapse or produce wildly inaccurate results when encountering slightly imperfect data. Mechanisms for data validation, anomaly detection at the input stage, and gracefully handling missing or erroneous data points are essential. For example, a civil engineering pipeline analyzing bridge stress might incorporate checks to flag strain gauge readings that exceed physically plausible limits or that exhibit sudden, impossible jumps, preventing these erroneous values from unduly influencing structural integrity assessments.

Beyond data quality, robustness also pertains to
**operational resilience**. Engineering systems often operate in environments with unreliable power, intermittent network connectivity, or physical disruptions. A robust pipeline needs to be designed with fault tolerance in mind. This might involve deploying redundant components, implementing graceful degradation strategies (where the system continues to operate with reduced functionality during failures), and ensuring that data is persisted reliably to avoid loss during outages. For a chemical plant process control pipeline, this could mean having fallback control logic that ensures safe operation even if the primary AI model or its data feeds become unavailable.

**Model robustness** is another critical aspect. Models trained on historical data might struggle when faced with novel conditions or subtle shifts in the operating environment. Techniques such as adversarial training, where models are exposed to intentionally crafted "difficult" data samples during training, can improve their resilience. Ensemble methods, which combine predictions from multiple different models, can also enhance robustness by averaging out individual model weaknesses. In an aerospace context, a model predicting engine performance would ideally be robust enough to handle variations in fuel quality, atmospheric pressure, and component wear without significant performance degradation.

Furthermore, a robust pipeline must be robust against **security threats**. Engineering systems, especially those connected to networks, can be targets for cyberattacks. This necessitates implementing strong authentication and authorization mechanisms, encrypting sensitive data, and employing intrusion detection systems. A compromised decision-making pipeline could have catastrophic consequences, leading to incorrect commands, data manipulation, or denial of service. Imagine a power grid management system where decisions about load balancing are compromised; the potential for widespread blackouts is significant.

The **explainability and interpretability** of the pipeline's decisions also contribute to its robustness. When a system makes a critical recommendation, engineers need to understand the reasoning behind it. This is not just for debugging; it's for building trust and ensuring accountability. If a model recommends a costly repair, an engineer needs to be able to verify that the recommendation is based on sound data and logic. Pipelines that provide clear explanations for their outputs, using techniques like feature importance or rule extraction, are inherently more robust because they allow for human oversight and validation. This is particularly important in safety-critical applications where human judgment remains an indispensable component of the decision-making process.

The lifecycle management of a robust pipeline also demands attention to **versioning and reproducibility**. Every component of the pipeline – from the data preprocessing scripts to the trained models and the inference code – should be version-controlled. This allows for easy rollback to previous stable versions if issues arise and ensures that experiments can be precisely reproduced. Reproducibility is a cornerstone of scientific and engineering rigor, and it is essential for debugging, auditing, and continuous improvement. Imagine needing to reconstruct the exact conditions under which a particular anomaly was detected months ago; without proper versioning, this would be an impossible task.

In practice, building these robust pipelines involves a deep understanding of both data science and software engineering principles. It requires a shift from a purely model-centric view to a system-centric perspective, where the entire workflow is considered as a cohesive entity. The choice of architecture, the selection of tools and frameworks, and the operational practices all play a significant role in achieving robustness. For example, adopting a microservices architecture can improve modularity and fault isolation, making it easier to update or replace individual components without affecting the entire system. Containerization technologies like Docker can further enhance reproducibility and simplify deployment across different environments.

Moreover, a robust pipeline is not a static artifact; it is a living system that requires continuous attention. The operational environment changes, data patterns evolve, and new insights are gained. Therefore, continuous integration and continuous deployment (CI/CD) practices are highly relevant. CI/CD pipelines can automate the process of testing, building, and deploying updates to the decision-making pipeline, ensuring that improvements are integrated efficiently and reliably. This iterative approach is fundamental to maintaining the long-term effectiveness and robustness of the system.

Ultimately, the goal of defining and building robust decision-making pipelines in engineering is to create systems that can be trusted. Trust in these systems allows engineers to delegate complex analytical tasks, automate critical processes, and make more informed, data-driven decisions. This trust is earned through a rigorous and disciplined approach to design, implementation, and ongoing management, ensuring that the pipelines are not only functional but also reliable, secure, and maintainable in the demanding environments of engineering practice. The following chapters will explore specific methodologies and tools that empower engineers to build such trustworthy pipelines, transforming raw data into confident engineering decisions. This detailed exploration of what constitutes a robust decision-making pipeline sets the stage for understanding the practical implementation challenges and solutions discussed in the subsequent sections of this book.

The transformation of raw engineering data into actionable intelligence is not a mere technical process; it is a fundamental shift in perspective—a transition from observing phenomena to understanding and influencing them. This journey is the very essence of data engineering in practice, bridging the often-perceived chasm between the abstract world of numbers and the concrete realm of engineering decisions. It requires a deliberate framework, a structured approach that guides us from the initial collection of sensor readings, logs, and measurements to the confident execution of a strategic action. At its heart, this transformation is about extracting meaning, discerning patterns, and translating them into directives that can improve efficiency, enhance safety, reduce costs, and foster innovation.

The conceptual framework for this data-to-insight pipeline is built upon a series of interconnected stages, each designed to refine and enrich the

information. It begins with the recognition that data, in its raw form, is often a collection of symptoms rather than diagnoses. A vibration sensor on a turbine might report fluctuating amplitude and frequency, but what does this
*mean* for the health of the turbine? This is where the critical role of domain expertise comes into play. Engineers, with their deep understanding of the physical principles governing a system, its expected behaviors, and its potential failure modes, are indispensable in interpreting this raw data. They provide the context, the "why" behind the numbers, allowing us to formulate hypotheses about the underlying causes. This expertise guides the selection of relevant data sources, helps in identifying noise and artifacts, and is crucial for feature engineering – the art of creating new variables that capture the essential characteristics of the system's state. Without this specialized knowledge, data can remain a jumbled collection of facts, devoid of the insights needed for effective decision-making.

Consider, for example, a civil engineering project involving the monitoring of a large concrete dam. Raw data might include temperature readings from embedded sensors, water pressure at various depths, and strain gauge measurements on the dam's structure. Individually, these might appear as simple time-series datasets. However, a dam engineer understands that the relationship between these variables is complex and dynamic. They know that thermal expansion and contraction of the concrete will cause stress, that hydrostatic pressure will increase with reservoir levels, and that these factors can interact. This domain knowledge informs the pipeline design: it dictates which sensors are most critical, the frequency at which data should be collected, and how anomalies in one sensor reading might be explained or exacerbated by readings from another. Feature engineering in this context might involve calculating the rate of temperature change, the stress induced by a specific water pressure at a given temperature, or the deviation of strain readings from expected thermal expansion models. These engineered features provide a much richer representation of the dam's state than the raw sensor outputs alone, making it far more likely that potential issues, such as developing cracks or excessive seepage, can be detected early.

This reliance on domain expertise extends beyond initial data processing and into the realm of model development and interpretation. While machine learning algorithms can uncover complex, non-linear relationships that might elude human analysis, their output must still be grounded in physical reality and engineering principles. An algorithm might identify a correlation between two variables, but it is the engineer who can determine if this correlation represents a genuine physical phenomenon or is merely a spurious artifact of noisy data or a limited training set. This interplay is vital for building trust in the automated decision-making process. When a pipeline flags a potential issue, the accompanying explanation, powered by domain-informed feature importance or interpretable model architectures, allows engineers to validate the finding and decide on the appropriate course of action with confidence. It's this human-in-the-loop validation, guided by deep understanding, that transforms a probabilistic prediction into a reliable decision.

The process of transforming data into actionable insights is therefore an iterative one, deeply interwoven with the engineering lifecycle. It's not a one-time setup but a continuous cycle of data collection, analysis, interpretation, decision-making, and feedback. Each decision made based on the pipeline's output provides new data points, either by confirming the accuracy of the prediction or by revealing discrepancies that require further investigation and refinement of the pipeline itself. This continuous learning loop is what allows engineering systems to adapt to changing conditions, to optimize performance over time, and to proactively address potential problems before they escalate.

The initial hurdle in this journey is often the sheer volume and heterogeneity of data. In modern engineering, data streams pour in from countless sources: IoT sensors embedded in industrial machinery, GPS trackers on logistics fleets, performance logs from complex software systems, environmental monitoring stations, and even crowdsourced data from field technicians. These datasets come in various formats – structured tables, unstructured text logs, time-series measurements, images, and video feeds. The first critical step is thus establishing robust **data ingestion** mechanisms. This isn't merely about collecting data; it's about doing so reliably, efficiently, and with an awareness of data quality. For instance, a predictive maintenance pipeline for an aircraft engine needs to ingest data from hundreds of sensors sampling at high frequencies. Robust ingestion means handling potential network interruptions, ensuring data synchronization across sensors, and flagging any readings that fall outside expected ranges due to sensor malfunction, rather than blindly processing them as valid. This initial cleaning and validation are foundational; garbage in, garbage out is a stark reality in data engineering.

Following ingestion, the data must be **preprocessed and feature-engineered**. Raw data is seldom directly usable. It requires cleaning (handling missing values, correcting outliers), transformation (scaling, normalization, encoding categorical variables), and crucially, feature engineering. This is where domain expertise shines. For example, in analyzing the performance of a wind turbine, raw wind speed and direction data might be less informative than derived features like the effective wind power available at the turbine rotor (considering wind shear and turbulence), or the consistency of wind direction over a short period. These engineered features capture nuances of the operational environment that directly impact energy generation and mechanical stress. Similarly, for a traffic management system, raw sensor counts of vehicles might be enhanced by features representing traffic density, average speed, or the rate of change of these metrics. The goal is to distill the essence of the data into a format that highlights meaningful patterns relevant to the decision at hand. This stage is often the most time-consuming and requires iterative refinement based on model performance and engineering intuition.

With well-prepared data, the next step involves **model development and selection**. This is where statistical and machine learning techniques are applied to build predictive or analytical models. The choice of model depends heavily on the specific engineering problem: regression for predicting component lifespan, classification for identifying fault types, clustering for grouping similar operational states, or anomaly detection for spotting deviations from normal behavior. However, the emphasis in a robust pipeline is not solely on achieving high accuracy scores in a lab environment. It's about selecting models that are not only predictive but also interpretable, especially in safety-critical applications. An engineer needs to understand *why* a model predicts a failure, not just *that* it predicts a failure. Techniques like SHAP (SHapley Additive explanations) or LIME (Local Interpretable Model-agnostic Explanations) are invaluable here, providing insights into which features contributed most to a particular prediction. Model robustness itself is also a key consideration; models must perform reliably under varying conditions and be resistant to adversarial inputs or data drift.

Once a model is trained and validated, it moves into the **inference and decision engine**. This component is responsible for applying the trained model to new, incoming data to generate predictions in real-time or in batches. More importantly, it acts as the decision-making hub, translating these predictions into concrete actions. This might involve setting thresholds for alerts, automatically adjusting control parameters in an industrial process, recommending maintenance schedules, or even triggering safety protocols. The "engine" part signifies that this isn't just about outputting a number; it's about embedding business logic and engineering rules around the model's predictions. For instance, a prediction of a critical component failure might trigger an immediate shutdown command *only if* certain safety conditions are met, such as confirmed absence of personnel in the vicinity. This layer of logic ensures that automated decisions align with operational policies and safety regulations.

The journey doesn't end with a decision; it loops back through **monitoring and feedback**. This is a crucial, often underestimated, phase in ensuring the long-term effectiveness and reliability of the data-to-insight pipeline. Continuous monitoring of both the data streams and the model's performance is essential. Data drift – changes in the statistical properties of incoming data that can invalidate a model – and concept drift – changes in the underlying relationships between variables – are common challenges in dynamic engineering environments. Automated systems must detect these shifts and trigger alerts for retraining or model updates. Furthermore, user feedback from engineers interacting with the system is invaluable. Did the alert lead to a correct diagnosis? Was the recommended action effective? This feedback loop is what enables the pipeline to evolve and adapt, ensuring that it remains relevant and continues to provide accurate, actionable insights over its entire lifecycle.

Finally, overarching principles of **scalability and maintainability** must be integrated from the outset. Engineering systems and the data they generate can grow exponentially. A pipeline that works for a single machine might collapse under the load of an entire factory or a city's infrastructure. Therefore, the architecture must be designed to scale efficiently, often leveraging cloud computing and distributed systems. Maintainability ensures that the pipeline can be easily updated, debugged, and managed by engineering teams over time. This involves well-documented code, modular design, automated testing, and clear operational procedures. A complex, brittle pipeline, even if initially accurate, can become a significant burden, hindering innovation and increasing operational risk.

In essence, the process of bridging the gap from data to actionable insights is an engineering discipline in itself. It demands a blend of technical prowess in data science and software engineering, combined with the deep contextual understanding that only domain experts can provide. The goal is to build systems that are not just analytical tools but intelligent partners, guiding engineers toward better decisions, more efficient operations, and safer systems. This transforms data from a passive record of events into an active driver of progress, empowering engineers to tackle increasingly complex challenges with confidence and precision. It is about empowering engineers to ask not just "what happened?" but "why did it happen?", "what will happen next?", and most importantly, "what should we do about it?". This shift in inquiry is the ultimate value proposition of a well-engineered data pipeline.

The successful application of this framework hinges on cultivating a data-centric mindset across engineering disciplines. It requires a cultural shift where data is viewed not as a byproduct, but as a primary asset. Engineers must be encouraged to think about how their systems generate data, how this data can be collected and utilized, and how insights derived from it can feedback into design and operational improvements. This collaborative approach, where data engineers work hand-in-hand with domain experts, is crucial. A data engineer might be adept at building efficient data pipelines and training sophisticated models, but without the input of a mechanical engineer on the specific failure modes of a pump, or an electrical engineer on the nuances of power grid fluctuations, the resulting insights may be superficial or even misleading.

The "actionable" aspect of actionable insights is paramount. An insight is only truly valuable if it leads to a tangible improvement or a decisive action. A prediction of imminent equipment failure is only actionable if it can be translated into a maintenance order, a spare parts request, or a temporary operational adjustment. A model identifying an anomaly in structural stress is only useful if engineers can interpret the severity of the anomaly and determine if structural reinforcement or immediate inspection is required. This often involves defining clear decision rules and workflows that integrate the pipeline's output directly into existing operational processes. For example, in a manufacturing setting, if a quality control pipeline detects a recurring defect pattern, the system should automatically alert the relevant production line supervisor, providing them with the specific data and analysis that led to the alert. This ensures that the insight is not lost in an email inbox or a forgotten report, but is acted upon promptly.

Furthermore, the concept of "actionable" also implies accessibility. The insights generated by the pipeline must be presented in a manner that is easily understood by the intended audience. A highly complex statistical output might be meaningless to a plant operator, whereas a simple visual dashboard showing key performance indicators and highlighting areas of concern can be immediately grasped. Therefore, the output layer of the pipeline – the visualization and reporting tools – is as critical as the data processing and modeling stages. Interactive dashboards, custom reports, and even natural language generation can be employed to convey complex information effectively. For instance, a fleet management system might use a dashboard to show real-time vehicle locations, estimated arrival times, and alerts for any vehicles experiencing potential mechanical issues, with drill-down capabilities for each vehicle to access more detailed diagnostic data.

The journey from data to actionable insight is also intrinsically linked to the concept of continuous improvement. Engineering systems are rarely static. They are subject to wear and tear, environmental changes, evolving operational demands, and the introduction of new technologies. A data pipeline that provides actionable insights today might become outdated tomorrow if it does not adapt. This necessitates a proactive approach to monitoring and retraining models, as well as a willingness to re-evaluate the entire pipeline architecture as needs evolve. This can involve incorporating new data sources, refining feature engineering techniques based on new understanding, or adopting more advanced modeling approaches. For example, as a fleet of autonomous vehicles accumulates more driving miles, the data generated can be used to retrain and improve the vehicle's navigation algorithms, leading to safer and more efficient operation. This cyclical process of data collection, insight generation, action, and feedback is the engine of continuous improvement in data-driven engineering.

Ultimately, the aim of bridging the gap from data to actionable insights is to empower engineers with a level of understanding and predictive capability that was previously unattainable. It allows them to move from reactive problem-solving to proactive optimization and risk mitigation. By leveraging the power of data engineering, we can unlock new levels of efficiency, enhance the reliability and safety of critical infrastructure, and drive innovation across all sectors of engineering. This fundamental transformation of raw data into a strategic asset is what defines the modern data-driven engineering landscape. It requires a thoughtful integration of technology, domain expertise, and a clear focus on the ultimate goal: making better, more informed decisions that shape the future of engineering.

The integration of machine learning (ML) into the fabric of modern engineering represents a paradigm shift, moving beyond empirical rules and static models to dynamic, adaptive systems capable of learning from data. This symbiotic relationship allows engineers to tackle problems of unprecedented complexity and scale, unlocking efficiencies and insights that were once the realm of science fiction. At its core, ML provides a powerful toolkit for extracting nuanced patterns and making probabilistic predictions from vast, intricate datasets, thereby augmenting human intuition and analytical capabilities. This subsection delves into the multifaceted roles ML plays in contemporary engineering, illustrating how its application is not merely an enhancement but a fundamental transformation of how we design, operate, and maintain complex systems.

One of the most impactful applications of ML in engineering is **predictive maintenance**. Traditionally, maintenance schedules were based on fixed intervals (time-based) or reactive repairs after a failure occurred (reactive maintenance). Both approaches are often suboptimal. Time-based maintenance can lead to premature component replacement, incurring unnecessary costs and downtime, or insufficient maintenance if components fail before their scheduled service. Reactive maintenance, by definition, results in unexpected downtime, potential cascading failures, and higher repair costs. Predictive maintenance, powered by ML, offers a proactive alternative. By analyzing sensor data from machinery—such as vibration patterns, temperature fluctuations, acoustic emissions, oil analysis, and electrical signals—ML models can learn the signatures of normal operation and, more importantly, the subtle precursors to failure. Algorithms like Support Vector Machines (SVMs), Random Forests, and Recurrent Neural Networks (RNNs) are adept at identifying these anomalies. For instance, a slight, consistent increase in vibration frequency combined with a minor temperature rise in a rotating bearing might be imperceptible to a human observer but can be flagged by an ML model as a strong indicator of impending wear or lubrication failure. The model can then predict the Remaining Useful Life (RUL) of the component, allowing maintenance to be scheduled precisely when needed, minimizing downtime and preventing catastrophic failures. This not only saves costs but also significantly enhances the reliability and safety of critical assets, from aircraft engines and industrial turbines to manufacturing robots and public transportation systems. The ability to anticipate failures before they occur transforms maintenance from a costly necessity into a strategic advantage, ensuring operational continuity and extending the lifespan of valuable equipment.

Closely related to predictive maintenance is

**anomaly detection**, a broader ML application crucial across many engineering disciplines. Anomaly detection involves identifying data points, events, or patterns that deviate significantly from expected or normal behavior. In civil engineering, for example, sensors embedded in bridges or dams can detect unusual strain, displacement, or seismic activity that might indicate structural compromise. ML models trained on historical data of normal structural responses can swiftly flag deviations, alerting engineers to potential issues long before they become critical. Similarly, in cybersecurity for industrial control systems (ICS), anomaly detection can identify unusual network traffic patterns that might signal a cyber-attack, protecting vital infrastructure from disruption. In the realm of material science, ML can be used to detect anomalies in manufacturing processes that could lead to defects in materials, ensuring consistent quality and performance. Even in software engineering, anomaly detection can monitor application logs to identify unusual error rates or performance degradations that point to bugs or operational issues. The power of ML in anomaly detection lies in its ability to identify subtle, multi-variate deviations that might be missed by simple threshold-based systems or human inspection, especially in systems with a vast number of monitoring points.

**Design optimization** is another area where ML is making significant inroads. Traditionally, engineering design involved extensive simulations, prototyping, and iterative refinement, which can be time-consuming and resource-intensive. ML, particularly through techniques like reinforcement learning and Bayesian optimization, can accelerate and enhance this process. Reinforcement learning agents can learn to navigate complex design spaces, iteratively adjusting parameters to achieve optimal performance based on defined objectives, such as maximizing structural integrity, minimizing energy consumption, or optimizing aerodynamic efficiency. For instance, in aerospace engineering, ML can be used to design more efficient aircraft wings by exploring a vast parameter space of airfoil shapes and structural layouts, learning which combinations yield the best lift-to-drag ratios under various flight conditions. In automotive engineering, ML can optimize vehicle designs for fuel efficiency and crash safety simultaneously. Bayesian optimization, on the other hand, is particularly effective when evaluating design performance is computationally expensive (e.g., complex finite element analysis simulations). It intelligently selects the next set of design parameters to evaluate, minimizing the number of simulations required to find an optimal solution. This drastically reduces the time and cost associated with the design cycle, enabling engineers to explore more innovative and high-performing designs.

ML is also revolutionizing
**control systems**. Traditional control systems often rely on well-defined mathematical models and PID (Proportional-Integral-Derivative) controllers, which work well for systems with predictable dynamics. However, many real-world engineering systems are highly complex, non-linear, and subject to unpredictable environmental changes or component degradation. ML-based control, particularly reinforcement learning, allows systems to learn optimal control strategies directly from interaction with the environment. This is invaluable for autonomous systems like self-driving cars, where complex decision-making is required in dynamic and uncertain scenarios. For example, a reinforcement learning agent can learn to navigate traffic, make lane changes, and react to unexpected events more effectively than a rule-based system. In industrial automation, ML can enable adaptive control of manufacturing processes, adjusting parameters in real-time to maintain product quality despite variations in raw materials or ambient conditions. This leads to more robust, efficient, and responsive control, pushing the boundaries of what automated systems can achieve.

Furthermore, ML is proving instrumental in
**diagnostics and prognostics** beyond simple maintenance predictions. In fields like medical engineering, ML algorithms analyze medical images (X-rays, MRIs, CT scans) to detect subtle signs of disease that might be

missed by the human eye, aiding in early diagnosis. In the energy sector, ML can analyze grid performance data to predict load demand, identify potential network instabilities, and optimize power generation and distribution for maximum efficiency and reliability. For materials engineers, ML models can predict the long-term performance and degradation of materials under various environmental stresses, informing the selection of appropriate materials for specific applications and estimating their service life. This predictive capability extends to complex systems like bridges, pipelines, and buildings, where ML can forecast their structural health and inform interventions needed to ensure public safety.

The success of these ML applications hinges on several critical factors, including the availability of high-quality data, the development of robust feature engineering techniques, and the careful selection and validation of appropriate ML models. As discussed in the previous context, domain expertise remains paramount. An ML model is only as good as the data it is trained on and the features it utilizes. Engineers, with their deep understanding of the physical principles, operational constraints, and failure modes of their systems, are indispensable in guiding the data collection process, identifying relevant features, and interpreting the outputs of ML models. For instance, when building a predictive maintenance model for a pump, a mechanical engineer can provide crucial insights into which operating parameters (e.g., flow rate, pressure, temperature, vibration) are most indicative of specific failure mechanisms (e.g., impeller wear, seal leakage, bearing failure). This domain knowledge informs the feature engineering process, ensuring that the ML model receives inputs that are physically meaningful and directly relevant to the problem.

The interpretability of ML models is another crucial aspect, especially in safety-critical engineering applications. While complex "black box" models like deep neural networks can achieve high predictive accuracy,

their opaque nature can be a barrier to adoption if engineers cannot understand
*why* a particular prediction or decision is being made. This is where explainable AI (XAI) techniques come into play. Methods such as SHAP (SHapley Additive exPlanations) and LIME (Local Interpretable Model-agnostic Explanations) allow engineers to understand the contribution of each input feature to a model's prediction. For example, if an ML model predicts an imminent failure in a turbogenerator, XAI can highlight that the prediction is primarily driven by specific patterns in vibration data from a particular bearing and a slight increase in exhaust gas temperature. This level of insight allows engineers to validate the prediction, build confidence in the model, and take targeted corrective actions, rather than blindly following a recommendation.

The implementation of ML in engineering also necessitates new skill sets and interdisciplinary collaboration. Data engineers, ML engineers, and domain experts must work in close partnership. Data engineers are responsible for building and maintaining the robust data pipelines that feed ML models, ensuring data quality, and managing data infrastructure. ML engineers focus on selecting, training, tuning, and deploying ML models, often collaborating closely with domain experts to define the problem, engineer features, and validate results. Domain experts provide the crucial contextual knowledge that grounds the ML development process in physical reality and engineering principles. This collaborative ecosystem is essential for translating the theoretical potential of ML into practical, reliable engineering solutions.

The evolution of ML in engineering is also driving advancements in the tools and platforms available. Cloud computing platforms offer scalable infrastructure for data storage, processing, and model training, enabling engineers to tackle larger and more complex problems. Specialized ML libraries and frameworks (e.g., TensorFlow, PyTorch, scikit-learn) provide powerful algorithms and functionalities, abstracting away much of the low-level complexity. Furthermore, MLOps (Machine Learning Operations) practices are emerging to streamline the deployment, monitoring, and management of ML models in production environments, ensuring that ML-powered engineering systems remain reliable and effective over time. The development of automated machine learning (AutoML) tools is also democratizing access to ML, allowing engineers with less specialized ML expertise to build and deploy models for specific tasks.

The impact of ML on engineering is not confined to incremental improvements; it is enabling entirely new ways of thinking and operating. It fosters a more proactive, data-driven approach to problem-solving, shifting the focus from reacting to failures to anticipating and preventing them. It allows for the design and operation of systems that are more resilient, efficient, and adaptive. By uncovering hidden patterns and making sophisticated predictions, ML empowers engineers to push the boundaries of innovation, creating solutions that are not only functional but also optimized for performance, sustainability, and safety. The journey from raw engineering data to intelligent, automated decisions is increasingly being guided by the sophisticated capabilities of machine learning, ushering in an era of unprecedented engineering advancement. The continuous feedback loops between data, ML models, and engineering actions create a virtuous cycle of improvement, ensuring that engineering systems become smarter and more effective over their lifecycles.

This book is designed to be your comprehensive guide to the world of engineering data and decision pipelines. We've structured the content to take you on a clear and progressive learning journey, starting from the fundamental building blocks and gradually advancing to the sophisticated construction and deployment of robust pipelines. Our core philosophy centers on a hands-on, project-based approach. We believe that true understanding and mastery come not just from absorbing theoretical concepts, but from actively applying them. Therefore, throughout the book, you will encounter numerous practical examples, code notebooks, and case studies that mirror real-world engineering challenges.

Our learning approach is carefully curated to ensure you build a solid foundation before moving on to more complex topics. The initial chapters will delve into the essential concepts of engineering data—its types, characteristics, and the inherent challenges in its acquisition and preparation. We will explore the anatomy of a decision pipeline, breaking down each component and its role in transforming raw data into actionable insights. This foundational understanding is critical, as it underpins everything that follows. You'll learn about data ingestion, cleaning, transformation, feature engineering, and the various stages of model development and integration.

As you progress, we will introduce you to the tools and technologies that power modern data pipelines. This includes exploring popular programming languages like Python, along with essential libraries and frameworks that facilitate data manipulation, analysis, and machine learning. We will demystify concepts such as data warehousing, data lakes, and the cloud-based infrastructure that often supports these systems. The emphasis will always be on practical application, demonstrating how these tools are used in conjunction with engineering data to solve specific problems.

A significant portion of this book is dedicated to the practical implementation of decision pipelines. We will guide you through the process of designing, building, and testing these pipelines, with a strong focus on modularity, scalability, and reliability. You will learn how to select appropriate algorithms, tune model parameters, and integrate them seamlessly into a larger workflow. The goal is to equip you with the skills to not only understand existing pipelines but also to confidently design and build your own.

To further solidify your learning and bridge the gap between theory and practice, we have incorporated a capstone project: a structural health monitoring (SHM) system. This project will serve as a practical application of all the concepts and techniques you will have learned throughout the book. You will have the opportunity to work with real or simulated SHM data, build a data pipeline to process it, develop and integrate a machine learning model for anomaly detection or performance prediction, and ultimately deploy a system that can continuously monitor the integrity of a structure. This project is not just an exercise; it's a tangible demonstration of your acquired expertise.

The code notebooks accompanying this book are an integral part of your learning experience. These notebooks provide executable code examples that you can run, modify, and experiment with. They are designed to illustrate the concepts discussed in each section in a clear and interactive manner. We encourage you to actively engage with these notebooks, run the code, change parameters, and observe the outcomes. This active participation is key to developing a deep, intuitive understanding of the material. Think of them as your digital laboratory, where you can safely explore and experiment with data pipeline concepts.

We have carefully structured the progression of these notebooks to align with the book's narrative. They begin with fundamental data manipulation tasks and gradually build up to more complex pipeline construction and model deployment scenarios. For instance, early notebooks might focus on data cleaning and exploratory data analysis for a simple sensor dataset, while later ones will involve orchestrating multiple processing steps, training advanced machine learning models, and setting up monitoring mechanisms. Each notebook is accompanied by explanations and comments to guide you through the code and its purpose.

The culminating structural health monitoring project will be particularly intensive, involving multiple interconnected notebooks. These will guide you through the entire lifecycle of developing and deploying an SHM pipeline. You'll start by setting up the data ingestion process for sensor readings, followed by data preprocessing and feature extraction. Then, you'll move on to model selection and training, experimenting with different machine learning algorithms suitable for time-series analysis and anomaly detection. The final stages will involve deploying the trained model as part of a functional pipeline, complete with monitoring and alerting capabilities. This comprehensive project provides a holistic view of what it takes to build and manage a real-world data-driven engineering system.

Beyond the code notebooks, the book is filled with practical examples drawn from various engineering domains. These examples are designed to showcase the versatility and power of data pipelines in solving diverse engineering challenges. Whether it's optimizing manufacturing processes, predicting equipment failures in a power plant, or analyzing traffic flow in a smart city, these case studies illustrate how data pipelines can drive efficiency, improve reliability, and enhance decision-making. We aim to demonstrate that the principles you learn are not confined to a single discipline but are broadly applicable across the engineering landscape.

We also emphasize the importance of understanding the context and domain knowledge when building data pipelines. While the tools and techniques are important, they are most effective when guided by a deep understanding of the engineering problem at hand. Our examples and discussions will consistently highlight how domain expertise informs data collection, feature engineering, model selection, and interpretation of results. This perspective is crucial for developing pipelines that are not only technically sound but also practically relevant and impactful.

To ensure a smooth learning curve, we have adopted a layered approach. We introduce concepts progressively, building upon previously acquired knowledge. Each chapter is designed to be largely self-contained, but also to seamlessly connect with the chapters that precede and follow it. This structure allows you to grasp individual concepts thoroughly before seeing how they fit into the larger picture. We recommend following the chapters in order to maximize your learning and avoid any gaps in understanding.

Throughout the book, we will encourage critical thinking and problem-solving. We will present challenges and prompt you to consider different approaches and solutions. The goal is not just to teach you how to use specific tools or algorithms, but to develop your ability to think analytically and creatively about engineering data and the pipelines that process it. You will learn to ask the right questions, identify potential pitfalls, and design robust, scalable, and maintainable solutions.

In essence, this book is more than just a technical manual; it's a guided expedition into the exciting intersection of engineering and data science. We are confident that by engaging with the material, working through the code, and tackling the capstone project, you will emerge with a profound understanding of engineering data pipelines and the confidence to apply your newfound skills to solve complex, real-world engineering problems. This journey will equip you to leverage the power of data to drive innovation and make more informed, intelligent decisions in your engineering endeavors. We are excited to have you join us on this transformative learning experience.

## Chapter 2: Understanding the Nature of Engineering Data

Engineering data, in its myriad forms, is rarely static or isolated. Instead, it is deeply interwoven with the fabric of time and space. This inherent temporal and spatial dimensionality is not merely an incidental characteristic; it is a fundamental property that profoundly influences how we collect, store, process, and analyze this data, and crucially, how we build effective decision pipelines. Ignoring these dimensions can lead to flawed insights, inaccurate predictions, and ultimately, suboptimal engineering decisions.

Consider, for instance, the vast streams of data generated by sensors embedded within physical systems. These sensors, whether monitoring the vibration of a wind turbine blade, the strain on a bridge's support structure, the temperature within a chemical reactor, or the flow rate in a pipeline, are invariably recording measurements over time. This results in time-series data, a ubiquitous form of engineering data. Each data point is not just a number; it is a snapshot of a system's state at a specific moment. The sequence of these snapshots, the temporal dependencies between them, is where much of the valuable information resides. A sudden spike in vibration might be an anomaly, but its significance is amplified if it follows a period of increasing amplitude, or if it occurs during a specific operational phase. Similarly, a gradual increase in temperature might indicate an impending failure, but understanding the rate of increase and its historical context is critical for timely intervention.

The temporal nature of engineering data means that the order of observations matters. Unlike independent, cross-sectional data, where the arrangement of data points is arbitrary, time-series data carries an intrinsic order. This order can reveal trends, seasonality, cyclical patterns, and sudden shifts, all of which are vital for understanding system behavior, predicting future states, and diagnosing problems. For example, in structural health monitoring, detecting fatigue in a material might involve observing a subtle but consistent change in its response to applied loads over many cycles. This change is not apparent in any single measurement but emerges from the accumulation of temporal information. Similarly, predicting the remaining useful life of a piece of equipment often relies on extrapolating degradation patterns observed over extended periods.

The analysis of time-series data necessitates specialized techniques. Traditional statistical methods that assume independence between observations can be misleading. Instead, we employ methods that explicitly model temporal autocorrelation – the correlation of a variable with itself at different points in time. Techniques such as moving averages, exponential smoothing, ARIMA (AutoRegressive Integrated Moving Average) models, and various forms of spectral analysis are designed to capture these temporal dependencies. In the realm of machine learning, recurrent neural networks (RNNs), Long Short-Term Memory (LSTM) networks, and Gated Recurrent Units (GRUs) are specifically architected to process sequential data, maintaining an internal state that reflects the history of observations. When building decision pipelines for applications involving time-series data, the choice of data structures, storage mechanisms, and processing algorithms must account for this sequential nature. Efficiently querying and aggregating data over time, handling irregular sampling rates, and managing potentially vast volumes of historical data are significant engineering challenges.

Beyond the temporal dimension, engineering data frequently exhibits spatial characteristics. This arises from the physical distribution and arrangement of components, sensors, or environments. Consider a network of sensors deployed across a bridge, each measuring strain at a different location. The readings from sensors that are physically close to each other are likely to be correlated. A localized stress concentration might affect nearby sensors, while a more distributed load might influence sensors across a wider area. This spatial correlation, or autocorrelation, is another critical aspect of engineering data.

Spatial data is prevalent in many engineering disciplines. Geographic Information Systems (GIS) are built around spatial data, mapping features and phenomena across the Earth's surface. In civil engineering, analyzing the structural integrity of a building involves understanding the spatial arrangement of beams, columns, and load-bearing elements. In environmental engineering, monitoring pollution levels or water quality across a river basin requires understanding the spatial distribution of sources and sinks. In manufacturing, optimizing the layout of a factory floor or analyzing defects on a product's surface involves spatial considerations.

The spatial nature of data implies that observations made at nearby locations are more likely to be similar than observations made at distant locations. This principle, often referred to as Tobler's First Law of Geography, is fundamental to spatial analysis. When dealing with spatially correlated data, we employ techniques that leverage these correlations. Spatial statistics, geostatistics, and spatial econometrics provide frameworks for analyzing such data. Interpolation techniques, like Kriging, are used to estimate values at unobserved locations based on the values at nearby known locations, explicitly modeling the spatial covariance.

In the context of decision pipelines, spatial data introduces unique challenges. Storing and querying spatial data efficiently often requires specialized databases, such as PostGIS, that support spatial indexing and query operations. Visualizing spatial data is crucial for understanding patterns and identifying areas of interest, leading to the use of tools like QGIS, ArcGIS, or custom mapping libraries. When building predictive models, incorporating spatial features – such as distance to a known source of pollution, proximity to a fault line, or the relative position within a network – can significantly improve performance. Furthermore, spatial models may need to account for phenomena that propagate or interact across space, such as the spread of a contaminant or the propagation of vibrations through a structure.

Often, engineering data possesses both temporal and spatial dimensions simultaneously. A network of weather stations, for example, collects temperature readings over time at various geographical locations. A fleet of autonomous vehicles generating sensor data involves readings from multiple sensors (spatial within the vehicle) collected over time. Monitoring a vast oil and gas pipeline involves pressure and flow measurements from numerous points along its length, recorded continuously. This spatio-temporal data is inherently complex and requires sophisticated analytical approaches.

Analyzing spatio-temporal data allows us to understand how phenomena evolve and interact across both time and space. For instance, tracking the movement of a weather front involves understanding its trajectory (spatial) and its progression over time (temporal). Predicting the impact of an earthquake requires modeling how seismic waves propagate through the Earth's crust (spatial) and how their intensity changes as they travel over time (temporal). In an industrial setting, understanding the spread of heat in a large manufacturing process involves considering how temperature changes at different points on the machinery (spatial) and how these changes evolve over the duration of the process (temporal).

The challenges in handling spatio-temporal data are compounded. Not only must we account for temporal dependencies, but we must also model spatial dependencies, and often, the interplay between them. This can lead to complex statistical models and machine learning architectures. Techniques such as spatio-temporal autocorrelation analysis, graph neural networks (GNNs) applied to sensor networks, and specialized deep learning models designed for spatio-temporal forecasting are employed. Decision pipelines designed for such data must be capable of ingesting, processing, and analyzing data that is indexed by both time and location, often requiring distributed computing frameworks and efficient data management strategies.

The implications for engineering decision pipelines are profound. When dealing with time-series data, a pipeline designed for static data will fail to capture critical temporal patterns. Similarly, a pipeline that ignores spatial correlations might miss localized anomalies or misinterpret regional trends. For spatio-temporal data, the challenge is even greater, demanding architectures that can handle multidimensional dependencies.

Consider a system for predicting equipment failure in a large factory. If the factory has numerous identical machines, and the failure of one machine tends to precede the failure of others in close proximity due to shared environmental factors or cascading effects, then spatial correlations are at play. If, furthermore, failures tend to occur after specific operational sequences or over a period of gradual degradation, temporal dependencies are also present. A robust decision pipeline for this scenario must not only process the sensor readings from each machine over time but also consider the spatial relationships between machines and the temporal evolution of system-wide behavior. The data might include timestamps, machine IDs, sensor readings (vibration, temperature, current), and the spatial coordinates of each machine on the factory floor.

The data ingestion component of the pipeline needs to handle time-stamped, potentially high-frequency data streams from multiple sources. The data cleaning and preprocessing stages might involve time-based filtering, anomaly detection within individual time series, and spatial smoothing to reduce noise. Feature engineering could involve creating temporal features like rolling averages, time since last maintenance, or rate of change, as well as spatial features like distance to the nearest failing machine or average sensor reading in the local neighborhood. Model selection would then need to consider algorithms capable of learning from spatio-temporal patterns, such as spatio-temporal graph convolutional networks or complex recurrent models. Finally, the output of the pipeline – a prediction of equipment failure – needs to be actionable, perhaps by alerting maintenance teams about specific machines or predicting potential factory-wide disruptions.

The practical challenges in implementing pipelines for temporal and spatial data are significant. Data volume can be immense, especially for high-frequency sensors or large spatial grids, requiring scalable storage and processing solutions like data lakes and distributed computing frameworks (e.g., Spark). Data quality issues, such as sensor drift, missing readings, or inaccurate location data, are common and require robust handling strategies. Synchronization of data from different sources, especially when dealing with distributed sensor networks, can be difficult. Furthermore, the complexity of the models required for accurate spatio-temporal analysis can strain computational resources and require specialized expertise.

In summary, recognizing and accounting for the temporal and spatial characteristics of engineering data is not an academic exercise; it is a practical necessity for building effective and reliable decision pipelines. Whether it's understanding the evolution of a physical process over time, analyzing the geographical distribution of environmental impacts, or modeling complex phenomena that unfold across both dimensions, these characteristics dictate the choice of tools, techniques, and architectural designs. Ignoring them leads to blind spots, inaccurate models, and ultimately, flawed engineering intelligence. A deep understanding of temporal and spatial dependencies empowers engineers to extract richer insights, make more accurate predictions, and build more resilient and intelligent systems. This understanding forms a crucial pillar in our journey to master engineering data and decision pipelines.

The preceding discussion has illuminated the critical importance of temporal and spatial dimensions in engineering data. However, the nature of data in engineering applications extends far beyond mere time-stamped or geographically indexed measurements. A fundamental characteristic, and often a significant hurdle, in harnessing engineering data lies in its inherent heterogeneity and multimodality. Engineering systems are rarely monolithic, nor do they typically rely on a single type of observation to characterize their state or performance. Instead, they are complex assemblages of diverse components, each contributing its unique informational signature, often through distinct sensing modalities.

Data heterogeneity refers to the variations in the characteristics of data collected from different sources or even from the same source under different conditions. This heterogeneity can manifest in several ways, profoundly impacting data integration and analysis. One common form is the diversity of sensor types. A single manufacturing plant, for instance, might employ thermocouples for temperature measurement, piezoelectric sensors for vibration analysis, pressure transducers for fluid dynamics, and optical sensors for dimensional checks. Each of these sensor types produces data with specific properties, ranges, resolutions, and sensitivities. A thermocouple might output a voltage proportional to temperature, requiring calibration and conversion, while a vibration sensor might produce an acceleration signal, which, when integrated, yields velocity and displacement. Differences in measurement units (e.g.,

Celsius versus Fahrenheit, Pascals versus psi, millimeters versus inches) are a straightforward, yet crucial, aspect of heterogeneity that must be addressed through rigorous unit conversion and standardization.

Beyond sensor types and units, data granularity also contributes to heterogeneity. Data can be collected at vastly different frequencies. A high-frequency vibration sensor might capture thousands of data points per second, providing a detailed picture of transient mechanical events. In contrast, a temperature sensor monitoring ambient conditions might sample only once every few minutes or hours, focusing on slower, more gradual changes. This disparity in sampling rates means that combining data from such sources requires careful consideration of temporal alignment and aggregation strategies. Should we downsample the high-frequency data to match the low-frequency data, potentially losing critical information about rapid events? Or should we upsample or interpolate the low-frequency data, introducing assumptions and potential inaccuracies? The choice depends heavily on the specific engineering problem and the desired level of detail. Furthermore, data might also vary in its conceptual granularity. For example, a sensor might provide a direct measurement of a physical quantity like pressure, while another might provide an indirect indicator, such as the motor current, which is correlated with load and thus pressure. Integrating these different levels of abstraction requires domain expertise and careful feature engineering.

The presence of multiple data granularities and types necessitates a robust approach to data preprocessing and fusion. Simply concatenating disparate data streams is rarely effective. Instead, a thoughtful strategy must be devised. This often begins with a comprehensive data cataloging effort, documenting each data source, its origin, sensor type, units, sampling rate, expected range, and any known limitations or biases. Standardization is a key step, involving the conversion of all data to a common set of units and potentially a common temporal resolution.

Techniques like resampling (upsampling or downsampling) and aggregation (e.g., calculating moving averages or taking the maximum/minimum over a time window) become essential tools. However, these operations must be performed with caution, as they can introduce artifacts or mask important phenomena. For instance, downsampling high-frequency vibration data might smooth over a critical, short-duration impact event, leading to a missed diagnosis of potential damage. Conversely, naively upsampling low-frequency data might create a false sense of detail and temporal resolution.

The challenge of heterogeneity is further amplified by the concept of multimodality. Multimodality arises when data from an engineering system is not confined to numerical sensor readings but encompasses information from entirely different types of sources, such as images, audio, text, or even more abstract representations. This is increasingly common as engineering systems become instrumented with cameras for visual inspection, microphones for acoustic monitoring, and sophisticated logging systems that generate textual error messages or operational notes.

Consider an automated inspection system for manufactured parts. It might combine:

1. **Numerical sensor data**: Readings from lasers or contact probes to measure precise dimensions.
2. **Image data**: High-resolution images captured by cameras to detect surface defects like scratches, cracks, or discoloration.
3. **Textual logs**: Error messages or quality reports generated by other automated systems involved in the manufacturing process.

Integrating these diverse data modalities presents a unique set of challenges. Each modality requires specialized techniques for processing, feature extraction, and analysis. Image data, for instance, demands techniques from computer vision, such as image segmentation, object detection, and feature descriptors (e.g., SIFT, SURF, or deep learning-based embeddings). Audio data might require spectral analysis, Mel-frequency cepstral coefficients (MFCCs), or other audio feature extraction methods. Textual data can be processed using natural language processing (NLP) techniques, including tokenization, stemming, sentiment analysis, and topic modeling.

The true power, however, lies in fusing these modalities to gain a more comprehensive understanding than any single modality could provide. For example, in monitoring the health of rotating machinery, combining vibration sensor data (numerical, temporal) with acoustic data (audio, spectral) and thermal imaging (image, spatial) can provide a much more robust diagnostic capability. A specific type of bearing failure might manifest as a particular pattern in vibration, an unusual acoustic signature (e.g., grinding or squealing), and a localized increase in temperature. Detecting these correlated patterns across modalities can lead to earlier and more accurate fault detection.

The integration of multimodal data typically involves several stages. First, each modality is processed independently using its tailored techniques to extract relevant features. For numerical sensor data, this might involve statistical features, time-domain analysis, or frequency-domain analysis. For images, it could be texture analysis, shape descriptors, or deep learned features. For text, it might be TF-IDF scores or word embeddings.

The second stage is feature fusion. This is where the extracted features from different modalities are combined into a unified representation. There are broadly two approaches to feature fusion: early fusion and late fusion.

**Early fusion** (also known as data-level fusion) involves combining the raw or minimally processed data from different modalities before feeding them into a single model. This is often challenging due to the disparate nature and dimensionality of raw data from different sources. For instance, trying to directly combine pixel values from an image with voltage readings from a sensor is generally not feasible or meaningful.
**Late fusion** (also known as decision-level fusion or model-level fusion) involves training separate models for each modality and then combining their outputs (e.g., predictions or confidence scores) to make a final decision. This is often more practical and robust, allowing each modality to be analyzed by its most suitable algorithms. For example, one model might predict bearing health based on vibration data, another based on acoustic data, and a third based on thermal images. The final prediction could be a weighted average of these individual predictions or a meta-classifier that takes the individual predictions as input.
A **mid-level fusion** approach involves extracting features from each modality using modality-specific models (e.g., CNN for images, RNN for time series) and then concatenating these feature vectors to form a richer, combined feature representation. This combined feature vector is then fed into a final classifier or regressor. This approach often strikes a good balance between leveraging modality-specific strengths and achieving a unified representation.

Let's consider a concrete example in industrial automation: predictive maintenance for a robotic arm.

**Numerical Data**: Joint torques, motor currents, encoder positions, and vibration sensors attached to the arm's links. These provide insights into the mechanical load, kinematic state, and dynamic behavior.
**Image Data**: Cameras mounted near the robotic arm capture its movements and the objects it interacts with. These images can reveal issues like unusual arm posture, collisions, or deviations from the intended path.

**Audio Data**: Microphones can capture the sounds of the robotic arm's operation. Grinding noises might indicate wear in a gear, while unusual buzzing could signify an issue with a motor or controller.
**Textual Logs**: The robot's control system generates logs detailing its operational status, error codes, and diagnostic messages.

To build a predictive maintenance system for this robotic arm, we would need to:

1. **Collect and synchronize data**: Ensure that data from all sensors and sources are timestamped accurately and collected concurrently.
2. **Preprocess each modality**:
**Numerical**: Filter noise, normalize values, extract time-domain features (e.g., RMS, peak-to-peak) and frequency-domain features (e.g., FFT analysis of vibration).
**Image**: Resize, normalize pixel values, potentially use pre-trained CNNs to extract image embeddings representing the arm's pose or any visual anomalies.
**Audio**: Convert to a standard format, perform spectral analysis, and extract features like MFCCs or power spectral densities.
**Text**: Tokenize logs, remove stop words, and convert to numerical representations using techniques like TF-IDF or word embeddings.
3. **Feature Fusion**: Concatenate the feature vectors extracted from each modality into a single, comprehensive feature representation. For instance, a feature vector might include the mean joint torque, the dominant frequency component of vibration, an image embedding of the arm's current pose, spectral features from the audio, and numerical representations of key log entries.
4. **Model Training**: Train a machine learning model (e.g., a support vector machine, a random forest, or a deep neural network) on this fused feature representation to predict different failure modes or estimate the remaining useful life of the robotic arm.

The challenge of multimodality extends to the very nature of the underlying phenomena being observed. In many physical systems, different phenomena manifest through different sensing modalities. Temperature changes might be primarily captured by thermal sensors, while structural stress is best observed through strain gauges. Degradation might be visually apparent in an image but also produce subtle acoustic emissions. A decision pipeline designed to handle only one modality would be inherently limited, potentially missing crucial indicators of system health or performance degradation.

The engineering of decision pipelines for heterogeneous and multimodal data requires a shift in mindset. It moves away from the assumption of a single, uniform data stream and embraces the complexity and richness of diverse information sources. This necessitates a modular design for the pipeline, where individual components are responsible for handling specific data types or modalities. For example, a data ingestion module might be capable of receiving data from various protocols and formats. Preprocessing modules could be specialized for image processing, time-series analysis, or text parsing. Feature engineering and fusion modules would then act as integrators, bringing together insights from these specialized components.

Furthermore, the choice of machine learning models becomes critical. While traditional models might struggle with highly diverse feature sets, deep learning architectures offer significant flexibility. Convolutional Neural Networks (CNNs) excel at image data, Recurrent Neural Networks (RNNs) and Transformers are adept at sequential data (time series, text), and various other specialized architectures can be employed for graph data or audio. Increasingly, researchers are developing multi-input deep learning models that can directly accept and process data from multiple modalities simultaneously, learning cross-modal interactions within the network's layers. These architectures can learn intricate relationships between, for example, how a visual defect in a manufactured component corresponds to a specific acoustic signature during its production.

The practical implications of dealing with heterogeneity and multimodality are profound for engineering decision-making. By effectively integrating diverse data sources, engineers can achieve:

**Enhanced diagnostic accuracy**: Combining evidence from multiple sensors and modalities can lead to more precise identification of faults and anomalies, reducing false positives and negatives.
**Earlier fault detection**: Subtle indicators of impending failure that might be missed by a single sensor type can be amplified when observed across multiple modalities. For example, a slight increase in temperature combined with a subtle change in acoustic emission might signal an early stage of bearing wear that neither observation alone would clearly indicate.
**Improved system understanding**: Multimodal data provides a richer, more holistic view of system behavior. Engineers can gain deeper insights into the interplay between different physical phenomena and their representations across various data types.
**More robust predictions**: Models trained on fused multimodal data are often more resilient to noise or missing information in a single modality, as other modalities can compensate.

However, the journey towards effective multimodal data integration is not without its obstacles. The increased complexity of data management and processing can lead to higher computational costs and longer processing times. Developing and maintaining models that can effectively handle multiple data types requires expertise across several domains, including signal processing, computer vision, natural language processing, and machine learning. Ensuring data quality, synchronization, and a common understanding of semantics across disparate data sources remains a significant challenge.

In conclusion, the heterogeneity and multimodality of engineering data are not mere footnotes to the temporal and spatial dimensions, but rather fundamental characteristics that define the landscape of modern engineering data analysis. Recognizing and systematically addressing these aspects through appropriate preprocessing, feature engineering, fusion techniques, and advanced modeling approaches is indispensable for building powerful, insightful, and reliable engineering decision pipelines. The ability to synthesize information from diverse sources – numerical streams, visual representations, auditory cues, and textual narratives – unlocks a far more profound understanding of complex engineering systems, paving the way for smarter, safer, and more efficient operations.

The pristine, idealized data sets often presented in introductory textbooks are a far cry from the messy reality encountered in engineering practice. In the real world, data is almost invariably tainted by imperfections. These imperfections fall broadly into three interconnected categories: noise, inherent uncertainty, and missing values. Recognizing, understanding, and strategically mitigating these issues is paramount for any successful engineering data analysis or machine learning endeavor. Ignoring them can lead to flawed conclusions, unreliable predictions, and ultimately, poor engineering decisions.

Noise, in the context of engineering data, refers to random fluctuations or systematic distortions that obscure the true underlying signal or measurement. Its origins are manifold and deeply rooted in the physical processes of data acquisition. Sensors, the primary conduits through which we observe the physical world, are not perfect transducers. They are subject to a host of environmental influences and internal limitations. For instance, temperature variations can cause sensor components to expand or contract, leading to a drift in their calibration and introducing spurious readings. Electromagnetic interference (EMI) from nearby electrical equipment, power lines, or even radio transmissions can induce unwanted signals into sensitive measurement circuits, particularly affecting low-level analog signals. Vibrations, often present in industrial environments, can physically shake sensors, leading to spurious oscillations in the recorded data. Even the very act of measurement can sometimes perturb the system being observed, a phenomenon particularly relevant in highly sensitive scientific instruments or delicate biological systems. For example, inserting a thermometer into a liquid might slightly alter the liquid's temperature distribution before a stable reading is achieved. In digital systems, quantization error, inherent in the analog-to-digital conversion process, introduces a form of noise as continuous analog values are mapped to discrete digital levels. The resolution of the analog-to-digital converter (ADC) dictates the granularity of this approximation, and signals smaller than the smallest discrete step will be lost or misrepresented.

Beyond external influences, internal sensor limitations contribute to noise. Electronic components have finite lifetimes and can degrade over time, leading to increased internal resistance, capacitance, or other electrical properties that alter their response. This degradation can manifest as a gradual shift in the sensor's baseline reading or an increased susceptibility to external noise. Furthermore, the manufacturing process itself introduces variability. Even identical sensor models from the same batch will exhibit slight differences in their performance characteristics due to tolerances in component manufacturing. This inherent variability contributes to the "noise floor" of the measurement system. For example, a batch of strain gauges might have slightly different gauge factors or temperature coefficients, leading to variations in their sensitivity and response.

The distinction between noise and uncertainty, while subtle, is important. Uncertainty is a more formal concept that quantifies the doubt about a measurement's accuracy. While noise often refers to the random fluctuations observed *around* a true value, uncertainty encompasses all potential deviations from the true value, including systematic errors (biases) and random errors (noise). Every measurement inherently possesses some degree of uncertainty. This uncertainty arises from a combination of factors: the limitations of the measuring instrument (its precision and accuracy), the variability of the phenomenon being measured, and the conditions under which the measurement is taken. For example, when measuring the length of an object with a ruler, there is uncertainty associated with the resolution of the ruler's markings (e.g., millimeters), the user's ability to align the ruler precisely with the object's edges, and potential parallax errors if the ruler is not viewed directly from above. In a chemical analysis, uncertainty might stem from the purity of reagents, the calibration of the analytical instrument (e.g., a spectrophotometer), and the variability in sample preparation.

Metrologists and metrically inclined engineers often distinguish between different sources of uncertainty. Type A uncertainty is evaluated by statistical methods from an observed series of measurements, effectively quantifying the random variations. Type B uncertainty is evaluated by other means, such as by the specifications of measuring instruments, calibration certificates, manufacturer's data, or by general knowledge of the physical and chemical properties of materials and phenomena. For instance, a manufacturer might specify that a particular digital multimeter has an accuracy of ±0.1% of reading plus 5 counts. This specification represents Type B uncertainty. The statistical spread of readings taken from that multimeter for a stable voltage would represent Type A uncertainty. The total uncertainty of a measurement is typically a combination of these sources, often calculated using root-sum-of-squares methods. Quantifying uncertainty is crucial for making informed decisions. If a component's measured dimension falls close to a critical tolerance limit, understanding the uncertainty associated with that measurement is vital to determine if the component is truly within specification or if it might be on the verge of being out of tolerance. This is especially important in safety-critical applications where even small deviations could have catastrophic consequences. For example, in aerospace or nuclear engineering, exceeding tolerance limits by even a tiny margin can render a component unusable or compromise the safety of an entire system.

Missing values represent another pervasive challenge in engineering data. These are simply data points that were not recorded or are unavailable for analysis. The reasons for missing data are diverse and often depend on the specific engineering context. In systems with distributed sensors, intermittent network connectivity can lead to data dropouts. If a sensor is temporarily disconnected from the network due to a faulty cable, a switch failure, or a network congestion event, the data it would have produced during that period will be missing. This is particularly common in large-scale IoT deployments or remote monitoring systems. In applications involving human interaction, such as the input of maintenance logs or operational notes, missing entries can occur due to oversight, human error, or incomplete data entry procedures. For instance, a technician might forget to record a specific parameter after performing a maintenance task, or a particular sensor reading might not be logged if the associated system component is powered down for maintenance.

Sensor malfunctions, even if they don't introduce noise, can lead to missing data. A sensor might fail completely, ceasing to transmit any data. Alternatively, a sensor might enter a fault state where it produces invalid or nonsensical readings that are subsequently flagged and excluded from the dataset. This exclusion, while a sensible data cleaning step, results in missing values for those specific time points or events. In batch processing or laboratory experiments, sample degradation or incomplete experimental runs can also lead to missing data. If a chemical sample deteriorates before analysis, or if an experiment is interrupted before all planned measurements are taken, the corresponding data will be absent. The phenomenon of "data poisoning" in machine learning, where malicious actors inject incorrect data, can also lead to values that are so erroneous they are effectively treated as missing.

The presence of noise, uncertainty, and missing values can have a profound impact on subsequent data analysis and model performance. Noise can mask underlying trends, making it difficult to discern genuine patterns from random fluctuations. If a signal is heavily contaminated by noise, statistical measures like averages or variances can become unreliable. For instance, estimating the average operating temperature of a machine with noisy temperature sensor readings might yield a value that is significantly different from the true average, leading to incorrect conclusions about its thermal performance. High levels of noise can also degrade the performance of machine learning models, causing them to learn spurious correlations or fail to generalize to unseen data.

Measurement uncertainty, when not properly accounted for, can lead to misinterpretations of system behavior. If a critical parameter is measured with high uncertainty, and its value is close to a design threshold, a decision based on that measurement might be wrong. For example, if a structural integrity analysis relies on precise measurements of strain, and these measurements have substantial uncertainty, the safety margin might be overestimated, leading to a risk of failure. Failing to account for uncertainty also makes it challenging to perform rigorous statistical inference, such as hypothesis testing or confidence interval estimation.

Missing values pose a direct challenge to many analytical techniques. Algorithms that expect complete data matrices will simply fail or produce erroneous results if confronted with missing entries. Imputation strategies, discussed later, are often employed to fill in these gaps, but the chosen method can introduce its own biases or assumptions. For example, simply replacing missing values with the mean of the available data might distort the data's distribution and reduce the variance, potentially leading to an underestimation of variability and an overestimation of model confidence. Moreover, the *pattern* of missingness itself can be informative. If data is missing more often under certain operational conditions, this might indicate an underlying issue with the data acquisition system or even a symptom of the system being monitored. Ignoring this pattern and simply imputing the values can lead to a loss of potentially valuable diagnostic information.

Identifying and quantifying the impact of these imperfections is the crucial first step in addressing them. For noise, techniques like visual inspection of time series plots, spectral analysis (e.g., using Fourier Transforms to identify dominant frequencies of interference), and statistical measures like standard deviation can offer initial insights. For instance, a sudden, sharp increase in the standard deviation of a signal might indicate the onset of a new source of noise. Moving averages or Savitzky-Golay filters can be used to smooth noisy data and reveal underlying trends, while the difference between the raw and smoothed signal can provide an estimate of the noise component.

Quantifying uncertainty often involves consulting instrument specifications, performing calibration checks, and analyzing the statistical spread of repeated measurements. Understanding the limitations of the measuring instruments is key. A ruler marked only in centimeters will have a higher inherent uncertainty for fine measurements than a caliper with micrometer precision. For missing values, the initial step is to identify their presence and frequency. Data profiling tools can quickly summarize the extent of missingness per feature or per time period. Visualizations such as missingness matrices or heatmaps can reveal patterns in where data is missing. For example, a heatmap might show that data from a particular sensor is consistently missing during nighttime hours, suggesting a power supply issue or a scheduled shutdown.

The impact on subsequent analysis can be gauged by performing preliminary analyses on both the raw, imperfect data and on versions of the data where certain imperfections have been addressed (e.g., noisy data smoothed, missing values imputed). Comparing the results of these analyses can highlight the sensitivity of the conclusions to the imperfections. For instance, training a predictive model on a dataset with and without imputation for missing values can reveal how much the model's predictions change. If the model's performance drastically improves after imputation, it underscores the significance of the missing data. Similarly, comparing model performance on raw noisy data versus filtered data can indicate the detrimental effect of noise. This initial assessment guides the choice of appropriate mitigation strategies, ensuring that resources are focused on addressing the most impactful issues. Ultimately, a robust engineering data pipeline must be designed with the expectation that data will be imperfect, and it must include mechanisms to detect, quantify, and manage noise, uncertainty, and missing values to ensure the reliability and validity of its outputs.

The digital revolution has fundamentally reshaped engineering, not only in how designs are conceived and simulations are run but, crucially, in how operational systems are monitored, maintained, and optimized. This transformation is intrinsically linked to the exponential growth in the volume of data generated by engineering applications. What was once a manageable stream of information, perhaps measured in kilobytes or megabytes, has ballooned into an ocean of data, frequently spanning gigabytes and terabytes, and in some extreme cases, even petabytes. This sheer scale of data presents a distinct set of challenges and opportunities for the engineering data professional.

Consider the realm of large-scale infrastructure. A modern bridge, equipped with thousands of sensors monitoring strain, vibration, temperature, and humidity at various points, generates a continuous stream of readings. Each sensor might transmit data every few seconds. Over the lifespan of the bridge, and across all its sensors, this data accumulates at an astonishing rate. Similarly, in advanced manufacturing environments, the proliferation of Industrial Internet of Things (IIoT) devices on the factory floor – from robotic arms and CNC machines to environmental sensors and quality control cameras – creates a high-velocity, high-volume data flow. Each machine component's operational parameters, its energy consumption, its diagnostic alerts, and images captured for visual inspection all contribute to a colossal dataset. In the aerospace industry, flight data recorders, alongside myriad sensors monitoring engine performance, structural integrity, and environmental conditions, accumulate terabytes of information over a single long-haul flight. The analysis of this data is not merely for operational efficiency or predictive maintenance; it is often critical for safety, regulatory compliance, and the continuous improvement of design and performance.

The implications of this data scale are profound, impacting both the computational resources required for processing and the infrastructure needed for storage. When dealing with data measured in megabytes, traditional desktop computers and standard relational databases often suffice. A dataset of a few hundred megabytes can typically be loaded into memory, allowing for rapid iteration with common data analysis tools and libraries. Operations like filtering, aggregation, and even training moderately complex machine learning models can be performed with relative ease on a single machine. Storage is also less of a concern; a few gigabytes of readily accessible storage are usually ample.

However, as we transition into the gigabyte and terabyte scales, the paradigm shifts dramatically. A dataset of several gigabytes might strain the memory capacity of a typical workstation, necessitating techniques that process data in chunks or utilize distributed computing frameworks. Storing terabytes of data requires dedicated storage solutions, often involving Network Attached Storage (NAS) devices, Storage Area Networks (SANs), or cloud-based object storage services. The cost of such storage, while decreasing, can still be a significant consideration, especially when dealing with historical data that may be accessed less frequently but still needs to be retained for compliance or long-term trend analysis.

The challenges intensify when data volumes reach petabytes, though this is more common in specialized scientific research (like genomics or particle physics) or massive-scale simulations rather than typical engineering operations, it's worth noting the principles extend. Processing petabytes of data is fundamentally impossible on a single machine. It necessitates a distributed computing infrastructure, employing clusters of machines working in parallel. This is where technologies like Hadoop Distributed File System (HDFS) for storage and MapReduce or its successors (like Apache Spark) for processing become indispensable. These frameworks are designed to partition data across multiple nodes and execute computations in parallel, dramatically reducing processing times from weeks or months to hours or days.

Efficient data management becomes paramount at these scales. Traditional database indexing strategies may become inefficient or unwieldy. For instance, indexing a terabyte-scale table on a single server would be prohibitively slow and resource-intensive. Instead, data engineers must consider distributed indexing mechanisms or employ alternative data structures and storage formats. Columnar storage formats, such as Apache Parquet or ORC, are often preferred for analytical workloads involving large datasets. These formats store data column by column rather than row by row, which significantly improves query performance for analytical queries that typically access only a subset of columns. This is because the system only needs to read the relevant columns from disk, rather than the entire row. Furthermore, these formats often include sophisticated compression techniques that reduce storage footprint and I/O bottlenecks.

Data partitioning is another critical strategy for managing large datasets. Data can be partitioned based on various criteria, such as time (e.g., daily, monthly, yearly partitions), geographical location, or sensor ID. This allows query engines to prune irrelevant partitions, drastically reducing the amount of data that needs to be scanned. For example, if a query is only interested in data from the last month, a time-partitioned table can direct the query to only access the partition corresponding to that month, ignoring all historical data. This concept of "predicate pushdown" is a cornerstone of efficient querying on large, distributed datasets.

When considering the computational challenges, the sheer amount of data means that any operation, even a simple aggregation, can take a considerable amount of time and processing power. Simple loops in Python that iterate over millions or billions of rows are no longer feasible. This is where optimized libraries and distributed processing frameworks come into play. Libraries like NumPy and Pandas in Python, while highly optimized for single-machine in-memory operations, have limitations when datasets exceed available RAM. For larger datasets, transitioning to tools like Apache Spark, which is designed for distributed data processing, is often necessary. Spark allows engineers to write code in familiar languages like Python (PySpark), Scala, or Java, but executes these operations across a cluster of machines. It employs in-memory caching and lazy evaluation to optimize performance. Lazy evaluation means that Spark operations are not executed immediately but are built up into a plan, which is then optimized and executed when an action (like collecting results or writing to storage) is called. This allows Spark to optimize the entire computation graph before execution.

The choice of processing techniques also depends on the nature of the engineering task. For batch processing, where data is collected over a period and then processed, technologies like Spark batch jobs or traditional ETL (Extract, Transform, Load) pipelines are suitable. For real-time or near-real-time analytics, where data needs to be processed as it arrives, stream processing frameworks like Apache Kafka Streams, Apache Flink, or Spark Streaming become essential. These frameworks can handle continuous data ingestion and processing with low latency, enabling applications such as real-time anomaly detection in machinery or dynamic adjustment of manufacturing parameters.

The concept of "data gravity" also becomes increasingly relevant with larger datasets. Data gravity refers to the phenomenon where as data accumulates, it becomes harder and more expensive to move. The sheer size of terabytes or petabytes of data means that moving it across networks or between storage systems can take days or even weeks, and incur significant network egress costs, especially in cloud environments. This often leads to a strategy of bringing compute to the data, rather than moving the data to the compute. Distributed processing frameworks are designed with this principle in mind, executing computations on the nodes where the data resides. This minimizes data movement and hence improves efficiency and reduces costs.

Furthermore, the complexity of the data itself can exacerbate the challenges of scale. In engineering, data is often multi-modal, comprising not just numerical sensor readings but also time-series data, images, video, textual logs, and even 3D models. Integrating and processing these diverse data types at scale requires sophisticated data pipelines and specialized tools. For example, analyzing video feeds from a manufacturing line for quality control requires integrating computer vision libraries with distributed processing frameworks. The storage of these large, unstructured or semi-structured data assets often utilizes object storage services like Amazon S3, Azure Blob Storage, or Google Cloud Storage, which are designed for scalability and cost-effectiveness.

The iterative nature of data engineering and machine learning development also presents challenges at scale. When developing a new model or refining an existing one, engineers typically perform numerous experiments, retraining models with slightly different parameters or data subsets. On a terabyte-scale dataset, each training run can take hours or days. This necessitates efficient experiment tracking, hyperparameter optimization strategies that minimize the number of full training runs, and techniques like transfer learning or model distillation to speed up the development cycle. Cloud-based machine learning platforms offer managed services that can orchestrate these complex workflows, manage compute resources, and track experiments, mitigating some of the operational overhead.

In summary, the transition from megabyte-scale to terabyte-scale data in engineering applications necessitates a fundamental shift in how data is managed, stored, and processed. It moves beyond single-machine capabilities to embrace distributed systems, specialized storage formats, and optimized processing frameworks. Efficient data management strategies, including partitioning and columnar storage, become crucial for query performance and cost-effectiveness. Scalable processing techniques, such as those offered by Apache Spark and other distributed computing platforms, are essential for handling the computational demands. Understanding and leveraging these technologies are no longer optional but are core competencies for engineering data professionals operating in the modern, data-rich landscape. The ability to design, implement, and maintain data pipelines that can effectively handle such vast quantities of information is a defining characteristic of successful engineering data initiatives.

The raw, unadulterated stream of data originating from engineering systems, while vast, is rarely a perfect reflection of the underlying phenomena it seeks to capture. Beyond the general "noise" that can obscure meaningful patterns, engineering datasets are replete with anomalies and outliers that are not merely statistical curiosities but often potent indicators of crucial events, subtle equipment malfunctions, or significant shifts in environmental conditions. These domain-specific deviations from the expected, the normal, or the predicted are of paramount importance because their timely and accurate detection is frequently the linchpin for maintaining system integrity, ensuring operational safety, and preventing catastrophic failures.

Consider, for instance, the realm of industrial machinery and manufacturing. A high-speed rotational component, such as a turbine rotor or a high-precision spindle in a CNC machine, is expected to operate within a specific vibration signature. This signature is a complex waveform that, when healthy, exhibits predictable frequencies and amplitudes corresponding to the rotational speed, bearing quality, and balance of the component. However, the emergence of a bearing defect, a microscopic crack, or an imbalance caused by material accumulation can introduce subtle but detectable changes to this vibration pattern. A sudden, sharp spike in amplitude at a particular frequency band, or the appearance of new, unexpected harmonic frequencies, might not be statistically extreme in the context of the entire dataset's range, but within the domain of vibration analysis, such a deviation is a loud alarm bell. This isn't a random blip; it's the physical manifestation of incipient failure. The ability to identify this specific type of anomaly – a change in spectral content indicative of wear or damage – is critical. Without this domain-specific understanding, such a change might be dismissed as statistical noise or an artifact of sensor calibration, leading to a missed opportunity for proactive maintenance. The cost of such a failure could range from expensive downtime and component replacement to, in severe cases, catastrophic mechanical disintegration.

Similarly, in the context of process engineering, temperature readings from a chemical reactor are fundamental to controlling reaction rates, ensuring product quality, and preventing runaway reactions. A steady, predictable temperature profile is the norm during stable operation. However, an unexpected surge in temperature can signal a variety of issues: a malfunctioning cooling system, an incorrect feedstock mixture leading to an exothermic runaway, or even a sensor failure that is reporting erroneously high values. The anomaly here isn't just a value that is statistically different; it's a deviation from the expected thermodynamic behavior of the system. A sudden spike, even if it falls within the absolute maximum recorded temperature over years of operation, is critically important if it occurs under circumstances where it is thermodynamically impossible or indicates a loss of control. Detecting this specific anomaly type – a thermal excursion that violates process physics or control objectives – is essential for immediate intervention. The consequences of not detecting it can include compromised product quality, environmental contamination from uncontrolled releases, or severe safety hazards.

In structural engineering and civil infrastructure monitoring, anomalies can manifest in ways that directly relate to the physical integrity of a structure. Consider a bridge equipped with strain gauges and accelerometers. Under normal traffic and environmental loads (wind, temperature fluctuations), the structure will experience predictable deformations and vibrations. An anomaly might be a sudden, localized increase in strain that is significantly higher than what the applied load would typically induce, or a persistent, low-amplitude vibration pattern that deviates from the structure's known natural frequencies. Such deviations can be early indicators of material fatigue, the loosening of critical fasteners, or even subtle structural damage from an impact or seismic event. The domain-specific knowledge here lies in understanding how mechanical stress propagates through the structure and how different types of damage or degradation will alter its dynamic response. An outlier in the strain gauge data might not be an extreme value in isolation, but when correlated with other sensor readings or with the expected load conditions, it becomes a critical anomaly signaling potential structural compromise. Ignoring such anomalies could lead to a gradual weakening of the structure, culminating in a sudden and potentially catastrophic failure.

The automotive industry provides another rich area for domain-specific anomalies. In advanced driver-assistance systems (ADAS) or autonomous driving systems, sensors like lidar, radar, and cameras are constantly collecting data about the vehicle's surroundings. An anomaly might be a radar return that, under clear visibility, mimics the signature of a solid object but is located in an area where no physical object should be, potentially indicating a sensor spoofing attempt or a peculiar environmental reflection. Or consider the thermal management of an electric vehicle's battery pack. While a general rise in battery temperature might be expected during fast charging or hard acceleration, a localized, rapid increase in the temperature of a single battery module, while others remain within normal operating ranges, is a critical anomaly. This could indicate an internal short circuit within that specific module, a precursor to thermal runaway. The anomaly is defined by its spatial localization and its divergence from the otherwise homogeneous behavior of the battery pack.

In the field of aerospace, the stakes are incredibly high, and the data generated by aircraft systems is meticulously monitored for anomalies. During flight, engine performance parameters such as thrust, fuel flow, exhaust gas temperature (EGT), and rotational speeds are continuously tracked. A deviation from the expected correlation between these parameters, even if individual readings are within their absolute historical ranges, can signify an anomaly. For example, an increase in EGT for a given level of thrust might indicate a degradation in the turbine blades' efficiency or an issue with the fuel injection system. This is not a random spike; it's a thermodynamic or mechanical inefficiency manifesting as a subtle but persistent shift in correlated variables. Similarly, in the structural health monitoring of an aircraft, the detection of micro-cracks or delamination in composite materials might be signaled by changes in the structure's acoustic emission signatures or its resonant frequencies. These are highly specialized anomalies that require an understanding of material science and structural dynamics to interpret.

The core principle across these diverse engineering disciplines is that anomalies are not always about extreme values in isolation. They are often about:

1.
**Deviations from expected physical or chemical behavior:** For instance, a temperature rising without an apparent heat source, or a pressure dropping in a sealed system without any detected leakage.
2. **Changes in the relationships between variables:** When two sensors that are normally correlated (e.g., engine RPM and fuel flow) begin to diverge, it signals an issue.
3. **Emergence of unexpected patterns:** The appearance of new frequencies in vibration data, or unusual noise signatures in audio recordings from machinery.
4. **Spatial or temporal discontinuities:** A sudden localized failure in a system where components are expected to degrade uniformly, or a signal that abruptly disappears and reappears.

5. **Violations of operational constraints or safety envelopes:** Readings that, while perhaps not historically unprecedented, occur under conditions where they are fundamentally unsafe or indicative of a loss of control.

Detecting these domain-specific anomalies requires more than just applying generic outlier detection algorithms like Z-score or Isolation Forests without context. While these methods can identify statistically unusual data points, they often fail to distinguish between benign outliers and critical indicators of system distress. For example, a simple Z-score approach might flag a brief, harmless surge in a sensor reading during a transient system startup as an anomaly, while completely missing a slow, insidious drift in a critical parameter that is still within the sensor's typical range but indicative of creeping degradation.

To effectively identify these crucial deviations, engineering data professionals must collaborate closely with domain experts – the mechanical engineers, chemical engineers, civil engineers, and physicists who understand the systems intimately. This collaboration allows for the development of anomaly detection strategies that are tailored to the specific physics, chemistry, and operational characteristics of the system under scrutiny. This might involve:

**Feature Engineering based on domain knowledge:** Instead of using raw sensor readings, engineers might create new features that capture specific physical phenomena. For vibration analysis, this means calculating power spectral densities, identifying specific frequency bands associated with known failure modes, or analyzing the envelope of vibration signals. For process control, it might involve calculating derived quantities like mass flow rates, energy balances, or reaction conversion rates.

**Physics-Informed Machine Learning:** Employing models that incorporate physical laws or constraints into their learning process. This could involve using differential equations to model system behavior and detecting deviations from the predicted trajectories, or using generative models that learn the distribution of "normal" system states based on physical principles.
**Contextual Anomaly Detection:** Evaluating an anomaly not just in isolation but within its operational context. A high temperature reading might be acceptable during a high-load operation but critically anomalous during idle. This requires incorporating contextual variables (e.g., operational mode, load, environmental conditions) into the anomaly detection framework.
**Time-Series Specific Techniques:** Many engineering data streams are time-series in nature. Advanced time-series anomaly detection methods, such as those based on Recurrent Neural Networks (RNNs), Long Short-Term Memory (LSTM) networks, or Transformer models, are adept at learning temporal dependencies and identifying deviations from expected sequences. However, even these powerful models benefit immensely from domain-specific feature engineering and careful interpretation of their outputs.
**Multi-sensor Fusion:** In complex systems, a single sensor anomaly might be ambiguous, but the convergence of anomalies across multiple, related sensors can provide a much stronger signal. Fusing data from different sensor types (e.g., combining vibration, temperature, and acoustic data from a pump) can reveal complex failure modes that would be invisible to individual sensor analysis.

The paramount importance of detecting these domain-specific anomalies cannot be overstated. It forms the bedrock of predictive maintenance, allowing for interventions
*before* a component fails, thereby minimizing downtime and reducing repair costs. It is fundamental to safety-critical systems, where early detection of deviations can prevent accidents. It is also crucial for ensuring product quality, optimizing operational efficiency, and enabling

continuous improvement in engineering designs. As systems become more complex and the data they generate grows in volume and velocity, the ability to intelligently identify and interpret these specialized anomalies will only become more critical for the engineering data professional. It moves the role beyond mere data processing to becoming an active participant in the operational intelligence and risk management of engineering enterprises.

# Chapter 3: Foundational Signal Processing Techniques

Signals and systems form the fundamental vocabulary for describing and analyzing how information propagates and is processed within engineering applications. At its core, a signal is a function that conveys information about the behavior or attributes of some phenomenon. Think of it as a carrier of data, a manifestation of an underlying physical process that we can measure and record. This could be anything from the fluctuating voltage across a resistor in an electronic circuit, the changing pressure within a pipeline in a chemical plant, the acceleration experienced by a vehicle's suspension system, or the intensity of light captured by a camera in an autonomous driving system. These phenomena are rarely static; they evolve over time, and it is this evolution that the signal represents.

In engineering, we commonly encounter two primary categories of signals: continuous-time signals and discrete-time signals. A **continuous-time signal**, often denoted as $x(t)$, is defined for all values of time $t$ within a given interval. This means that the signal's value is known at every instant, no matter how infinitesimally small the time difference. Such signals are often direct representations of physical processes that occur continuously in nature. For example, the temperature of a room measured with a high-precision thermometer over an hour would be a continuous-time signal. The voltage output from an analog microphone capturing a sound wave is another classic example. The very essence of these signals is their uninterrupted flow of information.

In contrast, a **discrete-time signal**, often denoted as $x[n]$, is defined only at specific, distinct points in time. These time points are typically indexed by an integer, $n$. Discrete-time signals are not usually directly observed from physical phenomena but are rather the result of sampling a continuous-time signal at regular intervals. The sampling process converts the continuous flow of information into a sequence of discrete values.

Imagine taking snapshots of the room's temperature every minute. Each measurement is a discrete value representing the temperature at that specific minute. The time interval between these snapshots is called the sampling period, and its inverse, the sampling frequency, determines how often we capture the signal's state. In digital signal processing, all signals are ultimately discrete-time signals because computers can only process a finite number of values at discrete points in time. The bridge between continuous and discrete signals is the sampling theorem, which, under certain conditions, guarantees that we can perfectly reconstruct the original continuous-time signal from its sampled discrete-time representation.

Beyond the nature of their time dependence, signals can also be characterized by other properties, such as their energy or power. The **energy** of a signal $x(t)$ is defined as the integral of its squared magnitude over all time: $Ex = \int{-\infty}^{\infty} |x(t)|^2 dt$. For discrete-time signals, this becomes a summation: $Ex = \sum{n=-\infty}^{\infty} |x[n]|^2$. Signals with finite energy are often transient or decay rapidly. The **power** of a signal $x(t)$ is defined as the average energy over time: $Px = \lim{T \to \infty} \frac{1}{2T} \int{-T}^{T} |x(t)|^2 dt$. For discrete-time signals, this is $Px = \lim{N \to \infty} \frac{1}{2N+1} \sum{n=-N}^{N} |x[n]|^2$. Signals that are periodic or have constant amplitude over time often have finite power but infinite energy. Understanding these properties is crucial for designing appropriate signal processing algorithms, particularly when dealing with noise reduction or signal detection in the presence of interfering signals.

The concept of a
**system** in engineering is intrinsically linked to signals. A system is any process or device that takes one or more signals as input and produces one or more signals as output. Systems are the mechanisms through which signals are modified, transformed, or analyzed. This transformation could be as simple as amplifying a weak audio signal or as complex as filtering out unwanted noise from a sensor reading before it's fed into a

control algorithm. For instance, a radio receiver is a system that takes an electromagnetic signal as input and produces an audio signal as output. A control system in a chemical plant takes sensor readings (signals) as input and adjusts actuators (producing output signals) to maintain desired process conditions.

When analyzing systems, engineers often focus on a particular class of systems known as
**Linear Time-Invariant (LTI) systems**. These systems possess two fundamental properties: linearity and time-invariance. A system is **linear** if it satisfies the principles of superposition and homogeneity. Superposition means that if the system produces output $y1(t)$ for input $x1(t)$ and output $y2(t)$ for input $x2(t)$, then for an input that is a linear combination of $x1(t)$ and $x2(t)$, say $a x1(t) + b x2(t)$, the output will be the same linear combination of the individual outputs, $a y1(t) + b y2(t)$, where $a$ and $b$ are constants. Homogeneity, a special case of superposition where $a=b=1$, implies that scaling the input by a factor scales the output by the same factor. Linearity is a powerful property because it allows us to break down complex input signals into simpler components, analyze the system's response to each component, and then combine the individual responses to determine the overall output. This greatly simplifies analysis.

A system is
**time-invariant** if its behavior does not change over time. This means that if we apply an input signal $x(t)$ at some time and obtain an output $y(t)$, then if we apply the exact same input signal $x(t - t0)$ but shifted in time by $t0$, the output will be the identical output signal, but also shifted by the same amount in time, $y(t - t_0)$. In essence, the system's characteristics—its parameters, its response—are constant, and it doesn't "remember" when it was subjected to a particular input. A simple example is a resistor; its resistance value does not change with time, so applying the same voltage at different times will always result in the same current.

The combination of linearity and time-invariance makes LTI systems mathematically tractable and incredibly useful in modeling many real-world engineering phenomena. For continuous-time LTI systems, the input-output relationship is fundamentally characterized by the **impulse response**, denoted by $h(t)$. The impulse response is the system's output when the input is the Dirac delta function, $\delta(t)$. The Dirac delta function is a theoretical signal that is zero everywhere except at time $t=0$, where it has infinite amplitude, but its integral over all time is unity. It represents an infinitely short, infinitely intense input pulse.

The profound significance of the impulse response $h(t)$ for LTI systems lies in the fact that *any* input signal $x(t)$ can be represented as a superposition of scaled and shifted impulse functions. Specifically, using the sifting property of the Dirac delta function, $x(t) = \int_{-\infty}^{\infty} x(\tau) \delta(t-\tau) d\tau$. Because the system is linear and time-invariant, its output $y(t)$ to this input $x(t)$ can be found by applying the same operations to the system's response to the impulse. This leads to the fundamental equation for continuous-time LTI systems: the **convolution integral**: $y(t) = x(t) h(t) = \int_{-\infty}^{\infty} x(\tau) h(t-\tau) d\tau$.

This convolution integral tells us that the output of an LTI system at any time $t$ is the sum (integral) of the products of the input signal at earlier times $\tau$ and the system's impulse response evaluated at the time difference $(t-\tau)$. It means the current output depends on all past inputs, weighted by how the system responds to impulses at those past times. The impulse response $h(t)$ completely characterizes the behavior of a continuous-time LTI system. If we know $h(t)$, we can predict the output for any input signal $x(t)$.

For discrete-time LTI systems, the analogous concept to the impulse response is the
**impulse response sequence**, denoted by $h[n]$. This is the system's output when the input is the Kronecker delta sequence, $\delta[n]$, which is 1 at $n=0$ and 0 for all other integer values of $n$. Similar to the continuous-time case, any discrete-time input signal $x[n]$ can be represented as a superposition of scaled and shifted delta sequences: $x[n] = \sum_{k=-\infty}^{\infty} x[k] \delta[n-k]$. The output $y[n]$ of a discrete-time LTI system is then given by the **convolution sum**: $y[n] = x[n] h[n] = \sum_{k=-\infty}^{\infty} x[k] h[n-k]$.
Again, the impulse response sequence $h[n]$ completely characterizes the discrete-time LTI system.

The mathematical operations of convolution, both the integral and the sum, are central to signal processing. They represent the fundamental mechanism by which LTI systems modify signals. Many common signal processing operations, such as filtering, echo cancellation, and equalization, are realized as LTI systems, and their design relies heavily on understanding and manipulating impulse responses.

The significance of this signal and system framework cannot be overstated. It provides a unified mathematical language to describe a vast array of engineering problems. Whether we are dealing with the transmission of radio waves, the dynamics of mechanical structures, the processing of audio or image data, or the analysis of financial time series, the underlying principles of signals and systems apply.

Consider an example from communications engineering. A radio transmitter modulates an information signal (e.g., voice) onto a carrier wave, creating a signal that can be transmitted through the air. The transmission medium (air, atmosphere) acts as a channel, which can be modeled as a system. This channel might introduce distortions, attenuation, or noise. The radio receiver is another system designed to receive the transmitted signal, undo the modulation (demodulate), and recover the original information signal, ideally minimizing the effects of the channel's distortion. The channel's behavior can often be approximated as an LTI system, characterized by its impulse response. Understanding this impulse response allows engineers to design filters and equalization techniques in the receiver to compensate for the channel's impairments, thereby improving the quality of the received information.

In control systems engineering, signals are used to represent system states, sensor measurements, and control commands. For example, in an automotive cruise control system, the speed of the car is a signal, the driver's set speed is another signal, and the signal sent to the engine throttle is a control signal. The car's engine, drivetrain, and dynamics form a complex system. The cruise control algorithm itself is a signal processing system that takes the measured speed (input signal) and the desired speed (reference signal) and generates a control signal to adjust the throttle to minimize the error between them. If we model the car's dynamics as an LTI system, then the control system design becomes a problem of designing a feedback controller, which is also a signal processing system, to achieve desired performance characteristics (e.g., fast response, minimal overshoot, stability).

In seismic data analysis, geophysicists record ground vibrations caused by earthquakes or artificial sources. These recorded vibrations are signals, often called seismograms. The Earth's subsurface layers act as a complex propagation system, filtering and altering the seismic waves. The recorded seismogram is the result of the source signal convolved with the Earth's impulse response. By analyzing the characteristics of the recorded signals and employing signal processing techniques like deconvolution (effectively trying to "undo" the convolution), geophysicists can infer properties of the subsurface, such as the location of oil and gas reservoirs or the structure of geological faults.

The theoretical framework of signals and systems, particularly the concepts of linearity and time-invariance, provides a powerful set of tools for analyzing and designing a wide range of engineering systems. It allows engineers to move beyond simply observing data to understanding the underlying mechanisms that generate and transform that data. This foundational knowledge is indispensable for anyone seeking to work with, analyze, or develop sophisticated engineering systems, especially in the era of big data where the ability to extract meaningful information from complex signal streams is paramount. The study of these fundamental concepts prepares us to delve into more advanced signal processing techniques, enabling us to solve intricate problems across various engineering disciplines. The elegance of LTI system theory lies in its ability to simplify complex real-world phenomena into manageable mathematical models, paving the way for predictable and reliable system design and analysis. This theoretical underpinning is not merely academic; it is the bedrock upon which much of modern engineering technology is built.

The direct examination of a signal in its temporal progression, known as time-domain analysis, offers an intuitive and fundamental approach to understanding the information embedded within it. This perspective allows us to observe how a signal changes moment by moment, revealing its underlying characteristics without the need for transformations into other domains, such as frequency. It is akin to watching a movie unfold frame by frame, where the sequence of events and their progression are directly apparent. This approach is often the initial step in signal processing, providing a foundational understanding before more complex analytical techniques are applied.

One of the most immediate observations in the time domain is the presence of
**trends**. A trend represents a general direction or movement in the signal over an extended period. This could be an upward trend, indicating a gradual increase in the signal's value, a downward trend signifying a decrease, or a relatively flat trend suggesting stability. Identifying trends is crucial in many applications. For example, in financial markets, an upward trend in a stock price might indicate growing investor confidence, while a downward trend could signal potential problems. In environmental monitoring, a rising trend in global average temperature is a key indicator of climate change. In manufacturing, a trend in sensor readings from a piece of machinery might foreshadow an impending failure, allowing for preventative maintenance. Mathematically, a trend can often be approximated by a linear function, where the signal's value increases or decreases at a roughly constant rate over time. More complex trends might involve polynomial functions or other non-linear models. The process of trend analysis often involves smoothing the signal to remove short-term fluctuations and highlight the longer-term movement. Techniques like moving averages or polynomial fitting can be employed for this purpose. A simple moving average, for instance, calculates the average of the signal over a sliding window of time, effectively smoothing out abrupt changes and revealing the underlying trend.

Beyond gradual trends, signals frequently exhibit
**patterns**, which are recurring or predictable structures within the data. The most common and significant type of pattern is periodicity. A **periodic signal** repeats itself exactly after a fixed interval of time, known as the period. Think of the regular rise and fall of tides, the oscillation of a pendulum, or the alternating current supplied to our homes. The time-domain representation of a periodic signal clearly shows these repeating cycles. For instance, a daily temperature profile might show a pattern of rising during the day and falling at night, repeating every 24 hours. In audio signals, musical notes are characterized by their fundamental

frequency and its associated waveform, which repeats periodically. Even complex signals like speech can exhibit periodic components related to vocal cord vibrations (voicing).

Detecting and analyzing these periodic patterns is a cornerstone of time-domain analysis. The

**period** ($T$) is the duration of one complete cycle. The **frequency** ($f$) is the inverse of the period ($f = 1/T$), representing the number of cycles per unit of time. For discrete-time signals, we often speak of the number of samples in a period or the sampling frequency, which relates to how often samples are taken. Visual inspection of a time-domain plot can often reveal periodicity if the pattern is clear and the duration is not excessively long. For more subtle or complex periodicities, mathematical tools are employed. Autocorrelation is a powerful technique that measures the similarity of a signal with a time-shifted version of itself. High correlation at a specific time shift indicates a repeating pattern with a period corresponding to that shift. For example, if we have a signal representing daily sales data, computing its autocorrelation might reveal a strong peak at a lag of 7 samples (days), indicating a weekly sales cycle.

Not all patterns are perfectly periodic. Many signals exhibit **quasi-periodic** behavior, where patterns repeat with some variation or irregularity. Biological signals, like heart rate, can be quasi-periodic. While there's a general rhythm, the exact timing between beats can vary slightly due to physiological factors. Identifying and quantifying these variations can be as important as identifying the underlying rhythm itself. Other non-periodic patterns might include transient events, such as spikes or dips, that occur irregularly. These could represent specific occurrences, like a sudden surge in network traffic or a momentary drop in sensor readings due to interference. Characterizing these events requires defining their duration, amplitude, and frequency of occurrence.

In addition to trends and patterns, understanding the overall distribution and variability of the signal's amplitude is crucial. This is where

**descriptive statistics** come into play. These statistics provide a quantitative summary of the signal's behavior in the time domain.

The
**mean** (or average) of a signal provides a central tendency, representing the typical value of the signal over the observed period. For a continuous-time signal $x(t)$ over an interval $[-T, T]$, the mean is calculated as:
$\mux = \frac{1}{2T} \int{-T}^{T} x(t) dt$.
For a discrete-time signal $x[n]$ over $N$ samples (e.g., from $n=0$ to $N-1$), the mean is:
$\mux = \frac{1}{N} \sum{n=0}^{N-1} x[n]$.
The mean is a fundamental measure of the signal's DC (direct current) component – its steady-state offset. For example, in an audio signal, the mean is typically close to zero, as sound waves oscillate around ambient pressure. However, if there's a constant background hum or bias, the mean will reflect that. In sensor data, a non-zero mean might indicate a calibration offset or a baseline operating level.

While the mean tells us the signal's center, it doesn't tell us anything about how spread out the signal's values are. This is where measures of **dispersion** or **variability** become essential. The **variance** ($\sigma^2_x$) quantifies the average squared difference of the signal values from the mean. It indicates how much the signal tends to deviate from its average. For a continuous-time signal:
$\sigma^2x = \frac{1}{2T} \int{-T}^{T} (x(t) - \mu_x)^2 dt$.
And for a discrete-time signal:
$\sigma^2x = \frac{1}{N} \sum{n=0}^{N-1} (x[n] - \mu_x)^2$.
A high variance suggests that the signal's values fluctuate widely around the mean, indicating significant variability or noise. A low variance means the signal values are tightly clustered around the mean, suggesting a stable or predictable signal. For instance, a temperature sensor in a climate-controlled room would likely have a low variance, while a sensor measuring outdoor temperature during a storm would exhibit high variance.

The
**standard deviation** ($\sigma_x$) is the square root of the variance: $\sigmax = \sqrt{\sigma^2x}$.
It is often preferred because it is in the same units as the original signal, making it easier to interpret. A standard deviation of 5 degrees Celsius, for example, provides a more direct sense of temperature fluctuation than a variance of 25 (degrees Celsius)$^2$. Together, the mean and standard deviation offer a concise statistical description of a signal's amplitude distribution. They are particularly useful for understanding the signal-to-noise ratio. If the standard deviation is large compared to the mean, it implies that noise or variability is a significant component of the signal.

Consider a practical example from the field of manufacturing. Imagine monitoring the vibration levels of a critical machine component. The vibration signal is collected over time.

Initially, we plot the raw vibration signal. We might observe that the overall level of vibration seems to be slowly increasing over the past week – this is a **trend**. Upon closer inspection of the waveform, we might notice a distinct oscillatory pattern repeating with a regular frequency, perhaps indicative of a rotating part. This is a **periodic pattern**. To quantify the typical vibration level, we calculate the **mean** of the signal. If the machine is operating normally, this mean might be relatively stable. However, if there are sudden jolts or impacts, these would cause temporary spikes, increasing the signal's **variance** and **standard deviation**. A sudden increase in the standard deviation, even if the mean remains constant, could signal a developing problem, such as a bearing wear or an imbalance, that is causing increased erratic motion without necessarily shifting the average vibration level. Analyzing these statistics over time can provide early warnings of potential equipment failure, allowing for scheduled maintenance and preventing costly downtime.

Another example can be found in biomedical engineering, specifically in analyzing electrocardiogram (ECG) signals. An ECG records the electrical activity of the heart. In its time-domain representation, we observe a series of waveforms corresponding to different phases of the cardiac cycle: P wave, QRS complex, and T wave. The regular repetition of these complexes signifies a healthy, rhythmic heartbeat – a clear **periodic pattern**. The time interval between successive R peaks (the R-R interval) is a critical measure. If this interval is relatively constant, it indicates a stable heart rate. Deviations from this regularity, known as heart rate variability (HRV), can be analyzed. While the overall mean heart rate might be within normal limits, changes in the variance and standard deviation of the R-R intervals can reveal important information about the autonomic nervous system's control over the heart. For instance, a decrease in HRV (lower variance in R-R intervals) can be an indicator of stress or an underlying medical condition. Furthermore, in some cardiac arrhythmias, the shape or timing of the P, QRS, or T waves might exhibit subtle changes or deviations from the norm – these are deviations from the expected periodic pattern that require careful detection.

In audio signal processing, time-domain analysis is fundamental for understanding characteristics like loudness and transient events. The **amplitude** of an audio signal directly corresponds to its perceived loudness. However, loudness is not simply the instantaneous amplitude, as it is perceived logarithmically by the human ear. Instead, measures like the Root Mean Square (RMS) amplitude are often used as a proxy for loudness over short time intervals. Calculating the RMS amplitude involves squaring the signal values, averaging them over a short window, and then taking the square root. This effectively smooths out rapid fluctuations and provides a more stable measure of the signal's energy or intensity. For instance, in an audio recording of speech, the RMS amplitude would increase during louder syllables and decrease during softer ones. Sudden, sharp increases in amplitude, like those produced by a drum hit or a clap, are known as **transients**. Detecting and analyzing these transients is important in tasks like beat detection in music or identifying specific sounds in a soundscape.

The
**peak amplitude** of a signal represents the maximum absolute value it reaches within a given time interval. This is important for avoiding signal clipping in amplification or transmission systems. If a signal's peak amplitude exceeds the dynamic range of a device, it will be distorted. Therefore, understanding the peak amplitude helps in setting appropriate gain levels.

Beyond simple amplitude measures, the
**zero-crossing rate** (ZCR) is another time-domain statistic that can provide insights into the signal's characteristics. The ZCR is the rate at which the signal changes sign, i.e., crosses the zero amplitude axis. For a continuous-time signal, it is the number of times $x(t)$ crosses zero per unit time. For a discrete-time signal, it's the number of times $x[n]$ changes sign from positive to negative or vice versa. A high ZCR often indicates a signal with high-frequency components or significant activity, while a low ZCR suggests a signal that is relatively constant, slowly varying, or has a dominant DC component. For example, in speech processing, voiced sounds tend to have a lower ZCR than unvoiced sounds because the vocal cords produce more regular, lower-frequency oscillations. In analyzing machine vibrations, a sudden increase in ZCR might correlate with the onset of new, higher-frequency vibrations.

The
**instantaneous amplitude** of a signal can also be thought of in terms of its envelope. The envelope of a signal describes the overall shape of its amplitude variations, often by tracking its peaks or by using techniques like the Hilbert transform. For example, a modulated signal, like an amplitude-modulated radio wave, has a carrier wave that oscillates rapidly, but its amplitude is varied according to an information-bearing signal. The envelope of the modulated signal would precisely follow this

lower-frequency information signal. Extracting this envelope allows us to recover the original transmitted information. In speech, the envelope of the speech signal reflects the changing characteristics of the vocal tract, which are crucial for distinguishing different phonemes.

In summary, time-domain analysis provides a direct and intuitive window into the nature of a signal. By examining how a signal evolves over time, we can identify fundamental characteristics such as long-term **trends**, recurring **patterns** (especially periodicity), and quantify its overall behavior through **descriptive statistics** like the mean, variance, and standard deviation. Furthermore, analyzing **amplitude variations**, including peak values, RMS levels, and the signal's envelope, along with measures like the zero-crossing rate, provides deeper insights into the signal's dynamic range, energy, and spectral content without explicit frequency decomposition. These techniques are the initial, essential steps in extracting meaningful information from raw data, forming the bedrock for more sophisticated signal processing applications across diverse engineering and scientific disciplines. Whether it's monitoring industrial machinery, analyzing physiological signals, or processing communication waveforms, the ability to interpret and quantify a signal's temporal behavior is paramount.
While time-domain analysis offers an intimate view of a signal's evolution, it can sometimes obscure the fundamental building blocks that constitute its complexity. Many signals, especially those arising from physical phenomena, are inherently periodic or composed of multiple periodic components operating at different rates. Observing these underlying frequencies directly in the time domain can be challenging, particularly when they are masked by noise, transient events, or when the signal is a superposition of many such components. This is where the powerful paradigm of **frequency-domain analysis** comes into play. Instead of examining how a signal changes over time, frequency-domain analysis shifts our perspective to ask: what frequencies are present in this signal, and what are their respective strengths?

The cornerstone of frequency-domain analysis is the **Fourier Transform**, named after the brilliant French mathematician Jean-Baptiste Joseph Fourier. Fourier's groundbreaking insight was that virtually any signal, regardless of its apparent complexity, can be represented as a sum of simple sinusoidal (sine and cosine) waves of different frequencies, amplitudes, and phases. This decomposition is immensely powerful because sinusoids are well-understood and mathematically tractable. By transforming a signal from its time-domain representation, $x(t)$, to its frequency-domain representation, $X(f)$, we gain access to a new dimension of information – the spectral content of the signal. This frequency spectrum, $X(f)$, essentially tells us "how much" of each frequency is present in the original signal.

The mathematical formulation of the Fourier Transform for a continuous-time signal $x(t)$ is given by:

$X(f) = \int_{-\infty}^{\infty} x(t) e^{-j2\pi ft} dt$

where:

- $X(f)$ is the Fourier Transform of $x(t)$, a complex-valued function representing the amplitude and phase of each frequency component $f$.
- $x(t)$ is the time-domain signal.
- $f$ is the frequency in Hertz (Hz).
- $t$ is time.
- $e^{-j2\pi ft}$ is Euler's formula, $e^{-j\theta} = \cos(\theta) - j\sin(\theta)$, where $j$ is the imaginary unit ($\sqrt{-1}$). The integral essentially correlates the signal $x(t)$ with complex exponentials at each frequency $f$. The imaginary unit $j$ signifies that the result of the transform is a complex number, which carries both magnitude (amplitude) and phase information for each frequency component.

For discrete-time signals, which are ubiquitous in digital systems, a related transform called the **Discrete Fourier Transform (DFT)** is used. If we have a sequence of $N$ samples $x[n]$ (where $n=0, 1, \ldots, N-1$), the DFT is defined as:

$X[k] = \sum_{n=0}^{N-1} x[n] e^{-j2\pi kn/N}$

where:

- $X[k]$ is the DFT of $x[n]$, representing the amplitude and phase at discrete frequency bins $k$.
- $k$ is the frequency index, ranging from $0$ to $N-1$.
- $N$ is the total number of samples.

The DFT is computationally intensive, leading to the development of the highly efficient **Fast Fourier Transform (FFT)** algorithm, which computes the DFT much faster, especially for large $N$. In practice, the FFT is the workhorse for spectral analysis in digital signal processing.

The output of the Fourier Transform, $X(f)$, is generally a complex-valued function. The **magnitude** of $X(f)$, often denoted as $|X(f)|$, represents the amplitude of the frequency component at $f$. This is typically what we refer to when we talk about the "spectrum" of a signal – a plot of $|X(f)|$ versus $f$ reveals the dominant frequencies and their relative strengths. The **phase** of $X(f)$, denoted as $\arg(X(f))$, provides information about the timing or alignment of each frequency component relative to a reference. While magnitude is often the primary focus for identifying spectral content, phase information is crucial for reconstructing the original signal accurately or for analyzing how different frequency components interact.

Let's consider a simple example. Imagine a signal that is a pure sine wave: $x(t) = A \sin(2\pi f
*0 t)$. In the time domain, this signal oscillates smoothly between $+A$ and $-A$ with a period of $1/f*0$. If we apply the Fourier Transform to this signal, we would find that it contains only two frequency components: one at $+f*0$ and another at $-f*0$. (The negative frequency arises from the mathematical representation of sine waves using complex exponentials, and it's related to the direction of rotation in the complex plane. For real-valued signals, the spectrum is typically symmetric around zero frequency). The magnitude spectrum $|X(f)|$ would show two sharp peaks, one at $f*0$ and one at $-f*0$, both with an amplitude proportional to $A$. All other frequencies would have a magnitude of zero.

Now, consider a signal that is a sum of two sine waves: $x(t) = A
*1 \sin(2\pi f*1 t) + A*2 \sin(2\pi f*2 t)$. In the time domain, this signal appears more complex, as the two oscillations interfere with each other. However, its Fourier Transform would reveal two distinct peaks, one at $f*1$ with magnitude proportional to $A*1$, and another at $f*2$ with magnitude proportional to $A*2$. This demonstrates the power of the Fourier Transform: it can disentangle a complex signal into its fundamental sinusoidal constituents, making the underlying periodicities explicitly visible.

This ability to reveal hidden periodicities is invaluable. For instance, in mechanical engineering, analyzing the vibration of machinery is crucial for diagnostics and prognostics. A rotating shaft with an imbalance will generate vibrations at a specific frequency corresponding to its rotation speed. If there are gear meshes, their interaction will produce vibrations at multiples of the gear's rotational frequency. By taking the Fourier Transform of vibration sensor data, engineers can create a **vibration signature** of the machine. Peaks in the spectrum at known characteristic frequencies can indicate specific faults. For example, a dominant peak at the shaft's rotational frequency might suggest an imbalance, while a peak at a different frequency could point to bearing wear or gear damage. Identifying **resonant frequencies** of a structure is another critical application. If a structure is subjected to vibrations at its natural resonant frequency, the amplitude of vibrations can grow dangerously large, potentially leading to catastrophic failure. Spectrum analysis can pinpoint these resonant frequencies, allowing engineers to design systems that avoid excitation at these critical frequencies or to implement damping mechanisms.

In acoustics and audio processing, frequency-domain analysis is fundamental. The human ear perceives sound based on its frequency content. A musical instrument's unique timbre or sound quality is largely determined by the combination and relative strengths of its fundamental frequency and its
**harmonics** (integer multiples of the fundamental frequency). The Fourier Transform allows us to analyze the harmonic spectrum of a note played by an instrument, which is a key characteristic for sound synthesis, identification, and manipulation. For example, the difference in the harmonic content between a clarinet and a violin playing the same note allows us to distinguish them. Analyzing the spectrum of speech can reveal information about the fundamental frequency of vocal cord vibration (pitch) and the resonant frequencies of the vocal tract (formants), which are crucial for distinguishing vowels and consonants.

Consider a scenario in civil engineering where a bridge is being subjected to wind loads. The wind can induce vibrations in the bridge structure. While the wind itself might have a complex, seemingly random temporal pattern, it can contain gusts at various frequencies. If any of these wind-induced frequencies match a natural frequency of the bridge, resonance can occur, leading to excessive oscillations. By performing a frequency analysis on vibration data collected from the bridge, engineers can identify which frequencies are most strongly excited. If these match predicted natural frequencies, it signals a potential risk. The magnitude of the spectral components at these frequencies indicates the severity of the excitation. This allows for targeted interventions, such as adding dampers or modifying the bridge's aerodynamic profile to reduce the amplification of vibrations at critical frequencies.

Another practical application is in electrical engineering, particularly in analyzing power systems and signal filtering. When dealing with AC (alternating current) power, the fundamental frequency is typically 50 Hz or 60 Hz, depending on the region. However, non-linear loads or switching power supplies can introduce harmonics – frequencies that are integer multiples of the fundamental frequency (e.g., 100 Hz, 150 Hz, 200 Hz, etc.). These harmonics can cause problems like increased heating in transformers and conductors, interference with sensitive electronic equipment, and distortion of the voltage and current waveforms. Spectrum analysis, often using the FFT, is used to measure the level of these harmonics and assess the power quality of the system. This information is crucial for designing filters to mitigate harmonic distortion and ensure reliable operation of electrical equipment.

In the realm of communications, frequency-domain analysis is indispensable. Radio waves are transmitted and received at specific carrier frequencies. A communication channel, however, doesn't transmit just a single frequency perfectly; it has a certain bandwidth, meaning it can effectively pass a range of frequencies. Modulation techniques, like Amplitude Modulation (AM) and Frequency Modulation (FM), encode information by altering the amplitude or frequency of a carrier wave. The resulting modulated signal occupies a certain bandwidth in the frequency domain. Analyzing the spectrum of a transmitted signal is essential for channel allocation, interference detection, and ensuring that the signal stays within its allocated frequency band. For example, when multiple radio stations transmit simultaneously, their signals must occupy distinct, non-overlapping frequency bands to avoid interfering with each other.

Spectrum analyzers are used to monitor these bands and ensure compliance.

The concept of a **power spectral density (PSD)** is closely related to the Fourier Transform and is widely used to describe the distribution of signal power over frequency. For a wide-sense stationary random process, the PSD, $S_x(f)$, provides the power per unit frequency. It is often computed using the FFT of segments of the signal. A plot of PSD versus frequency clearly shows where the signal's energy is concentrated. For example, a noisy signal might have a relatively flat PSD across a wide range of frequencies, indicating that noise is present uniformly. A signal with a strong periodic component will have sharp peaks in its PSD at the corresponding frequencies.

The inverse relationship between the time and frequency domains is also a fundamental concept. A signal that is very short in duration (a sharp pulse) will have a very wide frequency spectrum, containing many different frequencies. Conversely, a signal that is very spread out in time and changes slowly will have a narrow frequency spectrum, concentrated around low frequencies. This is an illustration of the uncertainty principle as applied to signals. A signal cannot be simultaneously arbitrarily narrow in both the time domain and the frequency domain. This has practical implications. For instance, to precisely localize an event in time (e.g., detect a very short transient), we typically need to analyze a wide range of frequencies. Conversely, to isolate a very specific frequency (e.g., filter out a narrow band of interference), the resulting filtered signal will be spread out more in time.

The Fourier Transform, and by extension the FFT, allows us to perform operations in the frequency domain that might be difficult or impossible in the time domain. For example, filtering a signal to remove unwanted frequencies is often more efficiently and effectively achieved by transforming the signal to the frequency domain, multiplying its spectrum by a filter's frequency response, and then transforming back to the time domain (using the Inverse Fourier Transform). This is particularly true for linear filtering operations.

Let's delve into a more detailed example. Suppose we have an audio recording that contains a persistent, annoying hum at 60 Hz, a common artifact from electrical interference. In the time domain, this hum is mixed with the desired audio signal, making it difficult to isolate and remove. However, in the frequency domain, this 60 Hz hum will appear as a distinct peak in the magnitude spectrum. We can then design a **notch filter** – a filter that attenuates a specific narrow band of frequencies. In the frequency domain, this notch filter is represented by a frequency response that is close to 1 for most frequencies but drops sharply to near 0 at 60 Hz. By multiplying the FFT of the audio signal by this notch filter's frequency response, we effectively suppress the 60 Hz component. Transforming the result back to the time domain yields an audio signal with the annoying hum significantly reduced or eliminated, while ideally preserving the desired audio content. This process is known as frequency-domain filtering.

The concept of the **spectrum analyzer** is a practical implementation of FFT-based frequency-domain analysis. These instruments take an input signal, often an electrical waveform, and display its frequency spectrum in real-time. They are crucial tools in fields ranging from telecommunications and radio frequency engineering to acoustic analysis and scientific research. Users can visually inspect the spectrum to identify signal components, measure their amplitudes and frequencies, detect interference, and verify system performance.

When analyzing signals that are not perfectly periodic or stationary (i.e.,

their statistical properties change over time), more advanced techniques are often employed. The
**Short-Time Fourier Transform (STFT)** is a modification of the Fourier Transform designed for non-stationary signals. Instead of transforming the entire signal at once, the STFT divides the signal into short, overlapping segments (windows) and computes the Fourier Transform of each segment. This results in a time-frequency representation of the signal, often visualized as a **spectrogram**. A spectrogram plots time on one axis, frequency on another, and the intensity or color at each point represents the magnitude of the frequency component at that specific time. Spectrograms are incredibly useful for visualizing how the spectral content of a signal evolves over time. For example, in speech analysis, a spectrogram can clearly show the transitions between different phonemes as changes in frequency patterns over short time intervals. In analyzing musical signals, a spectrogram can reveal how the fundamental frequencies and harmonics of notes change as a melody progresses. The choice of window size in the STFT involves a trade-off: a shorter window provides better time resolution (allowing us to pinpoint when a frequency appears or disappears) but poorer frequency resolution (making it harder to distinguish between closely spaced frequencies). Conversely, a longer window provides better frequency resolution but poorer time resolution.

Another powerful tool for analyzing non-stationary signals is the **wavelet transform**. Unlike the STFT, which uses fixed-size windows for all frequencies, the wavelet transform uses windows of varying sizes. It employs short windows for high frequencies (to capture rapid changes) and long windows for low frequencies (to capture slow variations). This adaptive nature often provides a more nuanced time-frequency representation, especially for signals with transient features or abrupt changes. Wavelets are particularly adept at analyzing signals with fractal properties or those exhibiting self-similarity across different scales, a common characteristic in natural phenomena.

In summary, frequency-domain analysis, powered by the Fourier Transform and its efficient implementation, the FFT, offers a profound shift in perspective from examining how signals evolve over time to understanding their constituent frequencies. It allows us to decompose complex signals into simpler sinusoidal components, revealing underlying periodicities, harmonic structures, and spectral characteristics that are often hidden in the time domain. This capability is fundamental to a vast array of applications, including diagnosing mechanical faults through vibration analysis, understanding acoustic signatures, designing and analyzing communication systems, ensuring power quality, and processing complex biological signals. By analyzing the magnitude and phase of these frequency components, we gain deep insights into the physical processes that generate the signals, enabling more accurate modeling, effective filtering, and robust detection of critical information. The transition from the time domain to the frequency domain unlocks a richer understanding of the signal's fundamental nature.

The previous discussion highlighted the power of the frequency domain, enabling us to decompose complex signals into their fundamental sinusoidal components. While this spectral view reveals the "what" of a signal's frequency content, it also opens the door to manipulating that content. Often, raw signals from sensors or experimental setups are corrupted by unwanted disturbances, such as random electrical noise, power line hum, or transient spikes. These imperfections can obscure the underlying signal of interest, making subsequent analysis or feature extraction unreliable. This is where the art and science of **filtering** come into play. Filtering, in essence, is the process of selectively attenuating or amplifying certain frequency components of a signal, thereby modifying its spectral characteristics to enhance desirable features or remove undesirable ones.

In the digital realm, filtering is implemented using algorithms that operate on sequences of sampled data. These algorithms, known as

**digital filters**, are designed to achieve specific frequency-selective behaviors. The most fundamental types of digital filters are characterized by their response to different frequency ranges:

**Low-Pass Filters (LPFs):** These filters allow frequencies below a certain cutoff frequency to pass through relatively unimpeded while significantly attenuating frequencies above it. Imagine trying to read a newspaper on a windy day; the wind gusts are analogous to high-frequency noise that can obscure the text. A low-pass filter acts like a gentle shield, smoothing out these rapid fluctuations and allowing you to focus on the slower-varying features of the text. In practice, low-pass filtering is often used for **smoothing** noisy data. For instance, a temperature sensor might exhibit rapid fluctuations due to electrical interference or minor environmental changes. Applying a low-pass filter can smooth out these erratic variations, revealing the underlying trend of the temperature change more clearly. This is particularly useful when the signal of interest is expected to change slowly over time, and high-frequency components are likely to be noise. Consider a financial time series: while daily fluctuations can be significant, the underlying long-term trend might be what an analyst is interested in. A low-pass filter can help to reveal this trend by removing the short-term noise.

Mathematically, a simple form of a digital low-pass filter can be implemented using a moving average. For a signal $x[n]$, a simple moving average filter of length $M$ computes the output $y[n]$ as:

$y[n] = \frac{1}{M} \sum_{i=0}^{M-1} x[n-i]$

This operation effectively averages $M$ consecutive samples, which inherently smooths out rapid variations. The larger the value of $M$, the more pronounced the smoothing effect, but also the greater the attenuation of higher frequencies. The cutoff frequency of this moving average filter is inversely related to $M$. While intuitive and easy to implement, the moving average filter has some limitations, such as a gradual rolloff (the transition from passing to attenuating frequencies is not abrupt) and a phase shift that can be undesirable in certain applications. More sophisticated digital low-pass filters, such as Butterworth, Chebyshev, or Elliptic filters, offer sharper transitions and more controlled phase responses, but they involve more complex mathematical design.

**High-Pass Filters (HPFs):** Conversely, high-pass filters allow frequencies above a certain cutoff frequency to pass while attenuating frequencies below it. These filters are useful for **feature enhancement** by highlighting rapid changes or transient events. If our signal of interest is a sudden event, like a brief spike or a sharp transition, and it's masked by a slow drift or a constant offset, a high-pass filter can effectively remove the low-frequency components, making the transient feature more prominent. For example, in analyzing the impact sound of a collision, the initial sharp acoustic event carries crucial information. A high-pass filter can help isolate this event by removing the ambient, lower-frequency background noise. In some image processing contexts, high-pass filtering can be used to detect edges or fine details by emphasizing high-frequency spatial variations.

A simple digital high-pass filter can be conceived as the complement of a low-pass filter. For instance, if we have a smoothed signal $y[n]$ (obtained using a low-pass filter), the original signal $x[n]$ can be thought of as the sum of the smooth component $y[n]$ and the high-frequency "detail" component $d[n]$ (i.e., $x[n] = y[n] + d[n]$). Therefore, the detail component, which represents the high-frequency content, can be approximated by $d[n] = x[n] - y[n]$. This difference operation, when applied with a smoothing filter, acts as a high-pass filter.

**Band-Pass Filters (BPFs):** These filters allow frequencies within a specific range (a band) to pass through, while attenuating frequencies both below and above this band. Band-pass filters are essential when we are interested in a particular frequency component or a narrow range of frequencies within a signal that might contain energy across a wide spectrum. For instance, in telecommunications, a receiver is tuned to a specific carrier frequency. A band-pass filter is used to isolate the desired signal at that carrier frequency and reject signals at other frequencies, as well as out-of-band noise. In audio processing, if we want to isolate a specific instrument's frequency range in a musical piece, a band-pass filter is the tool of choice.

A band-pass filter can often be realized by cascading a low-pass filter with a high-pass filter, where the cutoff frequency of the low-pass filter is higher than the cutoff frequency of the high-pass filter. The band between these two cutoff frequencies is then allowed to pass.

**Band-Stop Filters (BSFs) or Notch Filters:** These are the inverse of band-pass filters. They attenuate frequencies within a specific range (a band) while allowing frequencies outside this band to pass. Notch filters are a common type of band-stop filter that targets a very narrow band of frequencies for attenuation. Their most prominent application is in removing specific, persistent interfering frequencies. A classic example is removing the 50 Hz or 60 Hz hum generated by electrical power lines, which often contaminates biological signals (like ECGs or EEGs) or audio recordings. A notch filter designed to target precisely 60 Hz can effectively eliminate this unwanted component without significantly affecting the rest of the signal.

Designing effective digital filters involves understanding their characteristics in the frequency domain, specifically their **frequency response**. The frequency response of a filter describes how the filter affects the amplitude and phase of different frequency components of the input signal. It is typically represented by two functions: the **magnitude response** (which shows the gain or attenuation at each frequency) and the **phase response** (which shows the phase shift introduced at each frequency). The goal of filter design is to shape these responses to achieve the desired filtering action.

The trade-off between the sharpness of the filter's transition band (the region between the passband, where frequencies are allowed to pass, and the stopband, where frequencies are attenuated) and the complexity of the filter is a crucial consideration. Filters with very sharp transitions are often referred to as "brick-wall" filters, but achieving such ideal behavior digitally can lead to significant computational complexity and undesirable artifacts like ringing (oscillations) in the time-domain output. Therefore, a balance is usually struck between ideal performance and practical implementation constraints.

Beyond these basic types, filters can be classified based on their implementation:

**Finite Impulse Response (FIR) Filters:** These filters have an impulse response that is of finite duration. Their output is a weighted sum of current and past input samples. FIR filters are known for their stability and for their ability to have a linear phase response, which is critical in applications where phase distortion must be minimized (e.g., preserving the waveform of audio signals or preventing timing errors in communication systems). However, achieving sharp frequency selectivity with FIR filters often requires a large number of coefficients, leading to higher computational cost.

**Infinite Impulse Response (IIR) Filters:** These filters have an impulse response that theoretically lasts forever. Their output depends not only on current and past input samples but also on past output samples. IIR filters can achieve sharper frequency selectivity with fewer coefficients compared to FIR filters, making them computationally more efficient. However, they can be prone to instability if not designed carefully, and their phase response is generally non-linear, which can be a drawback. Popular IIR filter designs include Butterworth, Chebyshev, and Elliptic filters, which are often derived from their analog counterparts.

The process of
**smoothing** noisy sensor readings is a prime example where low-pass filtering is indispensable. Imagine a sensor measuring the position of a robotic arm. Due to mechanical vibrations, electrical noise in the sensor itself, and quantization errors from the analog-to-digital converter, the raw position data might appear as a jagged line, making it difficult to determine the arm's actual trajectory or to use it for precise control. Applying a low-pass filter, such as a moving average or a more sophisticated digital filter, can effectively reduce these high-frequency fluctuations. The output will be a smoother curve that better represents the intended motion of the arm. The degree of smoothing is controlled by the filter's cutoff frequency or its order (which relates to the number of filter coefficients or the complexity of its design). A lower cutoff frequency or a higher-order filter will result in more aggressive smoothing, but it will also attenuate legitimate high-frequency components of the signal, potentially leading to a loss of detail or introducing lag.

Conversely,
**denoising** can sometimes involve more than just low-pass filtering. If the noise has a specific spectral characteristic that is different from the signal,

we might use band-stop or notch filters. For instance, if we are recording the sound of a musical instrument in a room with fluorescent lights, we might encounter a distinct buzzing sound at twice the mains frequency (e.g., 100 Hz or 120 Hz) due to the lights. A notch filter specifically tuned to this frequency can remove this buzz without significantly altering the music.

**Feature enhancement** is another crucial application domain for filtering. Consider analyzing seismic data to detect subtle earthquake tremors. These tremors might be characterized by specific frequency bands. Background noise, such as seismic activity from distant sources or human-made disturbances, might occupy different frequency ranges. By applying a band-pass filter tuned to the expected frequency range of the tremors, we can amplify the signal of interest and suppress irrelevant noise, making the tremors easier to detect and analyze. Similarly, in medical imaging, specific filters can be applied to highlight certain tissue characteristics or to suppress artifacts. For example, a filter might be designed to enhance the visibility of fine vascular structures in an MRI scan by emphasizing signals within a particular frequency range that corresponds to the blood flow.

The choice of filter and its parameters (cutoff frequencies, filter order, type of filter design) depends heavily on the specific application and the characteristics of the signal and noise. This often involves a process of experimentation and iterative refinement. We might start with a filter design based on our prior knowledge of the signal and noise, analyze the filtered output, and then adjust the filter parameters to achieve a better result. For example, if after applying a low-pass filter for smoothing, the resulting signal appears too "laggy" or has lost too much detail, we might increase the cutoff frequency or switch to a filter with a gentler rolloff.

It's also important to note that filtering is often just one step in a larger data processing pipeline. The output of a filter is typically fed into subsequent stages, such as feature extraction, classification, or visualization. The effectiveness of these later stages is highly dependent on the quality of the data produced by the filtering process. Therefore, a thorough understanding of filtering techniques and their implications is fundamental for any data engineer or machine learning practitioner. The ability to selectively shape a signal's frequency content provides a powerful tool for extracting meaningful information from otherwise noisy or cluttered data, paving the way for more accurate analyses and robust system designs.

While the Fourier Transform excels at revealing the global frequency content of a signal, it operates under a fundamental limitation: it assumes that the signal's frequency composition remains constant over its entire duration. This assumption, while valid for many steady-state signals, falters when dealing with phenomena where the spectral characteristics evolve over time. Such signals, often termed **non-stationary**, are prevalent in numerous engineering domains. Consider the acoustic signature of a machine undergoing different operational phases, the changing electrical activity in a biological system, or the dynamic response of a mechanical structure under varying loads. In these scenarios, the frequencies present in the signal are not fixed; they emerge, disappear, and shift, painting a dynamic picture that a static frequency spectrum struggles to capture effectively.

The Fourier Transform, by decomposing a signal into an infinite sum of sinusoids, inherently loses the temporal information associated with each frequency component. While it tells us *which* frequencies are present, it is silent on *when* they are present. This is where the **Wavelet Transform** emerges as a powerful and complementary tool. Unlike the Fourier Transform, which uses infinitely long sine and cosine waves as its basis functions, the wavelet transform employs a set of specially designed, localized functions called **wavelets**.

The key innovation of wavelets lies in their inherent **time-frequency localization**. Imagine a wavelet as a "tiny wave" – it is short in duration and has a finite frequency bandwidth. By using these localized building blocks, the wavelet transform can analyze a signal at different scales and positions in time. This is analogous to using a magnifying glass with adjustable zoom levels to examine a complex image: you can zoom in to see fine details at a specific location (high resolution in time, narrow frequency band) or zoom out to get a broader overview (low resolution in time, wide frequency band).

At its core, the wavelet transform decomposes a signal into a series of scaled and translated versions of a mother wavelet. The **scale** parameter controls the degree of compression or stretching of the wavelet, which in turn relates to the frequency content being analyzed. Larger scales correspond to stretched wavelets, which are sensitive to lower frequencies and capture broader features of the signal. Smaller scales correspond to compressed wavelets, which are sensitive to higher frequencies and can detect rapid, localized events. The **translation** parameter shifts the wavelet along the time axis, allowing us to analyze the signal at different points in time.

Mathematically, the continuous wavelet transform (CWT) of a signal $x(t)$ is defined as:

$$W(a, b) = \frac{1}{\sqrt{|a|}} \int_{-\infty}^{\infty} x(t) \overline{\psi\left(\frac{t-b}{a}\right)} dt$$

Here, $\psi(t)$ is the mother wavelet, and $\overline{\psi(\cdot)}$ denotes its complex conjugate. The parameter $a$ is the

**scale**, and $b$ is the **translation** (time shift). The $\frac{1}{\sqrt{|a|}}$ term is a normalization factor that ensures the energy of the wavelet remains constant across different scales.

The CWT results in a two-dimensional representation of the signal, where one axis represents time (or translation $b$) and the other represents scale (or frequency, as scale is inversely related to frequency). This time-scale (or time-frequency) representation is what gives wavelets their power. It allows us to pinpoint precisely when a certain frequency component (or a feature associated with a particular scale) appears or disappears in the signal.

The choice of the mother wavelet is crucial and depends on the nature of the signal being analyzed and the features one aims to detect. There are many families of wavelets, each with different properties:

**Haar Wavelet:** The simplest wavelet, it is a square pulse. It is excellent for detecting abrupt changes or discontinuities but has limited smoothness, which can lead to blocky representations.

**Daubechies Wavelets (dbN):** A family of orthogonal wavelets that are widely used. They are characterized by their vanishing moments, which relate to their ability to represent polynomial signals exactly. Higher-order Daubechies wavelets are smoother and have better frequency localization but are also more spread out in time.

**Morlet Wavelet:** A complex wavelet, essentially a modulated Gaussian. It is very popular for time-frequency analysis because it offers a good balance between time and frequency resolution. It is well-suited for detecting oscillatory patterns.

**Mexican Hat Wavelet:** The second derivative of a Gaussian function. It is real-valued and good for detecting peaks and edges.

**Meyer Wavelets:** Infinitely differentiable, providing excellent smoothness, but their construction is more complex.

The practical implementation of the wavelet transform often involves a **discrete wavelet transform (DWT)**, which is computationally more efficient. The DWT typically uses filter banks to decompose the signal into different frequency sub-bands. This process, known as **multi-resolution analysis**, iteratively breaks down the signal into a coarse approximation (low frequencies) and detail coefficients (high frequencies).

In a typical DWT implementation using filter banks, the signal is passed through a low-pass filter (associated with approximation coefficients) and a high-pass filter (associated with detail coefficients). The output of these filters is then downsampled by a factor of two. This process is then recursively applied to the approximation coefficients, effectively analyzing the signal at progressively finer scales. For instance, at the first level of decomposition, the signal $x[n]$ is split into:

**Approximation Coefficients ($cA_1[n]$):** Representing the low-frequency components.
**Detail Coefficients ($cD_1[n]$):** Representing the high-frequency components.

This process can be repeated on the approximation coefficients $cA

*1[n]$ to obtain $cA*2[n]$ and $cD_2[n]$, and so on. Each subsequent level of decomposition analyzes the signal at a coarser scale (lower frequency range).

The power of the DWT lies in its ability to perform signal denoising and compression. When a signal is corrupted by noise, the noise often manifests as high-frequency components. By applying a DWT and then thresholding (setting to zero) the detail coefficients at certain levels (especially those that are likely to contain noise), and then reconstructing the signal using the inverse DWT, we can effectively remove the noise while preserving the essential low-frequency structure of the original signal. This is often more effective than traditional low-pass filtering because it can achieve better separation of signal and noise across different time scales.

**Signal Denoising with Wavelets:**
Consider a sensor signal that contains a critical low-frequency trend but is marred by high-frequency random noise. If we were to use a simple low-pass Fourier-based filter, we might smooth out the noise but also risk attenuating some of the important high-frequency variations within the signal itself or introduce undesirable phase shifts. The DWT offers a more nuanced approach. By decomposing the signal into multiple levels of approximation and detail coefficients, we can identify which coefficients correspond to the underlying signal and which are likely to be noise. Typically, the detail coefficients at finer scales (higher frequencies) will contain a larger proportion of noise. A common denoising strategy involves:

1.
**Decomposition:** Apply the DWT to the noisy signal up to a chosen decomposition level. This results in a set of approximation and detail coefficients at various scales.

2. **Thresholding:** For each set of detail coefficients, apply a thresholding rule.
**Hard Thresholding:** Coefficients whose magnitude is below a certain threshold are set to zero. Coefficients above the threshold remain unchanged.
**Soft Thresholding:** Coefficients whose magnitude is below a threshold are set to zero. Coefficients above the threshold are shrunk by the threshold value. Soft thresholding generally leads to smoother results.
The choice of threshold value is critical and can be determined through various methods, such as estimating the noise standard deviation from the finest detail coefficients.
3. **Reconstruction:** Apply the inverse DWT using the modified detail coefficients and the original approximation coefficients to reconstruct the denoised signal.

This process allows for adaptive denoising; it can remove noise more aggressively where it is prevalent (typically at higher frequencies and finer scales) without significantly distorting the signal in frequency bands where the signal energy is dominant.

**Feature Detection and Transient Analysis:**
The ability of wavelets to provide time-frequency localization makes them exceptionally well-suited for detecting transient events – short-lived phenomena that are characterized by a sudden change in frequency content. Examples include:

**Detection of micro-fractures in materials:** These might appear as sudden, sharp impulses in acoustic emission signals.
**Identification of R-peaks in ECG signals:** The R-peak is a distinct, transient spike in the electrocardiogram.

**Analysis of power system disturbances:** Short-circuit events or switching transients in electrical grids produce rapid changes in voltage and current waveforms.
**Localization of anomalies in seismic data:** Earthquakes or other geological events can generate transient wave packets.

In these cases, the wavelet transform will show a high-amplitude response at the specific time and scale that corresponds to the transient event. For instance, a sharp spike in the time domain might correspond to a concentrated energy distribution across a range of finer scales (higher frequencies) at a specific time point in the wavelet transform's time-scale plane. By analyzing the coefficients at different scales and times, one can effectively isolate and characterize these transient features, which might be missed or poorly resolved by traditional Fourier analysis.

Consider a signal containing both a slowly varying trend and a short, high-frequency burst. A Fourier transform would show the dominant low-frequency components and perhaps a broad band of higher frequencies representing the burst, but it wouldn't clearly indicate *when* the burst occurred. A wavelet transform, however, would reveal a localized peak of energy in the time-scale plane, specifically at the time the burst happened and across the scales corresponding to its frequency content. This temporal pinpointing is invaluable for understanding the dynamics of events.

**Comparison with Fourier Transforms:**
While Fourier analysis provides an excellent "what" (which frequencies are present), wavelet analysis offers a more comprehensive "what and when" (which frequencies are present and at what times).

**Time-Frequency Resolution:** Fourier transform offers perfect frequency resolution but zero time resolution. Wavelet transform provides a trade-off: it has finite time and finite frequency resolution. The resolution is often inversely proportional – a narrow wavelet in time will have a broad frequency content, and vice versa. This is sometimes referred to as the **Heisenberg Uncertainty Principle** applied to time-frequency analysis: you cannot simultaneously have arbitrarily precise time and frequency localization. Different wavelets offer different trade-offs in this regard.

**Stationarity Assumption:** Fourier is best for stationary signals, where frequency content is constant. Wavelets are ideal for non-stationary signals, where frequency content changes over time.

**Basis Functions:** Fourier uses sine and cosine waves (sinusoids) that extend infinitely. Wavelets use localized, scaled, and translated versions of a mother wavelet that are finite in duration.

**Applications:** Fourier is fundamental for spectral analysis, steady-state system analysis, and filtering based on fixed frequency bands. Wavelets shine in transient detection, signal denoising, time-varying spectral analysis, data compression, and feature extraction from non-stationary signals.

The ability to analyze signals at multiple resolutions (scales) is a cornerstone of wavelet theory. This
**multi-resolution analysis** allows us to examine a signal at different levels of detail. At a coarse resolution (large scales), we capture the overall trends and slow variations. As we move to finer resolutions (smaller scales), we can detect more subtle features, rapid fluctuations, and localized events. This hierarchical decomposition is akin to inspecting

an object first from a distance and then progressively closer, revealing more and more intricate details.

For example, imagine analyzing vibration data from a complex mechanical system. At a coarse scale, we might identify the fundamental operating frequencies of the main components. As we refine the analysis to finer scales, we could potentially detect higher-frequency harmonics, resonances, or even the signature of a developing fault, such as a bearing defect, which might manifest as specific, intermittent, higher-frequency signals. The wavelet transform provides a rich, multi-dimensional view of this data, enabling a deeper understanding of the system's behavior across different temporal and spectral regimes.

In essence, wavelet transforms provide a powerful lens through which to view signals that possess a dynamic nature. They allow engineers and scientists to decompose complex, time-varying signals into their constituent parts, revealing not just *what* frequencies are present but also *when* they appear and disappear. This temporal and spectral richness is invaluable for diagnosing problems, understanding complex phenomena, and developing more sophisticated signal processing algorithms in fields ranging from mechanical engineering and acoustics to biomedical signal analysis and geophysics. The transition from static spectral analysis to time-frequency analysis, enabled by wavelets, represents a significant advancement in our ability to interpret and manipulate signals from the real world.

# Chapter 4: Feature Engineering for Engineering Data

The journey from raw, unprocessed data to a set of variables that can effectively inform a machine learning model is a crucial one, often dictating the success or failure of an entire project. This transformative process is known as **feature engineering**. At its core, feature engineering is the art and science of selecting, manipulating, and creating features from raw data to improve the performance of predictive models. It's not merely about data cleaning or transformation; it's about leveraging an understanding of the data and the problem domain to craft variables that are more predictive, more discriminative, and ultimately, more useful for the learning algorithm.

In the realm of engineering, data often originates from complex physical processes, intricate machinery, or sophisticated simulations. This data, in its raw form, might be noisy, redundant, or not directly aligned with the specific patterns a model needs to learn. For instance, a time-series of temperature readings from a reactor might contain high-frequency noise that masks the underlying trend of increasing temperature. Simply feeding this raw series into a model might lead to poor predictions or require an overly complex model to overcome the noise. Feature engineering, in this context, would involve techniques to extract a smooth trend, capture the rate of temperature change, or identify anomalies that indicate deviations from normal operation.

The efficacy of feature engineering is deeply intertwined with **domain expertise**. A data scientist with a background solely in machine learning might struggle to uncover the most impactful features from engineering data. Conversely, an experienced engineer who understands the physics of a system, the mechanics of a machine, or the underlying principles of a process can guide the feature engineering process with invaluable insights. This synergy between domain knowledge and data science is what elevates feature engineering from a mechanical data preparation step to a strategic advantage. It allows practitioners to ask the right questions of the data, to hypothesize about what relationships might be important, and to create features that are not just statistically relevant but also physically meaningful.

Consider the example of predictive maintenance for industrial pumps. Raw data might include vibration readings, motor current, temperature sensors, and operational speed. A purely algorithmic approach might involve creating lagged features or rolling averages of these sensor readings. However, an engineer understands that the *interaction* between these variables is often more telling. For instance, an increase in motor current combined with a specific vibration signature at a particular operational speed could be a strong indicator of bearing wear. Feature engineering, guided by this domain knowledge, could involve creating interaction terms (e.g., current speed), ratios (e.g., vibration amplitude / motor current), or transforming variables based on physical principles (e.g., calculating power consumption from current and voltage, if available, which might be more indicative of efficiency degradation than current alone).

The process of feature engineering is inherently iterative. It's rarely a one-shot operation. It often begins with an initial understanding of the problem and the data, leading to the creation of a set of candidate features. These features are then used to train a model, and the model's performance is evaluated. Based on this evaluation, and often in conjunction with further domain exploration or hypothesis testing, new features are created, existing ones are refined, or irrelevant ones are discarded. This cycle of creation, evaluation, and refinement continues until a satisfactory level of model performance is achieved.

The types of features that can be engineered are vast and depend heavily on the nature of the data and the problem. For time-series data, common engineering techniques include:

**Lagged Features:** Values of a variable from previous time steps. For example, the motor current at the previous minute might be a good predictor of the current minute's performance.
**Rolling Statistics:** Aggregations of a variable over a defined window of time. This can include rolling means, medians, standard deviations, minimums, and maximums. A rolling standard deviation of vibration, for instance, can highlight periods of instability.
**Rate of Change (Derivatives):** The difference between consecutive time steps, or more sophisticated numerical derivatives, can capture how quickly a variable is changing. A sudden increase in the rate of temperature rise might be more significant than the absolute temperature itself in predicting a failure.
**Frequency Domain Features:** As discussed in previous contexts, transforms like the Fourier Transform or Wavelet Transform can be used to extract features related to the frequency content of signals. For vibration analysis, dominant frequencies and their amplitudes can indicate specific types of mechanical issues.
**Interaction Features:** Combinations of two or more raw features. As mentioned with the pump example, multiplying or dividing features can reveal synergistic or antagonistic relationships.
**Polynomial Features:** Creating features that are powers of existing features (e.g., temperature squared) can help models capture non-linear relationships.
**Indicator/Binary Features:** Creating binary flags based on thresholds. For example, a feature indicating whether the motor current exceeded a critical threshold for a sustained period.

For tabular data, feature engineering might involve:

**One-Hot Encoding:** Converting categorical variables into binary vectors.

**Target Encoding:** Replacing a categorical variable with the average of the target variable for that category. This can be a powerful way to capture the relationship between a category and the target.
**Binning/Discretization:** Grouping continuous variables into discrete bins. For example, categorizing pressure into "Low," "Medium," and "High."
**Ratio and Difference Features:** Similar to time-series, creating new features by dividing or subtracting existing numerical features. For a structural analysis, the ratio of stresses in different parts of a component might be more telling than the absolute stress values.
**Aggregation:** If the data has a hierarchical structure (e.g., multiple sensor readings per machine), aggregating these readings (e.g., average vibration per machine) can create meaningful features at a higher level.

The process of selecting which features to engineer is as important as the engineering itself. It's about creating features that are **informative** (i.e., they contain signals relevant to the target variable) and **discriminative** (i.e., they help the model distinguish between different classes or predict different values). Redundant or irrelevant features can not only increase computational cost but also lead to overfitting and reduced model generalization. Techniques like correlation analysis, feature importance scores from tree-based models, or dimensionality reduction methods can assist in this selection process.

Moreover, feature engineering needs to be performed with an awareness of the potential for introducing data leakage. Data leakage occurs when information from the future or from outside the training data is inadvertently included in the features used for training. For instance, when calculating rolling statistics for time-series data, ensuring that the calculation for a given time point only uses data from *before* that time point is critical. Similarly, when using target encoding, the target variable's average should be computed only on the training data, and then applied to both training and testing sets.

The art of feature engineering also lies in its creativity. It often involves looking at the problem from different perspectives and hypothesizing about how the underlying physical or operational processes manifest in the data. For instance, in analyzing the performance of an internal combustion engine, raw data might include fuel injection timing, manifold pressure, and exhaust gas temperature. An engineer might hypothesize that the *efficiency* of combustion, which is not directly measured, is a crucial factor. They might then try to engineer a feature that approximates this efficiency, perhaps by combining metrics like the ratio of fuel injected to air mass, or by looking at the rate of temperature increase in the cylinder. This is where the "art" comes into play, transforming seemingly unrelated numerical values into abstract representations that capture essential underlying dynamics.

The science aspect of feature engineering comes from the systematic and empirical validation of engineered features. Once a feature is hypothesized and created, its usefulness needs to be tested. This involves:

1. **Hypothesis Generation:** Based on domain knowledge or exploratory data analysis, hypothesize a relationship between raw data and the target variable, and how it can be best represented by an engineered feature.
2. **Feature Creation:** Implement the transformation or combination of raw data to create the new feature.
3. **Model Training:** Train a model using a baseline set of features and then retrain it with the newly engineered feature(s).
4. **Performance Evaluation:** Quantitatively assess the improvement (or degradation) in model performance using appropriate metrics (e.g., accuracy, precision, recall, AUC, RMSE).

5. **Validation:** For time-series or sequential data, ensure that the feature engineering process does not introduce look-ahead bias. Cross-validation techniques that respect the temporal order of data are essential here.

The development of powerful feature engineering techniques has been greatly accelerated by the advent of more sophisticated machine learning models, particularly deep learning. While deep learning models are often touted as "end-to-end" learning systems that can learn features directly from raw data, this does not diminish the importance of feature engineering, especially in domains with strong physical principles. In fact, domain-specific feature engineering can often lead to:

**More Data-Efficient Models:** When informative features are manually crafted, deep learning models might require less data to achieve good performance, as they are guided towards relevant patterns from the outset.
**More Interpretable Models:** Features that have a clear physical or operational meaning make it easier to understand why a model is making certain predictions. This is crucial in safety-critical engineering applications where explainability is paramount.
**Improved Performance with Simpler Architectures:** Well-engineered features can often allow simpler and faster models to outperform complex deep learning models trained on raw data.

For instance, in computer vision applied to engineering diagnostics (e.g., inspecting welds or structural integrity from images), while CNNs learn hierarchical features automatically, pre-processing steps like edge detection, texture analysis, or color space transformations (which are forms of feature engineering) can still significantly enhance the quality of features learned by the network.

Furthermore, the concept of feature engineering extends beyond simply creating new variables. It also involves the careful selection and transformation of existing variables to better suit a particular model. For example:

**Scaling and Normalization:** Many machine learning algorithms, especially those based on distance calculations or gradient descent (like SVMs, neural networks, and linear regression), are sensitive to the scale of input features. Scaling features to a common range (e.g., [0, 1] or with zero mean and unit variance) is a fundamental part of feature preparation that can be considered a form of feature engineering.
**Log Transformations:** For variables with highly skewed distributions (e.g., component failure counts), applying a logarithmic transformation can often normalize the distribution, making it more amenable to linear models.
**Box-Cox Transformations:** A more generalized power transformation that can handle a wider range of distributions and find an optimal transformation to stabilize variance and improve normality.

The choice of transformation depends on the underlying distribution of the data and the assumptions of the model being used. Understanding these assumptions is key to selecting the appropriate transformation.

A significant challenge in feature engineering for engineering data is the sheer volume and complexity of the data generated by modern systems. Sensor networks can produce terabytes of data daily. Extracting meaningful features from such high-dimensional and high-velocity data streams requires efficient algorithms and a robust computational infrastructure. Techniques like distributed computing (e.g., Spark) and specialized libraries for time-series analysis are often employed to manage this scale.

Moreover, the temporal nature of much engineering data presents unique challenges. Features that are predictive in one operational regime might be irrelevant or even misleading in another. This necessitates the development of adaptive feature engineering strategies that can change as the operating conditions of a system evolve. This might involve building models that can dynamically select or re-engineer features based on current system state.

In conclusion, feature engineering is not a peripheral task but a central pillar of successful machine learning in engineering. It bridges the gap between raw sensor readings and actionable insights by creating data representations that are both statistically powerful and physically interpretable. It demands a blend of analytical rigor, domain-specific knowledge, and creative problem-solving. By investing time and effort in thoughtfully crafting features, engineers and data scientists can unlock the true potential of their data, leading to more accurate predictions, deeper understanding of complex systems, and ultimately, better engineering solutions. The continuous evolution of this discipline, driven by new data sources, advanced algorithms, and a deeper understanding of engineering processes, ensures its enduring importance.

The temporal nature of data in many engineering applications presents a rich landscape for feature extraction. Raw time-series data, such as sensor readings from machinery, environmental monitoring, or process control systems, often exhibits complex patterns that are not immediately apparent without careful transformation. These patterns can relate to the overall health of a system, the occurrence of specific events, or deviations from normal operating conditions. Effectively engineering features from these sequential datasets allows us to represent dynamic behaviors, transient phenomena, and evolving trends in a manner that is more digestible and informative for machine learning algorithms. This subsection delves into practical methodologies for deriving such features, moving beyond simple time lags or basic aggregations to capture more nuanced aspects of temporal data.

One of the most fundamental and widely applicable techniques for feature engineering from time-series data involves the use of
**rolling statistics**. Instead of considering individual data points in isolation or computing a single aggregate over the entire series, rolling statistics compute a measure over a defined, moving window of data. This approach is invaluable for smoothing out noise, identifying local trends, and capturing the variability within a specific period. Common rolling statistics include the mean, median, standard deviation, variance, minimum, maximum, and range. For instance, a rolling mean of vibration data from a motor can provide a smoothed representation of its average vibration level over a short period, making it easier to discern slow increases indicative of wear. Conversely, a rolling standard deviation can highlight periods of increased instability or erratic behavior. If we are monitoring the temperature of a chemical reactor, a rolling standard deviation might reveal when the temperature fluctuations are becoming unusually large, potentially signaling an unstable reaction.

Beyond these basic statistics, more advanced rolling measures can provide deeper insights. The
**rolling skewness** and **rolling kurtosis** are particularly useful for understanding the shape of the data distribution within the window. Skewness measures the asymmetry of the distribution, indicating whether the data points tend to cluster more on one side of the mean. For example, a rapidly increasing positive skew in pressure readings within a pipeline might suggest a blockage that is causing pressure to build up unevenly. Kurtosis, on the other hand, quantifies the "tailedness" of the distribution – how prone it is to outliers. A high positive kurtosis (leptokurtic) indicates a distribution with heavy tails and a sharp peak,

meaning extreme values are more likely than in a normal distribution. Monitoring changes in rolling kurtosis for sensor readings could help detect the onset of anomalous events that produce occasional, but significant, spikes.

The choice of window size for rolling statistics is a critical hyperparameter. A small window will be more sensitive to short-term fluctuations and noise, while a large window will capture longer-term trends but might smooth over important transient events. The optimal window size often depends on the characteristic timescales of the phenomena being investigated. For example, when analyzing the performance of a batch process, a window size corresponding to the typical duration of a batch might be appropriate for capturing batch-to-batch variations, while for continuous processes, shorter windows might be preferred to detect rapid changes. It is often beneficial to experiment with multiple window sizes or even to create features using a set of different window sizes to capture information at various temporal resolutions.

Another powerful set of features can be derived by focusing on the **peak characteristics** of time-series signals, especially when dealing with event-driven phenomena or transient responses. For instance, in analyzing the impact of a specific input stimulus or the response to a disturbance, identifying the maximum value a signal reaches is often of paramount importance. This could be the maximum vibration amplitude during a specific operational cycle, the peak current draw of a motor when starting up, or the maximum temperature rise after a specific process event.

Beyond the peak value itself, the
**time-to-peak** can be a highly informative feature. This is the duration from a reference point (e.g., the start of an event, the beginning of a time window) until the signal reaches its maximum amplitude. A system's

response time, indicated by how quickly it reaches its peak, can be a strong indicator of its health or performance. For example, if a control system is supposed to respond to a setpoint change within a certain time, a delay in reaching the peak output could signal sluggishness or a fault. Similarly, in seismic data analysis, the time it takes for a seismic wave to reach its peak amplitude at a sensor can provide information about the geological layers it has traversed.

Furthermore, the
**width of the peak** at certain amplitude levels (e.g., half-maximum, often referred to as Full Width at Half Maximum or FWHM) can characterize the duration of an event or response. A sharp, narrow peak might represent a brief, intense event, while a broad, rounded peak might indicate a more sustained or diffuse phenomenon. In signal processing, FWHM is a common metric for pulse duration. For engineering data, this could translate to the duration of an abnormal vibration spike or the time a system remains above a certain operational threshold.

The
**area under the curve (AUC)** within a specified time window or around a peak can also be a valuable feature. It represents the cumulative effect of a signal over time. For example, the AUC of a current sensor reading during a motor startup phase might quantify the total energy consumed during that transient period. Similarly, the AUC of a temperature rise curve could indicate the total thermal stress experienced by a component. This cumulative measure can sometimes be more robust than peak values, as it is less sensitive to minor fluctuations in the signal's amplitude.

To capture the overall
**trend** and **directionality** of a time series, we can engineer features that quantify its progression over time. While rolling means provide a local trend, more explicit trend indicators can be beneficial. One simple approach is to calculate the difference between the value at the end of a

window and the value at the beginning, or between the end of the window and a rolling mean. This directly estimates the local slope. More sophisticated methods involve fitting a linear regression line to the data within a rolling window and extracting the slope of that line as a feature. This slope directly quantifies the rate of increase or decrease.

For longer time horizons, the **change in trend** itself can be an important feature. This can be captured by calculating the second derivative of the signal, or by computing the difference between consecutive slopes if using a rolling linear regression. A significant change in the second derivative might indicate a shift in the underlying dynamics of the system, such as a sudden degradation in performance or a change in operating regime.

Another perspective for time-series feature engineering involves looking at the **distribution of values within a window** in more detail. Beyond skewness and kurtosis, we can extract quantiles (e.g., 10th percentile, 90th percentile) to understand the spread of typical values. The **interquartile range (IQR)**, which is the difference between the 75th and 25th percentiles, is a robust measure of dispersion that is less sensitive to outliers than the standard deviation. Features derived from quantiles can effectively describe the central tendency and spread of the data in a way that is resilient to extreme values.

For intermittent or event-based data, such as the occurrence of alarms, faults, or specific operational states, features related to **event frequency** and **duration** are crucial. If an alarm system logs every instance of an alarm, we can engineer features like:

**Number of events within a time window:** How many times did a particular alarm trigger in the last hour, day, or week?

**Time between events:** The duration from one event occurrence to the next. A decreasing time between events might indicate a worsening problem.
**Duration of events:** If events have a defined start and end, how long do they typically last? Long-duration events might require different mitigation strategies than short bursts.
**Rate of events:** The number of events per unit of time, which normalizes frequency over different observation periods.

These event-based features are particularly powerful for predicting future occurrences or understanding the overall reliability of a system. For example, in a manufacturing plant, a machine that experiences a high frequency of minor faults might be a precursor to a major breakdown.

In situations where data is sampled at irregular intervals, standard rolling window techniques need adaptation. For such **irregularly sampled time series**, one common approach is to interpolate the data onto a regular grid using methods like linear interpolation, spline interpolation, or nearest-neighbor interpolation. Once regularized, standard rolling statistics can be applied. Alternatively, specialized techniques for irregular time series exist, such as Gaussian Processes, or adaptations of rolling statistics that consider the time gaps between points. For instance, a time-weighted average could be computed, where points closer in time to the current point contribute more to the average.

When dealing with cyclical or periodic phenomena, such as daily, weekly, or seasonal patterns, features can be engineered to capture these cycles. This can involve:

**Time of day/week/year features:** Creating cyclical features that represent the position within a day (e.g., hour of day, sine and cosine transformations of hour), week, or year. These can help models learn diurnal or seasonal effects.
**Lagged values at specific periodic intervals:** For example, comparing the current temperature to the temperature exactly 24 hours ago, or the temperature one week ago. Significant deviations from historical values at the same point in the cycle can be indicative of anomalies.
**Harmonic features:** Using Fourier transforms or related techniques to decompose the time series into its dominant frequency components. The amplitudes and phases of these frequencies can serve as features, capturing the strength and timing of cyclical patterns.

For complex signals, especially those exhibiting characteristics of resonance or vibration, features extracted from the **frequency domain** become indispensable. While not strictly "time-domain" features in the sense of direct temporal manipulation, they are derived from the time-series data and represent its spectral content. Applying a Fast Fourier Transform (FFT) to a time window of the signal transforms it from the time domain to the frequency domain, revealing the amplitudes of different frequencies present in the signal.

Key features that can be extracted from the frequency spectrum include:

**Dominant frequencies:** The frequencies with the highest amplitudes. These often correspond to natural frequencies of the system or rotational speeds of machinery.
**Amplitude of specific frequencies:** The magnitude of energy at particular frequencies of interest. For example, in rotating machinery, vibrations at the fundamental rotational frequency and its harmonics can indicate specific types of faults (e.g., imbalance, bearing defects).

**Spectral energy in frequency bands:** Summing the power spectral density over predefined frequency ranges. This can capture broad-band noise or energy associated with specific types of phenomena (e.g., high-frequency vibrations indicating cavitation).
**Spectral entropy:** A measure of the "randomness" or "disorder" of the frequency spectrum. A low spectral entropy suggests a few dominant frequencies, while high entropy indicates a more spread-out, noise-like spectrum.
**Peak frequency and its width:** Similar to time-domain peaks, but applied to the frequency spectrum, characterizing the sharpness or breadth of resonant peaks.

Wavelet transforms offer an even more powerful approach by providing time-frequency localization. Unlike FFT, which gives an average frequency content over an entire window, wavelets can decompose a signal into components at different frequencies and different points in time, allowing us to see how frequency content changes over time. Features derived from wavelet analysis might include:

**Energy coefficients at different scales (frequencies) and locations (time):** These coefficients quantify the presence and strength of specific patterns at specific times and frequencies.
**Dominant wavelet coefficients:** Similar to dominant frequencies in FFT.
**Time-localized spectral features:** By analyzing wavelet coefficients at different time points, we can capture transient frequency components.

When dealing with multivariate time-series data, where multiple sensors are recording simultaneously, the relationships *between* these series become critical. Feature engineering can then extend to capture **cross-correlations**, **co-variances**, and other forms of inter-series dependency.

**Cross-correlation:** Measures the linear relationship between two time series as a function of the lag applied to one of them. A high cross-correlation at a certain lag might indicate that a change in one sensor reading is predictive of a change in another sensor reading with a time delay.
**Co-variance/Correlation matrices:** Over a rolling window, the co-variance or correlation matrix between all pairs of sensors can be computed. Features derived from these matrices, such as eigenvalues or specific off-diagonal elements, can capture emergent relationships between variables. For example, if two temperature sensors that are normally uncorrelated suddenly become highly correlated, it might signal a shared underlying issue.
**Granger Causality:** A statistical hypothesis test used to determine if one time series is useful in forecasting another. If series X "Granger-causes" series Y, then past values of X can predict future values of Y, beyond what can be predicted by past values of Y alone. Engineered features could represent the strength of Granger causality between different sensor pairs.

The process of deriving these features requires careful consideration of the specific engineering domain and the problem at hand. For instance, in the context of structural health monitoring, features related to modal frequencies (natural vibration frequencies) and damping ratios, extracted from vibration time series, are paramount. For financial time series, features like volatility (often measured by rolling standard deviation or GARCH models) are critical. In the realm of signal processing for communication systems, features like signal-to-noise ratio (SNR), error rates, and synchronization metrics derived from raw waveforms are essential.

In summary, the extraction of meaningful features from time-series engineering data is a multifaceted endeavor. It moves beyond basic transformations to capture the dynamic, transient, and cyclical behaviors inherent in these datasets. By employing techniques such as rolling statistics (including advanced measures like skewness and kurtosis), analyzing peak characteristics (value, time-to-peak, width), quantifying trends and their changes, characterizing event occurrences, and exploring the frequency and time-frequency domains, we can construct a rich set of features. Furthermore, for multivariate time series, capturing inter-series dependencies through cross-correlation and other statistical measures adds another layer of analytical power. The thoughtful application of these techniques, guided by domain knowledge, is fundamental to building predictive models that accurately reflect the underlying physical processes and operational states of engineered systems.

The inherent oscillatory nature of many physical and mechanical systems means that their behavior, when observed over time, is often a superposition of various underlying frequencies. While time-domain analysis excels at capturing the temporal evolution of these signals, it can sometimes obscure the distinct contributions of these constituent frequencies. This is where the power of the **frequency domain** comes into play. By transforming a time-series signal into its frequency components, we gain a new perspective that can reveal characteristics otherwise hidden. This transformation allows us to understand *what frequencies are present* in the signal and *how strong their presence is*. This is crucial for diagnosing issues related to vibrations, resonances, material fatigue, and even certain types of electrical or acoustic anomalies that manifest as specific frequency signatures.

The most fundamental tool for venturing into the frequency domain is the **Fast Fourier Transform (FFT)**. The FFT is an efficient algorithm for computing the Discrete Fourier Transform (DFT), which decomposes a finite sequence of data points into a sum of sinusoidal components of different frequencies. When we apply an FFT to a segment of our time-series data (often referred to as a "window"), we obtain a spectrum. This spectrum is typically represented as a series of bins, each corresponding to a specific frequency, and the value in each bin represents the amplitude (or power) of the signal at that frequency. For engineering applications, this transformation is akin to dissecting a complex sound into its individual musical notes or analyzing a mechanical vibration into its fundamental modes of oscillation.

From this frequency spectrum, a rich set of features can be engineered. One of the most direct and informative features is the identification of **dominant frequencies**. These are the frequencies that exhibit the highest amplitudes in the spectrum. In machinery diagnostics, for example, a dominant frequency might correspond to the rotational speed of a motor shaft, indicating the presence of imbalance or a looseness in a component rotating at that speed. Other prominent frequencies can point to bearing defects, gear mesh issues, or the natural resonant frequencies of the structure itself. Detecting shifts or the emergence of new dominant frequencies over time can signal a change in the system's condition or the development of a fault.

Beyond identifying the single most prominent frequency, it is often beneficial to extract the amplitudes of several
**dominant frequencies**. For instance, in rotating machinery, faults can manifest at the fundamental rotational frequency (1x) and its integer multiples or sub-multiples (harmonics and sub-harmonics). An imbalance might show up strongly at 1x, while a bearing defect could manifest at specific frequencies related to the bearing geometry and its rotational speed. Therefore, engineers might extract the amplitudes of the 1st, 2nd, and 3rd harmonics, along with any other frequencies that are known to be indicative of specific failure modes within their domain.

Another critical set of features relates to the
**spectral power within specific frequency bands**. Instead of focusing on individual peaks, we can aggregate the energy of the signal over predefined ranges of frequencies. For instance, in analyzing acoustic

emissions from a material under stress, we might be interested in the total energy present in a high-frequency band that is characteristic of micro-fracture events. Similarly, in analyzing engine combustion, specific frequency bands might be associated with different combustion phenomena. Calculating the sum of the squared amplitudes (or the power spectral density) within these bands provides a robust measure of the signal's energy distribution across different parts of the spectrum. This approach is particularly useful for detecting broadband noise or diffuse phenomena that don't manifest as sharp, distinct peaks. For example, analyzing the spectral power in very high-frequency bands (ultrasonic range) could be used to detect cavitation in pumps or leaks in pressurized systems, as these events often generate broadband noise.

The concept of
**spectral entropy** offers a more abstract but powerful way to characterize the "noisiness" or "randomness" of the frequency spectrum. Mathematically, spectral entropy is derived from the probability distribution of the normalized spectral power. A spectrum dominated by a few strong peaks will have low spectral entropy, indicating a more ordered or tonal signal. Conversely, a spectrum that is relatively flat or spread out, with many frequencies contributing similar amounts of energy, will have high spectral entropy, suggesting a more random or broadband signal. Changes in spectral entropy over time can be indicative of evolving system dynamics. For instance, a system that transitions from a stable operating state with clear tonal components to a more chaotic state with broadband noise might exhibit an increase in spectral entropy, potentially signaling the onset of instability or increased friction.

To move beyond simple frequency domain representations and capture time-varying spectral characteristics, more advanced signal processing techniques are employed. The
**Short-Time Fourier Transform (STFT)** is one such method. The STFT applies the FFT to short, overlapping windows of the time-series data. This allows us to analyze how the frequency content of the signal changes

over time. The output of the STFT is often visualized as a **spectrogram**, which plots frequency on one axis, time on another, and the amplitude (or power) of each frequency component at each point in time using color intensity. Features derived from a spectrogram can include the time of occurrence of specific spectral events, the duration of frequency components, or the trajectory of dominant frequencies over time. For instance, a spectrogram of a gear meshing signal might reveal the characteristic spectral patterns of healthy operation, and any deviation – such as the appearance of sidebands around the gear mesh frequency – could indicate a developing fault, its timing observable on the spectrogram.

While the STFT provides a window into time-varying frequency content, it suffers from a fundamental trade-off inherent in the Heisenberg uncertainty principle: a more precise localization in time means less precise localization in frequency, and vice versa. The choice of window length in the STFT dictates this trade-off. A short window provides good temporal resolution but poor frequency resolution, while a long window offers good frequency resolution but smears out transient events in time.

This is where
**wavelet transforms** offer a significant advantage, particularly for analyzing signals with transient features or non-stationary characteristics. Unlike the Fourier transform, which uses fixed-size sine and cosine waves to decompose a signal, the wavelet transform uses "wavelets" – small, wave-like functions that are localized in both time and frequency. By scaling and shifting these wavelets, the transform can analyze the signal at different scales (corresponding to different frequencies) and at different points in time. This results in a **time-frequency representation** that offers a more adaptive resolution. For transient events, wavelets can provide excellent temporal localization. For broadband phenomena, they can offer good frequency resolution.

The output of a wavelet transform is a set of coefficients, often represented as a
**scalogram** (similar to a spectrogram). These coefficients quantify the similarity between the signal and the wavelet at different scales and times. Features engineered from wavelet coefficients can include:

**Energy distribution across scales:** Summing the squared magnitudes of coefficients at different scales can reveal which frequency bands contain the most energy. This is analogous to spectral power in frequency bands from FFT, but with the added dimension of time localization.
**Dominant wavelet coefficients:** Identifying the largest coefficients can point to the presence of specific patterns or events at particular times and scales.
**Time-localized spectral features:** By analyzing wavelet coefficients corresponding to specific time intervals, one can extract frequency information for transient events. For example, a sudden impact on a structure might produce a transient vibration that is well-captured by specific wavelet coefficients at the time of impact.
**Decomposition into approximation and detail coefficients:** Wavelet decomposition can recursively break down a signal into a lower-resolution "approximation" component and a "detail" component representing the lost information. Features can be derived from the statistics (e.g., variance, energy) of these detail coefficients at different decomposition levels, which correspond to different frequency ranges.

The choice of the "mother wavelet" is crucial in wavelet analysis and depends on the nature of the signal being analyzed. Different wavelets (e.g., Haar, Daubechies, Morlet) have different shapes and properties that make them more suitable for detecting different types of features. For instance, wavelets with sharp transitions might be good for detecting abrupt changes, while smoother wavelets might be better for analyzing oscillatory behavior.

In the context of engineering data, spectral features are invaluable for understanding the physics of a system. For example, in analyzing the vibration signatures of rotating machinery, the **frequency spectrum** can reveal:

**Imbalance:** Typically appears as a strong peak at the rotational frequency (1x).
**Misalignment:** Can manifest at the rotational frequency (1x) and its second harmonic (2x), sometimes with high magnitudes.
**Bearing defects:** Produce characteristic "BPFI" (Ball Pass Frequency Inner race), "BPFO" (Ball Pass Frequency Outer race), and "BSF" (Ball Spin Frequency) frequencies, which are dependent on the bearing geometry and rotational speed.
**Gear mesh problems:** Generate a fundamental gear mesh frequency, along with sidebands whose spacing is related to the rotational frequency of the meshing gears, indicating issues like wear, cracks, or eccentricity.
**Resonance:** If a dominant frequency matches a natural frequency of the machine structure or components, the vibration amplitude can be amplified significantly, potentially leading to damage.

Beyond these direct fault indicators, spectral analysis can also inform us about the material properties and the overall health of a component. For instance, changes in the stiffness or damping characteristics of a material due to fatigue or thermal degradation can lead to shifts in its natural frequencies. By monitoring these frequencies in vibration data, one can infer the progression of material damage or changes in operating conditions.

Consider a scenario in aerospace engineering where analyzing the acoustic emissions from an aircraft engine is critical for detecting early signs of component degradation. The engine's operation generates a complex soundscape, and FFT analysis of recorded audio over specific flight phases can reveal characteristic frequency patterns. For example, an increase in the spectral power within a specific ultrasonic band might indicate the onset of turbine blade flutter, a potentially catastrophic failure mode. Similarly, shifts in the dominant frequencies of engine combustion noise could signal issues with fuel injection or ignition. Wavelet analysis could further refine this by pinpointing *when* these anomalous frequency components appear, allowing for more precise diagnosis and proactive maintenance.

Another domain where spectral features shine is in structural health monitoring. Accelerometers placed on bridges, buildings, or wind turbine blades measure vibrations. FFT of these vibration signals can reveal the **modal frequencies** (natural frequencies) and mode shapes of the structure. Changes in these modal frequencies over time can indicate structural damage, such as cracks or loosening of connections, which alter the stiffness and mass distribution of the structure. For example, a bridge experiencing increased traffic load or environmental stress might exhibit a slight decrease in its fundamental natural frequency, detectable through spectral analysis of its ambient vibrations. Wavelet analysis can be particularly useful here for identifying transient responses to specific events like a heavy truck passing or a strong gust of wind, and analyzing how the structure's resonant frequencies respond to these dynamic loads.

In material science and manufacturing, spectral analysis can be used to characterize materials or monitor processes. For instance, the acoustic signal emitted during a grinding or polishing operation can be analyzed to infer the quality of the surface finish. Different types of surface irregularities or material removal mechanisms will produce distinct frequency signatures. By transforming the acoustic signal into the frequency domain, operators can monitor the grinding process in real-time and detect deviations that might indicate tool wear or improper settings.

When dealing with signals that are inherently periodic, such as the output of a rotating sensor or a regular sampling clock, spectral analysis can also be used to isolate and characterize these periodicities. The FFT will show strong peaks at the fundamental frequency and its harmonics. Understanding these inherent frequencies is crucial for distinguishing them from signals of interest. For example, if a sensor is intended to measure ambient temperature but is mounted on a rotating shaft, the FFT will reveal a strong peak at the shaft's rotational frequency. This information allows us to either filter out this unwanted component or to use it to infer the shaft's speed.

The practical implementation of spectral feature extraction often involves several steps. First, the raw time-series data is segmented into smaller, overlapping windows. The choice of window size is critical: it must be long enough to contain sufficient cycles of the lowest frequency of interest but short enough to capture the desired temporal resolution. Overlapping windows help to smooth out transitions and ensure that events occurring at window boundaries are captured. Second, each window is typically multiplied by a
**windowing function** (e.g., Hamming, Hanning, Blackman) before the FFT is applied. This is done to reduce "spectral leakage," an artifact where the energy of a single frequency component "leaks" into adjacent frequency bins due to the abrupt truncation of the signal at the window edges. The windowing function tapers the signal towards zero at the edges of the window, mitigating this effect.

After applying the FFT, we obtain a complex-valued frequency spectrum. For many applications, we are interested in the magnitude (amplitude) or power of these frequency components. The
**amplitude spectrum** is obtained by taking the magnitude of the complex FFT output, and the **power spectrum** is obtained by squaring the

magnitudes. For real-valued input signals, the spectrum is symmetric around the Nyquist frequency, and we typically only consider the first half of the spectrum (from 0 Hz up to the Nyquist frequency).

From these amplitude or power spectra, numerous features can be calculated. These include:

**Mean/Median of the spectrum:** A measure of the average spectral content.
**Variance/Standard Deviation of the spectrum:** Indicates the spread or flatness of the spectrum.
**Spectral flatness:** A ratio that quantifies how flat the spectrum is, often calculated as the geometric mean divided by the arithmetic mean of the power spectrum. A value close to 1 indicates a flat spectrum, while values close to 0 indicate a more tonal spectrum.
**Spectral centroid:** The "center of mass" of the power spectrum. It indicates where the bulk of the spectral energy is located.
**Spectral spread:** A measure of how spread out the spectrum is around the spectral centroid.
**Skewness and Kurtosis of the spectrum:** Similar to their time-domain counterparts, these can describe the shape of the spectral distribution.

For instance, in audio signal processing, spectral centroid is often related to the perceived "brightness" of a sound. In machinery diagnostics, a shift in the spectral centroid might indicate a change in the dominant vibration frequencies.

The application of these spectral features is highly dependent on the engineering domain. In telecommunications, frequency domain analysis is fundamental to understanding signal bandwidth, channel capacity, and the presence of interference. In medical engineering, analyzing the frequency content of biological signals like EEG (electroencephalogram) or ECG (electrocardiogram) can reveal disease states or physiological conditions. For example, specific frequency bands in EEG are associated with different brain states (e.g., alpha waves during relaxation, delta waves during deep sleep).

In summary, transforming engineering time-series data into the frequency domain unlocks a powerful set of analytical capabilities. Techniques like the Fast Fourier Transform (FFT) and its time-localized variants such as the Short-Time Fourier Transform (STFT) and wavelet transforms allow us to decompose complex signals into their constituent frequencies. From these representations, we can engineer features such as dominant frequencies, spectral power within defined bands, spectral entropy, spectral centroid, and coefficients from wavelet decompositions. These spectral features are instrumental in diagnosing faults in machinery, monitoring structural integrity, characterizing materials, analyzing complex physical phenomena, and understanding the periodic components within signals. Their utility stems from the fact that many physical systems exhibit characteristic responses at specific frequencies, and by analyzing the spectral content of observed data, we can directly infer underlying physical processes, system states, and potential anomalies that might be obscured in the time domain. The thoughtful selection and application of spectral features, guided by domain expertise, are therefore indispensable tools in the feature engineering arsenal for a wide range of engineering disciplines.

The journey into understanding and quantifying engineering data doesn't end with dissecting its frequency content. While the frequency domain reveals the underlying oscillatory components and their strengths, a complementary set of features emerges from examining the **statistical properties and distributional characteristics** of the data. These features offer a different lens through which to view signal behavior, providing a compact yet powerful summary that can be highly informative for tasks such as classification, anomaly detection, and system monitoring. Rather than focusing on *what frequencies* are present, this approach investigates *how the signal's values are distributed* over time and the inherent variability within those distributions.

At the core of statistical feature extraction are the **moments of a distribution**. These are fundamental mathematical properties that describe the shape and characteristics of a dataset. The first moment is the **mean**, representing the average value of the signal within a given time window or segment. It provides a baseline measure of the signal's central tendency. In many engineering applications, changes in the mean can signal a shift in operating conditions, a drift in sensor calibration, or the introduction of a constant offset. For instance, in monitoring the temperature of a critical component, a sustained increase in the mean temperature might indicate insufficient cooling.

The second moment is the **variance**, a measure of how spread out the data points are from the mean. A high variance indicates that the data points are widely dispersed, while a low variance suggests they are clustered closely around the mean. In the context of vibration analysis, for example, a sudden increase in variance might correspond to the onset of erratic behavior or the excitation of new, high-amplitude vibration modes. Variance is often a sensitive indicator of increased signal activity or instability. The **standard deviation**, which is simply the square root of the variance, is more intuitively interpretable as it is in the same units as the original data.

Moving beyond the basic measures of central tendency and spread, the third and fourth moments provide insights into the **asymmetry and "tailedness"** of the distribution, respectively. The **skewness** quantifies the asymmetry of the probability distribution of a real-valued random variable about its mean. A positive skewness indicates that the tail on the right side of the distribution is longer or fatter than the left side, meaning the distribution is shifted to the left.

Conversely, a negative skewness indicates that the tail on the left side is longer or fatter, with the distribution shifted to the right. In engineering, a signal exhibiting significant skewness might indicate the presence of occasional large spikes or drops that deviate from the typical behavior. For example, in analyzing the stress on a material, a highly positively skewed distribution of stress values might suggest intermittent, high-stress events that could lead to fatigue failure over time.

The
**kurtosis**, the fourth moment, measures the "tailedness" of the probability distribution. It describes how heavily the tails of a distribution differ from the tails of a normal distribution. High kurtosis (leptokurtic distribution) means that the tails are heavier and the peak is sharper than that of a normal distribution, indicating a higher probability of extreme values. Low kurtosis (platykurtic distribution) means that the tails are lighter and the peak is flatter, indicating a lower probability of extreme values. In signal analysis, kurtosis can be a crucial indicator of impulsive noise or extreme events. A high kurtosis value might signify the presence of impacts, shocks, or other transient phenomena that generate unusually large deviations from the mean, even if the overall variance is not exceptionally high. For example, in monitoring the acoustic emissions from a bearing, a high kurtosis might point to the presence of discrete impact events associated with spalling or debris.

These four moments—mean, variance, skewness, and kurtosis—collectively provide a robust statistical profile of a signal segment. They are relatively easy to compute and can be very effective in distinguishing between different operational states or identifying deviations from normal behavior. For instance, consider a manufacturing process where a machine operates in three distinct states: normal operation, slight wear, and imminent failure. Each state might be characterized by a unique combination of these statistical moments in its vibration signature. Normal operation might exhibit low variance and near-zero skewness and kurtosis (approximating a Gaussian distribution). As wear progresses, the variance might increase, and perhaps some positive skewness appears due to occasional impacts. In the imminent failure state, kurtosis could become very high, indicating frequent, large-amplitude impacts.

Beyond the moments, other statistical measures offer valuable insights. **Quantiles**, also known as percentiles, divide the data into contiguous intervals with equal probabilities. The median, for instance, is the 50th percentile, representing the middle value of a dataset when ordered. Other quantiles, such as the 10th, 25th, 75th, and 90th percentiles, provide information about the distribution's spread and identify potential outliers. The **interquartile range (IQR)**, defined as the difference between the 75th and 25th percentiles, is a measure of statistical dispersion that is less sensitive to outliers than the range (difference between maximum and minimum values). By examining specific quantiles, one can understand the range of typical values and the frequency of extreme observations. For example, in analyzing the flow rate of a fluid in a pipe, the 95th percentile of flow rate might be used to define a threshold for acceptable performance, while a sudden increase in the 5th percentile could indicate a blockage.

Measures of
**dispersion and spread**, besides variance and IQR, include the **range** itself (max - min), and more robust measures like the **median absolute deviation (MAD)**. MAD is the median of the absolute deviations from the median of a dataset. It is a highly robust measure of variability, meaning it is not significantly affected by extreme outliers, making it suitable for datasets with potential anomalies.

Furthermore, we can directly attempt to characterize the underlying **probability distribution** of the data segment. If we assume that the signal within a specific operational state follows a known probability distribution (e.g., Gaussian, Exponential, Weibull), we can estimate the parameters of that distribution and use them as features. For instance, if the vibration signal under normal conditions is expected to be Gaussian, we can estimate its mean and variance. If the signal exhibits exponentially distributed durations of events, we can estimate the rate parameter. In mechanical systems, the **Weibull distribution** is frequently used to model the lifetime of components or the distribution of stress cycles, as it can capture increasing, constant, or decreasing failure rates. Extracting the shape and scale parameters of a fitted Weibull distribution can provide powerful insights into the component's degradation process.

The process of fitting a distribution typically involves:

1. **Selecting a candidate distribution:** Based on domain knowledge or initial data exploration, a plausible distribution is chosen.
2. **Estimating parameters:** Methods like Maximum Likelihood Estimation (MLE) or method of moments are used to find the parameters that best fit the data to the chosen distribution.
3. **Assessing goodness-of-fit:** Statistical tests (e.g., Kolmogorov-Smirnov test, Anderson-Darling test) can be used to evaluate how well the fitted distribution represents the observed data.

The estimated parameters of the fitted distribution serve as the engineered features. For example, if we fit a Weibull distribution to the amplitude of vibration signals, its shape and scale parameters can indicate the nature of the underlying vibration sources and their growth over time. A changing shape parameter might suggest a shift in the dominant vibration-generating mechanisms.

These statistical and distributional features are particularly valuable when dealing with signals that might not have clear, distinct frequency peaks but exhibit changes in their overall variability, asymmetry, or the likelihood of extreme events. Consider the analysis of sensor readings from a complex chemical process. While frequency-domain analysis might reveal vibrations from pumps or agitators, statistical features can capture subtle shifts in the process variables themselves. For instance, an increase in the skewness of a temperature sensor reading might indicate an unstable reaction, even if no new significant frequencies appear in the vibrational spectrum. Similarly, a decrease in the kurtosis of a pressure sensor might suggest that extreme pressure fluctuations, which could indicate a potential safety hazard, are becoming less frequent or less pronounced.

The application of these features often involves segmenting the continuous time-series data into smaller, non-overlapping or overlapping windows. The choice of window size is critical: it must be large enough to capture statistically meaningful patterns but small enough to adequately track changes over time. For stationary signals (where statistical properties do not change over time), a single set of statistical features extracted from the entire signal might suffice. However, most engineering signals are non-stationary, meaning their statistical properties evolve. Therefore, extracting these features from a series of moving windows allows us to create time series of statistical features, which can then be used for monitoring and analysis.

For example, in the context of monitoring a robotic arm's joint torque, we might segment the torque data into 1-second windows. From each window, we would compute the mean, variance, skewness, and kurtosis of the torque values. This would result in four time series: mean torque over time, variance of torque over time, skewness of torque over time, and kurtosis of torque over time. An anomaly might manifest as a sudden spike in the variance or kurtosis series, even if the mean torque remains relatively stable. This could indicate a temporary jamming or a loss of control within the joint.

When combined with domain expertise, statistical features can offer profound insights. For instance, in the automotive industry, the analysis of engine knock signals often relies heavily on statistical properties. Knock events are characterized by sudden, high-amplitude pressure pulses within the cylinder, which contribute to a non-Gaussian distribution of pressure signals, often exhibiting high kurtosis. By monitoring these statistical moments, engineers can detect and mitigate engine knock, which can cause significant damage.

In geotechnical engineering, analyzing the statistical properties of seismic signals or soil displacement data can reveal important information about material behavior under stress. For example, the distribution of strain values in a soil sample might become skewed or develop heavy tails under certain loading conditions, indicating non-linear behavior or the onset of failure mechanisms.

The robustness of statistical features makes them particularly attractive for handling noisy data. While frequency-domain analysis can be sensitive to noise that can spread across different frequency bins, statistical measures like the median or MAD are inherently more resilient to outliers and random noise. This makes them excellent candidates for initial feature extraction or for use in environments where sensor noise is a significant concern.

Furthermore, statistical features can serve as powerful discriminators in classification tasks. Imagine distinguishing between normal operating conditions of a pump and conditions indicative of cavitation. Cavitation often introduces a broadband, somewhat random noise, which might not always manifest as a distinct frequency peak but rather as a general increase in signal variability and a shift towards more impulsive behavior. A higher variance and kurtosis in the vibration or acoustic signal could effectively differentiate a cavitating pump from a normally operating one, even if the dominant frequencies of the pump's mechanical components remain the same.

To illustrate the practical application, consider a scenario in industrial process control where temperature readings from a reactor are critical. The ideal state might be a stable, near-Gaussian distribution of temperature around a setpoint, characterized by low variance and kurtosis. However, if an exothermic reaction starts to become unstable, the temperature might exhibit oscillations or bursts of high activity. This could translate into an increase in the variance of the temperature readings and potentially a change in skewness if the oscillations are asymmetric. If the instability leads to sudden, large temperature spikes, the kurtosis would dramatically increase, signaling a potentially dangerous runaway reaction. By continuously monitoring these statistical features, operators can receive early warnings and take corrective actions.

The choice of which statistical features to extract should always be guided by an understanding of the underlying physical system and the expected failure modes or operating states. For example, if a system is known to be prone to impulsive events, kurtosis will likely be a highly relevant feature. If the system is expected to exhibit slow drift or changes in its average behavior, the mean will be a primary feature. If subtle changes in the signal's variability are key indicators, variance and MAD will be important.

In conclusion, statistical and distributional features offer a rich vocabulary for describing and understanding engineering data. By quantifying the central tendency, dispersion, asymmetry, and tail behavior of signals, we gain valuable insights into the operational state, health, and behavior of the system under observation. Moments like mean, variance, skewness, and kurtosis, along with quantiles, measures of dispersion, and parameters from fitted probability distributions, provide a compact, interpretable, and often robust way to characterize complex time-series data. These features are not merely descriptive statistics; they are powerful discriminators that can be directly leveraged for anomaly detection, fault diagnosis, and classification, complementing and often providing a different, but equally important, perspective compared to frequency-domain analysis. Their computation is straightforward, and their interpretability, especially when grounded in the physics of the problem, makes them indispensable tools in the feature engineering toolkit for any data-driven engineering application.

The preceding discussion has established the foundational statistical moments and distributional properties that offer a powerful lens for understanding engineering time-series data. While these general principles are broadly applicable, their true utility is unlocked when they are applied within the context of specific engineering disciplines. Different domains present unique phenomena, sensor modalities, and failure mechanisms, each demanding a tailored approach to feature engineering. This section delves into concrete examples across various engineering fields, illustrating how domain-specific knowledge is integrated with general feature extraction techniques to create highly effective, problem-tailored features.

Consider the field of
**Structural Health Monitoring (SHM)**. In this domain, the primary goal is to assess the integrity and performance of structures, such as bridges, buildings, aircraft, or mechanical components, often by analyzing vibration data. Vibrations are inherently sensitive to changes in structural properties like stiffness, mass, and damping, which can be affected by damage, wear, or environmental factors.

One of the most fundamental features extracted from vibration sensor data (often accelerometers) is the

**Root Mean Square (RMS)** value. The RMS value, calculated over a specific time window, provides a measure of the overall signal energy or intensity. For an acceleration signal $a(t)$, its RMS over a window of duration $T$ is given by:

$$
\text{RMS} = \sqrt{\frac{1}{T} \int_{0}^{T} a(t)^2 dt}
$$

In SHM, an increase in the RMS acceleration can indicate increased vibration levels, which might be associated with the onset of damage, such as cracks initiating or propagating, or the loosening of connections. For instance, in monitoring a bridge, elevated RMS values in response to traffic loads could signal a developing structural weakness. The RMS feature is a simple yet effective indicator of the overall dynamic activity.

Complementary to the RMS, the
**Peak-to-Peak Value** is another simple yet informative feature. This is simply the difference between the maximum and minimum amplitude values within a given time segment:

$$
\text{Peak-to-Peak} = \max(a(t)) - \min(a(t))
$$

A sudden surge in the peak-to-peak acceleration can be a strong indicator of transient events, such as impacts, sudden jolts, or the occurrence of sharp, high-amplitude oscillations. In aircraft monitoring, a significant increase in peak-to-peak acceleration could alert to a sudden aerodynamic event or a component experiencing extreme stress.

Beyond these time-domain amplitude measures, the **frequency domain** remains critically important in SHM. While we previously discussed its general principles, in SHM, specific spectral features are of paramount interest. These often relate to the **natural frequencies** of the structure. Every structure has a set of frequencies at which it will naturally vibrate when disturbed. These natural frequencies are directly dependent on the structure's material properties, geometry, and boundary conditions. Damage, by altering these properties, will typically cause a shift in these natural frequencies.

To extract these features, a common approach is to compute the **Power Spectral Density (PSD)** of the vibration signal. The PSD shows how the signal's power is distributed across different frequencies. Features can then be engineered to capture:

**The amplitude of spectral peaks at known natural frequencies:** If a structure's first natural frequency is known to be around 20 Hz, a feature could be the magnitude of the PSD at precisely 20 Hz. A reduction in this amplitude might indicate damage that has softened the structure.
**The shift in dominant frequencies:** Features can be designed to track the center of mass of the power distribution within specific frequency bands. A shift in this center of mass can indicate changes in natural frequencies. For example, a bridge designed to have its dominant vibration modes in the 1-5 Hz range might show a decrease in these frequencies if its support structures degrade.
**The presence of new spectral peaks:** Unexpected peaks appearing in the PSD can indicate the excitation of new vibration modes or the presence of localized defects. A feature could be a binary indicator (0 or 1) for the presence of a peak above a certain threshold in a specific frequency range where no peaks are expected under normal conditions.

Another class of features relevant to SHM, particularly for materials exhibiting non-linear behavior or undergoing fatigue, are related to **non-linearities**. These can be captured through advanced statistical measures or by analyzing the system's response to specific excitation signals. For instance, the **Bissell spectrum** or **Volterra series expansions** can quantify non-linear system behavior, though these are computationally intensive. Simpler proxies include higher-order moments (skewness and kurtosis), as discussed previously, or the analysis of **harmonic components**, which are multiples of the fundamental excitation frequency. The presence and amplitude of these harmonics can reveal non-linear stiffness characteristics.

Moving to
**Manufacturing and Process Monitoring**, the focus shifts to the stability, efficiency, and quality of production processes. Here, features are often derived from sensors measuring parameters like temperature, pressure, flow rate, voltage, current, vibration of machinery, or even visual inspection data.

**Process Stability** is a key concern. Features are designed to quantify how much a process parameter deviates from its desired operating point or its average behavior.

**Drift Rate:** For sensors measuring critical process variables (e.g., temperature in a chemical reactor), the rate at which the mean value changes over time can be a crucial feature. A steadily increasing temperature might indicate a control system issue or a change in reaction kinetics. This can be approximated by the slope of a linear regression line fitted to the sensor data over a moving window.

**Rate of Change:** Similar to drift, the instantaneous rate of change (first derivative) of a parameter can signal sudden shifts. For example, a rapid drop in fluid pressure might indicate a leak or a valve failure.
**Deviation from Setpoint:** The difference between the measured value and the target setpoint is a direct indicator of control performance. Features can include the mean of this deviation, its variance, or the number of times the deviation exceeds a predefined tolerance.

**Sensor Health and Calibration** are also critical. Sensors can drift, become noisy, or fail.

**Sensor Noise Level:** Features can quantify the variability (e.g., standard deviation or MAD) of a sensor reading when the physical process is expected to be stable. A sudden increase in this variability might indicate sensor malfunction or electrical interference.
**Cross-Sensor Consistency:** If multiple sensors are measuring related physical quantities, features can be engineered to capture their consistency. For example, in a multi-stage process, the ratio of flow rates between stages should remain within a certain range. A deviation from this expected ratio could indicate a problem in one of the stages or its associated sensors.
**Correlation between sensors:** Measuring how two or more sensor readings co-vary can reveal underlying process relationships or detect anomalies where these relationships break down.

**Machine Health Monitoring** within manufacturing is another prime area for feature engineering. This often overlaps with SHM but with a specific focus on the operational state of machinery like motors, pumps, gears, and conveyors.

**Bearing Fault Detection:** Vibrations from bearings are a classic example. Features might include:
**Specific frequency bands:** Faults in bearings often generate characteristic frequencies related to the ball pass frequency outer race (BPFO), ball pass frequency inner race (BPFI), and ball spin frequency (BSF). Features can be the amplitude of the PSD within these specific frequency bands.
**Envelope analysis features:** For detecting impacts within bearings, the envelope of the vibration signal is often analyzed. Features derived from the envelope can include its RMS, peak values, or spectral content.
**Kurtosis:** As mentioned, high kurtosis in vibration signals is often indicative of impulsive events, which are common in bearing defects.
**Gearbox Health:** Similar to bearings, gearboxes have characteristic frequencies related to gear mesh frequencies, sidebands, and impacts from tooth damage. Features would include amplitudes at these specific frequencies and their associated sidebands.
**Electric Motor Health:** Features can include analysis of vibration signals, but also electrical signals like current and voltage. Anomalies in current can indicate rotor bar issues, stator winding faults, or bearing problems. Features might include the amplitude of specific frequencies in the current spectrum (e.g., slip frequency sidebands) or measures of current imbalance.

Consider a
**chemical process**. Here, sensors might measure temperature, pressure, pH, concentration of reactants, and flow rates. The goal is to ensure the reaction proceeds safely and efficiently, producing the desired product with high yield and purity, while minimizing waste and avoiding hazardous conditions.

**Reaction Rate Indicators:** Features related to the rate of change of temperature or concentration can directly indicate the speed of the reaction. For exothermic reactions, a rapid increase in temperature might signal a runaway reaction.

**Mixing Efficiency:** In stirred tanks, features derived from vibration sensors on the impeller shaft or flow sensors can indicate the effectiveness of mixing. Changes in these features might suggest issues with the agitator, increased viscosity of the fluid, or the formation of lumps or precipitates.

**Product Purity Indicators:** If sensors can directly measure product concentration or impurity levels, features could include the mean concentration, its variability, or the rate of change. More indirectly, features from other sensors (e.g., a sudden change in pressure drop across a filter bed) might indicate build-up of byproducts or fouling, which can affect product purity.

**Safety Monitoring:** Features designed to detect hazardous conditions are paramount. This could include:

**Pressure spikes:** High kurtosis in pressure readings might indicate sudden gas evolution or cavitation.

**Temperature oscillations:** Significant variance or skewness in temperature might signal unstable reaction dynamics.

**Detection of specific chemical signatures:** If a fault condition leads to the production of a known byproduct or the decomposition of a reagent, spectral features from chemical sensors (e.g., mass spectrometry, infrared spectroscopy) can be engineered to detect its presence.

In the

**Automotive Industry**, feature engineering is applied across many areas, from engine diagnostics to autonomous driving.

**Engine Knock Detection:** As briefly touched upon, engine knock is a detrimental phenomenon where fuel ignites prematurely in the combustion chamber. This generates sharp, high-amplitude pressure waves. Features include:

**High kurtosis** of cylinder pressure signals.

**Amplitude of specific frequencies** in the acoustic or vibration signal, corresponding to the characteristic frequencies of knock events.
**Duration and energy of pressure pulses.**
**Powertrain Efficiency:** Features can monitor parameters like fuel injection timing, throttle position, engine speed, and exhaust gas recirculation (EGR) rates to assess combustion efficiency and identify potential issues with emission control systems. For example, deviations in oxygen sensor readings under specific engine load conditions might indicate inefficient combustion or catalyst degradation.
**Brake System Monitoring:** Features related to brake pedal pressure, wheel speed, and deceleration can be used to detect anomalies like brake fade, uneven braking, or ABS activation. For instance, a mismatch in deceleration between front and rear wheels during braking could indicate an issue with the brake distribution system.
**Autonomous Driving Sensors:** For systems like LiDAR, RADAR, and cameras, feature engineering is a cornerstone of object detection, tracking, and scene understanding. While deep learning has automated much of this, traditional engineered features are still relevant for specific tasks or as inputs to simpler models. Examples include:
**For LiDAR:** Point cloud density, intensity variations, geometric features of clusters (e.g., dimensionality, linearity, planarity).
**For RADAR:** Doppler shift (for velocity estimation), signal-to-noise ratio (SNR), coherence.
**For Cameras:** Edge detection (e.g., Canny), texture features (e.g., Local Binary Patterns - LBP), color histograms, optical flow.

In
**Aerospace Engineering**, the emphasis is on reliability, safety, and performance under extreme conditions.

**Aircraft Engine Health Monitoring (EHM):** Vibration, temperature, pressure, and flow rate sensors across engine components (compressors, turbines, combustion chambers) generate vast amounts of data. Features

are engineered to detect early signs of component degradation or malfunction:
**Vibration signatures:** Changes in vibration RMS, specific spectral peaks related to rotating machinery imbalances, bearing faults, or blade damage.
**Thermodynamic parameters:** Deviations in exhaust gas temperature (EGT), pressure ratios across stages, or fuel flow rate from expected values for a given engine setting. A common feature is EGT margin, which indicates how close the engine is to its operational limit.
**Performance parameters:** Features that capture the engine's overall efficiency, such as specific fuel consumption.
**Aircraft Structural Monitoring:** Beyond vibration, features might be derived from strain gauges, displacement sensors, or even acoustic emission sensors to detect structural fatigue, cracks, or delamination, especially in composite materials. Features can include the rate of strain accumulation, changes in stiffness (inferred from dynamic response), or the characteristics of acoustic emission signals (e.g., amplitude, duration, energy of events).
**Flight Control Systems:** Features can be engineered from actuator positions, control surface deflections, and sensor feedback loops to monitor system health and detect anomalies that could affect flight stability or safety. For instance, excessive jitter in an actuator's position or a discrepancy between commanded and actual position could signal a problem.

In
**Geotechnical Engineering**, analyzing soil and rock behavior under stress is critical for infrastructure projects like tunnels, dams, and foundations.

**Seismic and Vibration Analysis:** Similar to SHM, vibration data from sensors on structures or boreholes can be analyzed. Features can capture:

**Shear wave velocity:** Inferred from seismic signals, changes in shear wave velocity can indicate changes in soil stiffness or pore water pressure.
**Attenuation characteristics:** How seismic waves lose energy as they travel through the ground. Changes in attenuation can relate to soil layering, saturation, or damage.
**Pore Water Pressure Monitoring:** In dams and slopes, pore water pressure is a critical parameter affecting stability. Features could include the mean pressure, its rate of increase, or its distribution within the soil mass. High and rapidly increasing pore pressures can lead to landslides or dam failures.
**Inclinometer and Extensometer Data:** These sensors measure lateral movement and deformation. Features can include the rate of movement, the curvature of the deformed profile, or the total displacement accumulated over time, which are direct indicators of slope instability or settlement.

Across all these domains, several overarching principles guide the selection and engineering of features:

1.
**Domain Knowledge is Paramount:** The most effective features are almost always derived from a deep understanding of the physical system, the underlying phenomena being measured, and the specific failure modes or operational states of interest. Simply applying generic statistical features without this context can lead to suboptimal results.
2. **Link to Physical Meaning:** Features should ideally have a clear physical interpretation. This aids in model debugging, understanding model decisions, and gaining actionable insights. For example, a feature representing "rate of change of bearing temperature" is more directly interpretable than a high-order polynomial fit to temperature data.
3. **Capture Characteristic Signatures:** Many engineering problems involve detecting specific patterns or "signatures" associated with certain

events (e.g., fault frequencies in rotating machinery, specific chemical reaction kinetics). Feature engineering aims to highlight and quantify these signatures.

4. **Robustness to Noise and Variability:** Engineering sensors are often deployed in harsh environments, leading to noisy data. Features should be chosen or engineered to be as robust as possible to expected types of noise and normal operational variability, while still being sensitive to the anomalies of interest.

5. **Dimensionality Reduction:** While complex features can be informative, engineers often aim for a parsimonious set of features that captures most of the relevant information. Overly numerous or highly correlated features can lead to model complexity and overfitting. Techniques like Principal Component Analysis (PCA) or feature selection algorithms are often employed after initial feature engineering.

6. **Consider the Time Scale:** Features can be designed to capture phenomena occurring at different time scales, from instantaneous events (e.g., impact detection using peak amplitude) to slow drifts over hours or days (e.g., sensor calibration drift). The choice of window size for feature extraction is critical in this regard.

In essence, domain-specific feature engineering is an art and a science that blends mathematical rigor with practical engineering insight. It involves moving beyond generic statistical descriptors to craft features that are deeply attuned to the nuances of the problem at hand, ultimately enabling more accurate and reliable data-driven decision-making in a wide array of engineering applications. This iterative process of understanding the system, hypothesizing relevant physical indicators, engineering features to capture these indicators, and evaluating their effectiveness is central to successful applied data science in engineering.

# Chapter 5: Ensuring Data Quality and Integrity

The integrity and trustworthiness of engineering applications are inextricably linked to the quality of the data they process. In domains where the stakes are high—from ensuring the structural integrity of a bridge to optimizing the efficiency of a power plant, or guaranteeing the safety of an autonomous vehicle—even minor data inaccuracies can cascade into significant, potentially catastrophic, failures. Therefore, understanding and proactively managing data quality is not merely a procedural step; it is a critical engineering discipline in itself, forming the bedrock upon which all subsequent analysis, modeling, and decision-making must rest.

The journey of data from its source to its final application within an engineering system is fraught with potential pitfalls that can degrade its quality. Sensors, the primary conduits of real-world information into the digital realm, are susceptible to a myriad of issues. Calibration drift is a ubiquitous problem where a sensor's output gradually deviates from the true physical quantity it is measuring due to aging components, environmental exposure, or improper handling. This drift can be subtle, manifesting as a slow, almost imperceptible bias, or it can be more pronounced, rendering the sensor's readings completely unreliable. Imagine a temperature sensor in a critical chemical reactor. If its calibration drifts by just a few degrees Celsius, it could lead to misjudgments about reaction rates, potentially causing an exothermic reaction to go into a runaway state, with severe safety implications.

Noise is another pervasive adversary. Sensor noise can originate from various sources: thermal noise within electronic components, electromagnetic interference from nearby equipment, mechanical vibrations affecting sensitive measurement devices, or even atmospheric disturbances impacting remote sensing equipment. While some noise is inherent to the measurement process, excessive or non-random noise can obscure genuine signals, making it difficult to discern true patterns or anomalies. For instance, in a structural health monitoring system using accelerometers, high levels of random noise might mask the subtle vibrational signatures indicative of incipient structural damage, delaying or preventing timely intervention. Similarly, structured noise, such as 50/60 Hz electrical hum, can overpower weaker, yet more critical, signals if not properly filtered.

Furthermore, data can be lost or corrupted during transmission or storage. Network outages, faulty cables, or disk errors can lead to gaps in time-series data, corrupted data packets, or entirely lost files. These gaps are not just inconveniences; they represent missing pieces of the operational puzzle. If a critical sensor reading is missing during a period of high stress on a mechanical component, the system might fail to detect an impending failure. Similarly, corrupted data can introduce spurious values that, if not identified, can lead to incorrect inferences. Consider the process of analyzing performance data from a fleet of wind turbines. If data from a specific turbine is intermittently lost due to network issues during periods of high wind, the performance assessment for that turbine might be skewed, leading to suboptimal maintenance scheduling or power output predictions.

Data redundancy and inconsistencies introduce further complexities. In systems with multiple sensors measuring similar physical phenomena (e.g., multiple temperature sensors in different locations of a large industrial furnace), discrepancies can arise. These can be due to differing sensor characteristics, their placement, or local variations in the physical environment. Without a mechanism to reconcile these differences, downstream analyses can become ambiguous. Which temperature reading should be trusted if two sensors report significantly different values? This decision-making process, reliant on data quality, directly impacts control strategies and safety protocols.

Missing values, whether due to sensor malfunctions, transmission errors, or incomplete data collection, present a significant challenge. Simply ignoring rows with missing data can lead to biased models, especially if the missingness is not random. For example, if a sensor fails precisely when a critical event occurs, the data representing that event would be missing, and a model trained on the remaining data might never learn to recognize or respond to such events. Imputation techniques—methods for filling in missing data—are often employed, but the choice of imputation strategy can itself introduce bias if not carefully considered. A simple mean imputation might smooth over crucial variations, while more sophisticated methods require assumptions about the data that may not always hold true.

Outliers, extreme values that deviate significantly from the norm, are another critical data quality concern. While outliers can sometimes represent genuine, albeit rare, events (e.g., a sudden surge in pressure indicating a critical failure), they can also be artifacts of errors. Distinguishing between these two cases is vital. Unchecked, outliers can disproportionately influence statistical calculations (like means and variances) and machine learning model training, leading to skewed interpretations and predictions. For instance, an outlier in vibration data might be mistaken for a genuine bearing fault, leading to unnecessary maintenance, or conversely, a true failure event might be dismissed as an outlier if the system is not designed to treat extreme values with appropriate suspicion.

The downstream consequences of poor data quality in engineering applications are profound and far-reaching. In predictive maintenance, where models aim to forecast equipment failures, inaccurate sensor readings can lead to either false alarms (predicting a failure that doesn't occur, resulting in wasted resources and downtime) or missed predictions (failing to predict a genuine failure, leading to catastrophic breakdowns, safety hazards, and significant financial losses). Imagine a scenario where a key vibration sensor on a turbine experiences significant noise. A predictive maintenance algorithm might interpret this noise as an anomaly and schedule an unnecessary overhaul, incurring costs. Conversely, if a calibration drift makes the sensor consistently report lower vibration levels, a developing fault might go undetected until it results in catastrophic failure.

In process control, where data is used to dynamically adjust operational parameters to maintain stability and efficiency, faulty data can lead to instability. If a temperature sensor in a chemical reactor begins to read falsely high, the control system might reduce cooling, inadvertently exacerbating an overheating situation. This can cascade into reduced product quality, increased energy consumption, or, in worst-case scenarios, hazardous conditions. The precision required in many industrial processes means that even small deviations in input data can have amplified effects on the output.

Even in less critical applications, poor data quality erodes confidence and trust in the system. If an energy management system consistently overestimates or underestimates building energy consumption due to noisy or inaccurate sensor readings, occupants may experience discomfort, and operational inefficiencies will persist. The perceived reliability of the entire engineering solution diminishes when its underlying data foundation is shaky.

Recognizing the criticality of data quality, engineering workflows must incorporate robust data validation and cleaning procedures as an integral, non-negotiable part of the data lifecycle, not as an afterthought. This begins at the point of data acquisition. Implementing redundant sensors, where multiple sensors measure the same parameter, can provide a baseline for comparison and anomaly detection. If two out of three temperature sensors in a critical zone report similar values, and a third reports a wildly different value, it immediately flags the third sensor for investigation.

Sensor diagnostics and automated health checks are also essential. Modern sensors often come with built-in self-testing capabilities that can report their status, identify internal errors, or signal calibration issues. These diagnostic signals should be actively monitored. Regular, automated recalibration routines, comparing sensor readings against known standards or against the collective readings of a trusted sensor network, can help mitigate calibration drift.

During data transmission, error detection and correction codes (EDAC) can be employed to identify and, where possible, correct corrupted data packets. Protocols that ensure data integrity and provide acknowledgments of successful data reception are crucial. For data storage, employing reliable storage solutions with mechanisms for data redundancy (e.g., RAID configurations) and regular integrity checks can prevent data loss and corruption.

Upon data ingestion into an analysis pipeline, rigorous data validation checks must be performed. These checks should encompass a range of criteria:

**Range Checks:** Verifying that sensor readings fall within physically plausible limits. For example, a temperature sensor in a room should not report absolute zero or temperatures exceeding the melting point of steel

under normal operating conditions. Any reading outside these bounds is immediately suspect.
**Sanity Checks:** Evaluating the logical consistency of data. For instance, if a flow meter reports zero flow, the pressure drop across that section should also be zero (or within a very narrow, expected range for static fluid). A discrepancy here suggests an issue with one or both sensors or the underlying physics model.
**Rate of Change Checks:** Monitoring how quickly a variable changes. A sudden, unrealistic jump or drop in a temperature or pressure reading might indicate a sensor glitch rather than a genuine physical event. Defining acceptable rates of change for each parameter is crucial.
**Statistical Outlier Detection:** Employing statistical methods to identify values that deviate significantly from the expected distribution. Techniques like Z-scores, Modified Z-scores (using Median Absolute Deviation for robustness), or interquartile range (IQR) methods can help flag potential outliers. However, as noted, these flagged values require further investigation rather than automatic removal.
**Missing Value Analysis:** Quantifying the extent and pattern of missing data. Decision-making on how to handle missing data (imputation, interpolation, or exclusion) should be based on this analysis and the specific context of the data and the application.

The process of data cleaning and transformation must be carefully documented. Every step taken to address data quality issues—whether it's removing a corrupted data point, imputing a missing value, or filtering out noise—should be recorded. This audit trail is essential for reproducibility, debugging, and understanding how the data quality process might have influenced the final results. Transparency in data cleaning is paramount in engineering, where decisions based on data can have safety and operational implications.

Moreover, defining data quality metrics and establishing thresholds for acceptability is crucial for proactive monitoring. Metrics such as the percentage of missing data, the number of detected outliers, the average deviation from calibration standards, or the signal-to-noise ratio can be continuously tracked. When these metrics cross predefined thresholds, automated alerts can be triggered, prompting engineers to investigate and address the underlying data quality issues before they impact critical operations.

In essence, data quality management in engineering applications is a continuous, multi-faceted endeavor. It requires a combination of technical safeguards at the hardware and transmission levels, intelligent algorithms for validation and cleaning, and a vigilant human oversight informed by deep domain expertise. By treating data quality not as a mere prerequisite but as an ongoing, integral aspect of the engineering process, we can build more robust, reliable, and trustworthy systems that harness the full potential of data analytics and machine learning. This diligent approach ensures that the insights derived are not just statistically sound but also physically meaningful and operationally relevant, ultimately safeguarding the performance, safety, and efficiency of engineered systems.

The previous sections have laid the groundwork for understanding the pervasive challenges to data quality in engineering applications, from sensor inaccuracies and transmission errors to missing values and inconsistencies. Now, we delve into a critical aspect of data quality: the detection and handling of outliers and anomalies. In engineering, these extreme or unusual data points can signal either critical system events that demand immediate attention or erroneous measurements that could derail analysis if not properly managed. The distinction between these two scenarios is paramount.

### Detecting Outliers and Anomalies

Outliers are data points that deviate significantly from the majority of the data. Anomalies, a broader term, can encompass outliers but also include patterns or sequences of data that are unusual. For instance, a single, extreme temperature reading might be an outlier. However, a sustained period of slightly elevated, yet not extreme, temperature readings in an area that is typically cool could be considered an anomaly, perhaps indicating a developing issue not captured by individual extreme values.

One of the most straightforward statistical methods for outlier detection is the
**Z-score**. The Z-score measures how many standard deviations a data point is away from the mean of the dataset. For a given data point $x$, with a dataset mean $\mu$ and standard deviation $\sigma$, the Z-score is calculated as:

$Z = \frac{x - \mu}{\sigma}$

A common rule of thumb is to consider data points with a Z-score greater than a certain threshold (e.g., 2 or 3) as potential outliers. A Z-score of 3 means the data point is three standard deviations away from the mean. In a normal distribution, data points beyond 3 standard deviations are relatively rare, making this a reasonable heuristic. However, this method is sensitive to the presence of outliers themselves, as extreme values can inflate the standard deviation, thereby masking other outliers or making the Z-scores of existing outliers appear less extreme. Furthermore, the Z-score assumes a normally distributed dataset, which is not always the case in engineering contexts.

A more robust statistical approach, less sensitive to extreme values, is the

**Interquartile Range (IQR)** method. The IQR is the difference between the 75th percentile (Q3) and the 25th percentile (Q1) of the data.

$IQR = Q3 - Q1$

The IQR represents the spread of the middle 50% of the data. Outliers are typically defined as data points that fall below $Q1 - 1.5 \times IQR$ or above $Q3 + 1.5 \times IQR$. The factor 1.5 is a commonly used multiplier, but it can be adjusted (e.g., to 3 for "extreme" outliers) depending on the desired sensitivity. The IQR method is effective because it relies on percentiles, which are not affected by the magnitude of extreme values. This makes it a preferred choice when dealing with skewed distributions or datasets where outliers are expected.

For time-series data, which is ubiquitous in engineering, specific techniques are often more appropriate.
**Statistical Process Control (SPC)** charts are a powerful tool. These charts, like the X-bar and R charts, or individuals and moving range (I-MR) charts, monitor a process over time and display data points along with control limits. These limits are typically set at three standard deviations above and below the process mean. Data points falling outside these control limits are flagged as potential anomalies, indicating that the process may be out of statistical control. SPC charts are not only for detecting deviations but also for understanding process variability and identifying trends that might not be apparent from static statistical summaries. For example, a temperature sensor in a manufacturing process might consistently report values within the acceptable range but start a gradual upward trend. An SPC chart would visually highlight this trend, allowing for proactive adjustments before a critical threshold is breached.

Beyond traditional statistical methods, machine learning offers advanced techniques for outlier and anomaly detection.
**Isolation Forests** are an ensemble learning method that isolates anomalies by randomly selecting a feature and then randomly selecting a split value between the minimum and maximum values of the selected feature. The intuition is that anomalies are few and different, making them easier to "isolate" in fewer splits. The algorithm builds multiple isolation trees, and the anomaly score of a data point is based on the average depth at which it is isolated across all trees. Anomalies will typically be isolated at a shallower depth than normal data points. This method is particularly effective for high-dimensional datasets and does not require data to be normally distributed.

Another class of machine learning methods involves
**density-based approaches**, such as Local Outlier Factor (LOF). LOF measures the local density deviation of a given data point with respect to its neighbors. A data point is considered an outlier if its local density is significantly lower than that of its neighbors. This is useful when dealing with datasets where the density of normal data points varies.

For sequence data, such as vibration signatures of rotating machinery or sensor readings over time,
**Recurrent Neural Networks (RNNs)** and **Long Short-Term Memory (LSTM) networks** can be trained to learn the normal patterns of the sequence. Once trained, these models can predict the next data point in a sequence. If the actual data point deviates significantly from the prediction, it can be flagged as an anomaly. This approach is powerful for detecting subtle deviations in temporal behavior that might be missed by static outlier detection methods.

When dealing with multivariate data, where multiple sensor readings are correlated,

**Principal Component Analysis (PCA)** can be employed. PCA reduces the dimensionality of the data by identifying the principal components that capture most of the variance. Normal data points will lie close to the subspace spanned by the principal components, while anomalies, which often do not conform to the dominant patterns of variation, may have larger reconstruction errors when projected back into the original space.

The choice of detection method depends heavily on the nature of the data, the domain knowledge, and the specific goals. For instance, in a control system for a chemical reactor, rapid detection of extreme pressure spikes is critical and might favor methods that are highly sensitive to individual extreme values. In contrast, monitoring the long-term health of a bridge using strain gauges might benefit from methods that can identify subtle, evolving anomalies in vibration patterns over time.

### Strategies for Handling Outliers and Anomalies

Once potential outliers and anomalies have been detected, the next crucial step is deciding how to handle them. It is rarely appropriate to blindly remove all detected outliers, as they can sometimes represent genuine, albeit rare, events that are of utmost importance. For example, a sudden, massive power surge in a distributed energy grid might be an outlier in normal operational data, but it could signify a critical fault or a cyber-attack. Ignoring such data would be detrimental.

The decision-making process for handling outliers should be guided by domain expertise and the specific context of the engineering application.

**1. Removal:** This is the most straightforward approach but also the riskiest. Data points identified as outliers are simply deleted from the dataset. This is often justified when there is strong evidence that the outlier is a result of a measurement error, a sensor malfunction, or a data entry mistake, and it is unlikely to provide any valuable information about the system's behavior. For example, if a temperature sensor momentarily reported an impossible value (e.g., absolute zero or a value above the material's melting point), that specific data point could be safely removed if it's a single spurious reading. However, if multiple data points in a row exhibit this behavior, it might indicate a persistent sensor issue requiring more than just removal.

**2. Capping (Winsorizing):** Instead of removing outliers, capping involves replacing them with a specified maximum or minimum value. For example, if a data point is above the upper threshold (e.g., $Q3 + 1.5 \times IQR$), it might be replaced by $Q3 + 1.5 \times IQR$. Similarly, values below the lower threshold are replaced by $Q1 - 1.5 \times IQR$. This technique retains the data point but limits its extreme influence on statistical measures and model training. It's a compromise that acknowledges the existence of extreme values without letting them disproportionately skew results. This is particularly useful when the outlier might represent a real event but its precise value is uncertain or highly noisy.

**3. Transformation:** Data can be transformed using mathematical functions to reduce the impact of outliers. Common transformations include logarithmic, square root, or Box-Cox transformations. For example, a logarithmic transformation can compress the scale of very large values, making the distribution more symmetrical and less sensitive to extreme points. However, transformations can sometimes make the interpretation of the results more complex, especially in a direct engineering context where physical units and direct relationships are crucial. The choice of transformation needs careful consideration to ensure it aligns with the underlying physical processes being modeled.

**4. Imputation:** In some cases, detected anomalies might indicate a failure or interruption that is characteristic of the system's behavior. For instance, a sudden drop in pressure in a hydraulic system might indicate a leak. Instead of removing this data, it might be more informative to analyze the event. If the goal is to build a predictive model that can handle such events, one might choose to impute the missing or anomalous data in a way that captures the nature of the anomaly. For example, if a sensor fails during an event, the data might be missing, and imputation could be used to fill it based on other correlated sensors or a simplified model of the event's progression. However, this requires sophisticated imputation strategies beyond simple mean or median imputation.

**5. Treat as a Special Event:** In many engineering disciplines, outliers are not just errors but can be critical indicators of system state changes or potential failures. A sudden surge in vibration on a turbine, a rapid temperature increase in a reactor, or an unusual current draw in an electrical motor are all outliers that might signal an imminent failure. In such cases, the goal is not to remove or suppress these values but to detect them, classify them, and trigger appropriate responses. This might involve sophisticated anomaly detection algorithms that identify patterns indicative of specific fault modes, leading to alarms, diagnostic routines, or automatic safety shutdowns. The data point itself becomes a valuable piece of information signaling an event of interest.

**6. Investigation and Re-measurement:** The most prudent approach, especially in safety-critical applications, is to investigate detected outliers. This might involve reviewing sensor logs, checking environmental conditions, examining nearby sensors for corroborating evidence, or even scheduling a physical inspection or re-calibration of the sensor in question. If the investigation confirms a faulty reading, then removal or capping might be appropriate. If it confirms a genuine extreme event, the data point should be preserved and analyzed.

**Contextual Anomaly Detection:** It's vital to differentiate between global outliers (extreme values compared to the entire dataset) and contextual anomalies (values that are normal in general but unusual in a specific context). For example, a temperature reading of 25°C might be normal for an office environment but anomalous for a cryogenic storage unit. Advanced anomaly detection techniques often incorporate contextual information, such as time of day, operating mode, or other sensor readings, to identify these context-specific anomalies. Handling these requires understanding the specific conditions under which the data point was recorded.

**The role of Machine Learning Models:** When using machine learning models, the decision on how to handle outliers can also depend on the model itself. Some models, like tree-based algorithms (e.g., Random Forests, Gradient Boosting), are inherently more robust to outliers than others, such as linear regression or support vector machines with certain kernels. If a model is known to be sensitive, pre-processing steps to address outliers become more critical. It's also possible to train models to explicitly predict the probability of a data point being an outlier or an anomaly, providing a nuanced score rather than a binary classification.

The ultimate goal in handling outliers and anomalies is to preserve the integrity of the data and the reliability of the subsequent analysis or model. This requires a thoughtful, context-aware approach, blending statistical rigor with deep domain knowledge. It’s not just about finding the "wrong" numbers, but about understanding what those numbers signify within the complex operational landscape of engineering systems.

A proactive strategy for detecting and appropriately handling these data quality issues is a cornerstone of building trustworthy and effective engineering applications.

The methodology for dealing with outliers and anomalies should be clearly documented as part of the data processing pipeline. This documentation ensures reproducibility and transparency, allowing other engineers or stakeholders to understand how data quality was managed and how it might have influenced the final outcomes. In safety-critical systems, this level of rigor is not optional; it is a fundamental requirement for ensuring system reliability and safety. By systematically addressing these data quality challenges, we can build a more robust foundation for all engineering endeavors that rely on data-driven insights.

The presence of missing data is a ubiquitous issue encountered in virtually every domain of data engineering and machine learning, and its prevalence in engineering applications is no exception. Whether due to sensor malfunctions, data transmission interruptions, incomplete recording, or deliberate exclusion of certain data points, missing values can significantly compromise the integrity and utility of a dataset. Ignoring missing data or handling it improperly can lead to biased analyses, inaccurate predictions, and flawed decision-making. This section delves into the critical process of addressing missing data through imputation strategies, exploring a range of techniques from the simplest to the more advanced, and discussing their applicability and limitations within the context of engineering data.

### Understanding the Nature of Missing Data

Before embarking on imputation, it's crucial to understand why data might be missing. The mechanism of missingness can influence the choice of imputation technique and the potential biases it might introduce. Broadly, missing data can be categorized as:

**Missing Completely at Random (MCAR):** In this ideal scenario, the probability of a value being missing is independent of both the observed and unobserved values in the dataset. For instance, a data entry error that randomly affects a few records would be MCAR.
**Missing at Random (MAR):** Here, the probability of a value being missing depends only on the observed values of other variables, not on the missing value itself. For example, if men are less likely to answer a survey question about their weight (i.e., missingness depends on the observed 'gender' variable), but not dependent on their actual weight (the unobserved missing value), it's MAR.
**Missing Not at Random (MNAR):** This is the most problematic category, where the probability of a value being missing depends on the missing value itself or on unobserved factors. For example, individuals with very high incomes might be less likely to report their income, making the missingness dependent on the unobserved income value.

The imputation strategy often needs to consider these underlying mechanisms. While MCAR and MAR data can often be handled with standard imputation methods, MNAR data often requires more sophisticated modeling or domain-specific assumptions, as simple imputation techniques can introduce significant bias.

### Basic Imputation Strategies

The simplest approaches to imputation involve replacing missing values with a single, representative statistic derived from the observed data.

These methods are computationally inexpensive and easy to implement, making them a common starting point, especially for large datasets where computational efficiency is paramount.

### Mean Imputation

One of the most straightforward methods is **mean imputation**, where each missing value in a particular feature is replaced by the mean of the observed values for that feature.

For a feature $X$, with observed values $x_1, x_2, \dots, x_n$, the mean $\mu$ is calculated as:

$$\mu = \frac{1}{n} \sum_{i=1}^{n} x_i$$

Then, any missing value $x_{missing}$ for this feature is replaced by $\mu$.

**Advantages:**

**Simplicity:** Very easy to understand and implement.
**Computational Efficiency:** Fast, especially for large datasets.
**Preserves Mean:** The mean of the imputed feature remains unchanged.

**Disadvantages:**

**Distorts Variance:** Mean imputation reduces the variance of the feature because it replaces a range of values with a single value. This can lead to underestimation of variability and a loss of information.
**Biases Correlations:** It can distort relationships (correlations) between variables, as it doesn't account for relationships between features.
**Ignores Feature Relationships:** It treats each feature independently, failing to leverage information from other features that might be correlated.

**Engineering Context:** Consider a dataset of temperature readings from multiple sensors in a manufacturing plant. If one sensor intermittently fails, replacing its missing readings with the average temperature of all sensors might seem logical. However, if different sensors monitor different zones with distinct temperature profiles, the overall average might not accurately reflect the local conditions, leading to skewed performance assessments or control adjustments.

### Median Imputation

Similar to mean imputation,
**median imputation** replaces missing values with the median of the observed data for that feature. The median is the middle value of a dataset when it is ordered.

**Advantages:**

**Robustness to Outliers:** The median is less sensitive to extreme values (outliers) compared to the mean. This makes it a better choice for features with skewed distributions or the presence of outliers.
**Simplicity and Efficiency:** Easy to implement and computationally inexpensive.

**Disadvantages:**

**Distorts Variance:** Like mean imputation, it reduces variance.
**Biases Correlations:** It can still distort correlations between variables.
**Ignores Feature Relationships:** Does not leverage relationships between features.

**Engineering Context:** Imagine a dataset of vibration readings from rotating machinery. If a particular sensor reading is missing due to a transient electrical glitch, and the vibration data is often characterized by occasional high-amplitude spikes (outliers), using the median vibration level would be more appropriate than the mean. This prevents a few exceptionally high readings from unduly influencing the imputed value and subsequently distorting the statistical representation of normal operation.

### Mode Imputation

**Mode imputation** is used for categorical or discrete features. The mode is the most frequently occurring value in a feature. Missing values are replaced by the mode of the observed values.

**Advantages:**

**Suitable for Categorical Data:** The only sensible imputation for nominal or ordinal categorical features among the simple methods.
**Simple and Efficient:** Easy to implement.

**Disadvantages:**

**Can Create Bias:** If the mode is heavily dominant, imputing it can still misrepresent the data distribution.
**Ignores Feature Relationships:** Does not consider relationships with other features.

**Engineering Context:** In a system that logs fault codes (e.g., 'Error*A', 'Error*B', 'No*Error'), if a specific fault code is missing for a particular operational cycle, imputing it with the most common fault code ('No*Error') might be the simplest approach. However, if this missingness is correlated with specific operational states where certain errors are more probable, this simple imputation would be misleading.

### Advanced Imputation Strategies

While simple imputation methods are quick, their tendency to reduce variance and ignore relationships between variables can lead to biased results. More sophisticated techniques attempt to address these limitations by leveraging the information contained within other features of the dataset.

### K-Nearest Neighbors (KNN) Imputation

**K-Nearest Neighbors (KNN) imputation** is a non-parametric method that imputes a missing value for a data point based on the values of its $k$ nearest neighbors. The "nearest" neighbors are determined in the feature space using a distance metric (e.g., Euclidean distance).

The process for imputing a missing value for a feature $X$ in a data point $p$ is as follows:

1. Identify the $k$ data points that are closest to point $p$ based on the other (non-missing) features.

2. Consider the values of feature $X$ in these $k$ neighbors.
3. Impute the missing value for $X$ in point $p$ by taking a weighted average (or simple average) of the $X$ values of its $k$ neighbors. For numerical features, a weighted average, where closer neighbors have more influence, is often preferred. For categorical features, the most frequent value among the neighbors is used.

**Advantages:**

**Leverages Feature Relationships:** Accounts for correlations between features, providing more accurate imputations than univariate methods.

**Handles Non-linear Relationships:** Can capture complex, non-linear relationships between variables.
**No Distribution Assumption:** Does not assume a specific distribution for the data.

**Disadvantages:**

**Computational Cost:** Can be computationally expensive, especially for large datasets or when $k$ is large, as it requires calculating distances between data points.
**Sensitivity to $k$ and Distance Metric:** The choice of $k$ and the distance metric can significantly impact the imputation quality.
**Curse of Dimensionality:** Performance can degrade in high-dimensional spaces, as distance measures become less meaningful.
**Requires All Other Features:** Requires all other features to be present and in a suitable format for distance calculation.

**Engineering Context:** Consider a complex industrial process monitored by numerous sensors measuring pressure, temperature, flow rate, and voltage. If a single temperature sensor fails for a short period, KNN imputation can use the readings from nearby sensors (e.g., pressure and flow rate in the same unit, or temperature from adjacent units) to estimate the missing temperature. If the process exhibits strong correlations (e.g., increased flow rate leading to increased temperature under normal conditions), KNN can effectively use these relationships to provide a much more informed imputation than simply using the average temperature from all sensors. The choice of $k$ would need to be tuned; a small $k$ might be too sensitive to noisy neighbors, while a large $k$ might smooth out important local variations.

## Regression Imputation

**Regression imputation** uses a regression model to predict the missing values. It involves building a predictive model where the feature with missing values is the target variable, and the other features are predictors.

The process typically involves:

1. Select a feature with missing values, say $Y$.

2. Use the subset of data where $Y$ is observed to train a regression model (e.g., linear regression, polynomial regression, or even more complex models) to predict $Y$ based on other available features ($X_1, X_2, \dots, X_m$).
3. Use the trained model to predict the values of $Y$ for the data points where $Y$ is missing.

**Advantages:**

**Leverages Feature Relationships:** Explicitly models the relationship between the target variable and predictor variables.
**Can be Accurate:** Potentially more accurate than simple imputation methods if strong linear or non-linear relationships exist.

**Disadvantages:**

**Assumes a Model:** Assumes that the relationship between variables can be captured by the chosen regression model. If the model is misspecified (e.g., using linear regression for a non-linear relationship), the imputation can be biased.
**Reduces Variance (Potentially):** Similar to mean imputation, if the model has high predictive power and the errors are small, it can still reduce the observed variance.
**Requires Careful Model Selection:** The choice of regression model is critical.
**Computational Cost:** Training regression models can be computationally intensive, especially with many features or complex models.

**Engineering Context:** Suppose we have a dataset for an electrical grid including voltage, current, and power factor measurements. If the power factor for a particular measurement period is missing, and we know that power factor is often strongly correlated with voltage and current, we could train a regression model (e.g., a linear regression) to predict the power factor using voltage and current as predictors. The missing power factor values would then be filled in by the predictions from this model. This method is more sophisticated than simply using the average power factor, as it accounts for the specific operating conditions (voltage and current) at the time the data was recorded.

### Multiple Imputation (MI)

**Multiple Imputation (MI)** is a more advanced technique that addresses the uncertainty associated with imputation. Instead of filling in missing values with a single plausible value, MI creates multiple complete datasets, each with different imputed values.

The general MI process involves three steps:

1.
**Imputation:** Generate $m$ complete datasets. For each missing value, instead of imputing a single value, a plausible value is drawn from a distribution that reflects the uncertainty about the true value. This distribution is typically estimated from the observed data. Common imputation methods within MI include MCMC (Markov Chain Monte Carlo) methods or predictive mean matching.
2. **Analysis:** Perform the desired statistical analysis (e.g., calculating means, regression coefficients, hypothesis tests) on each of the $m$ complete datasets independently. This results in $m$ sets of results.
3. **Pooling:** Combine the results from the $m$ analyses into a single summary result. This pooling process accounts for both the within-dataset variance and the between-dataset variance (which reflects the uncertainty due to imputation), providing standard errors and confidence intervals that are more accurate than those from single imputation.

**Advantages:**

**Accounts for Uncertainty:** Properly accounts for the uncertainty introduced by imputation, leading to more valid statistical inferences.
**Reduced Bias:** Generally produces less biased estimates compared to single imputation methods, especially under MAR assumptions.
**Flexibility:** Can be used with various statistical models.

**Disadvantages:**

**Complexity:** Significantly more complex to implement and understand than single imputation methods.
**Computational Cost:** Requires generating multiple datasets and performing analyses on each, which can be computationally intensive.
**Requires Specific Software:** Often requires specialized statistical software or packages.

**Engineering Context:** Consider a structural health monitoring system for a bridge, where strain gauges and accelerometers collect data. Due to intermittent power or communication issues, some strain readings might be missing. Using Multiple Imputation here would involve creating, say, 50 slightly different versions of the complete strain dataset. Each version would have plausible values for the missing strains, reflecting the variability in what those strains *could* have been. Then, analysis (e.g., calculating the average stress or estimating the fatigue life) would be performed on each of these 50 datasets. Finally, these results would be pooled to provide a single estimate of stress or fatigue life, along with a realistic confidence interval that reflects not only the measurement noise but also the uncertainty from filling in the missing strain data. This ensures that the engineers are aware of the potential range of outcomes due to missing data.

### Deep Learning-Based Imputation

With the rise of deep learning, neural networks are increasingly being used for imputation, especially for complex, high-dimensional, or sequential data. Techniques such as autoencoders and recurrent neural networks (RNNs) can learn intricate patterns and dependencies within data.

**Autoencoders:** These neural networks are trained to reconstruct their input. By corrupting the input (e.g., by masking some values, simulating missing data), an autoencoder can learn to "denoise" or "fill in" the missing parts. The encoder compresses the input into a lower-dimensional representation, and the decoder reconstructs the original input from this representation. For imputation, the decoder part can be used to reconstruct the masked or missing values.
**Recurrent Neural Networks (RNNs) and LSTMs:** For time-series data, RNNs and their variants like LSTMs are well-suited. They can learn temporal dependencies. For imputation, an RNN can be trained to predict a sequence, and when parts of a sequence are missing, the network can generate plausible values based on the learned temporal patterns.

**Advantages:**

**Powerful for Complex Data:** Can capture highly non-linear and complex relationships, especially in high-dimensional or sequential data.
**Context-Aware:** Deep learning models can learn rich contextual information from the data.

**Disadvantages:**

**Data Hungry:** Typically require very large datasets to train effectively.
**Computationally Intensive:** Training deep learning models is resource-heavy and time-consuming.
**Black Box Nature:** Can be difficult to interpret how specific imputations are made, which might be a concern in critical engineering applications.
**Requires Careful Tuning:** Hyperparameter tuning can be challenging.

**Engineering Context:** In a scenario involving continuous monitoring of a complex chemical reactor using a multitude of sensors, deep learning-based imputation could be highly effective. For example, if the readings from a specific sensor are lost for several hours due to a network issue, an LSTM network trained on the historical sensor data could predict the missing values by considering the dynamic interactions between all other sensors and the temporal evolution of the process. This approach can capture subtle changes that might be missed by simpler methods, providing more accurate process state estimates during the outage, which is crucial for maintaining safe and efficient operation.

### Choosing the Right Imputation Strategy

The selection of an appropriate imputation strategy is not a one-size-fits-all decision. It depends on several factors:

1.
**Nature of the Data:** Is it numerical or categorical? Is it time-series or cross-sectional? Is the distribution skewed or normal?
2. **Mechanism of Missingness:** Is it likely MCAR, MAR, or MNAR? If MNAR is suspected, imputation might be less reliable, and domain expertise or specialized modeling may be required.
3. **Proportion of Missing Data:** If only a tiny fraction of data is missing (e.g., less than 1-5%), simple methods might suffice. As the proportion increases, more sophisticated methods become necessary to avoid significant bias.
4. **Goal of the Analysis:** Is the primary goal descriptive statistics, predictive modeling, or causal inference? Different imputation methods have varying impacts on these goals. For predictive modeling, preserving

relationships between variables is key. For inference, accounting for imputation uncertainty (as in MI) is crucial.
5. **Computational Resources:** The available time, processing power, and memory will dictate the feasibility of complex imputation techniques.
6. **Domain Expertise:** Understanding the engineering system from which the data originates is invaluable. It can inform assumptions about data relationships and the plausibility of imputed values. For example, knowing that certain parameters should never exceed physical limits is important.

**A Practical Workflow:**

A common and pragmatic approach to handling missing data involves:

**Initial Assessment:** Identify missing values, their patterns, and their proportion. Visualize missingness to understand if it's random or patterned.
**Consider Simple Methods First:** For small amounts of missing data or as a baseline, try mean, median, or mode imputation. Evaluate their impact on key statistics and simple models.
**Explore Advanced Methods:** If simple methods are insufficient or introduce noticeable bias, move to KNN, regression, or deep learning imputation. Compare their performance using appropriate metrics (e.g., by artificially removing data, imputing, and comparing imputed values to original ones, or by evaluating the performance of downstream models).
**For Inference, Use Multiple Imputation:** If statistical inference (e.g., hypothesis testing, confidence intervals) is critical, MI is generally the preferred method.
**Validate and Document:** Whichever method is chosen, it's essential to validate its impact and document the process thoroughly. Understanding how imputation affects results is key to trustworthy data analysis.

In engineering, where data quality directly impacts safety, efficiency, and reliability, addressing missing data with appropriate imputation strategies is not merely a procedural step; it is a fundamental requirement for building robust and dependable systems. The choice of method should be a deliberate one, informed by a deep understanding of the data, the problem at hand, and the potential consequences of imputation choices.

The integrity of data is not merely a matter of filling in the gaps, as explored in the previous discussion on imputation. It extends critically to the active process of **Data Validation and Verification Techniques**. These are the systematic procedures and checks put in place to ensure that the data entering, traversing, and residing within our engineering systems is not only complete but also accurate, consistent, and meaningful. Without robust validation and verification, even the most sophisticated imputation techniques or analytical models can be built upon a foundation of flawed information, leading to erroneous conclusions and potentially catastrophic failures in real-world applications. This section delves into the core methodologies employed to rigorously assess and confirm the quality and trustworthiness of engineering data.

At its heart, data validation is the process of confirming that data is "fit for purpose." It's about asking: Does this data adhere to the defined rules, constraints, and expectations? Verification, on the other hand, often involves a comparison or corroboration against an independent source or known truth. Together, they form a crucial defense mechanism against a multitude of data quality issues.

One of the most fundamental aspects of data validation is ensuring **data conformity to expected formats and types**. In engineering, data streams are often characterized by specific data types: sensor readings might be expected as floating-point numbers representing measurements in volts or meters, status indicators as integers or enumerated types, and timestamps in a precise datetime format. A failure here can mean that a numerical reading is incorrectly interpreted as a string, or a date is parsed in the wrong timezone. This can lead to immediate errors in calculations or downstream processing. For instance, imagine a control system attempting to calculate a rate of change for a temperature sensor. If a batch of temperature readings was mistakenly ingested as text strings, the system would fail to perform the necessary mathematical operations, halting production or triggering an unnecessary safety shutdown. Implementing strict type checks at the point of data ingestion—ensuring a numerical field contains only numbers, a boolean field only true or false values, and a date field a valid date—is a primary line of defense. This often involves defining schemas that specify the expected data type, length, and any character restrictions for each data field. Regular expressions are a powerful tool for validating string formats, such as ensuring that a unique equipment identifier adheres to a specific alphanumeric pattern.

Beyond basic types, data must also conform to **predefined ranges and constraints**. Most engineering parameters have inherent physical or operational limits. A pressure sensor in a particular vessel might be designed to operate between 0 and 10 bar, with an absolute maximum tolerance of 12 bar. Any reading outside this range, such as -1 bar or 15 bar, is almost certainly erroneous. Such out-of-range values can arise from sensor malfunctions, transmission errors, or even incorrect calibration. Validation rules must be established to flag or reject data points that fall outside these permissible boundaries. For example, in a system monitoring a hydroelectric dam's turbine speed, a reading of 5000 RPM when the maximum operational speed is 500 RPM would immediately be flagged. The action taken upon detecting such an anomaly can vary: it might be to log the data point as suspect, to replace it with a null value (triggering imputation processes), or to halt the data flow and alert an operator for immediate investigation. The choice depends on the criticality of the data and the potential impact of erroneous values.

**Consistency checks** are another vital component, particularly in systems where data originates from multiple sources or is aggregated over time. Data should be consistent both internally within a single record and externally across related records or datasets.

**Internal Consistency:** This refers to the logical relationships between different fields within the same data record. For example, in a dataset logging vehicle performance, if the 'engine RPM' is recorded as 2000 and 'vehicle speed' is recorded as 0 km/h, and the transmission is in 'Drive', this might indicate an internal inconsistency (unless it's a hybrid vehicle in an electric-only mode, for instance). In manufacturing, if a 'production batch ID' is recorded with a 'completion timestamp' that precedes its 'start timestamp', this is a clear internal inconsistency. These checks require understanding the domain and the relationships between different attributes.

**External Consistency (Cross-Source Validation):** This involves comparing data from one source with data from another source that is expected to represent the same or a related phenomenon. For instance, if a plant's central control system receives temperature readings from an individual sensor and also from a separate diagnostic module that aggregates data from multiple sensors in the same vicinity, these two sources should largely agree. Discrepancies can point to issues with one of the sensors, the communication links, or the aggregation logic. Consider a scenario where a conveyor belt system's speed is reported by the motor controller and independently by an optical encoder mounted on the belt. If these two measurements consistently differ by more than a defined tolerance, it signals a potential problem with either the motor controller's reporting, the encoder's accuracy, or the belt's slippage. This often involves setting up "golden records" or reference datasets against which incoming data is validated.

Establishing
**automated validation rules** is paramount for operationalizing data quality assurance. Manual checks are insufficient for the volume and velocity of data in modern engineering systems. These rules can be implemented at various stages of the data pipeline:

**At the Point of Data Ingestion:** As data arrives from sensors, devices, or external systems, immediate checks for format, type, range, and basic consistency can be performed. This prevents "bad" data from entering the system in the first place.
**During Data Transformation:** As data is cleaned, enriched, or aggregated, validation rules can ensure that these operations are performed correctly and do not introduce new errors. For example, after calculating a moving average, a rule might check if the averaged value falls within a plausible range based on the raw data used.
**Before Data Storage:** A final set of validation checks before data is committed to a data warehouse or data lake can act as a safeguard.

These rules can range from simple conditional statements (e.g., "IF `pressure` < 0 THEN FLAG_ERROR") to more complex statistical checks or even machine learning models trained to detect anomalous patterns. The rules should be documented clearly, version-controlled, and regularly reviewed to ensure they remain relevant as the system evolves.

**Cross-referencing with known benchmarks and historical data** provides a powerful layer of verification. In engineering, historical performance data often establishes a baseline for what constitutes "normal" operation. When new data arrives, it can be compared against these historical patterns. For example, a production line's output rate might historically fluctuate within a certain standard deviation. If a new batch of data shows a significantly higher or lower rate without a corresponding change in operating parameters (like input material quality or machine settings), it warrants investigation. This is akin to **statistical process control (SPC)** principles, where control charts are used to monitor process performance over time and detect deviations from expected variability.

Using established industry standards or expert-defined benchmarks is also a form of verification. For example, the energy consumption of a specific type of industrial pump under standard operating conditions is often well-documented. If the data shows a particular pump consuming significantly more energy than expected for its operational load, it suggests a potential issue with the pump itself, its control system, or the measurement of its performance.

Furthermore,
**data profiling** plays a crucial role in understanding the existing characteristics of data and identifying potential validation needs. Data profiling involves analyzing data to summarize its characteristics, such as:

**Value distributions:** Understanding the frequency of different values for a given attribute.
**Uniqueness:** Identifying unique values and potential duplicates.
**Missingness patterns:** Confirming the extent and nature of missing data.
**Data types and lengths:** Verifying the actual types and lengths against expectations.
**Outlier detection:** Identifying values that deviate significantly from the norm.

By profiling data regularly, engineers can uncover unexpected patterns or deviations that might indicate underlying data quality problems or the need for new validation rules. For instance, a data profile might reveal that a specific error code, which was historically rare, has suddenly become very frequent. This could prompt an investigation into a new system issue or a change in how error codes are logged.

The process of verification also extends to ensuring **data lineage and provenance**. Knowing where data originated, how it has been transformed, and who or what has accessed it is critical for debugging data quality issues. If a validation check fails, tracing the data's journey helps pinpoint the source of the error. Was it a faulty sensor at the source? A bug in a transformation script? An unauthorized manual alteration? Robust data lineage tracking provides this essential audit trail.

In sophisticated engineering systems, particularly those involving complex simulations or predictive maintenance, **model-based validation** is employed. Here, the data itself is used to validate a model, and conversely, a validated model can be used to validate incoming data. For example, if a physics-based model predicts a certain outcome based on current sensor readings, and the actual observed outcome differs significantly, it could indicate either an issue with the model or, more likely in this context, erroneous sensor data. Conversely, if an anomaly detection model, trained on historical "good" data, flags an incoming data point as highly unusual, this data point is a strong candidate for further verification.

**Data quality dashboards and reporting** are essential for providing visibility into the ongoing state of data integrity. These dashboards can track key metrics such as:

The number of records failing validation rules per day/week.

The types of validation errors most frequently encountered.
The percentage of data points that were imputed.
Trends in data quality over time.

Such reports enable proactive management of data quality, allowing teams to identify recurring issues, prioritize remediation efforts, and demonstrate the effectiveness of data quality initiatives.

Finally, it is crucial to recognize that data validation and verification are not one-time activities but rather **continuous processes**. As systems evolve, new sensors are added, operating parameters change, or external factors influence data patterns, the validation rules must be adapted. A culture of data quality, where every team member understands their role in maintaining data integrity, is more valuable than any set of automated checks alone. This proactive and iterative approach ensures that the data powering engineering decisions remains a reliable and trustworthy asset.
The ongoing health of any data-driven engineering system hinges not just on the initial validation of data, but on a vigilant, continuous process of monitoring. Once data has passed through the initial gates of validation and verification, the vigilance cannot cease. Systems change, sensors drift, external factors evolve, and new anomalies can emerge that were unforeseen during the initial setup. To navigate this dynamic landscape, the implementation of **Data Quality Dashboards and Monitoring** becomes not merely a best practice, but an operational imperative. These tools provide a crucial lens through which to observe the state of data integrity in real-time, empowering teams to detect, diagnose, and rectify issues before they cascade into significant problems.

At the core of effective monitoring lies the concept of **visualizing key data quality metrics**. Raw numbers and logs, while informative for deep dives, often fail to convey the overall health of the data ecosystem at a glance. Data quality dashboards transform these metrics into easily digestible visual representations, such as charts, graphs, and status indicators. These dashboards act as a central command center, offering a consolidated view of critical data quality dimensions. For instance, a dashboard might display the percentage of **data completeness** over a specific period, using a trend line to show whether more data is going missing. It could highlight **accuracy**, perhaps by comparing a sample of ingested sensor readings against a trusted, manually verified reference set or a physically plausible model, flagging any significant deviations. **Consistency metrics** can be visualized, such as the rate of records failing cross-field validation rules or the discrepancy levels between redundant data sources. The **timeliness** of data, crucial in real-time control systems or time-sensitive analytics, can be represented by the average latency of data ingestion or the percentage of data arriving within its expected window. By presenting these dimensions visually, even non-technical stakeholders can gain an intuitive understanding of the data's reliability, fostering a shared sense of responsibility for its quality.

Establishing and maintaining these dashboards requires a clear definition of what constitutes "good" and "bad" data for each metric. This involves setting appropriate
**thresholds and benchmarks**. For example, a manufacturing process might tolerate up to 1% missing readings from a non-critical sensor, but require near 100% completeness for a sensor that directly influences product quality. Similarly, a deviation of 5% in a critical temperature reading might be acceptable, while a 20% deviation warrants immediate attention. These thresholds should be dynamic, adapting to changes in operational conditions or system requirements. The dashboard should clearly indicate when a metric crosses these predefined thresholds, often through color-coding (e.g., green for acceptable, yellow for caution, red for critical) or distinct visual cues. This immediate feedback loop is fundamental to proactive data quality management.

Beyond mere visualization, the true power of monitoring lies in its ability to trigger
**automated alerts for data quality issues**. When a metric breaches a critical threshold, the system should not passively wait for an operator to notice it on the dashboard. Instead, it should proactively notify the relevant personnel. These alerts can be configured to be delivered through various channels, such as email, SMS, instant messaging platforms, or integrated into ticketing systems. The specificity of these alerts is key to effective intervention. An alert should not just say "data quality issue detected," but should ideally provide context: which dataset, which metric, which threshold was breached, and potentially, a link to drill down into the specifics.

Consider a scenario in a chemical processing plant where a flow rate sensor in a critical reaction stream begins to report values that are consistently outside the expected operational range and far from historical norms. Without automated alerts, this faulty data could be used to adjust reagent levels incorrectly, leading to a degraded product or even a safety hazard. However, with a robust monitoring system, the moment the sensor's readings fall below a lower bound threshold or exhibit an unusually high rate of change, an alert is automatically dispatched to the process control engineers. This allows them to immediately investigate the sensor, recalibrate it, or switch to a redundant sensor, preventing the propagation of erroneous data and safeguarding the process.

The design of these alerts is a nuanced process. Alert fatigue is a genuine concern; if systems generate too many non-critical alerts, operators may begin to ignore them. Therefore, a tiered alerting strategy is often employed. Low-priority issues might trigger a summary report at the end of the day, while critical breaches result in immediate, high-priority notifications. The alert system should also allow for intelligent grouping and correlation of events. For example, if multiple sensors in close proximity begin reporting anomalous values simultaneously, the system might infer a localized environmental issue or a network problem, rather than treating each sensor anomaly as an isolated incident. This sophisticated alerting can significantly reduce noise and focus attention on genuine problems.

The impact of these dashboards and alerts extends beyond immediate issue resolution to inform **preventative maintenance and continuous improvement**. By analyzing the historical trends on the dashboard, engineering teams can identify patterns in data quality degradation. For instance, if a specific sensor consistently shows drift in its readings after a certain period of operation, it might indicate that the sensor's calibration is decaying faster than anticipated, prompting a review of the maintenance schedule. If a particular type of data validation error (e.g., format errors for a specific incoming data feed) appears frequently, it suggests a need to revisit the data source's configuration or the ingestion logic. This historical data acts as a feedback loop, guiding efforts to improve the data collection infrastructure and processes, thereby reducing the occurrence of future quality issues.

Furthermore, data quality dashboards can be invaluable for **auditing and compliance**. In many industries, regulatory bodies require demonstrable evidence of data integrity and quality control. A well-maintained dashboard, with its auditable logs of metrics, thresholds, and triggered alerts, can serve as direct evidence of these efforts. It shows that the organization is actively monitoring its data, has established mechanisms for identifying and rectifying issues, and is committed to maintaining reliable information. This can be crucial during regulatory audits or for internal governance reviews.

The implementation of data quality dashboards and monitoring also necessitates clear

**ownership and accountability**. Who is responsible for setting up the dashboards? Who responds to alerts? Who analyzes the trends to drive improvements? Defining these roles and responsibilities ensures that the monitoring process is not a theoretical exercise but a practical, operational function. This often involves collaboration between data engineers, system operators, and domain experts who understand the context and criticality of the data.

To ensure that these monitoring systems themselves remain effective, regular review and refinement are essential. As systems evolve, new data sources are added, or business requirements change, the metrics, thresholds, and alert configurations may need to be updated. A process for periodically reviewing the performance of the monitoring system itself—evaluating the effectiveness of alerts, the relevance of displayed metrics, and the accuracy of thresholds—is crucial. This iterative approach ensures that data quality monitoring remains a dynamic and valuable component of the overall data governance strategy, fostering a robust and trustworthy data environment for engineering decision-making and operational control.

## Chapter 6: The Art of Data Labeling

In the realm of supervised machine learning, a fundamental concept underpins its predictive power: the **label**. Without these meticulously assigned markers, a model is akin to a student attempting to learn from a textbook with no answers to the practice problems. Supervised learning, by its very definition, requires a dataset where each data point is associated with a "correct" answer, or label. This allows the algorithm to learn the underlying patterns and relationships between the input features and the desired output. In engineering contexts, these labels are not abstract concepts; they translate directly into actionable insights and crucial system behaviors.

The indispensable role of labels becomes vividly clear when we consider the core objective of supervised learning: to train a model that can generalize its learning to unseen data. Imagine an engineering system designed to predict the onset of a specific type of equipment failure. The input data might consist of sensor readings (temperature, pressure, vibration, current), operational parameters (load, speed, duty cycle), and historical maintenance logs. For supervised learning to be effective here, each historical data point—each set of sensor readings and operational parameters at a given time—must be accompanied by a label indicating whether that specific condition was associated with the failure mode in question. This label could be a binary indicator: "Failure Imminent" or "Normal Operation." Alternatively, it could be a more granular classification, such as "Bearing Wear," "Overheating," or "Electrical Short," each representing a distinct failure mode. The quality and accuracy of these labels are paramount. If the historical data is incorrectly labeled—if a period of "Normal Operation" is mistakenly marked as "Failure Imminent," or vice versa—the model will learn a distorted representation of reality. This can lead to inaccurate predictions, potentially causing the system to either flag non-existent issues (leading to unnecessary maintenance and downtime) or, more critically, miss genuine precursors to failure, resulting in catastrophic breakdowns and safety risks.

Consider the application of supervised learning in image-based defect detection for manufacturing. High-resolution images of manufactured components are captured. The task is to automatically identify and classify defects like cracks, scratches, or inclusions. Here, the "label" is the annotation applied to each image. This could be a bounding box around the defect, a segmentation mask highlighting its exact shape, or simply a class label assigned to the entire image, indicating whether a defect is present and what type it is. For instance, an image of a circuit board might be labeled as "No Defect," "Solder Bridge," "Component Misalignment," or "Trace Break." The process of generating these labels involves human inspectors or specialized automated systems that meticulously examine each image, drawing precise boundaries or assigning the correct classification. If an inspector mistakenly marks a small scratch as a crack, or fails to identify a critical solder bridge, the model trained on this data will inherit these errors. The model might then learn to ignore minor scratches, potentially overlooking a precursor to a larger issue, or it might become overly sensitive to features that resemble solder bridges, leading to false positives. The precision of the label directly correlates with the precision of the model's detection capabilities.

In the domain of predictive maintenance for infrastructure, such as bridges or pipelines, labels can signify the presence and severity of structural anomalies. Sensor data from strain gauges, accelerometers, and visual inspection logs are collected. For a supervised learning model to predict structural integrity, historical data points need to be labeled with information about the condition of the structure at that time. A label might indicate "No Visible Damage," "Minor Corrosion," "Stress Crack Detected," or "Structural Fatigue." A more sophisticated labeling scheme could involve assigning a numerical score representing the severity of the anomaly. If an early stage of corrosion is missed during a manual inspection and the data is labeled as "No Visible Damage," the predictive model will not learn the subtle patterns associated with this early degradation. Consequently, it might fail to forecast the need for maintenance until the corrosion has advanced significantly, potentially compromising the structural safety of the bridge. The accuracy and consistency of these labels, often derived from expert human judgment or subsequent detailed analysis, are absolutely critical for the reliability of any predictive maintenance system.

The nature of labels can vary significantly depending on the specific supervised learning task. In
**classification problems**, labels are discrete categories. For example, in classifying the operational state of a pump in a water treatment plant, labels could be "Running," "Idle," "Priming," or "Under Maintenance." In **regression problems**, labels are continuous numerical values. An engineering example might be predicting the remaining useful life (RUL) of a component, where the label is a number representing hours or cycles until failure. The target variable in a regression task is the numerical label itself.

Furthermore, the dimensionality of labels can also differ. In many basic classification tasks, each data point has a single label. However, in more complex scenarios, data points might be associated with multiple labels, a situation known as multi-label classification. For instance, a single image of a complex industrial machine might exhibit signs of both overheating in one component and abnormal vibration in another. A multi-label approach would assign both "Overheating" and "Abnormal Vibration" as labels to that image. Similarly, in object detection, not only is an image classified as containing certain objects, but each object is also assigned a label and a bounding box, representing its type and location.

The economic and operational implications of label quality cannot be overstated. Poorly labeled data introduces noise into the training process, forcing the model to contend with conflicting information. This can lead to:

**Reduced Model Accuracy:** The most direct consequence is a decline in the model's ability to make correct predictions. The model might consistently misclassify certain types of events or under-predict the severity of issues.
**Increased Training Time and Cost:** Models trained on noisy data often require more training epochs and larger datasets to achieve a reasonable level of performance. This translates to higher computational costs and longer development cycles.
**Poor Generalization:** A model trained on inaccurate labels may overfit to the specific errors present in the training data, failing to perform well on new, unseen data that follows the true underlying patterns.
**Loss of Trust and Adoption:** If a deployed model frequently makes incorrect predictions, engineers and operators will lose confidence in the system, hindering its adoption and undermining the benefits of AI in engineering applications.
**Safety and Financial Risks:** In critical engineering applications, inaccurate predictions stemming from poor labels can lead to equipment damage, environmental incidents, or even harm to personnel, resulting in significant financial losses and reputational damage.

Consider a practical scenario in aerospace engineering where supervised learning is used for anomaly detection in flight data. Sensors on an aircraft generate vast amounts of telemetry data. For training a model to detect unusual sensor behavior that might indicate an impending issue, historical flight data is meticulously reviewed. Each segment of flight data—a period of time characterized by a specific set of sensor readings—is labeled by expert aviation engineers. These labels might indicate "Normal Operation," "Minor Turbulence Encountered," "Engine Performance Anomaly Detected," or "Unusual Control Surface

Movement." If, during the labeling process, an engineer fails to notice a subtle but significant deviation in a gyroscope's readings during a period of otherwise routine flight, and labels it as "Normal Operation," the supervised model will not learn to associate that specific pattern with any form of anomaly. When this pattern re-occurs in future flights, the model might miss it, potentially overlooking a critical precursor to a more serious flight control issue. The cost of such an oversight in aviation is immeasurable.

The creation of high-quality labels is an art that requires domain expertise, meticulous attention to detail, and robust processes. It often involves:

**Clear Definition of Labeling Guidelines:** Establishing precise criteria for what constitutes each label. For instance, defining the exact characteristics of a "crack" versus a "surface imperfection" in a manufacturing defect detection task. This ensures consistency among multiple labelers.
**Expert Domain Knowledge:** Engaging engineers and subject matter experts who possess deep understanding of the system or phenomenon being modeled. Their insights are crucial for accurately interpreting data and assigning appropriate labels, especially for complex or subtle patterns.
**Quality Control and Validation:** Implementing multiple layers of review for the labeled data. This can include having multiple labelers annotate the same data points and comparing their outputs (inter-annotator agreement), or having senior experts review a subset of the labels.
**Iterative Refinement:** Recognizing that the labeling process is not static. As the understanding of the problem evolves or as the model encounters new types of data, the labeling guidelines and the labels themselves may need to be revisited and refined.

**Tools and Infrastructure:** Utilizing specialized labeling platforms that streamline the annotation process, offer visualization tools, and facilitate quality checks. These tools can significantly improve efficiency and accuracy.

The impact of labels extends beyond just training a model; they are also critical for evaluating its performance. Metrics like accuracy, precision, recall, and F1-score are calculated by comparing the model's predictions against the ground truth labels in a held-out test dataset. If the test dataset itself is poorly labeled, these evaluation metrics will be misleading, providing a false sense of the model's real-world performance.

In summary, data labels are the bedrock of supervised learning in engineering. They are the "answers" that guide the learning process, enabling algorithms to distinguish between normal and anomalous states, classify different types of events, or predict continuous values. The quality, accuracy, and consistency of these labels directly dictate the reliability, safety, and effectiveness of the resulting AI models. As engineering applications increasingly rely on data-driven decision-making, the art and science of data labeling become not just a prerequisite, but a critical factor in unlocking the full potential of machine learning. Investing in robust labeling strategies and ensuring the integrity of labels is, therefore, a non-negotiable aspect of building trustworthy and high-performing AI systems in engineering.

The endeavor of data labeling, particularly within the intricate landscape of engineering applications, is far from a trivial exercise. While the previous discussion underscored the paramount importance of accurate labels as the bedrock of supervised learning, the practical implementation of acquiring these labels presents a spectrum of challenges and necessitates well-defined strategies. The quest for high-quality, consistent, and cost-effective labels drives the adoption of various methodologies, each with its own strengths, weaknesses, and applicability depending on the specific engineering domain and the nature of the data. Understanding these strategies is crucial for any practitioner aiming to deploy reliable machine learning models in engineering contexts.

One of the most direct, albeit often resource-intensive, approaches to data labeling is
**manual labeling by domain experts**. In engineering, this often involves enlisting the knowledge and discerning eye of seasoned engineers, technicians, or subject matter specialists. For instance, consider a scenario in aerospace where engineers are tasked with labeling high-frequency sensor data from an aircraft to detect subtle anomalies indicative of potential mechanical stress. These experts, possessing years of experience with flight dynamics and component behavior, would meticulously review segments of data, identifying patterns that might be imperceptible to an untrained observer. They might mark a specific sequence of vibration readings as "precursor to bearing wear," or a deviation in hydraulic pressure as "transient anomaly due to control surface flutter." Similarly, in civil engineering, structural health monitoring relies heavily on expert interpretation of sensor data. An engineer might examine acoustic emission data from a bridge and label specific signal patterns as "initiation of micro-cracking," or "evidence of bolt slippage." The value of this approach lies in the depth of understanding that domain experts bring. They can discern nuances, understand context, and make judgments that are not easily captured by simple rules or algorithms. However, this method is inherently limited by scalability and cost. Expert time is expensive, and the sheer volume of data generated in many engineering applications can make manual labeling an insurmountable bottleneck. Furthermore, inter-annotator agreement, or the consistency between different experts labeling the same data, can be a challenge. Even seasoned professionals may have slightly different interpretations of borderline cases, necessitating clear, detailed labeling guidelines and robust quality control mechanisms to ensure uniformity.

To mitigate some of the limitations of purely manual labeling, **semi-supervised learning** strategies have emerged as powerful tools. These methods leverage a small set of meticulously labeled data, often painstakingly curated by domain experts, to "teach" a model how to label a much larger corpus of unlabeled data. The core idea is to train an initial model on the limited labeled data. This model then makes predictions (labels) on the unlabeled data. These predictions, especially those made with high confidence, can then be added to the training set, and the model can be retrained. This iterative process, sometimes referred to as self-training or co-training, allows the model to progressively improve its labeling capabilities by learning from its own predictions. In an industrial automation context, imagine labeling images of manufactured parts for defect detection. A few hundred images might be manually labeled by an inspector, identifying defects like scratches, dents, or contamination. A deep learning model is then trained on this small labeled set. This model can then process thousands of unlabeled images, predicting the presence and type of defects. High-confidence predictions—for example, images where the model is virtually certain there is a scratch of a certain size—can be automatically added to the training set. The human expert then only needs to review and correct the low-confidence predictions or a random sample of the high-confidence ones. This significantly reduces the burden on the expert, allowing them to focus their attention where it is most needed. Another variant is **active learning**, where the model actively queries the human expert for labels on the data points that it is most uncertain about. This strategic selection of data to be labeled ensures that the expert's time is spent on the most informative samples, leading to more efficient learning and labeling. For example, in identifying anomalous sensor readings in a power grid, an active learning system might present the operator with data points that exhibit unusual but ambiguous patterns, asking for a definitive label to improve its understanding of rare fault conditions.

A third significant approach is

**programmatic labeling**, which involves using code, heuristics, rules, or existing knowledge bases to automatically assign labels to data. This method is particularly effective when there are well-defined patterns or logical relationships that can be expressed programmatically. For instance, in financial engineering, labeling transactions as "fraudulent" or "legitimate" can be partially automated by defining rules such as "if transaction amount exceeds $10,000 and is from an unusual location, label as potentially fraudulent." In the context of sensor data analysis for predictive maintenance, a rule could be established: "if the temperature of component X exceeds 150°C for more than 10 minutes, label the data as 'overheating event'." These rules can be derived from historical expert knowledge, engineering specifications, or observed data patterns. Frameworks like Snorkel have popularized the concept of "labeling functions," which are programmatic functions that encode heuristics or simple models to generate noisy labels. These labeling functions can then be combined using a generative model that learns to denoise and aggregate the outputs of multiple functions into a single, high-quality probabilistic label. This is incredibly powerful for engineering data where domain knowledge is abundant. For example, in manufacturing process optimization, one might define labeling functions based on different physical principles or quality control checks. One function might flag data points associated with high energy consumption; another might flag those with a high rate of material waste; a third might flag data where a specific machine parameter deviates from its optimal range. The programmatic labeling system can then combine these noisy signals to generate a more robust label indicating the overall "process inefficiency" or "quality risk." The advantage of programmatic labeling is its scalability and speed. Once the rules or functions are defined, they can process vast amounts of data almost instantaneously. However, the quality of the labels is entirely dependent on the accuracy and completeness of the heuristics or rules. These methods often struggle with subtle, complex, or context-dependent patterns that are difficult to codify explicitly. Moreover, developing and maintaining a comprehensive set of effective labeling functions can itself be a complex task, requiring significant effort and iteration.

When considering these strategies, several practical challenges and considerations come to the forefront, regardless of the chosen method. **Data preprocessing and feature engineering** are foundational. Before any labeling can occur, the raw engineering data must be cleaned, structured, and potentially transformed into features that are amenable to machine learning. For example, time-series data from sensors might need to be aggregated into fixed-length windows, or images might require normalization and augmentation. The quality of these preprocessed features directly impacts the effectiveness of the subsequent labeling process, whether manual, semi-supervised, or programmatic.

**Defining clear and unambiguous labeling guidelines** is paramount, especially for manual and semi-supervised approaches. Ambiguity in guidelines leads to inconsistent labels, which are detrimental to model training. For instance, in labeling images of structural cracks in concrete, guidelines must precisely define what constitutes a "crack" versus a "surface irregularity" or "construction joint." Should a crack of a certain width or depth be labeled? Should hairline cracks be included? Without such specificity, different annotators will label similar features differently, introducing noise and reducing the reliability of the labeled dataset. This necessitates a collaborative effort between data scientists and domain experts to create comprehensive documentation.

**Quality control and validation** are non-negotiable components of any robust labeling strategy. For manual labeling, this can involve multiple annotators labeling the same subset of data and measuring **inter-annotator agreement (IAA)**. Metrics like Cohen's Kappa or Fleiss' Kappa can quantify the level of agreement. Low IAA suggests issues with the labeling guidelines or the inherent subjectivity of the task, signaling a need for refinement. For semi-supervised and programmatic methods, validation is crucial to ensure that the automatically generated labels are sufficiently accurate. This often involves having domain experts review a statistically significant sample of the generated labels, or comparing the performance of models trained on different labeling strategies. A common technique is to use a small, high-quality manually labeled validation set to evaluate the accuracy of programmatic or semi-supervised labeling pipelines.

The
**cost-benefit analysis** of each labeling strategy is also a critical consideration. Manual labeling by domain experts offers the highest potential for accuracy but is the most expensive and slowest. Programmatic labeling is fast and cheap to scale but may sacrifice accuracy for complex tasks. Semi-supervised methods offer a middle ground, balancing cost and accuracy by optimizing the use of expert time. The choice of strategy often depends on the project's budget, timeline, the availability of domain experts, and the criticality of the application. In safety-critical engineering systems, where errors can have severe consequences, investing in higher-quality, albeit more expensive, manual labeling might be justified. For less critical applications, a more automated or programmatic approach might be sufficient.

Furthermore, the
**iterative nature of labeling** cannot be overstated. It is rarely a one-time activity. As models are developed and deployed, new data arrives, and performance is monitored. This process often reveals edge cases, new patterns, or previously unconsidered scenarios that require updates to the labeling guidelines or the addition of new labeled data. For example, a model trained to detect specific types of equipment failures might encounter a novel failure mode in the field. The data associated with this new mode will need to be collected, analyzed, and labeled by experts to retrain and improve the model's capabilities. This continuous feedback loop ensures that the labeling process remains aligned with the evolving needs of the engineering system and the machine learning models.

The
**choice of labeling tools and platforms** can significantly impact the efficiency and effectiveness of the entire process. Specialized data labeling platforms offer features such as intuitive user interfaces for annotators, project management tools, quality control workflows (e.g., consensus mechanisms, review queues), and integrations with data storage and model training pipelines. For image-based labeling, these tools provide sophisticated annotation capabilities like bounding boxes, polygons, and segmentation masks. For time-series data, they might offer specialized viewers for visualizing waveforms and highlighting specific events. For text-based data (e.g., maintenance logs), they provide interfaces for entity recognition and relationship extraction. Selecting the right tools can streamline the workflow, reduce human error, and facilitate collaboration among labeling teams.

In conclusion, acquiring high-quality labels for engineering data is a multifaceted challenge that demands careful strategic planning. Whether opting for the deep insights of domain experts through manual labeling, the efficiency gains of semi-supervised techniques that blend human intelligence with machine learning, or the scalability of programmatic labeling that leverages encoded heuristics, each approach presents a unique set of trade-offs. The key to success lies in a thorough understanding of these strategies, coupled with a rigorous approach to defining guidelines, implementing quality control, considering costs, and embracing an iterative refinement process. The integrity of the labels directly underpins the reliability, safety, and performance of engineering AI systems, making the art and science of data labeling a critical, non-negotiable investment.

The practical execution of data labeling, especially in sophisticated engineering domains, hinges significantly on the selection and adept utilization of appropriate tools and platforms. These technological enablers are not mere conveniences; they are integral components of a robust labeling workflow, directly influencing efficiency, accuracy, scalability, and overall project success. The landscape of data labeling solutions is diverse, encompassing a spectrum from nimble open-source projects to comprehensive, enterprise-grade commercial platforms, each designed to address different facets of the annotation challenge. Understanding these offerings and their respective strengths is paramount for any team tasked with preparing high-quality labeled datasets for machine learning in engineering applications.

At the foundational level, open-source tools offer a cost-effective and highly customizable entry point into data labeling. These projects, often driven by community collaboration, provide core functionalities that can be adapted to specific needs. For image annotation, projects like **LabelImg** are widely recognized. This Python-based graphical image annotation tool supports various object detection formats such as YOLO and Pascal VOC. Its straightforward interface allows users to draw bounding boxes around objects of interest in images, assign class labels, and export the annotations in formats compatible with many popular machine learning frameworks. For tasks involving more complex image segmentation, where pixel-level accuracy is required, tools like **CVAT (Computer Vision Annotation Tool)**, originally developed by Intel, stand out. CVAT is a web-based tool that supports bounding boxes, polygons, polylines, points, and cuboids, making it versatile for 3D data annotation as well. Its collaborative features, including user management and task assignment, make it suitable for small to medium-sized teams. For text annotation, **doccano** is a popular open-source option. It provides a user-friendly interface for sequence labeling, text classification, and sequence-to-sequence tasks, supporting formats like BIO (Begin, Inside, Outside) for named entity recognition. The advantage of these open-source tools lies in their flexibility; teams can often modify the source code to integrate custom logic, build specific annotation interfaces, or connect them to existing internal systems. Furthermore, they eliminate licensing costs, making them particularly attractive for academic research, startups, or projects with tight budgets. However, deploying and maintaining these tools often requires in-house technical expertise, and they might lack the sophisticated project management, advanced quality control, and enterprise-level support found in commercial solutions.

Transitioning from open-source to commercial data labeling platforms reveals a more integrated and feature-rich ecosystem designed for professional data annotation workflows. These platforms typically offer end-to-end solutions that manage the entire lifecycle of a labeling project, from data ingestion and workforce management to quality assurance and export. Companies like
**Amazon SageMaker Ground Truth**, **Google Cloud Vertex AI Data Labeling**, and **Microsoft Azure Machine Learning data labeling** provide managed services that integrate directly with their respective cloud ecosystems. SageMaker Ground Truth, for instance, allows users to build datasets for various machine learning tasks, including image, video, text, and 3D point clouds. It offers built-in workforce options (private, vendor, or public) and sophisticated automated labeling capabilities (using active learning) to accelerate the process. These cloud-based platforms simplify infrastructure management, allowing data scientists to focus on the labeling task rather than server maintenance. They often include robust quality control mechanisms, such as consensus labeling (requiring multiple annotators to label the same data point, with disagreements flagged for review) and inter-annotator agreement (IAA) metrics.

Beyond the major cloud providers, a host of specialized commercial data labeling platforms cater to diverse needs.
**Labelbox** is a prominent example, offering a comprehensive suite of tools for managing large-scale labeling projects across various data modalities. It emphasizes collaboration, workflow automation, and advanced quality assurance features. Labelbox's platform allows for the creation of custom annotation interfaces, supports complex labeling tasks like semantic segmentation and video object tracking, and provides detailed analytics on annotator performance and project progress. For engineering

applications, particularly those involving sensor data or time-series analysis, platforms like **Scale AI** have demonstrated strong capabilities. Scale AI provides a managed workforce and a technology platform designed for high-accuracy data labeling, including tasks like time-series anomaly detection, where precise event marking and categorization are critical. Their expertise in handling complex data types and ensuring data privacy is a significant advantage for sensitive engineering projects.

Another category of commercial tools focuses on specific types of data or industries. For instance, platforms specializing in **autonomous vehicle data labeling** often offer advanced functionalities for annotating lidar point clouds, video streams with intricate object tracking, and sensor fusion data. Similarly, platforms focused on medical imaging provide tools for precise segmentation of organs and tumors, crucial for training diagnostic AI models. While these specialized tools might be highly effective for their niche, general-purpose platforms like **SuperAnnotate**, **CVAT (which also has a commercial enterprise version)**, and **Keymakr** aim for broader applicability, supporting a wide range of data types and annotation tasks relevant to engineering, from manufacturing quality control to infrastructure inspection.

The selection of an appropriate data labeling tool or platform is a strategic decision that impacts project timelines, budget, and the ultimate quality of the labeled dataset. Several key factors should guide this choice. **Data Modality and Complexity** is perhaps the most critical. If the project involves only image annotation for object detection, a simpler tool might suffice. However, if it requires multi-modal data (e.g., combining sensor readings with video), complex 3D point cloud annotation, or intricate semantic segmentation of industrial equipment, a more advanced platform with specialized features will be necessary. For engineering tasks involving time-series sensor data, the platform must offer robust visualization tools, the ability to mark specific time intervals, and support for categorizing events or anomalies within those intervals.

**Scalability and Workforce Management** are also crucial considerations. For projects requiring millions of data points to be labeled, a platform that can effectively manage a large, distributed workforce (whether in-house or outsourced) is essential. Features like task distribution, progress tracking, and performance monitoring become paramount. Commercial platforms often excel here, offering sophisticated dashboards and reporting tools. For teams working with external labeling services, the platform's ability to integrate with or manage these vendors is a key benefit.

**Quality Control and Assurance Mechanisms** are non-negotiable for engineering applications where accuracy is often directly tied to safety and reliability. The chosen tool should support robust QA processes. This can include features like:

**Consensus Labeling:** Multiple annotators label the same data, and disagreements are highlighted.

**Review Queues:** A dedicated workflow for senior annotators or domain experts to review and correct labels.

**Inter-Annotator Agreement (IAA) Metrics:** Built-in calculation of metrics like Cohen's Kappa or Fleiss' Kappa to measure consistency among annotators.

**Golden Datasets:** A subset of pre-labeled data used to test annotator accuracy and identify training needs.

**Data Auditing and Versioning:** The ability to track changes to labels over time and revert to previous versions if necessary, which is invaluable for iterative development and debugging.

**Workflow Integration and Automation** is another significant advantage offered by many platforms. The ideal tool should seamlessly integrate with the broader machine learning pipeline. This includes easy data import from cloud storage (e.g., S3, GCS) or databases, integration with model training frameworks (e.g., TensorFlow, PyTorch), and support for exporting labels in standard formats (e.g., COCO, Pascal VOC, JSON, CSV). Features like active learning integration, where the platform uses a preliminary model to suggest labels or prioritize data for human review, can dramatically accelerate the labeling process and reduce costs by focusing human effort on the most informative data points.

**User Experience and Customization** contribute significantly to annotator efficiency and morale. An intuitive interface reduces the learning curve and minimizes errors. For specialized engineering tasks, the ability to customize the annotation interface—adding specific tools, defining custom shortcuts, or integrating domain-specific terminology—can be a critical differentiator. Open-source tools often provide greater flexibility for deep customization, while commercial platforms typically offer a balance of user-friendliness and configurability.

Finally,
**Cost and Licensing Model** must be evaluated. Open-source tools are free to use but may incur higher operational and development costs. Commercial platforms typically operate on subscription models, often priced based on features, number of users, or data volume. A careful cost-benefit analysis, considering not only the licensing fees but also the potential savings in time, labor, and improved model performance due to higher label quality, is essential. For large-scale, ongoing labeling efforts, enterprise-level solutions might offer better long-term value through dedicated support, advanced features, and managed services.

In summary, the choice of tools and platforms for data labeling in engineering is a multifaceted decision. Whether leveraging the adaptability of open-source projects like LabelImg or CVAT for specific tasks, or opting for the integrated workflows and advanced quality control of commercial platforms such as Labelbox, Amazon SageMaker

Ground Truth, or Scale AI, the goal remains the same: to create high-fidelity labeled datasets efficiently and reliably. The best-in-class solutions provide not just annotation interfaces, but comprehensive environments that foster collaboration, ensure data integrity, and streamline the path from raw data to deployable machine learning models, thereby laying a solid foundation for the success of any data-driven engineering initiative.

Ensuring the integrity and accuracy of labeled data is paramount, particularly when the performance of machine learning models hinges on the quality of the input. In engineering applications, where precision can translate directly to safety, efficiency, and reliability, the stakes are even higher. A dataset riddled with inconsistent or incorrect labels can lead to models that misinterpret sensor readings, incorrectly identify structural defects, or fail to predict critical equipment failures, with potentially severe consequences. Therefore, establishing and maintaining rigorous quality control mechanisms throughout the labeling process is not merely a best practice; it's a fundamental requirement for successful deployment.

The journey towards high-quality labeled data begins with the bedrock of clear, comprehensive annotation guidelines. These guidelines serve as the authoritative reference for every annotator, a codified set of rules and examples that define what constitutes a correct label for every possible scenario. For instance, when labeling images of industrial machinery for defect detection, the guidelines must meticulously define what qualifies as a "scratch" versus a "dent," the minimum size or severity to be considered a "defect," and how to handle partially obscured objects. This involves providing abundant visual examples: images clearly illustrating each class, along with edge cases and ambiguous situations, accompanied by explanations of how they should be labeled. Ambiguity is a common adversary in data labeling, and the guidelines must proactively address it. For example, a guideline might state, "If a crack is less than 0.5mm in length, do not label it as a defect. If it is greater than 0.5mm but less than

2mm, label it as 'Minor Crack.' If it is 2mm or longer, label it as 'Major Crack.'" This level of granularity minimizes subjective interpretation.

Beyond textual descriptions, visual aids are indispensable. Screenshots from annotation tools demonstrating correct bounding box placement, polygon drawing, or attribute selection are far more effective than words alone. For complex engineering data, such as time-series sensor data, guidelines might need to include specific protocols for marking events. For example, how to differentiate between a "transient anomaly" and a "sustained fault" in vibration data, or the precise start and end points for labeling a "power surge" event. The language used in the guidelines must be precise and unambiguous, avoiding jargon where possible or clearly defining it if it is essential. Furthermore, the guidelines should evolve; as new edge cases or common errors are identified during the labeling process, they should be incorporated into an updated version of the guidelines, ensuring continuous improvement. This iterative refinement process is crucial, turning a static document into a living, breathing standard that adapts to the complexities of the data.

One of the most effective strategies for ensuring label consistency, especially when multiple annotators are involved, is the implementation of consensus mechanisms. The core idea is simple yet powerful: if multiple individuals independently label the same piece of data, and their labels align, there's a significantly higher probability that the label is correct. Conversely, discrepancies signal potential issues that warrant further investigation. The most common form of consensus is **majority voting**. In this approach, each data point is assigned to multiple annotators (typically three or five). If, for instance, three annotators label an image, and two of them draw a bounding box around the same object with the same class label, that label is accepted. If all three disagree, or if there's a tie, the data point is flagged for review by a senior annotator or a domain expert.

The effectiveness of majority voting is directly proportional to the number of annotators assigned to each item. While assigning a higher number of annotators increases confidence, it also increases costs. The optimal number often depends on the complexity of the task and the required level of confidence. For critical engineering applications, a higher consensus threshold (e.g., 4 out of 5 annotators agreeing) might be necessary. Beyond simple majority, more sophisticated consensus methods can be employed.

**Adjudication**, for example, involves a designated reviewer who resolves all disagreements. This reviewer might be a project manager, a senior data scientist, or a domain expert who has the final say. This method ensures a single, authoritative label but places a significant burden on the adjudicator. Another valuable approach is **inter-annotator agreement (IAA) metrics**. Metrics like Cohen's Kappa, Fleiss' Kappa, or Krippendorff's Alpha can quantify the level of agreement among annotators. Low IAA scores serve as an early warning system, indicating that either the guidelines are unclear, the annotators require more training, or the task itself is inherently too subjective. Regularly monitoring IAA not only highlights potential quality issues but also provides insights into the clarity of the annotation guidelines and the proficiency of the labeling team.

To objectively assess annotator performance and calibrate their understanding against a known standard, the use of **gold standard datasets** is invaluable. A gold standard dataset, also known as a ground truth dataset or a reference set, comprises data points that have been meticulously labeled by one or more highly trusted domain experts. These labels are considered the definitive truth. When annotators begin a project, or at regular intervals, they are tasked with labeling a subset of this gold standard data. Their performance is then compared against the pre-defined correct labels. This comparison yields objective metrics on accuracy, precision, recall, and consistency. For example, if an annotator consistently misclassifies a specific type of sensor anomaly in the gold standard data, it signals a need for targeted retraining or clarification of the relevant guideline. Gold standard datasets also play a crucial role in identifying potential biases in the guidelines or the annotator pool. If a significant portion of the annotators struggle with a particular type of data or labeling scenario within the gold standard, it might indicate an oversight in the initial guideline creation or a pervasive misunderstanding that needs to be addressed across the team. The creation and maintenance of gold standard datasets require significant investment of expert time, but the insights they provide into labeler calibration and overall data quality are indispensable for high-stakes applications.

Continuous monitoring and
**regular quality audits** are essential to maintain high standards throughout the labeling lifecycle. This is not a one-time check but an ongoing process. Audits can take various forms. **Random sampling** of labeled data is a common and effective method. A statistically significant portion of the completed labels is randomly selected and reviewed by an independent auditor or a quality assurance team. This review assesses adherence to guidelines, correctness of labels, and consistency across different annotators. Any identified errors are logged, analyzed for patterns, and used to provide feedback to the annotators. If a specific annotator or a group of annotators shows a higher error rate, targeted retraining or closer supervision is initiated.

Beyond random sampling,
**performance-based audits** can be implemented. This involves focusing audits on data points that were flagged by consensus mechanisms, rejected during adjudication, or where annotator agreement was low. These are areas where errors are statistically more likely to occur. Furthermore, audits can be conducted by domain experts who are not directly involved in the day-to-day labeling but can provide a critical expert perspective. For instance, a civil engineer might audit the labeling of structural integrity images, or a process control engineer might audit

the labeling of industrial process data. This expert review is particularly vital for engineering applications where subtle nuances can significantly impact the interpretation of data. The audit process should not be perceived as punitive but as a constructive feedback loop aimed at collective improvement. The findings from audits should be transparently communicated to the labeling team, fostering a culture of shared responsibility for data quality.

**Addressing labeler bias and ambiguity** is a nuanced challenge that requires proactive management. Bias can creep into labeling in several ways. Annotators might unconsciously favor certain interpretations based on their prior experiences, assumptions, or even fatigue. For instance, in an autonomous driving scenario, an annotator might be more prone to labeling uncertain pedestrian detections as "false positives" if they have previously encountered many misleading signals, even if the current data point is borderline. Similarly, if the training data used to prepare the annotators had a disproportionate representation of certain scenarios, annotators might over- or under-apply labels to data exhibiting those characteristics. Mitigating bias involves several strategies. First, ensuring diversity in the annotator pool can help by bringing different perspectives to the task. Second, carefully designed guidelines that explicitly address potential biases and provide clear instructions for handling ambiguous situations are critical. For example, if there's a risk of bias in identifying certain types of manufacturing defects, the guidelines should include specific instructions on how to label borderline cases objectively, perhaps by assigning a confidence score or a "neutral" category.

Ambiguity in data itself is also a significant hurdle. Engineering data, especially from complex systems, is often inherently noisy or incomplete. A sensor reading might be noisy, making it difficult to definitively classify an event. An image might have poor lighting or be partially obscured. In such cases, the annotation guidelines should provide a clear protocol for handling uncertainty. This could involve:

**Confidence Scores:** Allowing annotators to assign a confidence score (e.g., on a scale of 1-5) to each label. Low-confidence labels can then be prioritized for expert review.
**Ambiguity Flags:** Providing a specific "ambiguous" flag that annotators can apply when they are genuinely unable to make a confident decision based on the provided guidelines and data. These flagged items can then be routed to a higher-tier review.
**Iterative Clarification:** Establishing a feedback loop where annotators can pose questions about ambiguous cases to project managers or domain experts. These questions can lead to clarifications or updates to the annotation guidelines.

The process of creating and managing labeled data for engineering applications is an intricate dance between human judgment and technological tools, guided by the unwavering pursuit of accuracy and consistency. It demands meticulous planning, clear communication, and a commitment to continuous improvement. By establishing robust annotation guidelines, implementing effective consensus mechanisms, leveraging gold standard datasets, conducting regular quality audits, and proactively addressing bias and ambiguity, teams can build the high-fidelity datasets that are the bedrock of reliable and performant machine learning models in the demanding field of engineering. This dedication to quality in the labeling phase directly translates to confidence in the models that are ultimately deployed.

The previous sections have underscored the critical importance of robust data labeling practices for engineering applications, emphasizing the foundational elements like clear guidelines, consensus mechanisms, gold standards, and quality audits. This foundational work is essential for any data labeling endeavor, but it takes on a more specialized form when dealing with data that possesses inherent temporal or structural complexity. Engineering disciplines often grapple with data that is not a static snapshot, but rather a dynamic sequence of measurements or a multi-dimensional representation of a physical object. Labeling such data requires techniques that can capture these intricate characteristics, moving beyond simple point-in-time classifications or single-image object identification. This subsection explores the unique challenges and specific methodologies employed when labeling time-series sensor data and complex structural data, illustrating how established labeling principles are adapted and extended to suit these data types.

Time-series data, ubiquitous in engineering, is characterized by observations recorded sequentially over time. This can range from the continuous stream of readings from a vibration sensor on a rotating machine to the discrete temperature measurements taken at regular intervals within a chemical reactor. The inherent sequential nature means that the context of a particular data point is heavily influenced by its preceding and succeeding values. Labeling this type of data often involves identifying specific events, patterns, or anomalies within these temporal sequences.

One fundamental annotation technique for time-series data is **point annotation**. This is the simplest form, where a specific timestamp or data point is assigned a label. For instance, a single vibration reading might be labeled as "normal operation," while a single temperature spike could be flagged as "overheating event precursor." However, point annotations alone often lack the necessary context to be fully informative. An isolated spike might be a transient noise artifact rather than a genuine operational issue. Therefore, point annotations are frequently used in conjunction with other methods or as a starting point for more granular labeling.

A more informative approach for time-series data is **interval labeling**, also known as **segment labeling**. Here, a contiguous range of time is assigned a single label. This is particularly useful for identifying sustained states or distinct operational phases. For example, a period of high-frequency vibration might be labeled as "bearing wear detected," or a prolonged period of elevated pressure in a pipeline could be marked as "pressure anomaly sustained." Defining the precise start and end points of these intervals is crucial. The annotation guidelines must provide clear criteria for when an event begins and ends. This might involve thresholds for signal amplitude, rate of change, or duration. For instance, a guideline for labeling "pump cavitation" in acoustic sensor data might specify that the interval begins when the signal amplitude exceeds a certain decibel level and exhibits a characteristic spectral signature, and ends when both conditions are no longer met for a continuous period of 100 milliseconds. This granular definition helps ensure consistency among annotators.

Consider the example of monitoring the structural health of a bridge using strain gauges. Over time, these gauges record minute deformations. A labeling task might involve identifying periods of unusual stress. A simple point annotation could flag a single high reading, but interval labeling would be more effective for identifying sustained periods of elevated strain that might indicate a developing structural issue. The annotator would define the start of the interval when the strain gauge readings consistently exceed a predetermined safe threshold and continue to do so for a significant duration, and the end of the interval when the readings return to normal levels. The label assigned to this interval might be "high stress event" or "potential fatigue indicator."

Beyond simple states, time-series data often requires labeling of **event sequences**. Here, the focus is on identifying distinct, often transient, occurrences within the data stream. These events might have a specific duration and characteristic shape. For example, in industrial process control, an "actuator fault" might manifest as a sudden spike followed by a gradual return to baseline. Labeling such an event would involve marking its beginning, its approximate duration, and its type. This could be achieved through bounding boxes drawn over the event's waveform in a time-series plot, or by defining start and end timestamps along with an event type.

The complexity increases when dealing with **multivariate time-series data**, where multiple sensors are recording data simultaneously. For instance, a jet engine might have hundreds of sensors monitoring temperature, pressure, airflow, and vibration. An anomaly might not be apparent in any single sensor but could be a subtle correlation or divergence across several. Labeling such data often requires sophisticated visualization tools that can overlay or align different time series. Annotators might need to identify an "engine surge" by observing a specific pattern across temperature, fuel flow, and RPM sensors, and then label the corresponding time interval across all relevant sensor streams. This necessitates tools that can display synchronized views of multiple data channels and allow for synchronized labeling across them.

For engineering applications, time-series labeling is critical for tasks such as predictive maintenance, anomaly detection, and performance monitoring. For instance, in a manufacturing plant, labeling vibration data from a conveyor belt motor could help train a model to predict bearing failure. The labels might include "normal," "imminent failure," and "failure detected." These labels would correspond to specific time segments where the vibration patterns exhibit characteristics indicative of these states. The quality of these labels directly impacts the model's ability to accurately forecast future failures, thereby preventing costly downtime.

Moving from temporal data to spatially complex structures, we encounter data like 3D models, point clouds, or detailed schematics. These representations are common in fields such as computer-aided design (CAD), robotics, and civil engineering, where understanding the geometry and composition of objects is paramount. Labeling this data requires annotations that capture spatial relationships, geometric properties, and material attributes.

One common form of annotation for 3D data is **point annotation**. Similar to time-series data, this involves assigning a label to individual points. In the context of 3D point clouds, this could mean labeling each point with the object it belongs to (e.g., "car," "pedestrian," "road") for applications in autonomous driving perception, or assigning a material property to each point, such as "steel" or "concrete," in a 3D scan of a building for structural analysis.

A more prevalent technique for 3D object detection and segmentation is **bounding box annotation**. This involves enclosing an object of interest within a three-dimensional rectangular box. For 3D models or point clouds, these are often referred to as "3D bounding boxes." The annotator defines the box by specifying its center coordinates, dimensions (length, width, height), and orientation in 3D space. This is crucial for tasks like inventory management in warehouses using 3D scans, or for identifying and locating components in complex machinery. For example, in a scan of a factory floor, each piece of equipment—a robot arm, a CNC machine, a workbench—would be enclosed in its own 3D bounding box, along with its class label.

**Semantic segmentation** is another vital labeling technique for complex structures, especially for point clouds and 3D meshes. Unlike bounding boxes that enclose objects, semantic segmentation assigns a class label to *every* point or surface element within the data. This provides a highly detailed understanding of the scene or object. For example, in a scanned environment for urban planning, every point could be labeled as "building," "road," "tree," "sky," or "vehicle." This allows for detailed analysis of urban landscapes, calculation of green space, or identification of road surfaces for maintenance planning. Similarly, in medical imaging, segmenting a 3D MRI scan of a human organ would involve labeling each voxel (3D pixel) to delineate the boundaries of the organ.

**Instance segmentation** takes semantic segmentation a step further by differentiating between individual instances of the same object class. If a scene contains multiple identical objects, like several chairs, semantic segmentation would label all points belonging to chairs as "chair." Instance segmentation, however, would assign a unique identifier to each individual chair, labeling points of chair 1, chair 2, chair 3, and so on. This is important in robotics for grasping and manipulating specific objects or in augmented reality to place virtual objects correctly in relation to real-world instances.

For engineering drawings or CAD models,
**part-based labeling** is common. This involves identifying and labeling individual components or sub-assemblies within a larger structure. For instance, in a CAD model of an engine, each valve, piston, crankshaft, and gasket would be identified and labeled. This can be done using bounding boxes around 2D projections or by directly selecting and labeling the corresponding 3D geometry. This type of labeling is essential for design validation, manufacturing process planning, and creating intelligent component libraries.

A more advanced form of annotation for 3D data involves capturing geometric or physical properties. This can include labeling surfaces with **material properties** (e.g., density, thermal conductivity), **surface normals** (indicating the direction a surface is facing), or **curvature**. Such labels are critical for finite element analysis (FEA) simulations or for generating realistic rendering of objects. For example, in a scanned model of a bridge component, annotators might label different surfaces with their material composition (steel, concrete, asphalt) and their physical properties, which are then used as input for structural stress simulations.

When dealing with engineering schematics, such as electrical circuit diagrams or piping and instrumentation diagrams (P&IDs), the task involves identifying and classifying symbols, lines, and their connections. For example, in a P&ID, annotators would identify and label each piece of equipment (pumps, valves, heat exchangers), instruments (pressure transmitters, flow meters), and piping lines, along with their flow direction and properties. The connections between these elements are also critical and would be labeled to represent the functional flow of the system. This is crucial for understanding complex industrial processes, training operators, and performing safety analyses.

The challenges in labeling time-series and complex structural data are amplified by the sheer volume of data and the subtle nature of many events or features. For time-series, identifying a "precursor anomaly" that occurs days before a critical failure might involve sifting through massive datasets, where the anomaly itself is a faint deviation from normal behavior. Similarly, in 3D point clouds, distinguishing between noise and actual small features, or correctly segmenting objects that are partially occluded, requires significant expertise and careful annotation.

To address these challenges, the principles of robust labeling discussed earlier become even more critical. Annotation guidelines for time-series data must meticulously define temporal relationships, event boundaries, and criteria for distinguishing signal from noise. For 3D data, guidelines need to be precise about occlusion handling, definition of object boundaries in complex geometries, and criteria for differentiating similar object classes. Consensus mechanisms are vital, perhaps even more so, as subtle differences in interpretation can lead to significant discrepancies in labels for complex data. Gold standard datasets for these types of data often require extensive expert review and validation, making their creation a significant undertaking.

Furthermore, specialized annotation tools are indispensable. For time-series data, these tools need to offer interactive plotting, zooming, panning, and the ability to draw and manipulate time intervals. They should also support visualization of multiple synchronized sensor streams and potentially offer automated tools to suggest event boundaries that annotators can then refine. For 3D data, annotation platforms must handle large point clouds and complex meshes, providing tools for drawing bounding boxes, performing semantic and instance segmentation (often with the aid of semi-automatic or AI-assisted tools), and visualizing data from different angles. The ability to work with different 3D file formats (e.g., .pcd, .ply, .stl, .obj) and integrate with simulation or analysis pipelines is also highly beneficial.

In summary, labeling time-series sensor data and complex structural data necessitates specialized techniques that move beyond basic classification or object detection. Interval labeling, event sequencing, 3D bounding boxes, semantic segmentation, and instance segmentation are crucial methodologies tailored to the inherent temporal and spatial complexities of engineering data. The successful application of these techniques relies heavily on detailed annotation guidelines, rigorous quality control, and sophisticated annotation tools, all aimed at capturing the nuanced information critical for building accurate and reliable machine learning models in demanding engineering domains.

# Chapter 7: Data Augmentation for Robustness

In the realm of engineering, where data often dictates critical decisions and shapes the performance of complex systems, the robustness of machine learning models is not merely a desirable trait but an absolute necessity. Real-world engineering scenarios are rarely static; they are dynamic, unpredictable, and rife with variations that can significantly impact the performance of a model trained on a limited or idealized dataset. This is precisely where the strategic application of data augmentation emerges as a powerful and often indispensable technique. The core principle is elegantly simple yet profoundly effective: to artificially expand the size and diversity of our training datasets by creating modified versions of existing data. By doing so, we expose our models to a wider spectrum of potential inputs, thereby rendering them more resilient to the inevitable noise, distortions, and unforeseen variations encountered during deployment. This proactive enhancement of the training data directly translates into models that are less prone to overfitting, generalize better to unseen data, and ultimately perform more reliably in the demanding operational environments characteristic of engineering applications.

The imperative for data augmentation stems from a fundamental challenge in many engineering domains: the scarcity of comprehensive and representative data. Acquiring and meticulously labeling engineering data, as discussed in previous sections, is a resource-intensive process. Sensor malfunctions, rare operational events, or the sheer cost of instrumentation can lead to datasets that are not only limited in size but also imbalanced, with certain critical scenarios being severely underrepresented. Imagine training a model to detect anomalies in a manufacturing process. If the dataset predominantly consists of 'normal operation' data and contains only a handful of examples of actual critical failures, the model will likely struggle to identify these rare but crucial events when they occur in practice. Data augmentation acts as a powerful equalizer in such situations. By applying transformations to the existing 'normal' data, we can generate plausible variations that simulate different operating conditions, environmental factors, or minor sensor fluctuations. This artificially increased diversity helps the model learn the distinguishing features of anomalies without requiring an unfeasibly large collection of actual failure instances.

Furthermore, engineering systems are constantly subjected to real-world imperfections that are often absent in meticulously curated laboratory datasets. Vibration, temperature fluctuations, electrical noise, varying lighting conditions in visual inspection tasks, or slight variations in material properties are all commonplace. A model trained solely on pristine data will be brittle; it will falter when faced with these unavoidable perturbations. Data augmentation provides a mechanism to systematically introduce these real-world variations into the training process. For example, in the context of analyzing images from a thermal camera inspecting electrical components, augmenting the dataset with images that have added random noise, slight blur, or variations in contrast can help a model become invariant to these common imaging artifacts. This ensures that a slightly noisy thermal image of an overheating component is still correctly identified, even if the noise level differs from what was present in the original training set.

The benefit of data augmentation extends beyond simply increasing the volume of data; it is about enriching its quality and representational capacity. By generating variations that mirror potential real-world scenarios, we are essentially teaching the model to be invariant to certain types of changes. For instance, if we are training a system to recognize different types of mechanical failures from audio signals, augmenting the data with variations in background noise, different microphone sensitivities, or slight speed variations in the machinery helps the model focus on the intrinsic acoustic signatures of the failures rather than superficial environmental factors. This leads to a more generalized understanding, where the model can reliably diagnose issues regardless of minor deviations in the recording conditions.

Consider the critical field of autonomous vehicle development. The sensors on a self-driving car—cameras, LiDAR, radar—are exposed to an unimaginably vast array of conditions: different times of day, varying weather (rain, snow, fog), diverse road surfaces, and a multitude of object appearances. It is practically impossible to collect and label training data for every conceivable scenario. Data augmentation becomes a cornerstone of training robust perception systems. For camera data, this can involve geometric transformations like random cropping, flipping, rotation, and scaling to simulate different viewing perspectives and distances. Photometric transformations, such as adjusting brightness, contrast, saturation, and hue, can simulate different lighting conditions and camera settings. For LiDAR data, techniques like random point dropping, jittering, and rotation can mimic sensor noise or slight changes in vehicle orientation. These augmentations allow the model to learn to detect pedestrians, vehicles, and road signs accurately, even under challenging and varied environmental conditions.

In predictive maintenance, identifying subtle precursors to equipment failure is paramount. These precursors often manifest as minor deviations in sensor readings that can be easily masked by operational noise or temporary environmental changes. For instance, a slight increase in vibration amplitude at a specific frequency might indicate incipient bearing damage. If this subtle signature is occasionally obscured by the inherent variability of normal machine operation or slight calibration drift in the sensor, a model trained on limited data might miss it. Data augmentation can help by introducing controlled levels of noise and simulating slight drifts, forcing the model to learn to discern the true signal of degradation amidst these perturbations. This is crucial because real-world deployment will inevitably involve such variations.

The concept of robustness, in the context of machine learning, directly correlates with a model's ability to perform well across a wide distribution of data, not just on the specific samples it was trained on. Data augmentation is a powerful, computationally efficient strategy to bridge the gap between the training distribution and the real-world deployment distribution. By systematically introducing variations that are representative of the expected operational environment, we are effectively making the model more robust. This means the model becomes less sensitive to minor deviations, more tolerant to noise, and better equipped to handle situations it has not encountered in its exact form during training. This is particularly vital in engineering applications where failures can have significant safety, economic, or environmental consequences, making a robust and reliable model a non-negotiable requirement.

Furthermore, data augmentation can play a role in mitigating the impact of data bias. If a dataset was collected under specific conditions, a model trained on it might perform poorly when deployed in environments that differ from those conditions. For example, a vision system trained to identify components on a production line might be highly optimized for the consistent lighting of that factory. If this system is to be deployed in a different factory with different lighting, or even used for quality control on parts that are stored under varying light before inspection, its performance might degrade. Augmentation techniques that simulate a range of lighting conditions can help create a more generalized model, less susceptible to the specific environmental biases present in the original training data. This is a proactive measure to ensure wider applicability and reliable performance across diverse operational contexts.

The effectiveness of data augmentation hinges on the careful selection and application of transformation techniques. These transformations must be relevant to the types of variations expected in the real-world deployment environment. Applying irrelevant or overly aggressive augmentations can distort the data to the point where it no longer represents the underlying phenomenon, potentially harming model performance. For example, excessively rotating images of machine parts might create unrealistic perspectives that confuse the model. The key is to generate plausible variations that enhance the model's ability to learn the underlying patterns and invariances, thereby building a more robust and generalizable system capable of withstanding the complexities of real-world engineering applications.

In the intricate world of engineering, where data streams flow continuously from sensors and monitoring systems, the temporal dimension of data is not just a sequence but a narrative of system behavior. This narrative, however, is rarely perfect. Real-world operational environments introduce a myriad of subtle and not-so-subtle distortions to these time-series signals. These distortions can arise from a multitude of sources: the inherent stochastic nature of physical processes, environmental fluctuations like temperature or humidity, electromagnetic interference, sensor drift, or even minor variations in the speed of an underlying process. When we train machine learning models on data that does not fully capture this spectrum of temporal variations, we risk creating systems that are brittle, prone to misinterpretation, and ultimately unreliable in their operational deployment. This is where the targeted application of augmentation techniques specifically designed for time-series data becomes paramount. These methods aim to artificially expand the training dataset by creating realistic, yet modified, versions of existing time-series observations. By exposing the model to these synthesized variations, we imbue it with a greater capacity to generalize and maintain performance under the diverse and often unpredictable conditions encountered in real engineering scenarios.

One of the most fundamental and widely applicable techniques for augmenting time-series data is the introduction of **random noise**. Sensor readings, by their very nature, are seldom perfectly clean. They are constantly affected by random fluctuations, often referred to as sensor noise. This noise can be additive, multiplicative, or a combination of both. To simulate these real-world imperfections, we can add a carefully controlled amount of random noise to the original time-series data. The characteristics of this noise—its mean, variance, and distribution (often Gaussian)—should ideally be chosen to reflect the expected noise profile of the sensors in the target deployment environment. For instance, if a sensor is known to exhibit Gaussian noise with a certain standard deviation, we would sample from a Gaussian distribution with that standard deviation and add it to each data point in the time series. This process helps the model learn to be invariant to minor signal perturbations. Imagine a vibration sensor on a rotating machine. Even during normal operation, there will be inherent vibrations and sensor noise. By adding artificial noise, we teach the model that small deviations from the 'ideal' signal are not necessarily indicative of an anomaly. This makes the model more robust to the sensor's inherent limitations and environmental interference, preventing it from falsely flagging normal operations as problematic. The amplitude and frequency content of the added noise can also be varied to simulate different types of interference or signal degradation. A more sophisticated approach might involve adding noise that is correlated over time, mimicking the behavior of certain types of persistent electrical interference or sensor drift. The key is to introduce noise that is plausible within the operational context, thereby enhancing the model's ability to distinguish true signals from background stochasticity.

Another powerful technique is **time warping**. Real-world processes do not always proceed at a perfectly constant pace. For example, a manufacturing process might experience slight variations in conveyor belt speed, or a chemical reaction might proceed at a slightly different rate due to subtle temperature fluctuations. These variations manifest as stretches or compressions along the time axis of the recorded data. Time warping techniques aim to simulate these temporal distortions. One common approach involves non-linearly stretching or compressing segments of the time series. This can be achieved by defining a set of control points along the time axis and then warping the time axis based on these points. For example, we could randomly select a segment of the time series and then stretch it by a certain factor, effectively slowing down the process in that segment. Conversely, we could compress it, speeding up the process. This transformation requires careful consideration to ensure that the warped time series remains physically plausible. For instance, if we are analyzing heart rate data, excessively stretching or compressing the signal could result in biologically impossible heart rates. Therefore, the degree of warping must be constrained by domain knowledge. Time warping is particularly effective for tasks where the shape of the temporal pattern is important, but its exact timing is less critical. Consider a system designed to detect a specific sequence of events in a complex industrial process. If the entire sequence occasionally unfolds slightly faster or slower due to variations in the upstream or downstream operations, a model trained without time warping might fail to recognize it. By augmenting the data with time-warped versions, we train the model to identify the characteristic pattern irrespective of minor temporal variations in its execution. This is achieved by creating synthetic time series where the sampling rate effectively changes over time, allowing for gradual stretching or shrinking of the temporal features.

**Amplitude scaling** is another straightforward yet effective augmentation technique. This involves multiplying the entire time series, or segments of it, by a random scaling factor. This operation directly affects the magnitude of the signal. In engineering applications, variations in amplitude can arise from several sources. For instance, the intensity of a measured phenomenon might vary due to changes in the input stimulus, distance from the source, or the gain setting of a sensor. In audio analysis of machinery, a louder engine might produce higher amplitude vibrations. In spectral analysis of electrical signals, the amplitude of certain harmonics might vary depending on the load conditions of a machine. By randomly scaling the amplitude of the training data, we train the model to be robust to these variations in signal intensity. For example, if a model is trained to detect a specific type of equipment failure based on its vibration signature, amplitude scaling ensures that it can still detect the failure whether the machine is operating at a higher or lower intensity. The scaling factor is typically chosen from a predefined range, ensuring that the scaled signal remains within physically plausible limits. It's important to note that amplitude scaling can be applied uniformly across the entire time series or selectively to specific frequency bands, depending on the nature of the variations expected. If the scaling is expected to affect all frequency components equally, a simple uniform multiplier is sufficient. However, if certain frequency components are more prone to amplitude variations (e.g., due to resonance effects), a more targeted approach might be necessary.

**Time shifting**, also known as translation, involves shifting the entire time series forward or backward by a random amount of time. This technique is particularly useful when the absolute timing of an event is not as critical as its occurrence relative to other events or its overall pattern. For example, if a model is designed to detect a specific fault signature that occurs within a longer operational sequence, a slight delay or advance in the onset of that signature might not change its fundamental characteristics. By applying random time shifts, we train the model to recognize the pattern regardless of its precise temporal placement within the broader context. This is akin to teaching the model to identify a melody without being overly sensitive to when the melody starts within a musical piece. The magnitude of the time shift is typically constrained to prevent events from overlapping unnaturally or shifting outside the boundaries of the observation window. For example, if we are analyzing a

10-second segment of data and shift it forward by 5 seconds, the original start of the segment is lost, and 5 seconds of new data would be needed at the end to maintain the segment length. Alternatively, the segment can be truncated or padded. Padding can be done with zeros, the mean value of the series, or by repeating the last observed value. The choice of padding strategy can itself introduce variations that contribute to robustness.

Combining segments of existing time series, often referred to as **segment recombination** or **mixup for time series**, offers a more advanced form of augmentation. This involves taking two or more existing time series (or segments thereof) and creating a new synthetic time series by concatenating or interpolating between them. For instance, one could take the first half of time series A and the second half of time series B to create a new sequence. Alternatively, techniques inspired by the mixup algorithm from image augmentation can be adapted. This involves creating a new sample as a convex combination of two existing samples: $\tilde{x} = \lambda xi + (1-\lambda) xj$, where $xi$ and $xj$ are two time series, and $\lambda$ is a random weight. This effectively creates synthetic data points that lie on the line segment connecting the two original data points in the feature space. For time series, this can be applied point-wise along the temporal dimension. For example, for each time step $t$, the value in the augmented series is $\tilde{y}t = \lambda y{i,t} + (1-\lambda) y{j,t}$, where $y{i,t}$ and $y_{j,t}$ are the values at time $t$ for the two original time series. This encourages the model to learn smoother decision boundaries and exhibit more linear behavior between samples, which can improve generalization. When applying segment recombination, it's crucial to ensure that the concatenated segments represent plausible transitions. For example, if combining data from two different operating states, the transition point should ideally reflect a realistic change in state. This technique can be particularly useful for creating data that represents transitions between different operational modes or for generating longer sequences from shorter ones.

Beyond these fundamental techniques, more specialized methods cater to the unique characteristics of time-series data.
**Frequency domain augmentation** is one such area. While time-domain techniques directly manipulate the signal's amplitude and time axis, frequency-domain methods operate on the spectral representation of the data, often obtained through Fourier Transforms. We can augment time series by manipulating their frequency components. For example, we could randomly attenuate or boost certain frequency bands. This might simulate changes in system dynamics that affect specific frequencies, such as the introduction of new resonant frequencies or the dampening of existing ones. Alternatively, we could introduce synthetic frequency components to simulate interference or signal artifacts that manifest at specific frequencies. This approach requires a good understanding of the underlying physical processes and the expected spectral characteristics of the signals.

Another nuanced approach is
**permutation or shuffling of segments**. While a complete shuffling of time points would destroy the temporal order, we can divide a time series into several contiguous segments and then permute the order of these segments. For instance, a time series representing a multi-stage process could be divided into segments corresponding to each stage. Permuting these segments would create a synthetic sequence where the stages occur in a different order. This technique is most applicable when the temporal dependencies between segments are less critical than the characteristics of the segments themselves, or when simulating scenarios where process steps might be reordered. For example, in a complex manufacturing workflow, a quality check might sometimes be performed before a specific assembly step. Permuting segments can help a model learn to identify component failures regardless of their position in the overall sequence of operations.

**Random cropping** of time series, similar to its application in image augmentation, involves selecting a random sub-sequence from the original time series. If the original time series is significantly longer than what is needed for analysis, random cropping can generate multiple shorter samples from a single long observation. This is useful when the temporal context beyond a certain window is not crucial, or when training models that operate on fixed-length sequences. It also helps the model focus on local patterns within the data rather than relying on the global structure. For instance, if a model is designed to detect anomalies that manifest over a few seconds, cropping a longer recording to different 5-second windows can create diverse training examples. The size of the crop window is a hyperparameter that needs to be tuned based on the expected duration of the phenomena of interest.

**Jittering**, a technique often applied to sensor data, involves adding small random perturbations to the data points. This is conceptually similar to adding noise but can be thought of as a very low-level form of perturbation that simulates the imprecision of measurement devices. Each data point $y_t$ *might be replaced by* $y_t + \epsilon_t$, *where* $\epsilon_t$ is a small random value drawn from a narrow distribution. This can help the model become less sensitive to minute variations in the signal, reinforcing the learned patterns.

When dealing with multivariate time series, where multiple sensors are recorded simultaneously, augmentation can also be applied across dimensions. For example,
**channel shuffling** or **channel dropping** can be employed. Channel shuffling involves randomly permuting the order of the channels (sensor readings) for a given time step or segment. This can help the model learn that the identity of a specific sensor might not be as important as the combination of signals it receives. Channel dropping, on the other hand, involves randomly setting the values of one or more channels to zero for a certain duration. This simulates scenarios where sensors might fail or

become temporarily unavailable, forcing the model to rely on information from the remaining sensors. This is particularly important for building robust systems that can tolerate partial sensor failures.

The choice and implementation of these augmentation techniques are not arbitrary. They must be guided by an understanding of the specific engineering domain and the expected real-world variations. Applying transformations that are physically implausible can lead to the generation of misleading data, which can degrade model performance rather than enhance it. For example, excessively distorting a time series representing a critical control system's parameters might create scenarios that could never occur in reality, thus providing no useful training signal. The goal is to mimic the types of noise, distortions, and variations that the system is likely to encounter during its operational life. This often involves collaborating with domain experts to identify the most relevant and impactful transformations.

Furthermore, the extent of augmentation—the magnitude of noise, the degree of warping, the range of scaling factors—is crucial. Overly aggressive augmentation can obscure the underlying signal, making it difficult for the model to learn the true patterns. Conversely, insufficient augmentation may not provide enough diversity to achieve the desired level of robustness. This often necessitates an iterative process of experimentation and hyperparameter tuning. Techniques like grid search, random search, or Bayesian optimization can be employed to find the optimal augmentation parameters that yield the best performance on a validation set.

The synergy between different augmentation techniques can also be powerful. Applying multiple transformations sequentially or in combination can create more complex and diverse synthetic data. For instance, one could apply time warping followed by amplitude scaling and then add random noise. The order of operations can matter, and careful consideration should be given to how these transformations interact. This combinatorial approach can significantly expand the effective size and diversity of the training dataset, leading to more resilient and generalizable machine learning models.

In summary, augmentation techniques for time-series data are indispensable tools for enhancing the robustness of engineering models. By intelligently introducing variations such as random noise, time warping, amplitude scaling, time shifts, segment recombination, frequency manipulations, and channel modifications, we can create synthetic data that better reflects the complexities of real-world operational environments. This proactive approach equips models with the ability to handle unseen data, tolerate sensor imperfections, and generalize across varying conditions, ultimately leading to more reliable and trustworthy engineering systems. The careful selection, implementation, and tuning of these techniques, guided by domain expertise, are key to unlocking their full potential.

The preceding discussion has underscored the critical importance of augmenting time-series data to foster robustness in machine learning models deployed in engineering contexts. However, engineering data is not confined to temporal sequences; it frequently encompasses visual information captured by cameras, imaging sensors, or even spectral data derived from various analytical instruments. These data modalities present their own unique challenges and opportunities for augmentation, necessitating distinct strategies to enhance model resilience. This subsection delves into these specialized augmentation techniques, focusing on image and spectral signal processing applications.

For image data, commonly encountered in visual inspection systems for quality control, automated defect detection, or monitoring the physical state of machinery and infrastructure, geometric transformations are fundamental. These transformations mimic the variations in viewpoint, scale, and orientation that an object or scene might present in a real-world scenario.

**Rotation** is a prime example. A camera capturing an object might be positioned at a slightly different angle, or the object itself might be rotated. Applying random rotations to training images, within a plausible range defined by the application (e.g., ±15 degrees for a standard inspection task), teaches a convolutional neural network (CNN) to identify features irrespective of their orientation. Consider an automated system for inspecting circuit boards for solder joint defects. A defect might appear slightly differently depending on the precise angle from which the image is captured. By augmenting the dataset with rotated versions of defect images, the model becomes less sensitive to these minor positional variations and more likely to detect the defect consistently.

**Flipping**, both horizontally and vertically, is another potent geometric augmentation. Horizontal flipping is particularly relevant for objects with bilateral symmetry. For instance, an inspection system looking for cracks on a component might benefit from horizontally flipped images if the crack could appear on either the left or right side of a symmetrically designed part. Vertical flipping is less universally applicable and depends heavily on the nature of the object and its typical orientation. A system inspecting aerial imagery of infrastructure, for example, might not benefit from vertical flipping if the "top" of the image consistently represents a specific geographical direction. However, for certain types of objects or patterns, it can introduce valuable diversity.

**Cropping** is a versatile technique for images. Random cropping involves extracting a random sub-image from the original. This serves multiple purposes. Firstly, it can simulate the effect of a sensor focusing on a particular region of interest, effectively creating multiple training samples from a single larger image. Secondly, it can help the model learn to identify objects or features even when they are partially occluded or appear at different scales within the frame. For example, in an automated visual inspection of manufactured parts, if a small scratch is the anomaly of interest, randomly cropping around potential scratch locations can help the model learn to identify such defects even if they occupy only a small portion of the overall image. The size of the crop window is a critical hyperparameter, determining the scale at which the model learns to recognize features. A related technique is **random resizing and cropping**, where an image is first resized to a larger dimension, then a random crop is taken, which can simulate objects appearing at varying distances from the camera.

**Shearing**, also known as skewing, distorts the image along an axis, mimicking perspective distortions or slight angular displacements. Applying a horizontal shear to an image shifts pixels horizontally in proportion to their distance from a reference line. This can simulate scenarios where the camera is not perfectly perpendicular to the object's surface, leading to a slight "leaning" appearance. For example, if inspecting the surface of a flat panel display, slight variations in the camera's angle might introduce shear. Augmenting with sheared images helps the model generalize to these perspective shifts.

Beyond these basic geometric transformations, more advanced techniques can manipulate the pixel values directly while preserving their spatial relationships to a degree.
**Brightness, contrast, and saturation adjustments** are common for color images. Randomly altering these parameters can simulate changes in lighting conditions, camera settings, or the inherent color properties of the material being inspected. A system designed to detect color variations in painted surfaces, for instance, needs to be robust to subtle shifts in hue, saturation, and brightness that might arise from different ambient light or minor variations in the paint application. Similarly, **color jittering** can

randomly alter the color channels (e.g., RGB values) independently, simulating subtle color casts or sensor imbalances.

For applications involving spectral data, such as Raman spectroscopy, infrared spectroscopy, or hyperspectral imaging, augmentation strategies often focus on mimicking variations in measurement conditions, sample preparation, or inherent spectral noise.
**Frequency-domain perturbations** are a key area. If the spectral data is represented in the frequency domain (e.g., after a Fourier Transform), augmentation can involve selectively amplifying or attenuating certain frequency bands. This could simulate changes in the underlying physical processes that affect specific spectral features, such as the introduction of spurious signals at particular frequencies or the dampening of characteristic peaks. For example, in analyzing the chemical composition of a material using spectroscopy, certain functional groups might exhibit characteristic peaks in specific frequency ranges. Augmenting by slightly altering the intensity of these ranges can help the model become less sensitive to minor variations in concentration or measurement noise.

Another approach for spectral data is
**adding spectral noise**. Similar to time-series noise addition, this involves introducing random fluctuations to the spectral intensity values. The nature of this noise can be tailored to mimic common sources of interference, such as electronic noise in the detector, cosmic rays, or variations in excitation intensity. Different noise models, such as Gaussian noise or Poisson noise (which is often more appropriate for photon-counting detectors), can be employed. This technique helps the model learn to distinguish true spectral signatures from random fluctuations.

**Baseline correction variations** can also serve as an augmentation strategy. In spectroscopy, the baseline of a spectrum (the slowly varying background signal) can be influenced by various factors, including scattering, instrument artifacts, or sample matrix effects. Augmenting the data by applying different baseline correction algorithms or by adding artificial baseline drifts (e.g., polynomial drifts) can help the model become more invariant to these baseline variations. This is particularly useful when the primary task is to identify specific peaks or spectral features that might be obscured or distorted by a non-ideal baseline.

**Filtering variations** are also relevant for spectral data. Applying different types of low-pass, high-pass, or band-pass filters with varying cut-off frequencies or kernel sizes can simulate changes in the resolution or smoothness of the spectral data. This can help the model learn to identify features across a range of resolutions and degrees of smoothing. For instance, if the spectral acquisition process sometimes results in sharper peaks and other times in broader ones, augmenting with data smoothed to different degrees can prepare the model for this variability.

Furthermore, for hyperspectral images, which combine spatial and spectral information, augmentation techniques can be applied independently or jointly to the spatial and spectral dimensions. Spatial augmentations like rotation and cropping can be applied to the image planes, while spectral augmentations can be applied to the spectral signatures extracted from pixels or regions of interest. Advanced techniques might involve
**spectral mixing**, where the spectral signatures of different materials are linearly combined to simulate mixed pixels, or **spectral band subset selection**, where only a random subset of spectral bands is used for training, forcing the model to learn from a sparser spectral representation.

When dealing with multivariate imaging or spectral data, akin to multivariate time series,
**channel shuffling** or **channel dropping** can also be applicable. For multispectral or hyperspectral images, "channels" refer to the different spectral bands. Randomly dropping certain spectral bands or shuffling

their order (if the order is not inherently meaningful) can create more robust models. Similarly, if multiple spectral measurements are taken from different locations or under different conditions, these can be treated as different channels.

The overarching principle for all these augmentation strategies, whether applied to time-series, images, or spectral data, is to create synthetic data that is
*plausible* within the operational context. Unrealistic transformations can do more harm than good. For instance, rotating a medical image of an organ by 180 degrees might be physically impossible or might fundamentally alter the interpretation of anatomical landmarks. Domain expertise is paramount in defining the bounds and types of transformations that are both beneficial for training and reflective of real-world variability. This ensures that the augmented data effectively serves its purpose: to imbue machine learning models with the robustness needed to perform reliably in the unpredictable environments of engineering applications. The careful selection and judicious application of these diverse augmentation techniques form a cornerstone of building resilient and trustworthy intelligent systems in engineering.
The preceding discussions have highlighted the indispensable role of data augmentation in fortifying machine learning models against the inherent variability and noise encountered in engineering applications, extending beyond temporal and basic visual data. However, the true power of augmentation is unlocked when these techniques are not applied generically but are meticulously crafted to reflect the specific nuances of a given engineering domain. This domain-specific approach moves beyond simulating general data variations to replicating the precise physical phenomena, operational conditions, and potential failure modes that a system is likely to encounter in its real-world deployment. By doing so, we imbue models with a deeper, more contextual understanding, leading to significantly enhanced robustness and reliability.

Consider the realm of structural engineering and civil infrastructure monitoring. Systems designed to assess the integrity of bridges, buildings, or pipelines often rely on sensor data, including strain gauges, accelerometers, or acoustic emission sensors. These sensors are subjected to a myriad of load conditions, ranging from routine traffic or wind loads to extreme events like earthquakes or impact damage. Augmenting sensor data for such applications demands simulating these varied load scenarios. Instead of simply adding random noise or applying generic transformations, we can generate synthetic data that mimics the expected strain or vibration patterns under different load magnitudes and types. For instance, a model trained to detect structural fatigue in a bridge might benefit from augmented data representing various levels of traffic density, wind gusts of differing intensities, or even simulated seismic tremors. This can be achieved by using finite element analysis (FEA) models to predict sensor responses under these diverse conditions and then using these simulated responses as training data. Furthermore, introducing realistic noise profiles characteristic of specific sensor hardware under these varying loads—such as electromagnetic interference during high-current operational phases or thermal drift during extreme temperature fluctuations—adds another layer of domain-specific realism. This ensures the model learns to discern genuine structural anomalies from sensor-induced artifacts that are correlated with specific operating conditions.

In the domain of manufacturing and industrial automation, machinery operates under a spectrum of environmental and operational parameters. Take, for example, a predictive maintenance system for a complex industrial robot arm. The performance of its actuators, sensors, and power systems can be significantly affected by ambient temperature, humidity, and the specific tasks the robot is performing. Domain-specific augmentation would involve generating training data that reflects these variations. If the robot arm is known to experience increased motor strain and potential overheating when performing heavy lifting tasks at elevated ambient temperatures, the augmentation process should synthesize sensor readings that capture this synergy. This could involve collecting baseline operational data and then applying physics-informed transformations or generating synthetic data using digital twins that simulate the robot's behavior under combined stresses of mechanical load and thermal effects. For instance, temperature-dependent resistance in electrical components or viscosity changes in lubrication fluids can be modeled and incorporated into the augmented data. Similarly, if a particular machining process generates a unique type of vibration signature that could be mistaken for a developing fault, augmenting data to specifically highlight or mask these process-specific signatures is crucial. This involves understanding the vibrational modes of the machinery and the expected outputs of the specific manufacturing task.

Communication networks, particularly those in industrial settings like wireless sensor networks (WSNs) for monitoring environmental conditions or controlling processes, are prone to various forms of communication interference. In these scenarios, robustness against packet loss, latency, and corrupted data is paramount. Domain-specific augmentation here would involve simulating realistic communication noise patterns. Instead of generic Gaussian noise, we might simulate fading effects characteristic of wireless channels (e.g., Rayleigh fading, Rician fading), introduce intermittent connectivity issues that mimic network congestion or device failures, or model the impact of specific sources of electromagnetic interference prevalent in industrial environments (e.g., from high-power machinery or radio frequency devices). For a WSN monitoring agricultural fields, augmentation might involve simulating signal attenuation due to rain, wind-blown foliage, or the presence of large metallic farm equipment. Techniques like Generative Adversarial Networks (GANs) can be trained on real-world examples of corrupted communication data to generate synthetic, yet realistic, corrupted packets, or data with altered timings and sequences, forcing the model to learn robust communication protocols and data recovery mechanisms.

The automotive industry presents a wealth of opportunities for domain-specific augmentation, particularly in the development of autonomous driving systems and advanced driver-assistance systems (ADAS). Perception models, for instance, need to be robust to a wide array of visual conditions. Augmenting camera data for these systems involves more than just random brightness or contrast changes. It requires simulating specific weather conditions like heavy rain, snow, fog, or glare from sunlight at dawn or dusk. These conditions not only affect image intensity and color but also introduce specific types of visual artifacts, such as reduced visibility range, blurring, the appearance of water droplets on lenses, or lens flare. Techniques like physically based rendering can be used to generate synthetic images that accurately capture the light scattering and absorption properties of different atmospheric particles. Similarly, for radar and LiDAR systems, augmentation must simulate effects like multi-path reflections off various surfaces (e.g., guardrails, other vehicles), attenuation due to precipitation, or interference from other sensors. Models for object detection and tracking need to generalize to partially occluded objects (e.g., a pedestrian partially hidden behind a parked car), objects seen at extreme ranges or angles, and objects with unusual appearances due to dirt, damage, or camouflage.

In the field of robotics, particularly in environments like warehouses or manufacturing floors, manipulators and mobile robots interact with objects and navigate complex spaces. Augmentation for these systems can involve simulating variations in object properties like friction, weight, and surface texture, which directly impact grasping and motion planning. If a robotic gripper is to handle a variety of objects, from smooth metal parts to irregularly shaped, textured plastic components, augmented data should reflect these tactile and visual differences. This can be achieved by synthetically altering the material properties in simulation environments and generating corresponding sensor data (e.g., force-torque sensor readings, camera images). Furthermore, simulating variations in lighting within a factory setting, or the presence of dynamic obstacles like moving humans or other robots, is crucial for navigation and interaction tasks. Generative models can be employed to create diverse object poses and configurations, and to simulate plausible human-robot interactions, ensuring the robot's decision-making algorithms are robust to the inherent unpredictability of real-world robotic operations.

Even in seemingly straightforward applications like quality control in food processing, domain-specific augmentation can be powerful. Imagine a system designed to detect surface defects on fruits or vegetables. While generic image augmentations like rotation and scaling are useful, domain-specific augmentation would involve simulating the natural variations in shape, size, color, and texture that are characteristic of that specific produce. It would also involve mimicking common types of defects relevant to that product, such as bruises, mold growth, insect damage, or cosmetic imperfections, and introducing these realistically. For example, a model for apple defect detection might be augmented with synthetic bruises that vary in size, color intensity, and shape, or with simulated mold patches that mimic the appearance and spread of fungal growth. This requires a deep understanding of the biological and physical characteristics of the produce and the common failure modes encountered during cultivation, harvesting, and storage.

The underlying principle across all these examples is the translation of domain knowledge into data augmentation strategies. This involves close collaboration between machine learning engineers and domain experts (e.g., structural engineers, manufacturing specialists, automotive engineers, roboticists, food scientists). Domain experts can identify the most critical sources of variability, potential failure modes, and the physical principles governing system behavior. This information is then used to guide the design of augmentation techniques that generate synthetic data that is not just statistically diverse but also physically and contextually plausible. This might involve incorporating physics-based simulations, leveraging digital twins, or using generative models trained on domain-specific data distributions. By moving beyond generic augmentation and embracing domain-aware approaches, we create training datasets that are far more representative of the complexities and challenges of real-world engineering scenarios, ultimately leading to machine learning models that are more dependable, resilient, and trustworthy.

The preceding discussions have underscored the paramount importance of data augmentation in enhancing the resilience of machine learning models, particularly within the intricate landscape of engineering applications. We've explored how domain-specific augmentation moves beyond generic transformations to capture the nuanced realities of real-world operations, from structural integrity monitoring and industrial automation to autonomous systems and agricultural technology. Yet, the introduction of augmentation techniques, while conceptually sound and practically valuable, necessitates a rigorous evaluation framework. The mere application of these methods does not inherently guarantee an improvement in model performance; rather, it is the judicious selection and implementation, followed by thorough assessment, that unlocks their true potential. This section delves into the critical methodologies for evaluating the impact of data augmentation on model performance, ensuring that these sophisticated data manipulation strategies translate into tangible benefits for the specific engineering task at hand.

To begin, a fundamental approach to evaluating augmentation's efficacy involves a direct comparison of model performance metrics on distinct validation sets. Typically, a machine learning project will involve a training set, a validation set (used for hyperparameter tuning and model selection), and a test set (used for a final, unbiased evaluation). When employing data augmentation, the training set is enhanced with

synthetically generated data. However, it is crucial to evaluate the model's performance on
*unaugmented* validation and test sets to understand how well the model generalizes to unseen, real-world data. This comparison is often framed as follows: first, a baseline model is trained *without* any augmentation. Its performance is then measured on the validation set using relevant metrics. Subsequently, the same model architecture (or an optimized one) is trained with the chosen augmentation strategies applied to the training data. The performance of this augmented model is then evaluated on the *same, unaugmented* validation set.

The selection of evaluation metrics is, of course, context-dependent and dictated by the specific engineering problem. For classification tasks, such as identifying defects in manufactured parts or classifying different types of structural anomalies, metrics like accuracy, precision, recall, F1-score, and the Area Under the Receiver Operating Characteristic Curve (AUC-ROC) are standard. A significant improvement in these metrics for the augmented model on the unaugmented validation set is a strong indicator of augmentation's positive impact. For instance, if a model trained with augmented sensor data for fault detection in rotating machinery shows a 5% increase in F1-score and a notable reduction in false positives (improving precision) on the validation set, it suggests that the augmentation helped the model better distinguish between normal operational noise and genuine fault signatures. Similarly, if an object detection system for autonomous vehicles, trained with augmented visual data simulating various weather conditions, demonstrates higher recall for pedestrians partially obscured by fog, this directly translates to improved safety.

Beyond classification, regression tasks are common in engineering. For example, predicting the remaining useful life (RUL) of equipment or estimating the load-bearing capacity of a structure. Here, metrics such as Mean Squared Error (MSE), Root Mean Squared Error (RMSE), Mean

Absolute Error (MAE), and R-squared are employed. If a model predicting RUL, trained with augmented operational data reflecting diverse usage patterns and environmental stresses, shows a lower RMSE and MAE on the validation set, it implies that the augmentation has enabled the model to make more accurate predictions across a wider range of operational conditions.

However, simply observing an improvement in standard metrics on a single validation set may not fully capture the benefits of augmentation, especially concerning robustness. Data augmentation is specifically designed to improve a model's ability to handle variations and noise. Therefore, evaluating robustness requires a more nuanced approach. One critical aspect is to assess the model's performance under conditions that are intentionally challenging or dissimilar to the bulk of the training data. This can involve creating specific "stress test" subsets of the validation or test data. For example, if the augmentation focused on simulating extreme weather for an automotive perception system, a stress test subset could consist entirely of images captured during heavy rain or snow. The augmented model's performance on this subset, compared to the baseline model, will reveal its enhanced resilience to these specific adverse conditions.

Another powerful method for evaluating robustness is to analyze the model's sensitivity to different types and levels of noise or perturbations. This can be achieved by systematically adding controlled noise to the validation set examples and observing how the model's predictions degrade. A model that has been effectively augmented should exhibit a slower degradation in performance as noise levels increase, or it should maintain higher accuracy even in the presence of significant noise. For instance, if the augmentation strategy for a communication system involved simulating various forms of packet loss and bit errors, the evaluation should include testing the model on validation data where packet loss rates and bit error rates are progressively increased. The augmented model's ability to maintain a low error rate in its output, even at higher noise levels, is a direct testament to the effectiveness of the augmentation.

Furthermore, the concept of generalization is intrinsically linked to robustness. While validation set performance gives an indication, assessing generalization often involves examining performance across different domains or datasets that the model has not been exposed to during training or validation. This could involve evaluating the model on data collected from a different sensor suite, a different geographical location, or under slightly different operational protocols, provided these variations are still within the general scope of the engineering task. If the augmented model performs consistently well across these diverse, unseen scenarios, it demonstrates superior generalization capabilities, a key outcome of effective augmentation.

The quantification of improvements can also be framed by comparing the model's performance on the *augmented* validation set versus the *unaugmented* validation set. While the primary goal is generalization to real, unaugmented data, this comparison can reveal how well the augmentation strategy aligns with the validation data's characteristics. If the augmented model performs significantly better on an augmented validation set compared to the unaugmented one, it suggests that the augmentation successfully introduced useful variations that are also present, albeit perhaps in a less pronounced form, in the real data. Conversely, if performance on the augmented validation set *decreases* significantly, it might indicate that the augmentation introduced unrealistic or irrelevant variations.

Statistical significance testing is a crucial step in confirming that observed improvements are not merely due to random chance. Techniques like paired t-tests or Wilcoxon signed-rank tests can be applied to compare the performance metrics (e.g., accuracy scores, error values) of the baseline and augmented models on the same set of validation examples. If the statistical test indicates a p-value below a chosen significance level (e.g., 0.05), we can confidently conclude that the augmentation had a statistically significant positive impact on the model's performance.

For complex engineering systems, evaluating the impact of augmentation might also involve analyzing the model's behavior in terms of its confidence scores or uncertainty estimates. A model that has learned from well-augmented data, representing a wider range of scenarios, might exhibit more calibrated confidence levels. That is, it should be more confident in its predictions for data points that are similar to those seen during training and less confident for novel or ambiguous cases. Evaluating this calibration can be done using metrics like Expected Calibration Error (ECE) or by plotting reliability diagrams. If the augmented model shows improved calibration, it means it provides more trustworthy predictions, which is invaluable in safety-critical engineering applications.

In some cases, it might be beneficial to perform ablation studies on the augmentation techniques themselves. If multiple augmentation methods were applied, one can systematically remove or alter specific techniques to understand their individual contributions to the overall performance improvement. This process helps in identifying the most impactful augmentation strategies for a given problem and can lead to a more efficient and effective augmentation pipeline. For example, if both random cropping and color jittering were applied to image data, an ablation study might involve training models with: (a) no augmentation, (b) only random cropping, (c) only color jittering, and (d) both techniques. Comparing the performance of these models would reveal the relative importance of each augmentation.

Finally, the long-term impact and practical implications of augmentation must be considered. This extends beyond immediate validation set performance. Does the augmented model require more computational resources for inference? Is the deployment process more complex? While these are not direct performance metrics of the model itself, they are critical considerations for the overall success of implementing an augmented model in an engineering context. The goal is to achieve a balance between performance gains and practical deployability. Therefore, a holistic evaluation considers not just statistical improvements but also the operational and economic feasibility of the augmented solution. By employing a combination of these evaluation methodologies, engineers can move beyond simply applying data augmentation to confidently demonstrating its value and impact on model performance, ensuring that the deployed systems are indeed more robust, reliable, and effective in their intended applications. This diligent evaluation process is what truly transforms data augmentation from a theoretical possibility into a powerful, practical tool for building superior machine learning solutions in engineering.

# Chapter 8: Building Production-Ready ML Pipelines: An Overview

In the realm of engineering, the transition of a machine learning model from a research prototype to a fully operational system is a journey marked by a fundamental shift in requirements. This shift is encapsulated by the concept of a 'production-ready' ML pipeline. It's not merely about achieving high accuracy on a held-out test set; it's about building a robust, reliable, and efficient system that can consistently deliver value in a real-world environment. Defining what constitutes such a pipeline requires us to look beyond the model's predictive capabilities and consider the entire lifecycle of its operation.

At its core, a production-ready ML pipeline is an automated, end-to-end system designed to perform a specific machine learning task. This task could range from predicting equipment failures in a manufacturing plant to optimizing energy consumption in a smart grid, or detecting anomalies in sensor data from a bridge. The emphasis on "automated" is critical. Manual steps in data ingestion, preprocessing, model training, evaluation, deployment, and inference are significant bottlenecks and sources of error in production. Therefore, a production-ready pipeline seeks to minimize or eliminate human intervention in these recurring processes. Automation ensures consistency, reduces the chance of human error, and enables rapid response to changing conditions.

Scalability is another non-negotiable attribute. Engineering systems often operate at a scale that dwarfs typical research experiments. This can mean processing vast volumes of data in real-time, serving predictions to a large number of users or devices concurrently, or training models on massive datasets. A production-ready pipeline must be architected to handle these demands efficiently. This involves choosing appropriate infrastructure, such as distributed computing frameworks, scalable databases, and cloud services, and designing the pipeline components to be horizontally scalable – meaning capacity can be increased by adding more machines rather than upgrading existing ones. For instance, a pipeline processing sensor data from thousands of industrial machines must be able to ingest, preprocess, and generate predictions for all these streams simultaneously without performance degradation.

Reliability is paramount, especially in safety-critical engineering applications. A production-ready pipeline must be resilient to failures. This means incorporating mechanisms for error handling, fault tolerance, and graceful degradation. If a component fails, the system should ideally continue to operate, perhaps with reduced functionality, rather than crashing entirely. This might involve redundant processing paths, automated recovery mechanisms, and robust logging to diagnose issues quickly. For a pipeline used in autonomous vehicle navigation, any failure must be handled with extreme caution, potentially triggering a safe fallback mode. The system's ability to withstand unexpected data anomalies, network outages, or hardware issues is a defining characteristic of its readiness for production.

Maintainability is often overlooked in the initial rush to deploy. However, a production-ready pipeline is one that can be easily updated, debugged, and managed over its entire lifespan. This involves adopting best practices in software engineering, such as modular design, clear documentation, version control for code and models, and standardized deployment procedures. As the underlying data distributions drift or new insights emerge, the pipeline will need to be retrained or updated. A maintainable pipeline allows these updates to be performed efficiently and with minimal disruption. It also makes it easier for new team members to understand and contribute to the system.

Monitoring forms the eyes and ears of a production-ready pipeline. Once deployed, the system operates in a dynamic environment. Data characteristics can change (data drift), the relationship between features and the target variable can evolve (concept drift), and the model's performance can degrade over time. Comprehensive monitoring is essential to detect these changes. This includes tracking not only operational metrics like latency and throughput but also data quality metrics, model performance metrics (on live or near-live data), and system health indicators. Automated alerts should be configured to notify the engineering team when predefined thresholds are breached, triggering investigations and potential interventions. For example, a pipeline predicting component wear might monitor the distribution of incoming sensor readings; a significant shift could indicate a change in operating conditions or a sensor malfunction, necessitating a review of the model or data processing.

Reproducibility is a cornerstone of scientific and engineering rigor, and it extends to production ML pipelines. Every step, from data preprocessing to model training and deployment, should be reproducible. This means that given the same input data and the same version of the pipeline code, one should be able to achieve the exact same results. This is crucial for debugging, auditing, and for ensuring that future iterations of the model are built upon a solid, understood foundation. Techniques like rigorous version control, containerization (e.g., Docker), and artifact management (e.g., storing trained models and datasets) are key enablers of reproducibility.

Furthermore, a production-ready pipeline must consider security. In engineering applications, data can be sensitive, and the ML system itself might be a critical infrastructure component. Protecting the data from unauthorized access, ensuring the integrity of the model, and preventing malicious attacks are vital. This involves implementing access controls, encrypting sensitive data, and securing the deployment environment. For systems controlling physical processes, security breaches could have severe consequences, making this an essential aspect of production readiness.

The concept of continuous integration and continuous deployment (CI/CD) is often synonymous with production-ready ML pipelines, especially when these pipelines are part of a larger software development ecosystem. CI/CD automates the process of integrating code changes, testing them, and deploying them to production. For ML, this extends to continuous training (CT), where models are retrained automatically as new data becomes available or when performance monitoring indicates a need for it. The pipeline integrates these stages, allowing for frequent, reliable updates to the ML system without manual orchestration.

Model versioning and rollback capabilities are also critical. In production, it's inevitable that a newly deployed model might perform worse than the previous version, or introduce unexpected issues. The pipeline should support the ability to easily revert to a known good version of the model or the entire pipeline if problems arise. This provides a safety net and reduces the risk associated with deploying updates.

Finally, the definition of production-ready includes efficient resource management. In engineering, operational costs can be a significant factor. A production-ready pipeline is optimized to use computational resources (CPU, GPU, memory, storage) and cloud services in a cost-effective manner, without compromising performance or reliability. This often involves selecting appropriate instance types, optimizing code for efficiency, and implementing auto-scaling strategies that adjust resource allocation based on demand.

In essence, a production-ready ML pipeline in engineering is a well-engineered, automated, scalable, reliable, maintainable, observable, and secure system that delivers consistent and valuable machine learning capabilities within its operational context. It transforms a theoretical model into a practical, deployed asset that can be trusted to perform its intended function over time. Achieving this state is a multidisciplinary effort, requiring collaboration between data scientists, ML engineers, software engineers, and domain experts, all working towards the common goal of robust, impactful deployment. It represents the culmination of rigorous development, thorough testing, and a deep understanding of the operational environment. The following sections will delve into the specific components and strategies required to build such pipelines.

The journey from a promising machine learning model developed in a research environment to a fully operational, value-generating system in an engineering context is a transformative one. This metamorphosis is fundamentally defined by the requirements of a 'production-ready' ML pipeline. It transcends the mere achievement of high accuracy on isolated datasets; it embodies the creation of a resilient, dependable, and efficient system capable of consistently delivering tangible benefits within a real-world operational setting. To truly grasp what constitutes such a pipeline, we must broaden our perspective beyond the model's predictive prowess to encompass its entire operational lifecycle.

At its conceptual core, a production-ready ML pipeline is an automated, end-to-end framework engineered to execute a specific machine learning task. This task could manifest in diverse engineering applications, such as forecasting equipment failures in industrial manufacturing, optimizing energy distribution within smart grids, or identifying subtle anomalies in the continuous streams of sensor data emanating from critical infrastructure like bridges. The emphasis on "automated" is not merely a desirable attribute but a critical necessity. Manual interventions at any stage – be it data acquisition, preprocessing, model training, performance assessment, deployment, or inference – introduce significant friction points and are fertile grounds for errors in a production setting. Consequently, a production-ready pipeline strives to minimize or entirely eliminate human involvement in these recurring processes. Automation fosters consistency, drastically reduces the likelihood of human oversight or mistakes, and enables swift responses to evolving operational conditions.

Scalability represents another non-negotiable prerequisite. Engineering systems often operate at scales that vastly dwarf typical experimental setups. This can translate to processing immense volumes of data in near real-time, serving predictions concurrently to a multitude of users or devices, or training models on datasets of astronomical proportions. A production-ready pipeline must be architected to handle these demands with utmost efficiency. This necessitates the selection of appropriate infrastructure, including distributed computing frameworks, highly scalable databases, and sophisticated cloud services. Furthermore, pipeline components must be designed for horizontal scalability – the ability to enhance capacity by adding more resources (e.g., servers) rather than upgrading existing ones. For instance, a pipeline responsible for processing real-time sensor data from thousands of interconnected industrial machines must possess the capability to ingest, preprocess, and generate predictions for all these data streams simultaneously without any perceptible degradation in performance.

Reliability is of paramount importance, particularly in engineering applications where safety and operational integrity are critical. A production-ready pipeline must exhibit resilience in the face of potential failures. This implies the incorporation of robust error-handling mechanisms, fault tolerance strategies, and provisions for graceful degradation. Should a component encounter an issue, the system should ideally be able to continue functioning, perhaps with diminished capabilities, rather than ceasing operation entirely. This might involve implementing redundant processing pathways, automated recovery protocols, and comprehensive logging systems to facilitate rapid diagnosis of issues. For a pipeline integral to the navigation systems of autonomous vehicles, any failure must be addressed with extreme vigilance, potentially triggering a secure fallback operational mode. The system's capacity to withstand unforeseen data anomalies, transient network interruptions, or hardware malfunctions is a defining characteristic of its readiness for deployment in a production environment.

Maintainability, while sometimes relegated to a lower priority during the initial deployment phase, is a crucial long-term consideration. A production-ready pipeline is one that can be effortlessly updated, meticulously debugged, and efficiently managed throughout its entire operational lifespan. This requires adherence to established software engineering best practices, such as modular design principles, clear and comprehensive documentation, stringent version control for both code and trained models, and the adoption of standardized deployment procedures. As the underlying data distributions inevitably shift over time or new operational insights emerge, the pipeline will require periodic retraining or updates. A maintainable pipeline ensures that these updates can be executed smoothly and with minimal disruption to ongoing operations. It also significantly simplifies the process for new team members to onboard and contribute effectively to the system.

Monitoring serves as the indispensable sensory apparatus for a production-ready pipeline. Once deployed, the system operates within a dynamic and often unpredictable environment. The statistical characteristics of incoming data can change (a phenomenon known as data drift), the underlying relationships between features and the target variable can evolve (concept drift), and consequently, the model's predictive performance may gradually degrade. Comprehensive monitoring is therefore essential to detect and flag these alterations. This monitoring must encompass not only operational metrics such as latency and throughput but also data quality indicators, model performance metrics (evaluated on live or near-live data streams), and critical system health signals. Automated alerts should be meticulously configured to notify the engineering team when predefined thresholds are crossed, thereby initiating investigations and potential corrective actions. For example, a pipeline tasked with predicting the remaining useful life of industrial components might continuously monitor the statistical distribution of incoming sensor readings; a significant deviation could signify a change in operating conditions or a sensor malfunction, prompting a review of the model or the data preprocessing steps.

Reproducibility is a fundamental tenet of scientific and engineering rigor, and its importance extends directly to production ML pipelines. Every operation, from the initial data transformation and preprocessing through to model training and final deployment, must be capable of being precisely reproduced. This means that given identical input data and the same version of the pipeline code, one should consistently achieve identical outcomes. This capability is absolutely vital for effective debugging, for auditing purposes, and for ensuring that subsequent iterations or improvements to the model are built upon a thoroughly understood and stable foundation. Techniques such as rigorous version control systems, containerization technologies (like Docker), and robust artifact management practices (which involve storing trained models, datasets, and other critical outputs) are indispensable enablers of reproducibility.

Furthermore, a production-ready pipeline must inherently address security concerns. In many engineering applications, the data being processed can be highly sensitive, and the ML system itself may constitute a critical component of the overall operational infrastructure. Protecting data from unauthorized access, ensuring the integrity and authenticity of the deployed model, and safeguarding against potential malicious attacks are of paramount importance. This typically involves implementing stringent access controls, employing encryption for sensitive data both in transit and at rest, and securing the entire deployment environment. For systems that control or influence physical processes, security breaches can have severe and far-reaching consequences, underscoring the critical nature of this aspect of production readiness.

The principles of continuous integration and continuous deployment (CI/CD) are frequently interwoven with the concept of production-ready ML pipelines, especially when these pipelines are integrated into broader software development ecosystems. CI/CD automates the intricate process of merging code changes, subjecting them to comprehensive testing, and subsequently deploying them into the production environment. In the context of machine learning, this paradigm extends to continuous training (CT), where models are automatically retrained as new data becomes available or when performance monitoring systems indicate a need for recalibration. The pipeline seamlessly integrates these distinct stages, facilitating frequent and reliable updates to the ML system without requiring manual orchestration.

Robust model versioning and the capability for rollback are also indispensable features. In a production setting, it is an inevitable reality that a newly deployed model might, in practice, perform less effectively than its predecessor or introduce unforeseen operational issues. A well-designed pipeline must incorporate the ability to effortlessly revert to a previously validated, stable version of the model or even the entire pipeline if problems are detected. This provides an essential safety net and significantly mitigates the inherent risks associated with deploying updates or new model iterations.

Finally, the comprehensive definition of production readiness encompasses efficient resource management. In the operational context of engineering, the associated costs can represent a significant consideration. A production-ready pipeline is meticulously optimized to utilize computational resources – including CPU, GPU, memory, and storage – in a cost-effective manner, without compromising its performance, reliability, or responsiveness. This often involves judicious selection of appropriate instance types in cloud environments, optimizing code for maximum computational efficiency, and implementing intelligent auto-scaling strategies that dynamically adjust resource allocation based on real-time demand fluctuations.

In summation, a production-ready ML pipeline within an engineering framework is a sophisticated, highly engineered, automated, scalable, dependable, maintainable, and observable system, secured against unauthorized access, that consistently delivers valuable machine learning capabilities tailored to its specific operational context. It effectively transforms a theoretical model, conceived in a research setting, into a practical, deployed asset that can be trusted to fulfill its intended function reliably over extended periods. Achieving this sophisticated state is inherently a multidisciplinary undertaking, demanding close collaboration among data scientists, ML engineers, traditional software engineers, and domain experts, all united by the common objective of achieving robust and impactful deployment. It represents the culmination of rigorous development methodologies, exhaustive testing protocols, and a profound comprehension of the operational environment in which the system will function. The subsequent sections will meticulously dissect the specific components, architectural patterns, and strategic considerations essential for constructing such advanced pipelines.

The construction of a production-ready machine learning pipeline involves the orchestration of several distinct yet interconnected components, each playing a crucial role in the end-to-end workflow. Understanding these building blocks is fundamental to designing and implementing a robust and scalable ML system.

**Data Ingestion and Validation**: This initial stage is the gateway for all data that fuels the ML pipeline. It involves reliably collecting raw data from various sources, which could include databases, message queues, APIs, streaming platforms, or flat files stored in distributed file systems. The sources are diverse, reflecting the complexity of engineering environments: sensor readings from industrial equipment, telemetry data from vehicles, logs from network devices, or records from operational databases. Once ingested, the data must undergo rigorous validation. This is not merely about checking for missing values, but a much deeper examination. Data validation ensures that the incoming data conforms to expected schemas, adheres to predefined data types, falls within acceptable ranges, and maintains expected statistical properties. For instance, if a pipeline processes temperature readings from a series of sensors, validation might check that temperatures are within a physically plausible range (e.g., not absolute zero or impossibly high) and that the frequency of readings is consistent with expected sensor behavior. Anomalous or malformed data can have catastrophic effects on downstream processes, leading to incorrect feature calculations, biased model training, or erroneous predictions. Therefore, robust data validation mechanisms are critical for maintaining data integrity and trust in the pipeline's outputs. This stage often involves data profiling to understand the characteristics of incoming data and establishing baseline expectations against which future data can be compared. Error handling is paramount here; corrupted or invalid data should be quarantined, flagged for investigation, or rejected gracefully, preventing it from contaminating the rest of the pipeline.

**Feature Engineering**: Following ingestion and validation, the raw data is transformed into features that are suitable for consumption by machine learning algorithms. This stage is often highly domain-specific and can significantly impact model performance. Feature engineering involves creating new features from existing ones, selecting the most relevant features, and transforming features into a format that the model can effectively learn from. In engineering applications, this might include calculating moving averages of sensor data to smooth out noise, deriving time-based features like 'hour of day' or 'day of week' for time-series forecasting, creating interaction terms between variables, or encoding categorical variables. For example, in a predictive maintenance scenario for an engine, features might be engineered from raw vibration data to capture characteristics like peak amplitude, frequency components (using Fourier transforms), or trends over time. Dimensionality reduction techniques, such as Principal Component Analysis (PCA), might also be employed here to reduce the number of features, thereby mitigating the curse of dimensionality and improving training efficiency, especially when dealing with high-dimensional sensor data. The output of this stage is a clean, structured dataset where each row represents an instance and each column represents a meaningful feature, ready for model training. Reproducibility is key; the exact same feature engineering steps must be applied consistently to both training and inference data.

**Model Training and Evaluation**: This is the core machine learning component where the model learns patterns from the prepared data. The process typically involves selecting an appropriate model architecture based on the problem type (e.g., regression, classification, time-series forecasting), initializing the model, and then iteratively updating its parameters using an optimization algorithm to minimize a defined loss function. In a production pipeline, this stage is usually automated and parameterized, allowing for easy retraining with new data or adjusted hyperparameters. Crucially, this stage is not just about training; it also encompasses rigorous evaluation. This involves assessing the model's performance on a separate validation or test dataset using a suite of relevant metrics (e.g., accuracy, precision, recall, F1-score for classification; Mean Squared Error (MSE), R-squared for regression; Root Mean Squared Error (RMSE) for time-series). The choice of evaluation metrics is critical and must align with the business objectives and the specific engineering application. For instance, in a safety-critical system, minimizing false negatives might be prioritized over overall accuracy. Beyond standard evaluation, advanced techniques like cross-validation are often employed during development to ensure the model generalizes well. Furthermore, this stage often involves hyperparameter tuning – the process of finding the optimal set of hyperparameters that yield the best model performance. This can be done using techniques like grid search, random search, or more sophisticated Bayesian optimization methods. The outcome of this stage is a trained and evaluated model, along with its performance metrics and associated artifacts (like feature importance scores or learned weights).

**Model Deployment**: Once a model has been trained, evaluated, and deemed suitable for production, it needs to be deployed so that it can be used to make predictions on new, unseen data. Model deployment is a critical engineering challenge that bridges the gap between development and operation. There are various strategies for deployment, each with its own trade-offs. A common approach is to package the trained model and its dependencies into a deployable artifact, such as a containerized application (e.g., using Docker). This artifact can then be deployed to an inference server or a dedicated machine learning serving platform. Alternatively, models can be embedded directly into applications, or deployed as microservices that can be called via an API. For real-time applications, low-latency serving is paramount, often requiring specialized infrastructure and optimization techniques. For batch processing, the model might be applied to large datasets periodically.

Versioning of deployed models is essential, allowing for easy rollbacks if a new model proves problematic. Continuous deployment (CD) practices are often applied here, automating the release of new model versions to production after they pass automated testing and validation gates. The goal is to make the model accessible and operational in a reliable and scalable manner, ready to serve predictions.

**Prediction Serving**: This component is responsible for generating predictions from the deployed model in response to incoming requests. When a new data instance arrives (e.g., a new sensor reading), it is first subjected to the same preprocessing and feature engineering steps that were applied during training. This ensures that the input data format is consistent with what the model expects. The prepared data is then fed to the deployed model, which performs inference and returns a prediction. The serving layer needs to be highly available, scalable, and performant, especially for real-time applications where low latency is critical. This might involve employing techniques like load balancing to distribute requests across multiple model instances, caching frequently requested predictions, or using specialized hardware like GPUs for faster inference. The output of the serving layer is the prediction itself, which can then be consumed by other systems, trigger alerts, inform decision-making, or be stored for later analysis. Robust logging of requests and predictions is vital for monitoring and debugging purposes.

**Monitoring and Feedback Loop**: The operational life of an ML pipeline does not end with deployment; it is an ongoing process. The monitoring component is responsible for observing the pipeline's performance in the production environment. This includes tracking not only system health metrics (e.g., uptime, latency, error rates) but also data quality, model performance, and potential drifts in data distributions or model behavior. As mentioned earlier, data drift and concept drift are natural phenomena that can degrade model performance over time. Monitoring systems should be configured to detect these drifts by comparing production data characteristics and model predictions against historical baselines or ground truth data (when available). Upon detecting significant drift or performance degradation, alerts are triggered, notifying the engineering team. This often initiates a feedback loop that leads back to earlier stages of the pipeline, such as data re-validation, feature re-engineering, or retraining the model with fresh data. This continuous feedback mechanism is crucial for maintaining the model's accuracy and relevance over its lifecycle. It ensures that the ML system remains a valuable asset and adapts to the evolving real-world conditions. This loop might involve human-in-the-loop components where domain experts review flagged predictions or data anomalies to provide crucial insights that inform model updates or pipeline adjustments.

These key components, when integrated and automated effectively, form the backbone of an end-to-end production-ready ML pipeline in engineering applications, enabling the reliable and scalable delivery of machine learning-driven insights and actions.

The selection of the right tools and technologies is not a mere supplementary consideration; it forms the bedrock upon which a resilient and effective production-ready ML pipeline is constructed. In the complex and demanding landscape of engineering applications, the choices made at this juncture have profound implications for scalability, maintainability, performance, and ultimately, the cost-effectiveness of the entire system. It is a process that demands a thorough understanding of project-specific needs, a keen awareness of the technological ecosystem, and a forward-looking perspective that anticipates future growth and evolving requirements. The temptation to default to familiar tools or the latest hyped technology must be resisted in favor of a principled, requirements-driven approach. This involves a systematic evaluation of various categories of tools, each serving a distinct but interconnected purpose within the ML pipeline.

One of the most fundamental decisions revolves around data storage. Engineering environments often generate vast quantities of data, ranging from high-frequency sensor readings to historical operational logs and complex simulation outputs. The chosen data storage solution must be capable of handling these diverse data types and volumes efficiently, while also supporting the specific access patterns required by the ML pipeline. Relational databases, while excellent for structured transactional data, may struggle with the sheer scale and variety of time-series sensor data or unstructured log files. For such scenarios, distributed file systems like Hadoop Distributed File System (HDFS) or cloud-based object storage solutions such as Amazon S3, Google Cloud Storage, or Azure Blob Storage become indispensable. These solutions offer immense scalability, cost-effectiveness, and durability, making them ideal for storing raw and processed data at petabyte scales. Furthermore, specialized time-series databases (e.g., InfluxDB, TimescaleDB) can offer optimized performance for ingesting and querying time-stamped data, which is ubiquitous in engineering applications like monitoring and predictive maintenance. Data lakes, built upon object storage and often integrated with cataloging and governance tools, provide a flexible approach to storing all types of data in their raw format, allowing downstream processing and analysis to be performed as needed. When considering data storage, it's crucial to evaluate not only raw storage capacity and cost but also ingestion rates, query performance, data durability, and the ease with which the storage layer integrates with subsequent processing and compute frameworks. The ability to store data in formats optimized for analytical workloads, such as Apache Parquet or ORC, can also significantly improve read performance for processing frameworks, thereby reducing overall pipeline execution times.

The processing framework is another critical pillar of the ML pipeline. In engineering, data often exists in distributed systems and requires parallel processing capabilities to handle large datasets efficiently. Apache Spark has emerged as a dominant force in this domain. Its ability to perform in-memory computations across distributed clusters makes it exceptionally well-suited for large-scale data transformations, feature engineering, and even distributed model training. Spark's rich ecosystem, including Spark SQL for structured data processing, Spark Streaming for real-time data ingestion and processing, and MLlib for machine learning algorithms, offers a comprehensive toolkit for many data engineering and ML tasks. When dealing with massive datasets that exceed the capacity of a single machine, Spark's distributed nature allows the workload to be spread across a cluster of machines, drastically reducing processing times. For instance, calculating statistical features across terabytes of sensor data or performing complex data cleansing operations on historical operational logs can be accomplished orders of magnitude faster with Spark compared to single-machine processing. However, Spark's resource requirements can be substantial, and its operational complexity might be an overhead for smaller-scale projects. Alternatives, such as Dask for Python-centric distributed computing, can offer a more Pythonic interface and integrate seamlessly with existing Python libraries, making it an attractive option for teams already heavily invested in the Python ecosystem. For stream processing, frameworks like Apache Flink or Kafka Streams provide robust capabilities for handling real-time data, enabling low-latency event processing and complex event detection, which are often critical in industrial control systems or real-time anomaly detection. The choice of processing framework should align with the data volume, velocity, and the complexity of the transformations required, as well as the team's existing skill set and infrastructure.

Orchestration platforms are essential for automating and managing the complex workflows that constitute an ML pipeline. These platforms enable the definition, scheduling, execution, and monitoring of sequences of tasks, ensuring that data flows correctly between different components and that the entire pipeline operates smoothly. Kubeflow, built on top of Kubernetes, offers a powerful and flexible platform for deploying and managing ML workloads, leveraging the scalability and portability of containerized applications. It provides components for data preparation, model training, hyperparameter tuning, and model serving, all orchestrated within a Kubernetes environment. MLflow is another popular choice, providing a unified platform for managing the ML lifecycle, including experiment tracking, code packaging, model registry, and deployment. Its ability to log experiments, parameters, and artifacts makes it invaluable for ensuring reproducibility and facilitating collaboration. Other orchestration tools, such as Apache Airflow, are more general-purpose workflow management systems that can be adapted to orchestrate ML pipelines. Airflow's strength lies in its flexibility and its ability to define complex dependencies between tasks using directed acyclic graphs (DAGs). When selecting an orchestration tool, consider factors such as ease of use, scalability, integration capabilities with other tools in your stack, and the level of automation and monitoring features provided. For pipelines that involve frequent retraining or complex branching logic, a robust orchestration platform is not just beneficial, but indispensable. The ability to visualize the pipeline, monitor task status, and receive alerts on failures are critical features for maintaining operational stability.

Containerization technologies, most notably Docker, have revolutionized the deployment and management of software, including ML pipelines. Docker allows developers to package an application and its dependencies into a standardized unit called a container. This ensures that the ML pipeline and all its components (libraries, frameworks, custom code) run consistently across different environments, from a developer's laptop to a production server or a cloud platform. This level of consistency is crucial for eliminating "it works on my machine" issues and simplifying deployment. For ML pipelines, containers are particularly useful for isolating different stages of the pipeline, managing dependencies for specific models or libraries, and ensuring that the exact environment used for training is replicated for inference. This greatly enhances reproducibility and reduces the risk of errors introduced by environmental discrepancies. Kubernetes, an open-source container orchestration system, often works hand-in-hand with Docker to automate the deployment, scaling, and management of containerized applications at scale. For complex ML pipelines involving multiple microservices or distributed training jobs, Kubernetes provides the necessary infrastructure for managing these containerized workloads efficiently. The adoption of containerization and orchestration platforms not only simplifies deployment but also enhances the portability and scalability of ML pipelines, allowing them to be moved between different cloud providers or on-premises infrastructure with minimal friction.

Cloud infrastructure has become an integral part of building production-ready ML pipelines, offering a vast array of services that accelerate development and deployment. Cloud providers like Amazon Web Services (AWS), Google Cloud Platform (GCP), and Microsoft Azure offer managed services for data storage (e.g., S3, GCS, Blob Storage), data processing (e.g., EMR, Dataproc, HDInsight), machine learning platforms (e.g., SageMaker, Vertex AI, Azure ML), container orchestration (e.g., EKS, GKE, AKS), and specialized hardware like GPUs and TPUs for accelerated training. Leveraging these managed services can significantly reduce the operational overhead associated with setting up and maintaining infrastructure. For example, using a managed Kubernetes service simplifies the deployment and scaling of containerized ML workloads. Similarly, managed ML platforms often provide integrated tools for data labeling, model training, hyperparameter tuning, and deployment, streamlining the entire ML lifecycle. The scalability and elasticity of cloud infrastructure allow pipelines to adapt to fluctuating demands, scaling resources up or down as needed, thereby optimizing costs. When choosing a cloud provider, consider the specific services offered, their pricing models, regional availability, and the level of integration with your existing technology stack. Hybrid cloud and multi-cloud strategies are also becoming increasingly prevalent, offering flexibility and avoiding vendor lock-in. A careful evaluation of compute options (e.g., CPU-based instances, GPU-accelerated instances), networking capabilities, and security features is crucial. For instance, real-time inference tasks might benefit from low-latency compute instances and optimized network configurations, while large-scale model training might leverage specialized GPU clusters. The choice of cloud services should be guided by the specific requirements of the pipeline, including performance, cost, security, and compliance mandates.

Beyond these core categories, a multitude of specialized tools and libraries can enhance the functionality and efficiency of an ML pipeline. For version control, Git is the de facto standard, essential for tracking code changes, managing different branches of development, and facilitating collaboration. Tools for experiment tracking, such as Weights & Biases or Comet.ml, offer sophisticated dashboards for visualizing and comparing model training runs, which is invaluable during the model development and tuning phases. For monitoring and logging, Elasticsearch, Logstash, and Kibana (the ELK stack) or cloud-native logging services can provide centralized log management and powerful visualization capabilities for troubleshooting pipeline issues. Security tools and practices, including identity and access management, encryption, and vulnerability scanning, must be integrated throughout the pipeline to protect sensitive data and prevent unauthorized access. The selection of these auxiliary tools should complement the core technology stack and address specific needs related to collaboration, debugging, security, and operational visibility.

In making these critical technology choices, a pragmatic approach is paramount. It is often beneficial to start with a well-defined set of requirements, prioritizing those that are most critical for the immediate deployment and future scalability. Consider the trade-offs between open-source solutions and proprietary managed services. Open-source tools often offer greater flexibility and cost advantages but may require more in-house expertise to manage and maintain. Managed services can reduce operational burden and accelerate deployment but might come with higher costs and less customization. Furthermore, the existing skill set of the engineering team should be a significant factor. Adopting technologies that the team is already familiar with can reduce the learning curve and speed up development. However, it is also important to foster a culture of continuous learning and be open to adopting new technologies that offer substantial advantages. Proof-of-concept projects and pilot deployments can be invaluable for testing and validating technology choices before committing to a large-scale implementation. Ultimately, the goal is to assemble a technology stack that is not only capable of meeting current needs but is also adaptable, scalable, and cost-effective for the long term, enabling the continuous delivery of value from ML-driven applications in engineering environments. This careful curation of tools and technologies forms the backbone of a robust and future-proof ML pipeline.

Workflow orchestration and automation are the cornerstones of a robust and efficient production-ready ML pipeline. Once the individual components and technologies have been selected, the challenge shifts to harmonizing them into a cohesive, automated system. This is where workflow orchestration platforms shine, transforming a collection of disparate scripts and processes into a well-oiled machine capable of executing complex sequences of tasks with minimal human oversight. The primary goal of orchestration is to manage the flow of data and control through the various stages of the ML lifecycle, ensuring that each step executes reliably, in the correct order, and with appropriate error handling.

At its core, workflow orchestration involves defining the dependencies between different tasks within the ML pipeline. These dependencies are crucial; for example, data preprocessing cannot begin until raw data has been successfully ingested, and model training cannot commence until the data has been appropriately cleaned and feature-engineered.

Orchestration tools allow these relationships to be explicitly defined, typically using a directed acyclic graph (DAG) or a similar visual representation. This graph illustrates the flow of execution, showing which tasks must complete before others can start, and which tasks can run in parallel. For instance, in a predictive maintenance pipeline for industrial machinery, the ingestion of sensor data might be a prerequisite for a feature extraction task. This feature extraction, in turn, might be a prerequisite for a model training task, which could then feed into a model evaluation task, and finally, a model deployment task. By defining these dependencies, the orchestrator ensures that operations occur in a logical sequence, preventing errors that would arise from attempting to process data that isn't yet available or training a model with incomplete features.

Scheduling is another fundamental aspect of workflow orchestration. Production ML pipelines often need to run at regular intervals - daily, hourly, or even in real-time - to incorporate new data, retrain models, and update predictions. Orchestration platforms provide sophisticated scheduling capabilities, allowing users to define precise execution times or intervals. This can range from simple cron-like schedules (e.g., "run every night at 2 AM") to more complex event-driven triggers. For example, a pipeline might be triggered to run only when a new batch of data arrives in a designated storage location, or when a specific performance metric of a deployed model drops below a certain threshold. This dynamic scheduling capability ensures that the pipeline operates in sync with the dynamic nature of the data and the business requirements, rather than relying on manual initiation. Imagine a scenario where a financial institution needs to retrain its fraud detection models daily based on the previous day's transactions. An orchestration tool can be configured to automatically trigger this retraining process every morning, ensuring the models are always up-to-date with the latest transactional patterns, a task that would be highly prone to human error and delays if performed manually.

Error handling and retries are critical for achieving reliability in automated workflows. No pipeline is immune to transient failures, such as network glitches, temporary resource unavailability, or issues with external service dependencies. Orchestration platforms provide mechanisms to define how the system should respond to these failures. This typically includes configurable retry policies, where a failed task can be automatically re-executed a specified number of times with a defined delay between attempts. This simple yet powerful feature can resolve a significant portion of execution issues without requiring human intervention. Beyond simple retries, sophisticated error handling can involve alerting specific teams when a task fails after multiple retries, or even triggering a rollback to a previous stable state. For example, if a data ingestion task consistently fails due to an issue with a third-party API, the orchestrator can be configured to retry the task several times. If it continues to fail, it can then trigger an alert to the data engineering team, providing them with the necessary logs and context to diagnose and fix the problem, while preventing downstream tasks from running with potentially incomplete or corrupted data.

Furthermore, orchestration platforms offer robust monitoring and logging capabilities. This is indispensable for understanding the health and performance of the ML pipeline. They provide dashboards and interfaces to visualize the execution status of various tasks, identify bottlenecks, and pinpoint the root cause of failures. Detailed logs are captured for each task, providing a trace of its execution, including any errors encountered, performance metrics, and the input/output of the operation. This comprehensive logging is invaluable for debugging, auditing, and ensuring compliance. For instance, in a pharmaceutical research setting where ML models are used to predict drug efficacy, auditors might require a complete, immutable record of every model retraining run, including the exact data used, parameters, and execution times. An orchestration platform, coupled with proper logging and versioning, can provide this auditable trail.

The concept of idempotency is also crucial when designing automated ML workflows. An idempotent operation is one that can be performed multiple times without changing the result beyond the initial application. In the context of ML pipelines, ensuring that tasks are idempotent is vital for safe retries and consistent execution. For example, a data loading task should ideally be idempotent; if it's retried, it shouldn't duplicate records or corrupt existing ones. Instead, it should ensure that the data is in the desired state, whether it was run once or multiple times. This often involves checking if the data already exists or has been processed before attempting to load or transform it again. While not all tasks can be made perfectly idempotent, striving for this property in critical stages like data ingestion and transformation significantly enhances the robustness of the automated workflow.

The choice of an orchestration tool often depends on the specific requirements of the ML pipeline and the existing infrastructure. Apache Airflow is a widely adopted open-source platform that excels at defining, scheduling, and monitoring complex workflows as DAGs. Its Python-based definition language makes it highly flexible and allows engineers to leverage the full power of Python for defining tasks. Airflow's extensive community support and rich feature set, including a user-friendly web interface for monitoring, make it a popular choice for many organizations. For instance, a large e-commerce company might use Airflow to orchestrate a daily pipeline that ingests sales data, updates customer segmentation models, and then deploys these updated models to personalize website recommendations, all scheduled to run overnight.

Another prominent contender, particularly in cloud-native environments, is Kubeflow Pipelines. Built on top of Kubernetes, Kubeflow Pipelines allows users to build and deploy portable, scalable ML workflows that leverage the power of containerization and Kubernetes orchestration. This is particularly advantageous for teams already invested in the Kubernetes ecosystem, as it allows them to manage their ML pipelines using the same paradigms and tools they use for other applications. Kubeflow Pipelines offers a visual interface for designing pipelines, which are composed of containerized steps. This approach ensures consistency across development, testing, and production environments, and facilitates easy scaling of individual pipeline components. For a startup developing a computer vision-based quality control system for manufacturing, using Kubeflow Pipelines could allow them to easily scale the image processing and model inference components on demand, leveraging the elastic nature of Kubernetes.

Cloud providers also offer their own managed orchestration services. For example, AWS Step Functions allows developers to coordinate distributed applications and microservices using visual workflows. It integrates seamlessly with other AWS services, making it a natural choice for pipelines built within the AWS ecosystem. Similarly, Google Cloud Composer, a managed Apache Airflow service, and Azure Data Factory provide robust orchestration capabilities tailored for cloud environments. These managed services often abstract away much of the operational overhead associated with managing the orchestration infrastructure itself, allowing teams to focus more on defining and building their ML pipelines. A company leveraging Azure for its data analytics could use Azure Data Factory to orchestrate a pipeline that pulls data from various Azure data sources, performs transformations using Azure Databricks, trains a model using Azure Machine Learning, and then deploys it as an API endpoint, all within a managed, scalable environment.

When considering orchestration, it's important to think beyond just the workflow definition and execution. The ability to manage different environments is also crucial. For instance, a pipeline might need to be tested in a staging environment before being deployed to production. Orchestration tools can facilitate this by allowing different configurations and deployments for different environments. Furthermore, the concept of CI/CD (Continuous Integration and Continuous Deployment) extends to ML pipelines. Continuous integration involves automatically testing code changes whenever they are committed, and continuous deployment involves automatically releasing those changes to production if they pass all tests. In the context of ML, this means that changes to model code, data preprocessing scripts, or even pipeline definitions can be automatically tested and, if successful, deployed. This drastically speeds up the iteration cycle and ensures that the pipeline is always running the latest, most tested version of the code and models.

For instance, imagine a team working on an NLP model for sentiment analysis. Every time a data scientist commits new code that improves the model's accuracy on a validation set, a CI/CD pipeline, orchestrated by a tool like Airflow or Kubeflow, could automatically trigger a series of steps: pull the latest code, run unit tests, ingest a fresh batch of training data, retrain the model, evaluate it against a hold-out test set, and if it meets predefined performance criteria, automatically deploy the new model to a production inference service. This level of automation not only reduces manual effort but also minimizes the risk of human error during deployment, leading to a more stable and reliable production system.

The orchestration of ML pipelines also plays a critical role in enabling MLOps practices. MLOps aims to bring DevOps principles to the machine learning lifecycle, emphasizing collaboration, automation, and continuous delivery. Workflow orchestration tools are the backbone of MLOps, enabling the automation of tasks such as data versioning, model training, model validation, and deployment. By automating these processes, MLOps platforms, powered by orchestration engines, allow for faster experimentation, more reliable deployments, and continuous monitoring and improvement of ML models in production. The ability to track lineage – understanding which version of the data was used to train which version of the model, and which experiments led to the current production model – is a key benefit enabled by well-orchestrated and logged pipelines.

In summary, workflow orchestration and automation are not just about convenience; they are fundamental requirements for building production-ready ML pipelines. They ensure that complex, multi-stage processes can be executed reliably, reproducibly, and efficiently. By defining dependencies, enabling intelligent scheduling, managing errors and retries, and providing comprehensive monitoring, orchestration platforms empower engineers and data scientists to move beyond ad-hoc scripts and build robust, scalable, and maintainable ML systems that can deliver continuous value. The selection and implementation of an appropriate orchestration tool is a critical step in the journey towards operationalizing machine learning.

As ML pipelines mature from experimental prototypes to critical production systems, their ability to scale and perform under increasing demands becomes paramount. The transition from a proof-of-concept that processes a few thousand data points to a system that handles millions, or even billions, requires a fundamental shift in architectural thinking. This section delves into the engineering considerations that underpin scalable and high-performance ML pipelines, moving beyond the logic of the workflow to the mechanics of efficient execution.

One of the most significant levers for achieving scalability in ML pipelines is the adoption of
**distributed computing**. When a single machine can no longer hold the data in memory or process it within a reasonable timeframe, distributing

the workload across multiple machines becomes not just beneficial, but essential. This involves breaking down large tasks into smaller, independent units that can be processed in parallel. Frameworks like Apache Spark have revolutionized this space for data processing. Spark's ability to perform in-memory computation and its resilient distributed dataset (RDD) abstraction allow it to handle massive datasets far more efficiently than traditional disk-based MapReduce. For instance, a data aggregation task that might take hours on a single machine could be completed in minutes on a Spark cluster, by partitioning the data and processing each partition concurrently on different nodes. This not only accelerates data preparation but also scales to accommodate growing data volumes without requiring a proportional increase in the processing time per data point. Similarly, for model training, distributed training frameworks such as TensorFlow Distributed or PyTorch DistributedDataParallel allow the training process to be spread across multiple GPUs or even multiple machines, drastically reducing the time it takes to train complex models on large datasets. Imagine training a deep neural network for image recognition; distributing this training across hundreds of GPUs can make previously infeasible training times a reality, enabling faster experimentation and more frequent model updates.

Beyond the computation itself, the efficiency of **data serialization and deserialization** plays a crucial role in pipeline performance, especially in distributed environments. When data is moved between different processes, services, or machines, it needs to be converted into a format suitable for transmission (serialization) and then reconstructed on the receiving end (deserialization). The choice of serialization format can have a profound impact on speed and efficiency. Traditional formats like JSON or XML are human-readable but can be verbose and slow to parse. For high-throughput, low-latency scenarios, binary serialization formats are often preferred. Protocol Buffers (protobuf) and Apache Avro are popular choices. Protobuf, developed by Google, is known for its efficiency and speed, generating compact serialized data and fast parsers. Avro, on the other hand, is well-suited for evolving schemas, making it a robust choice for data pipelines where data structures might change over time. For example, if an ML pipeline needs to pass feature vectors from a preprocessing service to a model serving service, using a highly efficient serialization format like protobuf can reduce network latency and CPU overhead, thereby improving the overall throughput of the system. This is particularly critical in real-time inference scenarios where milliseconds matter.

**Parallel processing** is a fundamental technique for enhancing performance, and it extends beyond just distributed computing. Within a single machine, modern CPUs have multiple cores, and many ML libraries are designed to leverage this parallelism. For instance, libraries like NumPy and scikit-learn often use multi-threading to accelerate operations like matrix multiplication or hyperparameter tuning. When tuning hyperparameters for a model, instead of trying one combination at a time, a parallel approach can evaluate multiple combinations concurrently across different CPU cores. This can significantly shorten the time required for hyperparameter optimization. Furthermore, within a pipeline, different stages might be designed to run in parallel if they are independent. For example, if a pipeline involves feature extraction from two different data sources and then combining these features for model training, the feature extraction steps from each source could potentially run in parallel, with the results being joined only before the training stage. Orchestration tools are key here, as they can identify these opportunities for parallel execution and manage the dependencies, ensuring that independent tasks are launched concurrently.

Optimizing
**model inference speed** is another critical aspect of performance, especially for applications requiring real-time or near-real-time predictions. This can involve several strategies. One common approach is **model quantization**, which reduces the precision of the model's weights and activations (e.g., from 32-bit floating-point numbers to 8-bit integers).

This can significantly reduce the model's size and speed up computation with minimal loss in accuracy. For example, deploying a large convolutional neural network for real-time object detection on an edge device might necessitate quantization to fit within the device's memory and processing constraints. Another technique is **model pruning**, where less important weights or connections in a neural network are removed, leading to a smaller, faster model.

The choice of
**inference serving infrastructure** also impacts performance. Dedicated inference servers, such as NVIDIA's Triton Inference Server or TensorFlow Serving, are optimized for high-throughput, low-latency model serving. These servers can handle concurrent requests, manage model versions, and leverage hardware acceleration (like GPUs) efficiently. For instance, a recommendation system that needs to serve millions of users concurrently would benefit immensely from a robust inference server that can scale horizontally and efficiently manage the underlying computational resources. Techniques like **batching inference requests** can also dramatically improve throughput. Instead of processing each request individually, requests can be grouped into batches, allowing the model to perform computations on multiple inputs simultaneously, thereby utilizing hardware more effectively. This is particularly beneficial when latency requirements are not strictly single-digit milliseconds, and a slight delay for batching is acceptable in exchange for higher overall throughput.

Furthermore, considering the
**hardware** on which models are deployed is essential for performance. For CPU-bound inference, optimizing the code for specific CPU architectures or using specialized libraries can yield significant gains. For GPU-bound inference, ensuring that the model is compatible with the GPU architecture and that the data transfer between CPU and GPU is minimized is crucial. In cloud environments, selecting the right instance types with appropriate CPU, GPU, and memory configurations is a direct

way to influence inference performance. For instance, deploying a natural language processing model that relies heavily on matrix operations would benefit from instances equipped with powerful GPUs, whereas a simpler model for tabular data might perform adequately on CPU-optimized instances.

**Caching** strategies can also play a vital role in improving the perceived performance of ML pipelines. If certain computations or feature sets are frequently reused, caching their results can avoid redundant processing. For example, in a customer churn prediction pipeline, if the process of generating a set of core customer features is computationally intensive and these features are used by multiple downstream models or for different prediction tasks, caching these precomputed features can save considerable time and resources. The cache could be implemented using in-memory data stores like Redis or Memcached, or even file-based caching mechanisms. Similarly, if model predictions themselves are relatively stable over short periods for certain user segments, caching these predictions can reduce the need for repeated inference calls, especially for less dynamic queries.

The scalability of the
**data storage and retrieval layer** is another often-overlooked aspect. If the pipeline needs to access massive amounts of data, the underlying data stores must be able to handle the read and write throughput. Databases that support distributed querying, data lakes optimized for large-scale analytical workloads (like data warehouses or data lakes built on object storage), and efficient indexing strategies become critical. For example, if a model retraining job requires reading terabytes of historical data daily, the choice of storage system and its ability to serve this data quickly and in parallel to the training cluster will directly impact the retraining time. Using columnar storage formats like Parquet or ORC can significantly improve read performance for analytical queries, as only the necessary columns are read, reducing I/O.

Finally,
**profiling and monitoring** are indispensable for understanding and optimizing performance. Without accurate insights into where bottlenecks occur, efforts to improve scalability can be misdirected. Profiling tools can identify slow-running functions or I/O-bound operations within the code. Monitoring systems, such as Prometheus and Grafana, can provide real-time dashboards of key performance metrics like request latency, throughput, CPU/GPU utilization, and memory usage. By continuously monitoring these metrics, engineering teams can proactively identify performance degradations, understand the impact of new code deployments, and make data-driven decisions about resource allocation and architectural adjustments needed to maintain and enhance the scalability and performance of the ML pipeline. For instance, observing a sudden spike in CPU utilization during peak inference hours might prompt an investigation into whether the models need optimization, more resources are required, or if a different serving strategy is needed. Similarly, noticing an increase in data loading times might indicate a need to optimize database queries or consider a more scalable data storage solution. This continuous feedback loop is essential for evolving an ML pipeline from a functional system to a truly production-ready, high-performing one.

# Chapter 9: Data Ingestion and Preparation Pipelines

The journey of any machine learning endeavor begins with data. Before algorithms can learn, patterns can be identified, or predictions can be made, that raw, unadulterated information must first enter our systems. This initial phase, known as data ingestion, is far from a simple act of copying files. It is a complex, nuanced process that demands robustness, reliability, and a deep understanding of the diverse sources from which data originates. The design of our data ingestion mechanisms is the bedrock upon which the entire machine learning pipeline is built. A shaky foundation here will inevitably lead to instability and failure downstream, regardless of how sophisticated our models or how powerful our processing capabilities may be.

We must first acknowledge the sheer variety of data sources an organization might interact with. These can range from the highly structured world of relational databases (SQL Server, PostgreSQL, MySQL) and data warehouses (Snowflake, BigQuery, Redshift) to the semi-structured formats found in logs, JSON files, or XML documents, and the rapidly flowing, often unbounded streams from IoT devices, user clickstreams, or social media feeds. Each of these presents unique challenges. Connecting to a traditional database might involve managing credentials, understanding table schemas, and efficiently querying large volumes of data without overwhelming the source system. Ingesting data from files stored in object storage like Amazon S3, Azure Blob Storage, or Google Cloud Storage requires handling different access patterns, dealing with potential network latency, and ensuring that we only process new or updated files.

The real complexities emerge when we consider real-time or near-real-time data streams. Internet of Things (IoT) devices, for instance, can generate telemetry data at an extraordinary rate, potentially millions of events per second. These events might come from sensors on industrial machinery, smart home devices, or wearable fitness trackers. SCADA

(Supervisory Control and Data Acquisition) systems, common in manufacturing and utilities, also produce continuous streams of operational data. Effectively ingesting this data requires specialized tools and architectures designed for high throughput and low latency. Message queues and streaming platforms like Apache Kafka, Amazon Kinesis, or Google Cloud Pub/Sub are indispensable in such scenarios. These platforms act as intermediaries, decoupling the data producers (the devices or systems generating data) from the data consumers (our ingestion pipelines). They provide buffering, fault tolerance, and a mechanism for multiple downstream services to consume the same data streams independently.

Beyond the origin and velocity of data, its format is another critical consideration. Data can arrive in a multitude of formats: CSV, JSON, Avro, Parquet, Protobuf, plain text, or even proprietary binary formats. Our ingestion mechanisms must be capable of parsing these diverse formats accurately. This often involves employing specific deserialization libraries or tools tailored to each format. For example, a pipeline might need to read comma-separated values from a daily batch file, parse intricate JSON payloads from a web API, and consume compact binary messages from a Kafka topic. The ingestion layer must be flexible enough to handle this heterogeneity gracefully, transforming raw data into a standardized internal representation that can be processed by subsequent stages of the ML pipeline. Often, converting data into an efficient columnar format like Apache Parquet or ORC during or immediately after ingestion can significantly benefit downstream analytical and machine learning workloads by improving read performance and reducing storage costs.

Ensuring data completeness during transfer is paramount. Data loss at the ingestion stage is akin to losing crucial ingredients before cooking a meal; the final product will be fundamentally flawed. Network interruptions, temporary outages of source systems, or errors during data transmission can all lead to missing data points or incomplete records. Robust ingestion mechanisms must incorporate strategies to mitigate these issues. This includes implementing retry mechanisms for transient failures, employing acknowledgments to confirm successful data reception, and potentially using idempotent ingestion processes to prevent duplicate data if retries occur. For streaming data, mechanisms like Kafka's offset management are crucial for ensuring that data is processed exactly once or at least once, allowing consumers to track their progress and resume from the last successfully processed message even after a failure.

Handling potential connection failures is an inherent part of designing reliable data ingestion. Systems go down, networks become unreliable, and credentials can expire. A well-designed ingestion pipeline should not simply crash when a connection is lost. Instead, it should be designed with resilience in mind. This involves implementing robust error handling, graceful degradation, and, where possible, automated recovery. For batch ingestion from databases, this might mean implementing connection pooling and timeout strategies, alongside logic to retry connections after a back-off period. For streaming sources, it could involve using client libraries that automatically handle reconnections or maintaining state to resume consumption from where it left off. Alerting mechanisms should also be in place to notify operators when persistent connection issues arise, allowing for timely intervention.

Furthermore, the concept of
**data validation** at the point of ingestion cannot be overstated. While some validation may occur in later stages, performing basic checks early can catch significant issues before they propagate. This includes schema validation (ensuring the data conforms to expected structures), data type checks (e.g., ensuring a numerical field actually contains numbers), and range checks (e.g., verifying that a timestamp falls within a reasonable

period). For example, if an IoT device is expected to send temperature readings between -50 and 150 degrees Celsius, a simple validation rule at the ingestion layer can flag or discard readings outside this range, preventing erroneous data from corrupting downstream analysis or model training. This proactive approach saves considerable debugging time and improves data quality from the outset.

When dealing with large volumes of data, **performance optimization** in ingestion becomes critical. Simply reading every byte and writing it to a new location can be a bottleneck. Strategies such as parallel ingestion, where multiple connections or threads read from different partitions or segments of the source data simultaneously, can dramatically increase throughput. Similarly, utilizing efficient data transfer protocols and compression techniques can reduce network bandwidth consumption and speed up data movement. For instance, ingesting large log files from a distributed file system can be significantly accelerated by distributing the read operations across multiple nodes in the ingestion cluster and writing the data in parallel to the target storage.

The choice of **ingestion patterns** also plays a vital role. Two primary patterns are batch ingestion and stream ingestion. Batch ingestion is suitable for data that can be collected and processed at discrete intervals (e.g., hourly, daily, weekly). This is common for transactional data, report generation, or periodic updates to analytical datasets. Tools like Apache Sqoop for transferring data between Hadoop and relational databases, or custom scripts leveraging database connectors, are often used here. Stream ingestion, on the other hand, is designed for continuous, real-time data flows. It requires a different set of tools and architectures, typically involving message queues and stream processing engines like Apache Flink or Spark Streaming. The decision between batch and stream ingestion depends heavily on the business requirements for data freshness and the nature of the data source. Sometimes, a hybrid approach is employed, where real-time streams are captured and processed for immediate insights, while also being batched for historical analysis or long-term storage.

Moreover,
**handling schema evolution** gracefully is a significant challenge in modern data pipelines. Data sources and their schemas are not static; they change over time as applications are updated or business requirements evolve. A rigid ingestion mechanism that breaks every time a schema changes will lead to constant pipeline failures. Therefore, ingestion systems should be designed to accommodate schema drift. This might involve using data formats like Apache Avro, which explicitly store schema information with the data and support schema evolution through compatibility rules. Alternatively, flexible parsing logic that can handle missing fields or newly added columns, perhaps by logging warnings or applying default values, can provide a degree of resilience. The key is to ensure that minor schema changes do not halt the entire ingestion process, allowing for controlled updates to the pipeline as schemas evolve.

**Security and access control** are also fundamental aspects of designing ingestion mechanisms. Data often contains sensitive information, and access to it must be carefully managed. Ingestion pipelines need to securely connect to source systems using appropriate authentication and authorization mechanisms. This might involve using API keys, OAuth tokens, IAM roles, or encrypted credentials. Data should be encrypted in transit using protocols like TLS/SSL to prevent eavesdropping. Furthermore, strict access controls should be in place to ensure that only authorized pipelines and services can read from sensitive data sources. Regularly auditing access logs and rotating credentials are essential security practices to maintain the integrity and confidentiality of the data being ingested.

Finally,

**monitoring and alerting** for the ingestion layer are indispensable. Just as with other components of an ML pipeline, the ingestion process needs to be observed to ensure it is functioning correctly. Key metrics to monitor include ingestion throughput, latency, error rates, and resource utilization (CPU, memory, network). Setting up alerts for anomalies, such as a sudden drop in throughput, a spike in error rates, or prolonged connection failures, allows for proactive problem detection and resolution before data quality is significantly impacted or the entire pipeline grinds to a halt. Comprehensive logging of ingestion activities, including successful transfers, encountered errors, and any data validation failures, is crucial for debugging and auditing purposes. This continuous oversight ensures that the vital first step of bringing data into the system is performed reliably and efficiently.

The choice between processing data in real-time or in batches is a fundamental decision that shapes the architecture of any data pipeline, particularly in the realm of machine learning. Each approach caters to different needs regarding data freshness, latency tolerance, and processing complexity, leading to distinct technological choices and operational considerations. Understanding these differences is paramount for designing an effective and efficient system.

Batch processing, the more traditional of the two, involves collecting data over a period and then processing it in discrete chunks or "batches." Imagine gathering all the sales transaction records from a retail store throughout an entire day. These records are then collected and processed together at the end of the day to update inventory, generate sales reports, or train a model to predict future sales based on historical patterns. This method is well-suited for tasks where immediate insights are not critical, and the value lies in analyzing aggregated historical data. For instance, if you're training a recommendation engine that needs to understand user preferences based on weeks or months of browsing history, batch processing is often sufficient and more cost-effective. The data can be accumulated in a data lake or data warehouse, and then a sophisticated processing job can be scheduled to run periodically, perhaps nightly or weekly. This allows for complex transformations, joins across multiple large datasets, and computationally intensive model training without impacting operational systems.

Architecturally, batch processing often relies on tools designed for handling large volumes of data stored in persistent repositories. Data warehouses like Snowflake, Google BigQuery, or Amazon Redshift are prime examples of infrastructure optimized for batch analytics. They can efficiently query and aggregate massive datasets stored in columnar formats. For processing that requires more complex transformations or machine learning model training, distributed computing frameworks like Apache Spark are commonly employed. Spark can read data from various sources (HDFS, S3, databases), perform intricate transformations, and train machine learning models in a distributed fashion, processing entire datasets in one go. Tools like Apache Sqoop were historically used to efficiently transfer data between relational databases and Hadoop-based systems for batch processing, though modern cloud data warehouses and object storage have often superseded this. The core idea is that data is ingested, stored, and then processed in scheduled, complete cycles.

The advantages of batch processing are numerous. Firstly, it is often more cost-effective for large-scale data analysis, as resources can be provisioned and scaled for specific processing windows, rather than being kept on standby for continuous operation. Secondly, it simplifies processing logic for many use cases, as the entire dataset is available at once, eliminating the need to manage state across an infinite stream of incoming data. This makes debugging and reasoning about the results more straightforward. Furthermore, batch processing is ideal for tasks that require deep, complex analysis across vast historical datasets, such as training sophisticated machine learning models that learn from years of data, performing end-of-period financial reconciliations, or generating comprehensive reports. The ability to access the entire dataset allows for powerful analytical queries and computations that might be infeasible or prohibitively expensive in a real-time setting.

However, batch processing has significant drawbacks, primarily its inherent latency. Because data is processed in chunks after a delay, insights derived from batch jobs are always out of date. If a business needs to react to events as they happen – for example, detecting fraudulent transactions in real-time, monitoring critical infrastructure for anomalies, or personalizing a user's experience on a website as they browse – batch processing is simply too slow. The delay between data generation and its availability for analysis can range from minutes to hours or even days, making it unsuitable for time-sensitive applications. This lack of immediacy means that opportunities might be missed, and critical issues might go unnoticed for extended periods.

This is where real-time or stream processing comes into play. In contrast to batch processing, stream processing deals with data as it arrives, continuously and often in very small, individual events or micro-batches. Think of the constant stream of data from sensors on a self-driving car, user clickstreams on an e-commerce website, or financial market tickers. These data sources generate events that need to be processed and acted upon almost instantaneously. The goal of stream processing is to provide low-latency insights and enable immediate responses to events. For instance, if a credit card transaction occurs, a stream processing system can analyze it in milliseconds and flag it as potentially fraudulent, blocking the transaction before it's fully authorized. Similarly, a social media platform might use stream processing to identify trending topics as they emerge, or an IoT platform might monitor sensor readings from industrial machinery to predict potential failures before they happen.

The architecture for stream processing is fundamentally different from batch processing. It typically involves a message queue or a streaming platform to act as a buffer and distributor for the incoming data streams. Apache Kafka is a de facto standard for this role. Kafka allows producers (e.g., IoT devices, web servers) to publish data streams, and consumers (e.g., stream processing applications) can subscribe to these streams. Kafka provides high throughput, fault tolerance, and durability, ensuring that data is not lost even if downstream processing applications temporarily fail. On top of Kafka, stream processing engines like Apache Flink, Apache Spark Streaming (which processes data in small micro-batches), or cloud-native services like Amazon Kinesis Data Analytics or Google Cloud Dataflow are used to process the data in motion. These engines are designed to operate on unbounded streams of data, maintaining state and performing computations as events arrive, often with latencies measured in milliseconds.

The primary advantage of stream processing is its speed and ability to provide near-instantaneous insights. This is critical for applications that demand immediate action or a real-time view of operations. Detecting anomalies, fraud detection, real-time analytics dashboards, personalized recommendations delivered on-the-fly, and alerting systems are all prime candidates for stream processing. By processing data as it's generated, businesses can react to changing conditions, opportunities, and threats in real-time, leading to improved customer experiences, reduced losses, and enhanced operational efficiency. The ability to continuously monitor and analyze data streams allows for proactive decision-making and dynamic adjustments to business processes.

However, stream processing introduces its own set of complexities and challenges. Managing state across an infinite stream of data is significantly more difficult than working with finite batches. Applications must be designed to handle out-of-order events, late arrivals, and potential reprocessing scenarios. Developing and debugging stream processing applications can be more complex, requiring a different mindset and specialized tools. Furthermore, achieving high throughput and low latency often requires significant computational resources and careful system tuning. Cost can also be a consideration, as stream processing engines may need to be running continuously, consuming resources even during periods of lower activity. Ensuring exactly-once processing semantics (where each event is processed exactly one time, even in the face of failures) is a non-trivial task and often requires careful configuration of the underlying streaming platform and processing engine.

The choice between batch and stream processing is rarely a binary one; many modern data architectures employ a hybrid approach, often referred to as "Lambda Architecture" or "Kappa Architecture" patterns. In a Lambda Architecture, both batch and stream processing paths are maintained. The stream processing path provides low-latency, but potentially less accurate or aggregated, results for real-time dashboards and immediate actions. The batch processing path, on the other hand, provides highly accurate, comprehensive results by reprocessing historical data periodically, which are then used to serve historical queries or retrain machine learning models. This offers the best of both worlds: real-time responsiveness and the accuracy of batch analysis. The Kappa Architecture simplifies this by aiming to handle all processing, both real-time and historical, using a single stream processing engine. Data is first ingested into a streaming platform, and then processed by the stream processor. For historical reprocessing, the stream processor can re-read data from the beginning of the stream or from a durable log.

When deciding between batch and stream processing, several factors should be considered. The first is the
**latency requirement**. How quickly does the data need to be available for analysis or action? If minutes or hours are acceptable, batch processing

might suffice. If milliseconds or seconds are required, stream processing is necessary. The second factor is the **nature of the data source**. Does the data arrive in a continuous flow, or is it collected and delivered in discrete chunks? IoT devices and user activity logs are typically continuous streams, while daily sales reports are inherently batched. Third is the **complexity of the processing logic**. While both batch and stream processing can handle complex logic, some operations, like training deep learning models on massive historical datasets, are more naturally suited to batch environments due to resource requirements and the need for the entire dataset. Conversely, tasks like real-time anomaly detection are inherently stream-based.

The
**cost implications** are also crucial. Continuous processing of high-volume streams can be expensive, requiring robust infrastructure and potentially higher operational costs. Batch processing, with its scheduled execution, can often be more resource-efficient. **Data volume and velocity** also play a role. While both approaches can scale, the engineering effort to build and maintain a high-throughput, low-latency stream processing system for massive data volumes can be substantial. Finally, **the availability of tools and expertise** within an organization is a practical consideration. Organizations might already have significant investments and expertise in batch processing tools and may need to invest in new technologies and training for stream processing.

For machine learning pipelines, the choice significantly impacts model training and deployment. Models that require frequent retraining with the latest data might benefit from stream processing capabilities or a robust batch retraining schedule. For instance, a fraud detection model that needs to adapt to evolving fraud patterns might be retrained daily or even hourly using batch processing on newly labeled data, or it could be updated incrementally using online learning techniques within a stream processing framework. Similarly, a recommendation engine might be trained weekly on a full batch of user interaction data, but also update user profiles in near real-time based on their current browsing session using stream processing.

Technologies like Apache Spark are versatile and can be used for both batch and stream processing. Spark's core engine can process large datasets in batch mode, while Spark Streaming allows it to process data in small, discrete time intervals (micro-batches), effectively bridging the gap between batch and true real-time streaming. Apache Flink, on the other hand, is designed from the ground up as a true stream processing engine, capable of handling unbounded streams with very low latency and sophisticated state management. Cloud providers offer managed services that abstract away much of the underlying complexity, allowing engineers to focus on the data processing logic. For example, AWS offers Kinesis for real-time data streaming and processing, and EMR (Elastic MapReduce) for managed Hadoop and Spark clusters for batch processing. Azure provides Event Hubs for streaming and Databricks or HDInsight for batch and stream processing. Google Cloud offers Pub/Sub for messaging and Dataflow for unified batch and stream processing.

Ultimately, the decision between real-time and batch processing is a trade-off between data freshness, processing complexity, and cost. A thorough understanding of the business requirements, the nature of the data, and the capabilities of available technologies is essential to make the right choice. Often, the most effective solution involves a combination of both, leveraging the strengths of each approach to build a comprehensive and responsive data pipeline. This nuanced approach ensures that data is processed in a way that maximizes its value, whether that value is derived from immediate action or from deep historical analysis. The continuous evolution of data processing technologies further blurs these lines, offering increasingly sophisticated tools for both batch and stream scenarios, pushing the boundaries of what's possible in data-driven decision-making.

The quest for reliable and actionable insights from data is inextricably linked to the quality of that data. Raw, unadulterated information is rarely ready for direct consumption by analytical models or decision-making processes. It is often riddled with inconsistencies, inaccuracies, and structural deficiencies that can lead to flawed conclusions, wasted computational resources, and ultimately, poor business outcomes. Recognizing this, the design of any robust data pipeline must incorporate mechanisms not only for ingesting data but also for meticulously preparing it. This preparation, often referred to as data cleaning and preprocessing, transforms raw data into a state that is consistent, accurate, and fit for purpose. The challenge, however, lies in performing these essential transformations efficiently and reliably, especially as data volumes grow and the rate of data arrival accelerates. Manual intervention for cleaning and preprocessing is simply not scalable or sustainable in modern data environments. Therefore, the automation of these critical steps is not merely a convenience; it is an imperative.

Automating data cleaning and preprocessing within a data pipeline means embedding these quality assurance and transformation processes directly into the regular flow of data. Instead of treating data cleaning as a separate, one-off task performed on a static dataset, it becomes an integral part of the pipeline's operational cycle. This approach ensures that every piece of data, as it moves through the system, undergoes the necessary validation and refinement. The objective is to build trust in the data by ensuring its consistency and accuracy at every stage, thereby empowering downstream applications, be they machine learning models, business intelligence dashboards, or analytical reports, to function optimally. This automation fosters a proactive approach to data quality, catching and correcting issues early in the pipeline, which is significantly more efficient and less costly than addressing them after they have propagated through multiple systems.

A foundational aspect of automated data cleaning involves handling missing values. In real-world datasets, it is common to encounter records where certain attributes are not recorded. These gaps can arise from various reasons: sensor failures, user input errors, or simply data collection limitations. The presence of missing values can disrupt analytical processes, as many algorithms cannot directly operate on them. Therefore, a robust pipeline needs to address this systematically. Common strategies for automated imputation include filling missing values with a predefined constant (e.g., 0 or a specific placeholder), using the mean or median of the available data for that feature, or employing more sophisticated methods like regression imputation, where the missing value is predicted based on other features in the dataset. The choice of imputation strategy can significantly impact the results of subsequent analyses, and the pipeline should be configured to apply the chosen method consistently and efficiently. For instance, when processing a stream of sensor readings from an industrial machine, if a temperature reading is missing, the pipeline might be configured to substitute it with the average temperature recorded over the last hour, or perhaps a value predicted by a simple time-series model trained on historical data. This ensures that analyses relying on temperature data can continue uninterrupted, albeit with a judiciously chosen approximation.

Outlier detection is another critical component of automated preprocessing. Outliers are data points that deviate significantly from the expected patterns or distributions of the rest of the data. They can arise from genuine extreme events, measurement errors, or data entry mistakes. If left unaddressed, outliers can disproportionately influence statistical measures, skew model training, and lead to misleading interpretations. Automated outlier detection techniques can be integrated into the pipeline to identify and flag or mitigate these anomalous data points. Simple methods include the Z-score or IQR (Interquartile Range) methods, which define thresholds based on statistical properties of the data. More advanced techniques might involve clustering algorithms or machine learning models trained to identify deviations from normal behavior. For example, in a financial transaction dataset, a transaction amount that is orders of magnitude larger than typical transactions might be flagged as a potential outlier. The pipeline could be set up to automatically flag such transactions for review, or in cases where the outlier is clearly a data entry error, it might be automatically corrected to a more plausible value or excluded from further analysis. This proactive identification and handling of outliers safeguard the integrity of the data used for downstream tasks.

Data type conversion is a seemingly simple but crucial preprocessing step that is often automated. Data sources can be inconsistent in how they represent information. Numbers might be stored as strings, dates in various formats, or categorical data in different encodings. For analytical engines and machine learning algorithms to process data effectively, it must be in a consistent and appropriate format. An automated pipeline can enforce these type conversions. For example, a column intended to store numerical quantities might initially arrive with some values as text due to stray characters. The pipeline can be configured to attempt conversion to a numeric type, coercing valid entries and handling or logging errors for invalid ones. Similarly, date fields, which might come in formats like "MM/DD/YYYY," "DD-MM-YY," or ISO 8601, can be standardized into a single, unambiguous datetime format. This standardization is essential for time-series analysis, aggregation by date, and ensuring compatibility with various data processing tools that are sensitive to data types.

Normalization and scaling are fundamental preprocessing techniques, particularly vital for many machine learning algorithms, especially those sensitive to the magnitude of input features. Algorithms like gradient descent-based models (e.g., linear regression, neural networks) and distance-based algorithms (e.g., K-Nearest Neighbors, Support Vector Machines) perform optimally when features are on a similar scale. Unscaled features can lead to slower convergence during training or biased model behavior. Automated pipelines can incorporate these transformations as standard steps. Common methods include Min-Max scaling, which rescales features to a specific range (e.g., 0 to 1), and Standardization (Z-score scaling), which transforms features to have a mean of 0 and a standard deviation of 1. The choice of method often depends on the specific algorithm and the distribution of the data. For instance, if a pipeline is preparing data for a customer churn prediction model, and one feature is "customer tenure" (measured in years) and another is "monthly charges" (measured in dollars), these features will likely have very different ranges. An automated scaler can bring them into a comparable range, ensuring that neither feature unduly dominates the model's learning process due to its scale. It's important that these scaling parameters (like the minimum, maximum, mean, and standard deviation) are learned from a representative training dataset and then applied consistently to both training and inference data to prevent data leakage and ensure correct application.

Beyond these core operations, automated data cleaning and preprocessing can extend to handling categorical data, text data, and ensuring data consistency across related fields. Categorical features, such as "product category" or "customer segment," often need to be converted into a numerical format that machine learning models can understand. Techniques like one-hot encoding or label encoding are commonly employed. An automated pipeline can ensure that the correct encoding strategy is applied and that new categories encountered in incoming data are handled gracefully, either by being assigned to a special "unknown" category or by triggering an alert. For text data, preprocessing steps like removing punctuation, converting text to lowercase, tokenization, and removing stop words are often necessary before applying natural language processing techniques. These text cleaning operations can be integrated seamlessly into the pipeline.

Furthermore, automated workflows can enforce business rules and constraints. This might involve checking for data integrity across related fields. For example, if a dataset contains both "order date" and "delivery date," a business rule might dictate that the delivery date must always be on or after the order date. An automated check can flag or correct instances where this rule is violated. Similarly, pipelines can enforce expected formats for identifiers, such as postal codes or phone numbers, ensuring that data adheres to predefined patterns. The automation of these checks reduces manual validation effort and ensures that data entering the system conforms to established business logic, preventing the propagation of erroneous data that could have significant downstream consequences.

The implementation of these automated cleaning and preprocessing steps within a data pipeline typically leverages modular design principles. Each cleaning or transformation task can be encapsulated as a distinct module or function. This modularity offers several advantages: it makes the pipeline easier to understand, debug, and maintain. Individual modules can be tested independently, and their configurations can be adjusted without affecting other parts of the pipeline. For example, the missing value imputation module can be swapped with a different strategy, or the outlier detection threshold can be fine-tuned, without requiring a complete redesign of the data ingestion or transformation logic. Orchestration tools play a crucial role here, managing the execution order of these modules, handling dependencies, and ensuring that data flows correctly from one processing step to the next.

Consider a scenario where a retail company is ingesting daily sales transaction data from multiple stores. The raw data arrives in various formats and may contain errors. An automated pipeline would:

1.
**Ingest Data**: Read the raw data files from various sources (e.g., S3 buckets, SFTP servers).
2. **Basic Validation**: Check file integrity and identify empty files or obvious structural issues.
3. **Data Type Conversion**: Ensure that transaction IDs are strings, dates are datetime objects, quantities are integers, and prices are floats. This might involve parsing different date formats and cleaning currency symbols from price fields.
4. **Missing Value Imputation**: If a "discount*percentage" is missing for a particular item, and the business rule is to assume no discount if not specified, the pipeline would fill these with 0. If a "customer*id" is missing, it might be replaced with a placeholder like "Guest" or "Unknown," depending on downstream requirements.
5. **Outlier Detection**: Flag transactions with exceptionally high total amounts, as these might indicate errors or fraudulent activity, or very low quantities that seem implausible for a given product. These might be put aside for human review.
6. **Categorical Encoding**: Convert product category names (e.g., "Electronics," "Clothing") into numerical representations, perhaps using one-hot encoding if the number of categories is manageable, or target encoding if dealing with a large number of categories.
7. **Normalization/Scaling**: If the data is being prepared for a sales forecasting model that uses features like "number of items sold" and "average item price," these features might be scaled to a common range to prevent the model from being biased by the differing magnitudes.
8. **Data Consistency Checks**: Verify that "delivery*date" is never before "order*date." Ensure that product IDs exist in a master product catalog.
9. **Output**: Save the cleaned and preprocessed data to a data warehouse or data lake, ready for analysis, reporting, or model training.

This end-to-end automation ensures that the data available for decision-making is consistently clean and well-structured, regardless of the initial state of the raw input.

The continuous monitoring and logging of these automated processes are also paramount. Pipelines should be equipped with mechanisms to track the execution of each cleaning and preprocessing step, record the number of records affected by each operation (e.g., how many values were imputed, how many outliers were detected), and log any errors encountered. This audit trail is invaluable for understanding data quality trends, diagnosing issues when they arise, and demonstrating compliance with data governance policies. Alerts can be configured to notify data engineers or stewards if certain thresholds are breached – for instance, if the percentage of missing values in a critical column exceeds a predefined limit, or if a disproportionate number of records are flagged as outliers.

The evolution of data processing frameworks has significantly empowered the automation of data cleaning and preprocessing. Libraries within languages like Python (e.g., Pandas, Scikit-learn) provide extensive functionalities for these tasks, which can be orchestrated using tools like Apache Airflow, Prefect, or Dagster. Cloud-based data processing services, such as AWS Glue, Google Cloud Dataflow, or Azure Data Factory, offer managed environments where these transformations can be defined and executed at scale, often with built-in capabilities for data profiling and quality checks. These platforms abstract away much of the infrastructure complexity, allowing data engineers to focus on defining the logic for cleaning and preprocessing.

In summary, automating data cleaning and preprocessing is not an optional add-on but a core requirement for building reliable and scalable data pipelines. By embedding checks for missing values, outlier detection, data type consistency, and feature scaling directly into the data flow, organizations can ensure that the data used for analysis and machine learning is accurate, consistent, and fit for purpose. This systematic approach minimizes manual effort, reduces the risk of human error, and builds trust in the data, ultimately leading to more informed and effective decision-making. The continuous refinement and monitoring of these automated processes are key to maintaining high data quality over time, enabling organizations to derive maximum value from their data assets.

The journey from raw data to actionable intelligence is often paved with intricate transformations, none more critical than feature engineering. While data cleaning and preprocessing lay the groundwork by ensuring data is accurate and consistent, feature engineering is where raw attributes are sculpted into meaningful representations that unlock the predictive power of analytical models. This process, historically a highly manual and often experimental endeavor, can become a significant bottleneck in the data pipeline. It requires domain expertise, creativity, and a deep understanding of how different data transformations can influence model performance. However, as datasets grow in complexity and volume, and the demand for rapid deployment of machine learning models intensifies, the automation of feature engineering becomes not just desirable, but an absolute necessity for scalable and reproducible data science workflows.

Integrating automated feature engineering directly into the data pipeline transforms it from a sequence of data ingestion and cleaning steps into a comprehensive engine for data readiness. This means that as data flows into the system, it doesn't just get cleaned; it actively gets enriched with new, derived features that are tailored for specific analytical tasks. This automation addresses several key challenges. Firstly, it significantly reduces the time and effort associated with manual feature creation, freeing up data scientists and engineers to focus on higher-level tasks like model selection, hyperparameter tuning, and interpreting results.

Secondly, it enforces consistency. When feature engineering steps are hardcoded or manually executed, there's a high risk of variations in application between different datasets or between the training and production environments. Automation ensures that the exact same transformations are applied every single time, regardless of when or where the data is processed. This is absolutely crucial for building trust in model predictions and ensuring that a model performs as expected in a live setting.

A foundational aspect of automated feature engineering involves the systematic application of pre-defined feature engineering logic. This logic can encompass a wide array of transformations, from simple arithmetic operations to complex aggregations and encodings. For instance, in a time-series dataset, creating features like "lagged values" (e.g., sales from the previous day or week) or "rolling averages" (e.g., average sales over the last 30 days) can be fully automated. If the pipeline identifies a timestamp column, it can be programmed to automatically generate features such as the hour of the day, day of the week, month, or year. Similarly, if numerical features represent quantities or monetary values, the pipeline can be configured to generate interaction terms (e.g., multiplying price by quantity to get total revenue) or polynomial features (e.g., squaring a feature to capture non-linear relationships). For categorical data, automated transformations like one-hot encoding or target encoding can be applied. The key is to define these transformation rules within the pipeline's code or configuration, allowing them to be executed repeatedly and reliably on incoming data.

Consider a scenario in e-commerce where customer behavior data is being processed. The raw data might include timestamps of website visits, product IDs viewed, and purchase amounts. Within an automated pipeline, we could define rules to generate valuable features:

**Time-based Features**: From the timestamp, extract features like \`hour*of*day\`, \`day*of*week\`, \`is_weekend\`. This helps in understanding if purchase patterns differ by time of day or day of the week.
**Session Features**: Group events by user and session to calculate metrics like \`session*duration\`, \`number*of*products*viewed*in*session\`, \`average*time*on_page\`. These can indicate user engagement.
**Purchase History Features**: For returning customers, aggregate past behavior such as \`total*spent*last*30*days\`, \`average*order*value\`, \`frequency*of*purchase\`, \`time*since*last_purchase\`. These are strong predictors of future purchasing intent.
**Product Interaction Features**: Create features related to product popularity or affinity, such as \`product*view*count*last7days\` or \`percentage*of*users*who*bought*product*X*after*viewing*product_Y\`.

These transformations, once defined, can be encapsulated in reusable modules within the pipeline. When new customer interaction data arrives, these modules are invoked, and the derived features are computed and appended to the dataset automatically. This eliminates the need for a data scientist to manually write and run scripts for each new batch of data or for each iteration of model development.

A critical aspect of automating feature engineering is managing feature versions. As models are retrained or as new insights lead to modifications in feature definitions, it's essential to keep track of which version of a feature was used for which model or experiment. This is where a feature store, often integrated with or complementary to the data pipeline, plays a pivotal role. A feature store acts as a centralized repository for curated features, providing a consistent way to define, store, serve, and discover features. When a pipeline generates a new feature or updates an existing one, it can register this new version in the feature store. This not only provides an audit trail but also allows other teams or models to easily access the latest, validated features. For example, if a feature engineering module is updated to use a more sophisticated method for calculating customer lifetime value, the new version of the `customer *lifetime*value` feature can be versioned in the feature store. Downstream models can then be pointed to use `customer*lifetime*value_v2`, ensuring that the transition is managed and traceable.

The ability to manage feature versions is paramount for reproducibility. In machine learning, reproducibility means that given the same data and the same code, one should be able to obtain the same results. Without proper versioning of features, if a pipeline is re-run months later, it might generate slightly different features if the underlying logic has changed, making it impossible to reproduce a previous model's performance or to debug historical issues. By versioning features, the pipeline can be configured to use a specific, historical version of a feature set, ensuring that the training data used for a particular model remains consistent and immutable. This is vital for regulatory compliance, A/B testing of models, and for maintaining production models that require consistent inputs.

Furthermore, ensuring consistency between features used during training and inference is a non-trivial challenge that automated feature engineering within a pipeline helps to solve. A common pitfall is the "training-serving skew," where the features generated for training a model are different from those generated when the model is deployed to make real-time predictions. This can happen if the feature generation logic is implemented separately in the training environment and the serving environment, leading to subtle discrepancies that can severely degrade model performance. By embedding feature engineering directly within the data pipeline, which is designed to operate consistently across different phases of the ML lifecycle (batch training, real-time inference), this skew is minimized.

For instance, imagine a pipeline that processes streaming user click data to predict purchase probability. The pipeline can be configured to perform feature extraction in near real-time for inference. When training data is prepared, the pipeline can be run in a batch mode over historical data, applying the exact same feature engineering logic to generate the training dataset. Features like `user *click*count*last*1*hour` or `time*since*last*click` would be calculated using the identical code path and logic, whether for training or serving. This is often achieved by defining feature engineering logic in a shared library that is accessible to both the training pipeline and the real-time inference service. A feature store can be instrumental here, providing a unified interface to retrieve the necessary feature definitions and logic for both contexts. When the pipeline needs to serve predictions, it can fetch the feature logic from the feature store, execute it on the incoming stream of data, and then pass the engineered features to the deployed model. This ensures that the features the model sees during inference are precisely the same as those it was trained on.

The automation of feature engineering also facilitates the discovery and application of complex feature transformations that might be too cumbersome or time-consuming to implement manually. Techniques such as embeddings (e.g., Word2Vec for text, or embeddings for categorical features in recommendation systems) or dimensionality reduction methods (like PCA) can be integrated as automated steps. For example, if a pipeline is processing textual product reviews, it can automatically include a step to generate TF-IDF vectors or dense embeddings from the review text. These embeddings then become new features that can be fed into a model for sentiment analysis or product recommendation. Similarly, for high-dimensional data, a PCA transformation can be applied to reduce the number of features while retaining most of the variance, making subsequent modeling more efficient. The pipeline orchestrates these transformations, ensuring that they are applied consistently and at scale.

Consider a scenario where a financial institution is building a fraud detection system. The raw data includes transaction details like amount, time, location, merchant ID, and user ID. Automated feature engineering within the pipeline can create sophisticated features such as:

**Velocity Features**: How many transactions has this user made in the last hour, day, or week? \`user*transaction*count*last*24h\`.
**Deviation Features**: How does this transaction amount compare to the user's average transaction amount? \`transaction*amountvsuser*avg_ratio\`.
**Geospatial Features**: If location data is available, calculate the distance between consecutive transactions for a user, or flag transactions occurring in unusual locations for that user. \`distance*from*previous_transaction\`.
**Temporal Features**: Time between consecutive transactions for a user. \`time*between*transactions*for*user\`.
**Merchant-based Features**: How often does this user transact with this merchant? \`user*transaction*count*with*merchant\`.

By automating the calculation of these complex, derived features, the pipeline can enrich the transaction data significantly. This transformed data then becomes the input for a fraud detection model. The automation ensures that these features are available for both training the model on historical data and for real-time scoring of new transactions. The feature store, in conjunction with the pipeline, can manage the state required for these calculations (e.g., storing the last known user transaction count or average amount) for real-time inference.

The operationalization of automated feature engineering requires robust tooling and infrastructure. Modern data pipelines are typically built using workflow orchestration tools like Apache Airflow, Prefect, or Dagster, which allow for the definition of complex directed acyclic graphs (DAGs) representing the sequence of operations. Within these DAGs, specific tasks can be dedicated to feature engineering. These tasks might leverage libraries like Pandas or Spark for data manipulation, Scikit-learn for transformations, or specialized feature engineering libraries. Cloud platforms also offer managed services that simplify this process. For example, AWS Glue, Google Cloud Dataflow, and Azure Databricks provide environments where data transformation and feature engineering logic can be defined and executed at scale, often with built-in connectors to various data sources and destinations.

The development process for automated feature engineering often starts with exploratory data analysis (EDA) and experimentation. Data scientists might experiment with different feature transformations in a notebook environment. Once promising features are identified, this logic needs to be translated into production-ready code that can be integrated into the pipeline. This transition phase is critical. It involves refactoring experimental code, ensuring it's efficient, robust, and handles edge cases. Moreover, the feature engineering code must be tested thoroughly. Unit tests can verify the correctness of individual transformations, while integration tests can ensure that features are generated as expected when the pipeline runs on sample data. The use of a feature store can simplify this by providing a standardized API for feature definition and retrieval, allowing teams to iterate on feature logic while maintaining a consistent interface for models.

One of the key benefits of a well-implemented automated feature engineering pipeline is its ability to adapt to changing data. For instance, if a new product category is introduced in an e-commerce system, the automated pipeline that generates category-based features can be updated to include this new category. If the feature engineering logic uses one-hot encoding, the pipeline can automatically update the set of generated columns to include the new category, or if it's designed to handle unseen categories gracefully, it can assign them to a designated "other" category. Similarly, if the business introduces new rules or metrics that need to be incorporated as features, these can be added as new transformation steps in the pipeline. This agility ensures that the data fueling analytical models remains relevant and captures the latest business dynamics.

The challenge of maintaining feature logic over time is also addressed by automation. As data sources evolve, or as requirements for features change, the feature engineering code within the pipeline will need updates. By keeping this logic codified and version-controlled, managing these changes becomes a software engineering problem, not a manual data wrangling task. This allows for more systematic deployment of updates, easier rollbacks if something goes wrong, and clearer documentation of the evolution of features. The integration with CI/CD (Continuous Integration/Continuous Deployment) practices further enhances this, allowing for automated testing and deployment of updated feature engineering modules.

In summary, feature engineering automation within the data pipeline is a crucial step towards building robust, scalable, and reproducible machine learning systems. It transforms a historically experimental and manual process into a reliable component of the data flow. By embedding pre-defined logic for feature creation, managing feature versions through tools like feature stores, and ensuring consistency between training and inference environments, organizations can significantly accelerate their time-to-insight and improve the reliability of their data-driven applications. This systematic approach to feature generation not only enhances efficiency but also builds a solid foundation of trust and traceability for the features that power critical analytical models. The continuous refinement and monitoring of these automated feature engineering processes are key to unlocking the full potential of data in dynamic and evolving business landscapes.

The very nature of data systems implies a continuous journey of evolution. As the underlying business processes that generate data change, as new data sources are integrated, or as analytical requirements deepen, the structure of the data itself—its schema—is inevitably altered. This dynamic reality presents a significant hurdle for data ingestion and preparation pipelines. A pipeline designed to process data in a specific format can become brittle, prone to failure, the moment that format shifts. Therefore, managing and evolving data schemas is not merely an operational concern; it's a fundamental aspect of building resilient and future-proof data infrastructure.

At its core, schema management is about understanding and controlling the blueprint of your data. This blueprint defines the names of fields, their data types, constraints (like whether a field can be null), and potentially relationships between different data entities. When this blueprint changes—a new field is added, an existing field is renamed, its data type is altered, or a field is deprecated—the pipelines that consume this data must be equipped to handle it. Ignoring these changes can lead to cascading failures: a new field that an ingestion process expects but doesn't find will halt the process; a field that has changed its data type (e.g., from string to integer) might cause parsing errors.

The primary challenge lies in maintaining backward compatibility. Ideally, when a schema evolves, existing pipelines should continue to function without modification, at least for a period. This allows for a graceful transition and minimizes disruption. A common strategy to achieve this is through additive schema changes. For instance, when introducing new attributes, these are typically added as optional fields. If a consumer of the data doesn't explicitly request or process this new field, it can simply be ignored. This approach is fundamental to extending data models without breaking existing consumers. Conversely, removing or renaming fields is inherently a breaking change. If a field is no longer needed, it should ideally be marked for deprecation first, with a clear communication plan to downstream users, before its actual removal. Renaming a field requires updating all references to that field in all consuming systems, which can be a complex and error-prone undertaking if not managed systematically.

Versioning schemas is a critical mechanism for managing these changes. Just as software code is versioned, so too should data schemas. Each significant modification to a schema can be assigned a new version number. This allows pipelines and applications to explicitly declare which version of a schema they are compatible with. For example, a data source might publish its schema as `customer
*v1.0` or `transaction*v2.3`. Downstream pipelines can then be configured to expect a specific version or a range of compatible versions. This explicit declaration provides a clear contract between data producers and consumers. When a schema producer releases `customer_v1.1`, they can document the changes relative to `v1.0` and specify that `v1.1` is backward-compatible with `v1.0`. Consumers can then decide when to upgrade their processing logic to take advantage of `v1.1` or continue using `v1.0` for a defined transition period.

Implementing backward-compatible data processing logic within the pipeline itself is paramount. This often involves techniques that make the pipeline robust to minor schema variations. For instance, when parsing incoming data, a pipeline can be designed to tolerate missing fields. If a field is expected but not present in a particular record, the pipeline can gracefully handle this by assigning a default value (like `null`, an empty string, or a specific placeholder) rather than throwing an error. This is particularly useful when dealing with data from various sources that might have slightly different update cycles or when a new field has been added to the source but not yet propagated to all data consumers. Similarly, if a field's data type is flexible, the pipeline might attempt type coercion where appropriate. For example, if a numerical field sometimes arrives as a string representation of a number (e.g., `"123.45"` instead of `123.45`), a robust pipeline could attempt to convert it to a numeric type. However, this must be done with caution to avoid unintended data loss or misinterpretation.

A more advanced approach to schema evolution involves using schema registries. These are centralized systems that store and manage schema definitions. When data is produced or consumed, it interacts with the schema registry to validate its schema or retrieve the expected schema. Apache Kafka, for instance, often integrates with schema registries like Confluent Schema Registry. In this setup, when a producer sends a message, it serializes the data according to a specific schema version. The schema registry then assigns a unique ID to this schema. The producer includes this schema ID with the message. When a consumer receives the message, it uses the schema ID to retrieve the corresponding schema from the registry and deserialize the data. If the producer evolves the schema (e.g., adds a new field), it registers the new schema version. The schema registry can be configured to enforce compatibility rules, such as "backward compatibility" or "forward compatibility."

Let's elaborate on compatibility rules within a schema registry context.

**Backward Compatibility**: This is perhaps the most commonly desired. A new schema version is backward-compatible if consumers using the previous *schema version can still read data produced with the* new schema version. This is typically achieved by making additive changes, such as adding new optional fields or setting default values for newly required fields. If a consumer expecting `schemav*1*` *reads data produced with*

`*schema*v2` (which has an added optional field), it will simply ignore the new field, and the read operation will succeed.
**Forward Compatibility**: A new schema version is forward-compatible if consumers using the new *schema version can still read data produced with the* previous schema version. This is often achieved by allowing the removal of fields that are not essential or by allowing the addition of new optional fields. If a consumer expecting `schema*v2*` *(which may have removed a field that existed in `schema*v1`) reads data produced with `schema_v1`, it must be able to handle the "missing" field gracefully, perhaps by assigning a default value.
**Full Compatibility (or No Breaking Changes)**: This is the strictest form, meaning the new schema is compatible with both older and newer versions. This often implies only adding optional fields.

The choice of compatibility rule is crucial and depends on the specific needs of the data ecosystem. For many real-time streaming pipelines, backward compatibility is the preferred mode, as it allows producers to evolve their data formats without immediately forcing all consumers to update their code. This provides flexibility and reduces the coordination overhead required for deployments.

Beyond compatibility rules, schema registries also facilitate schema discovery and governance. Teams can browse available schemas, understand their structure, and query historical versions. This transparency is vital for data teams to maintain a coherent understanding of the data landscape. Furthermore, integrating schema validation directly into the data pipeline during ingestion can catch schema deviations early. Before data is processed further, it can be checked against the expected schema. If a mismatch is detected, the pipeline can be configured to either reject the data, flag it for manual review, or attempt an automated remediation (if safe to do so). This early detection prevents downstream errors and makes troubleshooting significantly easier.

Consider a concrete example in an e-commerce data pipeline. Suppose we have a `product` dataset.

**Initial Schema (`product_v1`)**:
`product_id` (integer, required)
`product_name` (string, required)
`category` (string, required)
`price` (float, required)

**First Evolution (`product***v2*`)**: A new attribute, `description`, is introduced. The `productv2` schema is designed to be backward-compatible.
`product_id` (integer, required)
`product_name` (string, required)
`category` (string, required)
`price` (float, required)
`description` (string, optional)

A pipeline that uses `product
*v1` would read data produced with `product*v2` and simply ignore the `description` field. This is backward compatibility in action. The producer of the `product` data can now enrich their records with descriptions, and existing consumers continue to work.

**Second Evolution (`product***v3*`)**: The `category` field is being standardized. Some categories might become obsolete, and new ones introduced. Also, a `discountpercentage` field is added. The goal is again backward compatibility.
`product_id` (integer, required)
`product_name` (string, required)

`category` (string, required)
`price` (float, required)
`description` (string, optional)
`discount_percentage` (float, optional, default=0.0)

If a pipeline is still processing data intended for `product *v2`, it will read `product*v3` data and correctly process `product*id`, `product*name`, `category`, `price`, and `description`. It will encounter `discount_percentage` but, as an optional field it's not explicitly handled, so it would be ignored. This maintains backward compatibility.

However, if a pipeline needs to explicitly handle the `discount *percentage`, it must be updated to a version compatible with `product*v3`. For example, a data scientist might want to use the `discount*percentage` to calculate the `sale*price`. They would then update their pipeline to use `product*v3` and add a transformation step: `sale*price = price (1 - discount_percentage)`.

The challenge intensifies when schema changes are not additive, such as renaming a field or changing a data type. Renaming `price` to `unit *price` in `product*v4` would require an explicit update in any pipeline that uses the `price` field.
**Fourth Evolution (`product***v4`)*: Renaming `price` to `unitprice` and changing `product_id` to a UUID string.
`product_id` (string, required) - This is a breaking change if consumers expect an integer.
`product_name` (string, required)
`category` (string, required)
`unit_price` (float, required) - This is a breaking change if consumers expect `price`.
`description` (string, optional)
`discount_percentage` (float, optional, default=0.0)

To handle such breaking changes gracefully, a transition period is

essential. During this period, the data producer might publish data in both formats, or with a mapping that allows consumers to access the new field under the old name temporarily. For example, a data source could output `product
*v4` data but include a `price` field that is a direct alias or copy of `unit*price` for a transition phase. This allows downstream systems to migrate at their own pace. Automated pipelines can be configured to watch for specific schema versions or to dynamically adapt based on detected schema structures, although this adds complexity.

A robust approach to managing schema evolution within pipelines involves a combination of strategies:

1. **Schema Registry Integration**: Using a centralized schema registry (like Confluent Schema Registry for Avro/Protobuf, or a custom solution for JSON schemas) is foundational. It provides a single source of truth for schemas and enforces compatibility rules.
2. **Code-Level Resilience**: Within the pipeline's transformation logic, employ techniques like checking for field existence before accessing it, using default values for optional or newly introduced fields, and performing explicit type conversions with error handling.
3. **Versioned Processing Logic**: Design the pipeline code itself to be version-aware. This might involve using configuration files that specify the expected schema version or dynamically loading transformation modules based on the schema version of the incoming data.
4. **Monitoring and Alerting**: Implement comprehensive monitoring that tracks schema drift. Alerts should be triggered when data arrives with an unexpected schema or when a known schema deviates from its registered definition. This allows for proactive intervention before failures propagate.
5. **Deprecation Policies and Communication**: Establish clear policies for deprecating fields and entire schema versions. This involves a communication plan to notify data producers and consumers well in advance, providing them with sufficient time to adapt their systems.

Consider a scenario where data is ingested into a data lake. Different analytical tools and applications then consume this data. If the schema of a particular dataset in the data lake changes without proper management, all downstream applications relying on it might break. Using a schema registry and ensuring additive changes or employing a clear deprecation strategy helps avoid this. For instance, if a new attribute `customer *segment` is added to user profiles, the ingestion pipeline should add this as an optional field. All existing applications can continue to run, while new applications or updated versions can be developed to leverage this new `customer*segment` information.

When dealing with semi-structured or unstructured data (like logs or free-text fields), schema management takes a different form. While there might not be a strict, formal schema like in relational databases, there are still implicit structures or formats that evolve. For log data, the addition of new log fields or changes in log message formatting can disrupt parsing. In such cases, defining a schema for the parsed log data (e.g., in JSON format) and using a schema registry becomes crucial. The ingestion pipeline is responsible for parsing the raw logs into a structured format defined by a schema. If the raw log format changes, the parsing logic within the pipeline must be updated to match, and this update should be managed under a schema versioning strategy for the *parsed* data.

The concept of "schema-on-read" versus "schema-on-write" also plays a role. In schema-on-write systems (like traditional relational databases), the schema is strictly enforced at the time of data writing. Any deviation is rejected. In schema-on-read systems (like many data lakes), data is written as-is, and the schema is applied or inferred when the data is read. While schema-on-read offers flexibility, it shifts the burden of schema management to the consumers. To mitigate this, robust data pipelines can implement a hybrid approach: ingest data with minimal upfront schema enforcement (allowing for flexibility) but then apply schema validation and transformation to create a curated, schema-governed layer within the data lake. This curated layer ensures that downstream analytical processes work with predictable and consistent data structures.

The evolution of schemas also necessitates careful consideration of data governance and compliance. Regulations like GDPR or CCPA require specific handling of personal data. If the schema evolves to include or exclude certain types of sensitive data, or if the definition of what constitutes personal data changes, pipelines must adapt accordingly. Schema versioning and a well-documented schema registry provide an audit trail of how data fields have been defined and used over time, which is invaluable for compliance audits. For example, if a field containing personally identifiable information (PII) is deprecated and removed from the schema, schema versioning ensures that historical data processing jobs can still access it if needed for specific, approved purposes, while newer processing jobs will not encounter it.

Automated schema detection and evolution are emerging areas. Tools are being developed that can automatically detect changes in incoming data schemas and suggest or even automatically apply compatible schema updates. These tools can monitor data streams, compare the schema of new data batches against registered schemas, and, based on pre-defined rules, propose changes. For instance, if a new field appears consistently in incoming data, an automated system could flag this and propose adding it as an optional field to the registered schema. This can significantly reduce the manual effort involved in schema management, especially in large and dynamic data environments. However, human oversight remains critical to ensure that automated changes align with business intent and do not inadvertently break critical downstream processes.

In summary, managing and evolving data schemas is an indispensable part of building resilient data ingestion and preparation pipelines. It requires a proactive approach that embraces schema versioning, backward compatibility, and robust error handling. Leveraging schema registries and implementing clear deprecation policies are key to maintaining data integrity and pipeline stability as data sources and analytical needs evolve. By treating schema management as a first-class concern, organizations can build data pipelines that are not only efficient but also adaptable and dependable in the long run, minimizing the risk of costly failures and ensuring that data remains a reliable asset for decision-making.

# Chapter 10: Model Training and Evaluation Pipelines

The journey of a machine learning model doesn't end with its initial deployment. In fact, the deployment is merely a milestone in a much longer, iterative process. For models to remain effective and relevant, they must be continuously retrained and updated. Manually initiating these retraining cycles, managing the associated configurations, and tracking the outcomes is not only time-consuming but also prone to human error, especially as the number of models and their complexity grow. Automating model training workflows transforms this critical phase from an ad-hoc activity into a robust, reproducible, and integrated component of the broader machine learning lifecycle. This automation is key to achieving scalability, consistency, and agility in model development and deployment.

At its core, automating model training involves establishing triggers and systems that initiate the training process automatically. These triggers can be event-driven or schedule-based. An event-driven trigger might be activated by the arrival of a significant volume of new data, the completion of a data preprocessing pipeline, or a detected drift in the input data's statistical properties. For example, if a fraud detection model relies on daily transaction data, a new batch of validated transactions could automatically kick off a retraining job. Schedule-based triggers, on the other hand, execute training at predetermined intervals, such as weekly or monthly. This is common for models where data volumes might not fluctuate dramatically but performance might degrade subtly over time. A recommendation engine, for instance, might be scheduled for a weekly retraining to incorporate fresh user interaction data and adapt to evolving trends. The choice between event-driven and schedule-based triggers often depends on the model's sensitivity to new data, the acceptable latency for model updates, and the cost implications of frequent retraining. Robust automation requires a clear strategy for defining these triggers, ensuring they are aligned with business objectives and the model's operational requirements. This involves setting thresholds for data volume, defining acceptable drift metrics, and establishing appropriate retraining frequencies.

Beyond simply initiating training, the automation must encompass the entire training job lifecycle. This means programmatically defining the parameters, dependencies, and execution environment for each training run. A critical aspect of this is experiment tracking. Every training run is essentially an experiment, and meticulously recording its details is crucial for reproducibility, debugging, and future improvements. This involves tracking not just the hyper-parameters used (e.g., learning rate, number of layers, regularization strength) but also the specific version of the training code, the dataset version or split used, and any other configuration details that define the experiment. Equally important is tracking the resulting metrics. This includes performance metrics like accuracy, precision, recall, F1-score, AUC for classification models, or RMSE, MAE, R-squared for regression models. Beyond just the final metrics, it's also beneficial to log intermediate metrics during the training process, which can provide insights into convergence behavior and potential issues. Furthermore, the artifacts produced by a training run—such as the trained model weights, serialized model objects, feature importance scores, and visualizations of learning curves—must be systematically saved and versioned. This ensures that any trained model can be retrieved and reproduced later, facilitating auditing, rollback, and comparison with new models.

The infrastructure for effective experiment tracking is often provided by specialized tools, commonly referred to as MLOps platforms or experiment tracking systems. These platforms offer a centralized repository for logging, organizing, and visualizing experiment data. They allow data scientists and engineers to log parameters, metrics, and artifacts programmatically from their training scripts. Features like comparing multiple experiments side-by-side, filtering experiments based on specific criteria, and linking experiments to the code commits that produced them are invaluable. For example, a data scientist might train several variants of a neural network for an image classification task, varying the optimizer and learning rate. An experiment tracking system would allow them to log each combination of optimizer and learning rate as a separate experiment, along with its corresponding validation accuracy and the trained model file. Later, they can easily identify the best-performing model based on validation accuracy and retrieve its exact configuration and trained weights. This systematic approach to experiment tracking is a cornerstone of developing reliable and high-performing models.

To orchestrate these automated training workflows, Machine Learning Operations (MLOps) platforms and workflow orchestration tools play a pivotal role. These tools provide a framework for defining, scheduling, and monitoring complex pipelines that can span multiple steps, including data ingestion, preprocessing, feature engineering, model training, evaluation, and deployment. Popular examples include Kubeflow Pipelines, Apache Airflow, MLflow Projects, AWS SageMaker Pipelines, and Azure Machine Learning Pipelines. These platforms enable the definition of Directed Acyclic Graphs (DAGs) or similar structures, where each node represents a specific task or step in the workflow, and the edges define the dependencies between them.

Consider a typical automated training pipeline built using such a tool. The pipeline might begin with a data ingestion task that pulls the latest data from a data source. This data then flows into a data preprocessing task, which might involve cleaning, transforming, and splitting the data into training and validation sets. This task would typically be configured to use a specific version of the preprocessing code and potentially leverage a feature store to retrieve pre-computed features. The output of this stage, the prepared datasets, then feeds into the model training task. This task is where the core automation of model training is realized. It would be configured with the chosen model architecture, hyper-parameters (potentially fetched from a hyper-parameter optimization service or a predefined configuration), and the training dataset. The training task would also be instrumented to log all parameters, metrics, and artifacts to the experiment tracking system.

Upon completion of the training task, an evaluation task typically follows. This task uses the trained model to make predictions on the validation dataset and computes various performance metrics. These metrics are again logged to the experiment tracking system and can be used to trigger subsequent actions. For instance, if the evaluation metrics meet a predefined threshold (e.g., validation accuracy exceeds the current production model's accuracy by a certain margin), the pipeline might proceed to a model registration step. Here, the newly trained model is versioned and stored in a model registry, making it available for potential deployment. If the metrics do not meet the threshold, the pipeline might simply terminate, or it could trigger an alert to a human operator to investigate. This conditional execution based on performance is a powerful aspect of automated training workflows.

The orchestration tool manages the execution of these tasks, handling dependencies, resource allocation (e.g., spinning up compute instances for training), retries in case of transient failures, and overall pipeline monitoring. It provides a dashboard or interface where users can view the status of ongoing and completed pipelines, inspect logs for individual tasks, and understand the lineage of data and models. This visibility is critical for managing complex ML systems and ensuring that training processes are reliable and reproducible.

To further enhance the automation of model training, hyper-parameter optimization (HPO) can be integrated directly into the pipeline. Instead of manually selecting hyper-parameters, the pipeline can be configured to launch an HPO job. The HPO component, orchestrated by the workflow tool, would then systematically explore a defined search space of hyper-parameter values, launching multiple training tasks (often in parallel, leveraging distributed computing) for different combinations. Once the HPO job identifies the optimal set of hyper-parameters based on predefined search strategies (e.g., grid search, random search, Bayesian optimization), it outputs these parameters. The workflow then proceeds to a final training run using this optimal set, ensuring that the best possible model configuration is trained. This systematic exploration of the hyper-parameter space is a crucial step in maximizing model performance and is best managed programmatically within an automated workflow.

Furthermore, the concept of "model retraining pipelines" can be generalized to encompass concepts like model validation and A/B testing prior to full deployment. After a new model is trained and evaluated against a static validation set, it might undergo further testing against real-time production traffic. This could involve a shadow deployment where the new model runs in parallel with the existing production model, its predictions are logged, but not used to serve user requests. The outputs are then compared to ensure consistent behavior and identify potential discrepancies or regressions. Alternatively, a more aggressive A/B test might involve routing a small percentage of live traffic to the new model and comparing its performance metrics against the incumbent. These advanced testing phases can also be orchestrated as separate steps within the broader automated MLOps pipeline, ensuring that only thoroughly validated models are promoted to production.

The automation also extends to managing the environment in which training occurs. Containerization technologies like Docker are instrumental here. Each training task within a workflow can be executed within a Docker container that encapsulates all necessary libraries, dependencies, and even specific versions of frameworks like TensorFlow or PyTorch. This ensures that the training code runs consistently across different environments and that reproducibility is maintained. The workflow orchestration tool then manages the deployment and scaling of these containers on compute infrastructure, whether it's on-premises clusters or cloud-based services like Kubernetes. This abstract representation of the execution environment simplifies the process of setting up and managing training infrastructure, allowing data scientists to focus on model development rather than environment configuration.

Automating model training workflows is not a one-time setup but an ongoing process of refinement. As models evolve and new requirements emerge, the pipelines themselves need to be updated. This implies that the pipeline code, much like the model code, should be version-controlled, tested, and deployed using robust software engineering practices. CI/CD (Continuous Integration/Continuous Deployment) principles can be applied not just to model code but also to the MLOps pipelines themselves. This means that changes to the pipeline definition (e.g., adding a new step, modifying a trigger condition) are automatically tested and deployed, ensuring that the automation infrastructure itself remains agile and reliable.

In summary, the automation of model training workflows is a critical enabler for scalable, reliable, and efficient machine learning operations. It transforms the often manual and error-prone process of retraining into a robust, reproducible, and observable pipeline component. By establishing automated triggers, meticulously tracking experiments and their artifacts, and leveraging powerful MLOps orchestration tools, organizations can ensure that their machine learning models remain relevant and performant in dynamic production environments. This automation not only boosts productivity but also enhances the trustworthiness and agility of the entire machine learning lifecycle.

The journey from a raw dataset to a deployed, high-performing machine learning model is a complex and often iterative process. While automating the training execution itself is a significant step towards efficiency and reproducibility, the critical phases of selecting the most suitable model architecture and meticulously tuning its hyperparameters remain paramount for achieving optimal performance. These decisions can dramatically impact a model's accuracy, generalization ability, and robustness, and thus, their automation within the MLOps pipeline is not just a convenience but a necessity for any serious machine learning endeavor. This subsection delves into the strategies and techniques for automating model selection and hyperparameter tuning, transforming these previously manual and time-consuming tasks into streamlined, data-driven processes that can be seamlessly integrated into our automated training workflows.

At its heart, model selection involves choosing the appropriate algorithm or architecture for a given problem. While a data scientist's expertise is invaluable in narrowing down the initial set of candidates, the vast and ever-growing landscape of available models necessitates a systematic approach, especially when dealing with multiple potential solutions or when aiming for peak performance. Imagine a scenario where we are building a recommendation system. We might consider collaborative filtering techniques, content-based filtering, or even hybrid deep learning models. Each of these has different strengths and weaknesses, and determining which performs best requires more than just intuition; it requires empirical evidence. Automating this process means setting up a framework that can evaluate multiple candidate models on our specific dataset and objective metrics. This could involve training several distinct model types (e.g., a Logistic Regression, a Support Vector Machine, a Random Forest, and a basic Neural Network) for a classification task, each with a reasonable set of initial hyperparameter configurations. The results of these evaluations are then compared, allowing the pipeline to automatically identify the model type that demonstrates superior performance on the validation set. This initial model selection phase might not involve exhaustive hyperparameter tuning for each candidate, but rather a rapid assessment to prune less promising architectures before dedicating more resources to optimizing the top contenders. This form of automated model selection acts as a crucial early filter, preventing us from investing extensive tuning efforts into models that are fundamentally ill-suited for the task at hand.

Once a candidate model architecture (or a small set of promising ones) has been identified, the next crucial step is hyperparameter tuning. Hyperparameters are those parameters that are not learned from the data during training, but rather set beforehand. Examples include the learning rate in neural networks, the number of trees in a Random Forest, the regularization strength in linear models, or the kernel type in Support Vector Machines. These values have a profound influence on how a model learns and, consequently, on its performance. Finding the optimal combination of hyperparameters is often described as navigating a complex, multi-dimensional landscape where small changes can lead to significant shifts in performance. Manual tuning is typically an art form, relying on experience, intuition, and a lot of trial and error. However, in an automated pipeline, this needs to be a systematic exploration.

The most straightforward, albeit often computationally expensive, method for hyperparameter tuning is
**Grid Search**. In grid search, we define a discrete set of values for each hyperparameter we want to tune. The algorithm then exhaustively tries every possible combination of these values. For instance, if we are tuning the learning rate and the regularization strength for a model, we might define a grid: learning*rate = [0.1, 0.01, 0.001] and regularization*strength = [0.01, 0.1, 1.0]. Grid search would then train and evaluate the model for all

3x3 = 9 combinations. The advantage of grid search is its simplicity and guaranteed exploration of all specified points in the hyperparameter space. However, its major drawback is its scalability. The number of experiments grows exponentially with the number of hyperparameters and the number of values for each. If we have 5 hyperparameters, each with 5 possible values, that's 5^5 = 3125 combinations to test. This can quickly become computationally prohibitive, especially for complex models that take hours or days to train. Therefore, grid search is most effective when the number of hyperparameters to tune is small and the search space for each is limited. When integrating grid search into an automated pipeline, the workflow orchestrator would be instructed to launch a series of training jobs, each with a unique combination of hyperparameters from the defined grid, and then collect and compare the results.

A more efficient alternative to grid search, especially when the search space is large or when we have limited computational resources, is **Random Search**. Instead of exhaustively checking every combination, random search samples hyperparameter combinations from predefined distributions or ranges. For example, instead of specifying exact values for the learning rate, we might define a range, say, from 10^-4 to 10^-1, and randomly sample values from this range. Similarly, for a regularization parameter, we might sample from a log-uniform distribution. The key insight behind random search is that often, only a few hyperparameters truly influence the model's performance significantly, and the optimal values for these critical hyperparameters might not lie on the discrete grid points defined in grid search. Random search has been shown to be more efficient than grid search in finding good hyperparameter settings, especially in high-dimensional spaces, because it doesn't waste computation on unpromising regions of the hyperparameter space. It allows us to explore a wider variety of hyperparameter settings with the same computational budget. In a pipeline, random search would involve defining the distributions or ranges for hyperparameters and then launching a specified number of training jobs, each using randomly sampled hyperparameter values. The pipeline would then aggregate the results to identify the best-performing combination.

Moving beyond random sampling,
**Bayesian Optimization** offers a more intelligent and often even more efficient approach to hyperparameter tuning. Bayesian optimization builds a probabilistic model (a "surrogate model") of the objective function (e.g., validation accuracy) as a function of the hyperparameters. This surrogate model is updated iteratively as new hyperparameter configurations are evaluated. The algorithm then uses an "acquisition function" to decide which hyperparameter configuration to try next. The acquisition function balances exploration (trying hyperparameter values in uncertain regions) and exploitation (trying values that are predicted to yield the best performance). This makes Bayesian optimization particularly effective when evaluating each hyperparameter combination is expensive, as it aims to find the optimal settings with a minimal number of evaluations. For instance, if training a large deep learning model takes several hours, Bayesian optimization can significantly reduce the number of trials needed compared to grid or random search. Popular choices for surrogate models include Gaussian Processes, and common acquisition functions include Expected Improvement (EI) and Probability of Improvement (PI). Integrating Bayesian optimization into a pipeline involves a more complex orchestration: the workflow tool would manage the iterative process, calling the Bayesian optimization algorithm to propose the next set of hyperparameters, launching the training job, feeding the result back to the optimizer, and repeating until a stopping criterion (e.g., a maximum number of iterations or a satisfactory performance level) is met.

When implementing these tuning strategies within an automated pipeline, several practical considerations come into play. First, the **search space definition** is critical. This involves understanding which hyperparameters are most impactful and defining reasonable ranges or distributions for them. Domain knowledge and prior experience are invaluable here. Tools that support hyperparameter tuning often provide ways to specify these ranges, whether as discrete lists, continuous intervals, or more complex distributions. Second, **resource management** is key. Hyperparameter tuning, especially grid search and extensive random search, can be very parallelizable. Workflow orchestrators can be configured to launch multiple training jobs concurrently on available compute resources. For Bayesian optimization, while less parallelizable by nature (as each step depends on the previous), it can still be run in parallel by exploring multiple configurations proposed by the acquisition function simultaneously. The orchestration tool must be able to manage these parallel jobs, track their progress, and collect their results efficiently.

Third,
**stopping criteria** need to be defined. We cannot tune hyperparameters indefinitely. This might involve setting a maximum number of trials, a time limit for the tuning process, or a target performance metric that, if achieved, allows the tuning to stop early. For example, if we are using random search and after 100 trials, the performance hasn't improved significantly, we might decide to stop.

Fourth,
**reproducibility and logging** are paramount. Every experiment, with its specific hyperparameter combination, dataset version, and random seed, must be logged. The chosen hyperparameter configuration that yields the best performance should be clearly identified, and the corresponding trained model artifact must be saved and versioned. This ensures that we can reproduce the best result and understand exactly how it was achieved. The experiment tracking system mentioned in the previous context plays a crucial role here, capturing all these details automatically.

Let's consider an example of integrating random search into an automated pipeline for training a churn prediction model. Suppose we are

using a Gradient Boosting Machine (GBM). Key hyperparameters might include `n
*estimators` (number of trees), `learning*rate`, `max_depth`, and `subsample`. We could define our search space as follows:
- `n_estimators`: Uniform distribution between 100 and 1000.
- `learning_rate`: Log-uniform distribution between 0.001 and 0.1.
- `max_depth`: Integer distribution between 3 and 10.
- `subsample`: Uniform distribution between 0.6 and 1.0.

Our pipeline, orchestrated by a tool like Kubeflow Pipelines, would have a dedicated component for hyperparameter tuning. This component would take the defined search space and a `num_trials` parameter (e.g., 50). It would then launch 50 parallel or sequential training jobs, each sampling these hyperparameters. The training component itself would be configured to accept hyperparameter values as inputs and log the resulting validation AUC (Area Under the ROC Curve) to our experiment tracking system. After all 50 trials are complete, a post-processing step in the pipeline would query the experiment tracking system to find the hyperparameter combination that yielded the highest AUC. This "best" set of hyperparameters would then be passed to a subsequent "final training" component, which would retrain the GBM model using these optimal parameters on the entire training dataset (or a larger portion of it, depending on the strategy). The resulting model artifact would then be registered in the model registry.

For Bayesian optimization, the pipeline structure would be slightly different. Instead of launching a fixed number of trials, the tuning component would iteratively call the Bayesian optimizer. The optimizer, using a surrogate model and an acquisition function, would propose the next set of hyperparameters to try. The pipeline would then execute a training job with these proposed parameters, record the AUC, and feed it back to the optimizer. This loop would continue until, for example, 20 iterations are completed, or the improvement in AUC between iterations falls below a certain threshold. This iterative nature of Bayesian optimization is well-suited for scenarios where hyperparameter evaluations are costly and the goal is to find the optimum efficiently.

The integration of these tuning strategies into MLOps pipelines offers several significant advantages. Firstly, it **automates tedious manual work**, freeing up data scientists and engineers to focus on more strategic tasks. Secondly, it ensures **reproducibility**. By systematically logging all configurations and results, we can recreate any experiment and understand the decisions made. Thirdly, it leads to **better model performance**. By systematically exploring the hyperparameter space, we are more likely to find configurations that significantly outperform manually tuned models. Finally, it promotes **scalability and consistency**. Automated tuning can be applied consistently across numerous models and projects, leveraging distributed computing resources to handle large-scale tuning efforts without manual intervention.

It's important to note that the choice between grid search, random search, and Bayesian optimization often depends on the specific problem, the computational budget, and the number of hyperparameters. For a few hyperparameters and limited computational resources, random search might be sufficient. For more complex models where evaluations are very expensive, Bayesian optimization is often the preferred choice. Grid search, while conceptually simple, is typically reserved for very small search spaces or as a baseline. Advanced libraries and MLOps platforms often provide built-in support for these tuning strategies, allowing for their seamless integration into automated workflows. This automation is not just about executing training jobs; it's about intelligently navigating the vast space of possibilities to find the best performing models efficiently and reproducibly. This intelligent exploration of model choices and hyperparameter configurations is a cornerstone of building robust and high-performing machine learning systems in production.

The efficacy of any machine learning model hinges not solely on its training but, more crucially, on how rigorously it is evaluated and validated. Building robust automated frameworks for these critical post-training, pre-deployment stages is as vital as automating the training itself. This ensures that models not only perform well on unseen data but also meet the specific, often nuanced, requirements of the problem domain. A well-architected evaluation framework acts as a gatekeeper, preventing underperforming or unsuitable models from entering production and thereby mitigating risks associated with deployment failures, inaccurate predictions, and wasted resources.

At the core of any evaluation framework lies the selection of appropriate **performance metrics**. The choice of metric is deeply intertwined with the business objective and the nature of the problem. For instance, in a binary classification task, simply relying on accuracy can be misleading, especially in imbalanced datasets. Consider a fraud detection system where fraudulent transactions are rare. A model that predicts "no fraud" for every transaction might achieve 99% accuracy if only 1% of transactions are fraudulent. While the accuracy is high, the model completely fails at its intended purpose: detecting fraud. In such scenarios, metrics like **precision** (the proportion of correctly identified positive instances out of all instances predicted as positive) and **recall** (the proportion of correctly identified positive instances out of all actual positive instances) become paramount. Precision tells us how trustworthy our positive predictions are, while recall tells us how many of the actual positive cases we managed to catch. The **F1-score**, which is the harmonic mean of precision and recall, provides a balanced measure when both are important.

For regression problems, metrics like
**Mean Squared Error (MSE)** and **Root Mean Squared Error (RMSE)** are commonly used. MSE penalizes larger errors more significantly due to the squaring operation. RMSE, being the square root of MSE, is more

interpretable as it is in the same units as the target variable. However, these absolute error metrics can be sensitive to the scale of the target variable. For comparing models across datasets with different scales, or for understanding the error relative to the actual values, **Mean Absolute Percentage Error (MAPE)** or **Symmetric Mean Absolute Percentage Error (SMAPE)** might be more appropriate, though they can have issues with zero or near-zero actual values.

Beyond these common metrics, the specific domain may demand specialized ones. In natural language processing, for tasks like machine translation, BLEU (Bilingual Evaluation Understudy) scores are used. For image segmentation, the Intersection over Union (IoU) is a popular metric. For ranking or recommendation systems, metrics like Normalized Discounted Cumulative Gain (NDCG) are crucial. The automated evaluation framework must be flexible enough to accommodate these diverse metrics, allowing data scientists to configure the most relevant ones for their specific use case. When integrating this into a pipeline, the evaluation component would be responsible for calculating these metrics on a held-out validation dataset and reporting them. Crucially, these metrics need to be logged and stored in a way that allows for easy comparison and tracking over time, typically within the experiment tracking system.

A fundamental technique to ensure that a model's performance is not an artifact of a particular train-test split is
**cross-validation**. Instead of a single split of the data, cross-validation involves partitioning the dataset into multiple subsets, or "folds." The model is then trained and evaluated multiple times. In each iteration, one fold is used as the validation set, and the remaining folds are used for training. This process is repeated until each fold has served as the validation set exactly once. The final performance estimate is then the average of the performance across all folds.

The most common form of cross-validation is **k-fold cross-validation**, where the data is divided into 'k' equal-sized folds. For example, in 5-fold cross-validation, the data is split into five folds. The model is trained five times: first on folds 1-4 and validated on fold 5; then on folds 1-3 and 5, validated on fold 2; and so on. Averaging the performance across these five runs provides a more robust estimate of the model's generalization ability than a single train-validation split.

Another variant, particularly useful when dealing with small datasets, is **leave-one-out cross-validation (LOOCV)**. In LOOCV, 'k' is equal to the number of data points in the dataset. In each iteration, one data point is held out as the validation set, and the model is trained on all other data points. While this provides a nearly unbiased estimate of performance, it can be computationally very expensive, especially for large datasets, as it requires training the model as many times as there are data points.

For time-series data, standard k-fold cross-validation is inappropriate because it violates the temporal order of the data, leading to data leakage. Instead, techniques like **time-series cross-validation** or **walk-forward validation** are employed. In walk-forward validation, the data is split chronologically. The model is trained on an initial segment of data and validated on the subsequent period. Then, the training data is expanded to include the previous validation period, and the model is retrained and validated on the next subsequent period. This iterative process respects the temporal dependencies and ensures that predictions are always made on data that comes after the training data.

Automating cross-validation within an MLOps pipeline involves orchestrating these repeated training and evaluation cycles. The pipeline component responsible for evaluation would first split the training data into 'k' folds (or set up the walk-forward splits for time-series). It would then launch 'k' separate training and evaluation jobs, each using a different fold as the validation set. The results from these 'k' jobs would be collected, averaged to compute the final cross-validated performance metric, and then logged. This ensures that the performance estimate is not just a single number but a robust statistic reflecting the model's consistency across different data subsets. This also provides an indication of the variance in performance, which is crucial for understanding model reliability. High variance across folds might suggest that the model is sensitive to specific data points or configurations, warranting further investigation.

Beyond simply measuring performance, a critical aspect of a robust evaluation framework is establishing
**clear criteria for model acceptance or rejection**. This involves defining thresholds for the chosen performance metrics. Before a model can be considered for deployment, it must meet these predefined benchmarks. For example, a churn prediction model might be required to achieve an AUC of at least 0.85 on the validation set, a precision of at least 0.70 for the positive class (churners), and a recall of at least 0.60. If the model fails to meet any of these criteria, it is automatically rejected by the pipeline.

These thresholds should not be arbitrary. They are derived from a deep understanding of the business requirements, the cost of false positives and false negatives, and the acceptable level of risk. For instance, in a medical diagnosis system, the cost of a false negative (failing to detect a disease) is typically much higher than the cost of a false positive (flagging a healthy patient as sick, requiring further tests). Therefore, recall would likely be prioritized, and the acceptance threshold for recall would be set very high, possibly even at the expense of some precision.

Defining these criteria within the pipeline makes the decision-making process objective and automated. The evaluation component, after calculating the performance metrics, would compare them against these predefined thresholds. If all metrics exceed their respective thresholds, the model is marked as "accepted" and can proceed to the next stage, such as staging or A/B testing. If any metric falls below its threshold, the model is marked as "rejected," and the pipeline can halt, triggering an alert to the data science team. This automated gatekeeping mechanism is vital for maintaining the quality and reliability of models in production.

Furthermore, the acceptance criteria might not be static. They could evolve as the business needs change or as more data becomes available. The MLOps platform should provide mechanisms to update these criteria easily, ensuring that the evaluation framework remains aligned with current objectives. This dynamic nature of acceptance criteria is also a key differentiator of a mature MLOps system.

To further enhance the robustness of the evaluation, several advanced validation strategies can be integrated. One such strategy is **out-of-distribution (OOD) detection and validation**. Real-world data is rarely static; its statistical properties can drift over time. A model trained on data from one distribution might perform poorly when presented with data from a slightly or significantly different distribution. An OOD validation component can be introduced to test the model's behavior on data that is intentionally sampled from distributions different from the training data. This could involve using historical data from different time periods, data from different geographical regions, or synthetically generated data with modified characteristics. By evaluating the model on such data, we can identify potential vulnerabilities and understand its robustness to domain shifts.

Another important validation aspect is **bias and fairness testing**. Machine learning models can inadvertently learn and perpetuate societal biases present in the training data. An automated framework should include steps to assess whether the model exhibits unfair bias towards certain demographic groups (e.g., based on race, gender, age). This involves defining fairness metrics (such as demographic parity, equalized odds, or equal opportunity) and evaluating the model's performance across different sensitive attribute groups. If biases are detected, the model might be rejected or flagged for further bias mitigation techniques. Integrating these fairness checks directly into the validation pipeline ensures that ethical considerations are addressed proactively.

Finally,
**stress testing** can be employed to push the model to its limits. This involves feeding the model with challenging or adversarial inputs to see how it behaves under extreme conditions. For example, in image recognition, adversarial examples are subtly perturbed images that are misclassified by the model with high confidence. While creating such examples might be complex, a simpler form of stress testing could involve feeding the model with noisy data, incomplete data, or data with extreme values. The goal is to understand the model's failure modes and its performance ceiling.

Integrating these advanced validation techniques into the automated pipeline requires careful orchestration. Each validation step can be implemented as a distinct pipeline component. For OOD testing, the component would load specific OOD datasets and run predictions, comparing the results against expected behavior or performance bounds. For bias testing, it would segment the validation data by sensitive attributes, calculate performance metrics for each segment, and compare them using predefined fairness metrics. Stress testing components would generate or load specific stress-inducing data inputs and evaluate the model's output. The overall pipeline would then aggregate the results from all these validation stages. A model would only be deemed fully "validated" and ready for deployment if it passes all these rigorous checks. This comprehensive validation process, deeply embedded within the automated pipeline, is the cornerstone of building trustworthy and resilient machine learning systems. It transforms model evaluation from a reactive, ad-hoc process into a proactive, systematic, and integral part of the machine learning lifecycle.

The journey from raw data to a production-ready machine learning model is not a linear sprint, but rather an iterative expedition. Throughout this expedition, maintaining a clear and consistent record of every artifact — from the code that builds the model to the data it learns from and the resulting model itself — is not just good practice; it's a fundamental requirement for reproducibility, collaboration, and ultimately, trust in the ML system. This principle of comprehensive version control extends beyond just the model code. In a fully automated MLOps pipeline, ensuring that the exact dataset used for training a specific model version, and the trained model artifact itself, are meticulously versioned is as crucial as versioning the Python scripts or Jupyter notebooks. Without this, the very concept of reproducing an experiment or debugging a faulty model becomes an insurmountable challenge, akin to trying to reconstruct a complex recipe without knowing the exact ingredients or quantities used.

Consider a scenario where a model, initially performing well in validation, begins to degrade in production. To diagnose this, the team needs to ascertain precisely which version of the data was used to train the current production model, and which version of the code was responsible for its training. If the data has subtly changed over time — perhaps due to an upstream data pipeline update that introduced a new feature, a change in data schema, or even a data corruption event — then retraining the model on the "current" data might yield different results, and without knowing the original training data, it's impossible to replicate the initial successful state or understand the impact of the data change. Similarly, if the training code has evolved, a slight modification in hyperparameters, regularization techniques, or even the choice of loss function could lead to different model behaviors. Version control for datasets and models acts as the crucial audit trail, allowing engineers to rewind time and reconstruct the exact conditions under which a particular model was trained and evaluated.

For managing the versioning of the code that orchestrates the entire ML pipeline, including data preprocessing, feature engineering, model training, and evaluation, the ubiquitous tool of choice is **Git**. Git is a distributed version control system that allows developers to track changes to their codebase, revert to previous versions, and collaborate effectively with others. Every commit in Git represents a snapshot of the codebase at a specific point in time, along with a message describing the changes made. This granular tracking is indispensable for MLOps. When a new experiment is initiated, or a pipeline is updated, the associated code is committed to a Git repository. This ensures that for any given model artifact, there is a traceable link back to the exact version of the code that generated it. This is particularly important for reproducibility. If a specific model version is found to be performing exceptionally well, we can use its corresponding Git commit hash to retrieve the exact code that produced it, allowing for immediate retraining or further analysis without guesswork.

However, Git, in its native form, is designed for text-based files like source code. It is not optimized for handling large binary files, such as datasets or trained model weights. Storing multi-gigabyte datasets directly in a Git repository would quickly lead to enormous repository sizes, slow clone times, and an unwieldy workflow. This is where specialized tools come into play, bridging the gap between Git's code versioning capabilities and the need to manage large data assets.

One of the most prominent tools for versioning datasets and models in conjunction with Git is **Data Version Control (DVC)**. DVC works as a Git extension, enabling version control for data and models without bloating the Git repository. It operates on the principle of metadata tracking. Instead of storing the actual data files in Git, DVC stores small pointer files (typically with a `.dvc` extension) that contain metadata about the data artifact, such as its hash and location. The actual data files are stored externally, in a remote storage solution like Amazon S3, Google Cloud Storage, Azure Blob Storage, or even a local network drive.

When you use DVC, you `dvc add` your dataset or model files. DVC then calculates a hash of the file and creates a `.dvc` file that points to this hash. This `.dvc` file is what gets committed to Git. When you want to retrieve the actual data, you first check out the corresponding Git commit and then run `dvc checkout`. DVC reads the `.dvc` file, resolves the hash, and fetches the actual data from the configured remote storage, placing it in the expected location. This approach keeps the Git repository lean and fast, while still providing a complete history of data and model versions, tied directly to the codebase.

Imagine a data science team working on a fraud detection model. They have a large dataset of transaction records.

1. **Initial Setup**: The project is initialized with Git.
2. **Data Ingestion**: A version of the transaction data (e.g., `transactions_v1.csv`) is downloaded.
3. **DVC Initialization**: DVC is initialized within the Git repository, and a remote storage (e.g., S3 bucket) is configured.
4. **Adding Data to Version Control**: The team runs `dvc add data/transactions*v1.csv`. This creates `data/transactions*v1.csv.dvc` and stores the actual `transactions_v1.csv` in the configured S3 bucket.
5. **Committing to Git**: The team commits `data/transactions*v1.csv.dvc` to Git: `git add data/transactions*v1.csv.dvc && git commit -m "Add initial transaction data v1"`.
6. **Training Script**: A Python script `train.py` is developed using Git for version control.

7. **Model Training**: The `train.py` script uses `transactions*v1.csv` to train a model, producing `model*v1.pkl`.
8. **Adding Model to Version Control**: The team runs `dvc add models/model*v1.pkl`. This creates `models/model*v1.pkl.dvc` and stores `model_v1.pkl` in the S3 bucket.
9. **Committing Model to Git**: `git add models/model_v1.pkl.dvc && git commit -m "Add trained model v1"`.

Now, if the team later obtains an updated dataset (`transactions *v2.csv`) and retrains the model to produce `model*v2.pkl`:
1. **Add New Data**: `dvc add data/transactions*v2.csv` (creates `data/transactions*v2.csv.dvc`).
2. **Commit New Data**: `git add data/transactions_v2.csv.dvc && git commit -m "Add transaction data v2"`.
3. **Add New Model**: `dvc add models/model*v2.pkl` (creates `models/model*v2.pkl.dvc`).
4. **Commit New Model**: `git add models/model_v2.pkl.dvc && git commit -m "Add trained model v2"`.

At this point, Git history tracks the `.dvc` files, which in turn reference the specific versions of the data and models stored remotely. To reproduce the training of `model_v1.pkl`:

1. **Checkout Git**: `git checkout hashfor*v1*data*and*model>`. This will bring the correct `.dvc` files into the repository.
2. **Checkout Data and Model**: `dvc checkout`. This command reads the `.dvc` files and downloads the exact `transactions*v1.csv` and `model*v1.pkl` from S3.
3. **Checkout Code**: The Git commit hash also ensures that the version of `train.py` used at that time is checked out.

With all these components (code, data, model) precisely recreated, the training process for `model_v1` can be perfectly reproduced. This meticulous versioning is the bedrock of reproducible research and reliable MLOps.

Beyond DVC, another critical aspect of version control within MLOps pipelines is the management of
**experiment tracking and model registries**. While Git and DVC handle the versioning of code and data/model files, dedicated experiment tracking platforms provide a higher-level abstraction for managing model development iterations. Tools like **MLflow**, **Weights & Biases (W&B)**, **Comet ML**, or **Kubeflow Pipelines** offer functionalities to log metrics, parameters, artifacts, and crucially, to version trained models.

**MLflow**, for instance, is an open-source platform that provides a set of tools for managing the ML lifecycle, including experiment tracking, reproducibility, and model deployment. Within MLflow, an **experiment** is a collection of **runs**. Each **run** represents a single execution of a training script or an ML pipeline. During a run, MLflow can automatically log:
**Parameters**: The hyperparameters used for training (e.g., learning rate, batch size, number of epochs).
**Metrics**: Performance indicators calculated during or after training (e.g., accuracy, loss, precision, recall).
**Artifacts**: Any files generated by the run, such as trained model files (`.pkl`, `.h5`, TensorFlow SavedModel directories), data files, plots, or configuration files.

When a model is trained, MLflow can log the model artifact itself. This logged artifact is versioned within MLflow's artifact store. More importantly, MLflow provides a
**Model Registry**. The Model Registry is a centralized hub for managing the lifecycle of MLflow models. Models can be registered, transitioning through different stages like "Staging," "Production," and "Archived." Each

registered model is versioned, allowing you to easily track different iterations of a model and assign them to specific stages.

For example, after training `model
*v1.pkl` using the process described with DVC, the training script can be augmented to also log this model to MLflow. The script would initiate an MLflow run, log the parameters used, the metrics achieved on the validation set, and then log the `model*v1.pkl` file as an artifact. This artifact can then be registered as a new model in the MLflow Model Registry, potentially named "FraudDetectionModel." MLflow automatically assigns a version number to this registered model (e.g., Version 1). If `model_v2.pkl` is trained subsequently, it can be logged as Version 2 of the "FraudDetectionModel."

The integration of DVC and MLflow offers a powerful combination:

**DVC**: Versions the actual large data and model files, ensuring that the binary artifacts are traceable and retrievable. Git tracks the `.dvc` pointer files and the corresponding code.
**MLflow**: Tracks the experimental context — the parameters, metrics, and the specific run associated with a model version. It also provides a structured way to manage model lifecycles and promotes them through stages.

When a pipeline successfully trains a new model that meets the acceptance criteria defined in the evaluation stage, it can automatically:

1. Log the model artifact and associated metadata (parameters, metrics) to MLflow.
2. Register this model as a new version in the MLflow Model Registry.
3. Transition this newly registered model version to "Staging" for further testing in a pre-production environment.

This structured approach ensures that not only is the model artifact itself versioned, but its entire lineage — the code used, the data it was trained on, the hyperparameters, and the performance metrics — is meticulously recorded and made retrievable. This creates an auditable and reproducible record for every model artifact that passes through the MLOps pipeline.

The benefits of this comprehensive versioning strategy are manifold:

**Reproducibility**: As discussed, the ability to perfectly recreate any past experiment or trained model is paramount for debugging, auditing, and scientific integrity.
**Collaboration**: When multiple team members are working on a project, a shared and well-maintained version control system for code, data, and models ensures everyone is working with the same baseline and can easily understand each other's contributions.
**Debugging and Rollback**: If a deployed model starts exhibiting issues, version control allows for quick identification of the problematic model version and its associated training artifacts. This enables rapid rollback to a previously stable version or provides the necessary information to diagnose and fix the issue.
**Auditing and Compliance**: In regulated industries, maintaining an auditable trail of model development is often a strict requirement. Version control provides this necessary transparency and accountability.
**Efficiency**: By automating the tracking and versioning of artifacts, data scientists and engineers spend less time manually managing files and more time on developing and improving models.

Implementing effective version control for models and datasets requires a commitment to discipline and the adoption of appropriate tools. It's not a one-time setup but an ongoing practice that should be integrated into the daily workflow of the ML team. The pipeline itself becomes the enforcement mechanism, ensuring that every trained model artifact is automatically associated with its correct data version, code version, and experimental context. This holistic approach to versioning is a cornerstone of mature MLOps practices, enabling teams to build, deploy, and maintain machine learning systems with confidence and reliability. The ability to trace back the origin of any model, understand its training environment, and reproduce its results is what separates ad-hoc ML development from robust, production-grade MLOps.

The journey from raw data to a production-ready machine learning model is not a linear sprint, but rather an iterative expedition. Throughout this expedition, maintaining a clear and consistent record of every artifact — from the code that builds the model to the data it learns from and the resulting model itself — is not just good practice; it's a fundamental requirement for reproducibility, collaboration, and ultimately, trust in the ML system. This principle of comprehensive version control extends beyond just the model code. In a fully automated MLOps pipeline, ensuring that the exact dataset used for training a specific model version, and the trained model artifact itself, are meticulously versioned is as crucial as versioning the Python scripts or Jupyter notebooks. Without this, the very concept of reproducing an experiment or debugging a faulty model becomes an insurmountable challenge, akin to trying to reconstruct a complex recipe without knowing the exact ingredients or quantities used.

Consider a scenario where a model, initially performing well in validation, begins to degrade in production. To diagnose this, the team needs to ascertain precisely which version of the data was used to train the current production model, and which version of the code was responsible for its training. If the data has subtly changed over time — perhaps due to an upstream data pipeline update that introduced a new feature, a change in data schema, or even a data corruption event — then retraining the model on the "current" data might yield different results, and without knowing the original training data, it's impossible to replicate the initial successful state or understand the impact of the data change. Similarly, if the training code has evolved, a slight modification in hyperparameters, regularization techniques, or even the choice of loss function could lead to different model behaviors. Version control for datasets and models acts as the crucial audit trail, allowing engineers to rewind time and reconstruct the exact conditions under which a particular model was trained and evaluated.

For managing the versioning of the code that orchestrates the entire ML pipeline, including data preprocessing, feature engineering, model training, and evaluation, the ubiquitous tool of choice is **Git**. Git is a distributed version control system that allows developers to track changes to their codebase, revert to previous versions, and collaborate effectively with others. Every commit in Git represents a snapshot of the codebase at a specific point in time, along with a message describing the changes made. This granular tracking is indispensable for MLOps. When a new experiment is initiated, or a pipeline is updated, the associated code is committed to a Git repository. This ensures that for any given model artifact, there is a traceable link back to the exact version of the code that generated it. This is particularly important for reproducibility. If a specific model version is found to be performing exceptionally well, we can use its corresponding Git commit hash to retrieve the exact code that produced it, allowing for immediate retraining or further analysis without guesswork.

However, Git, in its native form, is designed for text-based files like source code. It is not optimized for handling large binary files, such as datasets or trained model weights. Storing multi-gigabyte datasets directly in a Git repository would quickly lead to enormous repository sizes, slow clone times, and an unwieldy workflow. This is where specialized tools come into play, bridging the gap between Git's code versioning capabilities and the need to manage large data assets.

One of the most prominent tools for versioning datasets and models in conjunction with Git is
**Data Version Control (DVC)**. DVC works as a Git extension, enabling version control for data and models without bloating the Git repository. It operates on the principle of metadata tracking. Instead of storing the actual data files in Git, DVC stores small pointer files (typically with a `.dvc` extension) that contain metadata about the data artifact, such as its hash and location. The actual data files are stored externally, in a remote storage solution like Amazon S3, Google Cloud Storage, Azure Blob Storage, or even a local network drive.

When you use DVC, you `dvc add` your dataset or model files. DVC then calculates a hash of the file and creates a `.dvc` file that points to this hash. This `.dvc` file is what gets committed to Git. When you want to retrieve the actual data, you first check out the corresponding Git commit and then run `dvc checkout`. DVC reads the `.dvc` file, resolves the hash, and fetches the actual data from the configured remote storage, placing it in the expected location. This approach keeps the Git repository lean and fast, while still providing a complete history of data and model versions, tied directly to the codebase.

Imagine a data science team working on a fraud detection model. They have a large dataset of transaction records.

1. **Initial Setup**: The project is initialized with Git.
2. **Data Ingestion**: A version of the transaction data (e.g., `transactions_v1.csv`) is downloaded.
3. **DVC Initialization**: DVC is initialized within the Git repository, and a remote storage (e.g., S3 bucket) is configured.
4. **Adding Data to Version Control**: The team runs `dvc add data/transactions*v1.csv`. This creates `data/transactions*v1.csv.dvc` and stores the actual `transactions_v1.csv` in the configured S3 bucket.

5. **Committing to Git**: The team commits `data/transactionsv*1.csv.dvc` to Git: `git add data/transactions*v1.csv.dvc && git commit -m "Add initial transaction data v1"`.
6. **Training Script**: A Python script `train.py` is developed using Git for version control.
7. **Model Training**: The `train.py` script uses `transactionsv*1.csv` to train a model, producing `model*v1.pkl`.
8. **Adding Model to Version Control**: The team runs `dvc add models/modelv*1.pkl`. This creates `models/model*v1.pkl.dvc` and stores `model_v1.pkl` in the S3 bucket.
9. **Committing Model to Git**: `git add models/model_v1.pkl.dvc && git commit -m "Add trained model v1"`.

Now, if the team later obtains an updated dataset (`transactions *v2.csv`) and retrains the model to produce `model*v2.pkl`:
1. **Add New Data**: `dvc add data/transactionsv*2.csv` (creates `data/transactions*v2.csv.dvc`).
2. **Commit New Data**: `git add data/transactions_v2.csv.dvc && git commit -m "Add transaction data v2"`.
3. **Add New Model**: `dvc add models/modelv*2.pkl` (creates `models/model*v2.pkl.dvc`).
4. **Commit New Model**: `git add models/model_v2.pkl.dvc && git commit -m "Add trained model v2"`.

At this point, Git history tracks the `.dvc` files, which in turn reference the specific versions of the data and models stored remotely. To reproduce the training of `model_v1.pkl`:

1. **Checkout Git**: `git checkout hashforv*1*data*and*model>`. This will bring the correct `.dvc` files into the repository.
2. **Checkout Data and Model**: `dvc checkout`. This command reads the `.dvc` files and downloads the exact `transactionsv*1.csv` and `model*v1.pkl` from S3.

3. **Checkout Code**: The Git commit hash also ensures that the version of `train.py` used at that time is checked out.

With all these components (code, data, model) precisely recreated, the training process for `model_v1` can be perfectly reproduced. This meticulous versioning is the bedrock of reproducible research and reliable MLOps.

Beyond DVC, another critical aspect of version control within MLOps pipelines is the management of
**experiment tracking and model registries**. While Git and DVC handle the versioning of code and data/model files, dedicated experiment tracking platforms provide a higher-level abstraction for managing model development iterations. Tools like **MLflow**, **Weights & Biases (W&B)**, **Comet ML**, or **Kubeflow Pipelines** offer functionalities to log metrics, parameters, artifacts, and crucially, to version trained models.

**MLflow**, for instance, is an open-source platform that provides a set of tools for managing the ML lifecycle, including experiment tracking, reproducibility, and model deployment. Within MLflow, an **experiment** is a collection of **runs**. Each **run** represents a single execution of a training script or an ML pipeline. During a run, MLflow can automatically log:
**Parameters**: The hyperparameters used for training (e.g., learning rate, batch size, number of epochs).
**Metrics**: Performance indicators calculated during or after training (e.g., accuracy, loss, precision, recall).
**Artifacts**: Any files generated by the run, such as trained model files (`.pkl`, `.h5`, TensorFlow SavedModel directories), data files, plots, or configuration files.

When a model is trained, MLflow can log the model artifact itself. This

logged artifact is versioned within MLflow's artifact store. More importantly, MLflow provides a
**Model Registry**. The Model Registry is a centralized hub for managing the lifecycle of MLflow models. Models can be registered, transitioning through different stages like "Staging," "Production," and "Archived." Each registered model is versioned, allowing you to easily track different iterations of a model and assign them to specific stages.

For example, after training `model
*v1.pkl` using the process described with DVC, the training script can be augmented to also log this model to MLflow. The script would initiate an MLflow run, log the parameters used, the metrics achieved on the validation set, and then log the `model*v1.pkl` file as an artifact. This artifact can then be registered as a new model in the MLflow Model Registry, potentially named "FraudDetectionModel." MLflow automatically assigns a version number to this registered model (e.g., Version 1). If `model_v2.pkl` is trained subsequently, it can be logged as Version 2 of the "FraudDetectionModel."

The integration of DVC and MLflow offers a powerful combination:

**DVC**: Versions the actual large data and model files, ensuring that the binary artifacts are traceable and retrievable. Git tracks the `.dvc` pointer files and the corresponding code.
**MLflow**: Tracks the experimental context — the parameters, metrics, and the specific run associated with a model version. It also provides a structured way to manage model lifecycles and promotes them through stages.

When a pipeline successfully trains a new model that meets the acceptance criteria defined in the evaluation stage, it can automatically:

1. Log the model artifact and associated metadata (parameters, metrics) to MLflow.

2. Register this model as a new version in the MLflow Model Registry.
3. Transition this newly registered model version to "Staging" for further testing in a pre-production environment.

This structured approach ensures that not only is the model artifact itself versioned, but its entire lineage — the code used, the data it was trained on, the hyperparameters, and the performance metrics — is meticulously recorded and made retrievable. This creates an auditable and reproducible record for every model artifact that passes through the MLOps pipeline.

The benefits of this comprehensive versioning strategy are manifold:

**Reproducibility**: As discussed, the ability to perfectly recreate any past experiment or trained model is paramount for debugging, auditing, and scientific integrity.
**Collaboration**: When multiple team members are working on a project, a shared and well-maintained version control system for code, data, and models ensures everyone is working with the same baseline and can easily understand each other's contributions.
**Debugging and Rollback**: If a deployed model starts exhibiting issues, version control allows for quick identification of the problematic model version and its associated training artifacts. This enables rapid rollback to a previously stable version or provides the necessary information to diagnose and fix the issue.
**Auditing and Compliance**: In regulated industries, maintaining an auditable trail of model development is often a strict requirement. Version control provides this necessary transparency and accountability.
**Efficiency**: By automating the tracking and versioning of artifacts, data scientists and engineers spend less time manually managing files and more time on developing and improving models.

Implementing effective version control for models and datasets requires a commitment to discipline and the adoption of appropriate tools. It's not a one-time setup but an ongoing practice that should be integrated into the daily workflow of the ML team. The pipeline itself becomes the enforcement mechanism, ensuring that every trained model artifact is automatically associated with its correct data version, code version, and experimental context. This holistic approach to versioning is a cornerstone of mature MLOps practices, enabling teams to build, deploy, and maintain machine learning systems with confidence and reliability. The ability to trace back the origin of any model, understand its training environment, and reproduce its results is what separates ad-hoc ML development from robust, production-grade MLOps.

Ensuring consistency and portability of training environments is a critical challenge in machine learning operations. The infamous "it works on my machine" problem arises from the myriad of dependencies, libraries, operating system configurations, and hardware differences that can exist between a developer's local setup and the environments where models are trained or deployed. This variability can lead to elusive bugs, inconsistent performance, and significant delays in the development and deployment lifecycle. To combat this, the practice of **containerization** has become an indispensable tool in the MLOps arsenal.

At its core, containerization provides a standardized way to package an application and its dependencies into a single, isolated unit called a container. This container encapsulates everything needed to run the application: the code, runtime, system tools, system libraries, and settings. By isolating the application and its environment, containers ensure that it behaves consistently regardless of the underlying infrastructure. The most widely adopted containerization technology is **Docker**.

Docker allows us to define the exact specifications of our training environment within a `Dockerfile`. This text file acts as a blueprint, detailing the base operating system image, the installation of necessary libraries (e.g., TensorFlow, PyTorch, Scikit-learn, Pandas), the copying of training scripts and helper modules, and the definition of the command to execute when the container starts. For instance, a simple `Dockerfile` for a PyTorch training job might look something like this:

```dockerfile

**Use an official PyTorch image as the base image**
FROM pytorch/pytorch:1.13.1-cuda11.6-cudnn8-runtime

**Set the working directory in the container**
WORKDIR /app

**Copy the requirements file into the container at /app**
COPY requirements.txt .

**Install any needed packages specified in requirements.txt**
RUN pip install --no-cache-dir -r requirements.txt
```

**Copy the rest of the application code into the container at /app**
COPY . .

**Define the command to run the training script when the container launches**
CMD ["python", "train.py"]
```

In this example:

`FROM pytorch/pytorch:1.13.1-cuda11.6-cudnn8-runtime` specifies a pre-built Docker image that already contains a specific version of PyTorch, along with CUDA and cuDNN libraries for GPU acceleration. This saves the immense effort of manually installing these complex dependencies and ensures consistency in the GPU driver and library versions.
`WORKDIR /app` sets the default directory for subsequent commands.
`COPY requirements.txt .` and `RUN pip install --no-cache-dir -r requirements.txt` install all Python package dependencies listed in `requirements.txt`. This is crucial for ensuring that the exact versions of libraries used during development are available during training.
`COPY . .` copies all files from the current directory (where the `Dockerfile` is located) into the container's `/app` directory. This includes the training scripts, utility functions, and any configuration files.
`CMD ["python", "train.py"]` defines the default command to be executed when a container based on this image is run. In this case, it's to execute the `train.py` script.

Once this `Dockerfile` is created, it can be used to build a Docker image:

```bash

docker build -t my-ml-training-image .
```

This command instructs Docker to build an image named `my-ml-training-image` using the `Dockerfile` in the current directory. The resulting image is a self-contained, immutable artifact that includes the Python environment, all necessary libraries, and the training code.

The benefits of using Docker for training environments are profound:

1.
**Reproducibility**: By defining the entire environment in a `Dockerfile`, we eliminate ambiguity. Any individual or any machine can pull this image and run the training job, guaranteeing identical software dependencies and configurations. This directly addresses the "it works on my machine" syndrome. If the training pipeline is orchestrated by a CI/CD system or a cloud ML platform, it will use this identical image, ensuring that the training run is precisely as intended.

2.
**Portability**: Docker containers are designed to run consistently across various environments. Whether it's a local laptop, a powerful on-premises server, a virtual machine in the cloud (AWS EC2, Google Compute Engine, Azure VM), or a managed Kubernetes cluster, the containerized training job will behave the same way. This portability simplifies the transition from development to staging to production, and allows for flexible resource allocation. Need more compute power? Spin up more instances of the same container on a distributed computing cluster.

3.
```

**Isolation**: Containers provide process-level isolation. This means that the dependencies and processes within a training container do not interfere with other containers or the host system. This prevents conflicts between different projects or library versions and enhances security by limiting the attack surface.

4.
**Dependency Management**: Managing complex software dependencies, especially those involving specific versions of libraries, compilers, and system packages, can be a significant headache. Dockerfile provides a declarative way to manage these dependencies. Once defined, the installation process is automated and consistent, reducing manual errors and setup time. For machine learning, this is particularly crucial due to the rapidly evolving nature of deep learning frameworks and their intricate dependencies on CUDA, cuDNN, and other hardware-specific libraries.

5.
**Scalability**: Containerization, when combined with orchestration platforms like Kubernetes, enables seamless scaling of training jobs. Multiple instances of the same training container can be launched in parallel to leverage distributed computing resources, accelerating the training process for large models or datasets. Orchestration platforms can manage the lifecycle of these containers, ensuring they are scheduled, monitored, and restarted if they fail.

6.
**Simplified CI/CD Integration**: Containerized training jobs fit naturally into Continuous Integration and Continuous Delivery (CI/CD) pipelines. The CI process can build the Docker image, run basic tests, and push it to a container registry. The CD process can then deploy this image to various training environments, triggering automated training runs. This automation reduces manual intervention and speeds up the iteration cycle.

When integrating containerization with version control systems like Git and DVC, a robust workflow emerges. The `Dockerfile` itself should be versioned alongside the training code in Git. This ensures that the exact definition of the training environment is tracked and associated with specific code commits. When a new training run is initiated, the pipeline first checks out the relevant Git commit (which includes the `Dockerfile` and training scripts) and then builds the Docker image from it. DVC is used to fetch the specific version of the dataset and any pre-trained model checkpoints that the training script requires.

For example, a typical MLOps pipeline might perform the following steps:

1. **Trigger**: A new dataset version is added (tracked by DVC), or a code change is committed to Git.
2. **Checkout Code**: The pipeline checks out the specific Git commit that contains the `Dockerfile`, training scripts, and `requirements.txt`.
3. **Build Docker Image**: A Docker image is built from the `Dockerfile`. This image will contain the precise versions of all software dependencies.
4. **Fetch Data/Model Artifacts**: DVC is used to download the specific version of the training data and any required model checkpoints as defined by the Git commit.
5. **Run Training Container**: The pipeline starts a Docker container using the built image. The container is instructed to use the fetched data and execute the training script. The training script, running within the isolated container, has access to all its defined dependencies and the correct data.
6. **Log Results**: The training script outputs logs, metrics, and potentially saves trained model artifacts. These outputs can be captured by the pipeline and logged to an experiment tracking system like MLflow. The model artifacts themselves might also be versioned using DVC and registered in a model registry.

This orchestrated approach ensures that every aspect of the training process is reproducible and consistent. The container acts as a portable, self-sufficient training capsule, guaranteeing that the software environment is identical every time, irrespective of where it's executed. This significantly reduces debugging time, builds confidence in the model development process, and accelerates the path to production. Furthermore, using container registries like Docker Hub, AWS ECR, Google GCR, or Azure ACR allows for centralized storage and management of these training images, making them easily accessible to different teams and environments. When deploying models, the same containerization principles can be applied, ensuring that the inference environment matches the training environment, thereby minimizing the risk of performance discrepancies between training and serving. This unified approach to environment management is a cornerstone of robust and scalable MLOps.

## Chapter 11: Model Deployment Strategies

The culmination of an extensive machine learning project is not the final model artifact itself, but its successful integration into a production system where it can deliver value. This transition from a trained model sitting in a development environment to a functioning component of a business process is known as model deployment. The strategy chosen for deployment dictates how predictions are generated, how requests are handled, and how the model interacts with the broader application ecosystem. Selecting the right deployment pattern is a critical engineering decision, influenced by factors such as the desired response time, the volume of requests, the available infrastructure, and the operational constraints of the application.

One of the most straightforward deployment patterns is **batch prediction**. In this approach, the model is used to process a large volume of data at once, typically on a scheduled basis. Instead of making individual predictions on demand, the system collects a batch of input data, feeds it to the model, and stores the generated predictions for later use. This pattern is particularly well-suited for scenarios where real-time inference is not a requirement, and where processing can be done offline.

Consider a retail company that wants to recommend products to its customers. It might not need to generate recommendations for every single user visit in real-time. Instead, it can run a batch prediction job overnight. This job would take the latest customer data (browsing history, purchase history, demographics) and generate a set of personalized product recommendations for each customer. These recommendations would then be stored in a database and served to customers the next day when they visit the website. This approach is computationally efficient because it allows for optimization of the processing workload. Instead of spinning up resources for each individual request, the system can allocate dedicated resources for a single, sustained batch job. This can also lead to cost savings, especially in cloud environments, by leveraging spot instances or reserved instances for predictable workloads. Furthermore, batch prediction simplifies the infrastructure requirements. It typically involves a processing environment (which could be a cluster of machines, a cloud-based data processing service like AWS Glue or Google Dataflow, or even a powerful single server) and a data store to hold both the input data and the output predictions. The model itself is loaded into memory within the processing environment for the duration of the batch job.

The workflow for batch prediction typically looks like this:

1. **Data Ingestion**: Raw data relevant for prediction is collected and stored, often in a data lake or warehouse.
2. **Data Preparation**: The collected data is preprocessed, transformed, and joined as needed to match the format expected by the model. This stage often mirrors the preprocessing steps used during model training to ensure consistency.
3. **Model Loading**: The trained model artifact (e.g., a saved Scikit-learn model, a TensorFlow SavedModel, or a PyTorch state dictionary) is loaded into the processing environment.
4. **Batch Inference**: The preprocessed data is fed to the loaded model in chunks or as a whole batch. The model generates predictions for each data point.
5. **Prediction Storage**: The generated predictions are stored in a structured format, such as a database table, a CSV file, or an object store, often linked back to the original input data or the entity it pertains to (e.g., a customer ID, a product ID).
6. **Downstream Consumption**: Other applications or services can then access these pre-computed predictions for various purposes, such as displaying recommendations, flagging items for review, or generating reports.

A key advantage of batch prediction is its suitability for applications where the cost of real-time computation is prohibitive or unnecessary. For instance, in marketing analytics, generating personalized email campaigns based on predicted customer churn or lifetime value can be effectively done via batch processing. The predictions are made once, and then the resulting lists of customers are used to segment audiences for targeted email blasts. This pattern also lends itself well to scenarios where complex feature engineering is required, which might be too computationally intensive to perform on-the-fly for every prediction request. The batch job can execute these complex transformations on large datasets efficiently.

However, batch prediction has limitations. The primary one is the lack of immediacy. If a user performs an action on a website and requires an immediate response based on that action (e.g., updating a fraud score as a transaction is being processed), batch prediction is not a viable option. The predictions are only as fresh as the last batch run, meaning there's an inherent latency between data changes and their impact on predictions. Additionally, managing the scheduling and orchestration of batch jobs can require robust job scheduling tools (like Apache Airflow, Luigi, or cloud-native schedulers) to ensure reliability and timely execution. Monitoring these jobs for failures, performance degradation, and resource utilization is also a critical operational concern.

In contrast to batch processing,
**real-time inference** delivers predictions on demand, responding to individual requests as they arrive. This is essential for applications requiring immediate feedback and dynamic interactions. The most common pattern for real-time inference is serving predictions via a **REST API**. In this model, the trained machine learning model is deployed as a microservice, accessible through a web API. Client applications send prediction requests (typically containing the input features for a single instance or a small batch) to a specific API endpoint, and the service returns the model's prediction in response.

A typical REST API deployment involves several components:

1. **Model Service**: A web server (e.g., Flask, FastAPI, Django in Python, or other frameworks in different languages) hosts the trained ML model. This service is responsible for receiving incoming requests, preprocessing the input data, performing inference using the loaded model, and formatting the output prediction.
2. **API Gateway**: Often, an API Gateway sits in front of the model service. It acts as a single entry point for all client requests, handling tasks such as authentication, authorization, rate limiting, request routing, and load balancing. This decouples the client from the backend services and adds a layer of security and manageability.
3. **Client Application**: This is the application that needs predictions. It could be a web application, a mobile app, another backend service, or even a data analysis tool. The client constructs a request with the necessary input features and sends it to the API endpoint.
4. **Model Registry/Storage**: The trained model artifact is stored in a central location, such as an object storage service (S3, GCS, Azure Blob Storage) or a dedicated model registry (MLflow, SageMaker Model Registry, Vertex AI Model Registry). The model service retrieves the appropriate model version from this storage when it starts up or when a model update is deployed.

Let's illustrate with a fraud detection system. When a user attempts to make a credit card transaction, the payment processing application needs to know instantly whether that transaction is fraudulent. The application would send the transaction details (amount, merchant, location, user's past behavior features, etc.) as a JSON payload to a `/predict` endpoint of the fraud detection API. The API service would then load the fraud detection model, preprocess the input features, run the model, and return a probability score indicating the likelihood of fraud. If the score exceeds a predefined threshold, the transaction might be blocked or flagged for manual review.

The technologies commonly used for building these real-time APIs are web frameworks like Flask or FastAPI in Python, which are lightweight and efficient for building microservices. For production environments, these frameworks are often deployed using containerization (Docker) and orchestrated by platforms like Kubernetes, which handle scaling, load balancing, and high availability. Tools like TensorFlow Serving, TorchServe, or ONNX Runtime can also be employed to serve models directly, offering optimized inference performance and management capabilities for specific ML frameworks.

The advantages of real-time API deployment are clear:

**Low Latency**: Predictions are generated almost instantaneously, enabling interactive and dynamic user experiences.
**Up-to-date Predictions**: The model can react to new information as it arrives, providing predictions based on the most current data available.
**Scalability**: With container orchestration, API services can be scaled automatically to handle fluctuating request volumes. If traffic surges, more instances of the model service can be spun up; if traffic decreases, instances can be scaled down to save resources.
**Decoupling**: The ML model service is independent of the client application, allowing for separate development, deployment, and scaling cycles. Updates to the model can be made without redeploying the entire client application.

However, real-time inference comes with its own set of challenges:

**Infrastructure Costs**: Maintaining always-on services, especially those that need to scale rapidly, can be more expensive than batch processing, which can utilize resources more flexibly.

**Complexity**: Setting up and managing a robust API infrastructure, including API gateways, load balancers, container orchestrators, and monitoring systems, adds significant operational complexity.
**Cold Starts**: In serverless or auto-scaling environments, there can be a delay (a "cold start") when the first request arrives after a period of inactivity, as the model and environment need to be loaded.
**Resource Management**: Ensuring that the model service has sufficient resources (CPU, memory, GPU) to handle peak loads without introducing unacceptable latency requires careful capacity planning and monitoring.
**Model Drift and Monitoring**: Continuous monitoring of model performance in production is crucial. Real-time systems must have mechanisms to detect performance degradation due to data drift or concept drift, triggering alerts for retraining or model updates.

Beyond traditional server-based deployments,
**edge deployment** represents another significant paradigm. In this pattern, the machine learning model is deployed directly onto the device where the data is generated, rather than sending the data to a central server for inference. This includes a wide range of devices, from mobile phones and smartwatches to IoT sensors, autonomous vehicles, and industrial machinery.

Edge deployment is driven by several key benefits:

**Reduced Latency**: By performing inference locally on the device, the round trip to a central server is eliminated, leading to extremely low latency. This is critical for applications like real-time object detection in autonomous driving or immediate response systems in robotics.
**Bandwidth Efficiency**: Sending raw sensor data or video streams to the cloud can consume significant bandwidth. Edge inference processes the data locally and only transmits relevant results or metadata, saving bandwidth costs and enabling operation in areas with limited connectivity.

**Privacy and Security**: Sensitive data can be processed and analyzed directly on the device without ever leaving it, enhancing user privacy and data security. This is particularly important for applications dealing with personal health information or proprietary industrial data.
**Offline Operation**: Devices equipped with edge ML models can continue to function and provide intelligent features even when disconnected from the network. This is vital for remote locations, unreliable network conditions, or critical safety systems.
**Cost Savings**: While edge devices might require more processing power, the reduction in cloud compute and bandwidth costs can often offset this, especially for large-scale IoT deployments.

The process of edge deployment typically involves optimizing the trained model for the target hardware. Large, complex models trained on powerful hardware (like GPUs) are often too resource-intensive for edge devices. Therefore, techniques such as:

**Model Quantization**: Reducing the precision of model weights and activations (e.g., from 32-bit floating-point to 8-bit integers) to decrease model size and computational requirements.
**Model Pruning**: Removing less important weights or connections in the neural network to reduce its complexity and size.
**Knowledge Distillation**: Training a smaller, "student" model to mimic the behavior of a larger, more accurate "teacher" model.
**Hardware-Specific Optimization**: Using specialized libraries and tools (e.g., TensorFlow Lite, PyTorch Mobile, Core ML for Apple devices, OpenVINO for Intel hardware, NVIDIA TensorRT for NVIDIA hardware) that are designed to run ML models efficiently on specific edge processors (CPUs, GPUs, NPUs, TPUs).

Once optimized, the model is packaged and deployed to the edge device. This deployment can be managed remotely through an over-the-air (OTA) update mechanism, similar to how mobile apps are updated.

Examples of edge deployment are abundant:

**Smartphones**: Running on-device voice assistants, camera features (e.g., portrait mode, scene recognition), predictive text, and personalized content feeds.
**IoT Sensors**: Smart home devices analyzing sensor data locally for anomaly detection (e.g., detecting water leaks), predictive maintenance in industrial equipment, or intelligent surveillance cameras performing object detection.
**Autonomous Vehicles**: Processing sensor data (cameras, LiDAR, radar) in real-time for perception, path planning, and control decisions, where even milliseconds of latency can be critical.
**Wearable Devices**: Monitoring health metrics, detecting irregular heart rhythms, or providing fitness insights directly on a smartwatch.

The challenges associated with edge deployment include the limited computational resources and battery life of edge devices, the complexity of managing and updating models across a large fleet of distributed devices, and the need for specialized expertise in model optimization and embedded systems development. Security of models and data on potentially less secure edge devices is also a significant concern. Furthermore, debugging issues on remote, inaccessible devices can be considerably more difficult than debugging a server-based API. Ensuring consistency across diverse hardware architectures and operating systems present on edge devices also adds complexity.

A closely related deployment pattern is **embedded systems**. While edge deployment can encompass a broad range of devices, embedded systems often refer to systems where the ML model is an integral part of a larger, specialized piece of hardware designed for a specific function. Think of a medical device that analyzes ultrasound images in real-time, or a robotic arm on a manufacturing line that uses computer vision to inspect parts. In these cases, the ML model isn't just an application running on a general-purpose device; it's tightly integrated into the hardware's core functionality.

This often means working with highly constrained environments, where memory, processing power, and energy consumption are severely limited. Models must be extremely efficient, and the deployment process might involve custom hardware acceleration or deeply optimized inference engines. For instance, deploying a computer vision model to a smart camera might involve custom ASICs (Application-Specific Integrated Circuits) or FPGAs (Field-Programmable Gate Arrays) tailored for neural network inference. The development cycle for embedded ML can be longer and more complex, requiring close collaboration between ML engineers, hardware engineers, and embedded software developers. The validation and testing process is also more rigorous, as failures can have more severe consequences in critical applications like healthcare or industrial automation.

**Choosing the Right Pattern**:

The selection of a deployment pattern is a strategic decision that significantly impacts the success and feasibility of an ML project. It's rarely a one-size-fits-all situation, and often, complex systems might employ a combination of these patterns. For example, a system might use edge devices for initial data filtering and real-time anomaly detection, sending only the most critical events or aggregated data to a cloud-based API for more in-depth analysis or archival.

When making this choice, several key questions must be addressed:

1.
**Latency Requirements**: Does the application need an immediate response to user actions, or can predictions be generated asynchronously? If real-time is critical (e.g., autonomous driving, high-frequency trading), edge or low-latency APIs are necessary. If batch processing is acceptable (e.g., weekly sales forecasts, personalized email campaigns), batch prediction might be more efficient.

2.
**Data Volume and Velocity**: How much data needs to be processed, and how frequently does it arrive? High-volume, high-velocity data might necessitate distributed batch processing or highly scalable real-time APIs. Edge devices can help manage large volumes of raw data locally.

3.
**Connectivity**: Is reliable network connectivity available at the point of data generation and prediction? If not, edge deployment becomes essential.

4.
**Computational Resources**: What are the available computational resources on the client devices or in the target deployment environment? Resource-constrained environments will require optimized models suitable for edge or embedded deployment.

5.
**Cost Considerations**: What is the budget for infrastructure, development, and maintenance? Batch processing can be cost-effective for predictable workloads, while scalable APIs and edge deployments have different cost structures.

6.

**Privacy and Security**: Are there strict privacy or security requirements for the data being processed? Edge deployment can enhance privacy by keeping data local.

7.
**Model Complexity and Size**: How large and computationally intensive is the trained model? Large models might be prohibitive for edge devices and might require powerful server-side infrastructure.

8.
**Maintainability and Updates**: How will the model be updated and maintained over time? Server-based deployments (APIs) generally offer more straightforward mechanisms for remote updates than managing thousands of individual edge devices.

Understanding these trade-offs allows engineering teams to select the deployment pattern that best aligns with the specific requirements of their ML application, ensuring that the model can be effectively and efficiently utilized to achieve its intended business objectives. This careful consideration of deployment strategies is a hallmark of mature MLOps practices, transforming a trained model from a research artifact into a reliable, valuable production asset. The journey doesn't end with deployment; it's just the beginning of a continuous cycle of monitoring, evaluation, and iteration.

The necessity for immediate, on-demand predictions in a multitude of modern applications — from e-commerce personalization and fraud detection to autonomous systems and interactive content platforms — necessitates a robust and scalable approach to model deployment. This is where the concept of building scalable prediction services comes to the forefront. Unlike batch predictions, which operate on pre-defined schedules and large datasets, or simple API deployments that might struggle with significant traffic fluctuations, scalable prediction services are designed to dynamically adapt to varying loads, ensuring consistent performance and availability. The architectural backbone of such services often relies on principles of microservices and sophisticated container orchestration platforms.

At its core, a scalable prediction service is an application designed to expose a machine learning model's inference capabilities through an API, typically a RESTful interface. However, the "scalable" aspect differentiates it from a basic API. This scalability is achieved through a combination of well-architected components and the intelligent use of infrastructure. A common and highly effective pattern involves packaging the model inference logic within a containerized application. Docker is the de facto standard for this, allowing developers to bundle the model, its dependencies, and the inference server (e.g., Flask, FastAPI, TensorFlow Serving, TorchServe) into a self-contained, portable unit. This containerization ensures that the service runs consistently across different environments, from local development machines to large-scale cloud deployments.

The true power of scalability emerges when these containers are managed by an orchestration platform. Kubernetes has become the dominant force in this domain. It provides a framework for automating the deployment, scaling, and management of containerized applications. For a prediction service, Kubernetes allows us to define a "Deployment," which specifies the desired state for our application – for instance, "we want at least three instances of our fraud detection model container running at all times." Kubernetes then ensures this state is maintained. If a container crashes, Kubernetes automatically restarts it. If the load increases, Kubernetes can be instructed to add more instances of the container, distributing the incoming requests across them.

Load balancing is a critical component in any scalable service. When multiple instances of the prediction service are running, a load balancer is needed to distribute incoming API requests evenly across these instances. This prevents any single instance from becoming overwhelmed and ensures efficient resource utilization. In a Kubernetes environment, this is often managed by a Service object, which provides a stable IP address and DNS name for the set of pods (running containers) belonging to a particular Deployment. Kubernetes then typically integrates with cloud provider load balancers or uses internal load balancing mechanisms to route traffic to the appropriate pods. For external access, an Ingress controller can be used to manage external access to the services within the cluster, often providing HTTP and HTTPS routing, SSL/TLS termination, and name-based virtual hosting.

Auto-scaling is the mechanism that allows the prediction service to automatically adjust the number of running instances based on demand. This is a cornerstone of building cost-effective and performant scalable services. Kubernetes offers two primary mechanisms for auto-scaling:

1. **Horizontal Pod Autoscaler (HPA)**: This scales the number of pods in a Deployment or ReplicaSet. The HPA monitors metrics like CPU utilization, memory usage, or custom metrics (e.g., requests per second, queue depth) and increases or decreases the number of pods accordingly. For a prediction service, if the average CPU utilization across all running pods exceeds a certain threshold (e.g., 70%), the HPA will instruct Kubernetes to create more pods. Conversely, if the utilization drops below a threshold, it will scale down the number of pods to save resources. This dynamic adjustment is crucial for handling spiky traffic patterns common in many real-world applications.

2. **Cluster Autoscaler**: While HPA scales the number of pods, the Cluster Autoscaler scales the number of nodes (physical or virtual machines) in

the Kubernetes cluster itself. If the HPA tries to schedule more pods but there aren't enough resources available on existing nodes, the Cluster Autoscaler will provision new nodes. Conversely, if nodes are underutilized for a sustained period, it will terminate them. This ensures that the underlying infrastructure can support the auto-scaling needs of the prediction services running on it.

The process of setting up a scalable prediction service typically involves several key steps:

First,
**model serialization and packaging**. The trained machine learning model needs to be saved in a format that can be loaded by the inference server. Common formats include `pickle` for Scikit-learn models, `SavedModel` for TensorFlow, or `.pth`/`.pt` for PyTorch. This serialized model artifact is then placed into a container image. The container image will include a web framework (like FastAPI or Flask) that defines API endpoints (e.g., `/predict`). This framework loads the model upon startup and exposes a POST endpoint that accepts input features, preprocesses them, feeds them to the model for inference, and returns the predictions, usually in JSON format.

Second,
**containerization**. Using a `Dockerfile`, we define how to build the container image. This typically involves:
Starting from a base image (e.g., a Python image).
Copying the model artifact and the inference application code into the image.
Installing all necessary dependencies (e.g., `requirements.txt` for Python packages).
Defining the command to run when the container starts (e.g., `uvicorn main:app --host 0.0.0.0 --port 80`).

Third,
**deployment to an orchestration platform**. The container image is pushed to a container registry (like Docker Hub, Google Container Registry, AWS Elastic Container Registry). Then, Kubernetes manifests (YAML files) are created to define the Deployment, Service, and potentially the HPA.
**Deployment**: Specifies the container image to use, the number of initial replicas, and update strategies.
**Service**: Defines how to access the pods managed by the Deployment, providing a stable endpoint.
**Horizontal Pod Autoscaler**: Configures the metrics and thresholds for scaling the number of pods.

These manifests are then applied to the Kubernetes cluster using `kubectl apply -f
`. The orchestration platform takes over, creating the pods, setting up load balancing, and ensuring the desired number of instances are running, while the HPA monitors performance and adjusts the pod count as needed.

Consider an example: a recommendation engine for an e-commerce platform. Users browse products, add items to their cart, and make purchases. The system needs to provide real-time product recommendations on product pages, in the shopping cart, and on the homepage.

1.
**Model Training**: A recommendation model (e.g., collaborative filtering, content-based filtering, or a hybrid approach) is trained offline using historical user interaction data.
2. **Model Packaging**: The trained model is saved. A Python application using FastAPI is developed to load this model. The API endpoint

`/recommendations` takes a `user*id` and a list of `context*products` (e.g., products currently being viewed) as input. It retrieves necessary user features, performs inference to generate a list of recommended product IDs, and returns them.
3. **Containerization**: A `Dockerfile` is created to build an image containing FastAPI, the recommendation model, and all dependencies.
4. **Kubernetes Deployment**:
A `Deployment` is defined to run multiple replicas of the recommendation service container image.
A `Service` of type `LoadBalancer` (or `ClusterIP` with an Ingress) is created to provide a stable network endpoint for the recommendation service.
An `HorizontalPodAutoscaler` is configured to monitor the average CPU utilization of the pods. If it exceeds 70%, the number of pods will increase; if it drops below 30%, it will decrease.
If the cluster runs out of node capacity to accommodate new pods requested by the HPA, the Cluster Autoscaler (if configured) will add more nodes.

When a user visits a product page, the frontend application makes a request to the recommendation service's API endpoint (e.g., `http://recommendations.example.com/recommendations?user_id=12345`). The load balancer routes this request to one of the available recommendation service pods. The pod processes the request, generates recommendations, and sends them back. If traffic spikes (e.g., during a flash sale), the HPA will automatically scale up the number of recommendation service pods, ensuring that all incoming requests are handled promptly. As traffic subsides, the HPA scales down the pods to conserve resources and reduce costs.

Beyond basic CPU/memory metrics, advanced auto-scaling can be implemented using custom metrics. For instance, if the prediction service enqueues requests into a processing queue before inference (perhaps for batching within the service instance itself or for integrating with other asynchronous components), the depth of this queue can serve as a powerful scaling metric. A growing queue indicates that the service is falling behind, triggering scaling up. Similarly, for real-time services that interact with external systems, the latency of those interactions or the rate of successful inferences per second could be used as scaling signals.

Managing multiple models or different versions of a model within a scalable service architecture also presents interesting challenges and opportunities. A common pattern is to use a
**model registry** as a central repository for trained models. This registry stores model artifacts, metadata (training parameters, performance metrics, versions), and often provides APIs for retrieving specific model versions. The scalable prediction service can then be designed to dynamically load different model versions based on configurations or A/B testing strategies. For instance, a new version of the recommendation model might be deployed to a small percentage of traffic (e.g., 5%) using a canary deployment strategy. The HPA and Kubernetes' deployment strategies ensure that traffic is gradually shifted to the new model as confidence grows, all while maintaining scalability and availability.

Another crucial aspect of building scalable prediction services is **observability**. This encompasses logging, metrics, and tracing.
**Logging**: Each prediction service instance should log relevant information, such as incoming request details, prediction results, any errors encountered, and model loading status. These logs are aggregated and stored in a centralized logging system (e.g., Elasticsearch, Splunk) for analysis and debugging.
**Metrics**: Beyond the metrics used for auto-scaling (CPU, memory), it's vital to collect application-specific metrics. For a prediction service, this includes metrics like request latency (P95, P99), throughput (requests per second), error rates (e.g., HTTP 5xx errors), and potentially model-specific metrics like inference time per request or the distribution of

prediction outputs. These metrics are typically exposed in a Prometheus-compatible format and visualized using dashboards (e.g., Grafana).
**Tracing**: Distributed tracing (e.g., using Jaeger or Zipkin) helps to understand the flow of a request across multiple services in a microservices architecture. For a prediction service, tracing can reveal how much time is spent on network communication, data preprocessing, model inference, and post-processing within the service itself, as well as how the service interacts with other upstream or downstream services. This is invaluable for diagnosing performance bottlenecks.

The deployment of prediction services also needs to consider **resiliency**. This involves designing the system to withstand failures. Kubernetes inherently provides a good level of resiliency through its self-healing capabilities and the ability to run multiple replicas. However, additional considerations include:
**Health Checks**: Kubernetes uses health checks (liveness and readiness probes) to determine if a pod is running and ready to receive traffic. A liveness probe checks if the application is still running, while a readiness probe checks if it's ready to serve requests. If a liveness probe fails, Kubernetes restarts the pod. If a readiness probe fails, Kubernetes stops sending traffic to the pod.
**Graceful Shutdowns**: When a pod is being terminated (e.g., during scaling down or updates), it should shut down gracefully, finishing any in-flight requests before exiting. This prevents abrupt disconnections and potential data loss.
**Circuit Breakers**: If the prediction service relies on other external services, implementing circuit breakers can prevent cascading failures. If an external service becomes unresponsive, the circuit breaker "opens," and requests are immediately failed or routed elsewhere, rather than waiting for a timeout and potentially overwhelming the prediction service or the failing service further.

For very high-throughput scenarios or latency-sensitive applications, more specialized inference servers or frameworks might be employed.

TensorFlow Serving, TorchServe, and NVIDIA Triton Inference Server are examples of dedicated inference servers optimized for performance. They often offer features like automatic model loading, multiple model support, batching of requests for improved GPU utilization, and support for various hardware accelerators. These can be deployed as containers within Kubernetes, managed and scaled in the same manner as custom-built services.

The scalability of prediction services is not solely an infrastructure concern; it also influences model development. Models designed for real-time inference should be efficient. This might involve:

**Feature Engineering**: Ensuring that features can be computed quickly at inference time. Complex, time-consuming feature computations might need to be pre-computed and stored, or optimized heavily.
**Model Complexity**: While deep learning models can be very powerful, extremely large or complex models might have inference times that are too high for real-time requirements, even with powerful hardware. Techniques like model quantization, pruning, or using more efficient architectures become critical.
**Data Formats**: Standardizing on efficient data formats for requests and responses (e.g., Protocol Buffers, Avro, or optimized JSON serialization) can significantly reduce overhead.

In summary, building scalable prediction services is a multi-faceted engineering challenge that moves beyond simply deploying a model. It involves architecting a resilient, adaptable system capable of handling dynamic workloads. By leveraging containerization with Docker and orchestration with Kubernetes, coupled with intelligent load balancing and auto-scaling mechanisms, organizations can deploy models that deliver consistent, real-time predictions. The continuous monitoring of performance through robust logging, metrics, and tracing, along with careful consideration of model efficiency and deployment strategies like canary releases, ensures that these services remain performant, cost-effective, and reliable as user demand evolves. This approach transforms a static ML model into a dynamic, business-critical component that can scale with the organization's needs.

Edge deployment represents a paradigm shift in how machine learning models are utilized, moving computation from centralized cloud or data center environments directly to the physical devices or local networks where data is generated. This approach is particularly relevant in scenarios involving Internet of Things (IoT) devices, autonomous vehicles, smart manufacturing equipment, and other distributed systems where real-time decision-making, reduced latency, and offline operation are paramount. Unlike the scalable prediction services discussed previously, which focus on serving models from powerful, centralized infrastructure, edge deployment tackles the unique constraints and opportunities presented by resource-limited, geographically dispersed hardware.

The primary drivers for adopting edge deployment are manifold. Firstly, **latency reduction** is often a critical factor. When decisions need to be made within milliseconds, sending data to the cloud for processing and then receiving a response introduces unacceptable delays. Consider an autonomous vehicle's perception system: a delay of even a few hundred milliseconds in identifying an obstacle could have catastrophic consequences. By performing inference directly on the vehicle's onboard computers, these critical decisions can be made almost instantaneously.

Secondly,
**bandwidth efficiency** is another significant advantage. IoT devices, especially those deployed in remote or mobile environments, may have limited or expensive network connectivity. Transmitting vast amounts of raw sensor data (e.g., high-definition video streams from surveillance cameras, or continuous sensor readings from industrial machinery) to the cloud can quickly consume available bandwidth and incur substantial

costs. Processing this data at the edge and only sending back critical insights or alerts significantly reduces the data transmission burden. For instance, a smart factory sensor monitoring vibration levels might only send an alert to a central server if an anomaly indicative of impending equipment failure is detected, rather than streaming continuous vibration data.

Thirdly,
**privacy and security** considerations often favor edge deployment. Sensitive data, such as personal health information from wearable devices or proprietary operational data from industrial sensors, can be processed locally without ever leaving the device or its immediate network. This minimizes the risk of data breaches during transmission or storage in the cloud and helps comply with stringent data privacy regulations. For example, a medical device that analyzes patient ECG data might perform initial anomaly detection on the device itself, only sending anonymized or aggregated reports to healthcare providers.

Fourthly,
**reliability and offline operation** are crucial for applications that cannot afford downtime. In environments with intermittent or unreliable network connectivity, relying solely on cloud-based inference would render the system inoperable. Edge devices can continue to perform their intelligent functions even when disconnected from the internet, ensuring uninterrupted operation. This is essential for applications like remote environmental monitoring stations that might operate for extended periods without network access, or critical infrastructure control systems.

However, deploying machine learning models at the edge comes with a distinct set of challenges that require specialized techniques and careful consideration. The most prominent challenge is
**resource constraints**. Edge devices, such as microcontrollers, single-board computers (like Raspberry Pi), or even specialized edge AI chips, typically have significantly less computational power (CPU, GPU),

memory (RAM), and storage compared to cloud servers. This necessitates the use of highly optimized models that can perform inference efficiently within these limitations.

**Model optimization** is therefore a cornerstone of successful edge deployment. This involves several strategies aimed at reducing model size and computational complexity without sacrificing too much accuracy.
**Model Quantization**: This is a technique that reduces the precision of the model's weights and activations. Instead of using 32-bit floating-point numbers, quantization uses lower-precision representations, such as 16-bit floats, 8-bit integers, or even binary values. This dramatically reduces the model's memory footprint and can speed up inference, especially on hardware that has specialized support for lower-precision arithmetic. For example, an image classification model quantized from float32 to int8 can become significantly smaller and run faster on embedded processors.
**Model Pruning**: Pruning involves removing redundant or unimportant connections (weights) or even entire neurons from a neural network. This can be done during or after training. By identifying and eliminating parameters that contribute little to the model's performance, the model becomes sparser, smaller, and faster. Techniques include magnitude pruning (removing weights with small absolute values) and structured pruning (removing entire channels or filters).
**Knowledge Distillation**: This is a training technique where a smaller, more efficient "student" model is trained to mimic the behavior of a larger, more complex "teacher" model. The student model learns to generalize not only from the ground truth labels but also from the "soft targets" (probability distributions over classes) produced by the teacher model. This allows the student model to achieve accuracy comparable to the teacher model while being much smaller and faster, making it suitable for edge deployment.
**Efficient Model Architectures**: Choosing or designing model architectures inherently suited for efficiency is crucial. Architectures like MobileNets, SqueezeNets, and EfficientNets are specifically designed for

mobile and embedded vision applications, balancing accuracy with computational cost and parameter count. These architectures often employ techniques like depthwise separable convolutions, which are more efficient than standard convolutions.
**Hardware-Aware Neural Network Design**: This involves designing or adapting neural network architectures to take advantage of specific hardware accelerators present on edge devices. For instance, if an edge chip has specialized hardware for matrix multiplication with 8-bit integers, the model design would be optimized to leverage this capability.

Beyond model optimization, the **deployment and management of models on a fleet of edge devices** introduce complex logistical challenges. Unlike a centralized service where updates are pushed to a single location, edge deployments involve managing potentially thousands or millions of devices scattered geographically.

**Firmware and software updates** for models are a critical aspect of the MLOps lifecycle at the edge. Models are not static; they may need to be retrained and updated as new data becomes available or as performance degrades over time. Delivering these updates to edge devices reliably and securely is a significant undertaking.
**Over-the-Air (OTA) Updates**: This is the standard mechanism for delivering software and model updates remotely. A robust OTA update system must be in place to ensure that updates are downloaded, verified for integrity and authenticity, and applied to the devices without causing disruption. This typically involves a secure communication channel between the central management system and each edge device.
**Version Control and Rollback**: Managing different versions of models on a distributed fleet requires careful tracking. If a newly deployed model introduces bugs or performance issues, the ability to quickly roll back to a previous stable version is essential. This necessitates a system that can

track which model version is deployed on which device and allows for selective or fleet-wide rollbacks.
**Delta Updates**: To minimize bandwidth consumption and update time, it's often beneficial to deliver only the changes (deltas) between model versions rather than the entire model file. This requires mechanisms to identify and package only the modified parts of the model.

**Device management and monitoring** are also crucial for maintaining the health and performance of edge ML deployments.
**Device Telemetry**: Edge devices need to report their status, including hardware health, resource utilization (CPU, memory, power), network connectivity, and the performance of the deployed model (e.g., inference latency, error rates). This telemetry data is essential for identifying potential issues before they cause failures.
**Remote Diagnostics and Debugging**: The ability to remotely diagnose problems on edge devices is invaluable. This might involve collecting logs, running diagnostic tests, or even establishing secure remote access for deeper troubleshooting.
**Security**: Edge devices are often more vulnerable to physical tampering and cyberattacks than centralized servers. Security must be a primary consideration throughout the entire lifecycle, from secure boot and encrypted communication to secure storage of models and credentials.

To illustrate the practical application of edge deployment, consider the example of
**predictive maintenance sensors on industrial equipment**. In a large manufacturing plant, numerous machines operate continuously. Traditional maintenance involves scheduled inspections or reacting to breakdowns, both of which can lead to costly downtime and production losses.

1.

**Problem Definition**: The goal is to predict potential equipment failures before they occur by analyzing sensor data (e.g., vibration, temperature, acoustic emissions, current draw) in real-time.

2. **Edge Device Selection**: Small, ruggedized edge devices equipped with microcontrollers or embedded processors are installed near the machinery. These devices have sensors attached to collect the necessary data.

3. **Model Development and Optimization**:

A machine learning model (e.g., an anomaly detection model, a time-series forecasting model, or a classification model to identify failure modes) is trained in a cloud environment using historical data.

This model is then heavily optimized for the target edge device. This might involve:

Using a framework like TensorFlow Lite or PyTorch Mobile to convert and optimize the model for mobile and embedded deployment.

Quantizing the model weights from float32 to int8.

Pruning less important connections.

Selecting or designing an efficient neural network architecture.

Ensuring that any feature engineering steps required by the model can be performed efficiently on the edge device.

4. **Deployment to Edge Devices**:

The optimized model, along with the necessary inference runtime and data acquisition software, is packaged and deployed to the edge devices, likely via an OTA update mechanism.

Each device is configured to continuously collect sensor data, preprocess it as needed, and feed it into the optimized ML model for inference.

5. **Inference and Alerting**:

The edge device performs real-time inference. For instance, it might analyze a window of vibration data and output a probability of an anomaly.

If the model detects a high probability of an anomaly or a specific failure pattern, the edge device triggers an alert. This alert is sent to a central monitoring system, which could be a cloud platform or an on-premises server.

Crucially, the raw sensor data is not constantly streamed. Only the anomaly detection result or a summary of the sensor readings around the detected anomaly is transmitted. This conserves bandwidth and reduces the load on the network.

6. **Centralized Monitoring and Action**:

The central monitoring system receives alerts from multiple edge devices. Maintenance personnel are notified, and they can then schedule inspections or repairs for the specific piece of equipment before a catastrophic failure occurs.

The system might also aggregate alerts and telemetry from all devices to provide an overall health status of the plant's machinery.

7. **Model Retraining and Updates**:

Periodically, or when new failure modes are identified, the models are retrained using updated data. This might involve collecting data from devices that experienced actual failures, or data from corrected operations.

The updated, optimized models are then pushed out to the fleet of edge devices using the OTA update system. This continuous feedback loop is essential for improving the accuracy and effectiveness of the predictive maintenance system over time.

This industrial predictive maintenance example highlights how edge deployment enables proactive interventions, reduces unplanned downtime, and optimizes maintenance schedules, all while operating within the constraints of distributed, potentially intermittent connectivity and limited on-device computational resources.

Another significant domain for edge deployment is **real-time video analytics**. Consider security surveillance systems, retail analytics, or autonomous driving.

**Smart Cameras**: Instead of sending raw video streams to the cloud for analysis, edge-enabled smart cameras can perform object detection, facial recognition, or activity analysis directly on the device. This significantly

reduces the amount of data that needs to be transmitted, enabling higher resolution video or more cameras to be supported with the same network infrastructure. For example, a smart camera in a retail store could count people entering and exiting, detect shelf stock-outs, or identify suspicious behavior, only sending alerts or aggregated statistics to a central server.
**Autonomous Vehicles**: As mentioned earlier, autonomous vehicles rely heavily on edge computing for processing sensor data from cameras, LiDAR, radar, and ultrasonic sensors. Models for object detection, lane keeping, and path planning must run on the vehicle's onboard computers in real-time to ensure safety. The sheer volume of data generated by these sensors requires powerful, specialized edge hardware and highly optimized ML models.
**Robotics**: In industrial robotics or autonomous mobile robots (AMRs) in warehouses, edge deployment enables sophisticated perception and navigation capabilities. Robots can use onboard cameras and depth sensors to navigate complex environments, identify and manipulate objects, and collaborate with other robots or humans, all powered by models running locally.

The challenges of managing distributed model instances at the edge are amplified by the diversity of hardware and software environments. Edge devices can range from powerful edge servers with GPUs to tiny microcontrollers with minimal processing capabilities. Ensuring that a model performs consistently and efficiently across this heterogeneous landscape requires careful consideration of:

**Hardware Abstraction Layers**: Using frameworks that provide hardware abstraction can simplify deployment across different edge platforms. Libraries like TensorFlow Lite, ONNX Runtime, and Apache TVM aim to provide optimized runtimes for a wide variety of hardware targets, including CPUs, GPUs, NPUs (Neural Processing Units), and specialized DSPs (Digital Signal Processors).
**Model Conversion Tools**: Tools that convert models trained in standard frameworks (like TensorFlow, PyTorch, or Keras) into formats optimized

for edge devices are essential. TensorFlow Lite converter, PyTorch Mobile exporter, and ONNX converters are examples of such tools. These tools often apply optimizations like quantization and operator fusion during the conversion process.

**Edge Orchestration Platforms**: While Kubernetes is dominant for cloud deployments, specialized orchestration platforms are emerging for managing fleets of edge devices. These platforms help with device provisioning, secure communication, software and model deployment, and monitoring. Examples include AWS IoT Greentepe, Azure IoT Edge, Google Cloud IoT Edge, and open-source solutions like K3s (a lightweight Kubernetes distribution) or solutions built on top of edge gateways. These platforms aim to bring some of the conveniences of cloud orchestration to the edge.

The concept of an
**edge gateway** often plays a crucial role in managing edge deployments. An edge gateway acts as an intermediary between a collection of edge devices and the central cloud or data center. It can perform several functions:

**Data Aggregation and Preprocessing**: The gateway can collect data from multiple local sensors, perform initial aggregation and filtering, and then send a more manageable data stream to the cloud.

**Protocol Translation**: Edge devices may use various communication protocols (e.g., MQTT, CoAP). The gateway can translate these into standard protocols understood by the cloud.

**Local Inference**: More powerful gateways can host and run ML models for local inference, offloading computation from simpler edge devices.

**Device Management**: The gateway can serve as a single point of contact for managing and updating devices within its local network.

Consider a smart building scenario:

**Edge Devices**: Numerous sensors (temperature, humidity, occupancy, light), smart thermostats, and connected lights are deployed throughout the building.
**Edge Gateway**: A powerful computer or server is installed in the building's network closet. This gateway connects to all the individual sensors and devices.
**ML Model**: An ML model for optimizing HVAC (Heating, Ventilation, and Air Conditioning) and lighting based on occupancy, time of day, external weather data, and user preferences is deployed on the edge gateway. This model might be trained in the cloud and then optimized for the gateway's hardware.
**Edge Inference**: The gateway continuously receives data from sensors. It runs the HVAC and lighting optimization model locally. Based on the model's predictions, it sends commands to thermostats and smart lights to adjust settings. For example, if occupancy sensors indicate a room is empty, the gateway might turn off lights and adjust the thermostat to a more energy-efficient setting.
**Cloud Connectivity**: The gateway periodically sends aggregated data (e.g., average temperature, total energy consumption) and performance metrics of the ML model to a central cloud platform for long-term storage, further analysis, and model retraining. It might also receive updated model versions or configuration changes from the cloud.
**Benefits**: This approach significantly reduces latency for real-time control of building systems, ensures continued operation even if the internet connection is temporarily lost, and reduces the amount of data transmitted to the cloud.

The evolution of specialized hardware accelerators for AI at the edge (e.g., Google Coral, NVIDIA Jetson, Intel Movidius) has further fueled the adoption of edge ML. These chips are designed for power efficiency and high performance in tasks like neural network inference, enabling more complex models to be run on devices with tight power budgets. This opens up new possibilities for applications in areas like mobile robotics, drones, and portable diagnostic devices.

In conclusion, edge deployment of machine learning models is a rapidly growing field that addresses the critical need for localized, low-latency, and bandwidth-efficient intelligence. It involves a distinct set of challenges compared to cloud deployment, primarily centered around resource constraints and the complexities of managing distributed fleets of devices. Success in edge ML hinges on rigorous model optimization techniques, robust OTA update and device management strategies, and often the use of specialized hardware and edge orchestration platforms. As IoT continues to expand and the demand for real-time, intelligent decision-making at the source of data generation grows, edge deployment will undoubtedly play an increasingly vital role in the broader landscape of machine learning applications.

The preceding discussion has illuminated the intricacies of deploying machine learning models at the edge, a domain characterized by resource constraints and distributed systems. Now, we pivot our attention to a foundational element for robust and scalable deployments in any environment, whether cloud-based or at the edge: **Infrastructure as Code (IaC)**. In the context of model deployment, IaC is not merely a best practice; it is a critical enabler of reliability, repeatability, and velocity.

The traditional approach to setting up and managing the infrastructure required to serve machine learning models involved manual configuration. This often meant a team of engineers logging into servers, installing software, configuring networks, and deploying models through a series of ad-hoc steps. While this might suffice for a single, static deployment, it quickly becomes unmanageable and error-prone as the scale and complexity of operations grow. Inconsistencies between development, staging, and production environments are common, leading to the dreaded "it worked on my machine" syndrome, but extended to the entire infrastructure. Furthermore, any attempt to scale up, replicate a deployment, or recover from a failure would necessitate repeating these often tedious and error-prone manual processes.

Infrastructure as Code fundamentally alters this paradigm by treating infrastructure—servers, databases, load balancers, virtual networks, and more—as code that can be written, versioned, tested, and managed just like application code. This approach brings several profound benefits to the deployment of machine learning models.

Firstly,
**repeatability and consistency** are paramount. When infrastructure is defined in code, the exact same configuration can be applied repeatedly, ensuring that development, staging, and production environments are identical. This eliminates a significant source of deployment-related bugs and simplifies troubleshooting. For instance, if a model behaves differently in production than it did in staging, one of the first checks would be to ensure the underlying infrastructure is precisely the same, a verification that IaC makes trivial by comparing version-controlled code. When deploying a new version of a model that requires a specific set of dependencies, updated libraries, or a particular network configuration for optimal performance, IaC ensures that these requirements are met consistently across all instances of the serving environment. This is crucial for maintaining model performance and reliability over time.

Secondly, IaC facilitates
**automation**. The code defining the infrastructure can be integrated into CI/CD pipelines. This means that whenever a new model version is ready or an infrastructure change is proposed, the deployment process can be entirely automated. This automation significantly reduces the time from model training to production deployment, accelerating the iteration cycle and allowing data science teams to deliver value more quickly. Imagine a scenario where a model needs to be deployed across multiple regions for

global availability. With IaC, this entire process—provisioning virtual machines, configuring load balancers, setting up security groups, and deploying the model serving application—can be triggered with a single command or a commit to a version control repository.

Thirdly, IaC enables
**version control and traceability**. By storing infrastructure definitions in a version control system like Git, every change made to the infrastructure is tracked. This provides a complete audit trail, allowing teams to see who made what changes, when, and why. This is invaluable for debugging, compliance, and rollback scenarios. If a particular infrastructure configuration leads to performance degradation or a security vulnerability, it's straightforward to revert to a previous, known-good state by simply checking out an older version of the infrastructure code. This granular control and historical record are critical for maintaining stable and secure ML deployment environments.

Fourthly, IaC fosters
**collaboration and knowledge sharing**. The infrastructure definition is no longer confined to the knowledge of a few individuals who manage servers manually. Instead, it becomes a shared asset within the engineering team, documented in code. This makes it easier for new team members to understand the deployment environment and for different teams (e.g., data science, MLOps, platform engineering) to collaborate effectively on the infrastructure. When a data scientist needs to request specific infrastructure resources for a new model, they can work with the platform team to define these requirements in code, which can then be reviewed and merged into the main infrastructure repository.

Finally, IaC contributes to
**cost management**. By clearly defining the resources required for a deployment, teams can better estimate and control infrastructure costs. Furthermore, IaC enables the creation of automated scripts to tear down environments when they are no longer needed, preventing resources

from being provisioned unnecessarily and incurring ongoing charges. For transient environments used for model testing or experimentation, IaC is particularly useful for ensuring that these resources are automatically provisioned for the duration of the test and then cleanly deprovisioned, optimizing cloud spend.

Several popular tools facilitate the implementation of Infrastructure as Code. Among the most widely adopted are HashiCorp's Terraform and Amazon Web Services' (AWS) CloudFormation. While other tools exist, such as Ansible, Chef, and Puppet (which often blur the lines between configuration management and provisioning), Terraform and CloudFormation are primarily focused on provisioning and managing cloud infrastructure resources.

**Terraform** is an open-source tool that allows users to define and provision infrastructure across a wide range of cloud providers (AWS, Azure, Google Cloud, etc.) and other services (like Kubernetes, Datadog, etc.) using a declarative configuration language called HashiCorp Configuration Language (HCL) or, alternatively, JSON. Terraform works by maintaining a state file that tracks the current state of the managed infrastructure. It then compares the desired state defined in the configuration files with the current state and generates an execution plan to make the necessary changes. This plan is reviewed by the user before being applied, ensuring control over the automated provisioning process.

When deploying ML models, Terraform can be used to define everything from the virtual machines or containers that will host the model inference servers, to the load balancers that distribute incoming traffic, the auto-scaling groups that manage the number of instances based on load, the networking components like VPCs and subnets, and the security groups that control access. For example, a Terraform configuration could define a set of EC2 instances (on AWS) or VMs (on Azure/GCP) with specific instance types and operating systems, configure an Elastic Load Balancer to route traffic to these instances, set up an Auto Scaling Group to ensure a minimum number of instances are always running and to scale up or down based on CPU utilization or custom metrics, and define IAM roles and policies to grant the necessary permissions for the model serving application. This declarative approach ensures that the entire ML serving environment, including its scaling and resilience mechanisms, is managed as code.

**AWS CloudFormation** is AWS's native IaC service. It allows users to model and provision AWS resources in a declarative way using JSON or YAML templates. Similar to Terraform, CloudFormation templates describe the desired state of the AWS resources, and CloudFormation then provisions and configures those resources accordingly. When you create or update a stack (a collection of AWS resources managed as a single unit), CloudFormation monitors the process and provides status updates. It also supports rollbacks, meaning if a stack creation or update fails, CloudFormation can automatically revert to the previous state.

Using CloudFormation for ML deployments on AWS, one could define an Elastic Beanstalk environment configured to deploy a Docker container running a model serving framework like Flask or FastAPI with a pre-trained model. Or, it could provision an EKS (Elastic Kubernetes Service) cluster, along with the necessary worker nodes, IAM roles, and networking configurations, to deploy models as Kubernetes pods. For serverless inference, CloudFormation can be used to define Lambda functions, API Gateway endpoints, and associated resources required to create a serverless ML inference API. The ability to define complex interdependencies between resources—for example, ensuring a database is created before an application that needs to connect to it—is a key strength of CloudFormation, making it suitable for orchestrating the entire infrastructure for an ML deployment.

Let's consider a practical scenario for deploying a real-time recommendation engine. The ML team has developed a Python model that takes user history and item features as input and outputs a list of recommended items. This model needs to be served with low latency and high availability.

Using
**Terraform**, the infrastructure could be defined as follows:

1.
**Virtual Private Cloud (VPC) and Subnets**: Define a VPC with public and private subnets across multiple availability zones for high availability.
2. **Security Groups**: Create security groups to allow inbound HTTP traffic (port 80/443) to the model serving instances and outbound traffic to necessary external services.
3. **EC2 Instances / EKS Cluster**:
**Option A (EC2 Instances with Auto Scaling Group)**: Define an EC2 launch template specifying an AMI with the necessary ML runtime (e.g., Python, TensorFlow Serving, TorchServe), user data scripts to download the model and start the serving application, and instance type suitable for inference. Then, define an Auto Scaling Group to manage the desired number of instances, min/max capacity, and scaling policies (e.g., scale based on CPU utilization of the serving containers).
**Option B (EKS Cluster)**: Define an EKS cluster, including the control plane and worker nodes. For ML serving, this would typically involve deploying the model within containers orchestrated by Kubernetes.
4. **Elastic Load Balancer (ELB)**: Configure an Application Load Balancer (ALB) to distribute incoming recommendation requests across the EC2 instances or EKS pods. The ALB would have listeners for HTTP/HTTPS and target groups pointing to the appropriate instances/pods.

5. **IAM Roles and Policies**: Define IAM roles for the EC2 instances or EKS nodes to allow them to access other AWS services if needed (e.g., S3 for model storage, CloudWatch for logging).

The Terraform code would look something like this (simplified example for EC2):

```hcl

Define AWS provider
provider "aws" {
region = "us-east-1"
}

VPC and Subnets (simplified)
resource "aws_vpc" "main" {
cidr_block = "10.0.0.0/16"
tags = {
Name = "ml-deployment-vpc"
}
}

resource "aws
subnet" "publica" {
vpcid = awsvpc.main.id
cidr_block = "10.0.1.0/24"
availability_zone = "us-east-1a"
tags = {
Name = "public-subnet-a"
```

```
}
}
```

**Security Group**

```
resource "awssecuritygroup" "ml_sg" {
name = "ml-serving-sg"
description = "Allow access to ML serving instances"
vpcid = awsvpc.main.id

ingress {

from_port = 80
to_port = 80
protocol = "tcp"
cidr_blocks = ["0.0.0.0/0"] In a real scenario, restrict this
}

egress {

from_port = 0
to_port = 0
protocol = "-1"
cidr_blocks = ["0.0.0.0/0"]
}

tags = {

Name = "ml-serving-sg"
}
}
```

**EC2 Launch Template (simplified)**

```
resource "awslaunchtemplate" "ml_template" {
name_prefix = "ml-serving-"
image_id = "ami-0abcdef1234567890" Replace with an appropriate AMI
instance_type = "t3.medium"
vpcsecuritygroupids = [awssecuritygroup.mlsg.id]
key_name = "my-ssh-key" Optional, for debugging

user_data = base64encode(<<-EOF

!/bin/bash
Install dependencies and start ML serving container
echo "Starting ML serving..."
Example: Docker setup
sudo apt-get update -y
sudo apt-get install docker.io -y
sudo systemctl start docker
sudo docker run -d -p 80:80 my-recommendation-model:latest
echo "ML serving setup complete."
EOF
)

tags = {

Name = "ml-serving-instance"
}
}
```

**Auto Scaling Group**

```
resource "awsautoscalinggroup" "ml_asg" {
desired_capacity = 2
max_size = 5
min_size = 1
vpczoneidentifier = [awssubnet.publica.id] Add more subnets for multi-AZ

launch_template {

id = awslaunchtemplate.ml_template.id
version = "$Latest"
}

target
grouparns = [awslbtargetgroup.mltg.arn]
healthchecktype = "ELB"
healthcheckgrace_period = 300

tags = [

{
key = "Name"
value = "ml-serving-asg"
propagateatlaunch = true
}
]
}
```

**Application Load Balancer (ALB)**

```
resource "awslb" "mlalb" {
name = "ml-recommendation-alb"
```

internal = false
load*balancer*type = "application"
security*groups = [aws*security*group.ml*sg.id]
subnets = [aws*subnet.public*a.id] Add more subnets for multi-AZ

enable
*deletion*protection = false

tags = {

Name = "ml-recommendation-alb"
}
}

resource "aws
*lb*target*group" "ml*tg" {
name = "ml-serving-tg"
port = 80
protocol = "HTTP"
vpc*id = aws*vpc.main.id

health_check {

enabled = true
interval = 30
path = "/health" Assuming a /health endpoint for the model server
port = "traffic-port"
protocol = "HTTP"
matcher = "200"
timeout = 5
unhealthy_threshold = 3
healthy_threshold = 3
}

tags = {

Name = "ml-serving-tg"
}
}

resource "aws
*lb*listener" "ml_listener" {
load*balancer*arn = aws*lb.ml*alb.arn
port = "80"
protocol = "HTTP"

default_action {

type = "forward"
target*group*arn = aws*lb*target*group.ml*tg.arn
}
}
```

In this example, running `terraform init`, `terraform plan`, and `terraform apply` would provision all the necessary AWS resources to host and serve the recommendation model, automatically managing scaling and load balancing.

Similarly, for
**AWS CloudFormation**, a template would define the AWS resources. For a deployment using ECS (Elastic Container Service) and Fargate for serverless container execution:

```yaml

AWSTemplateFormatVersion: '2010-09-09'
Description: CloudFormation template for ML recommendation service on ECS Fargate

Resources:

VPC and Subnets (can be defined here or referenced from existing)
VPC:
Type: AWS::EC2::VPC
Properties:
CidrBlock: 10.0.0.0/16
Tags:
- Key: Name
Value: ml-cfn-vpc

SubnetPublicA:

Type: AWS::EC2::Subnet
Properties:
VpcId: !Ref VPC
CidrBlock: 10.0.1.0/24
AvailabilityZone: !Select [ 0, !GetAZs '' ]
Tags:
- Key: Name
Value: public-subnet-a

ECS Cluster

EcsCluster:
Type: AWS::ECS::Cluster
Properties:
ClusterName: ml-recommendation-cluster

Task Definition for the ML serving container

EcsTaskDefinition:
Type: AWS::ECS::TaskDefinition
Properties:
Family: ml-recommendation-task
NetworkMode: awsvpc
RequiresCompatibilities:
- FARGATE
Cpu: '1024' 1 vCPU
Memory: '2048' 2 GB
ExecutionRoleArn: !GetAtt EcsTaskExecutionRole.Arn
ContainerDefinitions:
- Name: recommendation-service
Image: .dkr.ecr..amazonaws.com/ml-recommendation:latest Replace with your ECR image
PortMappings:
- ContainerPort: 80
HostPort: 80
LogConfiguration:
logDriver: awslogs
options:
awslogs-group: /ecs/ml-recommendation-cluster/recommendation-service
awslogs-region: !Ref AWS::Region
awslogs-create-group: 'true'
HealthCheck:
Command:
- "CMD-SHELL"
- "curl -f http://localhost:80/health || exit 1" Example health check

IAM Role for ECS Task Execution

EcsTaskExecutionRole:
Type: AWS::IAM::Role

```
Properties:
AssumeRolePolicyDocument:
Version: '2012-10-17'
Statement:
- Effect: Allow
Principal:
Service: ecs-tasks.amazonaws.com
Action:
- sts:AssumeRole
Path: /
Policies:
- PolicyName: AllowECSAccess
PolicyDocument:
Version: '2012-10-17'
Statement:
- Effect: Allow
Action:
- logs:CreateLogStream
- logs:PutLogEvents
Resource: ""
```

ALB Target Group

```
AlbTargetGroup:
Type: AWS::ElasticLoadBalancingV2::TargetGroup
Properties:
Name: ml-recommendation-tg
Port: 80
Protocol: HTTP
VpcId: !Ref VPC
TargetType: ip
HealthCheck:
Enabled: true
IntervalSeconds: 30
```

Path: /health
Port: 80
Protocol: HTTP
Matcher: '200'

ALB

ApplicationLoadBalancer:
Type: AWS::ElasticLoadBalancingV2::LoadBalancer
Properties:
Name: ml-recommendation-alb
Type: application
Scheme: internet-facing
Subnets:
- !Ref SubnetPublicA Add more subnets for multi-AZ
SecurityGroups:
- !Ref AlbSecurityGroup

ALB Listener

AlbListener:
Type: AWS::ElasticLoadBalancingV2::Listener
Properties:
DefaultActions:
- TargetGroupArn: !Ref AlbTargetGroup
Type: forward
LoadBalancerArn: !Ref ApplicationLoadBalancer
Port: 80
Protocol: HTTP

Security Group for ALB

AlbSecurityGroup:
Type: AWS::EC2::SecurityGroup

```
Properties:
GroupDescription: Allow HTTP traffic to ALB
VpcId: !Ref VPC
SecurityGroupIngress:
- IpProtocol: tcp
FromPort: 80
ToPort: 80
CidrIp: 0.0.0.0/0 Restrict in production

ECS Service

EcsService:
Type: AWS::ECS::Service
Properties:
Cluster: !Ref EcsCluster
ServiceName: ml-recommendation-service
TaskDefinition: !Ref EcsTaskDefinition
DesiredCount: 2
LaunchType: FARGATE
NetworkConfiguration:
AwsvpcConfiguration:
Subnets:
- !Ref SubnetPublicA Add more subnets for multi-AZ
SecurityGroups:
- !Ref AlbSecurityGroup This security group will be attached to the
Fargate tasks
LoadBalancers:
- TargetGroupArn: !Ref AlbTargetGroup
ContainerName: recommendation-service
ContainerPort: 80
HealthCheckGracePeriodSeconds: 300
```

When this CloudFormation template is deployed, AWS provisions the necessary ECS cluster, Fargate tasks, ALB, target groups, and networking components to serve the recommendation model. The ML team would simply need to ensure their Docker image with the model serving application is available in ECR.

The integration of IaC into the ML deployment workflow profoundly impacts the operational maturity of machine learning systems. It transforms infrastructure management from a reactive, manual endeavor into a proactive, automated, and auditable process. This is critical for building reliable, scalable, and maintainable ML systems that can evolve alongside the models they serve. As ML models become more integral to business operations, the underlying infrastructure must be as robust and agile as the models themselves, a goal that Infrastructure as Code helps to achieve. This foundation of codified infrastructure is essential for any serious MLOps strategy, providing the stable ground upon which advanced deployment automation, monitoring, and management techniques can be built.

The preceding discussion has underscored the indispensable role of Infrastructure as Code (IaC) in establishing robust and repeatable ML deployment environments. Building upon this foundation of codified infrastructure, we now transition to a crucial aspect of operationalizing machine learning at scale: **Continuous Integration and Continuous Delivery (CI/CD) pipelines for ML models**, often referred to under the umbrella of MLOps. This represents the next logical step in transforming the ML lifecycle from a series of manual, ad-hoc processes into an automated, efficient, and continuously improving system.

CI/CD, a practice long embraced by software engineering, aims to automate the build, test, and deployment phases of the software development lifecycle. When applied to machine learning, CI/CD pipelines become the engine that drives the transition of a trained and validated model from a data scientist's experimentation environment into a production-ready serving system. The core principle is to minimize human intervention and maximize automation, ensuring that changes – whether to model code, training data, or infrastructure – are integrated and deployed rapidly, reliably, and with a high degree of confidence.

The motivation behind integrating ML models into CI/CD pipelines is multifaceted. Firstly, it dramatically accelerates the pace of iteration. In traditional ML development, a new model version might take days or even weeks to deploy due to manual testing, packaging, and deployment procedures. CI/CD pipelines can reduce this to minutes or hours, allowing data science teams to experiment more rapidly, gather feedback, and deploy improvements much faster. This agility is critical in dynamic business environments where model performance can degrade over time due to concept drift or changes in data distributions.

Secondly, CI/CD pipelines enhance reliability and consistency. By automating the build, test, and deployment steps, each model deployment follows the exact same process, minimizing the risk of human error. This consistency is vital for ML systems where subtle variations in the deployment environment or process can lead to performance discrepancies or outright failures. Imagine a scenario where a model update is pushed to production. A CI/CD pipeline can automatically include a battery of tests – from unit tests on the model's code to integration tests with downstream services and performance tests against a validation dataset – before the model is made available to end-users. If any of these automated checks fail, the pipeline can halt the deployment, preventing a potentially faulty model from impacting users.

Thirdly, CI/CD pipelines foster collaboration and transparency. The pipeline itself serves as a visible and auditable record of how models are deployed. When a model is deployed, the pipeline logs provide a clear trace of which code was used, which data was involved in training and validation, which tests were executed, and what infrastructure was provisioned (thanks to IaC). This transparency is invaluable for debugging, compliance, and for enabling different teams (data scientists, ML engineers, operations) to understand and trust the deployment process.

Let's consider the typical stages of a CI/CD pipeline for machine learning, which can be broadly categorized into Continuous Integration (CI) and Continuous Delivery/Deployment (CD).

**Continuous Integration (CI) for ML:**
The CI phase focuses on automating the process of merging code changes from multiple developers into a shared repository, followed by automated builds and tests. For ML, this extends to integrating model training and validation logic.

1.
**Code Commit and Trigger:** The process typically begins when a data scientist or ML engineer commits changes to the model's source code, training scripts, feature engineering logic, or even configuration files stored in a version control system like Git. This commit event triggers the CI pipeline.

2.
**Automated Testing of Code:** Before any model training or complex deployment steps occur, the pipeline first runs standard software tests on the code itself. This includes:
**Unit Tests:** Verifying the correctness of individual functions and components (e.g., a data cleaning function, a feature transformation class).

**Integration Tests:** Ensuring that different modules of the ML pipeline work together as expected (e.g., the data loader integrates correctly with the feature transformer).
**Linting and Static Analysis:** Checking for code style violations and potential bugs without executing the code.

3.
**Model Training (Optional but Recommended for CI):** In some CI setups, a lightweight version of the model training process might be included. This could involve training on a small subset of data or for a reduced number of epochs. The goal is not to produce a production-ready model, but to catch potential errors in the training code itself, such as syntax errors, incorrect data loading, or issues with framework setup. This is sometimes referred to as "continuous training" within the CI context, though the full, iterative training process is typically part of the CD phase.

4.
**Model Validation and Testing:** Once the training code is deemed functional (or if a pre-trained model artifact is used), the pipeline proceeds to validate the model's performance. This is a critical step that differentiates ML CI from traditional software CI.
**Data Validation:** Ensuring that the input data used for validation adheres to expected schemas and distributions. Libraries like Great Expectations or custom scripts can be employed here to check for data quality issues, missing values, or unexpected value ranges.
**Model Performance Metrics:** Evaluating the trained model against a dedicated validation dataset using relevant metrics (e.g., accuracy, precision, recall, F1-score for classification; RMSE, MAE for regression; AUC for ranking). This evaluation is automated, and the pipeline can be configured to fail if the model's performance falls below a predefined threshold.

**Bias and Fairness Checks:** For models that impact users, it's increasingly important to include automated checks for bias against different demographic groups or other sensitive attributes.
**Model Explainability Checks:** In some cases, running automated explainability tools (like SHAP or LIME) on a sample of predictions to ensure the model's reasoning remains sensible.

5.
**Model Artifact Generation and Storage:** If all CI tests pass, the trained model is packaged into a deployable artifact. This artifact often includes the model weights, the inference code, and any necessary dependencies. This artifact is then versioned and stored in a model registry or a binary artifact repository (e.g., MLflow Model Registry, S3, GCS, Azure Blob Storage). This ensures that there is a traceable record of the model that passed the CI checks.

**Continuous Delivery/Deployment (CD) for ML:**
The CD phase focuses on automating the release of validated changes to a production or staging environment. For ML, this involves taking the validated model artifact and deploying it as a serving endpoint.

1.
**Triggering the CD Pipeline:** The CD pipeline is typically triggered after the CI pipeline successfully completes and a validated model artifact is registered. This trigger can be automatic or manual, depending on the organization's risk tolerance and deployment strategy.

2.
**Infrastructure Provisioning (IaC Integration):** As discussed previously, IaC plays a vital role here. The CD pipeline can invoke IaC tools (like Terraform or CloudFormation) to provision or update the necessary infrastructure for serving the model. This might involve spinning up new virtual machines, configuring Kubernetes deployments, or updating

serverless functions. The infrastructure configuration is version-controlled and managed alongside the model code.

3.
**Model Deployment:** The validated model artifact is then deployed to the provisioned infrastructure. This can take various forms:
**Containerization:** Packaging the model and its serving code into a Docker container. This container can then be deployed to orchestration platforms like Kubernetes (e.g., using Helm charts for managing deployments) or managed container services like AWS ECS or Azure Container Instances.
**Serverless Functions:** Deploying the model as a serverless function (e.g., AWS Lambda, Google Cloud Functions, Azure Functions) for event-driven or API-based inference.
**Dedicated ML Serving Platforms:** Utilizing specialized platforms like TensorFlow Serving, TorchServe, or NVIDIA Triton Inference Server, which are optimized for high-performance model serving. The CD pipeline would be responsible for configuring these servers, loading the model artifact, and ensuring they are running.

4.
**Staged Rollouts (Canary Deployments, Blue/Green Deployments):** To minimize risk during production deployments, CD pipelines often implement staged rollout strategies:
**Canary Deployments:** A new model version is first deployed to a small subset of users or traffic (e.g., 5% of requests). Performance and error rates are closely monitored. If the new model performs as expected, the traffic is gradually increased until 100% of traffic is routed to the new version. If issues are detected, the rollout is paused, and traffic is reverted to the old model.
**Blue/Green Deployments:** Two identical production environments are maintained: a "blue" environment running the current production model and a "green" environment where the new model is deployed. Once the green environment is fully tested and validated, traffic is switched from

blue to green. If any issues arise, traffic can be quickly switched back to the blue environment.

5.
**Automated Smoke Tests and Integration Tests in Staging/Production:** After deployment, the pipeline performs a final set of automated checks in the target environment. These "smoke tests" are crucial to ensure the deployed model is responding correctly and that basic functionality is intact. Integration tests with other services might also be run.

6.
**Monitoring and Rollback:** A critical component of CD is the ability to monitor the deployed model in production and automatically roll back to a previous stable version if performance degrades, error rates spike, or critical issues are detected. This monitoring often leverages metrics collected by dedicated ML monitoring tools, which track not only system health (e.g., latency, CPU usage) but also model-specific metrics (e.g., prediction drift, data drift, prediction bias).

**Tools and Technologies for ML CI/CD:**

The implementation of ML CI/CD pipelines often involves integrating a suite of specialized tools:

**Version Control Systems (VCS):** Git (e.g., GitHub, GitLab, Bitbucket) is the de facto standard for managing code and configuration.
**CI/CD Orchestrators:** Jenkins, GitLab CI, GitHub Actions, CircleCI, Azure DevOps Pipelines, AWS CodePipeline are popular choices for defining and running pipelines. These tools allow you to script the entire workflow.

**Containerization:** Docker is essential for packaging ML models and their dependencies into portable units.
**Container Orchestration:** Kubernetes (K8s), AWS Elastic Kubernetes Service (EKS), Google Kubernetes Engine (GKE), Azure Kubernetes Service (AKS) are widely used for deploying and managing containerized applications, including ML models.
**Model Registries:** Tools like MLflow Model Registry, SageMaker Model Registry, Vertex AI Model Registry provide a centralized repository for versioning, managing, and discovering trained ML models.
**Feature Stores:** For models that rely on curated features, feature stores (e.g., Feast, SageMaker Feature Store, Vertex AI Feature Store) can be integrated into the pipeline to ensure consistency between training and serving features.
**Infrastructure as Code (IaC):** Terraform, CloudFormation, Ansible, Pulumi for provisioning and managing the underlying infrastructure.
**MLOps Platforms:** End-to-end platforms like Kubeflow, SageMaker, Vertex AI, Azure Machine Learning provide integrated capabilities for model training, deployment, and management, often including built-in CI/CD features.
**Monitoring Tools:** Prometheus, Grafana, Datadog, New Relic, and specialized ML monitoring solutions (e.g., Evidently AI, Arize AI, Fiddler AI) are used to track model performance and detect drift in production.

## A Practical Example: CI/CD for an Image Classification Model

Let's walk through a simplified example of a CI/CD pipeline for an image classification model using Python, TensorFlow, Docker, Kubernetes, and GitLab CI.

**Scenario:** A data science team has developed an image classification model. They want to automate the process of retraining, validating, and deploying this model whenever new labeled images are added to their dataset or when improvements are made to the model architecture.

**Pipeline Stages:**

**1. Continuous Integration (CI) - Triggered by Git Push**

**Trigger:** A push to the `main` branch of the Git repository containing the model code, training scripts, and Dockerfile.
**Stage 1: Linting and Unit Tests:**
The pipeline starts by running `flake8` and `pytest` on the Python code for data loading, preprocessing, model definition, and training.
Example GitLab CI snippet:
```yaml
lintandtest:
stage: build
script:
- pip install -r requirements.txt
- flake8 .
- pytest tests/unit/
```
**Stage 2: Model Training (Lightweight):**
A small subset of the training data is used to train the model for a few epochs. This ensures the training script runs without errors and the model can be initialized.
The trained model weights (even if not optimal) are saved as an artifact for the next stage.
Example GitLab CI snippet:
```yaml
lightweight_train:
stage: test
```

script:
- python train.py --data*subset --epochs 5 --output*model*path*
*model*artifact.h5
artifacts:
paths:
- model_artifact.h5
```

**Stage 3: Model Validation:**
Using the `model_artifact.h5` generated in the previous step, the pipeline evaluates the model on a separate validation dataset.
Key metrics (e.g., accuracy, F1-score) are calculated.
The pipeline checks if the accuracy is above a predefined threshold (e.g., 85%). If not, the pipeline fails, and the data scientists are notified.
Example GitLab CI snippet:
```yaml
validate_model:
stage: test
script:
- python validate.py --model model*artifact.h5 --data validation*data/ --
threshold 0.85
dependencies:
- lightweight_train
```

**Stage 4: Containerize and Push Model:**
If validation passes, the pipeline builds a Docker image containing the model artifact (`model_artifact.h5`) and the inference script (`predict.py`). This Docker image is tagged with a unique version (e.g., Git commit SHA) and pushed to a container registry (e.g., GitLab Container Registry, Docker Hub, AWS ECR).
Example GitLab CI snippet:
```yaml
build*and*push_image:
stage: deploy_ci
script:

- docker build -t registry.gitlab.com/your-group/your-project/image-classifier:$CI*COMMIT*SHA .
- docker push registry.gitlab.com/your-group/your-project/image-classifier:$CI*COMMIT*SHA
only:
- main
```

**2. Continuous Delivery (CD) - Triggered by successful CI**

**Trigger:** The successful completion of the `build*and*push_image` stage in the CI pipeline.
**Stage 1: Provision/Update Kubernetes Deployment:**
The CD pipeline interacts with Kubernetes. It uses `kubectl` or a Helm chart to deploy the newly built Docker image.
This might involve updating an existing Kubernetes Deployment resource to use the new image tag.
**Infrastructure as Code (IaC) Integration:** The Kubernetes manifests themselves (or the Helm chart) are version-controlled, and any changes to the underlying infrastructure (e.g., requesting more CPU/memory for pods) would also be managed via IaC and integrated here.
Example GitLab CI snippet (using kubectl and a pre-defined manifest):
```yaml
deploy*to*staging:
stage: deploy_cd
script:
- export IMAGE*TAG=$CI*COMMIT_SHA
- sed "s|**IMAGE***TAG*|$IMAGETAG|g" kubernetes/deployment.yaml > kubernetes/deployment_new.yaml
- kubectl apply -f kubernetes/deployment_new.yaml
- kubectl rollout status deployment/image-classifier-deployment
environment: staging

```
only:
- main
```

**Stage 2: Staging Environment Testing:**
Once the new model is deployed to a staging environment, automated smoke tests are executed. These tests send sample requests to the deployed model and verify that it returns valid predictions. Integration tests with downstream services might also be performed.
Example GitLab CI snippet:
```yaml
teststagingdeployment:
stage: test_cd
script:
- python tests/integration/stagingsmoketest.py
environment: staging
needs: ["deploytostaging"]
```

**Stage 3: Production Deployment (Manual Approval or Automatic):**
If staging tests pass, the deployment can proceed to production. This stage might require manual approval to ensure human oversight. Similar to staging, the pipeline updates the Kubernetes Deployment resource to use the new image.
**Staged Rollout:** To implement a canary deployment, the pipeline could first update a smaller subset of replicas, monitor their performance, and then gradually scale up.
Example GitLab CI snippet (with manual approval):
```yaml
deploytoproduction:
stage: deploy_cd
script:
- export IMAGETAG=$CICOMMIT_SHA
- sed "s|IMAGETAG|$IMAGETAG|g" kubernetes/deployment.yaml >
kubernetes/deployment_prod.yaml
- kubectl apply -f kubernetes/deployment_prod.yaml
```

- kubectl rollout status deployment/image-classifier-deployment
environment: production
when: manual Requires manual click to proceed
only:
- main
needs: ["test*staging*deployment"]
```

**Stage 4: Post-Deployment Monitoring and Rollback:**
After deployment to production, continuous monitoring is crucial. The pipeline can trigger automated alerts based on model performance metrics or system health.
If issues are detected (e.g., accuracy drops below 80%, latency exceeds 500ms), the pipeline can be configured to automatically trigger a rollback to the previous stable version of the model. This rollback mechanism would involve updating the Kubernetes Deployment to use the previous image tag.

This example illustrates how CI/CD pipelines automate the journey of an ML model from code commitment to production deployment, incorporating testing, validation, and infrastructure management at each step. The key takeaway is that by embracing automation and integrating MLOps principles, organizations can significantly improve the speed, reliability, and efficiency of their ML initiatives. This iterative, automated approach is fundamental to building and maintaining high-performing ML systems in production.
```

## Chapter 12: Monitoring Deployed Models and Detecting Drift

The deployment of a machine learning model into a production environment marks a significant milestone, signaling the transition from experimentation and development to real-world application. However, this deployment is not an endpoint but rather the commencement of a continuous lifecycle. The inherent dynamism of the real world means that the conditions under which a model was trained and validated will invariably change, leading to a degradation in its predictive power and overall utility. This necessitates a robust and proactive approach to **continuous model monitoring**. Without vigilant oversight, even the most sophisticated models can silently falter, leading to flawed insights, suboptimal business decisions, and potentially significant financial or operational repercussions.

The core rationale behind continuous monitoring stems from the unavoidable reality of drift. Models are built upon assumptions about the data they will encounter and the relationships they are expected to capture. These assumptions, however, are often based on historical data. When deployed, models face live, evolving data streams. This evolution can manifest in several ways, broadly categorized as **data drift** and **concept drift**.

**Data drift**, also known as covariate shift, occurs when the statistical properties of the input features in the production environment change from those observed during training. Imagine a fraud detection model trained on transaction data from a specific holiday season. Post-holiday, consumer spending patterns, merchant types, and transaction volumes might significantly alter. If the model has not been updated or retrained to account for these new distributions, its ability to accurately flag fraudulent transactions will diminish. Similarly, a recommendation system trained on user behavior before a major product redesign might struggle to predict preferences once users adapt to the new interface and features. The underlying relationships between features and the target variable might remain the same, but the input data itself has changed. Detecting this shift is paramount. This can involve tracking the distributions of individual features (e.g., mean, median, variance, frequency of categorical values) and comparing them against baseline distributions established during training or a previous stable period. Statistical tests like the Kolmogorov-Smirnov test, Chi-squared test, or Population Stability Index (PSI) are common tools for quantifying the difference between two distributions.

**Concept drift**, on the other hand, is a more insidious form of degradation. It occurs when the relationship between the input features and the target variable itself changes over time. Consider a model predicting customer churn. Initially, factors like price increases might be strong predictors of churn. However, over time, a competitor might introduce a superior product, making product quality or feature sets the dominant drivers of churn. The concept of "what causes churn" has evolved, rendering the original model's learned relationships obsolete. This type of drift is harder to detect as the input data might not change drastically, but the underlying patterns that led to certain predictions are no longer valid. Detecting concept drift often requires monitoring model performance metrics (accuracy, precision, recall, AUC, etc.) on labeled production data (if available, which is often delayed or sparse) or by employing techniques that indirectly infer concept drift, such as analyzing the model's confidence scores or changes in prediction distributions over time. For instance, if a model that previously had high confidence in its predictions starts exhibiting lower confidence across the board, it might signal that the underlying concepts it learned are no longer holding true.

The imperative for continuous monitoring is further amplified by the nature of deployed ML systems. Unlike static software, ML models are inherently adaptive and susceptible to the environment they operate in. A model that performs impeccably today might be underperforming significantly by next week or next month, and this decline might go unnoticed without a dedicated monitoring system. This silent degradation can lead to a cascade of negative consequences:

**Erosion of Trust:** When users, stakeholders, or downstream systems repeatedly receive inaccurate or irrelevant outputs from an ML model, their trust in the system erodes. This can lead to the abandonment of the ML solution, despite its initial promise.
**Poor Business Decisions:** Many ML models are deployed to inform critical business decisions, such as credit scoring, marketing campaign targeting, inventory management, or medical diagnoses. If these models are providing flawed insights due to drift, the decisions based on them will also be flawed, potentially leading to financial losses, missed opportunities, or incorrect operational choices.
**Compliance and Regulatory Risks:** In regulated industries like finance and healthcare, ML models are often subject to stringent compliance requirements. A poorly performing model that exhibits bias or makes discriminatory predictions due to drift can lead to significant regulatory penalties and legal challenges.
**Suboptimal User Experience:** For customer-facing applications like recommendation engines, search result rankings, or personalized content delivery, model degradation directly impacts the user experience. Irrelevant recommendations or search results can lead to user frustration and disengagement.
**Increased Operational Costs:** Reactively fixing models that have already degraded significantly is often more costly and time-consuming than proactively monitoring and maintaining them. Debugging issues in a production system with subtle performance degradations can be a complex and resource-intensive task.

Therefore, establishing a continuous monitoring framework is not merely a best practice; it is a fundamental requirement for the responsible and sustainable operation of ML systems in production. This framework should encompass several key components:

First,
**defining clear performance baselines and thresholds** is crucial. Before deploying a model, extensive validation and testing are performed to establish expected performance metrics on a representative dataset. These established benchmarks serve as the initial reference point. Continuous monitoring involves comparing live performance against these baselines. Thresholds should be set for key metrics (e.g., accuracy, latency, error rate, prediction bias) and for drift indicators (e.g., PSI for feature drift). When these thresholds are breached, an alert should be triggered. These thresholds should be intelligently chosen, balancing the need for sensitivity to degradation with the desire to avoid excessive false alarms.

Second,
**collecting and storing relevant telemetry data** is indispensable. This includes not only the model's predictions and the input data it receives but also system-level metrics such as latency, throughput, error rates, and resource utilization (CPU, memory). For models that require labeled feedback, this feedback loop must also be captured. The volume of data can be substantial, necessitating scalable data pipelines and storage solutions. Techniques like data sampling or using feature stores can help manage this data deluge.

Third,
**automating the detection of anomalies and drift** is the core operational aspect. This involves implementing scheduled jobs or event-driven processes that analyze the collected telemetry data against predefined rules and models. These detection mechanisms should be capable of identifying both sudden drops in performance and gradual degradation over time. Machine learning techniques themselves can be

employed for drift detection, such as anomaly detection algorithms applied to prediction distributions or feature statistics.

Fourth,
**establishing an effective alerting and notification system** is vital to ensure that detected issues are promptly communicated to the relevant teams. Alerts should be actionable, providing sufficient context about the nature and severity of the problem. Integration with existing incident management systems (e.g., PagerDuty, Opsgenie) is often necessary. The alert should indicate *what* has drifted or degraded, *which* model or feature is affected, and *when* the issue was detected.

Fifth,
**implementing a robust rollback and retraining strategy** is essential for remediation. When drift or degradation is detected and confirmed, there must be a mechanism to quickly revert to a stable version of the model or to retrain and redeploy an updated model. This might involve automated rollback procedures triggered by critical alerts or a more deliberate process involving human review before retraining. The CI/CD pipelines discussed previously are instrumental in facilitating these remediation actions, ensuring that deploying a fix or a new model version is as automated and reliable as the initial deployment.

Finally, the monitoring process itself must be
**continuously reviewed and improved**. As the ML system evolves and business needs change, the monitoring strategy may need to be adapted. New features might be introduced, or the underlying data generation processes might shift, requiring adjustments to the drift detection algorithms or performance thresholds.

The transition from a one-off deployment to a continuously monitored ML system is a hallmark of mature MLOps practices. It acknowledges that ML models are not static software components but dynamic systems that require ongoing stewardship to remain effective and trustworthy. By embracing the imperative of continuous model monitoring, organizations can unlock the full, sustained value of their machine learning investments and ensure that their AI-powered systems continue to drive innovation and achieve desired outcomes reliably and responsibly. The insights gleaned from this monitoring not only help maintain existing models but also provide invaluable feedback for future model development, creating a virtuous cycle of improvement. Without this vigilance, the promise of AI can quickly turn into a liability, making continuous monitoring an indispensable pillar of any successful ML deployment strategy.

The preceding discussion has laid the groundwork for understanding why continuous monitoring of deployed machine learning models is not just a recommendation but a fundamental necessity for their sustained efficacy. We've explored the insidious nature of data and concept drift, the tangible consequences of ignoring these phenomena, and the essential components of a comprehensive monitoring framework. Now, we delve into a critical pillar of this framework: the direct and ongoing assessment of how well our models are actually performing in the wild. This is where we move beyond tracking the statistical properties of the data and begin to quantify the model's predictive power against reality.

At its heart, monitoring prediction performance is about answering a simple yet profound question: Is the model still doing what it was designed to do, and how well is it doing it? This involves a systematic and automated approach to measuring the model's output against actual outcomes, or reliable proxies for those outcomes. The key metrics used for this evaluation will naturally depend on the specific problem the model is intended to solve and the type of machine learning task it represents. For classification problems, this might include accuracy, precision, recall, F1-score, and the Area Under the Receiver Operating Characteristic Curve (AUC-ROC). For regression tasks, common metrics are Mean Squared Error (MSE), Root Mean Squared Error (RMSE), Mean Absolute Error (MAE), and R-squared. For more specialized applications like recommendation systems, metrics might involve Mean Average

Precision (MAP), Normalized Discounted Cumulative Gain (NDCG), or click-through rates.

The challenge in production environments is that obtaining the "ground truth" – the actual, definitive outcome that the model was trying to predict – can be a complex and often delayed process. In many scenarios, the ground truth is not immediately available. For instance, a model predicting customer churn might only have its predictions validated weeks or months later when a customer actually decides to leave. Similarly, a fraud detection model's accuracy can only be definitively assessed after a transaction has been thoroughly investigated, which can take time. This temporal gap between prediction and ground truth revelation is a significant hurdle that monitoring systems must be designed to overcome.

One of the primary strategies for dealing with this latency is to establish a robust feedback loop. This involves capturing the model's predictions alongside the input data and, as the ground truth becomes available, linking it back to the corresponding predictions. This can be achieved by augmenting the data pipelines that feed the model. When a new prediction is made, a record is created that includes the input features, the model's output (e.g., predicted class, probability score, regression value), a timestamp, and a unique identifier for the prediction. As ground truth data emerges – perhaps from manual review, downstream system confirmations, or user feedback – this data is collected and joined with the historical prediction records using the unique identifier or timestamps. This forms a valuable dataset of "prediction-outcome pairs" that can be used for retrospective performance analysis.

To make this process actionable, it's essential to define clear performance thresholds. These thresholds represent the minimum acceptable level of performance for the model. For example, a binary classification model might have a threshold for accuracy (e.g., 90%), precision (e.g., 85%), or recall (e.g., 92%). A regression model might have a threshold for RMSE (e.g., less than 10 units). These thresholds should not be arbitrary; they should be derived from the business objectives the model is intended to serve and the acceptable risk tolerance of the organization. A model that is critical for safety or compliance might require much stricter performance thresholds than a model used for exploratory analysis.

The process of calculating these performance metrics and comparing them against the defined thresholds should be automated. This typically involves scheduled jobs that run at regular intervals (e.g., daily, weekly, or even hourly, depending on the criticality and data velocity). These jobs would query the stored prediction-outcome pairs, compute the relevant performance metrics for the recent period, and then compare these calculated values against the established thresholds. If any metric falls below its designated threshold, an alert is triggered.

Consider a fraud detection system. The model predicts the probability of a transaction being fraudulent. The ground truth is obtained when a transaction is confirmed as either fraudulent or legitimate after investigation. The monitoring system would track metrics like:

**Precision:** Of all transactions flagged as fraudulent, what percentage were actually fraudulent? A drop in precision might indicate the model is issuing too many false positives, leading to customer annoyance and lost business due to unnecessary blocks.
**Recall (Sensitivity):** Of all actual fraudulent transactions, what percentage did the model correctly identify? A drop in recall means the model is missing more fraud, leading to financial losses.
**Accuracy:** The overall percentage of correct predictions (both fraudulent and legitimate). While seemingly straightforward, accuracy can be

misleading in imbalanced datasets, hence the importance of precision and recall.
**False Positive Rate:** The percentage of legitimate transactions incorrectly flagged as fraudulent.

The monitoring system would continuously calculate these metrics over a rolling window of recent transactions for which ground truth is available. If, for instance, the recall drops below a predefined acceptable level (e.g., 95%), signifying that the model is missing a significant number of actual fraud cases, an alert would be generated. This alert would ideally contain information about the specific metric that breached the threshold, the current value, the threshold value, the time period over which the degradation was observed, and potentially a link to a dashboard displaying the trend over time.

For regression models, such as a demand forecasting system, the metrics might include:

**RMSE:** The square root of the average of squared differences between predicted and actual demand. A rising RMSE indicates that the model's predictions are becoming less accurate.
**MAE:** The average of the absolute differences between predicted and actual demand. This metric is less sensitive to outliers than RMSE.
**MAPE (Mean Absolute Percentage Error):** The average of absolute percentage errors. This provides a relative measure of error and is useful for comparing performance across products with different demand scales.

A drop in performance, say an increasing RMSE beyond the acceptable limit, would trigger an alert. This could happen, for example, if a new competitor enters the market, drastically changing purchasing patterns in ways the original model did not anticipate. The monitoring system would detect this increased error and notify the relevant teams, prompting an investigation into whether retraining or feature engineering is necessary.

Crucially, these performance metrics should not just be viewed in isolation or at a single point in time. Visualizing these metrics over time is paramount. This is where automated dashboards become indispensable tools. These dashboards, powered by the same data pipelines that feed the monitoring jobs, can display trends of accuracy, precision, recall, RMSE, and other relevant metrics over days, weeks, and months. Visualizing these trends allows for the identification of gradual degradation that might not immediately breach a strict threshold but indicates a slow decline in performance. It also helps in correlating performance drops with external events or changes in the system. For example, a sudden dip in recommendation quality might coincide with a website redesign or a change in marketing strategy.

The design of these dashboards should prioritize clarity and immediate insight. Key performance indicators (KPIs) should be prominently displayed, often with color-coding to indicate status (e.g., green for within thresholds, yellow for approaching thresholds, red for breached thresholds). Historical trends should be easily accessible, allowing users to zoom in on specific periods or compare performance before and after a model update. Drill-down capabilities are also beneficial, enabling analysts to investigate the root cause of performance issues by examining specific segments of data or particular types of errors.

Beyond direct performance metrics, it's also valuable to monitor proxy metrics that can often serve as early indicators of performance degradation, especially when ground truth is significantly delayed or unavailable. These proxy metrics can include:

**Prediction Distribution:** Changes in the distribution of the model's output scores. For example, if a classification model's confidence scores (e.g., probabilities) suddenly become much lower across the board, it might suggest the model is becoming less certain about its predictions, which can often precede a drop in accuracy. Conversely, a sudden shift in the distribution of predicted values might also be a warning sign.
**Model Confidence Scores:** Tracking the average confidence score or the distribution of confidence scores for predictions. A general decline in confidence can be a precursor to concept drift.
**Outlier Predictions:** Monitoring the frequency of predictions that are significantly different from the typical predictions or that lie at the extreme ends of the prediction range. An increase in such extreme predictions might signal that the model is encountering data far outside its training distribution.
**User Feedback:** For systems with direct user interaction, metrics like user engagement, satisfaction ratings, or explicit feedback mechanisms (e.g., "thumbs up/down" on recommendations) can serve as vital, albeit subjective, performance indicators. A decline in positive user feedback can be an early warning that the model's output is no longer meeting user expectations.
**Downstream System Performance:** If the model's output is used by other systems, monitoring the performance of those downstream systems can sometimes reveal issues caused by the upstream model. For example, if a fraud detection model starts issuing more false positives, the customer service system that handles disputes might see an increase in inquiry volume and handling time.

Implementing a robust system for monitoring prediction performance and accuracy requires a thoughtful combination of automated processes, well-defined metrics, clear thresholds, insightful visualizations, and proactive alerting. It's an ongoing commitment that ensures the machine learning models deployed in production remain valuable assets, rather than silently deteriorating liabilities. By continuously measuring and reacting to actual model performance, organizations can maintain the integrity of their AI-driven operations, safeguard against costly errors, and ensure that their investments in machine learning continue to yield the intended benefits. This vigilance is not just about fixing problems; it's about understanding the dynamic relationship between our models and the ever-changing real world they are designed to serve.

The transition from a meticulously trained machine learning model to its deployment in a live, dynamic environment marks a crucial inflection point. While our previous discussions have emphasized the importance of monitoring model performance against ground truth and leveraging proxy metrics, a fundamental precursor to performance degradation often lies in changes to the very data the model consumes. This is the realm of *data drift*, a phenomenon where the statistical distribution of input features observed during inference deviates significantly from the distribution seen during model training. When such a divergence occurs, the model's ability to make accurate predictions can be severely compromised, even if the underlying relationships it learned remain theoretically valid. It's akin to asking a skilled chef to cook a meal using ingredients they've never encountered before; their technique might be perfect, but the outcome will likely be suboptimal.

Understanding and detecting data drift is therefore a cornerstone of proactive model monitoring. Unlike concept drift, which implies a change in the relationship between features and the target variable, data drift focuses solely on the characteristics of the input data itself. This means that even if the world's underlying logic hasn't changed, if the *way* we observe that world through our data does, our model can falter. Consider a model trained to predict housing prices using features like square footage, number of bedrooms, and average neighborhood income. If, over time, new luxury developments lead to a significant increase in the average square footage of homes on the market, or a major economic shift drastically alters average neighborhood incomes, the model will be exposed to feature values it hasn't seen much of, or at all, during training.

This misalignment between training and inference data distributions can lead to extrapolations that are unreliable and inaccurate.

The detection of data drift is primarily an exercise in statistical comparison. The core idea is to quantify the difference between the distribution of an input feature in a reference dataset (typically the training data or a representative sample of recent production data that exhibits good performance) and its distribution in the current inference data. A variety of statistical methods and metrics can be employed for this purpose, each offering a different lens through which to view distributional changes.

One of the most direct approaches is to compare the empirical cumulative distribution functions (ECDFs) of a feature. The Kolmogorov-Smirnov (K-S) test is a non-parametric statistical test that can be used to compare two samples to determine if they come from the same distribution. When applied to data drift detection, we compare the distribution of a feature from the training data against its distribution from recent inference data. The K-S test calculates the maximum absolute difference between the two ECDFs. A larger difference suggests a greater divergence between the two distributions. The test yields a p-value, which can be used to determine if the observed difference is statistically significant, indicating that the two samples likely originate from different distributions. This test is particularly useful for continuous numerical features.

However, the K-S test has limitations. It is generally more sensitive to differences in the location and scale of distributions rather than changes in their shape. For categorical features, or when we want to capture more nuanced distributional shifts, other measures become more appropriate. One such class of measures involves calculating divergence or distance metrics between probability distributions.

Kullback-Leibler (KL) divergence, often denoted as $D(P \| Q)$, is a measure of how one probability distribution P diverges from a second expected probability distribution Q. In the context of data drift, P would represent the distribution of a feature in the current production data, and Q would represent its distribution in the reference (training) data. A KL divergence of zero means the distributions are identical, while higher values indicate greater divergence. A significant challenge with KL divergence is that it is not symmetric ($D(P \| Q) \neq D(Q \| P)$) and is undefined if P assigns a non-zero probability to an event that Q assigns zero probability to. This latter point makes it sensitive to features that may appear in production data but were absent in training data.

A related and often more practical measure is Jensen-Shannon (JS) divergence. JS divergence is a symmetric and smoothed version of KL divergence. It is defined using the KL divergence as: $JS(P \| Q) = 0.5$ *D(P || M) + 0.5* $D(Q \| M)$, where $M = 0.5 (P + Q)$ is the average of the two distributions. JS divergence is always finite and bounded between 0 and 1 (or 0 and log 2, depending on the base of the logarithm used in KL divergence). A JS divergence of 0 indicates identical distributions, while a value of 1 (or log 2) indicates maximum divergence. This symmetry and boundedness make it a robust choice for comparing feature distributions.

Another powerful metric for assessing distributional differences is the Population Stability Index (PSI). PSI is widely used in credit risk modeling and is highly effective for detecting shifts in distributions of both continuous and categorical variables. For a given feature, PSI is calculated by comparing the proportion of data falling into specific bins or categories between a reference population (e.g., training data) and a comparison population (e.g., recent inference data). The formula for PSI is:

$PSI = \sum

{i=1}^{n} (Actual\%i - Expected\%i) \times \ln(\frac{Actual\%i}{Expected\%_i})$

where:

$n$ is the number of bins or categories.
$Actual\%_i$ is the percentage of data in the comparison population that falls into bin $i$.
$Expected\%_i$ is the percentage of data in the reference population that falls into bin $i$.

The interpretation of PSI values is generally as follows:

PSI < 0.1: Little to no significant shift.
0.1 ≤ PSI < 0.2: Moderate shift.
PSI ≥ 0.2: Significant shift.

When calculating PSI for continuous features, it is crucial to discretize the feature into a set of bins. The choice of the number of bins and the bin edges can influence the PSI value, so consistency in binning across comparisons is essential. For categorical features, each category can be treated as a bin. PSI is particularly appealing because it provides a single, interpretable number that quantifies the overall shift in distribution. It is also sensitive to both the magnitude and direction of shifts, and it penalizes bins with zero expected percentage more heavily.

When implementing these drift detection methods, it is imperative to establish clear thresholds for what constitutes a "significant" drift. These thresholds should not be universally fixed but rather tailored to the specific feature, the model's criticality, and the business context. For instance, a small shift in a feature that has a weak impact on the model's predictions might be inconsequential. Conversely, a moderate shift in a highly influential feature could be a serious warning sign. Typical thresholds for PSI, as mentioned, are often around 0.1 for moderate drift and 0.2 for significant drift. For K-S tests, thresholds are typically derived from the chosen significance level (alpha), leading to a critical value for the test statistic.

Beyond statistical tests and divergence measures, simpler, more heuristic approaches can also be valuable, especially for initial monitoring or as complementary checks. These might include tracking summary statistics for each feature: mean, median, variance, quantiles, number of unique values, and percentage of missing values. A sudden spike or drop in the mean or median, a dramatic change in variance, or an increase in the proportion of missing data for a particular feature can all be indicators of underlying data drift. For example, if a feature that typically has a mean of 50 and a standard deviation of 10 suddenly exhibits a mean of 80 and a standard deviation of 5, it's a strong signal that the data distribution has shifted.

When monitoring begins, the "reference" distribution is often established from the model's training data. However, as models operate in production for extended periods, the training data might become increasingly stale. It is often beneficial to periodically update the reference distribution. This can be done by selecting a recent period of production data that is known to have good model performance and using that as the new baseline. This adaptive reference window ensures that the drift detection is sensitive to changes relative to the most recent stable operating conditions, rather than being perpetually anchored to potentially outdated training data.

The process of detecting data drift is typically automated and integrated into the model monitoring pipeline. This involves:

1. **Feature Selection:** Identifying which input features warrant drift monitoring. It's not always necessary or cost-effective to monitor every single feature. Focus on features that are known to be important for model prediction (e.g., high feature importance in tree-based models, significant coefficients in linear models) or features that are expected to be volatile due to external factors.
2. **Data Collection:** Regularly sampling inference data and the corresponding reference data. This often involves logging all input features for predictions made within a specific time window (e.g., last 24 hours, last week).
3. **Distribution Comparison:** Applying the chosen statistical tests or divergence measures to compare the distributions of selected features between the current inference data and the reference data.
4. **Thresholding and Alerting:** Evaluating the test statistics or divergence scores against predefined thresholds. If a threshold is breached for a critical feature, an alert is triggered, signaling a potential issue.
5. **Visualization:** Presenting the drift metrics and trends over time through dashboards. This allows for visual inspection of degradation patterns and helps in understanding the severity and progression of the drift.

For instance, imagine a model that predicts customer lifetime value (CLV) based on customer demographics, purchase history, and engagement metrics. A key feature might be "average monthly spend." If the reference distribution shows an average monthly spend of $100 with a standard deviation of $30, but recent inference data reveals an average spend of $150 with a standard deviation of $20, this indicates a significant upward shift. This drift could be due to a successful marketing campaign that attracted higher-spending customers, or perhaps a change in pricing that has led all customers to spend more. Regardless of the cause, this drift in average spend might impact the model's ability to accurately predict CLV for both existing and new customer segments.

Similarly, consider a natural language processing (NLP) model deployed for sentiment analysis of product reviews. If the model was trained on data from a specific region or time period, and is now being used to analyze reviews from a different region that uses distinct slang or has a different cultural context for expressing sentiment, data drift in the word embeddings or feature representations could occur. A sudden increase in the frequency of certain keywords or phrases, or a change in their semantic meaning as perceived by the model, would constitute data drift. This might manifest as a drop in the accuracy of sentiment classification. Monitoring the distribution of word frequencies, n-gram occurrences, or even embeddings themselves for key terms would be crucial.

The choice of statistical test or metric often depends on the nature of the feature. For ordinal or interval features, K-S tests, PSI, and JS divergence are effective. For nominal features, PSI calculated on category proportions or chi-squared tests of independence (though less common for direct drift detection and more for association) are appropriate. It's also good practice to monitor for changes in missing value rates. An unexpected surge in missing values for a specific feature could indicate a problem with data ingestion or upstream data sources, which will inevitably affect model predictions.

It is vital to remember that detecting data drift is not an end in itself. It is a signal. The ultimate goal is to ensure the continued accuracy and reliability of the deployed model. Therefore, the alerts generated by data drift detection systems should trigger an investigation. This investigation might involve:

**Root Cause Analysis:** Determining why the drift is occurring. Is it a change in user behavior, a new product launch, seasonality, a change in data collection mechanisms, or an issue with data pipelines?

**Impact Assessment:** Quantifying how the detected drift is affecting model performance. This is where correlating drift metrics with performance metrics becomes critical. A significant PSI value for a feature might be acceptable if model performance remains high, but if it coincides with a drop in accuracy, it demands immediate attention.
**Remediation:** Deciding on the appropriate course of action. This could range from simply acknowledging the drift if its impact is negligible, to triggering a model retraining process, or even updating the feature engineering or data collection pipelines if the root cause lies there.

The concept of "model retraining" is intimately linked with data drift. When significant data drift is detected, it often implies that the model is operating on data that is substantially different from what it was trained on. In such cases, the model's learned patterns may no longer be as relevant or accurate. Retraining the model on a more recent, representative dataset that includes the observed drift is a common strategy to re-align the model with the current data distribution and, hopefully, restore its predictive performance. The frequency of retraining can be driven by a combination of scheduled intervals and triggered events, such as significant data drift alerts.

In summary, detecting input feature distribution changes – data drift – is a proactive measure essential for maintaining the health of deployed machine learning models. By employing statistical tests like the Kolmogorov-Smirnov test, divergence measures such as Jensen-Shannon divergence, and specialized metrics like the Population Stability Index, we can quantify deviations in feature distributions between training and inference data. Establishing clear, context-aware thresholds for these metrics allows for automated alerting when significant shifts occur. This detection mechanism serves as an early warning system, signaling the potential need for model retraining or other interventions, thus ensuring that models continue to perform optimally in the ever-evolving landscape of real-world data. The continuous, vigilant monitoring of feature distributions is a non-negotiable aspect of responsible and effective MLOps.

The previously discussed data drift centers on shifts in the statistical properties of the input features themselves. However, a more insidious, and often more impactful, form of drift is *concept drift*. Concept drift signifies a change not in the data the model sees, but in the fundamental relationship between that data and the outcome the model is trying to predict. It means the underlying rules or patterns that govern the target variable, based on the input features, have evolved. Imagine a model trained to predict loan default risk. If economic conditions change, leading to a different set of factors influencing a borrower's ability to repay, even if the applicant's profile (features) remains the same, their default risk might change. This is concept drift.

Detecting concept drift is inherently more challenging than detecting data drift because it often requires observing the consequences of the drift rather than directly measuring the changing inputs. We don't have a "ground truth" of the relationship to directly compare against. Instead, we typically infer concept drift by observing a degradation in the model's predictive performance over time, or by noticing anomalies in its prediction behavior. When the statistical distributions of input features might remain stable (data drift is minimal or absent), but the model's accuracy starts to fall, it's a strong indicator that the concept the model learned during training is no longer a faithful representation of reality.

One of the most straightforward, albeit indirect, methods for detecting concept drift is through the continuous monitoring of model performance metrics against actual observed outcomes (ground truth), as discussed in previous chapters. If a model that was once performing at 95% accuracy begins to consistently deliver predictions with only 80% accuracy, and this decline is sustained, it strongly suggests that the underlying relationship between features and the target has shifted. This requires having access to timely and accurate ground truth data, which is not always available in real-time for all applications. For instance, in a spam detection model, if the proportion of falsely identified legitimate emails (false positives) starts to increase significantly, it implies that what constitutes "spam" has changed in ways the model hasn't adapted to. The characteristics of legitimate emails might have evolved, or spammers might have developed new tactics that the model no longer recognizes as non-spam.

However, relying solely on aggregated performance metrics can sometimes mask the subtle onset of concept drift. A global performance drop might be the result of a sudden, severe concept drift event, or it could be a gradual erosion of accuracy. Furthermore, in scenarios where ground truth is delayed or scarce, these metrics might not be available for timely detection. This necessitates exploring more direct or sensitive indicators of concept drift.

Analyzing model residuals—the difference between the predicted value and the actual observed value—can offer deeper insights. If concept drift is occurring, the residuals are likely to exhibit a systematic pattern over time. For example, in a regression task, if the model consistently underpredicts for a specific range of input values after a period of accurate predictions, it suggests that the relationship for those values has changed, leading to an upward shift in the true outcome. Visualizing the distribution of residuals, or plotting residuals against time or key input features, can help reveal such systematic deviations. If the residuals, which were once seemingly random, start showing a discernible trend (e.g., always positive for a particular segment of data), it signals a breakdown in the model's assumptions about the relationship between inputs and outputs.

Specialized drift detection algorithms are designed to explicitly monitor a model's predictive power or internal state for signs of concept drift, often without direct reliance on ground truth in all cases. These algorithms can be broadly categorized into those that monitor model performance (often using proxy metrics or statistical tests on predictions) and those that directly monitor changes in the model's internal representation or decision boundaries.

One common approach in this category involves using statistical tests on the model's predictions. For instance, if we assume that the model's predictions should be independent of time (or some other ordering), we could perform time-series analysis on the sequence of predictions. A sudden change in the statistical properties of these predictions, such as a shift in their mean, variance, or autocorrelation, could indicate concept drift. More sophisticated methods often involve dividing the incoming data stream into segments (e.g., fixed-size windows or adaptive windows) and comparing the statistical properties of predictions made on consecutive segments. If the distributions of predictions on these segments diverge significantly, it suggests a change in the underlying concept. For example, a binary classification model that predicts a stable probability of around 0.5 for a certain class of inputs might suddenly start predicting probabilities consistently above 0.7, indicating that the concept of belonging to that class has shifted.

Another class of techniques involves analyzing the error rate of the model. Algorithms like the Drift Detection Method (DDM) and the Early Drift Detection Method (EDDM) are prominent examples. DDM works by monitoring the probability of error. It tracks the error rate and its standard deviation. If the current error rate exceeds a certain threshold (e.g., a specific number of standard deviations above the minimum error rate observed), it signals potential drift. EDDM builds upon DDM by also monitoring the distance between errors. If errors become more frequent or closer together, it suggests a more rapid drift. These methods are particularly useful when ground truth is available, even with a delay, as they directly leverage the accuracy of the model's predictions. The core idea is that a drift in the underlying concept will inevitably lead to an increase in prediction errors. By statistically analyzing the behavior of these errors, we can detect the drift.

Consider a customer churn prediction model. The model might have been trained on data where churn was primarily driven by high prices and poor customer service. Over time, new competitors might emerge, making price less of a differentiator, and instead, the availability of new features or a smoother user experience becomes the dominant factor for churn. If the model continues to prioritize price as the main churn predictor, its accuracy will decrease. DDM and EDDM would detect this by observing an increasing rate of false negatives (customers predicted to stay but who actually churn) or false positives (customers predicted to churn but who stay), and this increase would cross a statistically defined threshold.

Beyond analyzing error rates, some methods aim to detect concept drift by monitoring the model's internal decision-making process or by comparing the current data with what the model has learned. For instance, if a model uses ensemble methods, changes in the weights or contributions of individual base learners can sometimes indicate drift. However, for many complex models like deep neural networks, introspection into internal states is often difficult.

A more direct approach involves actively probing the model or using auxiliary models. One technique is to train a "drift detector" model that tries to distinguish between data points from the current period and data points from a reference period. If the drift detector can accurately classify these periods, it indicates that the data distributions have changed in a way that affects the model's inputs or the target concept. Another variant is to use a separate model trained to predict the target variable based on the same features. If the performance of this new model deviates significantly from the original deployed model, and both models are evaluated on similar incoming data streams, it can point to concept drift affecting the original model.

Another important consideration is the temporal nature of concept drift. Concept drift is often not a sudden, instantaneous event but rather a gradual process. The relationship between features and the target may slowly evolve. This gradual drift can be harder to detect with methods that look for abrupt changes. Adaptive learning methods and online learning algorithms are designed to inherently handle concept drift by continuously updating the model as new data arrives. However, even with adaptive models, monitoring for
*changes in the rate of adaptation* or *significant shifts in model parameters* can serve as indicators of drift. If a model's parameters need to be updated more frequently or by larger magnitudes than usual, it suggests that the underlying concept is undergoing substantial change.

For classification tasks, concept drift can manifest as a change in class separability. The decision boundary that the model learned might no longer effectively separate the classes. Techniques that analyze the confidence of predictions can be helpful here. If the model's confidence in its predictions decreases across the board, or specifically for certain data segments, it's a strong signal that the underlying patterns have shifted, making the classification task harder. For example, a model that was highly confident in classifying images of cats and dogs might become less confident if the types of cat and dog images it encounters in production begin to include breeds or poses that were rare or absent in the training data, and the fundamental visual cues it learned to rely on are no longer as discriminative.

In supervised learning, especially for regression problems, analyzing the distribution of
*predictions* themselves can be a form of concept drift detection, particularly when ground truth is scarce. If the model's predictions for a population of inputs suddenly shift their mean or variance, it implies that the expected outcome for that population has changed. For instance, a model predicting house prices might consistently produce lower estimates than observed sales prices for a particular neighborhood after a period of significant, unforeseen economic development. This deviation in the expected outcome, without a corresponding drastic change in the input features (e.g., the size of houses remaining similar), points to concept drift. The underlying concept of "what determines a house price" in that neighborhood has evolved.

The choice of drift detection technique for concept drift depends heavily on the specific application, the availability of ground truth, the type of model, and the desired sensitivity. In many real-world systems, a combination of approaches is employed:

1. **Performance Monitoring:** Continuously track key performance metrics (accuracy, precision, recall, AUC, RMSE, etc.) against ground truth. Establish thresholds for performance degradation that trigger alerts.
2. **Residual Analysis:** Analyze the distribution and behavior of model residuals. Look for systematic biases or trends that emerge over time.
3. **Prediction Monitoring:** Track statistical properties of model predictions. Detect shifts in their distribution, especially if ground truth is unavailable or delayed. For classification, monitor the distribution of predicted probabilities.
4. **Error Rate Monitoring:** Employ algorithms like DDM or EDDM to statistically analyze the rate and pattern of prediction errors, directly signaling concept drift when error rates exceed predefined limits.

5. **Data Segmentation and Comparison:** Divide incoming data into time windows and compare predictions or model behavior across these windows. Statistical tests can quantify divergence.
6. **Model-Specific Indicators:** For certain model architectures, internal metrics or parameter changes might be monitored. For ensemble models, changes in base learner contributions could be an indicator.

When concept drift is detected, the process of remediation typically involves model retraining or updating. Since the fundamental relationship the model learned is no longer accurate, the model needs to be re-educated on current data that reflects the new reality. This retraining process needs to be informed by the nature of the drift. Was it a sudden shift that requires immediate retraining on the latest data? Or was it a gradual evolution that can be addressed by periodically retraining on aggregated recent data?

It is crucial to distinguish concept drift from data drift, as the remediation strategies can differ. If data drift is the primary issue, retraining on new data might suffice, assuming the relationships remain valid. However, if concept drift is present, simply retraining on new data might not be enough if the underlying relationships themselves are fundamentally flawed or if the feature engineering is no longer appropriate. In such cases, revisiting the model architecture, feature selection, and feature engineering processes might be necessary, in addition to retraining.

For instance, consider an e-commerce recommendation system. A data drift might occur if the popular product categories on the platform change (e.g., from electronics to apparel). However, a concept drift would occur if customer preferences for
*how* they discover new products change. Initially, customers might have responded well to recommendations based on "customers who bought this also bought that." But over time, with the rise of social media

influence, recommendations based on trending items or curated lists might become more effective. If the recommendation engine continues to rely solely on past purchase correlations, its effectiveness will wane, indicating concept drift in user preference dynamics. Detecting this might involve monitoring click-through rates on recommendations and observing a decline, or analyzing the diversity and novelty of recommended items that users actually engage with.

The challenge with concept drift is its often elusive nature. It's a change in the "rules of the game" that the model is playing. Unlike data drift, where we can directly measure how the "playing field" (input data) has changed, concept drift requires us to infer the rule change from the outcomes. This makes robust monitoring systems that combine performance tracking, prediction analysis, and specialized drift detection algorithms essential. The goal is to catch these shifts early, before they lead to significant business impact, and to enable timely intervention, whether that's through model retraining, re-engineering, or even a complete re-evaluation of the modeling approach. The continuous vigilance against both data and concept drift is paramount for maintaining the long-term utility and reliability of deployed machine learning systems in dynamic real-world environments.

An integral component of any robust machine learning operations (MLOps) pipeline, particularly those focused on maintaining the performance of deployed models, is a well-defined and responsive alerting system. This system acts as the proactive guardian of your model's integrity, transforming raw monitoring data into actionable insights. Without it, the continuous streams of metrics and drift indicators would merely be passive observations, failing to trigger the necessary interventions to preserve model effectiveness. The primary objective of such a system is to distill complex monitoring signals into clear, timely notifications that alert relevant stakeholders to potential issues, ranging from minor performance dips to significant model decay.

The design of an effective alerting system hinges on several key principles. Firstly,
**threshold definition** is paramount. This involves establishing specific, quantifiable thresholds for the metrics being monitored. These thresholds should not be arbitrary; they must be grounded in a deep understanding of the model's business context and acceptable performance envelopes. For instance, a fraud detection model might have a very low tolerance for false negatives (undetected fraudulent transactions), meaning the threshold for the false negative rate might be set extremely low. Conversely, a recommendation engine's acceptable performance might be gauged by click-through rates or conversion rates, with thresholds set to reflect a healthy engagement level. The thresholds can be static, based on historical best performance, or dynamic, adapting to seasonal trends or known operational patterns.

Secondly,
**alert granularity and routing** are critical for ensuring that the right people are notified about the right issues. An alert indicating a slight, transient increase in prediction latency might be routed to a junior engineer for investigation, while a sharp drop in model accuracy that could lead to significant financial losses would warrant immediate escalation to senior data scientists, product managers, and potentially even business unit leaders. This often involves creating different alert severities (e.g., informational, warning, critical) and mapping these severities to specific communication channels (e.g., email, Slack, PagerDuty) and recipient groups. The goal is to avoid alert fatigue by only raising alarms when necessary and ensuring that critical alerts are impossible to miss.

Thirdly,
**alert context and explainability** are vital for efficient remediation. An alert that simply states "Model Accuracy Dropped Below 80%" is far less useful than one that provides additional context: "Model Accuracy for

'Product Category X' Dropped to 78% (Threshold: 85%) in the last 12 hours. This deviation is correlated with an increase in data drift for feature 'User*Engagement*Score' and a recent update to the 'Seasonal_Trends' data feed. Potential impact: decreased relevance of recommendations for this category." This richer alert allows the recipient to quickly grasp the severity, scope, and potential causes of the issue, significantly accelerating the diagnosis and resolution process. Incorporating links to relevant dashboards, logs, or automated diagnostic reports within the alert itself can further enhance this explainability.

The implementation of these principles often involves leveraging specialized tools and platforms. For threshold-based alerting on metrics, systems like Prometheus, Grafana, or cloud-native monitoring services (e.g., Amazon CloudWatch, Google Cloud Monitoring, Azure Monitor) are commonly used. These platforms can scrape metrics from deployed models, store them, and trigger alerts based on predefined rules. For more complex drift detection algorithms that might not directly translate to a simple metric threshold, custom alerting logic needs to be built. This could involve running statistical tests on model predictions or residuals at regular intervals and triggering an alert if the p-value falls below a certain significance level or if a drift detection score exceeds a threshold.

Beyond simply notifying humans, a sophisticated alerting system can serve as a powerful catalyst for
**automated remediation**, particularly in the realm of model retraining and updating. The same signals that trigger human alerts—performance degradation, significant data drift, or detected concept drift—can also be used to automatically initiate a model refresh. This closes the loop in the MLOps lifecycle, transforming the system from a reactive monitoring mechanism into a proactive self-healing one.

The decision to automate retraining is a critical one and should be carefully considered. For models where performance decay is a consistent and predictable threat, and where retraining is a relatively low-risk, low-cost operation, full automation can be highly beneficial. For example, a model predicting daily stock prices might be retrained nightly on the latest market data. If monitoring detects a significant deviation in the day's trading patterns from historical norms, the retraining process could be automatically triggered to incorporate these new patterns. This ensures the model is always working with the most current information, minimizing the window of vulnerability to drift.

When considering automation, the granularity of the trigger is crucial. Instead of waiting for a critical performance drop, alerts triggered by statistically significant drift in input data distributions or a sustained increase in prediction errors (even if still within acceptable performance bounds) can initiate a "preemptive" retraining. This is particularly valuable for concept drift, which can be insidious. By retraining when early signs of concept drift appear, before they significantly impact the model's accuracy, the system can prevent a more substantial degradation in performance.

The process of automated retraining typically involves several steps. First, the alert or drift detection signal acts as a trigger for an orchestration tool (e.g., Kubeflow Pipelines, MLflow, Apache Airflow). This orchestrator then initiates a predefined pipeline. This pipeline will typically fetch the latest relevant data, which might include recent incoming data, newly labeled data, or a combination thereof. It then feeds this data into the model training process. The exact training procedure—whether it's a full retraining from scratch, a fine-tuning of existing weights, or an incremental update—depends on the model architecture and the nature of the drift.

For instance, if a supervised learning model detects a significant shift in the distribution of a key feature, the retraining pipeline might first involve re-evaluating and potentially re-engineering that feature before retraining the model. If concept drift is suspected, the pipeline might focus on incorporating newly labeled data that reflects the evolved relationship between features and the target variable. In some cases, especially with deep learning models, a simple fine-tuning step using recent data can be sufficient to adapt to minor concept drifts, while more substantial shifts might necessitate retraining the entire network.

Crucially, automated retraining should not be a "black box" operation. The same principles of context and explainability that apply to human-facing alerts should also guide automated processes. The orchestration tool should log detailed information about why a retraining was triggered, what data was used, the parameters of the training run, and the performance of the newly trained model. This information is vital for debugging any issues that arise with the retrained model and for auditing the MLOps process.

Furthermore, a robust system will include a mechanism for **validation and rollback** of automatically retrained models. Before a newly trained model is automatically deployed to production, it must undergo rigorous validation. This typically involves evaluating its performance on a hold-out validation set and comparing it against the current production model. If the new model performs significantly worse than the incumbent, or if it fails to meet predefined quality gates (e.g., minimum accuracy, maximum error rate), the automated deployment should be halted. In such scenarios, the alert that triggered the retraining should be escalated to human review, and the system should be configured to automatically roll back to the previous stable version of the model. This "human-in-the-loop" approach for critical deployments safeguards against potentially problematic automated updates.

The concept of "triggers" extends beyond just retraining. In some dynamic environments, the detection of drift or performance degradation might trigger other automated actions. For example, if a model's output is used to drive dynamic pricing, a significant drop in prediction accuracy might trigger a temporary reversion to a simpler, rule-based pricing strategy or a manual pricing review. If a recommendation system's effectiveness declines, it might trigger an automated A/B test to evaluate alternative recommendation algorithms or feature sets. This broader interpretation of "retraining triggers" encompasses any automated action designed to mitigate the impact of model drift or performance issues.

The decision on what constitutes a sufficient trigger for automated retraining is often an empirical one, informed by the model's criticality, the cost of retraining, and the potential business impact of degraded performance. For a mission-critical system where even minor accuracy drops can have severe financial consequences, a lower threshold for triggering retraining is warranted. For less critical systems, a higher threshold might be acceptable to avoid the overhead and potential risks of frequent automated updates.

Moreover, the timing of retraining is an important consideration. If drift is detected in real-time, an immediate retraining might be initiated. However, for many applications, especially those dealing with large datasets or complex training procedures, retraining can take hours or even days. In such cases, the trigger might queue up a retraining job to be executed during off-peak hours or when sufficient computational resources become available. The alerting system should also inform stakeholders about the status of these automated processes, providing visibility into when a retraining was initiated, its progress, and its eventual outcome.

Consider the case of a natural language processing (NLP) model used for sentiment analysis in customer reviews. Over time, language evolves. New slang, idioms, or shifts in the way customers express positive or negative sentiment can render a previously accurate model obsolete. A data drift alert might detect a change in the frequency of certain words or phrases. However, concept drift might manifest as the model misinterpreting the sentiment of reviews that use new phrasing. An effective alerting system would monitor not only the statistical properties of the input text but also the distribution of sentiment scores. If a statistically significant shift in the average sentiment score for a particular product category is observed, or if the model's confidence in its sentiment predictions drops, this could trigger a retraining pipeline. This pipeline would incorporate recently labeled customer reviews, allowing the model to learn the new linguistic patterns and re-establish accurate sentiment classification. The automated retraining would ensure that the product team receives up-to-date insights into customer satisfaction, preventing misguided business decisions based on stale sentiment analysis.

Similarly, in a computer vision system used for quality control on a manufacturing line, a subtle change in the material composition of a product, or a new type of defect, could lead to concept drift. Initially, the model might be excellent at identifying known defects. However, if a new manufacturing process introduces subtle visual variations that the model was not trained on, its ability to correctly classify products as "good" or "defective" will degrade. An alerting system monitoring the model's precision and recall on a sample of newly produced items would flag any significant performance drop. This alert could then automatically trigger a retraining process using images of the newly produced items, potentially incorporating new defect categories if they can be identified and labeled. This ensures that the quality control system remains effective, preventing defective products from reaching customers and minimizing production waste.

In summary, a robust alerting system is not merely a passive monitor; it is an active orchestrator of model health. By defining clear thresholds, routing alerts effectively, providing contextual information, and intelligently triggering automated remediation processes like retraining and rollback, it forms the backbone of a resilient MLOps strategy. These automated triggers transform the reactive process of monitoring into a proactive loop of continuous improvement, ensuring that deployed models remain accurate, reliable, and valuable assets throughout their lifecycle in ever-changing production environments.

## Chapter 13: Case Study: Structural Health Monitoring System

The integrity and longevity of our built environment—the bridges that connect communities, the buildings that house our lives, and the dams that manage our water resources—are foundational to modern society. However, these massive structures are not immutable. They are subjected to relentless environmental stressors, dynamic operational loads, and the relentless march of time, all of which can contribute to degradation and potential failure. Recognizing this inherent vulnerability, the field of Structural Health Monitoring (SHM) has emerged as a critical discipline, employing advanced sensing, data acquisition, and analytical techniques to continuously assess the condition of civil infrastructure. The overarching goal of SHM is to transition from traditional, often reactive, maintenance strategies to a proactive, data-informed approach that ensures public safety, optimizes resource allocation for repairs, and extends the service life of these vital assets.

The imperative for SHM is underscored by the significant consequences of structural failure. Catastrophic events, such as bridge collapses or dam breaches, not only result in tragic loss of life but also inflict immense economic damage, disrupt essential services, and can have profound environmental impacts. Historically, infrastructure maintenance has relied on scheduled inspections, often visual, supplemented by periodic, intrusive testing. While valuable, these methods can be labor-intensive, costly, and may fail to detect subtle, developing damage that could progress to a critical state between inspection intervals. Furthermore, they often provide only a snapshot of the structure's condition at a specific point in time, offering limited insight into its real-time behavior or the cumulative effects of its operational history. This is where the principles of SHM offer a transformative paradigm shift. By embedding sensors directly into or onto the structure, SHM systems can capture a continuous or semi-continuous stream of data reflecting the structure's response to various stimuli. This data can then be analyzed to detect anomalies, diagnose potential damage, and predict future performance, enabling timely interventions before minor issues escalate into major problems.

The fundamental concept of SHM involves establishing a baseline of healthy structural behavior and then continuously comparing current operational data against this baseline. Deviations from the norm can indicate the presence of damage, such as cracks, corrosion, delamination, or material fatigue. However, SHM is far more than just damage detection. A comprehensive SHM system can provide a wealth of information, including:

**Operational Load Monitoring:** Understanding the actual forces and stresses a structure experiences during its service life (e.g., traffic loads on a bridge, wind loads on a building). This is crucial because design assumptions might differ significantly from real-world usage.
**Environmental Condition Sensing:** Monitoring factors like temperature, humidity, wind speed, seismic activity, and exposure to de-icing salts or corrosive agents, which all influence material degradation.
**Damage Detection and Localization:** Identifying whether damage exists, its type, and its approximate location within the structure.
**Damage Assessment and Prognosis:** Quantifying the severity of detected damage and predicting how it might evolve over time, including estimating the remaining useful life of the structure or its components.
**Performance Evaluation:** Assessing whether the structure is performing as intended and meeting its design specifications under current conditions.

The unique data characteristics inherent in SHM applications present distinct challenges and opportunities for data engineering and machine learning. Unlike many other domains, SHM data is often characterized by:

**High Volume and Velocity:** Modern SHM systems can deploy hundreds or even thousands of sensors, generating vast amounts of data continuously. This requires robust data acquisition, transmission, and storage infrastructure.

**Multi-Modal and Heterogeneous Data:** Data can come from a variety of sensor types, including strain gauges, accelerometers, displacement sensors, crack meters, acoustic emission sensors, fiber optic sensors, and even visual cameras. These sensors measure different physical phenomena, often at different sampling rates, leading to a complex and heterogeneous data landscape.

**Spatio-Temporal Correlation:** The behavior of a structure is inherently linked to its physical location and the sequence of events. Damage at one point can influence behavior at another, and the history of loading and environmental exposure is critical for understanding current conditions. This necessitates sophisticated analysis techniques that can account for both spatial dependencies and temporal evolution.

**Environmental Noise and Operational Variability:** SHM data is often contaminated by environmental noise (e.g., wind-induced vibrations on a bridge that are not indicative of damage) and operational variability (e.g., variations in traffic patterns). Distinguishing between true damage indicators and these extraneous factors is a significant analytical challenge.

**Limited Labeled Data for Damage:** While data from a healthy structure might be abundant, obtaining sufficient labeled data representing various types and severities of damage can be difficult and expensive. This is often because significant damage is rare by design, and deliberately inducing it for data collection purposes is impractical or unethical. This scarcity poses challenges for supervised machine learning approaches.

**Uncertainty and Imprecision:** Sensor readings inherently contain some level of uncertainty and imprecision. Furthermore, the relationship between sensor readings and structural damage is often complex and not perfectly understood, introducing further uncertainty into the analysis.

**Long-Term Monitoring Requirements:** SHM systems are designed for long-term operation, potentially spanning decades. This requires data management strategies that can handle historical data effectively, accommodate evolving sensor technologies, and maintain data integrity over extended periods.

Addressing these unique data characteristics is precisely where the methodologies and tools discussed in this book find their application. The challenges of high-volume, multi-modal data, coupled with the need to detect subtle anomalies in the presence of noise and variability, call for advanced data processing pipelines, robust feature engineering, and sophisticated machine learning models capable of learning complex spatio-temporal patterns. The scarcity of labeled damage data also pushes towards unsupervised learning techniques, anomaly detection algorithms, and transfer learning approaches that can leverage data from healthy states to infer potential issues.

The practical implementation of an SHM system typically involves several interconnected components. At the forefront are the **sensors**, strategically placed to capture relevant physical responses. These sensors are connected to data acquisition units (DAUs), which digitize the analog sensor signals and perform initial signal conditioning. The digitized data is then transmitted, often wirelessly or through wired networks, to a central data repository. This repository serves as the storage hub for raw and processed SHM data, requiring careful design to handle the volume, variety, and velocity of incoming information. Following data ingestion, **data processing and feature engineering** pipelines are crucial. This stage involves cleaning the data, filtering out noise, synchronizing data from different sensors, and extracting meaningful features that can characterize the structural state. These features might include statistical measures (e.g., mean, variance, RMS values), frequency domain characteristics (e.g., power spectral densities), or more advanced indicators derived from signal processing techniques.

The core of the SHM system lies in the **analytical engine**, where machine learning models are deployed to interpret the processed data. This engine is responsible for establishing baselines, detecting deviations, identifying potential damage, and ultimately providing actionable insights. As highlighted in previous sections, the development and deployment of these analytical models require robust MLOps practices, including version control, automated testing, and continuous monitoring. The outputs from the analytical engine—alerts, condition assessments, or damage predictions—are then communicated to stakeholders, such as structural engineers, maintenance managers, and regulatory bodies, through **reporting and visualization** tools. These tools often include dashboards that provide real-time overviews of the structure's health, historical trend analysis, and detailed reports on detected anomalies or identified risks. Finally, the entire system is underpinned by a framework for **system management and maintenance**, ensuring the reliability and operational readiness of sensors, data acquisition hardware, communication networks, and software components.

The transition from traditional inspection methods to data-driven SHM represents a significant leap forward in how we manage and preserve our critical infrastructure. It moves us from a reactive stance, often only addressing problems after they become visible or critical, to a proactive and predictive approach. This shift not only enhances safety by identifying potential threats early but also leads to more efficient and cost-effective maintenance strategies. By understanding the true condition of a structure in real-time, resources can be precisely allocated to address the most pressing issues, preventing unnecessary over-maintenance and avoiding the catastrophic costs associated with unexpected failures. The ability to monitor structures continuously allows for a deeper understanding of their behavior under various operating conditions, leading to better design practices for future infrastructure and more informed decisions about the lifecycle management of existing assets. As we delve deeper into the case study, the practical application of these SHM principles, and the specific data engineering and machine learning challenges involved, will become increasingly evident.

The efficacy of any Structural Health Monitoring (SHM) system is intrinsically tied to the quality, nature, and comprehensive understanding of the data it collects. For the specific case study we are examining, the primary data source revolves around vibration measurements, predominantly captured by accelerometers strategically deployed across the structure. These accelerometers are electromechanical transducers that measure acceleration, which in turn provides crucial insights into the dynamic response of the structure when subjected to various external forces. These forces can range from the mundane, like ambient traffic or wind gusts, to the more significant, such as seismic events or extreme weather conditions.

The data generated by these accelerometers is fundamentally time-series data. This means that each data point is associated with a specific timestamp, creating a sequential record of the structure's vibrational behavior over time. The nature of this time-series data is characterized by several key attributes that profoundly influence how it must be processed, analyzed, and ultimately used to infer the health of the structure. One of the most prominent characteristics is the high sampling rate. To accurately capture the dynamic responses of a structure, especially at higher frequencies, accelerometers are typically configured to record data at very high frequencies. This can range from tens of Hertz (Hz) to several kilohertz (kHz), depending on the expected dynamic characteristics of the structure and the phenomena being monitored. For instance, monitoring for the onset of brittle fracture or the propagation of fatigue cracks might necessitate sampling rates that can resolve very rapid oscillations, while monitoring for more gradual changes due to thermal expansion or slow crack growth might tolerate lower sampling frequencies. The consequence of these high sampling rates is a rapid accumulation of data. A network of even a modest number of accelerometers, each sampling at 1 kHz for 24 hours a day, can generate gigabytes of data daily. This necessitates robust data acquisition hardware, efficient data transmission protocols, and scalable data storage solutions. Simply put, the sheer volume of data generated by high-fidelity vibration monitoring poses a significant data engineering challenge from the outset.

Another critical characteristic of accelerometer data is its inherent susceptibility to noise. This noise can originate from a multitude of sources, both internal and external to the sensing system. Internal noise can arise from the electronic components of the accelerometer itself, digitization errors within the data acquisition unit, or electromagnetic interference affecting the signal transmission. External noise, which is often more pervasive and challenging to mitigate, stems from various environmental and operational factors. Ambient vibrations from sources like nearby traffic, construction activities, or even human footfall can introduce spurious signals that obscure the true structural response. Wind is a particularly significant source of noise for many civil structures, inducing vibrations that can be complex and highly variable. Similarly, operational loads, such as the passage of vehicles on a bridge, can introduce transient vibrations that are distinct from the structural degradation we aim to detect. The challenge for SHM practitioners is to distinguish between the subtle changes in vibrational patterns that signify structural damage and the transient, environmentally induced vibrations that are a normal part of the structure's operational life. This often requires sophisticated signal processing techniques, such as filtering, spectral analysis, and advanced noise reduction algorithms, to isolate the structural response of interest.

Furthermore, accelerometer data is often characterized by the presence of transient events. These are short-duration, high-amplitude signals that deviate significantly from the baseline ambient vibration levels. Examples include the impact of a heavy vehicle crossing a bridge, the sudden gust of wind, or even minor seismic tremors. While these events can provide valuable information about the structure's response under dynamic loading, they can also pose challenges for data analysis. If not handled appropriately, these transient spikes can skew statistical measures, saturate data buffers, or trigger false alarms if detection algorithms are not robust enough. Conversely, specific types of damage, such as the formation or propagation of a crack, might manifest as specific transient phenomena or subtle changes in the way the structure responds to these external events. For instance, the impact of a load on a cracked beam might produce a different acoustic signature or a different damping characteristic compared to an intact beam. Therefore, understanding and effectively processing these transient events, rather than simply discarding them as noise, is crucial for accurate structural health assessment.

The characteristics of vibration data also extend to its spatial and temporal correlations. Accelerometers are typically deployed in a spatially distributed manner across a structure to capture its global and local vibrational modes. The response measured at one accelerometer is not independent of the responses at other locations. This spatial correlation is fundamental to understanding the vibration modes of a structure – how it deforms and oscillates in specific patterns at certain frequencies. For example, the first bending mode of a bridge will exhibit characteristic patterns of displacement across its deck, and the accelerometers located there will reflect this. Damage, such as a crack or a change in stiffness, can alter these modes, leading to shifts in natural frequencies, changes in mode shapes, and variations in damping ratios. Analyzing these spatio-temporal correlations allows engineers to not only detect the presence of damage but also to localize it within the structure. The temporal aspect refers to the evolution of these patterns over time. A healthy structure will exhibit a relatively stable set of modal parameters under similar environmental and operational conditions. As damage accumulates, these parameters will gradually change. Monitoring these changes over extended periods is key to prognostication and understanding the rate of degradation.

The inherent variability of operational and environmental conditions further complicates the analysis of vibration data. A bridge, for instance, will experience different traffic loads depending on the time of day, day of the week, and even the season. Wind conditions can vary dramatically, from a gentle breeze to a gale. Temperature fluctuations can cause expansion and contraction of structural materials, affecting stiffness and vibration characteristics. These variations mean that a "normal" vibration signature is not a single, fixed pattern but rather a range of acceptable behaviors under different conditions. SHM systems must be designed to account for this variability. This can involve collecting data under a wide range of conditions to build a comprehensive understanding of normal behavior, or developing algorithms that can normalize or adapt to these external influences. For example, an algorithm might learn to differentiate between a change in a natural frequency caused by damage and a temporary change caused by a significant temperature increase. This is where machine learning techniques that can model complex, non-linear relationships and account for confounding factors become particularly valuable.

The "baseline" against which current structural behavior is compared is also a critical concept. Ideally, this baseline is established when the structure is in a known pristine or healthy condition. However, in practice, establishing a perfect baseline can be challenging. Structures may already have minor, unrecorded damage from their construction or early service life. Furthermore, the act of installing sensors and data acquisition systems can itself introduce minor perturbations. Therefore, SHM systems often rely on a "moving baseline" or a statistical representation of healthy behavior that accounts for inherent variability.

The data from healthy operational periods is used to define the expected range of responses, and deviations outside this range are flagged as potential anomalies. The robustness of this baseline and the sensitivity of the deviation detection algorithms are critical determinants of the SHM system's performance.

The physical characteristics of the sensors themselves also play a role in data quality. Accelerometers come in various types, each with its own specifications regarding sensitivity, bandwidth, range, and resolution. The choice of accelerometer depends on the specific application and the types of vibrations expected. MEMS (Micro-Electro-Mechanical Systems) accelerometers are often chosen for their cost-effectiveness, small size, and low power consumption, making them suitable for large-scale deployments. Piezoelectric accelerometers, on the other hand, might offer higher sensitivity and bandwidth, making them suitable for detecting finer details or higher-frequency vibrations. The mounting of the accelerometers is also paramount. A poorly mounted sensor can pick up spurious vibrations from its immediate surroundings, or fail to accurately capture the vibrations of the structural element it is intended to monitor. For example, if an accelerometer on a bridge deck is loosely attached, it might vibrate independently of the deck itself, leading to erroneous readings. Proper installation and regular checks of sensor mounting are therefore an integral part of maintaining data quality in an SHM system.

Moreover, the signal conditioning and digitization process introduces its own set of data characteristics. Analog signals from accelerometers are converted into digital form by Analog-to-Digital Converters (ADCs). The resolution of the ADC (e.g., 12-bit, 16-bit, 24-bit) determines the precision with which the analog signal can be represented. A higher resolution means finer granularity in the digital representation, reducing quantization error. The sampling rate, as mentioned earlier, must be at least twice the highest frequency of interest to avoid aliasing, according to the Nyquist-Shannon sampling theorem. However, in practice, sampling rates are often set significantly higher to provide a buffer and to facilitate digital filtering. Data acquisition units also often incorporate anti-aliasing filters, which are low-pass filters applied before digitization to remove frequencies above the Nyquist frequency, thus preventing aliasing. The characteristics of these filters (e.g., their cutoff frequency and roll-off) can also subtly influence the recorded data.

Finally, the transmission of this data from the sensors to a central processing unit introduces potential for data loss or corruption. Wireless transmission, while offering flexibility, can be susceptible to interference, signal degradation, or packet loss, especially in challenging environments like urban canyons or over long distances. Wired connections, such as Ethernet or fiber optics, generally offer higher reliability and bandwidth but can be more costly and complex to install, particularly for retrofitting existing structures. The protocols used for data transmission, such as TCP/IP or specialized industrial protocols, have their own error detection and correction mechanisms, but complete data integrity cannot always be guaranteed. Therefore, SHM systems must incorporate mechanisms for data validation, error detection, and potentially data recovery or imputation to handle missing or corrupted data segments. The sheer volume and complexity of vibration data in SHM systems, originating from high-frequency measurements, susceptible to environmental noise and operational variability, and requiring sophisticated spatio-temporal analysis, underscore the critical need for advanced data engineering and machine learning techniques to extract meaningful insights into the health of our vital infrastructure.

The journey from raw, high-frequency vibration data to actionable insights about a structure's health is a sophisticated one, heavily reliant on the art and science of feature engineering. This critical process transforms the dense, often noisy time-series signals into a more manageable and interpretable set of characteristics that can illuminate subtle changes in structural behavior, changes that might otherwise remain hidden within the overwhelming volume of raw measurements. Our focus now shifts to this pivotal stage, where we engineer features specifically designed to detect structural anomalies within the context of our Structural Health Monitoring (SHM) system. The goal is to distill the essence of the structure's dynamic response into a concise set of indicators that can effectively signal deviations from its healthy state.

One of the most fundamental approaches to feature engineering from vibration data involves temporal aggregation. Raw accelerometer readings provide a moment-by-moment account of motion, but often, it is the statistical tendencies over a period of time that reveal the structure's underlying dynamic properties. To this end, we segment the continuous time-series data into discrete, overlapping or non-overlapping time windows. The choice of window size is a crucial hyperparameter, influencing the trade-off between capturing short-term fluctuations and smoothing out transient noise. A window that is too short might be overly sensitive to momentary disturbances, while one that is too long might obscure evolving damage that manifests gradually. Within each time window, a suite of statistical features can be extracted. Common measures include the mean, median, variance, standard deviation, root mean square (RMS), skewness, and kurtosis of the acceleration signals. For instance, a steady increase in the RMS value of acceleration across multiple sensors on a particular structural element might suggest increasing stiffness or a change in its load-bearing capacity, potentially due to developing damage. Similarly, a significant increase in the variance or standard deviation could indicate an increase in the amplitude of vibrations, which might be a precursor to a loss of structural integrity. Skewness and kurtosis, being higher-order statistical moments, are particularly adept at capturing the shape of the distribution of acceleration values. An increase in kurtosis (leptokurtosis) might signal the presence of more frequent, high-amplitude excursions, potentially related to impacts or nonlinear behavior indicative of damage. Conversely, a decrease (platykurtosis) could suggest a smoother, more dampened response. These statistical features, when calculated across all sensors and tracked over time, provide a robust, albeit somewhat coarse, representation of the structure's dynamic state.

Beyond simple statistical aggregations, a deeper understanding of structural dynamics is achieved by analyzing the frequency content of the vibration signals. Every structure possesses a set of natural frequencies at which it preferentially vibrates when disturbed. These frequencies are intrinsic properties, largely determined by the structure's mass, stiffness, and boundary conditions. Damage, such as cracking, delamination, or loosening of connections, alters these physical properties, leading to measurable shifts in the natural frequencies. To extract these crucial parameters, we employ spectral analysis techniques, most commonly the Fast Fourier Transform (FFT). By applying the FFT to segments of the time-series data (often using the same time windows as for statistical features), we convert the signal from the time domain to the frequency domain, revealing the amplitude of vibrations at different frequencies. The dominant peaks in the resulting power spectral density (PSD) plot correspond to the structure's natural frequencies. Features engineered from the spectral analysis can include:

**Dominant Natural Frequencies:** The primary feature is simply identifying the frequencies at which the highest spectral power occurs. Monitoring trends in these frequencies over time is paramount. A decrease in a natural frequency typically indicates a reduction in stiffness, a common manifestation of damage. For example, if a critical bending mode of a bridge deck consistently shows a lower frequency than its established baseline, it might suggest the presence of cracks or material degradation affecting its flexural rigidity.
**Frequency Band Power:** Instead of just pinpointing the exact frequency, we can also quantify the total energy or power within specific frequency

bands known to correspond to certain vibration modes. For instance, a band representing the first bending mode might be monitored. An increase in power within this band, even if the peak frequency remains relatively stable, could indicate increased amplitude of oscillation for that mode, potentially due to increased excitation or altered damping characteristics.

**Spectral Centroid:** This feature represents the "center of mass" of the spectrum. It's calculated as the weighted average of frequencies, where the weights are the spectral amplitudes. A shift in the spectral centroid can indicate a general redistribution of energy across frequencies, which might be associated with changes in stiffness or damping.

**Spectral Spread (Bandwidth):** This feature quantifies the width of the spectral peaks. Damage can sometimes lead to a broadening of these peaks, indicating a less well-defined resonant frequency or increased damping.

**Harmonic Content:** For structures subjected to periodic loads or exhibiting certain types of nonlinearities, the presence and amplitude of harmonics (multiples of the fundamental frequency) can be informative. Changes in harmonic content might signal the development of nonlinear behavior, often a harbinger of damage.

The analysis of spectral content is not limited to the amplitude spectrum. The phase information, though often more challenging to interpret directly, can also yield valuable features related to mode shapes and wave propagation within the structure. However, for practical SHM, amplitude-based spectral features are more commonly employed due to their robustness against noise and ease of interpretation.

Another crucial aspect of structural dynamics that can be quantified is damping. Damping is the mechanism by which energy is dissipated from a vibrating system. It's responsible for the decay of oscillations after an excitation ceases. Damage can significantly affect a structure's damping characteristics. For example, a loose connection might introduce new damping mechanisms through friction, while the formation of a crack might alter the material's inherent damping properties or introduce energy dissipation through crack closure and opening. Features related to damping can be extracted through various methods:

**Logarithmic Decrement:** This classic method is applied to free vibration decay signals. After an impulse or sudden load release, the amplitude of vibration decays exponentially. The logarithmic decrement is calculated from the ratio of successive amplitudes of these decaying oscillations. A higher logarithmic decrement indicates higher damping. This feature is most effective when specific events trigger free vibrations that can be isolated and analyzed.

**Quality Factor (Q-factor):** In the frequency domain, the Q-factor is inversely related to damping. It can be estimated from the width of resonant peaks in the frequency response function. A lower Q-factor signifies higher damping.

**Damping Ratio (ζ):** For systems where the damping can be approximated as viscous damping, the damping ratio can be directly estimated from spectral analysis or time-domain decay. A damping ratio of 0 represents no damping, 1 represents critical damping, and values above 1 represent overdamping. Changes in this ratio are direct indicators of altered energy dissipation.

**Modal Damping Estimation:** More advanced techniques, such as the Frequency Domain Decomposition (FDD) or Stochastic Subspace Identification (SSI) methods, can simultaneously estimate natural frequencies, mode shapes, and modal damping ratios from ambient vibration data. Extracting these modal parameters as features provides a comprehensive view of the structure's dynamic state.

The process of extracting these modal parameters is often computationally intensive but yields highly informative features. For example, if the damping ratio associated with a particular vibration mode consistently increases over time, it might suggest the onset of energy dissipation mechanisms due to damage, such as friction at a newly formed crack or loosening of a bolted joint. Conversely, a decrease in damping could potentially indicate crack closure or stiffening in certain scenarios, though this is less common as a sign of deterioration.

The spatial distribution of sensors also opens avenues for feature engineering that capture how vibrations propagate across the structure. This is particularly relevant for detecting localized damage.

**Cross-correlation Functions:** By computing the cross-correlation between signals from pairs of accelerometers, we can quantify the degree of similarity and the time lag between their vibrations. Changes in cross-correlation patterns can indicate alterations in wave propagation paths, which might be caused by structural damage that obstructs or reroutes these waves.
**Coherence Function:** The coherence function measures the linear relationship between two signals as a function of frequency. A coherence value close to 1 indicates a strong linear relationship, while a value close to 0 suggests little or no linear relationship. Damage can disrupt this coherence, particularly for signals traveling across the damaged region.
**Wavelet Transforms:** Unlike the FFT, which provides a global frequency representation, the Continuous Wavelet Transform (CWT) and Discrete Wavelet Transform (DWT) offer time-frequency localization. This means they can decompose a signal into components that represent specific frequency bands localized in time. This is particularly useful for analyzing transient events and identifying the exact time and frequency at which anomalies occur. Features extracted from wavelet coefficients can include energy in specific time-frequency bins, or changes in the patterns of wavelet decomposition over time. For instance, a crack forming might introduce a localized disturbance that is clearly visible in the wavelet

spectrum at a specific time and frequency, which might be missed by traditional FFT.

When dealing with multi-input, multi-output (MIMO) systems, as is typical in SHM with numerous sensors, the concept of Operational Modal Analysis (OMA) becomes central. OMA techniques aim to extract modal parameters (frequencies, damping, mode shapes) from output-only vibration measurements, assuming the excitation is broadband and random (e.g., wind, traffic). Features derived from OMA, such as changes in modal frequencies, modal damping ratios, or alterations in modal curvature (which reflects mode shape changes), are powerful indicators of structural degradation. For example, if the modal curvature associated with the first bending mode of a bridge shows a significant deviation from its baseline in a specific location, it strongly suggests localized damage in that area.

The sheer volume of data necessitates efficient feature extraction. Techniques like Principal Component Analysis (PCA) or Independent Component Analysis (ICA) can be applied to reduce the dimensionality of the feature space, identifying the most significant underlying components of variation. These components themselves can then be monitored as features. For example, if the first principal component, which might capture the dominant global vibration modes, starts to change its temporal behavior, it could signal a global change in the structure's dynamics.

Furthermore, it's not just about extracting features from individual sensors or pairs of sensors; it's also about developing features that represent the
*interactions* between different parts of the structure. A damaged component might not only vibrate differently itself but also alter how it

influences the vibrations of adjacent components. This leads to features that capture spatial coherence and inter-sensor relationships.

The process of feature engineering is inherently iterative and domain-specific. The choice of features depends heavily on the type of structure, the expected failure modes, the sensor network configuration, and the available computational resources. For instance, in monitoring a slender structure like a wind turbine tower, features sensitive to bending modes and torsional vibrations would be prioritized. For a bridge, features related to its deck vibrations, pier responses, and potential for resonance under traffic loads would be crucial.

In summary, feature engineering for detecting structural anomalies transforms raw vibration data into meaningful indicators. This involves moving from basic statistical measures over time windows to sophisticated spectral analyses that identify natural frequencies, quantifying damping characteristics through various decay and spectral methods, and leveraging spatial information via cross-correlations and advanced OMA techniques. The ultimate aim is to create a compact, informative set of features that can reliably distinguish between normal operational variations and genuine signs of structural degradation, thereby enabling proactive maintenance and ensuring the safety of critical infrastructure. The success of any machine learning model deployed for anomaly detection hinges critically on the quality and relevance of these engineered features.

As we continue to extract and refine these features, it becomes imperative to consider the temporal dynamics not just of the structure itself, but also of the feature values. A single anomalous feature value might be a false alarm, but a consistent trend or a sustained deviation over multiple observation periods is a much stronger indicator of a problem. This leads to the consideration of time-series feature extraction techniques that look at the evolution of features themselves. For example, rather than just looking at the current standard deviation of acceleration, we might track the *trend* of the standard deviation over the past week, or the *rate of change* of the dominant natural frequency. These meta-features, derived from the primary engineered features, can provide an even higher level of abstraction and sensitivity to evolving structural conditions.

Moreover, the normalization and scaling of features are critical steps that often accompany feature extraction, especially when preparing data for machine learning algorithms. Features derived from different sensors or different physical quantities (e.g., frequency vs. variance) may have vastly different scales. Without appropriate scaling (e.g., min-max scaling to a [0, 1] range, or standardization to zero mean and unit variance), algorithms might inadvertently give undue weight to features with larger numerical values, regardless of their actual importance. This is particularly relevant when combining statistical features, spectral features, and damping estimates into a single feature vector for subsequent analysis.

The introduction of environmental and operational condition (EOC) data, such as temperature, wind speed, and traffic load, presents an opportunity for more sophisticated feature engineering through EOC-aware modeling. Instead of simply observing a change in a feature, we can engineer features that represent the *residual* change after accounting for the expected influence of EOC. For example, a feature could be engineered as: `(Observed Natural Frequency) - (Predicted Natural Frequency based on EOC)`. A significant residual would then be a stronger indicator of damage than the raw observed frequency, as it has been "cleaned" of environmental influences. This necessitates a model that can accurately predict structural behavior based on EOC, which itself can be a complex machine learning task.

The process of identifying and selecting the most informative features is also a form of engineering. Techniques like Recursive Feature Elimination (RFE), feature importance scores from tree-based models (e.g., Random Forests, Gradient Boosting), or statistical tests (e.g., ANOVA) can be employed to rank and select a subset of features that are most discriminative for anomaly detection. This dimensionality reduction not only improves model efficiency but also helps in interpretability by focusing on the most critical indicators of structural health. The iterative nature of this process—extracting features, evaluating their predictive power, refining them, and selecting the best ones—is a cornerstone of building an effective SHM system. It is this careful crafting of features that allows us to bridge the gap between raw sensor data and a clear understanding of the structure's integrity.

Having meticulously engineered a rich set of features from our structural vibration data, the next logical progression is to assemble these components into a robust and automated pipeline for anomaly detection. This section delves into the practical construction of such a pipeline, outlining the journey from raw data ingestion to continuous structural health monitoring. We will discuss the integration of various stages, from data acquisition and preprocessing to model training and deployment, emphasizing a hands-on approach guided by code notebooks.

The foundation of any operational anomaly detection system is the ability to reliably ingest data from the source – in our case, simulated sensor data representing the health of a virtual structure. This initial stage involves establishing a data ingestion mechanism that can efficiently receive and format the incoming streams of vibration measurements. For practical implementation, this often translates into reading data from files (e.g., CSV, Parquet) that simulate sensor outputs, or, in a more advanced setup, connecting to real-time data streams from sensors via protocols like MQTT or Kafka. The data must be parsed, cleaned of any obvious errors (e.g., corrupted readings, missing values beyond a certain threshold), and organized into a consistent format suitable for subsequent processing. For our virtual structure, we will assume the availability of time-series data from multiple simulated accelerometers, each timestamped and associated with a specific location on the structure. The data might be organized into daily or hourly batches, or it could be a continuous stream depending on the monitoring frequency requirements.

Once the raw data is ingested, it flows into the automated feature engineering module. This is where the principles discussed previously – statistical aggregations, spectral analysis, damping estimations, and spatial relationship features – are brought to life programmatically. The goal is to have a system that, given a segment of raw vibration data, can automatically compute the relevant features without manual intervention. This typically involves a series of scripts or functions, each responsible for calculating a specific set of features. For instance, a function might take a window of raw acceleration data from a single sensor, compute its mean, variance, RMS, skewness, and kurtosis, and return these values. Another set of functions would perform the FFT on similar windows to extract dominant frequencies, spectral centroids, and band powers. More complex functions might be dedicated to calculating cross-correlations between sensor pairs or applying wavelet transforms. The output of this stage is a feature vector (or a set of feature vectors) for each time window or observation period, representing the structural state at that moment. To maintain consistency and comparability, it's crucial that the feature extraction parameters (e.g., window size, overlap, FFT resolution, frequency bands) are fixed and applied uniformly across all incoming data.

A key consideration in automated feature engineering is handling the sheer volume and velocity of data. Efficient implementation using libraries like NumPy and SciPy for numerical computations, and potentially parallel processing frameworks like Dask or Spark for large-scale operations, becomes indispensable. Furthermore, the output of the feature engineering module needs to be stored in a way that facilitates efficient retrieval for model training and inference. A common approach is to store these feature vectors in a time-series database or a data lake, indexed by timestamp and sensor ID or location.

With the features engineered, the next critical step is to train an anomaly detection model. The choice of model depends on the nature of the anomalies we expect to detect and the characteristics of our feature data. Given that SHM often deals with deviations from a "normal" operational state, unsupervised or semi-supervised anomaly detection algorithms are particularly well-suited. These models learn the patterns of normal behavior from a dataset labeled as "healthy" and then identify instances that deviate significantly from these learned patterns.

One highly effective and interpretable algorithm for this purpose is the **Isolation Forest**. This ensemble method works by randomly partitioning the data space. Anomalies, being few and different, are often isolated in fewer partitions (shorter tree paths) compared to normal instances. The algorithm builds an ensemble of isolation trees. For each tree, a random feature is selected, and then a random split point within the range of that feature is chosen. This process is repeated recursively until all data points are isolated. The anomaly score for a data point is then calculated based on the average path length across all trees in the forest. Shorter average path lengths indicate a higher likelihood of the data point being an anomaly. Isolation Forest is computationally efficient and generally performs well without requiring extensive hyperparameter tuning, making it an excellent choice for our SHM pipeline.

Another robust option is the
**One-Class Support Vector Machine (OC-SVM)**. This algorithm aims to find a hyperplane that best separates the "normal" data points from the origin in a high-dimensional feature space, effectively creating a boundary around the normal data. Any data point falling outside this boundary is

considered an anomaly. OC-SVM is particularly effective when the normal data forms a compact cluster, and it can learn complex, non-linear boundaries using different kernel functions (e.g., radial basis function - RBF). However, it can be more computationally intensive than Isolation Forest, especially with large datasets.

For our implementation, we will focus on demonstrating the use of **Isolation Forest** due to its efficiency and effectiveness in identifying outliers in high-dimensional feature spaces, which is characteristic of our engineered feature sets. The training phase involves feeding the model with a substantial dataset of features computed from the structure operating under normal conditions. This "normal" dataset should ideally represent a wide range of operational states (e.g., varying load conditions, environmental factors) to ensure the model learns a comprehensive definition of healthy behavior.

Once trained, the anomaly detection model is ready for deployment. The deployment strategy for a continuous SHM system involves setting up a mechanism to feed new, incoming feature data to the trained model and receive anomaly scores or binary anomaly predictions. This is often implemented as a real-time or near-real-time processing loop. New sensor data arrives, is ingested, features are extracted, and these features are passed to the deployed model.

The output of the anomaly detection model is a score indicating the degree of abnormality. We then need to establish a threshold for this score. Data points with scores exceeding this threshold are flagged as potential anomalies. The selection of this threshold is critical and involves a trade-off between false positives (flagging normal behavior as anomalous) and false negatives (missing actual anomalies). This threshold can be determined empirically by analyzing the distribution of anomaly scores on a validation set of normal data, or it can be set based on acceptable risk levels for the structure. For instance, a higher threshold would lead to fewer false alarms but might miss subtle anomalies, while a lower threshold would catch more anomalies but increase the risk of false alarms, potentially leading to unnecessary investigations or downtime.

The deployment pipeline should also include a system for alerting and reporting. When an anomaly is detected (i.e., the score exceeds the threshold), an alert should be triggered. This alert could be sent to structural engineers or maintenance personnel via email, SMS, or a dedicated dashboard. The alert should include details about the anomaly, such as the timestamp, the location (if derivable from sensor data), the magnitude of the anomaly score, and potentially the specific features that contributed most to the anomaly score, providing valuable diagnostic information.

Furthermore, the pipeline should be designed for continuous learning and adaptation. Structural behavior can evolve over time even in the absence of damage due to factors like material aging, wear and tear, or changes in operational loads. Therefore, the anomaly detection model may need to be periodically retrained or updated to reflect these gradual changes. This could involve incorporating new "normal" data into the training set or using online learning techniques if the chosen model supports them. Mechanisms for version control of trained models and monitoring their performance over time are essential components of a robust deployment.

To facilitate the practical implementation of this entire process, we will provide code notebooks. These notebooks will guide the user through each stage: simulating sensor data, performing feature extraction, training an Isolation Forest model, setting an anomaly threshold, and simulating the deployment and alerting process. The notebooks will be structured to be modular, allowing users to experiment with different feature sets, model parameters, and thresholding strategies. For example, one notebook might focus solely on data ingestion and feature engineering, while another might take pre-computed features and demonstrate model training and evaluation. A final notebook could tie everything together, simulating a continuous monitoring scenario.

The simulation of sensor data is a crucial starting point for developing and testing our pipeline without access to a real-world structure. This simulation can range from simple synthetic data generation (e.g., adding noise to a baseline signal) to more complex physics-based models that mimic structural responses under various excitations and damage scenarios. For our purpose, we will start with a baseline "healthy" signal representing typical vibrations and then introduce simulated anomalies. These anomalies could manifest as sudden spikes, gradual shifts in frequency content, or changes in vibration amplitude, reflecting various types of structural degradation such as impacts, loosening of components, or material fatigue.

For example, a simulated impact event might introduce a short-duration, high-amplitude transient in the accelerometer data, which should be clearly distinguishable by our anomaly detection system. A gradual loosening of a bolted joint, on the other hand, might lead to a subtle increase in vibration amplitudes and a decrease in natural frequencies over time. Our feature engineering module, equipped with statistical and spectral analysis tools, should be capable of capturing these changes. The Isolation Forest, trained on data representing the structure before such degradation, should then flag these deviations as anomalous.

The process of training the Isolation Forest model will involve carefully curating the "normal" dataset. This dataset should be representative of the structure's behavior under expected operating conditions. If the structure experiences significant variations in temperature, wind, or load throughout its life, the training data should ideally encompass these variations. This helps the model learn that a certain level of fluctuation in vibration patterns is normal. For instance, wind can induce significant vibrations in a bridge or a wind turbine. A well-trained model will learn the relationship between wind speed and vibration characteristics and will not flag these wind-induced vibrations as anomalies. However, if the vibration amplitude under a specific wind speed suddenly increases beyond what is predicted by the wind speed alone, this deviation would be a strong candidate for an anomaly. This highlights the importance of considering environmental and operational conditions (EOC) in the training data.

The deployment stage is where the rubber meets the road. Here, the trained model is integrated into an operational framework. This could be a scheduled batch process that runs periodically (e.g., every hour, every day) to analyze recent data, or it could be a streaming process that analyzes data in real-time as it arrives. For a critical infrastructure like a bridge or a building, a near-real-time streaming approach is often preferred to ensure rapid detection of potential threats. The pipeline would look something like this:

1.
**Data Acquisition:** Receive streaming data from accelerometers.
2. **Data Buffering & Windowing:** Collect data into time windows for analysis.
3. **Feature Engineering:** Compute the predefined set of features from each window.
4. **Anomaly Scoring:** Feed the feature vector into the deployed Isolation Forest model to get an anomaly score.
5. **Thresholding:** Compare the anomaly score against a pre-defined threshold.

6. **Alerting/Reporting:** If the threshold is exceeded, generate an alert and log the event. If not, continue monitoring.

The alerting mechanism is a crucial part of the human-in-the-loop aspect of SHM. Simply detecting an anomaly is only the first step; the information needs to be communicated effectively to the right people who can then initiate further investigation. This might involve deploying human inspectors to the site, performing more detailed analyses with specialized equipment, or initiating repair procedures. The alert system should be designed to be informative and actionable, providing enough context for the recipient to understand the severity and nature of the potential issue.

Furthermore, the performance of the deployed pipeline needs to be continuously monitored. This involves tracking metrics such as the rate of detected anomalies, the rate of false alarms, and the timeliness of alerts. Over time, if the structure undergoes changes that are not considered damage (e.g., a minor refurbishment that alters its stiffness slightly), the model's performance might degrade. Periodic retraining with updated "normal" data, or perhaps a more sophisticated online learning approach, can help maintain the pipeline's effectiveness. This iterative refinement process is key to building a truly resilient and reliable SHM system. The notebooks will serve as practical blueprints for constructing and experimenting with such a pipeline, enabling a hands-on understanding of each component's role and interplay in achieving automated structural health monitoring. The emphasis will be on creating a clear, reproducible workflow that can be adapted to different structural types and monitoring objectives.

The output of our automated structural health monitoring (SHM) pipeline, after the anomaly detection model has processed new feature sets, is not merely a numerical score. It is, in essence, a diagnostic signal, a potential harbinger of change within the structure. The crucial next step, therefore, is the art and science of interpreting these results and translating them into a form that is comprehensible and actionable for structural engineers and asset managers. This phase moves beyond the algorithmic prediction and into the realm of practical decision-making, risk assessment, and intervention planning.

The anomaly scores generated by models like the Isolation Forest, as discussed previously, represent a degree of deviation from the established patterns of "normal" structural behavior. A score closer to 1 typically indicates a higher likelihood of anomaly, while scores closer to 0 suggest behavior well within the expected operational parameters. However, a raw score, without context, is of limited value. The immediate challenge is to define what constitutes a "significant" deviation – a deviation that warrants further investigation or potential action. This is where the concept of
**thresholding** becomes paramount.

Establishing an appropriate anomaly detection threshold is not a one-size-fits-all endeavor. It is a nuanced process that requires careful consideration of the structure's criticality, the potential consequences of failure, and the cost of false alarms. A very low threshold might lead to a high rate of false positives, triggering numerous unnecessary inspections and potentially causing operational disruptions due to over-cautiousness. Conversely, a very high threshold might allow subtle but developing damage to go undetected, increasing the risk of catastrophic failure.

The process of setting this threshold often begins with analyzing the distribution of anomaly scores generated from data known to represent the structure's healthy state. This could be data collected during its commissioning phase, or from periods where comprehensive inspections confirmed its integrity. By examining this distribution, engineers can identify a point beyond which anomaly scores become statistically improbable under normal operating conditions. Statistical methods, such as percentiles (e.g., the 95th or 99th percentile of normal scores), can serve as a starting point. For instance, if 99% of the anomaly scores from healthy data fall below 0.7, then a score exceeding 0.7 could be designated as a potential anomaly.

However, purely statistical approaches may not always suffice. The inherent complexity of structural behavior, coupled with the dynamic nature of environmental and operational conditions (EOCs), means that "normal" can sometimes exhibit significant variability. For example, a bridge will naturally exhibit different vibration characteristics under high wind loads compared to calm conditions, or under heavy traffic compared to light traffic. A well-trained anomaly detection model should account for this expected variability. When it flags an anomaly, it signifies a deviation *beyond* the expected range of normal variability for the given EOCs.

This leads to a more sophisticated approach: **context-aware thresholding**. Instead of a single global threshold, thresholds might be dynamic, adjusting based on real-time or near-real-time EOC data. For a bridge, the threshold for anomaly scores might be slightly higher during periods of strong winds or heavy traffic, acknowledging the increased baseline vibration levels. This requires not only correlating anomaly scores with EOCs but also having models that can predict expected anomaly scores based on these EOCs. If the actual anomaly score significantly exceeds the *predicted* normal score for the current EOC, then it becomes a stronger candidate for a genuine issue.

Another critical aspect of thresholding is the concept of **confidence levels and risk tolerance**. For a critical piece of infrastructure, such as a nuclear power plant containment structure or a major suspension bridge, the tolerance for false negatives (missed damage) is extremely low. In such cases, a lower threshold, accepting a higher rate of false positives, might be preferred, with robust protocols in place to handle these alarms efficiently. For less critical assets, or components where failure has less severe consequences, a higher threshold might be acceptable, prioritizing operational efficiency and minimizing false alarms.

The output of the anomaly detection pipeline, once an anomaly score crosses a predefined threshold, is the
**triggering of an alert**. This alert is the signal that initiates the SHM system's response mechanism. The design of this alert system is as crucial as the anomaly detection model itself. An effective alert should be:

**Timely:** Delivered with minimal delay after anomaly detection to allow for prompt investigation.
**Informative:** Providing sufficient detail to enable initial assessment by engineers. This typically includes:
**Timestamp:** When the anomaly was detected.
**Location/Sensor ID:** Which sensor or group of sensors flagged the anomaly. This is critical for pinpointing the potential issue.
**Anomaly Score:** The magnitude of the deviation, indicating severity.
**Contributing Features (if available):** Some advanced models can provide insights into which features contributed most to the anomaly score. This can offer strong clues about the nature of the problem (e.g., changes in spectral content might suggest looseness, while increased damping might indicate material degradation or added mass).
**Relevant EOC Data:** The environmental and operational conditions at the time of the anomaly.
**Actionable:** Guiding the recipient on the next steps.
**Prioritized:** Allowing for differentiation between minor deviations and potentially critical events.

The alert system can take various forms, depending on the operational context. It might manifest as:

**Dashboard Notifications:** A visual alert on a centralized SHM dashboard, often color-coded to indicate severity (e.g., green for normal, yellow for caution, red for alert).
**Automated Emails or SMS Messages:** Direct communication to assigned personnel for urgent issues.
**Integration with Work Order Systems:** Automatically generating a maintenance request or inspection ticket in a computerized maintenance management system (CMMS).

Beyond the immediate alert, the interpretation of results extends to defining subsequent
**investigation protocols**. When an alert is triggered, a structured response should follow. This protocol should outline:

1.
**Initial Verification:** A rapid assessment of the alert's validity. This might involve:
**Reviewing recent EOCs:** Was there an unusual event (e.g., a major storm, an earthquake, a significant load event) that could explain the deviation?
**Checking data quality:** Was there a sensor malfunction or communication error that might have produced a spurious reading?
**Looking for corroboration:** Do other nearby sensors or related systems show similar anomalies?

2.
**Detailed Analysis:** If the alert appears valid, a more in-depth investigation is required. This could involve:
**Expert review of anomaly data:** Structural engineers examining the time-series data, feature values, and the anomaly score in detail.
**Root cause analysis:** Using the provided information (location, features, EOCs) to hypothesize potential causes of the anomaly, such as crack initiation, bolt loosening, corrosion, or external impact.
**Comparison with historical data:** Examining trends and patterns of similar anomalies in the past.

3.
**Field Inspection:** If the analysis indicates a potential physical issue, a targeted field inspection by trained personnel becomes necessary. The SHM system's output should guide the scope and focus of this inspection, making it more efficient and effective than a general, routine check. For example, if the anomaly is strongly localized to a specific sensor on a bridge pier, the inspection team will focus their efforts on that precise area.

4.
**Further Diagnostics and Monitoring:** Depending on the findings of the field inspection, additional monitoring or specialized diagnostic techniques (e.g., ultrasonic testing, thermography, strain gauging) may be employed. The SHM system can then be used to track the evolution of the anomaly after any interventions.

5.
**Decision Making:** Based on the gathered evidence, a decision is made regarding the structural integrity and any required maintenance or repair actions. This decision-making process is the ultimate goal of the SHM system.

A key aspect of interpreting results and triggering alerts is understanding the
**types of anomalies** that the system is designed to detect. Our SHM pipeline, with its feature engineering and anomaly detection capabilities, is geared towards identifying deviations that suggest a change in the structure's physical state. These might include:

**Changes in Stiffness or Damping:** For instance, the onset of micro-cracking might subtly reduce stiffness, leading to shifts in natural frequencies or increased vibration amplitudes. Loose connections or the

degradation of damping materials would also manifest as changes in these parameters. Our spectral analysis features and damping estimation techniques are designed to pick up such changes.
**Increased Excitation or Response:** An anomaly could indicate that the structure is experiencing external forces or responding to them in an amplified manner beyond normal operational variations. This might be due to a new, unexpected load, or a change in the structure's geometry that alters its dynamic response.
**Structural Degradation:** Features related to signal distortion (e.g., skewness, kurtosis beyond normal ranges), or changes in the statistical distribution of vibration signals, could indicate material fatigue, corrosion, or internal damage.
**Localized Issues:** By correlating anomalies across multiple sensors, it becomes possible to infer localized problems. For example, if a cluster of sensors around a specific joint shows correlated anomalies, it strongly suggests an issue at that joint.

The interpretation also involves discerning between anomalies that represent
**potential damage initiation** and those that might indicate **increased structural risk** due to external factors or operational changes. For instance, a sudden, significant increase in vibration amplitude during a storm might be an indication of increased structural stress and therefore increased risk, even if no permanent damage has occurred yet. Similarly, a gradual drift in a key structural parameter over time might not immediately indicate a critical issue but represents a growing risk that needs to be managed.

The concept of
**model confidence** is also relevant here. While anomaly detection models aim to distinguish between normal and anomalous, there is always a degree of uncertainty. Some anomalies might be borderline – scoring just above the threshold. The interpretation phase should account for this. A

system could potentially categorize alerts based on the anomaly score's proximity to the threshold:

**Level 1 Alert (Low Confidence):** Score is slightly above the threshold. May warrant passive monitoring or a review of EOCs.
**Level 2 Alert (Medium Confidence):** Score is moderately above the threshold. Suggests a potential issue requiring further data review and possibly targeted inspection.
**Level 3 Alert (High Confidence):** Score is significantly above the threshold. Indicates a high probability of a structural problem, demanding immediate investigation and potential action.

This tiered alerting system allows for a more nuanced response, avoiding unnecessary overreaction to minor deviations while ensuring that critical issues are addressed promptly. The ability to drill down into the contributing features for each alert is paramount for this nuanced interpretation. If an anomaly is flagged, and the primary contributing features are those related to spectral content (dominant frequencies, band powers), a structural engineer might immediately consider hypotheses related to loose components, changes in material stiffness, or damage affecting modal characteristics. If features related to amplitude and variance are dominant, this might point towards issues with load transfer, excessive vibration amplitude under excitation, or localized stress concentrations.

Furthermore, the interpretation of results is not a static, one-time event. It is an ongoing process that informs the continuous improvement of the SHM system itself. Feedback from field inspections and subsequent repairs is invaluable. When an anomaly is detected, investigated, and found to be due to a specific cause (e.g., a particular type of bolt loosening), this information can be used to:

**Refine Feature Engineering:** Perhaps a new feature or a modification to an existing one could be more sensitive to this specific type of damage.
**Improve Thresholding:** The experience gained can help in adjusting thresholds for future detections of similar issues.
**Enhance Alerting Logic:** Understanding what information was most useful during the investigation can lead to improvements in the alert content and delivery.
**Update Model Training Data:** If the identified issue represents a new type of damage or a deviation from previously understood "normal" behavior, the system might need to be retrained with data that captures this new state, or with specific examples of this damage type to learn to flag it more effectively (if using semi-supervised or supervised approaches for specific known damage types).

The process of interpreting results and triggering alerts therefore forms a critical feedback loop, ensuring that the SHM system remains a living, evolving tool for ensuring structural safety. It bridges the gap between sophisticated data science and practical engineering decision-making, transforming raw data into actionable intelligence that protects valuable infrastructure and, most importantly, human lives. The goal is not simply to detect anomalies, but to provide insights that lead to informed, timely, and effective interventions, ultimately contributing to the long-term resilience and reliability of our built environment. This careful, iterative process of interpretation and action is what imbues the SHM system with its true value.

The increasing sophistication of machine learning (ML) models deployed in engineering applications, while offering unparalleled predictive power, has also introduced a significant challenge: the "black box" problem. When models, especially deep learning architectures, operate on complex datasets derived from sensors, simulations, or operational logs, their decision-making processes can become opaque. This opacity is problematic because engineering relies on a foundation of understanding, causality, and verifiable reasoning. Simply accepting a model's output – whether it's a prediction of imminent structural failure, a recommendation for operational adjustments, or a classification of a manufacturing defect – without comprehending the underlying rationale, erodes trust and limits the practical utility of these powerful tools. This is precisely where Explainable Artificial Intelligence (XAI) steps in, aiming to demystify ML models and provide transparent, interpretable insights into their workings.

XAI is not merely an academic pursuit; it is becoming an indispensable component for the responsible and effective deployment of AI in critical engineering domains. In fields like aerospace, civil infrastructure, automotive, and manufacturing, where safety, reliability, and regulatory compliance are paramount, the ability to explain *why* a model made a certain prediction is as important as the prediction itself. Engineers and domain experts need to understand the model's reasoning to:

**Build Trust and Confidence:** When an AI system flags a potential anomaly in a bridge's structural health monitoring (SHM) data, engineers need to trust that the alert is based on sound principles and not a spurious correlation or a misunderstanding of normal operating conditions. Explanations can validate the model's findings and build confidence in its ongoing operation.

**Debug and Improve Models:** If a model consistently makes incorrect predictions or exhibits biases, understanding the contributing factors behind these errors is essential for iterative improvement. XAI techniques can pinpoint specific features, data points, or model components that are leading to flawed outputs, guiding engineers in refining feature engineering, data preprocessing, or model architecture.

**Ensure Regulatory Compliance:** In many industries, regulations mandate that decisions affecting safety or public welfare must be justifiable and auditable. AI systems used in these contexts must be able to provide clear explanations for their decisions to satisfy regulatory bodies and ethical standards. For example, in autonomous vehicle systems, understanding why a car decided to brake or swerve is crucial for accident investigation and certification.

**Facilitate Human-AI Collaboration:** For AI to truly augment human expertise, it must communicate effectively. XAI bridges the gap by providing insights that enable human experts to collaborate with the AI, validate its findings, and make more informed decisions. This is particularly relevant in complex diagnostic tasks where an AI might identify subtle patterns that a human might miss, but a human expert can then use the AI's explanation to confirm or refute the finding based on their deep domain knowledge.

**Discover New Knowledge:** Sometimes, the explanations provided by XAI techniques can reveal unforeseen relationships or underlying mechanisms within the engineering system being studied. This can lead to new scientific discoveries or novel engineering approaches. For instance, an XAI analysis of sensor data in a chemical process might reveal an unexpected interaction between two variables that was previously not understood, leading to process optimization.

The core challenge in XAI is to extract meaningful insights from models that can be highly complex, often involving millions of parameters and non-linear interactions. The goal is not necessarily to fully reverse-engineer the model's internal workings to a level that would be equivalent to hand-coding the logic, but rather to provide sufficient interpretable information that allows a human to understand the *drivers* of a specific prediction. This is often framed as answering questions like: "Why did the model predict X?" or "What are the most important factors influencing this prediction?"

Several families of XAI techniques have emerged to address these needs. These can broadly be categorized into model-specific methods (which leverage the internal structure of a particular model type, like a decision tree or linear model) and model-agnostic methods (which can be applied to any ML model, treating it as a black box). For complex, black-box models prevalent in modern engineering AI, model-agnostic techniques are often the most practical starting point.

One of the most widely adopted and intuitive model-agnostic XAI techniques is
**Local Interpretable Model-agnostic Explanations (LIME)**. LIME's core idea is to explain an individual prediction of any black-box model by approximating its behavior around that specific prediction with a simpler, interpretable model (such as a linear model or a decision tree). The process works as follows:

1.
**Perturb the Instance:** For a given data point (e.g., a set of sensor readings from a structure at a particular time), LIME generates a number of perturbed versions of this data point. These perturbations involve slightly altering the input features. For instance, if the input is a time series of vibration data, LIME might slightly change the amplitude of certain frequency components or introduce minor shifts in time.
2. **Get Predictions from the Black-Box Model:** The original black-box model is used to predict the outcome for each of these perturbed data points.

3. **Weight the Perturbations:** The perturbed data points are then weighted based on their proximity to the original instance. Data points that are very similar to the original instance receive a higher weight, while those that are significantly different receive a lower weight. This ensures that the explanation is "local" to the specific prediction being investigated.
4. **Train an Interpretable Model:** A simple, interpretable model (e.g., a linear regression) is trained on these weighted, perturbed data points and their corresponding black-box model predictions. Because the interpretable model is trained locally around the instance of interest, it can effectively approximate the behavior of the complex black-box model in that specific region.
5. **Extract Explanations:** The coefficients or rules from the trained interpretable model are then used to explain the prediction. For a linear model, the coefficients indicate the impact of each feature on the prediction. For example, if LIME is used to explain why an SHM model predicted a high anomaly score for a particular sensor reading, the interpretable model might reveal that an increase in the power spectral density within a specific frequency band was the primary driver of that high score. LIME can then present these contributing features, often as a list of words or feature-value pairs with associated weights, indicating their importance.

Consider an application in predictive maintenance for industrial machinery. A complex deep learning model might be trained to predict the likelihood of a specific component failure (e.g., a bearing seizing) based on vibration, temperature, and acoustic data. When the model predicts a high probability of failure for a particular machine, LIME can be applied to explain this prediction. LIME might reveal that the most influential features for this specific prediction were a sudden spike in high-frequency vibrations in the acoustic data and a sustained rise in temperature from a sensor located near the bearing. This information is invaluable for maintenance engineers. Instead of a generic "failure likely" alert, they receive a specific indication of *why* the alert was triggered, allowing them to focus their inspection and diagnostics on the most probable causes. They might then check the bearing's temperature directly, perform acoustic analysis in the specified frequency range, or inspect the lubrication system, leading to a more efficient and accurate diagnosis.

Another powerful and increasingly popular XAI technique is **SHapley Additive exPlanations (SHAP)**. SHAP is grounded in cooperative game theory and provides a unified framework for interpreting predictions from any machine learning model. The core idea behind SHAP is to attribute the difference between a model's prediction for a specific instance and the average prediction (or baseline) to the individual features of that instance. It does this by calculating Shapley values, which represent the marginal contribution of each feature to the prediction, averaged over all possible combinations of features.

The calculation of Shapley values can be computationally intensive, especially for a large number of features. However, efficient approximations exist, such as KernelSHAP (which is model-agnostic and similar to LIME but with a more theoretically grounded way of calculating Shapley values) and TreeSHAP (an optimized version for tree-based models like Random Forests and Gradient Boosting Machines).

For a given prediction, SHAP values provide:

**Global Explanations:** By aggregating SHAP values across many instances, one can understand the overall impact of each feature on the model's predictions. For example, a SHAP summary plot can show the distribution of SHAP values for a feature across the dataset, revealing not only which features are important on average but also how their values (high or low) affect the model's output.

**Local Explanations:** For a single prediction, SHAP values explain how each feature contributed to pushing the model's output away from the baseline prediction. A positive SHAP value for a feature indicates that this feature's value for the current instance pushed the prediction higher (e.g., towards an anomaly alert), while a negative SHAP value indicates it pushed the prediction lower.

Let's revisit the SHM example. Suppose an Isolation Forest model, as discussed previously, flags a particular timestamp with a high anomaly score. Applying SHAP to this prediction would provide precise Shapley values for each input feature (e.g., specific frequency band powers, RMS values, damping ratios) that contributed to that high score.

A high positive SHAP value for "Power in 10-20 Hz band" would strongly suggest that the elevated energy in this frequency range was a primary reason for the anomaly detection.

A negative SHAP value for "Overall RMS vibration" might indicate that while some specific aspects were anomalous, the overall vibration level was within expected bounds, providing nuance to the alert.
The SHAP force plot is a particularly effective visualization tool. For a single prediction, it shows the baseline prediction (e.g., the average anomaly score) and how each feature's SHAP value pushes the prediction higher or lower, ultimately arriving at the final predicted anomaly score. This visual representation clearly illustrates the interplay of different factors influencing the model's decision.

In an engineering context, SHAP's ability to quantify the exact contribution of each feature is immensely valuable. For instance, if an AI model is used for defect detection in manufacturing based on images, SHAP can highlight the specific pixels or regions in an image that the model considered indicative of a defect. This allows quality control engineers to visually verify the model's reasoning and understand what visual cues are being recognized. If the model is focusing on irrelevant patterns (e.g., reflections on the surface instead of actual material flaws), SHAP can expose this, guiding retraining or feature selection.

Consider a more complex scenario involving a cyber-physical system, such as a smart grid. An AI model might be responsible for detecting anomalous power consumption patterns that could indicate equipment malfunction or a cyber-attack. When an anomaly is detected, SHAP values can pinpoint which combinations of sensor readings (e.g., voltage, current, frequency, time of day, neighboring grid segments' load) were most critical in triggering the alert. This level of detail enables grid operators to quickly differentiate between a false alarm, a genuine equipment issue, or a sophisticated cyber threat, allowing for a targeted and appropriate response.

Beyond LIME and SHAP, other XAI techniques are being explored and applied in engineering.
**Partial Dependence Plots (PDPs)** and **Individual Conditional Expectation (ICE) plots** can illustrate how a specific feature affects the model's prediction on average (PDP) or for individual instances (ICE), assuming other features are held constant. While simpler, they can offer valuable insights into feature importance and interaction. For understanding decision-making processes in tree-based models, **TreeSHAP** is particularly efficient, and visualization tools like **Tree-maps** can illustrate the decision paths taken by the model. For deep learning models, techniques like **saliency maps** (in computer vision) and **attention mechanisms** (in natural language processing and sequence models) can highlight which parts of the input data the model "focused on" to make its prediction.

The practical implementation of XAI in engineering workflows involves integrating these techniques into the ML pipeline. This typically means:

1.
**Selecting Appropriate XAI Methods:** The choice of XAI technique depends on the model type, the complexity of the data, the specific questions being asked, and the desired level of interpretability. For a general-purpose black-box model, LIME and SHAP are strong candidates. For interpretable models like linear regression or decision trees, the model itself is already explanatory, but XAI can still quantify feature importance.
2. **Generating Explanations:** This involves running the chosen XAI algorithms on the model and the data, either for specific predictions of interest or for a representative sample of data to understand general model behavior.
3. **Visualizing and Communicating Insights:** Raw XAI outputs (e.g., lists of feature importances, numerical Shapley values) need to be translated into understandable formats for engineers. Visualizations like SHAP summary plots, force plots, PDPs, and LIME's colored feature attribution are crucial for conveying these insights effectively.
4. **Acting on Explanations:** The ultimate goal is to use these explanations to improve decision-making, debug models, and build trust. This requires a feedback loop where engineers review the explanations, validate them against their domain knowledge, and use them to inform subsequent actions, whether it's a maintenance intervention, a model retraining, or a process adjustment.

In summary, Explainable AI is a critical enabler for the widespread and trustworthy adoption of advanced ML techniques in engineering. By providing mechanisms to understand
*why* an AI model makes a particular prediction, XAI techniques like LIME and SHAP empower engineers to build, deploy, and rely on AI systems with greater confidence. They transform opaque "black boxes" into transparent tools, fostering trust, facilitating debugging, ensuring compliance, and ultimately leading to safer, more efficient, and more

robust engineering solutions across a multitude of applications. The continued research and development in XAI promise even more sophisticated methods for demystifying AI, further accelerating its beneficial integration into the fabric of modern engineering practice. Reinforcement Learning (RL) represents a paradigm shift in how we approach automated decision-making and control in systems that evolve over time and interact with their surroundings. Unlike supervised learning, which relies on labeled datasets of input-output pairs, or unsupervised learning, which seeks patterns in unlabeled data, RL learns through trial and error. An "agent" interacts with an "environment," taking actions and receiving feedback in the form of rewards or penalties. The agent's objective is to learn a policy – a strategy for choosing actions – that maximizes its cumulative reward over time. This makes RL particularly well-suited for optimization and control problems where the optimal course of action is not immediately obvious and must be discovered through experience.

At its core, an RL system comprises several key components. The **agent** is the learner and decision-maker. It observes the state of the environment and selects an action based on its current policy. The **environment** is everything external to the agent that it interacts with. It receives actions from the agent, transitions to a new state, and provides a reward signal back to the agent. The **state** is a representation of the environment at a particular point in time. The agent uses this state information to inform its decisions. The **action** is what the agent does in response to a given state. Finally, the **reward** is a scalar value that the environment provides to the agent after each action, indicating how desirable that action was in that state. Positive rewards encourage the behavior, while negative rewards (penalties) discourage it. The ultimate goal of the agent is to learn a policy that maximizes the expected sum of future discounted rewards. The discount factor, often denoted by gamma ($\gamma$), determines the importance of future rewards relative to immediate ones. A $\gamma$ close to 1 means the agent is far-sighted, while a $\gamma$ close to 0 means it is myopic.

The learning process in RL often involves a delicate balance between **exploration** and **exploitation**. Exploration means trying out new actions to discover potentially better strategies, even if they might yield lower immediate rewards. Exploitation means using the currently known best strategy to maximize rewards. Without exploration, an agent might get stuck in a suboptimal policy. Without exploitation, it might never leverage its learned knowledge to achieve high rewards. Various strategies exist to manage this trade-off, such as epsilon-greedy policies, where the agent chooses a random action with a small probability ($\epsilon$) and the best-known action otherwise.

Several fundamental RL algorithms have been developed, each with its strengths and applications.
**Q-learning** is a model-free, off-policy algorithm that learns an action-value function, often denoted as $Q(s, a)$. This function estimates the expected future cumulative reward of taking action $a$ in state $s$ and then following the optimal policy thereafter. The agent updates its Q-values iteratively based on the Bellman equation:

$Q(s, a) \leftarrow Q(s, a) + \alpha [r + \gamma \max_{a'} Q(s', a') - Q(s, a)]$

where $\alpha$ is the learning rate, $r$ is the received reward, $s'$ is the next state, and $a'$ are possible actions in state $s'$. By learning the optimal Q-values, the agent can derive an optimal policy: at any state $s$, choose the action $a$ that maximizes $Q(s, a)$.

Another class of algorithms is based on
**policy gradients**. These methods directly learn a parameterized policy $\pi(a|s; \theta)$, which maps states to a probability distribution over actions. The goal is to adjust the policy parameters $\theta$ to maximize

the expected total reward. Algorithms like REINFORCE use the gradient of the expected reward with respect to the policy parameters to update $\theta$. Policy gradient methods are particularly useful when the action space is continuous or very large, as they do not require learning value functions for all possible actions.

More advanced algorithms, such as
**Actor-Critic methods**, combine the benefits of value-based and policy-based approaches. An "actor" network learns the policy, while a "critic" network learns a value function (e.g., a state-value function $V(s)$ or an action-value function $Q(s, a)$). The critic's value estimates are used to guide the actor's policy updates, often leading to more stable and efficient learning than pure policy gradient methods. Deep Reinforcement Learning (DRL) leverages deep neural networks to approximate these policies and value functions, enabling RL to tackle high-dimensional state spaces, such as those found in image or raw sensor data. This has led to remarkable successes in areas like game playing (AlphaGo) and robotics.

The applications of RL in engineering are vast and continue to expand. One prominent area is
**adaptive control systems**. In robotics, for instance, an RL agent can learn to control a robot's limbs to perform complex tasks like grasping objects or walking on uneven terrain. The agent observes the robot's joint angles, velocities, and sensor feedback (tactile, visual) as states, chooses motor commands (actions), and receives rewards based on task completion, efficiency, or stability. Unlike traditional control methods that rely on precise mathematical models of the robot and its environment, RL can adapt to uncertainties, wear and tear, and variations in the environment that might not be fully accounted for in a model. For example, an RL-controlled robotic arm might learn to compensate for slight inaccuracies in its calibration or adapt its grip strength based on the perceived slipperiness of an object, all through learned experience.

Smart grids offer another compelling use case for RL, particularly in

**optimizing energy consumption and distribution**. An RL agent can learn to manage energy flow in a complex network of power generators, storage devices, and consumers. The state could include real-time demand, electricity prices, renewable energy availability (solar, wind), and grid status. Actions might involve adjusting power generation from different sources, charging or discharging batteries, or even subtly influencing demand through smart appliance scheduling. The reward signal would be designed to encourage grid stability, minimize operational costs, maximize the use of renewable energy, and meet consumer demand reliably. For example, an RL agent could learn to predict peak demand periods and strategically charge large battery storage systems when electricity is cheap and abundant (e.g., from solar generation during the day) and then discharge them to meet demand during expensive peak hours, thereby reducing reliance on fossil fuel peaker plants and lowering overall costs.

**Autonomous navigation** in complex and dynamic environments is another domain where RL excels. For self-driving cars, drones, or autonomous underwater vehicles, RL agents can learn to navigate safely and efficiently. The state space can include data from cameras, LiDAR, radar, GPS, and inertial measurement units. Actions involve controlling steering, acceleration, braking, or flight surfaces. Rewards are typically designed to encourage reaching the destination, maintaining safety (avoiding collisions), adhering to traffic laws, and optimizing for metrics like travel time or energy efficiency. An RL agent can learn nuanced behaviors, such as merging into traffic smoothly, negotiating intersections with unpredictable human drivers, or planning optimal routes in real-time based on dynamic road conditions or obstacles. This learning can go beyond explicit programming, allowing the system to discover emergent behaviors that are robust to unforeseen situations.

In the realm of

**manufacturing and industrial processes**, RL can be employed for optimizing production lines, managing inventory, and controlling complex chemical reactions. For example, an RL agent could learn the optimal settings for a continuous manufacturing process, such as the temperature, pressure, and flow rates in a chemical reactor. The state would encompass sensor readings from the process, while actions would be adjustments to these control parameters. The reward function would be designed to maximize product yield, minimize energy consumption, and maintain product quality within specified tolerances. The agent would learn to discover intricate relationships between control parameters and process outcomes that might be difficult for human engineers to intuit or model precisely. Similarly, RL can optimize scheduling of jobs on a shop floor, dynamically reassigning tasks to machines to minimize idle time and maximize throughput based on real-time machine availability and job priorities.

Furthermore, RL is finding its way into **resource management and allocation** problems. Consider the dynamic allocation of computing resources in a cloud environment. An RL agent could learn to adjust the number of virtual machines or processing units allocated to different tasks based on their current computational demands and predicted future needs. The state might include current CPU/memory utilization, task queue lengths, and predicted workload. Actions would be to scale resources up or down. The reward would be a function of system performance (e.g., task completion times) and resource utilization cost. This allows for a more responsive and cost-effective allocation of computational power compared to static allocation schemes.

The development and application of RL in engineering also come with significant challenges.
**Sample efficiency** is a major hurdle; RL algorithms often require a vast number of interactions with the environment to learn an effective policy. This can be prohibitively expensive or time-consuming in real-world

engineering systems where interactions might involve physical processes, simulations that are computationally intensive, or even safety-critical operations. Techniques like **model-based RL**, where the agent learns a model of the environment's dynamics, can help improve sample efficiency by allowing the agent to "plan" or "simulate" experiences internally without directly interacting with the real world. **Transfer learning** and **meta-learning** are also crucial, aiming to enable RL agents to leverage knowledge gained from one task or environment to accelerate learning on new, related tasks.

**Safety and reliability** are paramount in engineering applications. For an RL agent to be deployed in a safety-critical system, it must be guaranteed to operate within safe boundaries and exhibit predictable behavior. This is an active area of research, with approaches including **constrained RL**, where the agent is penalized for violating constraints, and the use of **formal verification techniques** to provide assurances about the learned policy. Simulating the environment to a high degree of fidelity is often a prerequisite for safely training and testing RL agents before they are deployed in the real world.

The

**design of appropriate reward functions** is another critical aspect. A poorly designed reward function can lead to unintended behaviors or suboptimal outcomes, even if the RL algorithm itself is well-implemented. For instance, rewarding a self-driving car solely for reaching its destination quickly might lead it to drive recklessly. Engineers must carefully consider the multi-objective nature of many engineering problems and design reward functions that align with all desired criteria and constraints. This often involves careful tuning and iterative refinement of the reward signal based on observed agent behavior.

Finally,

**interpretability and explainability** remain significant challenges for complex DRL systems, similar to other deep learning models. While RL agents can learn highly effective control policies, understanding *why* they make specific decisions can be difficult, especially when deep neural networks are used as function approximators. Research in XAI for RL is crucial for building trust, enabling debugging, and ensuring that these systems can be understood and validated by human engineers. Techniques for visualizing learned policies, analyzing state-action affordances, or decomposing complex behaviors into simpler components are essential for practical deployment in demanding engineering fields. Despite these challenges, the potential of Reinforcement Learning to unlock new levels of performance and autonomy in control and optimization makes it an indispensable tool and a key area of future development in engineering AI.
In the realm of modern engineering, data is often a distributed asset. Whether it originates from numerous sensors across a vast manufacturing floor, individual smart devices within a city's infrastructure, or even across geographically dispersed research facilities, this data frequently presents a logistical and privacy challenge. Centralizing all this information into a single location for traditional machine learning model training can be impractical, costly, and sometimes impossible due to regulatory requirements, competitive concerns, or sheer data volume. This is precisely where the paradigm of **Federated Learning (FL)** emerges as a transformative approach, offering a path to collaborative intelligence without compromising data locality or privacy.

Federated Learning is a machine learning technique that enables the training of a shared global model across multiple decentralized edge devices or data silos, without the need to exchange raw data. Instead of bringing the data to the model, FL brings the model to the data. The core idea is to iteratively train a machine learning model on local datasets held by individual participants (clients), and then aggregate the learned model updates—such as parameter gradients or weights—at a central server.

This central server then combines these updates to create an improved global model, which is subsequently sent back to the clients for further local training. This cycle repeats until the global model converges to a satisfactory performance level.

Let's delve deeper into the mechanics of this process. Initially, a global model, often a neural network, is initialized either by the central server or collaboratively by the participants. This global model is then distributed to a selected subset of participating clients. Each client, possessing its own local dataset, trains this model using its private data. During this local training phase, the model's parameters are adjusted based on the specific characteristics and patterns present in the client's data. Crucially, the raw data itself never leaves the client's device or silo. Once local training is complete, each client sends only the
*updates* to the model parameters back to the central server. These updates represent what the model has learned from the local data.

The central server then undertakes the crucial step of **aggregation**. A common and effective aggregation algorithm is **Federated Averaging (FedAvg)**. In FedAvg, the server computes a weighted average of the model updates received from the participating clients. The weights are typically proportional to the size of the local dataset each client used for training, giving more influence to clients with more data. This aggregated update is then used to refine the global model. For instance, if the model is a neural network with parameters $\mathbf{w}$, and client $k$ has $n*k$ data samples, after a round of local training on its data $D*k$, it computes an update $\Delta \mathbf{w}*k$. The server then computes the global update as $\Delta \mathbf{w}*{\text{global}} = \sum*{k} \frac*{nk}{N} \Delta \mathbf{w}*k$, where $N = \sum*k n_k$ is the total number of samples across participating clients. This improved global model is then sent back to the clients for the next round of training.

This iterative process offers significant advantages, particularly in engineering contexts.

**Privacy preservation** is perhaps the most compelling benefit. By keeping sensitive raw data localized, FL inherently addresses concerns related to data breaches, regulatory compliance (like GDPR or CCPA), and the proprietary nature of industrial datasets. For instance, in a manufacturing setting, different factories owned by the same company might be reluctant to share their production line sensor data due to competitive advantages or trade secrets. FL allows these factories to collaboratively build a more robust predictive maintenance model without exposing their internal operational details.

**Reduced communication overhead** is another key advantage. Transmitting massive raw datasets can be bandwidth-intensive and costly, especially from edge devices with limited connectivity. FL only requires the transmission of model updates, which are typically much smaller in size than the raw data, leading to significant savings in communication costs and improved efficiency, especially in scenarios with a large number of clients or limited network capacity.

**Logistical feasibility** is also enhanced. In many engineering applications, data is generated at the edge—on robots, in vehicles, on smart meters, or within industrial control systems. These edge devices may not have the capability or the connectivity to upload large volumes of data to a central cloud. FL allows these devices to contribute to model training directly, leveraging their local processing power and data.

Consider the application of FL in **smart manufacturing**. A multinational automotive manufacturer might have multiple assembly plants around the world. Each plant collects data from its robotic assembly lines, quality control sensors, and supply chain management systems. To improve the overall efficiency and quality across all plants, they might want to train a model that can predict equipment failures, optimize robotic arm movements for precision, or identify potential quality defects in real-time. However, sharing proprietary production data between plants, or between different companies in a supply chain, is often not feasible due to competitive sensitivities or data ownership issues. With Federated Learning, each plant can train a local model on its own data. The learned insights—represented as model parameter updates—can then be securely aggregated at a central server to create a superior global model. This global model, incorporating the collective knowledge from all participating plants, can then be deployed back to each plant, leading to improved performance for everyone without any plant having to reveal its sensitive operational data. For example, if one plant experiences a unique type of failure in a specific robot model, its local training will capture this anomaly. This learning, when aggregated, can help other plants proactively identify and mitigate similar issues, even if they haven't encountered it themselves yet.

Similarly, in the domain of
**smart cities**, FL can be applied to a multitude of challenges. Imagine an urban traffic management system. Data on traffic flow, speed, and congestion patterns is generated by sensors, smart traffic lights, and connected vehicles across different districts. Centralizing all this data might be a privacy concern for citizens and raise logistical hurdles. Using FL, a distributed traffic prediction model can be trained. Each city district, or even individual traffic signal controllers, can train a local model on its observed traffic data. These local models are then aggregated to form a city-wide traffic prediction model. This global model can then be used to optimize traffic light timings dynamically across the entire city, reducing congestion, improving travel times, and lowering emissions. The privacy of individual vehicle movements or detailed sensor readings is preserved because only aggregated model updates are shared.

Another compelling use case is in **predictive maintenance for industrial equipment**. Across an energy utility company's vast network of power generation facilities, each facility collects sensor data from its turbines, generators, and transformers. The goal is to predict potential equipment failures before they occur, minimizing downtime and maintenance costs. However, each facility might have unique operational characteristics and maintenance logs that it considers confidential. FL enables a collaborative approach where each facility trains a local predictive maintenance model on its own historical sensor data and failure records. These local models are then aggregated to produce a robust global model that can predict failures more accurately by learning from the diverse operational contexts of all facilities. This shared intelligence allows the utility to preemptively address potential issues across its entire infrastructure, enhancing reliability and operational efficiency.

The application of FL in engineering extends to areas like **autonomous systems and robotics**. A fleet of delivery robots operating in different geographic locations or within various warehouses could collectively improve their navigation and object manipulation capabilities. Each robot, through its interactions with its local environment, gathers data on successful and unsuccessful navigation attempts, object grasping successes, and pathfinding challenges. Instead of uploading all this rich, but potentially large, sensory and operational data, each robot can train a local version of a navigation or manipulation policy. The updates from these local training sessions are then aggregated to refine a global policy. This aggregated policy can then be redistributed to all robots, enabling the entire fleet to benefit from the experiences of each individual unit, leading to faster learning and more robust performance in diverse operational settings.

However, federated learning is not without its challenges, especially in complex engineering environments.

**Statistical heterogeneity** among clients is a significant issue. In traditional FL, it's often assumed that data distributions across clients are similar (i.i.d. - independent and identically distributed). However, in real-world engineering scenarios, data from different factories, cities, or devices can vary drastically. For example, a manufacturing plant in a region with older machinery will have a different data distribution than a plant with state-of-the-art equipment. This heterogeneity can lead to model divergence and slow convergence, or even a degradation of the global model's performance. Advanced FL techniques are being developed to address this, such as personalized FL, where clients can fine-tune the global model to their specific local data characteristics, or clustered FL, where clients are grouped based on data similarity to train more specialized models.

**System heterogeneity** also poses a challenge. Participating devices in an FL network can have vastly different computational capabilities, network bandwidths, and battery life. Some devices might be powerful servers, while others are low-power edge sensors. This disparity can lead to stragglers—clients that take much longer to complete their local training or communication, slowing down the entire aggregation process. Strategies to mitigate this include selecting clients for training rounds based on their capabilities, using asynchronous update mechanisms, or employing model compression techniques to reduce the size of updates.

**Security and privacy concerns** persist even in FL. While raw data is not shared, model updates themselves can potentially leak information about the local data if not handled carefully. Techniques like **differential privacy** can be applied to the model updates before they are sent to the server, adding noise to obscure the contribution of any single data point. Secure multi-party computation (SMPC) and homomorphic encryption can also be used to ensure that the central server can perform aggregation without actually seeing the individual client updates. Ensuring that the central server itself is trustworthy is also paramount.

The
**choice of aggregation algorithm** is critical. While FedAvg is a good starting point, it might not be optimal for all scenarios, especially with highly heterogeneous data. Research into more sophisticated aggregation methods that can better handle non-i.i.d. data, such as FedProx, which adds a proximal term to the local objective function to limit the divergence from the global model, or SCAFFOLD, which uses control variates to correct for client drift, is essential for unlocking the full potential of FL in engineering.

Furthermore,
**model selection and architecture design** are important considerations. The complexity of the global model must be appropriate for the data available across all clients. An overly complex model might overfit to the data of a few dominant clients, while an undersized model might not capture the nuances present across the diverse datasets. Experimentation and iterative refinement are often required to find the right model architecture.

The practical implementation of FL in engineering systems requires careful orchestration. This involves:

1.
**Client Selection:** Deciding which clients participate in each training round. This can be random, or based on factors like data availability, device readiness, or network conditions.
2. **Local Training Strategy:** Determining the number of local epochs, the optimizer to use, and the learning rate for each client's local model training.

3. **Communication Protocol:** Establishing secure and efficient channels for model distribution and update transmission.
4. **Aggregation Strategy:** Choosing and implementing the aggregation algorithm, and deciding on the frequency of aggregation.
5. **Global Model Update:** Applying the aggregated update to the global model and distributing it for the next round.
6. **Termination Criteria:** Defining when the training process has converged, typically based on the global model's performance on a validation set or the stability of the model updates.

The iterative nature of FL makes it well-suited for continuous learning and adaptation in dynamic engineering environments. As new data becomes available at the edge, models can be incrementally updated, allowing systems to adapt to changing conditions, evolving operational parameters, or emerging patterns without the need for periodic, large-scale data collection and retraining cycles. This "always-learning" capability is invaluable for systems that operate in real-time, such as autonomous driving systems that encounter new road conditions or industrial processes that experience variations in raw material quality.

In summary, Federated Learning represents a powerful paradigm shift for machine learning in distributed engineering data scenarios. By enabling collaborative model training without centralizing raw data, it addresses critical challenges related to data privacy, security, communication costs, and logistical feasibility. Its applications in smart manufacturing, smart cities, predictive maintenance, and autonomous systems are vast and continue to grow. While challenges related to data and system heterogeneity, security, and aggregation remain active areas of research, ongoing advancements in FL algorithms and techniques are paving the way for its broader adoption, promising to unlock unprecedented levels of intelligence and automation across the engineering landscape by harnessing the collective power of distributed data.

The iterative nature of Federated Learning (FL) makes it well-suited for continuous learning and adaptation in dynamic engineering environments. As new data becomes available at the edge, models can be incrementally updated, allowing systems to adapt to changing conditions, evolving operational parameters, or emerging patterns without the need for periodic, large-scale data collection and retraining cycles. This "always-learning" capability is invaluable for systems that operate in real-time, such as autonomous driving systems that encounter new road conditions or industrial processes that experience variations in raw material quality.

In summary, Federated Learning represents a powerful paradigm shift for machine learning in distributed engineering data scenarios. By enabling collaborative model training without centralizing raw data, it addresses critical challenges related to data privacy, security, communication costs, and logistical feasibility. Its applications in smart manufacturing, smart cities, predictive maintenance, and autonomous systems are vast and continue to grow. While challenges related to data and system heterogeneity, security, and aggregation remain active areas of research, ongoing advancements in FL algorithms and techniques are paving the way for its broader adoption, promising to unlock unprecedented levels of intelligence and automation across the engineering landscape by harnessing the collective power of distributed data.

## The Role of Simulation in ML Pipeline Development

In the intricate tapestry of machine learning (ML) pipeline development, particularly within the demanding landscape of engineering applications, the ability to experiment, iterate, and validate is paramount. Real-world testing, while the ultimate arbiter of performance, often presents significant hurdles. These can range from prohibitive costs and logistical complexities to outright dangers associated with testing in live, critical systems. Imagine attempting to train an autonomous driving system by intentionally driving cars into unpredictable scenarios, or refining a robotic arm's precision by allowing it to make potentially damaging mistakes on an assembly line. These are scenarios where direct, real-world experimentation is not only inefficient but also irresponsible. This is precisely where the power of **simulation environments** emerges as an indispensable tool, acting as a virtual proving ground for the entire ML pipeline, from initial data generation to final model deployment.

Simulation allows us to create controlled, reproducible, and safe environments that mimic the complexities of the real world. This capability is transformative across multiple stages of ML pipeline development. One of the most immediate benefits is the ability to **generate synthetic data**. In many engineering domains, obtaining vast, diverse, and perfectly labeled datasets can be a monumental undertaking. Sensor failures, rare operational events, or specific environmental conditions might occur too infrequently in real-world data collection to adequately train a robust model. Simulations can be meticulously designed to generate data that captures these precise conditions. For instance, to train a model that predicts structural integrity failures in a bridge under various weather conditions, a simulation can generate data representing extreme wind speeds, heavy rainfall, seismic activity, and combinations thereof, along with their corresponding structural stress responses. This synthetic data, if generated with sufficient fidelity to reality, can supplement or even replace real-world data, especially in the early stages of development, enabling faster iteration and reducing reliance on hard-to-obtain real-world observations. Furthermore, simulations can be programmed to generate perfectly labeled data, eliminating the often tedious and error-prone manual labeling process, thereby accelerating the training phase significantly. The ability to control the parameters of data generation—such as the frequency of certain events, the level of sensor noise, or the specific types of anomalies—provides an unparalleled level of fine-tuning for model training.

Beyond data generation, simulation environments serve as robust **testbeds for the entire ML pipeline**. An ML pipeline is not just a single model; it's a complex orchestration of data preprocessing, feature engineering, model training, hyperparameter tuning, validation, and deployment. Each of these components can be individually developed and tested within a simulated environment before being integrated. For example, a data preprocessing module designed to handle noisy sensor readings from a robotic arm can be tested with simulated noisy sensor data generated by the same environment. This allows engineers to identify and fix bugs or inefficiencies in each stage independently, ensuring that the pipeline's components work harmoniously together. When developing a predictive maintenance model for industrial machinery, the pipeline might involve ingesting sensor data, performing Fourier transforms to identify vibration patterns, and then feeding these features into a recurrent neural network (RNN). Each of these steps can be simulated. We can generate synthetic sensor data exhibiting specific fault signatures, apply the Fourier transform in the simulation, and then feed the resulting spectral data into a simulated RNN. This end-to-end testing within a controlled simulation ensures that the entire workflow is functional and efficient.

A critical advantage of simulation is its ability to facilitate **comprehensive performance evaluation** under a wide spectrum of conditions. Real-world deployments are often constrained by the need to avoid risky scenarios. Simulations, however, can be programmed to push the boundaries. Engineers can evaluate how an ML model performs under extreme load, during rare fault conditions, or in the presence of adversarial inputs, all without any real-world consequences. For an autonomous vehicle's perception system, simulations can generate scenarios involving sudden, unexpected obstacles, poor visibility conditions (e.g., fog, heavy rain, snow), and complex lighting changes (e.g., entering/exiting tunnels). By systematically varying these parameters and observing the model's output (e.g., detection accuracy, latency), engineers can gain deep insights into the model's robustness, identify its failure modes, and quantify its reliability under stress. This systematic stress-testing is crucial for building trust and confidence in ML systems deployed in safety-critical applications. For example, testing an ML model designed to detect anomalies in power grid operations could involve simulating scenarios with cascading failures, sudden demand surges, or targeted cyber-attacks. The simulation can precisely control the timing and nature of these events, allowing for a precise measurement of the ML model's ability to detect and respond to each specific threat. This level of controlled experimentation is impossible to replicate in a live grid.

The ability to conduct
**what-if analyses** is another significant benefit of using simulations. Engineers can alter specific parameters within the simulation and observe their impact on the ML pipeline's performance. For instance, if a simulation environment is used to test an ML-driven control system for a chemical process, engineers can simulate the effect of using a different type of catalyst, altering the flow rate of a reactant, or introducing a minor temperature fluctuation. By observing how the ML controller adapts and what its resulting outputs are, engineers can make informed decisions about process design, parameter tuning, and the operational envelope for the ML system. This forward-looking capability allows for proactive design and optimization, rather than reactive adjustments after deployment.

Furthermore, simulations are instrumental in
**developing and refining control policies** for complex dynamic systems. Many engineering problems involve optimizing the behavior of a system over time. Reinforcement learning (RL) is a powerful ML paradigm for such tasks, but training RL agents directly in the real world is often impractical and dangerous. A robot learning to perform delicate surgery through trial and error in a live operating room is unthinkable. However,

a simulation of the surgical environment, complete with realistic tissue properties, instrument dynamics, and even simulated patient responses, provides a safe and effective training ground. The RL agent can explore a vast state-action space, learn from simulated rewards and penalties, and develop sophisticated control strategies without risking patient harm. Similarly, an RL agent tasked with optimizing energy consumption in a smart building can be trained in a simulated building environment that accurately models thermal dynamics, occupancy patterns, and HVAC system responses. The agent can learn to make optimal decisions regarding heating, cooling, and lighting, leading to significant energy savings once deployed in the actual building.

The fidelity of a simulation is a critical factor in its utility. A low-fidelity simulation might be quick to run but may not accurately reflect real-world dynamics, leading to models that perform poorly when deployed. Conversely, a high-fidelity simulation might be computationally expensive and slow, negating some of the speed advantages of using simulations. Therefore, there is often a trade-off between simulation complexity and computational cost. The development of
**hybrid approaches** is also gaining traction, where ML models are initially trained on synthetic data from a high-fidelity simulation, then fine-tuned using smaller amounts of real-world data, or where elements of real-world data are injected into simulations to increase their realism. Techniques like **domain randomization** are employed in simulation to expose the ML model to a wide variety of visual textures, lighting conditions, and object variations, making the learned policy more robust to discrepancies between the simulation and the real world.

For instance, consider the development of an ML system for inspecting manufactured parts for defects. A simulation could generate thousands of images of perfect parts, as well as parts with a variety of simulated defects: scratches, dents, misalignments, incorrect colorations, and so on. The simulation can precisely control the size, location, and severity of these defects, ensuring comprehensive coverage. This synthetic dataset can be used to train an image classification or object detection model. Subsequently, the model can be tested on a smaller, curated dataset of real-world images, and further fine-tuned if necessary. This simulation-driven approach significantly reduces the time and effort required to gather and label a sufficiently large and diverse dataset for defect detection.

The use of simulation is also vital for **ensuring the explainability and interpretability** of ML models in engineering. By controlling specific input variables in a simulation and observing how the model's predictions change, engineers can gain insights into which features are most influential for a given decision. For example, if an ML model is predicting the likelihood of material fatigue, a simulation could be used to systematically vary parameters like applied stress, temperature, and material composition. By observing the resulting changes in the predicted fatigue life, engineers can understand how sensitive the model is to each factor, which can be crucial for debugging and for gaining domain-specific knowledge. This is particularly important in regulated industries where understanding *why* a model makes a certain prediction is as important as the prediction itself.

In summary, simulation environments are not merely an optional add-on but a foundational element for the efficient, safe, and robust development of ML pipelines in engineering. They provide the means to generate diverse data, serve as safe environments for rigorous testing and validation, enable comprehensive performance evaluation under extreme conditions, facilitate sophisticated what-if analyses, and offer a practical platform for training complex control policies, especially through reinforcement learning. As ML models become increasingly integrated into critical engineering systems, the role of simulation in accelerating their development, enhancing their reliability, and ensuring their safety will only continue to grow in importance. It allows engineers to explore the design space, anticipate potential issues, and build more resilient and trustworthy intelligent systems.

The landscape of engineering and its associated computational methodologies is in a constant state of evolution, driven by the insatiable demand for greater efficiency, enhanced predictive capabilities, and more sophisticated control over complex systems. While the preceding discussions have illuminated foundational and advanced techniques in machine learning relevant to engineering, it is crucial to cast our gaze forward. The future promises a convergence of physical and digital realms, where intelligent algorithms are not merely analytical tools but integral components of dynamic, interactive, and self-optimizing systems. Among the most transformative of these emerging trends is the concept of **Digital Twins** and their profound integration with Artificial Intelligence (AI).

A Digital Twin, at its core, is a virtual replica of a physical asset, process, or system. It is not a static 3D model, but a living, dynamic representation that is continuously updated with real-time data from its physical counterpart. This data flows from sensors, operational logs, maintenance records, and other sources, creating a synchronized, data-rich mirror image. Imagine a jet engine, a wind turbine, a manufacturing plant, or even an entire city – each can have a digital twin. This twin evolves alongside its physical twin, reflecting its current state, historical performance, and operational context. The fidelity of a digital twin is paramount; the more accurately it mirrors the physical entity, the more reliable its insights and predictions become. This requires sophisticated data pipelines capable of ingesting, processing, and contextualizing vast streams of information from diverse sources.

The true power of digital twins, however, is unlocked when they are infused with the capabilities of Artificial Intelligence. AI, with its ability to learn from data, identify patterns, and make predictions, elevates a digital twin from a mere monitoring tool to a proactive, intelligent system. This integration allows for a paradigm shift in how we approach engineering challenges, moving from reactive problem-solving to predictive and prescriptive interventions.

One of the primary areas where AI-powered digital twins excel is in **predictive analytics and anomaly detection**. By analyzing historical data and real-time sensor feeds within the virtual environment, AI algorithms can identify subtle deviations from normal operating behavior that might precede a failure. For instance, in a manufacturing facility, a digital twin of a critical piece of machinery, coupled with an AI model trained on vibration, temperature, and pressure data, can predict an impending bearing failure weeks in advance. This allows for scheduled maintenance during planned downtime, avoiding costly and disruptive unplanned shutdowns. The AI doesn't just report that a parameter is slightly out of bounds; it learns the complex interdependencies of various parameters and forecasts the *consequences* of these deviations over time. It can distinguish between a transient anomaly and a precursor to a more significant issue. This predictive capability extends beyond simple equipment health to optimizing process parameters for yield, quality, or energy efficiency. The AI can explore scenarios within the digital twin to understand how minor adjustments to, say, a chemical reaction temperature or a robotic arm's speed, might impact overall throughput or defect rates.

Furthermore, AI integration transforms digital twins into powerful **simulation and "what-if" analysis platforms**. Traditional simulations often rely on predefined physics-based models, which can be computationally intensive and may not fully capture the nuances of real-world operation, especially when dealing with complex emergent behaviors or wear-and-tear effects. An AI-enhanced digital twin can leverage its learned models to run simulations with unprecedented speed and adaptability. Engineers can pose complex questions to the twin:

"What would be the impact on plant output if we increase the throughput of raw material X by 15% while simultaneously experiencing a 5% degradation in the efficiency of pump Y?" The AI, drawing upon its understanding of the interrelationships within the digital twin, can simulate these conditions, predict the outcome, and even suggest optimal adjustments to other parameters to mitigate any negative consequences. This capability is invaluable during the design phase of new products or processes, allowing for rapid iteration and optimization before any physical resources are committed. It also supports scenario planning for operational disruptions, such as supply chain interruptions or unexpected demand surges.

The synergy between digital twins and AI also extends to **intelligent control and optimization**. In many complex systems, direct human control or even traditional feedback control loops struggle to achieve optimal performance due to the sheer number of interacting variables and the dynamic nature of the environment. An AI agent, operating within or in conjunction with the digital twin, can learn to dynamically control the physical system. This is particularly relevant in areas like autonomous systems, smart grids, and advanced manufacturing. For example, an AI controlling a fleet of autonomous vehicles might use the digital twin of the city's traffic network to optimize routes in real-time, considering not only traffic congestion but also predicted road closures, weather events, and even the battery levels of the vehicles themselves. In a smart grid, an AI could use a digital twin of the power distribution network to optimize energy flow, balance supply and demand from diverse sources (solar, wind, conventional), and predict potential overloads, making micro-adjustments to minimize losses and ensure grid stability. The digital twin provides the AI with a safe, data-rich environment to learn and refine its control strategies without the immediate risks associated with experimenting on the live system.

The development and deployment of AI-powered digital twins are not without their challenges.

**Data quality and integration** remain paramount. The accuracy and reliability of the digital twin are directly dependent on the quality, completeness, and timeliness of the data it receives. Ensuring seamless integration of data from disparate sources, often with different formats and communication protocols, requires robust data engineering practices. **Scalability** is another significant consideration; as the complexity of the physical asset or system increases, so does the computational demand for maintaining and simulating its digital twin. Furthermore, **model interpretability and trustworthiness** are crucial, especially when AI is used for critical decision-making. Engineers need to understand *why* an AI makes a particular prediction or recommendation. While deep learning models can be powerful, their "black box" nature can be a barrier to adoption in safety-critical engineering applications. Research into explainable AI (XAI) is therefore closely linked to the advancement of AI-powered digital twins.

Moreover, the
**security of digital twins** is a growing concern. A digital twin represents a wealth of sensitive information about a physical asset or process. Unauthorized access or manipulation of the digital twin could lead to significant operational disruptions, intellectual property theft, or even physical damage. Robust cybersecurity measures are essential to protect these virtual replicas.

Despite these challenges, the trajectory is clear. The convergence of digital twins and AI represents a fundamental shift in engineering, moving towards systems that are not only monitored but also understood, predicted, and intelligently managed. This fusion enables unprecedented levels of optimization, resilience, and autonomy. It promises to accelerate innovation by allowing engineers to virtually prototype, test, and refine designs and operational strategies with greater speed and confidence. It enhances operational efficiency by enabling proactive maintenance and real-time adaptive control. It also fosters a deeper understanding of complex systems, providing insights that were previously inaccessible. As computational power continues to grow and AI algorithms become more sophisticated, the capabilities of AI-powered digital twins will expand, touching virtually every domain of engineering. We are on the cusp of an era where the virtual and physical worlds are inextricably linked, driven by intelligent, data-informed insights. This represents not just an advancement in technology, but a redefinition of what is possible in the design, operation, and maintenance of the engineered world around us. The continuous learning and adaptation facilitated by AI within these virtual mirrors will allow engineering systems to become more robust, responsive, and ultimately, more intelligent.

# Chapter 15: Best Practices and Your Engineering Data Journey

The journey towards truly intelligent engineering systems, as illuminated by the power of AI-infused digital twins, is not solely a technical undertaking. While sophisticated algorithms, robust data infrastructure, and advanced simulation techniques form the bedrock, the ultimate success hinges on a crucial, often underestimated, element: culture. Establishing a culture of data-driven engineering is not merely about adopting new tools; it is about fostering a fundamental shift in how teams think, collaborate, and make decisions. This cultural transformation is the essential precursor to effectively harnessing the full potential of advanced data pipelines and the insights they generate. Without this intrinsic embrace of data as a core asset, even the most cutting-edge technologies risk becoming underutilized or misunderstood.

At its heart, a data-driven culture means that decisions, from strategic planning to day-to-day operational adjustments, are informed by evidence derived from data, rather than solely relying on intuition, historical precedent, or anecdotal experience. This doesn't negate the value of expert judgment; rather, it augments it. Domain experts, with their deep understanding of the physical systems, processes, and their inherent complexities, are indispensable. However, in a data-driven environment, their expertise is combined with the objective insights provided by data analysis. This creates a powerful synergy where intuition guides the questions asked of the data, and data validates or refines those intuitions. For instance, a seasoned mechanical engineer might hypothesize that a particular vibration pattern indicates an impending failure in a pump. In a data-driven culture, this hypothesis is not acted upon immediately based on experience alone. Instead, it triggers a focused investigation of the sensor data associated with that pump. The data engineer or data scientist would then analyze historical vibration data, correlating it with known failure modes and operational parameters. If the data supports the hypothesis, a precise, data-backed maintenance recommendation can be made, specifying the type of failure, the estimated time to failure, and the optimal intervention strategy.

Conversely, if the data contradicts the hypothesis, the engineer is encouraged to explore other explanations, leading to a more thorough and accurate diagnosis.

This collaborative dynamic between domain experts and data specialists is a cornerstone of a thriving data-driven engineering culture. Traditionally, these groups might operate in silos, with engineers focused on physical design and operation, and data professionals concerned with information management. In a data-driven organization, these boundaries blur. Data scientists are encouraged to gain a foundational understanding of the engineering principles and operational realities of the systems they are analyzing, while engineers are empowered and encouraged to understand the capabilities and limitations of data analysis techniques. This mutual respect and shared understanding foster more effective problem-solving. For example, when developing an AI model for predicting the fatigue life of a material, the material scientist's knowledge of stress concentrations, material properties, and failure mechanisms is crucial. Simultaneously, the data scientist's ability to identify relevant features from sensor data, build predictive models, and quantify uncertainty is equally vital. A team that can effectively bridge these knowledge gaps will invariably develop more accurate, robust, and interpretable models than a team where these disciplines remain separate. This cross-pollination of knowledge can occur through formal training programs, informal knowledge-sharing sessions, or by embedding data scientists within engineering teams and vice-versa.

Promoting continuous learning and experimentation is another critical facet of establishing a data-driven engineering culture. The field of data science and AI is rapidly evolving, as are the systems and processes that engineering teams manage. What is considered best practice today may be outdated tomorrow. Therefore, an environment that encourages ongoing learning, exploration, and safe experimentation is essential. This means allocating time and resources for engineers and data professionals to stay abreast of new techniques, attend conferences, and pursue further education. More importantly, it involves creating a culture where experimentation is not viewed as a risky indulgence but as an inherent part of the innovation and improvement process. This can manifest in several ways. For instance, teams might be encouraged to set aside a portion of their time for "innovation sprints" where they can explore new datasets or test novel analytical approaches without the immediate pressure of immediate production deadlines. Failure during experimentation should be seen not as a setback, but as a valuable learning opportunity. A failed experiment can provide critical insights into what doesn't work, thereby guiding future efforts more effectively. Documenting these experiments, both successes and failures, and sharing the learnings widely within the organization, further strengthens the collective knowledge base and accelerates the adoption of effective data-driven practices.

The implementation of robust data pipelines, a prerequisite for advanced analytics and digital twins, is intrinsically linked to this cultural shift. Building and maintaining these pipelines requires a deep understanding of data lineage, quality, governance, and security. In a data-driven culture, there is a collective ownership of data quality. Engineers understand that the reliability of their predictive maintenance models, for example, is directly proportional to the accuracy and completeness of the sensor data fed into them. This awareness encourages greater diligence in ensuring that data acquisition systems are functioning correctly, that sensors are calibrated, and that data is validated at the point of entry. Data governance policies are not seen as bureaucratic hurdles but as essential frameworks for ensuring that data is used ethically, securely, and consistently across the organization. This includes establishing clear definitions for key metrics, defining access controls, and implementing data quality checks at various stages of the pipeline. When data is treated as a strategic asset, with clear ownership and well-defined processes for its management, the foundation for reliable data-driven decision-making is solidified.

Furthermore, a data-driven culture often involves a commitment to transparency and accessibility of data. While proprietary information must be protected, making relevant data available to those who need it to perform their roles can significantly accelerate innovation and problem-solving. This might involve creating centralized data repositories or data lakes, providing intuitive tools for data exploration and visualization, and establishing clear processes for requesting access to specific datasets. When engineers can easily access and explore the data related to their projects, they are more likely to identify trends, uncover anomalies, and formulate new hypotheses. For example, if an engineer responsible for optimizing the performance of a manufacturing line can readily access historical production data, quality control metrics, and machine uptime logs, they can more quickly identify bottlenecks, diagnose root causes of defects, and test potential improvements. This democratization of data, within appropriate security and governance frameworks, empowers individuals at all levels of the organization to contribute to data-informed decision-making.

The role of leadership in fostering this culture cannot be overstated. Leaders must not only champion the importance of data but also actively demonstrate its value through their own decision-making processes. This means allocating budget and resources to data initiatives, setting clear expectations for data utilization, and celebrating successes that arise from data-driven insights. Leaders should encourage a mindset of continuous improvement, where data is used not just to solve immediate problems but also to proactively identify opportunities for innovation and optimization. This might involve setting ambitious targets for reducing unplanned downtime, improving product quality, or enhancing energy efficiency, and then empowering teams to use data to achieve those targets. When leadership consistently prioritizes and rewards data-driven approaches, it sends a powerful message throughout the organization, encouraging widespread adoption and engagement.

Moreover, a data-driven culture thrives on a feedback loop. The insights generated from data analysis should not be a one-off report but should lead to actionable changes, the impact of which is then measured and fed back into the system. This iterative process of "measure, analyze, act, and learn" is fundamental to continuous improvement. For instance, if an AI model predicts an optimal operating temperature for a chemical reactor, and this recommendation is implemented, the subsequent performance of the reactor (e.g., yield, energy consumption, byproduct formation) should be meticulously monitored. This data then serves to validate the AI's prediction, refine the model, and inform future operational adjustments. This continuous cycle ensures that the organization is constantly learning and adapting, becoming more efficient and effective over time. Without this feedback mechanism, data analysis can become a purely academic exercise, failing to translate into tangible improvements.

Finally, cultivating a data-driven engineering culture is an ongoing process, not a destination. It requires consistent effort, adaptation, and a willingness to evolve. As new technologies emerge and data sources expand, the organization must remain agile, embracing new tools and techniques while staying true to the core principles of evidence-based decision-making. It is about building an organizational DNA where data is inherently interwoven into the fabric of every engineering endeavor, enabling a future where systems are not only designed and built with precision but are also continuously understood, optimized, and evolved through the intelligent application of data. This cultural imperative is the invisible yet indispensable scaffolding upon which the advanced capabilities of AI-powered digital twins and intelligent engineering systems are built.

The increasing reliance on data-driven approaches within engineering, particularly with the advent of sophisticated AI and digital twin technologies, brings with it a profound responsibility to consider the ethical implications of these practices. As we empower machines and algorithms to make or inform critical decisions that affect safety, efficiency, and even human well-being, a robust framework for ethical conduct becomes not just a best practice, but an absolute necessity. This subsection delves into the multifaceted ethical considerations that engineers and data scientists must navigate to ensure that their work is not only technically sound but also socially responsible and trustworthy.

One of the most prominent ethical concerns revolves around data privacy and security. Engineering systems, especially those incorporating IoT devices, sensor networks, and user interactions, often collect vast amounts of data, some of which may be sensitive or personally identifiable. While this data is invaluable for optimizing performance, predicting failures, and informing design, its collection, storage, and processing must adhere to stringent privacy regulations and ethical guidelines. Engineers must be acutely aware of the provenance of their data, ensuring that it has been collected with appropriate consent and anonymization where necessary. Furthermore, robust security measures are paramount to prevent unauthorized access, breaches, or misuse of this data. The potential consequences of a data breach in an engineering context can range from compromised intellectual property and financial loss to, in critical infrastructure or safety-sensitive applications, direct threats to public safety. Implementing principles of data minimization, where only necessary data is collected and retained, and employing state-of-the-art encryption and access controls are fundamental steps in safeguarding privacy. Moreover, transparency with stakeholders about data collection practices and how data is used builds trust and reinforces ethical stewardship.

Algorithmic bias represents another significant ethical hurdle. Machine learning models are trained on historical data, and if this data reflects existing societal biases, the resulting algorithms will likely perpetuate and even amplify these biases. In engineering, this can manifest in various ways. For example, an AI system designed to optimize traffic flow might inadvertently prioritize certain neighborhoods over others based on historical travel patterns that were themselves influenced by socioeconomic factors or discriminatory urban planning. Similarly, a predictive maintenance system for industrial machinery, if trained on data where certain equipment types were historically maintained differently based on implicit biases, could lead to disproportionate maintenance efforts or neglect. The ethical imperative here is to actively identify, measure, and mitigate bias in data and algorithms. This requires a proactive approach, including diverse data collection strategies, rigorous bias detection techniques during model development, and ongoing monitoring of model performance in real-world deployment to identify any emergent unfairness. Techniques like fairness-aware machine learning, which incorporate fairness constraints into the model training process, are crucial tools in this endeavor.

Fairness in automated decision-making is intrinsically linked to algorithmic bias. When engineering systems, powered by data and algorithms, make decisions that impact individuals or groups, it is essential that these decisions are perceived as fair and equitable. This concept of fairness can be complex and context-dependent, encompassing notions of equal opportunity, equal outcome, or other definitions tailored to the specific application. For instance, an automated system for resource allocation in a city's infrastructure maintenance might need to ensure that services are distributed equitably across different communities, regardless of their demographic composition. Engineers must engage in thoughtful deliberation about what constitutes "fairness" in their specific domain and translate these principles into quantifiable metrics and algorithmic constraints. This often involves interdisciplinary collaboration, bringing together engineers, ethicists, social scientists, and legal experts to define and operationalize fairness. It also necessitates a careful consideration of the trade-offs that may exist between different fairness definitions and between fairness and other performance objectives, such as efficiency or accuracy.

The responsible deployment of AI and data-driven systems is a broad ethical umbrella that covers numerous aspects. It begins with a thorough understanding of the potential risks and unintended consequences associated with any deployed system. This involves not just technical performance metrics but also the societal impact, potential for misuse, and long-term implications. For safety-critical engineering applications, such as autonomous vehicles or medical devices, the ethical bar is exceptionally high. Rigorous testing, validation, and verification processes are non-negotiable. Furthermore, there is an increasing emphasis on explainability and interpretability in AI. Black-box models, where the decision-making process is opaque, can be problematic from an ethical standpoint, especially when those decisions have significant consequences. Engineers should strive to develop and deploy systems whose reasoning can be understood and audited, allowing for accountability and trust. The development of "explainable AI" (XAI) techniques is a critical area of research and development that supports this ethical goal.

Accountability is another cornerstone of ethical data science in engineering. When an AI system makes an erroneous decision or causes harm, it is crucial to establish who is responsible. Is it the data scientist who trained the model, the engineer who deployed it, the organization that commissioned it, or the data itself? Clear lines of accountability need to be established, and this often requires careful documentation of the entire data lifecycle, from data acquisition and preprocessing to model development, validation, and deployment. This documentation should include the rationale behind design choices, the datasets used, the performance metrics achieved, and any known limitations. In the context of complex engineering systems, a multi-stakeholder approach to accountability is often necessary, where different parties share responsibility based on their roles and contributions.

The ethical considerations extend to the very design of engineering processes and systems. This includes fostering an organizational culture that prioritizes ethical thinking and providing engineers with the training and resources they need to navigate complex ethical dilemmas. Ethical review boards or dedicated ethics committees can play a vital role in scrutinizing new projects and technologies. Furthermore, engaging with the public and other stakeholders to understand their concerns and expectations is an important aspect of responsible innovation. Engineering solutions are rarely developed in a vacuum; they exist within a societal context, and their ethical implications must be considered in light of that context. This can involve conducting impact assessments, performing ethical risk analyses, and actively seeking diverse perspectives to ensure that systems are developed for the benefit of society as a whole, not just a select few.

The concept of "value alignment" is also critical. AI systems should be designed to align with human values and goals. In engineering, this means ensuring that automated systems are not only efficient but also safe, reliable, and contribute positively to human endeavors. For example, an AI system designed to optimize energy consumption in a building should do so without compromising occupant comfort or health. This requires a deep understanding of the intended purpose of the system and its potential broader impacts. It involves a continuous dialogue between the developers of the technology and the end-users, as well as the broader community affected by its deployment.

Moreover, the issue of unintended consequences must be addressed proactively. Even well-intentioned AI systems can have unforeseen negative effects. For instance, an AI system designed to automate certain engineering tasks might lead to job displacement, requiring careful planning for workforce transition and reskilling. Similarly, systems designed to enhance efficiency could inadvertently increase environmental impact if not carefully designed and monitored. A thorough risk assessment process, including scenario planning and "what-if" analyses, is essential to anticipate and mitigate these potential downsides. This proactive approach to risk management is a hallmark of ethical engineering.

The ongoing evolution of AI and data science means that ethical considerations are not a static checklist but a dynamic and evolving field. Engineers and data scientists must remain committed to continuous learning, staying abreast of new ethical challenges and best practices. This includes engaging with professional organizations, participating in ethical training, and contributing to the development of industry standards and guidelines. The goal is to build a future where engineering innovation is not only technologically advanced but also ethically robust, ensuring that the powerful tools we develop serve humanity's best interests and contribute to a more just and sustainable world. This commitment to ethical data science is as critical to the success of our engineering data journey as any technical skill or technological advancement. It is the foundation upon which trust is built, and without trust, the full potential of these transformative technologies cannot be realized responsibly.

The landscape of data engineering and machine learning is in a perpetual state of flux, characterized by an insatiable appetite for innovation and a relentless pace of change. To not merely survive but to thrive in this dynamic environment, a steadfast commitment to continuous learning and proactive skill development is not an option; it is an imperative. The technologies, methodologies, and best practices that are cutting-edge today can rapidly become antiquated tomorrow. Therefore, the discerning data professional must cultivate a mindset of lifelong learning, viewing each new development not as a threat, but as an opportunity to expand their toolkit and deepen their expertise.

Embarking on this journey of perpetual learning requires a strategic approach, one that leverages the abundance of resources available to the modern engineer. Online learning platforms have emerged as invaluable allies, offering structured courses on virtually every conceivable aspect of data engineering and machine learning. From foundational concepts in statistics and programming to advanced topics in distributed systems, deep learning architectures, and MLOps, these platforms provide flexible and accessible avenues for acquiring new knowledge. Platforms like Coursera, edX, Udacity, and fast.ai offer curated specializations and Nanodegree programs, often developed in collaboration with leading universities and industry experts. These courses typically combine theoretical instruction with practical, hands-on projects, allowing learners to immediately apply what they've learned and build a tangible portfolio. For instance, a data engineer looking to enhance their skills in cloud-native data warehousing might enroll in a specialization focused on Snowflake or BigQuery, while a machine learning engineer aiming to master natural language processing could delve into a deep learning course covering transformer models. The key is to identify areas where your current skill set can be augmented or where emerging trends suggest a future need, and then to seek out reputable courses that align with those goals.

Beyond structured online courses, the vast repository of research papers and academic publications represents a critical, albeit often more demanding, source of cutting-edge knowledge. Conferences, both in-person and virtual, serve as vital hubs for the dissemination of groundbreaking research and the latest industry trends. Attending or even virtually participating in events like NeurIPS, ICML, KDD, or industry-specific conferences focused on cloud computing or data management, offers a unique opportunity to gain insights directly from the researchers and practitioners pushing the boundaries of the field. These events are not just about attending talks; they are about networking with peers, engaging in discussions with thought leaders, and understanding the challenges and opportunities that are currently shaping the data ecosystem. Many conferences make their proceedings and even recorded talks publicly available, extending their reach beyond the event dates and providing a rich archive of knowledge. Staying abreast of papers published on platforms like arXiv, particularly in the subfields relevant to one's work, allows for an early understanding of theoretical advancements that may soon translate into practical tools and techniques.

However, knowledge acquisition is only one half of the equation; true mastery comes through application. Hands-on practice is the crucible in which theoretical understanding is forged into practical proficiency. This can take many forms, from contributing to open-source projects to building personal passion projects. Engaging with open-source communities allows engineers to collaborate with a diverse group of developers, learn from their code, and contribute to tools that are used by thousands worldwide. Projects like Apache Spark, TensorFlow, PyTorch, or various data pipeline orchestration tools are constantly evolving, and contributing to them provides invaluable experience with large-scale codebases and collaborative development workflows. For those who prefer a more self-directed approach, personal projects offer a low-stakes environment to experiment with new technologies. This could involve building a recommendation engine for a favorite streaming service, creating a data visualization dashboard for public datasets, or developing a small-scale predictive model for a hobby. The process of defining a problem, gathering data, selecting tools, implementing a solution, and iterating based on results is an incredibly effective learning mechanism. It exposes the nuances of real-world data, the challenges of implementation, and the iterative nature of engineering.

The rapid evolution of the field also necessitates a keen awareness of emerging trends and technologies. This includes not only the development of new algorithms and frameworks but also shifts in infrastructure, tooling, and best practices. For instance, the rise of cloud computing has fundamentally reshaped data engineering, leading to the widespread adoption of managed services for databases, data lakes, and processing engines. Similarly, the increasing maturity of containerization and orchestration technologies like Docker and Kubernetes has become central to deploying and managing data pipelines and ML models at scale. MLOps, the practice of applying DevOps principles to machine learning workflows, is another area that has rapidly gained prominence, focusing on the automation and streamlining of the entire ML lifecycle, from experimentation to production deployment and monitoring. Keeping a pulse on these overarching trends, perhaps by following industry blogs, subscribing to relevant newsletters, or participating in online forums, is crucial for maintaining a forward-looking perspective.

Furthermore, the very nature of data engineering and machine learning often involves dealing with complex, distributed systems. Understanding the principles behind distributed computing, data consistency, fault tolerance, and scalability is paramount. As datasets grow and computational demands increase, the ability to design and implement solutions that can efficiently process and analyze data across multiple machines becomes increasingly critical. This might involve delving into concepts like MapReduce, distributed databases, or message queuing systems. Similarly, as machine learning models become more sophisticated and are integrated into critical applications, a deep understanding of model evaluation, bias detection, interpretability, and ethical considerations becomes non-negotiable.

To foster this continuous learning, it's beneficial to establish a personal learning regimen. This could involve dedicating a certain amount of time each week to reading research papers, completing online course modules, or working on a personal project. Establishing learning goals, such as mastering a new programming language, understanding a specific ML algorithm, or becoming proficient in a new cloud service, can provide direction and motivation. Peer learning and knowledge sharing within teams or professional communities are also incredibly powerful. Regularly discussing challenges, sharing insights from new learnings, and conducting brown-bag sessions can accelerate the learning process for everyone involved. Teaching a concept to others, even informally, is one of the most effective ways to solidify one's own understanding.

The data engineering and machine learning domains are not static; they are living, breathing fields that are constantly being redefined by new discoveries and technological advancements. To remain relevant and effective, engineers must actively embrace a philosophy of continuous learning. This involves strategically leveraging online courses, engaging with academic research and industry conferences, dedicating time to hands-on practice and personal projects, and staying attuned to emerging trends and technologies. By cultivating a proactive and inquisitive mindset, data professionals can navigate the complexities of this ever-evolving field, ensuring their skills remain sharp and their contributions impactful for years to come. The journey of a data engineer or machine learning practitioner is, in essence, a journey of perpetual discovery and refinement, where the commitment to learning is as foundational as the algorithms they implement or the data they manage. This dedication to expanding one's knowledge base and honing practical skills is not just about professional growth; it's about building the resilience and adaptability required to tackle the complex, data-driven challenges of the future.

The operationalization of data pipelines and machine learning models extends far beyond the initial development and deployment phases. To ensure the long-term health, understandability, and evolvability of these critical systems, meticulous documentation is not merely a best practice; it is a foundational pillar of robust data engineering and machine learning operations. Without comprehensive documentation, systems can quickly become opaque enigmas, resistant to debugging, difficult to modify, and virtually impossible for new team members to grasp, leading to a detrimental loss of institutional knowledge and a significant increase in maintenance overhead.

The scope of documentation should encompass every facet of the data lifecycle and model lifecycle. For data pipelines, this begins with a clear articulation of their purpose and objectives. What business problem does this pipeline solve? What are the expected inputs and outputs? What are the critical performance indicators (KPIs) for its success, such as latency, throughput, or data freshness? Beyond these high-level descriptions, the technical details are paramount. Each stage of the pipeline should be documented, detailing the data sources, the transformations applied, the technologies utilized (e.g., specific SQL dialects, Python libraries, Spark configurations), and any dependencies on other systems or services. This includes documenting the schema of intermediate and final datasets, the logic behind data cleaning and validation steps, and the error handling mechanisms in place. For instance, a daily sales data aggregation pipeline might have a documentation entry detailing its connection to the transactional database, the SQL queries used to extract relevant data, the application of a Python script for currency conversion and aggregation, and its output to a data warehouse table. The documentation should also specify scheduling parameters, alerting configurations, and contact points for support. Version control information for the pipeline scripts and configurations is also indispensable, allowing for easy rollback to previous stable states if an issue arises.

Feature engineering, a critical bridge between raw data and machine learning model performance, demands equally rigorous documentation. For each feature created, its origin, transformation logic, and intended use case must be clearly recorded. This involves explaining how raw data attributes were combined, aggregated, or transformed to create new features. For example, if a "customer *lifetime*value" feature is engineered, the documentation should detail the formula used, the time window considered for historical purchases, and any discounting or inflation adjustments applied. The rationale behind feature selection or creation is also vital; why was this particular feature deemed important for the model? What hypotheses does it aim to capture? Documenting the statistical properties of engineered features, such as their distribution, mean, median, and variance, can also be highly beneficial for understanding their behavior and potential impact on model training. This includes noting any imputation strategies used for missing values within a feature and the justification for those choices. Furthermore, if features are generated dynamically or on-demand, the process and latency involved should be documented. This level of detail ensures that data scientists can understand and trust the features they are using, and that the feature engineering process itself is reproducible and auditable.

The documentation for model training procedures should be exhaustive. This includes detailing the specific algorithm chosen, the hyperparameters used, and the rationale behind their selection. If hyperparameter tuning was performed, the search space, the tuning method (e.g., grid search, random search, Bayesian optimization), and the performance metric used for evaluation should be clearly documented. The dataset splits used for training, validation, and testing must be specified, along with any data preprocessing steps applied specifically for model training, such as scaling, normalization, or encoding. For instance, a logistic regression model for customer churn prediction might have documentation specifying the use of StandardScaler on numerical features, OneHotEncoder for categorical features, and a train-test split of 80/20, with the random seed for reproducibility noted. Information about the training environment—such as the Python version, library versions (e.g., scikit-learn, TensorFlow, PyTorch), and hardware specifications—is also crucial for replicating the training process. The expected training time and any checkpoints saved during the training process should also be recorded.

Model evaluation is another area where comprehensive documentation is essential. This involves detailing the metrics used to assess model performance (e.g., accuracy, precision, recall, F1-score, AUC, RMSE) and the justification for choosing those specific metrics based on the problem context and business objectives. Confusion matrices, ROC curves, precision-recall curves, and other relevant visualizations should be generated, saved, and referenced in the documentation. It's also important to document any bias detection or fairness assessments performed on the model, along with the methodologies and findings. For example, if a model is being used for loan application review, documentation should detail whether fairness metrics were evaluated across different demographic groups and what the outcomes were. The version of the model being documented, along with its training date and the specific commit hash of the training code, creates a traceable lineage.

Deployment configurations also require meticulous documentation. This includes specifying the target environment (e.g., cloud platform, on-premises servers), the infrastructure requirements (e.g., CPU, memory, disk space), and the networking configurations. For models deployed as APIs, the API endpoint, request/response schemas, authentication mechanisms, and expected latency should be clearly outlined. Versioning of deployed models is critical, allowing for the management of multiple versions in production and the ability to roll back to a previous version if a new deployment introduces issues. Documenting the deployment process itself, including any CI/CD pipelines involved, the tools used for orchestration (e.g., Docker, Kubernetes, AWS SageMaker, Azure ML), and the configuration of monitoring and alerting systems, ensures that the deployment is repeatable and manageable. For example, a containerized model deployed to Kubernetes might have documentation detailing the Dockerfile used to build the image, the Kubernetes deployment YAML files, the service configuration, and the monitoring tools (e.g., Prometheus, Grafana) used to track its health and performance.

Beyond the technical specifics, documentation should also cater to different audiences. While data engineers and ML engineers will require detailed technical specifications, business stakeholders might need a more high-level overview of what a pipeline or model does, what its business impact is, and how to interpret its outputs. This necessitates a tiered approach to documentation, where summary documents are linked to more detailed technical guides.

To facilitate the creation and maintenance of documentation, adopting specific tools and practices is highly recommended. For code-related documentation, inline comments and docstrings within scripts are fundamental. These should explain complex logic, variable meanings, and function purposes. Tools like Sphinx can then be used to automatically generate comprehensive documentation from these docstrings. For pipeline definitions, tools like Apache Airflow, Dagster, or Kubeflow Pipelines offer features for documenting DAGs (Directed Acyclic Graphs), which can include descriptions of tasks, their dependencies, and their parameters. For model registries, platforms like MLflow or Weights & Biases provide structured ways to log model artifacts, parameters, metrics, and code versions, which can then be exported or linked to more formal documentation.

A centralized knowledge base, such as a wiki (e.g., Confluence, MediaWiki) or a shared documentation platform, is invaluable for consolidating all aspects of system documentation. This provides a single source of truth that can be easily searched and accessed by the entire team. Establishing clear guidelines and templates for documentation can also ensure consistency and completeness across different projects and teams. For instance, a template for documenting a data pipeline might include sections for: Overview, Data Sources, Data Schema, Transformations, Dependencies, Scheduling, Alerting, Monitoring, Contact Information, and Version History.

Regular review and updates are crucial for maintaining the relevance and accuracy of documentation. As systems evolve, so too must their documentation. Implementing a process where documentation updates are a mandatory part of the code review or release process can help ensure that it stays current. Outdated documentation can be as detrimental as no documentation at all, leading to misinformation and errors. Dedicating specific time for documentation grooming, perhaps as part of sprint retrospectives or dedicated work sessions, can help address this.

The benefits of comprehensive documentation are manifold and directly contribute to a more efficient, collaborative, and resilient data engineering and machine learning practice. It significantly reduces the onboarding time for new team members, enabling them to become productive more quickly. It fosters collaboration by providing a common understanding of systems, facilitating discussions and knowledge sharing among team members. It simplifies debugging and troubleshooting by offering clear insights into system behavior and potential failure points. It supports reproducibility by clearly defining the steps and configurations required to replicate results, which is essential for scientific rigor and regulatory compliance. It aids in auditing and governance by providing a transparent record of data lineage, model training, and deployment processes. Ultimately, investing in thorough documentation is an investment in the long-term success and sustainability of your data initiatives, preventing knowledge silos and ensuring that your complex data systems remain understandable and manageable for years to come. It is the bedrock upon which scalable, reliable, and collaborative data operations are built.

The journey through the intricate world of engineering data, from foundational principles to advanced best practices, culminates in this crucial juncture: the commencement of your own impactful projects. You've absorbed the methodologies, understood the imperative of robust documentation, and appreciated the architectural considerations that underpin successful data systems. Now, it's time to translate that knowledge into tangible outcomes, to transform the abstract concepts into concrete solutions that drive intelligent decision-making within your organization. This is not merely about replicating what you've learned; it's about adapting and innovating, applying these principles to your unique engineering challenges.

Embarking on your next engineering data project is an act of purposeful creation. It requires a blend of strategic foresight and tactical execution. The initial step, and arguably the most critical, is the meticulous definition of the problem you aim to solve. Resist the urge to dive straight into code or algorithms. Instead, dedicate time to deeply understand the business context and the specific pain point that necessitates a data-driven solution. Engage with stakeholders, ask probing questions, and ensure a shared understanding of the desired outcomes. What business metric are you trying to influence? What decisions will this project enable? What does success look like, not just in technical terms, but in terms of business value? This clarity will act as your compass, guiding every subsequent decision and preventing scope creep that can derail even the most promising initiatives. For instance, if the objective is to reduce customer churn, is the goal to identify at-risk customers for proactive intervention, or to understand the root causes of churn to inform product development? The answer to this question will dictate the data sources, feature engineering approaches, and model types you consider.

Once the problem is clearly articulated, the next phase involves scoping the project realistically. This means breaking down the grand vision into manageable phases or sprints. It's about identifying the minimum viable product (MVP) – the core functionality that delivers initial value and allows for early feedback – and then planning for iterative enhancements. Avoid the temptation to build everything at once. Instead, focus on delivering incremental value, allowing for agility and adaptation as you learn and gather feedback. Consider the data landscape: what data is readily available? What data needs to be acquired or synthesized? What are the potential challenges in data integration, quality, or accessibility? A phased approach allows you to tackle these challenges in manageable chunks, building momentum and demonstrating progress along the way. For a project aimed at optimizing inventory levels, the MVP might focus on predicting demand for a subset of high-value products, using historical sales data. Subsequent phases could incorporate external factors like seasonality, promotions, or supply chain disruptions.

Leveraging existing tools and frameworks, as discussed throughout this book, is paramount to accelerating your development process. Don't reinvent the wheel. Identify the technologies and platforms that best suit your project's needs, considering factors like scalability, maintainability, and your team's expertise. Whether it's leveraging cloud-based data warehousing solutions for efficient storage and querying, employing distributed computing frameworks for large-scale data processing, or utilizing managed machine learning services for model deployment, judicious selection of tools can significantly reduce development time and operational overhead. For example, if your project involves building a recommendation engine, rather than developing a custom recommendation algorithm from scratch, explore leveraging existing libraries like Surprise or cloud-based services that offer pre-built recommendation models and infrastructure.

The iterative nature of data engineering and machine learning projects cannot be overstressed. Your first attempt is unlikely to be perfect, and that's perfectly acceptable. Embrace experimentation and a culture of continuous learning. Build a robust testing and validation framework into your process from the outset. This includes unit tests for individual components, integration tests for pipeline flows, and rigorous evaluation metrics for any models developed. The insights gained from testing and evaluation should feed back into the development cycle, informing refinements and improvements. Remember the importance of version control for all your code, configurations, and even data schemas. This not only ensures reproducibility but also provides a safety net for experimentation, allowing you to easily revert to previous stable states if an iteration doesn't yield the desired results. Think of your project as a living entity, constantly evolving based on feedback, performance monitoring, and new insights.

Crucially, you are not alone on this journey. The data engineering and machine learning communities are vast, vibrant, and incredibly supportive. Don't hesitate to tap into this collective intelligence. Engage in online forums, attend meetups and conferences, and contribute to open-source projects. When you encounter a roadblock, chances are someone else has faced a similar challenge and shared their experience. Asking for help is a sign of strength, not weakness. Furthermore, consider contributing your own learnings and solutions back to the community.

This not only solidifies your own understanding but also helps others who are just beginning their journey. Platforms like Stack Overflow, Reddit communities dedicated to data science and engineering, and GitHub are invaluable resources for seeking and offering assistance. When posing a question, be clear, concise, and provide enough context for others to understand your problem.

Building strong internal collaborations is equally vital. Foster open communication with your colleagues, data scientists, domain experts, and business stakeholders. Share your progress, discuss challenges, and actively seek feedback. A collaborative environment where knowledge is shared freely accelerates problem-solving and leads to more robust and well-rounded solutions. When documenting your project, as previously emphasized, consider creating different levels of documentation tailored to various audiences. A high-level overview for business leaders, detailed technical specifications for fellow engineers, and clear usage guides for end-users will ensure that the value of your project is understood and accessible to all.

As you progress through your projects, continuously evaluate the performance and impact of your solutions. Establish key performance indicators (KPIs) that align with the initial project objectives and monitor them diligently. Are you achieving the desired outcomes? Is the system operating efficiently? Are there opportunities for optimization? This continuous monitoring and evaluation loop is essential for ensuring the long-term success and sustainability of your data initiatives. For example, after deploying a fraud detection system, regularly reviewing metrics like true positive rate, false positive rate, and the financial impact of prevented fraud is crucial. This data will inform future model retraining, threshold adjustments, or even entirely new feature development.

The act of initiating and completing an engineering data project is a powerful learning experience. Each project, regardless of its scale or complexity, will equip you with invaluable skills and insights. Embrace the challenges, celebrate the successes, and view every hurdle as an opportunity for growth. The principles and practices outlined in this book are not static rules; they are a framework for building intelligent, adaptable, and impactful data systems. Apply them with creativity, persistence, and a commitment to continuous improvement. The world of engineering data is dynamic, and your ability to navigate its complexities, build robust solutions, and drive meaningful change will be your greatest asset. Go forth, experiment, collaborate, and build the intelligent systems that will shape the future. Your engineering data journey is just beginning, and the potential for innovation and impact is limitless. Remember that the skills you hone extend beyond the technical realm; they foster critical thinking, problem-solving, and the ability to translate complex data into actionable insights that empower organizations to make smarter, more informed decisions. This is the essence of engineering data, and it is a skill set that will serve you throughout your career.

www.ingramcontent.com/pod-product-compliance
Lightning Source LLC
LaVergne TN
LVHW052015200926
848481LV00005B/1495

# *List of Figures*

# *List of Tables*

# *Preface*

What is research and who is a researcher? Why engage in research and what is its value? How do we come to know what we know? What can we *really* know? *Paradigms of Research for the 21st Century* opens the door for wondering about these and many other important questions pertaining to the nature and process of educational research. Conceived as a journey into the familiar and the uncharted territories of knowledge, this book offers an insightful and detailed account of Western and non-Western worldviews and perspectives on reality, knowledge, and values, many of which have been instrumental to the development of different research traditions and methods in North America.

This book demonstrates how essential components of educational inquiry such as ideas, theories, philosophies, ideologies, epistemologies, value statements, methodologies, and methods can be applied to conducting and implementing robust research projects. The aforementioned essential components form a *paradigm*—a system of inquiry, a model, and a way of knowing. Empirical-analytic, pragmatic, interpretive, critical, poststructuralist, and transcendental paradigms are delineated as alternatives to a more orthodox division of conceptualizing research as quantitative or qualitative. The discussions on the nature of science and scientific method shed light on a number of misconceptions of these notions in educational research. Resulting from these discussions is an exposure of misconceived and misrepresented links between positivism and quantitative research.

Venturing on a paradigm journey are the dedicated contributors to this edition who share their tales of learning to theorize and practice educational research. Their hope is that graduate students, professional researchers, and scholars will benefit from this project and it might be of interest to all lovers of wisdom.

Welcome to a paradigm journey!

## *A Preneopragmatic, Postmodern Ditty About Existential Phenomenon*

Walking in the classroom
I was feelin' fine.
Asked about some questions
What's a Paradigm?
Naturally my fears grew
I felt so abused.
Looked around for confidence
You all seemed so confused.

"Hey folks have some handouts."
"Take 'em, have a ball"
Rorty, Kant, and Hegel
Dewey and Foucault.
Habermas, Adorno, take Nietzsche
For some sparks.
What's a Timbred Research?
Giroux, Freire, and Marx

We climbed out from an Existential mineshaft.
There is no deny'n,
the class became Gemeinschaft.
Feyerabend tells us
"You can bend the rules.
Research call for
using all the tools"
Look beyond the task when
Conceptualizing Framework
The threads of solid research exist
On many spools

Now we've all survived it
ESR610
A world of information
Shall we do it all again?
Adapting Methodology will help us in our showing.
Hermeneutics finds a way,
Cartesian ways of knowing.
To make our journey forward,
we must use the past
To Bacon, Locke, and all the rest
Thanks I've had a blast
The courtesy of Kerry Muldowney, colleague and
former student of Paradigms of Research

Acknowledgments

I would like to express my warm gratitude to all contributors to this book—my colleagues and friends without whose assistance this manuscript would be an impossible undertaking. I am especially indebted to Baudelaire Ulysse and Eileen Kolich for sharing their talent and knowledge in our collaborative work.

To my former and current doctoral students—thank you for sustaining my sense of curiosity and inspiring me to pursue this project. I am grateful to Kerry Muldowney for supporting my first steps in teaching paradigms and sharing his big heart, wit, humor, and the gift of poetry and music with me.

I wish to acknowledge the support from the staff at Peter Lang Publishing: managing director Alison Jefferson, series editor Shirley Steinberg, editorial assistants, production managers, and all unnamed persons who have contributed to the production, marketing, and publication of this edition.

# *Introduction*

Antonina Lukenchuk

## *The Beginning—the Wondering*

This book has been writing itself for a number of years, at least since the time I started teaching a graduate course in paradigms of research at a Midwestern private university. However, I can probably trace the deeper roots of this project to as far back as my childhood memories. Faded and almost forgotten, they nonetheless elicit recollections imbued with enchanting images. I enjoyed a highly imaginative childhood. My less-than-exciting external surroundings led me to search for wonder in the realm of the transcendent. This imaginary land of myths, folk songs, and stories became my safeguard and a lovely haven in the midst of the crude and dreary reality of the outside world. Entrance into adulthood brought with it the experiences that demystified a great deal of my childhood's imaginings, but the wonderings about the world and what lies beyond its horizon has persisted.

My first encounter with the word *philosophy* during my undergraduate studies has turned into an affectionate and lasting affair, and throughout the years of academic training, philosophical inquiry has been sustaining my sense of curiosity and the purpose of my educational pursuits. I feel intuitively drawn to the word *philosophy* because it speaks to me in a female voice in the language of my origin. The affectionate words *phileo* (Greek for love) and *sophia* (Greek for wisdom) that comprise philosophy are, in fact, of a female gender. I am a lover of wisdom, that is, a woman who loves and seeks wisdom. I become a philosopher by default the moment I wonder who I am by nature or what the meaning of this project is. There is hardly a person in this world who is not a philosopher *by nature* (the drive to know is evidently intrinsic to a human being). The questions that Paul Gauguin (1848–1903) assigns to his painting are endemic to humankind: *Where do we come from? What are we? Where are we going?* These questions impel people to fly to the moon, to delve into the depths of the oceans, to penetrate the nuclear layers of energy and the human body, and to create ambitious social projects. What would our lives be like if it were not for some courageous individuals who dared to pursue unimaginable projects?

Education makes an inquiry attainable and, until fairly recently in Western modern history, education has been inseparable from philosophical pursuits. Seekers of wisdom in ancient Western and non-Western world cultural traditions have been philosophers, scientists, *and* educators—catalysts of intellectual, moral, and political transformations in their respective societies. The modern age of scientific and technological advancements in the West provided an impetus for a sharp division of sciences into "natural" and "human" and the ensuing methodological debates surrounding these sciences. Educational inquiry was forced to find its place within the new division of sciences and to develop methods best suited for its needs and purposes.

Since the nineteenth century in the West, education has been defined as a human, social, or behavioral science, depending on the object of its inquiry and its juxtaposition to natural sciences. The twentieth-century revolutionary theories of relativity and quantum mechanics overturned the Newtonian explanation of the universe as the only true scientific paradigm, and the discovery of DNA radically changed the understanding of living things (Grof, 1985). These revolutionary events also represented the strongest challenge to the positivistic assumption of science. Twentieth-century philosophy had to engage with a scientific world and rethink its role in providing the all-encompassing metaphysical systems of explanation of the universe and the predicament of a human being within it. Subsequently, the new conception of science was to be developed to account for the paradigm shifts in twentieth-century physics, biology, chemistry, and other natural sciences.

Contemporary science is no longer expected to produce certain knowledge, and scientific method is employed by natural sciences to generate alternative paradigms of knowledge, some of which can be accepted as the best explanations available, and in the long run, they can be discarded and replaced by new paradigms. The present-day philosophy of human and social sciences is concerned with the study of both the human realm and the natural realm, which until very recently were regarded as distinct and different and, therefore, required different methods of investigation. Moreover, natural science is viewed by today's scientists as an effectively human practice in which a researcher is actively engaged (Polkinghorne, 2004). Contemporary scientific, philosophical, and educational inquiries focus on a variety of issues pertaining to individual areas of study that can only incrementally contribute to the whole of the understanding of various phenomena. To keep up with the aforementioned changes in the conception of science, educational researchers need to reconsider the obsolete methodological debates still raving on the pages of some academic publications (e.g., Howe, 2009).

This book was conceived out of love of wisdom and the desire to provoke imaginative thinking about educational inquiry. Gaston Bachelard (1884–1962) once said that when imagination works, everything works. We first imagine things before we know them. Bachelard's (2004) poetic turn led him to reconsider his epistemology as a project of a scientific mind, thus, giving primacy to imagination in the process of inquiry. Scientific knowledge "emerges only after we use some imagination, both in formulating questions and in framing hypotheses to answer them" (Audi, 2003, p. 260). Bachelard's name is important to consider in context of this book because he was an originator of the theory of epistemological breaks (1938/2002) in the philosophy of science that was developed many years prior to the similar theory of paradigm shifts put forth by Thomas Kuhn (1962/2000).

This book intends to bring to light obscure, forgotten, or unknown facts pertaining to educational research that can be instrumental to its conceptual rigor and accuracy. Like any pursuit, this work represents an open-ended inquiry that is subject to critics' scrutiny and questioning, which we would welcome. This book is an invitation to readers to join the *paradigm journey* undertaken by a few dedicated persons with the purpose of gathering their patches of wisdom that are scattered around the world and sharing their love messages with others.

## Why This Book and What Is It About?

*Paradigms of Research for the 21st Century* contributes significantly to the field of educational research in the following ways: it is (1) filling in considerable gaps in the existing educational research publications, which lack philosophical foundations; (2) expanding on the definition of *paradigm* and its alternatives for educational research grounded in various philosophical traditions since most current definitions of paradigm are insufficient; (3) amplifying the importance of vital links between epistemological and methodological assumptions; (4) exposing and clarifying misconceived links between positivism and quantitative methods of analysis; (5) elucidating a new conception of science and its impact on educational research, information that is rarely, if ever, mentioned in current research sources; and (6) advocating epistemological and methodological pluralism be on equal footing in all educational inquiries.

For the past 20 years, I have been teaching a number of doctoral-level courses, including research methodology, primarily interpretive and critical, as well as theoretical courses that focus on epistemology and various ways of knowing, teaching, learning, and doing research within educational settings. These courses are designed to acquaint students with a broad range of philosophical, ideological, and theoretical perspectives on educational research as the tools to conceptualize research and scholarly projects such as dissertations.

The recurring discussions that I have with my colleagues who teach research courses and serve on dissertation committees reveal how ill-prepared some of our doctoral candidates are to conduct dissertation research projects, even after taking a number of research courses. The lack of students' knowledge and skills is especially apparent when they are faced with making appropriate choices regarding research methodologies and conceptual tools that adequately fit their research purposes. Our doctoral candidates often face the proverbial chicken or the egg conundrum and which comes first. In other words, should they first consider a paradigm and then a toolbox of methods, or vice versa? Students must be equipped to answer other related questions. What are the relationships between theoretical frameworks and specific methods of investigation? To what extent can a research project be successful in terms of properly made epistemological and methodological choices?

Most educational researchers agree that "methods of analysis do not emerge out of thin air. They are informed by, and extend out of, particular theoretical sensibilities" (Holstein & Gubrium, 2012, p. 5). All research is anchored to basic beliefs about the nature of the world, knowledge, and values. How each researcher "conceptualizes the best way to apprehend the social world is clearly dependent upon what she or he believes about the nature of existence. What constitutes data? What constitutes a pattern in data? What does the pattern mean?" (Pascale, 2011, p. 5). Theoretical models, frameworks, philosophies, ideologies, beliefs, or perspectives, the terms that can be housed under the umbrella definition of *paradigm*, provide a road map for successful research or scholarly projects. The definition of *paradigm* generates interesting discussions and debates among contemporary educational researchers (Anfara & Mertz, 2006; Creswell, 2003; Lather, 2004; Polkinghorne, 1983). The notion of paradigm permeates this book and renders its content relevant to the educational research process.

While the consensus on the importance of the role of paradigms in educational research is widely acknowledged, most research methods texts provide fairly limited space to philosophical discussions pertaining to educational inquiry. There are only a handful of current editions that offer in-depth accounts of the theoretical foundations of research (Anfara & Mertz, 2006; Cohen et al., 2008; Jackson & Mazzei, 2012; Merriam & Simpson, 2000;

Olsen, 2010; Pascale, 2011; St. Pierre & Pillow, 2000; Yu, 2006). Moreover, most of these sources focus exclusively on either theoretical frameworks of qualitative research (e.g., Anfara & Mertz) or particular areas of study such as, for instance, feminist poststructuralist theory (e.g., St. Pierre & Pillow). By comparison, *Paradigms of Research for the 21st Century* provides a more comprehensive and detailed historical and philosophical analysis of educational inquiries pertaining to all types of research: qualitative, quantitative, or mixed methods. This book abounds in philosophical terminology, which is rarely given proper attention in research methods textbooks (e.g., McMillan, 2008).

Despite an unequivocal repudiation of positivism in the mid-twentieth century, some contemporary researchers continue to misrepresent quantitative methods of analysis as positivistic (e.g., Hesse-Biber & Leavy, 2011; Pascale, 2011). The agreement has been reached by the philosophers of science that *all* of our knowledge is conditional and constructed within the contingent conceptual systems relative to time and place (Nelson, 2012). Given the contingency of truth/knowledge, what can educators count on as effective and critical methods of investigation? Paradigms of educational research represent a rich bricolage of methodological possibilities, and this book considers and discusses six of these.

The word *paradigm* is derived from the two Greek words *para* (beside) and *deigma* (example). The etymology of paradigm clearly presumes a relational construct, a pairing of sorts. Modern dictionary definitions elaborate on paradigm as follows: model, conjugation, giving all the inflections of a word, example, archetype, beau ideal, chart, criterion, ensample, exemplar, ideal, mirror, model, original, pattern, prototype, sample, standard (Kipfer, 2010). Kuhn's definition of paradigm is most frequently cited as "constellations of law, theory, application and instrumentation . . . ; models from which spring particular coherent traditions of scientific research" (Runes, 1983, p. 240).

Our conception of paradigm integrates its major existing definitions and the etymology of the word, all of which lead us to designate the following threefold meaning to paradigm: (1) a system of educational inquiry, (2) a model, and (3) a way of knowing. Chapter 3 elaborates on the justifications for this definition of paradigm. Figure 1 portrays a paradigm pyramid built on its multiple definitions.

Educational researchers tend to differentiate primarily between quantitative and qualitative research. While such distinction is valid in terms of data and methods of their analysis, paradigms as theoretical frameworks of research require more expanded philosophical renditions and more diverse

***PARADIGM***
***Par-a-digm***
archetype
example
pattern
sample
model
chart
ideal
theory
system
original
standard
exemplar
framework
worldview
belief system
way of knowing

*Figure I.1:* Paradigm Pyramid

differentiations. The construct of paradigm encompasses a number of conceptual tools (referred to in this book as "conceptual repertoire"), epistemological assumptions, and corresponding methods of analysis. Creswell (2003), for instance, distinguishes between the four "alternative knowledge claim positions": postpositivism, constructivism, advocacy/participatory, and pragmatism (p. 6). Lather (2004) proposes four paradigms in a slightly different configuration: prediction (positivist), understanding (interpretive), emancipatory (critical), and deconstruction (poststructuralist) (p. 207).

The analysis of various philosophical traditions of inquiry in Western and non-Western cultural traditions allows us to delineate six paradigms of educational research: empirical-analytic, pragmatic, interpretive, critical, poststructuralist, and transcendental. These six paradigmatic constellations do not exhaust all possibilities; however, they encompass major existing positions on knowledge, reality, and value statements in the philosophy of science. An important message intersecting the content of this book and being advocated by its contributors is that of an epistemological and methodological pluralism that recognizes and validates all Existing paradigms on equal ground.

## *Organization of the Book and What Is New in This Edition*

The book consists of two conceptually related parts foreshadowing the interconnectedness of theory *and* practice. The constructs of theory and practice are often conceived as separate entities. The word *theory*—via Late Latin from Greek, *theoria* (contemplation or speculation)—means a "system of ideas intended to explain something," a "set of principles on which the practice of an activity is based," or an "idea used to account for a situation or justify a course of action" (Stevenson & Lindberg, 2010, p. 1799). Polkinghorne (2004) renders practice as an "engaged action or activity," a "tradition, tacit knowledge, worldview, paradigm, ideology, framework, or presupposition" (pp. 6–7). More than two centuries ago, Immanuel Kant (1724–1804) emphasized that experience without a theory is blind, and theory without experience is mere intellectual play. Present-day philosophers of science consider the quest for knowledge as an activity in which a researcher is actively engaged, thus affirming the *reciprocity of theory-practice relationships.* Accordingly, Part I chapters of this book represent a theory component of this synergetic duo, and chapters 4 through 14 of Part II of this book exhibit its practice piece. Hence, paradigms and examples from practice should be understood as relational and mutually dependent constructs, whereby one informs the other and in turn is being informed and enriched by the other's experience. Examples from practice represent research and scholarly projects based on doctoral dissertations completed within various educational programs at three institutions of higher learning in the Midwest.

**Part I.** Chapter 1 takes readers on a fascinating philosophical journey across continents and traditions. It weaves the tales of ancient, modern, and postmodern worlds into a tapestry of beliefs that have been instrumental to the development of educational inquiry in North America. Chapter 2 amplifies the discussions on epistemology and philosophy of science and their relevance to educational research. It foregrounds the importance of methodological debates in natural and human sciences that have provided an impetus for radical changes in the conception of science and paradigm shifts in educational inquiry. New to this chapter is a number of additional sections that focus on the most recent developments within the context of digital technologies and artificial intelligence. Finally, Chapter 3 integrates the content of the preceding chapters in terms of relevant links among philosophical, epistemological, and methodological assumptions. Chapter 3 also provides a brief analysis of the Part II excerpts from the dissertation research exemplifying various theoretical perspectives and portrays a pluralistic paradigmatic image by means of graphical and textual representations.

**Part II.** The contributors to the scholarly work presented in Part II are persons of diverse socioeconomic, racial, ethnic, gender, and immigrant backgrounds, lifestyles, and political persuasions. What binds them together is a sheer love of and dedication to intellectual pursuits resulting in positive change in their immediate or global communities. Part II features six new chapters based on the content of recent dissertations defended with distinction and/or awarded with the title of the best dissertation of the year of graduation in a specific institution.

Research begins in wonder and thus bears an imprint of thousands of years of the human history recorded in tales, dialogues, teachings, myths, legends, and stories. Storytelling is the most primordial form of research and it continues to cast its spell on storytellers and their followers. The ancient art of storytelling gave rise to narrative research, which, since the 1960s, has been gaining considerable popularity among educational researchers (Goodall, 2008; Holstein & Gubrium, 2012; Riessman, 2008). As its critical component, counter-narrative allows for investigations of various critical issues in contemporary American education.

Thus, Part II opens with powerful research conducted by Thera Tilmon (Chapter 4) that focuses on the stories of elementary school teachers navigating the normative discourses of whiteness while advocating for African American students who may lack support and encouragement from their teachers. Thera calls on professional educators to commit their utmost support for connecting with and supporting Black students.

Matthew Woolsey (Chapter 5) presents an ethnographic investigation of first-generation Asian Indian immigrants who have attained senior-level leadership positions in U.S. higher education. Matthew explores the evolution of the field of leadership since the Industrial Revolution onward and its global perspectives. His purpose is to offer a "lantern" that sheds light on the unchartered territory of insight into the sociocultural contexts that enable Asian Indians to gain extraordinary heights in higher education leadership.

Joanne Yonan (Chapter 6) ventures on a complex case study of high school teachers dedicated to build classroom inclusion for LGBTQ+ students of color. Joanne asserts that these students represent the most bullied group of students in American high schools. Joanne calls on educational professionals to make schools welcoming places particularly for this group of students and to integrate the practices that can offset the oppression that LGBTQ+ students of color often experience.

Case studies provide ample opportunities for researchers to explore, in depth, classrooms and other settings as real-world contexts, or "natural" phenomena that bind time and space, individuals and environments, thus ensuring a comprehensive understanding of specific issues (Creswell, 2003). Thus, Amy Kendryna (Chapter 7) presents a compelling case study that explores adverse childhood experiences (ACEs) among elementary school students within the school district where she has been serving as school principal for several decades. Amy asserts that ACEs are potentially traumatic events that can have negative lasting effects on the health and well-being of children and in their later lives as adults. Amy's research has resulted in the development of the social-ecological model that can serve as a road map for all educators concerned with the students' academic performance and, more importantly, their well-being.

A grounded theory study by Regina Schurman (Chapter 8) demonstrates how the classical Glaserian approach can be applied to generate a model of sustainable professional employment for clinical exercise physiologists. Regina's research is firmly positioned within the pragmatic paradigm that enables her to recast Peirce's (1839–1914) method of rigorous scientific inquiry and his proverbial flash of insight. The pragmatist view allows the features of grounded theory to become clearer and more understandable in terms of generating substantive theory.

Cheryl Jean DeRoo (Chapter 9) invites readers on a passionate case-study journey to explore civically engaged curriculum within the elementary school district where she has been serving as school principal for several decades. The purpose of Cheryl's research is to investigate ways in which teachers can develop and implement civically engaged curriculum, which, in turn, can motivate students to understand the importance of civic responsibility and engagement in civic learning. Cheryl calls upon educational professionals to develop agency in order to advocate for action-oriented civic education.

Eirini Adamopoulou (Chapter 10) presents an empirical-analytic study of Greek parents' perceptions and experiences regarding their children's learning and social-emotional difficulties in elementary schools. Eirini employs the Test of Psychosocial Adaptation and the Parent Survey to identify Greek parents' perceptions of the causes and responsibility for solving their children's problems, the level and type of parental perceived burden due to their children's challenges, and their actions to support their children's learning and social-emotional difficulties, including their use of available community services.

Irene Garcia-Benavides (Chapter 11) ventures on a comprehensive case study to investigate barriers that prevent speech-language pathologists from providing appropriate services to deaf and hard of hearing children ages two to five. Irene is a dedicated professional and scholar whose research provides a compelling critique of a medical model of hearing loss. Based on her research findings, Irene passionately advocates for a sociocultural model and encourages her colleagues to develop culturally and linguistically informed practices from which both deaf and hard of hearing children and their parents can benefit.

Chapter 12, written by Baudelaire K. Ulysse, presents a sophisticated discourse analysis of the politics and economics of neoliberalism in local and global perspectives. Baudelaire poses the two following questions: In what way does neoliberalism embody imperialism and breed hegemony, exploitation, inequity, and inequality? Why does neoliberalism pervade education, and what effect does it have on the orientation of education? As an educator, Baudelaire has a deep conviction that it is his vocation to be involved in the political process and, more important, to shun political neutrality on issues that concern society and the human condition.

Toya Michelle Webb (Chapter 13) offers yet another unique example of a narrative study—the "narratives of grit" by African American women aspiring for community college senior leadership positions. Toya turns to the tradition of storytelling and counter-storytelling to portray the lives of nine extraordinary women paving their way to professional accomplishments while overcoming overt or hidden microaggressions, stereotypes, and racism. Reflecting on her own path to a senior leadership position, as well as the findings of the study, Toya appeals to educational professionals and the institutions that they represent to challenge their preconceived assumptions of African American women within the context of institutional practices.

Chapter 14 closes the circle of a constellation of examples from practice by dedicated educational professionals and scholars. Authored by Sharon Duncan, this chapter presents a generational phenomenological story of disability closes the circle of the storytelling tradition represented in this part of the book. Compelling, moving, and empowering, this study uncovers the meaning of the lived experiences of four individuals with intellectual disabilities and their families over three generations. Through the stories of resistance and resilience, the voices of the individuals with intellectual disabilities and their families reach out to the world beyond illusory or self-imposed fences, and gain prominence and power.

Finally, the postscript reflects on the experience of walking through the paradigm journey and offers a parting message to all lovers of wisdom.

## References

Anfara, V. A., Jr., & Mertz, N. T. (Eds.). (2006). *Theoretical frameworks of qualitative research*. SAGE Publications.

Audi, R. (2003). *Epistemology: A contemporary introduction to the theory of knowledge* (2nd ed.). Routledge.

Bachelard, G. (1938/2002). *The formation of the scientific mind: A contribution to a psychoanalysis of objective knowledge* (M. McAllester Jones, Trans.). linamen.

Bachelard, G. (2004). *The poetics of reverie: Childhood, language, and the cosmos* (D. Russell, Trans.). Beacon.

Cohen, L., Manion, L., & Morrison, K. (2008). *Research methods in education* (6th ed.). Routledge.

Creswell, J. W. (2003). *Research designs: Qualitative, quantitative, and mixed methods approaches* (2nd ed.). SAGE Publications.

Goodall, H. L. (2008). *Writing qualitative inquiry: Self, stories, and academic life*. Left Coast Press.

Grof, S. (1985). *Beyond the brain: Birth, death, and transcendence in psychotherapy*. SUNY Press.

Hesse-Biber, S. N., & Leavy, P. (2011). *The practice of qualitative research* (2nd ed.). SAGE Publications.

Holstein, J. A., & Gubrium, J. F. (Eds.). (2012). *Varieties of narrative analysis*. SAGE Publications.

Howe, K. R. (2009). Epistemology, methodology, and education sciences: Positivist dogmas, rhetoric, and the education science question. *Educational Researcher, 38*(6), 428–440.

Jackson, A. Y., & Mazzei, L. (2012). *Thinking with theory in qualitative research: Viewing data across multiple perspectives*. Routledge.

Kipfer, B. A. (Ed.). (2010). *Roget's international thesaurus* (11th ed.). Collins Reference.

Kuhn, T. (1962/2000). The structure of scientific revolutions. In S. Rosen (Ed.), *The philosopher's handbook* (pp. 503–519). Random House.

Lather, P. (2004). Critical inquiry in qualitative research: Feminist and poststructural perspectives: Science "after truth." In K. deMarrais & S. D. Lapan (Eds.), *Foundations for research: Methods of inquiry in education and the social sciences* (pp. 203–215). Lawrence Erlbaum.

McMillan, J. H. (2008). *Educational research: Fundamentals for the consumer* (5th ed.). Pearson.

Merriam, S. B., & Simpson, E. L. (2000). *A guide to research for educators and trainers of adults*. Krieger.

Nelson, G. (2012). Fighting for the humanities. *Academe, 98*(1), 16–21.

Olsen, W. (2010). *Realist methodology*. SAGE Publications.

Pascale, C.-M. (2011). *Cartographies of knowledge: Exploring qualitative epistemologies*. SAGE Publications.

Polkinghorne, D. E. (1983). *Methodology for the human sciences: Systems of inquiry*. SUNY Press.

Polkinghorne, D. E. (2004). *Practice and the human sciences: The case for a judgment-based practice of care*. SUNY Press.

Riessman, C. K. (2008). *Narrative methods for the human sciences*. SAGE Publications.

Runes, D. D. (Ed.). (1983). *Dictionary of philosophy*. Littlefield, Adams.

Stevenson, A., & Lindberg, C. A. (Eds.). (2010). *New Oxford American dictionary* (3rd ed.). Oxford University Press.

St. Pierre, E. A., & Pillow, W. S. (Eds.). (2000). *Working the ruins: Feminist poststructural theory and methods in education*. Routledge.

Yu, C. H. (2006). *Philosophical foundations of quantitative research methodology*. University Press of America.

# *Part I Paradigms of Research: Multiple Ways of Knowing*

# Chapter 1 Presaging Educational Inquiry: Historical Development of Philosophical Ideas, Traditions, and Perspectives

Baudelaire K. Ulysse and Antonina Lukenchuk

## *Inquiry and the Pursuit of Wisdom*

> Philosophy is a battle against the bewitchment of our intelligence through the means of language.
>
> —Ludwig Wittgenstein, *The Oxford Dictionary of Quotations*, 2001, p. 824

Inquiry has been a vital and constant element in the pursuit of knowledge. Education makes the pursuit or attainment of knowledge, whether directly or indirectly, one of its main objectives. Therefore, education must embrace inquiry as a perpetual ally to succeed in this pursuit. Hence, the term *educational research* ought to represent inquiries that are focused, albeit not exclusively, on pursuing knowledge and that are aimed at understanding knowledge of all types. The pursuit as well as the attainment of knowledge that is presumed in inquiry does not involve the teleological conjecture, as such conjecture varies from researcher to researcher and from project to project; rather, such pursuit aims to grasp the essence of, the process leading to, as well as the reliability of knowledge.

These aspects of knowledge—essence, process, and reliability—underscore the questions that have driven intellectual activities since the beginning of time. Moser (2006) discusses these aspects of knowledge respectively in terms of "defining features," "sources," and "justification" (p. 273). The essence of knowledge—that which comprises knowledge of any type—evokes the "what" question and is presumed to exist, unbeknownst to us or not, until that knowledge is accessed, uncovered, or discovered. Further, Moser breaks down the essence of knowledge into distinct kinds, which he labels "explicit" and "tacit":

> Explicit knowledge is self-conscious in that the knower is aware of the relevant state of knowledge, whereas tacit knowledge is implicit, hidden from self-consciousness. Much of our knowledge is tacit: it is genuine but we are unaware of the relevant states of knowledge, even if we can achieve awareness upon suitable reflection. (p. 273)

Moser's perceptive remarks seem to establish an equation that accounts for the link or the missing link between the known and the unknown, and evidently the nexus of the knower, the known, and the unknown. In addition, Moser (2006) asserts:

> Philosophers have identified various species of knowledge: for example, propositional knowledge (that something is so), non-propositional knowledge of something (i.e., knowledge by acquaintance, or by direct awareness), empirical (a posteriori) propositional knowledge, non-empirical (a priori) propositional knowledge, and knowledge on how to do something. (p. 273)

While the plethora of epistemic species might seem overwhelming, they, however, exude and underscore the cognitive diversity and relativity, which drives the vehicle of inquiry pertaining to the attainment of wisdom. This effectively led philosophers to surmise whether "extent of our a priori knowledge [was] relative to the extent of our a posteriori knowledge" (Moser, 2006, p. 273). Evidently, contemporary scholars and educators embrace inquiry as an effective method in the pursuit of knowledge. But the effective use of inquiry, particularly in educational research, requires a refined grasp of the history of inquiry as well as its historic contribution to the pursuit of knowledge. The Greek origin of the word *philosophy* means love of wisdom (Foley & Mohan, 2003; Ozmon & Craver, 2008). However abstract, this meaning is suggestive of a relentless and unrestrained pursuit of wisdom. This pursuit is neither characterized by aimless and desultory meandering in epistemological terrains, nor contained by ideological commitments; rather, it embodies a judicious and vigorous investigation of complex and open-ended questions regarding both the immaterial and the material realms.

Knowledge, in its variegated forms and sources, may exist independently of human existence, but the pursuit of knowledge by intelligent beings has largely been a human enterprise. There might be other intelligent beings that exist and inhabit places lying beyond earth's orbital threshold, but insofar as our general knowledge of the material world is concerned, one cannot assert with even the slightest degree of certainty that there are, in fact, intelligent beings inhabiting other planets or coexisting planet Earth with human beings. A concession must be made regarding the immaterial realm, which becomes largely a matter of speculation and belief as truth that can be deduced from reason (Plato), and/or experienced through faith and reason (Aquinas). While this concession is plausible, its subject lies outside the scope of the current project.

Granted knowledge writ at large is and has been a project of human enterprise, it follows then that the pursuit of knowledge as well as the grasp thereof remains inextricably linked to the human species. Further, knowledge writ at large, widely conceived as the objective of human intellectual enterprise or activity, is neither new nor old—it is evolving. Knowledge as such represents a diversely adorned and intricate tapestry with billions of pieces being potentially scattered across a wide array of intercontinental spaces that have been gathered by lovers of wisdom from distant and disparate lands. This creates a whole that is paradoxically unified and diversified. Each piece of this intricate and gigantic tapestry that is collected is valuable in time and space to the group of peoples living in those spaces, and it embodies answers to puzzling questions germane and relative to their material conditions and metaphysical assumptions. One might raise the question of whether the ultimate goal ought to be to find all these pieces and connect them so the big picture might become visible. Still, another might ask whether the ultimate goal ought to be for people in those respective places to use whatever piece or pieces they have culled from this intricate and beautifully adorned tapestry and direct them toward the creation of additional pieces based on what they already have in order to portray or convey their vision of that tapestry, however relative such vision might be in respect to their distinct perception.

## *Relevance of Philosophical Inquiries to Research*

Let us suppose that this painting referred to hitherto represents a tapestry embedding various forms and sources of knowledge. Assuming this is the case, whether symbolically or actually, the forms and sources would have to be both universal and evolutionary. This is to say then that there are forms of objective knowledge, both material and metaphysical, accessible to intelligent human beings from different places across all continents. Once accessed, these forms of knowledge are extracted, analyzed, interpreted, elaborated on, and applied by intelligent human beings to material conditions relative to these beings while at the same time metamorphosing into new forms and laying foundations for further investigations. Could this then be the way human beings have been interacting with their world? Are human beings always eager to grasp what is immediately available and known while at the same committing themselves to know more about that which has been grasped in order to develop a multidimensional view of it for further inquiry, elaboration, explication, and articulation?

The known always triggers the search for the unknown, creating an unending cycle of epistemological quest, at the core of which lies the assumption that knowledge is not final but evolutionary. Philosophers and scholars alike have conceptualized this epistemological cycle as the pursuit of wisdom, a pursuit that has continued to fascinate philosophers and scholars from all parts of the world. Hence, the pursuit of wisdom epitomizes research. By research is meant the inquisitive process that seeks to uncover and discover new phenomena as well as explain and expand existing ones. Research, being proper, may be qualified in accordance with the objectives or the disciplines, in which case such research could be educational, psychological, neurological, or economic. The process and the impetus of research do not change but are only varied by the methods used (e.g., empirical-analytic, interpretive, or mixed).

The cumulative work gathered within this book is geared toward research in the discipline of education; hence the focus is educational research. As the introductory chapter has stipulated, the objective of this project is to show how research in education is grounded in various enduring philosophical traditions of inquiry. Because educational research is grounded in the philosophical traditions of inquiry, it necessarily follows that properly conducted educational research must factor in the philosophical schools or paradigms that embody this inquiry and its pursuit of wisdom.

Properly situating academic works in these larger philosophical frameworks is the act of a skilled researcher. This postulate is consistent with the premise of this book and with the notion that knowledge of any type is somehow predicated upon previously known facts or proposed theories. Therefore, if an academic work should be considered credible, that work must reflect familiarity with or be interconnected to previous works. For instance, if one conducts research in political science using rationalism as a tool of analysis, that person will demonstrate a more refined knowledge of rationalism by tracing its origin to idealism and realism. By the same token, if another person conducts research in political science using liberalism as a tool of analysis, that person will provide a more rounded treatment of liberalism by tracing liberalism back to John Locke and rationalism. Countless other examples could be provided to illustrate the imperativeness for researchers to show the connection they claim to philosophical traditions that preceded, informed, and shaped contemporary tools, or the theoretical perspectives underpinning the respective researches of these researchers. It is for that reason that the focus of this book is on delineating the most influential philosophical schools in the history of ideas while showing their interlinks to tools and theories researchers currently employ. The understanding of these philosophical schools is vital for the effective use of tools and theories in research projects, but such understanding is best served with an introduction of philosophy writ at large, particularly considering its major components such as metaphysics, epistemology, and axiology.

## *Branches of Philosophy: Metaphysics, Epistemology, and Axiology*

Metaphysics is one of the branches of philosophy. The etymological makeup of the term *metaphysics* is telling and relevant to its meaning and focus. Two Greek words, *meta* and *phusia*, are joined to form the word metaphysics. *Meta* is a preposition, which could mean with, after, or behind. If it is accompanied with the genitive case, it could mean with, among, or against (Trenchard, 1998); if it is accompanied with the accusative case (direct object), then its meaning could be after or behind (Wallace, 2000). The term *metaphysics* does not provide sufficient syntactical context to determine whether the construction is genitive or accusative, but drawing from its emphases and orientations, we may infer that *meta* in metaphysics stands for after or behind.

Whereas the modern science of physics concerns itself primarily with the phenomena of "the natural world, that is, in the realm of things existing in space and time" (Lowe, 2002, p. 2), metaphysics, on the other hand, focuses on as well as investigates "the nature of things existing in space and time, with the nature of space and time themselves, and with the nature of causation" (p. 2). In addition, other abstract subjects such as being (ontology), mathematics, logic, time, space, and related aspects of the universe (cosmology) belong to the domain of metaphysics. Here lies the fine line between physics and metaphysics—the scope of physics is confined to the realm of natural phenomena, while metaphysics subsumes the realm of natural phenomena and assumes the existence of another realm beyond the natural one. In addition, metaphysics goes even deeper by investigating the nature/essence of those entities existing within both realms.

The philosophical concept, epistemology, is formed by two Greek words—*episteme* (knowledge/justified or proven knowledge) and *logos* (explanation/study). Epistemology has been conceptually posited as a branch of philosophy whose primary objective lies in "the study of the nature of knowledge and justification [thereof]" (Moser, 2006, p. 273). This study is both reflective and analytic, revolving around the questions of whether humans truly know, the nature of what humans really know, and the certainty of what humans claim to know. The emphases and orientations of epistemology make it a "theory of knowledge" (Moser et al., 1998). Philosophical reflection on the conditions of knowledge and sources of knowledge goes back at least to the ancient Greek philosophers Plato (c. 427–347 BC) and Aristotle (384–322 BC). Plato's *Theaetetus* and Aristotle's *Analytics*, more than any other writings, set the stage for epistemology "by delimiting the concept and the structure of human knowledge" (Moser et al., 1998, p. 4). Congruently, justification of knowledge, aimed at a high degree of certitude, has dominated the discourse on epistemology.

This need for the justification of knowledge has yielded two different schools of thought—foundationalism and non-foundationalism (Grayling, 1996). The former school maintains that knowledge can be justified in terms of finite claims or grounds. In other words, knowledge can be objective. Philosophers such as Rene Descartes (1596–1650), John Locke (1632–1704), and David Hume (1711–1776) shared that view. Those philosophers did not necessarily agree on the ground on which knowledge may be justified. For instance, Descartes posited that reason was the main purveyor of knowledge, while Locke and Hume posited experience as the source from which knowledge emanates. Locke, in particular, believed the human brain/mind is a blank slate until knowledge is wrought on it by experience, experience through the senses that forms the basis for the thesis of empirical knowledge. Similarly, Hume stressed the senses, particularly feeling or human emotion, as the purveyor of knowledge. Like Descartes, Kant (1711–1804) maintained knowledge can be sufficiently justified and stressed reason as an adequate tool by which objective knowledge may be accessed and interpreted. Both Descartes and Kant rejected the thesis of skepticism that challenges the claims of knowledge and suggested "proposed justification [for knowledge] might be insufficient" (Grayling, 1996, p. 47). The latter school, non-foundationalism, stems from skepticism and remains largely skeptical about the justification, the certainty, and the objectivity of knowledge. Foundationalism and non-foundationalism ultimately revolve around the question of whether knowledge can be objective or subjective.

The concept of axiology and its investigative orientations derive from the Greek etymology of the cognate. The Greek *axios* means value and its combination with logos (study/explanation/reason) forms this branch of philosophy, which investigates "the nature of value and what kinds of things have value" (Lemos, 2006, p. 949). Other scholars, like Scruton (1996), refer to this branch of philosophy as ethics and aesthetics. But there are many others who, like Lemos, view axiology as encompassing ethics, aesthetics, and other practical aspects that fit perfectly under this branch of philosophy.

## *Ancient and Classical Philosophical Traditions*

Thus far, this chapter has focused largely on delineating philosophical concepts, ideas, and thoughts that are particularly common in Western philosophy. It is often assumed that ancient Greeks were the first to develop speculative thought, yet a second-century Christian, Clement of Alexandria, claimed that the Greeks borrowed their ideas from the barbarians (in ancient times barbarians represented communities or tribes not belonging to the great civilizations of Greece and Rome). Whichever the truth might be, it is historically important to recognize the contributions of ancient Greeks to the subsequent development of Western philosophy, architecture, science, literature, and arts. No history of ancient thought "can avoid the mountain mass of Plato" (Kenny, 1997, p. 22). English mathematician and philosopher A. N. Whitehead (1861–1947) once said that the European philosophical tradition, generally speaking, consists of a series of footnotes to Plato. Plato was responsible for immortalizing his teacher Socrates (469–399 BC) in the dialogues that gave rise to Idealism. Aristotle of Stageira, a student of Plato and tutor of Alexander the Great, ushered in Realism and the development of natural sciences.

While Western civilizations have significantly contributed to the conceptualization as well as the systemization of the project of contemporary philosophy, philosophizing activities are not exclusive to the West. The philosophic temperament is "found throughout the world and may be assumed to have been present throughout the hundred thousand years of human being" (Kenny, 1997, p. 4). Furthermore, the questions that drive Western philosophy are not unique to Western societies either. By philosophizing activities, we mean the unflinching intellectual drive and quest by human beings that seeks to comprehend as well as explicate existence, and pertains to time and space, and includes the material and the immaterial world. The following sections feature Hinduism and Buddhism as ancient philosophical traditions in order to illustrate the claim that philosophy is not a project unique to Western societies. As such, the ensuing discussions should be construed as a continuity of the project of philosophy that engages metaphysical and physical questions, and more important, reflect the same intense human fascination with the pursuit of wisdom, as is evident in Western philosophical traditions.

## *Hindu Philosophical Inquiry,* Jñāna, *and* Moksha

The Hindu worldview assumes that all beings are caught in a cycle of painful existence where they are bound to experience multiple lifetimes. But this worldview also maintains that the duration of a person's experience in the cycle of existence is contingent upon his or her karma; to the degree that this person's karma has a quality lesser than the requisite to be liberated from the cycle, he or she may consider three different paths toward exiting—knowledge, devotion, and karma. Karma resurfaces, but it presupposes deeds of better quality.

The path of knowledge is of particular interest to the thesis of the pursuit of wisdom for the following reasons. The path of knowledge posits knowledge as a way out of the painful cycle of existence. Johnson (2009) suggests *jñāna* exudes the sense of gnosis as in "realization of ultimate reality" (p. 157). Further, he accurately identifies this path in Hinduism as "the quest for liberating knowledge, identified as the realization of the relationship between [B]rahman [*ultimate reality*] and atman [*human soul*], which informs much of the teaching of the Upanishads, and which subsequently becomes the characteristic means to liberation" (p. 157). While Johnson's view is accurate, the interpretive meaning he suggested is too narrow, limiting *jñāna* to spiritual enlightenment and excluding knowledge (episteme), the object of inquiry. In fact, Chethimattam (1971) offers a compelling case in favor of a more comprehensive view of *jñāna*, which encompasses but is not limited to knowledge (Greek equivalent gnosis) as a spiritual enlightenment. Chethimattam's interpretive meaning is, in our opinion, more accurate, considering *jñāna* is linked to the Vedas.

In fact, this postulation of knowledge as a way out of the cycle of existence presumes that something is lacking epistemologically, hence ignorance entrenches the human soul deeper into the cycle of ignorance (Chethimattam, 1971). Thus, knowledge becomes a requisite toward liberation. Particularly, it states that the acquisition of knowledge is potent enough to erase one's past that may include burdensome bad karma, at which point that person will be liberated from the cycle more quickly. Worth noting is that the knowledge a person is required to acquire is not a random or arbitrary kind of knowledge. Its object [*from the syntactical formulation: I know the Vedas*] is the Vedas; in other words, the Vedas are the content of this knowledge.

In Hinduism, the pursuit of wisdom is stressed, albeit confined, to the Vedas. Even then, the elevation of the Vedas in the Hindu pursuit of wisdom amplifies the thesis of inquiry that is espoused in the present work. The thesis maintains that the known and the unknown exist in an unending cycle of philosophical or scientific inquiry that continuously captures as well as captivates the interest of the human mind, even galvanizing the mind toward greater dimensions of epistemological depth and breadth. The Vedas are the most sacred and ancient texts in the Hindu worldview and were the primary texts in the earliest forms of Hinduism (Van Voorst, 2011). Fittingly, Veda in Sanskrit means "wisdom" or "vision," which underscores the notion of the pursuit of wisdom. The Hindu Vedas themselves are ritualistic and vastly metaphysical, embodying cosmological and ontological speculations, and as such are deeply philosophical, reflecting a profound interest in wisdom of all sorts.

While the Vedas remain vital to the current forms of Hinduism, the notion of knowledge as a pathway toward liberation represents a paradigm shift that was wrought by a series of new philosophical writings referred to as the *Upanishads.* The Upanishads infused the then-oldest forms of Hinduism, Vedism—whose relevance was threatened by the emergence of the vibrant and philosophically elaborate system of Buddhism—with new ideas as well as new deities. But, the *Upanishads* did not necessarily overhaul the Vedas. Instead, they deconstructed the Vedas, particularly the highly ritualistic and elitist elements thereof, while presenting more systematized and philosophical interpretations and elaborations of the Vedas (Chethimattam, 1971; Hiriyanna, 1975). Even with the turn of the philosophical tide, which is evident in the *Upanishads*, the search for enlightenment by the human mind through the grasp of wisdom has remained constant.

No other Hindu book best illustrates this claim than the *Bhagavad Gita.* Composed of 18 chapters and nestled in the epic war between the Pandavas and Kouravas, the *Bhagavad Gita* is replete with references to the infiniteness of wisdom and is infused with repeated calls for the human soul to yearn and search that infinite wisdom. Paradoxically, the call to seek such wisdom should by no means be construed as an indication that such wisdom might be grasped or attained. That wisdom is there but is not there, making it quite elusive. However elusive, it dwells in the Ultimate Reality. In other words, the Ultimate Reality is wisdom, but wisdom is embedded in the Vedas. So, grasping wisdom as such necessitates the seeker or the philosopher to search and to intellectually grapple with the Vedas. Once the seeker or the philosopher has attained a relatively perfect understanding or knowledge of the Vedas, he or she becomes liberated from *samsara* (cycle of reincarnation). That attainment in and of itself is, according to Hinduism, the consummate enlightenment, or realized relationship between the Brahman and that seeker. Worth noting is that this attained knowledge, albeit metaphysical, did not bypass inquiry.

## *Buddhist Philosophical Inquiry,* Prajna, *and* Nirvana

Emerging from the Hindu background, Siddhartha Gautama (586–466 BC) also stressed the pursuit of wisdom. As an Indian prince, Gautama grew up steeped in the Hindu system; like his contemporary Indian compatriots, he thought of himself as being caught in this cycle of painful existence. The difference between Gautama and many Indians of his generation was that Gautama had grown disenchanted as well as disillusioned about the viability of then existing Hindu ways for a person to escape the cycle of existence. Such disenchantment and disillusion later infused Gautama with indifference so intense that Gautama decided to abandon his domestic life, as he knew it then, so he could proceed to the third and fourth stages of life (respectively, forest dwelling and asceticism). His abandonment represented an act of non-attachment to what was as well as a striving toward reaching what had not yet been grasped.

That which Gautama pursued both sacrificially and passionately was wisdom, or *jñāna*. His quest, which was successful by his later claim, came to embody paradoxically the essence of what he had tried to vanquish—suffering. This is epitomized in his acknowledgment that suffering exists because of things we desire to grasp. Suffering he did experience, even as he strove to overcome suffering, for he nearly died from his extreme ascetic regimen of dieting and meditating, which illustrated his postulation that suffering, in fact, originates in the human heart. When he finally reached his goal, the attainment of a deep level of consciousness—nirvana or enlightenment—which supposedly brought him closest to ultimate reality or transported him deepest into realms of reality, he gasped in gratification and exulted subliminally as he shared his newly obtained wisdom with his followers:

> As long, O monks, as my knowledge and insight were not quite clear regarding each of Four Noble Truths, I was uncertain whether I had attained to the full insight of what wisdom that [is] unsurpassed in the heavens or on earth. But as soon as my knowledge and insight were quite clear regarding each of these Four Noble Truths, then I became certain that attained to the full insight of that wisdom that is unsurpassed in the heavens or on earth. Now this knowledge and this insight have arisen within me. The emancipation of my heart is immovable. This is my last existence. Now there will be no rebirth for me! (as cited in Van Voorst, 2011, p. 82)

Gautama's achievement has been conceived as *enlightenment* in and of itself—knowledge surpassing the bounds of earth and heavens. For his achievement to be properly understood, Gautama's inquiry must be placed within the Hindu cultural and religious background as discussed earlier. The discourse excerpted above introduces the Four Noble Truths that represent one of the major teachings of the Dharma. It was part of the Buddha's first sermon wherein he outlined this Buddhist Dharma that contains two major teachings—the three characteristics of existence (suffering, non-existent self, and impermanence) and the Four Noble Truths (knowledge of suffering, origin of suffering, cessation of suffering, and knowledge of the path) (Prebish & Keown, 2010; Van Voorst, 2011).

The knowledge of the path contains eight teachings or principles referred to as the *noble eightfold path*, of which the first two are *right view* and *right resolve/thought*. Right view and resolve/thought are particularly noted because they embody *prajna* (Prebish & Keown, 2010). Literally, *prajna* means wisdom. Thus, *prajna* can be said to embody intellectual activities, or to be manifest in intellectual activities (Murti, 2010). In other words, knowledge and *prajna*, as conceptualized in the Buddhist Madhyamika system, are coupled, if not inextricably linked, to create a type of dialectic. That dialectic is knowledge and thus philosophy itself.

The examples of Hinduism and Buddhism, as ancient ways of knowing, illustrate the close link between knowledge and philosophical inquiry (research). Evidently, fascination with wisdom and the quest to grasp wisdom are imprinted on the human psyche regardless of their geographical or geopolitical status. Philosophizing activities within Hinduism and Buddhism embody such fascination and quest.

## *Modern Western Philosophy*

Western classical systems of Plato's idealism and Aristotle's realism gave rise to the corresponding traditions of rationalism and empiricism. Stemming from metaphysics, idealism embodies a philosophical approach that separates the mind from the material world (Blackburn, 1996). In this philosophical tradition, "facts about mental life form the familiar class, and the ones about the physical world need some kind of certification from them" (Blackburn, p. 68). The idealist perspective has either informed or conceived various epistemological paradigms. In particular, the questions rationalism and empiricism have raised inevitably fall within the philosophical purview of idealism and realism.

Two philosophers tower over the emergence of rationalism and empiricism respectively—Descartes and Locke. Descartes and Locke were not necessary on the opposite side of the epistemological debate, but their respective ideas were different enough to yield polemical themes. For instance, Descartes postulated knowledge as "clear and distinct ideas," accessible through reason. To arrive at his conclusion, Descartes used the method of doubt. "He rejected as completely false any thought that could be doubted for any reason" (Bishop, 2011, p. 284). Descartes' principle, *cogito ergo sum*, became the basis of his ironic unwavering faith in reason (Bennett, 2001). Using the model inherent in his first principle, Descartes was able to infer "other perfectly clear and distinct ideas, including the existence of God, and the certainty of his own mathematical propositions" (Bishop, p. 285). Overall, Descartes' methodology for the certainty of scientific knowledge became the basis of modern *rationalism*, which maintains reason as the primary and "unique path to knowledge" (Garber, 2006, p. 771).

Like Descartes, Locke ushered in a new science of knowledge, and they both went on to etch lasting imprints on the Enlightenment Movement and, ultimately, on the history of intellectual ideas. Locke viewed knowledge as a product of experience. He argued that no ideas were innate to the mind and that all ideas came to the mind through sensuous experiences and "its own inner workings" (Bishop, 2011, p. 282). Finally, if we must have knowledge or acquire the certainty of knowledge, such knowledge must come "directly or indirectly through sensory experiences" (Moser & Nat, 1995, p. 22).

Philosophical schools of empiricism and rationalism have exerted a significant amount of influence on the history and development of ideas in the West and beyond its borders. These schools seldom agree with each other internally. Notwithstanding their lack of internal agreement, these schools share the profound preoccupation with understanding of both the material and the immaterial world. By the end of the nineteenth century, radical empiricism gave rise to logical positivism that embodies a philosophical approach that jettisons metaphysical claims. Otherwise known as the Vienna Circle, positivists were influenced by the empiricism of Hume and also by the *Tractatus Logico-Philosophicus* of Wittgenstein (1889–1951). The rejection of metaphysical claims by logical positivists was grounded almost entirely in their unequivocal commitment to empirical knowledge and to scientific method as the only tool that could access this knowledge. Any thought, knowledge, or tool outside the realm of empiricism and scientific method was deemed meaningless (Blackburn, 1996, p. 69).

## *Positivism*

Positivism is often identified with several traditions that share common threads in the philosophical, linguistic, and sociological movements of the end of the nineteenth and the beginning of the twentieth centuries: logical atomism, logical empiricism, logical positivism, and logical (or linguistic) analysis. Auguste Comte (1798–1857) appropriated logical positivism as the ground for the development of the science of sociology. Comte was convinced that human phenomena could and should be studied with the methods employed by natural sciences. He attempted to create a positive science of human beings as opposed to theological and metaphysical speculations. Comte claimed to discover an "evolutionary law of three stages" (Runes, 1983, p. 259) that all societies pass through: theological, metaphysical, and positive, the latter being associated with the advent of sociology as the highest positive science in the hierarchy of sciences. Such positive science was meant to result in the discovery of the laws and regulations of human behavior calculated by mathematical formulas. A "perfect" society based on these laws of behavior would subsequently ensue. John Stuart Mill (1806–1873) adhered to a similar positivistic view, yet unlike Comte, he did not claim that the science of sociology could be based on absolutely certain knowledge.

R. Avenarius (1843–1896) and E. Mach (1838–1916) created a more rigid version of positivism. Avenarius' *empiriocriticism* asserts that pure experience should be the ground for certain knowledge, and Mach defends the view that knowledge should be limited to sensations. These ideas found their ultimate expression in the works of the scientists and philosophers who banded together in the 1920s to form the Vienna Circle group, which included Rudolf Carnap, Otto Neurath, Herbert Feigl, Felix Kaufmann, and Kurt Gödel, under the leadership of Moritrz Schlick (1882–1936). Their purpose was to eliminate the so-called metaphysical and speculative errors. Fascinated by the progress of modern science, and especially by the theories of relativity and quantum mechanics, they elevated science to an insurmountable pedestal.

The Vienna Circle members were influenced by a number of prominent philosophers of the time: A. J. Ayer (1910–1989), G. E. Moore (1873–1958), B. Russell (1872–1970), G. Ryle (1900–1976), and especially L. Wittgenstein. Worth noting is the fact that Wittgenstein never associated himself directly with logical positivists and later made considerable revisions to his early philosophical works, particularly with regard to language, as will be discussed. One major preoccupation of logical positivists was with the language, the meaning of words, and how language statements reflect relations between words and the world. Logical positivists understood the link between language and the world as being directly related to sense data (Polkinghorne, 1983). *What you see is what you get!* This is a figurative expression that stands for the central principle of verification posited by logical positivism. The principle of verification, also known as *verificationism*, asserts that "no proposition can be accepted as meaningful unless it can be verified on formal grounds (through logic and mathematics) or verified on empirical or sense-data grounds" (Ozmon & Craver, 2008, p. 259). The only true and therefore meaningful propositions are either analytic (logical and mathematical) or synthetic (empirically verifiable), whereas claims such as "God is love," "This teacher is passionate about her job," or "The third-graders do not like taking tests" are considered nonsensical (Robinson & Groves, 2001).

Logical positivists encountered a series of problems associated with verificationism and other principles. Their disregard of the fact that there are unverifiable propositions in the language as well as some fundamental assumptions of science that cannot be verifiable led to a rapid decline and eventual refutation of positivism in the 1950s. Positivistic reliance on empirical sense data undermines the attempt to obtain an irrefutable knowledge precisely because these data depend on subjective perceptions. Despite its questionable reputation, positivism left an imprint on educational philosophy and research. In the 1950s, "Hardie and O'Connor criticized educational theories as vague and unscientific and hence as mere expressions of opinion" and recommended that educational research "become more scientific" (Kneller, 1984, p. 139). Positivism exerted considerable influence on behaviorism, cognitive science, and systems analysis.

Few professional philosophers can identify themselves with logical positivism today. Whereas positivism has been discarded as a scientific paradigm, it is often mistaken for "scientific" research in education. Yu (2006) points to the misconceived links between positivism and contemporary quantitative research, which might be due to the historical facts about the prominent founders of statistical methods such as Karl Pearson (1857–1936) and Ronald A. Fisher (1890–1962). The primetime of their careers coincided with the dominant position of positivism and fierce debates between evolutionary biologists and Mendel's (1822–1884) geneticists. While C. Darwin's (1809–1882) theory held that evolution is a result of accumulated small changes in traits over considerable periods of time, Mendel's theory of genetics contended that evolution is a discontinuous process and is driven by the mutation of genes. By the beginning of the twentieth century, both theories were blended into the so-called biometrics. Pearson initially adhered to Darwin's evolutionary biology, while Fisher came to support a blended view of a Mendelian-Darwinian-biometrician synthesis (Yu, 2006).

Arguably, statistics is not a subject-free methodology derived from timeless mathematical axioms: "biological themes and philosophical presumptions drove Karl Pearson and R. A. Fisher to develop their statistical schools" (Yu, 2006, p. 20). Different philosophies underlie the various schools of quantitative methods. It is certainly impossible to divorce the names of Fisher and Pearson from their association with positivism, yet it is equally inappropriate to regard the methods they developed and that were eventually accepted (with modifications) by quantitative researchers as positivistic. Yu presents compelling arguments in support of this thesis, which will be further elaborated in Chapters 2 and 3.

By the second half of the twentieth century, positivism had been largely rejected by the Anglo-American and Continental philosophers of science. Frederick Suppe, Willard Quine, Stephen Toulmin, and Michael Polanyi are among the most outspoken critics of positivist view on science (Polkinghorne, 1983). Positivism has "failed in its attempts to reconstruct science into a logically unified system of theoretical statements grounded in the certainty of sense experience" (Polkinghorne, p. 93). A number of anti-positivist movements (e.g., Gestalt psychology, linguistic philosophy, structuralism, poststructuralism, and Wittgenstein's later work) signaled a paradigm shift in the conception of science. These movements shared a common belief, namely, that it is impossible to obtain absolutely certain knowledge in social and human sciences because human beings cannot stand outside their language systems and cultures. A skeptical response to logical positivism captures this assumption through the *Weltanschauungen* (world outlook) analysis, the thesis of which runs as follows: "One never has access to reality: one can only look through the opaque spectacles of the cognitive apparatus of one's historically given *Weltanschauungen*" (Polkinghorne, p. 103). It was Wittgenstein's later work on language games that played a "catalytic role in the origin of the *Weltanschauungen* analysis [for subsequent philosophers of science]" (Polkinghorne, p. 103).

Wittgenstein's departure from his earlier, positivistic position is expressed in *Philosophical Investigations* (1953/2009). In it, Wittgenstein proposes the language game theory, which questions the possibility that there is a direct relationship between a word and an object (which is a positivistic position). The meanings of words, asserts Wittgenstein, are determined by various contexts, or rules of games (such as in a chess game), in which they are used. Wittgenstein maintains a position of radical pluralism on the possibility of different worldviews represented by many different languages, logics, and subsequently "truths"—all functioning within particular language games. It follows then that what we perceive and see as true depends on our world picture. In other words, human perception is fundamentally interpretive; it is always seeing something *as something*. Wittgenstein illustrates this principle of interpretive "seeing" by a duck-rabbit figure (see Figure 1.1) adopted from American psychologist Joseph Jastrow (1863–1944).

*Figure 1.1:* Jastrow's Duck-Rabbit Figure

With the decline and repudiation of positivism, philosophers of science abandoned the idea of searching for the foundations (or grounds) of knowledge and appropriated instead probabilistic and provisional "truth" statements conditioned by sociocultural and linguistic contexts. The metaphor of knowledge as an unbreakable foundation is often attributed to Descartes. As a counterpoint to this position, the twentieth-century philosophers of science W. Quine (1908–2000) and R. Rorty (1931–1650) proposed instead a net or spider web as a metaphor of knowledge, entertaining the idea that within the web of knowledge, some of its elements can be "weak" or "worn out" and we can subsequently "repair them while hanging on to the relatively stable parts, which still offer support" (Palmer, 2002, p. 108).

Subsequently, many philosophers of science turned to ideas developed prior to the reign of positivism in the 1920s. One of the richest sources of these ideas was American pragmatism and especially the philosophy of Charles S. Peirce, who claimed that science does not represent a "systematized knowledge but the pursuit itself in which scientists are engaged" (Polkinghorne, 1983, p. 119).

### *American Pragmatism*

The story of pragmatism begins in Cambridge, Massachusetts, in the 1870s, when several young and talented minds (C. S. Peirce, W. James, C. Wright, J. Fiske, and F. E. Abbot) who referred to themselves as members of "Metaphysical Club" would gather to discuss and debate philosophical problems. The most prominent of these thinkers, Charles S. Peirce (1830–1914) and William James (1842–1910), were considered the official founders of pragmatism. John Dewey (1859–1952) developed pragmatism further and made it central to his educational philosophy, which "encourages the process-oriented, problem-solving instruction that is so popular with American teachers" (Gutek, 2004, pp. 71–72).

James popularized pragmatism and applied it a great deal to his work in psychology, known as *functionalism.* James added a value component to the practicality thesis of ideas. From a pragmatic standpoint, one should not be concerned with whether ideas are true or false, but rather with the difference that they can make in our lives. The ideas should have "cash value" (James's famous expression).

Despite his major contributions to pragmatism, Peirce's name remained in obscurity until about the second half of the twentieth century when his collected works were published for the first time. Subsequently, Peirce's genius gained worldwide recognition. In his later career, Peirce became highly dissatisfied with the way James, Dewey, and others used the term *pragmatism*, which made him rename his original philosophy into *pragmaticism* (the word that he himself considered ugly). Peirce insisted that pragmatism is not a philosophy or a theory of truth, but rather a method to assist us in finding solutions to problems. His celebrated definition of pragmatism is expressed in the following passage:

> Our idea of anything *is* our idea of its sensible effects. It appears, then, that the rule for attaining the third grade of cleanness of apprehension is as follows: Consider what effects, that might conceivably have practical bearings, we conceive the object of our conception to have. Then, our conception of these effects is the whole of our conception of the object. (1998, p. 146)

Derived from the Greek word *pragma* (action or deed), pragmatism emphasizes the synergy of relations between theory and practice, knowledge and action. Pragmatism is said to be a distinctly American philosophy and a natural outgrowth of the American spirit and way of life (Sellars, 2010) that reflects the American experience of the early settlers in a new land and their demands for the ideas to solve everyday problems. American pragmatism emerged as a response to long-standing European philosophical influences that seemed too "abstruse and too remote from the immediate concerns of a young, vigorous nation" (Popkin & Stroll, 1993, p. 274) recovering from the devastation of the Civil War. There was a sense among many American philosophers that the European eschatological traditions exhausted themselves and were in need of a revival that would bring the new scientific discoveries to the forefront of philosophical inquiry.

Pragmatists embrace scientific inquiry as a radical departure from positivism. Peirce (1966) contends that although positivism has a "favorable influence upon scientific investigation, its fundamental position is false"

(p. 137). Peirce's essential position on knowledge, in contrast to positivism, was that our knowledge about the world of objects is fallible and that scientific knowledge has limits. Peirce revered science and thought of it as a living and breathing process. Peirce's (1998) consensus theory of truth elaborates on the process of validating true ideas by the community of scientists. It is the "COMMUNITY" [Peirce's emphasis] that has "definite limits, and [is] capable of a definite increase of knowledge" (1998, p. 115). Peirce firmly believed that scientists and philosophers are motivated by pure love of the pursuit of truth. An inquiry begins because of a genuine doubt: "The irritation of doubt causes a struggle to attain a state of belief. I shall term this struggle inquiry ... It is certainly best for us that our beliefs should be such as may truly guide our actions so as to satisfy our desires" (1998, p. 126).

Peirce's method of scientific inquiry translates perfectly into Dewey's problem-solving method. Known as instrumentalism, or experimentalism, Dewey's pragmatic philosophy combines a theory of logic and a principle of ethical analysis and criticism. His expression *warranted assertions* entered the philosophical and educational vocabulary to designate pragmatic truth. In his "Logic: The Theory of Inquiry" (1938), Dewey proposed the notion of intelligence as an essentially evaluative experience. We cannot separate experience as moral, scientific, practical, or theoretical, hence his notion of the reconstruction of human experience. The purpose of inquiry is thus to resolve a doubt or to solve a problem and, while doing so, to exhibit moral practical value of that experience. Dewey's philosophy connects the continuity of experience with the idea of education as growth: "The educative process can be identified with growth when that is understood in terms of active principle, *growing*" (as cited in Johnson & Reed, 2012, p. 111).

Dewey's instrumentalism and experimentalism are linked through the notion of evolutionary philosophy, which influenced a great number of thinkers of that time (Interestingly, Dewey was born in 1859, the year when Darwin's *The Origin of Species* was published). Dewey tested his ideas as the experimental method of education in the University of Chicago Laboratory School, which he directed from 1896 to 1904. It was against the metaphysical theories of reality and knowledge that Dewey defended his "unity of knowledge" system, designating the relation between knowing and doing and the active social conception of human intelligence (Gutek, 2004).

The recent revival of pragmatism finds its expression in the neo-pragmatist critique of normativity in Western analytic philosophy. Particularly, Richard Rorty is critical of the American philosophy as being greatly influenced by the search for objective knowledge and thus attempting to establish a "normal" discourse. As a counterpoint, Rorty proposes an "abnormal" discourse as a criticism of this position (Ozmon & Craver, 2008). Cornel West (b. 1953) advocates *prophetic pragmatism*, which merges the ideas of Emerson, liberation theology, and classical pragmatism (Ozmon & Craver). In Rorty's view, the current neo-pragmatists' agenda has to do with "reconciling the antimetaphysical antiabsolutist trends in twentieth-century English, American, and Continental philosophy" and with envisaging the role of philosophy as helping people and society to "break free from outworn vocabularies and attitudes, rather than to provide 'grounding' for the institutions and customs of the present" (as cited in Popkin & Stroll, 1993, p. 316).

The reconciliatory spirit of pragmatism makes itself manifest in educational inquiry through its attempts to do away with the so-called paradigm wars between quantitative and qualitative purists (see, e.g., Johnson & Onwuegbuzie, 2004). Wedded to this spirit are pragmatism's remarkable contributions to the theory of truth and the method of rigorous scientific inquiry that in turn have become instrumental to an overall nineteenth-century anti-positivist movement launched by European existential-phenomenological and hermeneutic philosophers.

## *Existential-Phenomenological and Hermeneutic Inquiries*

Where do we come from? What are we? Where are we going?

Several philosophical traditions developed in nineteenth-century Europe would make the existential questions central to their inquiry as well as part of a concerted effort to articulate the anti-positivist response to the excesses of rationalism and the disputes over the methods by which to approach the study of human phenomena. In 1858, the German historian Droysen distinguished between the terms *erklären* (explanation) and *verstehen* (understanding), which further marked an important distinction between the methods used in natural sciences based on the explanation of natural phenomena, and the methods employed in human sciences that relied on the understanding of human phenomena (Polkinghorne, 1983). Henceforth, *verstehen* becomes not only a legitimate source of knowledge, but more important, an alternative to a foundationalist epistemology way of knowing that is firmly embedded in historically particular and contingent vocabularies (Westphal, 2006).

Giambattista Vico (1668–1744) is said to be the forerunner of the anti-positivist response. Yet it was the German Romantic movement of the nineteenth century that contributed to the response most significantly. The Romantics were philosophers, poets, writers, and artists who questioned the ultimate authority of human reason and its privileged status as espoused by Enlightenment thinkers. Romantics turned their attention to human emotions and desires, the "perennial features of human existence that haunt those who celebrate the rational" (Oliver, 1997, p. 116). Finding a creative outlet in art and aestheticism, the Romantics launched an era of sensibility as a counter-current to a systematic rationalized approach to life. Their purpose was to achieve harmony between the intellect and passion.

Schelling (1775–1854), Novalis (1772–1801), and Hölderlin (1770–1843) are perhaps the most prominent names associated with German Romanticism. Schelling's identity philosophy represents a complex, dialectic ontological system that integrates subject and object, real and ideal, the *uni*verse and the *multi*plicity of being or self. Schelling resolves the internal struggle between artistic eros and systematic reason in favor of art as a unifying principle and the ground for the ultimate expression and realization of self. F. von Hardenberg (Novalis) reifies the unifying principle through poetry and attempts poetic philosophy—an understanding of the self and its world not in abstractions but by romanticizing them. Romanticizing is understood as a portrayal of the unexpected that interrupts our ordinary life and shows what we are *not*, what we are potentially: *Die Welt muß romantisirt werden* (The world must be romanticized), proclaims Novalis. In his major work, *Hyperion*, Hölderlin advances the All-Unity principle as the ultimate self-knowledge and self-expression through aesthetics. The Romantics inspired other philosophers of the anti-positivist response (e.g., Dilthey, Husserl, Heidegger, Merleau-Ponty, Gadamer, Ricoeur, and Habermas) whose philosophies of life laid foundations for the existential-phenomenological and hermeneutic inquiries.

As a systematic philosophy, existentialism was founded by Søren Kierkegaard (1813–1855) and Friedrich Wilhelm Nietzsche (1844–1900) and further developed by a number of European and American thinkers, psychologists, literary figures, and educators: Sartre, de Beauvoir, Buber, Jaspers, Marcel, Tillich, Rogers, Maslow, Camus, and Greene, to name a few most widely acclaimed. Existential themes of freedom, passionate choice, and an acute sense of responsibility for creating one's own destiny and meaning of life in a seemingly absurd and lonely world; living the values that one espouses; and overcoming the fear of death in the situations that require an ultimate choice and subsequently displaying courage and integrity of one's character run across the spectrum of existentialism in a variety of its representations.

Kierkegaard, the leading figure in Christian existentialism, contends that a true Christian lives a life of constant internal conflict in his or her search for God, and it is not through doctrine, theological studies, or regular church attendance, but instead through the leap of faith that he or she can find God, the God from within. Assuming that God exists and one can find Him, the human being is still in a precarious situation—still absolutely alone and abandoned in a seemingly indifferent and hostile world. Out of this complete isolation and despair comes the cry of one in the wilderness. But instead of God's answer, there is only silence: "the human being's experience of nothingness before God, which is at the same moment the complete fulfillment of human existence" (Gutek, 1997, p. 109).

Along comes Nietzsche who proclaims, "God is dead!"—the expression that does not have much to do with a theological argument but rather with Nietzsche's critique of modernity with its reliance on speculative philosophy and slave Christian morality. Nietzsche's concerns with the expression of truth and falsehood leads him to explore the Greek culture in the light of rational (embodied by Apollo) and irrational (embodied by Dionysus) principles. From the synthesis of these two principles arises "the beauty of an art in which life is contained but not destroyed, and in which the terrible and the irrational exist side by side with the serene" (Kenny, 1997, p. 217). Art and aesthetic, not knowledge, are given ontological priority in Nietzsche's existentialist project. Unless one creates something, it would be better that one had never been born. Existence, therefore, can be justified only artistically: only as an "aesthetic product can the world be justified to all eternity," and only as the "genius in the act of creation merges with the primal architect of the cosmos can he truly know something of the eternal essence of art" (Nietzsche, 2000, pp. 261–262).

Art owes its continuous evolution in the Apollonian-Dionysian duality. Being a moral deity, Apollo persistently attempts to retain his self-control in the midst of the warring spheres of influence [non-Apollonian Titans and extra-Apollonian barbarians], until the "effects of the Dionysiac spirit struck the Apollonian Greeks as Titan and barbaric . . . Their whole existence, with its temperate beauty, rested upon a base of suffering and *knowledge* which had been hidden from them until the reinstatement of Dionysos uncovered it once more. And lo and behold! Apollo found it impossible to live without Dionysos" (Nietzsche, 2000, p. 256). Nietzsche ultimately favors the Dionysian principle as an expression of will—the will to power, to be more precise. To put it differently, each and every one of us has the potential to become reborn into *Übermensch* (Superman), which is an unrealized potential within us, as long as we are *willing* to overcome the external limitations of our existence: "The individual, with his limits and moderations, forgot himself in the Dionysiac vortex and became oblivious to the laws of Apollo. Indiscreet extravagance revealed itself as truth, and contradiction, a delight born of pain, spoke out of the bosom of nature" (Nietzsche, p. 257).

Nietzsche's philosophy had a profound influence on twentieth-century thinkers, especially on Sartre and Heidegger. Existentialism as a European phenomenon became especially pronounced during and after WWII when philosophers, writers, and ordinary citizens questioned the rationality of the war machine and the sanity of decisions behind it that resulted in the death of millions of people, many of whom sacrificed their lives in the name of false and destructive ideologies. Jean-Paul Sartre's (1905–1980) existentialism was shaped by the anguish, atrocities, and devastation of war. Sartre was part of the French Resistance during WWII and experienced the confrontation with death directly when he was captured by the Nazis. Sartre explicitly positions himself as an atheistic existentialist. In "Existentialism and Humanism," he defines existentialism through his famous dictum, "existence precedes essence." What does he mean by that?

> Man first of all exists, encounters himself, surges up in the world—and defines himself afterwards ... There is no human nature, because there is no God to have conception of it. Man simply is. Man is nothing else but that which he makes of himself. (as cited in Ozmon & Craver, 2008, p. 249)

Regardless of God's presence or absence in our lives, we are doomed to freedom in our earthly existence with its little pleasures and sorrows, and with the burden of making our own choices and assuming full responsibility for them and for the world that we create. Sartre's lifelong partner and philosopher in her own rite, Simone de Beauvoir (1908–1986), created an original version of existential philosophy and became widely known for her feminist classic, *The Second Sex* (1949/1989). The book details the analysis of patriarchal societies and the predicament of woman as the Other within them:

> Humanity is male and man defines woman not in herself but as relative to him; she is not regarded as an autonomous being. For him she is sex, absolute sex, no less. She is defined and differentiated with reference to man and not he with reference to her. He is the Subject, he is the Absolute—she is the Other. (1989, p. xxii)

Beauvoir's celebrated credo, "one is not born but becomes a woman," reifies the existential condition that renders the choice for emancipation both possible and justified.

The beginnings and development of phenomenology are most commonly attributed to Husserl, Schutz, Heidegger, Sartre, Merleau-Ponty, and Freire. Edmund Husserl (1859–1938), notably the father of phenomenology, studied the structures of human consciousness and developed phenomenology along rationalist lines (transcendental phenomenology). Phenomenology literally means the study of appearances (Gr. < phenomena) that are being structured by our consciousness in specific patterns and come in different shapes as objects, ideas, memories, or images. The phenomenological process of uncovering the structures of consciousness can be compared with an archeologist excavating a prehistoric site. One has to carefully describe the various strata in order to reveal the meaningful structures that are taken for granted in everyday experience, which Husserl calls "lifeworld" (*Lebenswelt*). Lifeworld designates the everyday world of our affairs (family, work, pleasure, etc.). We may think of this world as "objective and independent, yet it is we who sustain it and give it meaning" (Kneller, 1984, p. 30). The task of phenomenological inquiry is, therefore, to describe the phenomena as they appear to our consciousness and to endow them with meaning.

Alfred Schutz (1899–1959) brought Husserl's phenomenology to the social world and made human action central to its inquiry. Maurice Merleau-Ponty (1908–1961) developed phenomenology along the lines of embodied consciousness. As embodied beings we relate to the world primarily through senses. Sense perceptions that originate in our thoughts are rooted in childhood, when we learn how to move and experience things in a "prereflective" manner. We think, act, and feel as we do "because of the omnipresent, prereflective stratum of [our] experience" (Kneller, 1984, p. 43). Our bodily perception of the world is "dehiscence, a splitting open of the body as touching and touched, as seer and seen that allows the body to experience things" (Low, 2000, p. 17).

Martin Buber (1878–1965) contributed immensely to the existential-phenomenological educational theory by advancing the argument of the *I-Thou* dialogue as an authentic and mutually appreciative form of relationships between individuals. *I-Thou* is counter-positioned with an *I-It* mode of objectified and self-interested relationships. Buber advocates the *I-Thou* relation among teachers and students and conceives of it as a communion of divine and human character, whereas "one's faith in God and in one's fellow human beings is witness to one's devotion to a higher end" (Ozmon & Craver, 2008, p. 227).

The tradition of hermeneutics has a long and fascinating history. The term comes from the Greek *hermeneuein*, "to interpret," and is linked to the name of Hermes, the Greek god messenger. Hermes was the son of Zeus and Maia, the daughter of Atlas, and was born out of wedlock. His regular duties included carrying messages to and from Zeus, between the other gods and mortals. Known for his devious character, Hermes was a protector of mischief makers (Couch, 1997). He is often portrayed as wearing winged-shoes or sandals, a round helmet-shaped hat, and carrying a staff entwined with serpents. Worth noting is the fact that Hermes has siblings in other cultural traditions, for instance, Mercury in Roman mythology, Garuda the mythical bird in Hinduism and Buddhism, and Slava the messenger bird of Perun (equivalent of Zeus) in Slavic mythology.

Hermeneutics acquired its revolutionary spirit from the Protestant Reformation of the sixteenth century when, in opposition to the Catholic Church's authority over biblical texts, the Protestants "called for a return to the text itself" (Polkinghorne, 1983, p. 219). With the spread of literacy and the printing press, it became possible for common people to have access to biblical texts. M. Luther's (1483–1546) translation of the Bible into modern German revolutionized and shifted the consciousness of the religious laity in Germany, and eventually throughout Europe, from the confines of church dogmas to the vast and open prairie of hermeneutics wherein they were able to read freely and interpret independently the word of God.

Wilhelm Dilthey (1833–1911) is recognized as the leading figure in hermeneutics, although he credited Friedrich Schleiermacher (1768–1834) with the development of the art. Dilthey attempted to shape hermeneutics as a human science capable of generating knowledge for social and political decisions. Dilthey realized that it would be impossible to gain certain and objective knowledge of the human realm, yet one could strive for approximation of such knowledge in which "there are degrees of truth which move closer to a sure understanding" (Polkinghorne, 1983, p. 223). Significant to the study of hermeneutics are also the philosophies of Martin Heidegger (1889–1976) and Hans-George Gadamer (1900–2002).

Heidegger's *Being and Time* (1927) marks a radical departure from conventional assumptions of knowledge and the ego-subject in Western philosophy. It is not about the way we know the world, but the way we *are*. The question of being, thus, acquires ontological priority over all other questions. Heidegger posits the question of being within the context of *Dasein*—the realm of our existence. Human existence constitutes the openness where being can be revealed. For something to be means for it to be revealed, uncovered, made manifest. We exist in the world because we understand what it means to be. Our authentic existence—being-in-the-world—is possible only when self as ego is eclipsed by the manifestation of our finitude. The modes of being in the world also include being-with-others and being-toward-death. "The being of *Dasein* means ahead-of-itself-being-already-in-(the world) as being-amidst (entities encountered in-the-world). This Being fills in the signification of the term '*care*' [Sorge]" (Heidegger, 1962, p. 237). I *am* care (Sorge), the unity of lived experiences, temporal transcendence, openness to and involvement with worldly affairs, my being "here" (the *Da* of *Dasein*). The more open and authentic I am, the more able I am to care for myself and others.

In his seminal work *Truth and Method* (1960/2004), Gadamer extended and applied the main concepts developed by Heidegger regarding the historical and interactive conditions of human understanding. As a model for his method, Gadamer suggests translation from one language to another. Interpretation is not just reconstruction of meaning, it also involves a fusion of horizons, an interaction between the interpreter and the meaning in the text. Interpretation is a mediated process that has a circular character. The parts of the text constitute a complex whole that is the meaning of the text. The horizon is "something into which we move and that moves with us. Horizons change for a person who is moving. Thus the horizon of the past, out of which all human life lives and which exists in the form of tradition, is always in motion" (Gadamer, 1992, p. 271). The process of movement from the first pre-judgmental notion of the meaning of the whole (in which the parts are understood) to a change in the sense of the meaning of the whole is called the *hermeneutic circle*. Hence, interpretation is never final, and the process of understanding does not result in finite and objective truth. Hermeneutic understanding is conditioned and mediated by language, culture, and context. Hermeneutic method aims at "maintaining the intersubjectivity of mutual understanding in ordinary-language communication and in action according to common norms" (Habermas, 1972, p. 176). More important, the philosophical hermeneutics of Heidegger and Gadamer call into serious question the very possibility of objective historical knowledge.

Existential-phenomenological and hermeneutic (life) philosophies have opened extraordinary venues for researchers to pursue the study of human phenomena as a multi-paradigmatic endeavor. Their emergence and development signaled a radical shift from a positivistic view of scientific knowledge to epistemological and methodological pluralism. The legacy of early hermeneutics and its rebellious spirit was inherited by the twentieth-century thinkers for whom it was not enough to understand the world—they ventured to change it. This iconoclastic spirit of the twentieth century emanating from a desire for change and a new voice might be framed as postmodernism.

## Critical and Postmodern Inquiries

The paradigm of postmodernism, which gave rise to various critical projects, particularly critical theory, is set against the postmodern backdrop. These critical projects originated in Western thought, focused on the notion of truth and the certainty thereof, and objected to the view of knowledge as neutral and rational. In addition, reflecting a shift away from modernism, as well as being heavily informed by the works of Karl Marx (1818–1883),

Friedrich Nietzsche (1844–1900), and Sigmund Freud (1856–1939), these critical projects conceived two important schools of thought—Frankfurt School and poststructuralism (Carrette, 2005).

While Michel Foucault and Jacques Derrida were the more prominent figures within poststructuralism, Frankfurt School featured Max Horkheimer, Marcus Adorno, and Habermas as its key thinkers. While these two critical schools had their differences, they nonetheless shared some basic assumptions about knowledge, society, and political institutions:

> Following Marx critical theory is aware that all knowledge is linked to economic and political ideology; following Nietzsche it understands that all knowledge is linked to the "will to power"; and following Freud it understands that all knowledge is linked to things outside our awareness (the unconscious). (Carrette, 2005, p. 28)

Traces of these critical pioneers are evident in almost every critical work that has been undertaken since then, and the fact that the three thinkers highlighted above viewed critical work from various prisms are also signs that critical project is neither monolithic nor homogeneous.

Grounded in the historical materialist tradition, critical theory embodies an unflinching interest in the social, political, spatial, and economic conditions of humans (Rush, 2004). From a Marxist standpoint, historical materialism is a philosophical perspective that is strongly grounded in all things physical and material, and even empirical in many ways (Smart, 1999), while the dialectic method represents a tool of analysis that views "every social system as having within it immanent forces that give rise to contradictions that can only be resolved by a new system" (Rush, 2004, p. 12). Thus, dialectic materialism is critical at its core and vies that agency is imperative for humans to determine and transform their respective material conditions, or the realities of their physical existence, or "sensuous existence" (Rush, p. 20).

Emanating from that background, critical theory "represents a sophisticated effort to continue Marx's transformation of moral philosophy into social and political critique, while rejecting orthodox Marxism as a dogma" (Bohman, 2006, p. 324). Critical theorists may have had varying degrees of perspectives on the unfolding of critical endeavor, but they were unequivocally united on the questions and issues that led to the conception of their critical enterprise:

> The motivation for this enterprise appears similar for each of the theorists—the aim being to lay the foundation for an exploration, in an interdisciplinary

> research context, of questions concerning the conditions which make possible the production and transformation of society, the meaning of culture, and the relation between the individual, society and nature. (Held, 1980, p. 16)

Held (1980) underscores this unity on the questions and concerns of critical theory as the central and melding theme that underlie collaboration and co-existence among the Frankfurt School scholars. Indeed, this unity has contributed to the success of critical theory, legitimizing it as a theoretical analysis that concerns itself with the actuality of life as it unfolds.

Geuss (1981) breaks down the fundamentals of critical theory and posits them as its central theses. The first thesis, according to Geuss, claims that critical theory is "aimed at producing enlightenment in the agents" who subscribe to the framework, in terms of "enabling those agents to determine what their true interests are" (p. 2). A second prong to the first thesis is that critical theory is "inherently emancipatory"; that is to say, it liberates "agents from a kind of coercion which is at least partly self-imposed, from self-frustration of conscious human action" (p. 2). The second thesis maintains that critical theory has a "cognitive content" that makes this theory intrinsically a "form of knowledge" (p. 2).

Flowing logically from the second thesis, the third one maintains that critical theory is dissimilar "epistemologically in essential ways from theories in the natural sciences": while "natural science is objectifying," critical theory is "reflective" (Geuss, 1981, p. 2). Objectifying refers to natural science making human beings the objects of its studies and embracing empirical standards that supposedly make findings about humans objective; but the "reflective" qualification of critical theory underscores its interest in understanding and interpreting the human condition and inspiring actions to improve it (Geuss, 1981). Critical theory seeks to transform human conditions materially while aiming to shift and balance power dynamics between the oppressed and their oppressors, between those in power and their subordinates. As such, critical theory has been established as an effective tool to critique dominant establishments or discourse, and to foster human emancipation (Bohman, 2006; Freire, 1971/1998; McLaren & Farahmandpur, 2005).

In this chapter, we endeavored to trace the historical development of philosophical ideas, traditions, and perspectives while highlighting their prevailing theme of pursuit of wisdom, including their significance to various paradigms of knowledge and to educational research. Thus, the preceding discussions fittingly preface the discussion of epistemology in the next chapter.

## *References*

Bennett, J. (2001). *Learning from six philosophers: Descartes, Spinoza, Leibniz, Locke, Berkeley, Hume* (Vols. 1–2). Oxford University Press.

Bishop, P. (2011). *Adventures in the human spirit* (6th ed.). Prentice Hall.

Blackburn, S. (1996). Metaphysics. In N. Bunnin & E. P. Tsui-James (Eds.), *Blackwell companion to philosophy* (pp. 64–89). Blackwell Publishing.

Bohman, J. (2006). Frankfurt school. In R. Audi (Ed.), *The Cambridge dictionary of philosophy* (2nd ed., pp. 324–325). Cambridge University Press

Carrette, J. (2005). Critical theory and religion. In C. Partridge (Ed.), *Introduction to world religions* (pp. 28–31). Fortress Press.

Chethimattam, J. B. (1971). *Patterns of Indian thought.* Geoffrey Chapman.

Couch, M. (Ed.). (1997). *Greek and Roman mythology.* Todtri.

de Beauvoir, S. (1989). *The second sex.* Vintage Books.

Foley, M., & Mohan, W. J. (2003). *Philosophic inquiry: An introduction.* Xlibris Corporation.

Freire, P. (1971/1998). *Pedagogy of freedom: Ethics, democracy, and civic courage* (P. Clarke, Trans.). Rowman & Littlefield.

Gadamer, H.-G. (1992). The historicity of understanding. In K. Mueller-Vollmer (Ed.), *The hermeneutics reader: Texts of the German tradition from the Enlightenment to the present* (pp. 256–292). Continuum.

Garber, D. (2006). Rationalism. In R. Audi (Ed.), *The Cambridge dictionary of philosophy* (2nd ed., pp. 771–772). Cambridge University Press.

Geuss, R. (1981). *The idea of a critical theory: Habermas and the Frankfurt School.* Cambridge University Press.

Grayling, A. C. (1996). Epistemology. In N. Bunnin & E. P. Tsui-James (Eds.), *The Blackwell companion to philosophy* (pp. 38–63). Blackwell.

Gutek, G. L. (2004). *Philosophical and ideological voices in education.* Pearson.

Habermas, J. (1972). *Knowledge and human interests* (J. J. Shapiro, Trans.). Beacon Press.

Heidegger, M. (1962). *Being and time.* Harper & Row.

Held, D. (1980). *Introduction to critical theory: Horkheimer to Habermas.* Athenaeum Press.

Hiriyanna, M. (1975). *Outlines of Indian philosophy* (10th ed.). Lewis Reprints.

Johnson, R. B., & Onwuegbuzie, A. J. (2004). Mixed methods research: A research paradigm whose time has come. *Educational Researcher, 33*(7), 14–26.

Johnson, T. W., & Reed, R. F. (2012). *Philosophical documents in education* (4th ed.). Pearson.

Johnson, W. J. (2009). *Oxford dictionary of Hinduism.* Oxford University Press.

Kenny, A. (Ed.). (1997). *The Oxford illustrated history of Western philosophy.* Oxford University Press.

Kneller, G. F. (1984). *Movements of thought in modern education.* Macmillan.

Lemos, N. L. (2006). Value theory. In R. Audi (Ed.), *The Cambridge dictionary of philosophy* (2nd ed., pp. 949–950). Cambridge University Press.

Low, D. (2000). *Merleau-Ponty's last vision: A proposal for the completion of "The visible and the invisible."* Northwestern University Press.

Lowe, E. J. (2002). *A survey of metaphysics.* Oxford University Press.

McLaren, P., & Farahmandpur, R. (2005). *Teaching against global capitalism and the new imperialism: A critical pedagogy.* Rowman & Littlefield.

Moser, P. K. (2006). Epistemology. In R. Audi (Ed.), *The Cambridge dictionary of philosophy* (2nd ed., pp. 273–278). Cambridge University Press.

Moser, P. K., Mulder, D. H., & Trout, J. D. (1998). *The theory of knowledge: A thematic introduction.* Oxford University Press.

Moser, P. K., & Nat, A. V. (1995). *Human knowledge: Classical and contemporary approaches* (2nd ed.). Oxford University Press.

Murti, T. R. V. (2010). *The central philosophy of Buddhism: A study of Madhyamika system.* Munshiram Manoharlal.

Nietzsche, F. (2000). The birth of tragedy and the geneology of man. In S. Rosen (Ed.), *The philosopher's handbook: Essential readings from Plato to Kant* (pp. 243–266). Random House.

Oliver, M. (1997). *History of philosophy.* Metro Books.

Ozmon, H. A., Craver, S. M. (2008). *Philosophical foundations of education* (8th ed.). Merrill Prentice Hall.

Palmer, D. (2002). *Does the center hold? An introduction to Western philosophy* (3rd ed.). McGraw-Hill.

Peirce, C. S. (1966). *Selected writings (Values in a universe of chance).* Dover.

Peirce, C. S. (1998). *The essential writings.* Prometheus Books.

Polkinghorne, D. E. (1983). *Methodology for the human sciences: Systems of inquiry.* SUNY Press.

Popkin, R. H., & Stroll, A. (1993). *Philosophy made simple* (2nd ed.). Broadway Books.

Prebish, C. S., & Keown, D. (2010). *Introducing Buddhism* (2nd ed.). Routledge.

Robinson, D., & Groves, J. (2001). *Introducing philosophy.* Totem Books.

Rush, F. (2004). Conceptual foundations of early critical theory. In F. Rush (Ed.), *The Cambridge companion to critical theory* (pp. 6–39). Cambridge Press.

Runes, D. D. (Ed.). (1983). *Dictionary of philosophy.* Littlefield, Adams.

Scruton, R. (1996). *Modern philosophy: An introduction and survey.* Penguin Books.

Sellars, R. W. (2010). *The essentials of logic.* Houghton Mifflin.

Smart, N. (1999). *World philosophies.* Routledge.

Trenchard, W. C. (1998). *Complete vocabulary guide to the Greek New Testament.* Zondervan.

Van Voorst, R. E. (2011). *Anthology of world scriptures* (7th ed.). Wadsworth.

Wallace, D. B. (2000). *The basics of New Testament syntax: An intermediate Greek grammar.* Zondervan.

Westphal, M. (2006). Hermeneutics as epistemology. In J. Greco & E. Sosa (Eds.), *The Blackwell guide to epistemology* (pp. 415–435). Blackwell.

Wittgenstein, L. (1953/2009). *Philosophical investigations* (4th ed., G. E. M. Anscomber, P. M. S. Hacker, & J. Schulte, Trans.). Blackwell.

Yu, C. H. (2006). *Philosophical foundations of quantitative research methodology.* University Press of America.

# Chapter 2 Epistemology and Philosophy of Science: Traditions, Perspectives, and Controversies

ANTONINA LUKENCHUK AND BAUDELAIRE K. ULYSSE

## Epistemology and Philosophy of Science: Overview

### Epistemological Legacies and Controversies

In Chapter 1, we defined epistemology as a branch of philosophy whose primary objective lies in "the study of the nature of knowledge and justification [thereof]" (Moser, 2006, p. 273). Kenny (2010) suggests that the Greek word for the term epistemology has special significance. According to Anthony, episteme "is often used to indicate a knowledge of a rather grand kind, so that one of its English equivalents is science" (p. 121). That is a valid point, considering the important role science has played in explaining and justifying knowledge; hence, epistemology has been conceptually defined as "the science of knowing" (Pojman, 1999, p. 1). Throughout Chapter 1, we perused the philosophical concept of epistemology and showed how various schools of thought in the history of philosophy have captivated the human mind and contributed to our understanding of knowledge and the pursuit thereof.

In the present chapter, we propose to focus primarily on knowledge—scientific knowledge of all sources. This primary focus immediately thrusts us into terrains that are already charted. This means that our intention is not to reinvent the wheel, but to account for the spokes that hold the wheel together. In other words, we will attempt to identify, review, analyze, and synthesize various theories of knowledge while guiding the reader/researcher to the shore where they could either coast, however comfortably and uncomfortably, or chart a new course. We hope, however, that readers will not settle comfortably, but that they will instead continue to navigate critically the various waves and currents ushered in their direction.

In addressing the theory of knowledge, Moser, Mulder, and Trout (1998) suggest that a theory of knowledge should first and foremost differentiate between "genuine knowledge and merely apparent knowledge, between the real thing and likely counterfeits" (p. 23). This suggestion raises a fundamental question that is rather recurring in the debates on the concept of knowledge. But is the supposed line between genuine knowledge and apparent knowledge real, or is it imaginary? Or, more importantly, could such a supposed line represent an unnecessary dichotomy? The philosophers, both past and present, who spent considerable time investigating knowledge were indeed interested in distinguishing among various types or kinds of knowledge. In the process, they focused on the following questions, among others. How do we know what we know? What counts as knowledge? Whose knowledge is of most worth? What is the scope of knowledge? What are its limits? In what ways might some types of knowledge be considered more credible than others?

Introducing his anthology of classical and contemporary readings on the theory of knowledge, Pojman (1999) highlights three different types of knowledge: *knowledge by acquaintance*, *competence knowledge*, and *propositional knowledge*. Pojman's types of knowledge are general categories that may be labeled differently in other literature, and we do not necessarily view them as exhaustive.

However, Pojman makes a compelling point about the connection between epistemology and propositional knowledge. Thus, he explains what comprises propositional knowledge:

> Person S knows that *p* (where *p* is some statement or proposition). Propositions have truth value; that is, they are true or false. They are the objects of propositional knowledge. When we claim to know that *p* is the case, we are claiming that *p* is true. Here are three examples of propositional knowledge: "I know that the sun will rise tomorrow," "I know that I have a mind," and "I know that Columbus discovered America in 1492." (p. 2)

All three examples of propositional statements provided above can be either verified or falsified. Logically, none of those statements can be both true and false simultaneously. Wherever one of such statements is false, then its opposite must be true; conversely, wherever one of such statements is true, then its opposite must be false. Thus, the verification process may use various methods that test both the "truth" value of knowledge claim and the source of that knowledge.

It should be noted that philosophers' attempts to distinguish among various kinds of knowledge is not new. The Greek language, which has immensely informed philosophical discourses of knowledge, features various Greek equivalents for the English verb "to know." In addition to "episteme," *oida* is also a Greek word for "to know" and it is suggestive of experiential knowledge. *Ginosko* is another Greek equivalent for "to know." Perhaps more important than the Greek words affecting our understanding of knowledge are the notions of knowledge, which have been extensively and judiciously treated in the works of Greek thinkers.

The list of Greek thinkers is without a doubt extremely long, featuring Protagoras, Pythagoras, Socrates, Plato, and Aristotle, along with other distinct groups of Greek thinkers such as the Sophists, the Epicureans, and the Stoics. All of the aforementioned Greek thinkers or groups have, in one way or another, contributed to modern concepts of knowledge or have contributed to projects seeking to answer questions related to the source, the essence, and the certainty of knowledge (Kenny, 2010). But we want to focus on the works of Plato, particularly the *Theaetetus* that casts Socrates and the *Republic* as well as the works of Aristotle in *Nicomachean Ethics* and *Posterior Analytics.*

The importance of Socrates, Plato, and Aristotle in understanding the concept of knowledge cannot be overstated. *Theaetetus*, for instance, focuses on answering the question "what is knowledge?" Most of the domains that are referred to as sources of knowledge—perception, reason, memory, and consciousness (Audi, 2003)—have their origins steeped in the works of Greek thinkers. For instance, according to Kenny (2010), *Theaetetus* proposes knowledge be viewed as geometry, astronomy, shoemaking, and carpentry, and he argues that "to know something is to perceive it with the senses" (p. 123). The notion of knowledge as perception was a position apparently held by Protagoras, but Plato set the stage where Socrates examined that position in considering its soundness (Kenny, 2010). In his evaluation of perception as knowledge, Socrates, as Kenny points out, readily granted that there are "ordinary cases" when this notion of knowledge as perception is not "erroneous," but denied these might be "cases of real knowledge" (p. 124).

Kenny (2010) skillfully breaks down the reasons why Socrates denied the notion of knowledge as perception:

> There are cases of perception without knowledge: we can hear a foreign language spoken, and yet do not the language (163b). There are cases of knowledge without perception: when we shut our eyes and recall something we have seen, we know what it looks like and yes are no longer seeing it (164a). But if knowing = perception, then both these must be cases of simultaneously knowing and not knowing, and surely that is an absurdity? (p. 124)

The dialogue continues between Theaetetus and Socrates, even after Theaetetus' proposition of knowledge as perception has been rejected. Determined to gain Socrates' assent on a definite understanding of knowledge, Theaetetus theorized once more that knowledge should be "thought (*doxa*), and thought is an activity of the soul by itself" (Kenny, 2010, p. 125). Theaetetus' proposition of knowledge as "thought" suggests that the thinking process of the mind is in and of itself "knowledge."

The assumption of this proposition is that when the mind thinks, it is engaging in an activity of questioning and answering different topics while "forming opinions" in the process. That, according to Theaetetus, equals to knowledge. According to Kenny, Socrates rejected that proposition on the basis that "there are false thoughts" (p. 125). Expanding on the notion of knowledge as thought, Theaetetus then added *logos* as a buffer, claiming that knowledge is "true thought, plus *logos*" (Kenny, 2010, p. 125). Theaetetus hoped to further qualify "true thought" with logos. This seems an apparent effort to capitalize on Socrates' slight willingness to grant "knowledge as true thought," as suggested by Kenny (2010). Hence, *logos* is expected to manifest in three different forms—expression, analysis, and description—which, in Socrates' assessment, turned out to be insufficient to support the proposition of knowledge as thought, plus logos (Kenny 2010).

Like Socrates and Plato, Aristotle spent considerable energy unraveling questions pertinent to the sources and the essence as well as the validity of knowledge claims. Aristotle's elaboration on these questions takes place primarily in the *Nicomachean Ethics. Arete*, *techne*, *episteme*, *phronesis*, *ergon*, *poiesis*, and *praxis* are recurring terms in the *Nicomachean Ethics* (Kenny, 2010). The ultimate question for Aristotle is how these seemingly varying terms could work to produce knowledge. Kenny (2010) captures how Aristotle synthesized these notions to conceive a knowledge that is deemed excellent:

> The nature of the *arete* of anything depends on its *ergon*, that is to say its job or characteristic output. The *ergon* of the mind and all its faculties is the production of true or false judgments (*NE* 6.2. 1139a29). That, at least is its *ergon* in the sense of its characteristic activity, its output whether it is working well or ill; its activity, when it is working well and doing its job, and therefore its *ergon* in the strict sense, is truth alone (2. 1139b12). The intellectual *aretai*, then, are excellences that make an intellectual part of the soul come out with truth. There are five states of the mind that have this effect—*techne, episteme, phronesis, sophia, nous*—which we may translate as skill, science, wisdom, understanding, and insight (3. 1139b16–17). (p. 132)

For Aristotle, insofar as knowledge of any subject regarding the world (both material and immaterial) is concerned, the human mind is always at work.

Hence, the mind plays a central role in understanding as well as obtaining knowledge whose object is related to the material and the immaterial world. *Logocentric* principle of knowledge in both Plato's and Aristotle's philosophies necessarily include a value component. Both philosophers sought proper ways to apply reason for the ultimate benefit of human beings—for them to live a fully satisfied life. Plato was convinced that his philosophy "could provide a science of the soul that would cure diseases of thought, judgment, and desire and deliver people from the sufferings of their ordinary lives" (Polkinghorne, 2004, p. 101). Conversely, Aristotle, although primarily agreeing with his mentor on the centrality of the reason-*logos* principle to make good judgments, claimed that living a fulfilling, happy and, therefore, a good life cannot be reduced to the skills of science-*techne* coupled with an ultimate ("true") knowledge-*episteme*. Aristotle believed that people know from experience what happiness and fulfillment are about and he conceived a human being as "fully embodied entity" with both reason and emotions involved in their "decisions about how to live the good life" (Polkinghorne, 2004, p. 109). Therefore, Aristotle's treatment of *phronesis* as "practical wisdom" acquires a more interesting and complex rendition than it does in Plato's philosophy.

Aristotle distinguished between three major tasks in human life and their corresponding activities. First, we need to develop a theory (*theoria*) which requires an application of mathematical and logical reasoning (*episteme*); then follows the task of *techne*, or the "scientific" skills of making artifacts which requires *poiesis*—the knowledge or wherewithal to produce objects; and finally, there is a need for *praxis*, or "acting for the good life of the other or the state," which requires the use of *phronesis* or practical reasoning (Polkinghorne, 2004, p. 112). *Praxis* acquires an important place in Aristotle's philosophy which intentionally connects the benefits that we can reap from proper application of reason to make good decisions which consequently lead to a fulfilled and happy life. Aristotle's principles of *phronesis* and *praxis* influenced the works of such twentieth-century thinkers as Arendt, Collingwood, Habermas, Heidegger, and Lyotard.

In *The Human Condition* (1998), Arendt expresses deep concerns about the decline of genuine political life in contemporary Western democracies and urges us "to think what we are doing," to invigorate a sense of the good and purposeful life through the synergy of *vita activa* (active life) and *vita contemplativa* (contemplative life). Arendt (1998) revitalizes the Aristotelian notion of *bios politikos*—the life "devoted to the matters of the *polis*," the "realm of human affairs," stressing action, or *praxis*, as the activity that will "establish and sustain it" (p. 7). Through acting and speaking, or "good deeds" and "good words," which Arendt associates with full engagement in social and political life, we can reclaim the lost meaning of *bios politikos* and can thus restore the notion of the good life. In the evolutionary process of re-awakening *bios politicos*, Arendt distinguishes between several fundamental human activities—"labor," "work," and "action," of which only "action" epitomizes genuine *praxis* and a fulfilled life. Although labor and work are worthwhile practices, they cannot satisfy our political aspirations, for it is only an action due to its condition of plurality that is "specifically *the* condition of all political life" (Arendt, 1998, p. 7).

The caveat of a logocentric principle in Western philosophy is that the mind must do its work well to arrive at any of its objectives such as skill, science, wisdom, understanding, and insight. Fast forwarding to the eighteenth century, these terms—skill, science, wisdom, understanding, and insight—which were wrought on the history of ideas by Greek philosophers, had continued to dominate the discourse on knowledge. Medieval philosophy is similarly important, but we consider it beyond the scope and objectives of this project; hence we have fast-forwarded to the eighteenth-century era, which might arguably be the stepping-stone or precursor to contemporary philosophy.

As stated earlier, Greek philosophical ideas, as enshrined particularly in the works of Socrates, Plato, and Aristotle, have had an immense influence on modern and contemporary Western ideas; however, the relationship between Greek philosophers and European philosophers during the eighteenth century is seldom consonant. Kenny (2010) illustrates this quite beautifully with his observation on the anticlimactic end of the discourses between Theaetetus and Socrates:

> Perhaps Theaetetus gave up too soon. If he had offered a fourth account [the three accounts he gave were words of expression, analysis, and description] of *logos* as meaning something like "justification," "reason," or evidence, then his definition of knowledge as true belief plus logos would have been found satisfactory by many a philosopher during the subsequent millennia of philosophy. (p. 126)

Indeed, Theaetetus would have found an eager audience among philosophers in the eighteenth century and today, not simply because "logos" is widely viewed as rational method to justify belief or ideas, but also because perception, which was rejected by Socrates, is widely accepted as a source of knowledge by contemporary philosophers. In this regard, Winkler (2006) writes:

> For the most part, eighteenth century philosophers viewed the understanding as one of several "faculties" or powers of the human mind; perception (or one

> of its cognates) was their preferred label for its characteristic or most basic act or operation. In this they followed the example set by Descartes, Malebranche, and Locke. The word perception was also used, however, as a synonym for idea—that is, as a label for the object of an act of understanding. (p. 236)

If Winkler is right about how eighteenth-century philosophers viewed perception, which he is, then the result of whatsoever the human mind attempted to understand would be understood. According to those philosophers, the mind would yield an epistemological product, which would have been "labeled" perception. This is not the only instance where modern or contemporary philosophers have departed from their Greek forefathers such as Socrates, Plato, and Aristotle. The Sophists espoused a view of knowledge which Socrates and Plato loathed. In particular, they emerged and thrived approximately in the same era as Socrates and Plato, although many prominent sophists preceded both Socrates and Plato. Sophists shared a deep skepticism about absolute knowledge and truth. Essentially, they rejected the existence of absolute knowledge and truth which they rendered relative (*cognitive relativism*). Sophists embraced and taught rhetoric as a special skill, and they emphasized "process, skill, and technique" (Johnson, 1998, p. 202). Sophists believed that special skill, rhetoric, could be applied to personal and social matters. Hence, rhetoric, for sophists, was the only skill that mattered and was worth teaching.

Perhaps, more important is the deep skepticism that was embedded in the notion of truth as subjective, as opposed to objective (Johnson, 1998). The philosophical commitment of the Sophists was devoid of absolute truths and ethical standards, which undermined what Socrates, Plato, and Aristotle taught and propagated. Particularly, Socrates contended that having expert knowledge is important and is in fact requisite for anyone to be able to teach genuinely and skillfully (Johnson, 1998, p. 208). Various modern and contemporary philosophers who have also raised reasonable doubt regarding the nature of knowledge have espoused this same philosophical commitment as the sophists.

In addition to reason and perception, many philosophers have proposed memory as a source of knowledge as well. Hartley and Hume placed varying degrees of reliability on memory. Winkler (2006) provides an insightful summary of how Hartley and Hume, along with other eighteenth-century philosophers, conceived memory:

> Memory was generally understood as a power to reproduce earlier ideas or representations. It was often described as a faculty of recalling sensations and the ideas derived from them—one that preserves the combination or order they had when they entered the mind. In Hartley, for example, traces of sensations

> and ideas are recalled "in the same order and proportion, accurately or nearly" (Observations). Like others who offered this standard definition, Hartley did not ask whether memory is a faculty that somehow aspires to accuracy or one that achieves it by definition. (p. 256)

The ability to reproduce and to represent ideas is posited as "a faculty of recalling sensations," but the mind plays a vital role in that it serves as the space housing objects, images, or ideas that might have crossed the mind at earlier stages. Interestingly, Hartley stops short of claiming the reproduction and representations engendered by these so-called "recalling sensations" are accurate. But there are many other philosophers who posit memory as a valid source knowledge capable of producing reliable understanding and knowledge. For instance, Audi (2003) claims: "Our beliefs are countless and varied. A vast proportion of them are stored in memory, though beliefs do not originate there" (p. 330). The caveat with memory is that it supposedly preserves beliefs but does not produce them. Furthermore, Audi goes on to elaborate:

> Metaphorically, [this] epistemological picture portrays both knowledge and justification as grounded in looking and thereby seeing. Perception looks outward, and through it we see the physical world. Memory looks backward, and through it we see the past, or at least some of the past. Introspection looks inward, and through it we see the stream of our own consciousness. Reason looks beyond experience of the world of space and time, and through it we see concepts and their relations. Testimony, our chief social source of knowledge, looks to others and thereby draws on all of these individual sources in those who convey their knowledge to us. (Audi, 2003, p. 332)

In the preceding quote, Audi elaborates on his perspective on memory as a source of knowledge. In addition, Audi briefly describes other sources of knowledge, such as reason, consciousness, and testimony, while showing their connectivity as well as their collective contribution to knowledge, or our grasp and certainty thereof. Also important in Audi's remarks is the notion of belief.

For many philosophers, knowledge is belief justified by reason or other evidence. In their piece "Knowledge: Undefeated Justified True Belief," Lehrer and Paxson (1999) advance the thesis of knowledge as belief. First, they use two different notions—justified true belief and undefeated justified true belief—to support their claim of knowledge as belief. Lehrer and Paxson begin their piece with the following explanation:

> If a man knows that statement is true even though there is no other statement that justifies his belief, then his knowledge is basic. Basic knowledge is completely justified true belief. On the other hand, if a man knows that a statement is true because there is some other statement that justifies his belief, then his knowledge is non-basic. Non-basic knowledge requires something in addition

> to completely justified true belief; for, though, a statement completely justifies a man in his belief, there may be some true statement that defeats his justification. So, we must add the condition that his justification is not defeated. (p. 153)

Hence, "undefeated justified true belief" represents something someone believes to be true and which has been justified by something or someone other than that thing believed to be true or justified by someone other than the claimer. The importance of justifying claims of knowledge and the persistence of the view of knowledge as belief have conceived two different philosophical frameworks—*foundationalism and non-foundationalism*—within which issues of subjectivity, relativeness, objectivity, validity, and truthfulness of knowledge are raised. Kuehn (2006) claims that the seventeenth-century philosophical issues related to knowledge and the certainty thereof are antecedents of the philosophical concerns of the eighteenth century. He elaborates:

> During the Middle Ages, the problem of knowledge and belief has been assimilated into the problem of knowledge versus (religious) faith. The thinkers of the eighteenth century tried to escape the problem connected with this religious dimension. In doing so, they were deeply influenced by developments of the preceding century (the beginning of the modern period). It has been argued that all of their problems had their roots in the seventeenth century. This is an exaggeration, but it is true that for understanding the framework in which the problem of knowledge and belief arose for the eighteenth century, it is necessary to know the broad outlines of the discussion of knowledge in the seventeenth century and especially theories of Rene Descartes and John Locke. (pp. 390–391)

Indeed, the mid-seventeenth century in Europe was marked by major paradigm shifts in the developments of philosophical ideas. Descartes and Locke indubitably represent two foremost and perhaps most influential thinkers of that era, and their ideas have laid the foundation for epistemological foundationalism. Conceptually, foundationalism embodies

> the view that knowledge and epistemic (knowledge-relevant) justification have a two-tier structure: some instances of knowledge and justification are non-inferential, or foundational; and all other instances thereof are inferential, or non-foundational, in that they derive ultimately from foundational knowledge or justification. (Moser, 2006, p. 321)

Thus, foundationalism represents a larger philosophical framework, which is underpinned by the presupposition that human beings can be certain of knowledge and that their knowledge claims can be objective. Both Descartes and Locke embraced scientific knowledge, but they disagreed sharply on the process to obtain such knowledge (method).

For Descartes, "knowledge was essentially independent of sense perception" (Kuehn, 2006, p. 391). The process leading to the grasp as well as the certainty of knowledge involves belief and subjectivity, but does not end at either one (Kuehn, 2006). However, Locke's view of knowledge was grounded in a deep and even unwavering commitment to sense perception, which one could say is empiricism at its purest. Essentially, Locke posited that the mind was an empty slate (tabula rasa) with knowledge of its own but has to rely on the experiences wrought on it by sensuous experiences. Moreover,

> Locke believed that there were basically three kinds of such perceptions, namely, intuition, demonstration, and sensation. Intuitive knowledge is based on immediate agreements and disagreements between ideas. In demonstrative knowledge, we must rely on intermediate ideas when we compare two ideas. It needs arguments and proofs, or demonstrations. Sensitive knowledge reaches "no farther than the Existence of Things" actually present to our Senses. (Kuehn, 2006, p. 393)

While Descartes and Locke obviously disagreed on the process and method to obtain knowledge, they shared the belief that human beings are able to acquire knowledge and be certain of that knowledge once acquired. For Descartes, the certainty of cognitive objectivity can be acquired by deduction (mathematical), and for Locke such certainty can be reached through sense perception. The legacies of Descartes and Locke, particularly they relate to the justification of knowledge, live on in the philosophy of science as well.

## *Philosophy of Science: Science Challenged and Redefined*

Philosophy of science deals with the application of epistemological concerns to a variety of areas of study and it proposes methods that can lead those areas of study to satisfactory results. Due to major scientific and technological advancements in nuclear physics, mathematics, neuroscience, chemistry, and biology, twentieth-century philosophy had to engage more vigorously with a scientific world to rethink its dominant role in liberal arts and sciences. Until about the seventeenth century, in the West, philosophy's domain included both physical and metaphysical concerns and its reign as *philosophia vero omnium mater* (from Latin, "the mother of all arts and sciences") was unquestionable. This started to change rapidly from the industrial revolution onward, and by the end of the twentieth century, philosophy clearly lost its ultimate authority in providing an all-encompassing picture of the world. This task was left to individual disciplines, whereas philosophy acquired a more supportive role in examining language statements and their meaning within these disciplines. Philosophers of science became preoccupied with the methods (and their critique) used by natural sciences and the analysis of a variety of concepts pertaining to scientific theories. It became apparent that a critical reexamination of scientific method was overdue. The very question of what counts as knowledge was subject to an unprecedented scrutiny by the twentieth-century advancements in theoretical physics.

According to Papineau (1996), two sets of concerns dominate the current philosophy of science, creating "two broad areas" (p. 290). The first broad area investigates the question "whether science ever uncovers permanent truths, whether objective decisions between competing theories are possible and whether the results of experiment are clouded by prior theoretical expectations" (p. 290). The last broad category, according to Papineau, focuses on "the metaphysics of science," examining scientific claims about the natural and related phenomena.

Contemporary philosophy of science features various philosophers, but we want to highlight the contributions of Gaston Bachelard (1884–1962) and Thomas Kuhn (1922–1996). Because of the fact that the translations of the works of Continental philosophers from a variety of their respective languages into English can be a matter of time, many of their works often become available to English-speaking audiences later than their original publications. This was the case with French philosopher Gaston Bachelard who in the 1930s developed a theory of "epistemological breaks," which was further elaborated in Thomas Kuhn's theory of paradigm shifts.

The corpus of Gaston Bachelard features work encompassing science, poetry, epistemology, and imagination. To Bachelard, imagination, more than reason, is a unifying force in the human soul. Bachelard's poetics is linked essentially to his epistemology and more general views on the history of arts and sciences. His widely acclaimed notion of *epistemological obstacle* (also known as *epistemological break* or, interchangeably, *epistemological rupture*) provides, on the one hand, a sharp criticism of positivism, and on the other, a solid justification for an integrated approach to knowledge and intuition, rational and irrational, and scientific and poetic.

Yet, another fascinating feature of Bachelard's work is the integration of epistemology and psychoanalysis. This integration of epistemology and psychoanalysis ends up functioning as a sort of "therapeutic" effect on "objective" knowledge, whereby utilitarian and mundane irrationalities that impede the progress of objective knowledge are removed. In addition, psychoanalysis helped him understand how "blockages" are formed in some people that prevent them from the formation of the scientific mind. He called these blockages "epistemological obstacles." Even a healthy mind, he thought, still has some "dark areas, traces of the old in our new ways of thinking" (Bachelard, 2002,

p. 20). Eventually, his study of "pre-scientific" texts led him to conclude that "the age of reason" was also marked by "unreason" as he determined how even some among the so-called "educated" people of his era displayed "disturbed" minds about some scientific discoveries such as electricity.

Bachelard posited that the formation of the scientific mind requires three stages of development: the concrete, the concrete-abstract, and the abstract. Having examined the epistemological obstacles to objective thought (2002), he changed his position on the primacy of the scientific mind. The impetus that caused the change in his position is that he came to understand that imagination is not an obstacle but an essential element of psychic dynamism. Epistemology thus represents two dialectical activities, intellectual and imaginative, which should form the rhythm of life (Bachelard, 2000). Hence, Bachelard (2004) claims, "Without the help of poets, what can a philosopher, weighted down with years, do if he persists talking about imagination? He has no one to test. He would immediately get lost in the labyrinth of tests and counter-tests" (Bachelard, 2004, p. 25).

Inspired by Bachelard's ideas, Kuhn developed a theory of paradigm shifts that shed additional light on a new conception of science and scientific knowledge. Kuhn spent about 15 years studying the history of science that resulted in his famous *The Structure of Scientific Revolutions* (1962). He came to the conclusion that the development of science is not a linear and cumulative process. Some theories can be contradictory. His central concept is that of a paradigm whose definition entered most etymological and philosophical dictionaries as a "constellation of beliefs, values, and techniques shared by the members of a given scientific community" (Runes, 1983, p. 240).

In his seminal work, *The Structure of Scientific Revolutions* (1962), Kuhn maintains that some paradigms are general and encompassing, while others guide scientific thinking within specific areas of study. A paradigm is essential in the process of observation and experiment:

> Paradigms provide scientists not only with a map but also with some of the directions essential for map-making. In learning a paradigm the scientist acquires theory, methods, and standards together, usually in an inextricable mixture. Therefore, when paradigms change, there are usually significant shifts in the criteria determining the legitimacy both of problems and of proposed solutions. (Kuhn, 2000, p. 519)

A scientist cannot avoid bringing a definite belief system into the area of study. Kuhn observed that early stages of most sciences went through "pre-paradigm periods" characterized by conceptual chaos and competing views of nature. Paradigm debates always involve the question: "Which problems is it more significant to have solved? Like the issue of competing standards, that question of values can be answered only in terms of criteria that lie outside of normal science altogether, and it is that recourse to external criteria that most obviously makes paradigm debates revolutionary" (Kuhn, 2000, p. 519). When the majority of the scientific community accepts a paradigm, this newly accepted paradigm becomes a "warrant"—a mandatory way of approaching problems ("normal science"). A new and radical theory is not an addition to the existing knowledge but its interruption.

Kuhn's theory of paradigm shifts reinforces the general assumptions held by the twentieth-century philosophers of science—that our knowledge of the world is essentially fallible and, if acquired, it can only represent the best explanation available. Any new discovery can potentially lead to a dramatic shift in our view of the world's picture. This new understanding of science proposes an expanded notion of reason supported by a hermeneutic and a pragmatic logic. Charles S. Peirce (see Chapter 2), for instance, regarded the knowledge of science not as "the truth" but only as its approximation. "Truth" thus represents the effectiveness of our knowledge as demonstrated by the effectiveness of our action. Peirce also believed that knowledge was a communal achievement and that the community ("scientific community," as he would have it) had to make a decision to accept or reject a given paradigm of knowledge.

Considering the multifaceted constellation of existing beliefs, epistemological pluralism is the position from which one ought to approach the question of methods in both natural and human sciences. Contemporary inquiry often represents *syncretic* research which "proposes something more than the use of multiple systems of inquiry: it proposes the additional step of syncretizing the results of the multiple inquiries into a unified and integral result" (Polkinghorne, 1983, p. 254). For instance, German philosopher Otto Apel (b. 1922) proposed syncretic research in psychoanalysis in a form of "tacking," or "zigzagging," whereby the researcher "first is engaged in the research process, then distances himself from it, analyzes and reevaluates his position, and then returns to be a participant of the research again" (Polkinghorne, 1983, p. 255). Jurgen Habermas (b. 1929) developed the project that syncretized hermeneutic and empirical sciences to create guidelines for the logic of a critical science, and this will be the focus of our further discussion.

## *The Fallen Skies of Epistemological Certainty*

### *"Positive" Knowledge Dethroned*

The foundationalist assumptions of scientific knowledge, as enshrined in the philosophical works of Descartes and Locke, dominated epistemological discourses in the West for a long time. These assumptions have culminated in the positivist conception of science which held that only those things of which we are absolutely certain can be counted as knowledge. However, at the turn of the twentieth century, the "fallen angels" of logical positivism were overpowered by the new forces coming from several movements in the philosophy of science (see Chapter 2). Logical positivism was dethroned as supposedly the only valid scientific paradigm by the new developments in nuclear physics and microbiology. The nature of science and its scope have changed dramatically through the expansion of the boundaries of scientific inquiry which shifted radically from positivistic and reductionist models. An understanding of science by Anglo-American and Continental philosophers shifted entirely from the positivist to the post-positivist conception of science. The pioneering philosophers of science who championed the cause of questioning the absolute certainty of positivistic science were Bachelard, Kuhn, Frank, Popper, and Feyerabend, among a few others. Karl Popper (1902–1994) was one of the first to contest the claims of positivistic science by raising questions of scientific method that posit observation as its stepping-stone leading to theoretical formulations.

Paul Feyerabend (1924–1994) provided radical criticism of positivistic scientific methodology in his seminal work, *Against Method: Outline of an Anarchistic Theory* (1978). *Against Method* begins with Feyerabend's celebrated quote: "Science is an essentially anarchic enterprise: theoretical anarchism is more humanitarian and more likely to encourage progress than its law-and-order alternatives" (Feyerabend, 2000, p. 493). Feyerabend insists on the fact that science is not and cannot be governed by a system of firm, unchanging, and absolute principles and that all methodologies have their limits. The history of science "does not just consist of facts and conclusions drawn from facts. It also contains ideas, interpretations of facts, problems created by conflicting interpretations, mistakes, and so on" (Feyerabend, 2000, p. 495). To put it differently, there is no single theory that agrees with all the facts in its domain. In agreement with Bachelard and Kuhn, Feyerabend asserts that history clearly shows us that "epistemological breaks" have been necessary to propel scientific progress. Accordingly, pluralistic methodology becomes a necessity when comparing rival theories and ideas. Feyerabend's principle of methodological anarchism finds its utmost expression in the following statement: "[T]he idea of a fixed method, or of a fixed theory of rationality, rests on too naïve a view of man and his social surroundings. [It is clear that] the only one principle that can be defended under *all* circumstances and in all stages of human development is the principle: *anything goes*" (Feyerabend, 2000, p. 502).

"Anything goes" is the principle that can be leveraged against the backdrop of the debate formulated by the skeptics who believed that there could be only two propositions of knowledge—apodictic and problematic (see the discussion above). It follows then that a proposition can be either "infallible and beyond doubt or dubious and, therefore, not *episteme*" (Polkinghorne, 1983, p. 12). However, and as Feyerabend so vigorously claims, there can be indeed "assertoric" propositions that stand between apodictic ("infallible") and problematic ("dubious"). Assertoric propositions, although "supported by evidence," still "remain open to future confirmation and correction as more experience is gained" (Polkinghorne, 1983, p. 12). It follows then that between the extremes of absolute certainly and absolute uncertainty, "statements of knowledge can be judged against each other, and some of them can be accepted and used as the base for action while others can be rejected" (Polkinghorne, 1983, p. 13). The acceptance of assertoric knowledge as a legitimate goal of science "has reopened a possibility for alternative epistemological frameworks" (Polkinghorne, 1983, p. 12). Pertaining to the disputable nature of knowledge claims is the fact that knowledge is being developed in a "historical and cultural context, and it is subject to the limitations of the conceptual and technical tools of its situation" (Polkinghorne, 1983, p. 242).

A new understanding of science based on the fallibilistic and conditional nature of knowledge ushered in the development of pluralistic epistemologies. Although originated much earlier in time (see Chapter 2), hermeneutics was perhaps one of the most potent movements that challenged the notion of knowledge that was restricted to specifically the rationalist domain. *Understanding* (*verstehen* in German) becomes hermeneutic knowledge. The upper-case letter "U" underscores the importance of the notion. Without a capital letter "U," understanding refers to any kind of comprehension. Yet when capitalized, the word denotes a "specific type of understanding, the comprehension of meaning" (Polkinghorne, 1983p. 217). *Understanding* thus becomes a way of knowing and a method whereby researchers apprehend the meaning and translate it into a variety of forms of data to serve the purposes of their research.

Hermeneutics emphasizes the "embededness of knowledge in historically particular and contingent vocabularies" (Westphal, 2006, p. 416). Philosophical hermeneutics of Heidegger and Gadamer represent, by far, one of the most influential anti-positivist responses. Heidegger, for instance, repudiates foundationalism in his account of the hermeneutic circle. He draws distinctions between linguistic and prelinguistic interpretation of the text. To him, interpretation is always *seeing-as*. There is, in other words, an a priori understanding before we enter the circle, and it is, in fact, our understanding of ourselves. Every act of interpretation thus presupposes our understanding of ourselves as a thrown projection in our dealings with things. Heidegger admits that knowledge does have foundations, but "the basis of the linguistic expressions that are the bearers of truth or falsity are not those representations that are epistemically privileged, [but rather] practices that are not truth bearing" (Westphal, 2006, p. 424). Heidegger makes practice foundational to his epistemology and looks for a more primordial conception of truth which he often labels as "unconcealment" (along with some other terms).

Jurgen Habermas extended the hermeneutic tradition to the study of social theory, thus providing a sharp criticism of positivistic science. Habermas' ideas, along with those of other twentieth-century critical and postmodern philosophers, represent a concerted effort to deconstruct the very notion of episteme as a hegemonic construct in advanced Western powers.

### *Episteme Deconstructed*

Critical hermeneutics positions Habermas within the milieu of the Continental postmodern/poststructuralist contemporary thinkers such as Jean-Francois Lyotard (1924–1998), Gille Deleuze (1925–1995), Michel Foucault (1926–1984), Jean Baudrillard (1929–2007), Jacques Derrida (1930–2004), and Julie Kristeva (b. 1941), among a few others, who have been performing deconstructive works and situated themselves within the postmodern outlook, which views itself as essentially different from modernism. Loyard's description of postmodernism as "incredulity toward metanarratives" (as cited in Rose, 1991, p. 55) puts deconstruction in perspective. Hence the project of deconstruction has been primarily about deconstructing metanarratives of any sort, including epistemological frameworks. Particularly, deconstructive works focus on delineating the political, social, and economic influences on what knowledge is accepted as valid and objective.

The history of postmodern outlook can be traced to nineteenth-century British artists. In the beginning of the twentieth century, the label of postmodernism was attached to a broad movement in art also known as "post-impressionist" or "post-industrial." Nietzsche is considered by many a presage of postmodern thought, which he expressed as the crisis of modernity [of his time] and the advent of a new age of *Übermensch* (see Chapter 2). The modern era is typically associated with the rise of natural sciences and the decline of the centralized power of Christendom (predominantly Catholicism). Secular movements within the Age of Enlightenment are also referred to the modern era. A modernist was regarded as a person committed to the modern age who believed that "traditions must be overthrown or redefined in order to do justice to the new forms of experience" (Scruton, 1996, p. 2). English-speaking philosophy is "modern, but not modernist. French philosophy [. . .] (e.g., Derrida, Foucualt) is modernist, without being particularly modern, i.e., without basing itself in the assessment of arguments, or in the desire to build on established truths" (Scruton, 1996, p. 2). At the turn of the twentieth century, the label "postmodern" was adopted by several French thinkers who had been sparking the debates of the "arching questions of the human spirit" (Scruton, 1996, p. 3).

The concern with these debates was unavoidable for Jurgen Habermas. In his opus magnum *Knowledge and Human Interests* (1972), Habermas brings forth the following three major theses: that (1) "*achievements of the transcendental subject have their basis in the natural history of the human species;*" (2) that "*knowledge equally serves as an instrument and transcends mere self-preservations;*" and (3) that "*knowledge-constitutive interests take form in the medium of work, language, and power*" (Habermas, 1972, pp. 312–313).

Especially important for educational inquiry, Habermas further draws distinctions regarding the three different modes of research associated with human interests. First, in the *empirical-analytic sciences*, "knowledge is [...] predictive knowledge. However, the *meaning* of such predictions, that is their technical exploitability, is established only by the rules according to which we apply theories to reality" (Habermas, 1972, p. 308). Further, the *historical-hermeneutic sciences*

> gain knowledge in a different methodological framework. Here the meaning of the validity of propositions is not constituted in the frame of reference of technical control. [. . .] Theories are not constructed deductively and experience is not organized with regard to the success of operations. Access to the facts is provided by the understanding of meaning, not observation. (Habermas, 1972, p. 309)

And finally, the "systematic *sciences of social action*, that is economics, sociology, and political science, have the goal [. . .] of producing nomological knowledge" (Habermas, 1972, p. 310). Habermas vehemently emphasizes that a critical social science will never be satisfied with such an outcome. It should be "concerned with going beyond this goal to determine when theoretical statements grasp invariant regularities of social action as such and when they express ideologically frozen relations of dependence that can in principle be transformed" (Habermas, 1972, p. 310). The methodological framework that Habermas proposes for determining the meaning of the validity of critical propositions of this type of inquiry is established by *self-refection* ("reflexivity"). Self-reflection designates an emancipatory cognitive interest.

Habermas' emancipatory and self-reflective practices incite social imaginations of postmodern and poststructuralist thinkers. Foucault (1967), for instance, proposes a metaphor of *heterotopia*, denoting a concept of human geography (place, space, dwelling, etc.). Heterotopia represents a *real* space (as opposed to utopia) which allows for generating non-hegemonic conditions of "otherness." Foucault maintains that there are *real* places in every culture and in every civilization that are formed in the very founding of society, which are "something like counter-sites, a kind of effectively enacted utopia in which the real sites, all the other real sites that can be found within the culture, are simultaneously represented, contested, and inverted" (Foucault, 1967, p. 3). Foucault's concern is with the spirit of individual and social imagination that should spur the societal and political change in an oppressive society.

Jacques Derrida, another prominent figure in postmodern and poststructuralist movement, is known for his radical hermeneutics. Derrida's main thesis is, "nothing is outside the text." This means, epistemologically, that "being must always already be conceptualized," and, ontologically, that "the thing itself is a sign" (Westphal, 2006, p. 430). In maintaining that there will always be at least two interpretations of interpretation [of the text], Derrida not just overcomes metaphysics, he essentially abolishes it. The critique of logocentric principle in the history of Western philosophy finds its ultimate expression in the philosophy of Derrida that can be briefly captured in the notions of identity and difference, or in other words, of continuity and being *deferred*. Derrida coins the word *differance* to convey both the difference and deferral. There is no knowledge as such, concludes Derrida, and its use-value becomes a mere production for "sale."

Jean Baudrillard's (1929–2007) postmodern critique of social realities in advanced Western powers is expressed through his extravagant images of simulacra and hyperreality. Assuming that we are the inhabitants of a postmodern world where the demarcation lines between what is real and what is not are simply impossible to draw, then, as Baudrillard suggests, most of us are confined to a hyperreality of Disneyland, a "perfect model of all the entangled orders of simulation":

> This imaginary world is supposed to be what makes the operation successful. But, what draws the crowds is undoubtedly much more the social microcosm, the miniaturized and *religious* reveling in real America, in its delights and drawbacks. [...] The objective profile of the United States [...] may be traced throughout Disneyland [...]. All its values are exalted here, in miniature and comic-strip form. Embalmed and pacified. Whence the possibility of an ideological analysis of Disneyland: ... digest of the contradictory reality. But this conceals something else, and that "ideological" blanket exactly serves to cover a *third-order simulation*: Disneyland is there to conceal the fact that it is the "real" country, all of "real" America, which *is* Disneyland. (Baudrillard, 1999, p. 485)

Baudrillard urges individuals to reawaken their self-consciousness and break away from illusions, deceptions, and oppressive influences of omnipotent and transcendent powers of politics, ideology, religion, or consumerism.

The domino effect of critical poststructuralist Continental philosophers produced a vibrant constellation of Anglo-American thinkers. Critical feminists who followed in the footsteps of their foremothers such as Simone de Beauvoir (1908–1986) ushered in several movements critical to the development of gender and identity issues in contemporary educational inquiry. Sociologist Dorothy Smith (b. 1926), for instance, argued that women experience the world differently from men, since men encounter the world "already processed" (e.g., meals prepared, laundry done), while the work of women is "the processing of the raw material" into a form "suitable for consumption" (Longino, 2006). Psychologist Carol Gilligan "criticized her colleague Lawrence Kohlberg's account of moral development as resting too much on a pattern ascertained from male samples" (Longino, 2006, p. 330). Educational psychologist Mary Belenky and her colleagues suggest that "women learn through connection rather than separation"; and they claim this as a "way of knowing" (Longino, 2006, p. 330).

One of the consistent themes running through the feminist rethinking of the subject of knowledge is the "insistence on its embodiment" (Longino, 2006, p. 331), which concerns the mind-body problem in Western philosophy. The disembodied self is a "Cartesian masculine subject." It is in fact displaced onto the bodies of "feminized and primitivized Others—European women and nonwhite women and men—who are thereby epistemologically disfranchised" (Longino, 2006, p. 332).

Haraway (1999) contributed to the feminist and postmodern critique of the philosophy of science as an essentially masculine project. Along with this critique, Haraway deconstructs the mythology of a unified women's movement on the basis of her argument of our "fractured identities":

> There is nothing about being "female" that naturally binds women. There is not even such a state as "being" female, itself a highly complex category constructed in contested sexual scientific discourses and other social practices. Gender, race, or class consciousness is an achievement forced on us by the terrible historical experience of the contradictory social realities of patriarchy, colonialism, and capitalism. (p. 540)

Haraway's concern is with feminists' "lapsing into boundless difference" and "giving up on the confusing task of making partial, real connections"; some differences are "playful; some are poles of world historical systems of domination. 'Epistemology' is about knowing the difference" (p. 543).

Embodiment is an important construct to delineate standpoint epistemologies championed by Donna Haraway in her essay, *Situated Knowledges* (1988). Standpoint epistemology represents an analysis of some Marxist ideas regarding the position of workers as opposed to "capitalists." Workers' understanding of their condition gave them privilege over capitalists, and this superiority could be regarded as both epistemological and political. Additionally, sexual division of labor in childbearing provided the basis for the opposed structuring of material life of women and men. Although the standpoint epistemological assumptions shared the above Marxist-based ideology, they failed to account for women's diversity and particular locations of female oppression (Longino, 2006).

Another dimension of the embodiment of the knower is the denial of any essential difference between subjects and objects of knowledge. With this regard, reflexivity takes on an especially important dimension, i.e., "the knower's awareness of her assumptions and values and of the ways in which these affect her beliefs and theorizing" (Longino, 2006, p. 334). Feminist epistemologists are convinced that current social arrangements "assign epistemic privilege to occupants of one social position," and that feminist standpoint theory "seeks to reverse the assignment and grants epistemic privilege to those in subordinated, socially unprivileged positions" (Longino, 2006, p. 338). Whichever the case, the postructuralist feminists are working vehemently toward to the demise of the positivistic rhetoric of science (Lather, 2004).

Worth noting is the fact that poststructuralist position steers away from feminism's tendency to make generalizations based on the experiences and accounts of Western, white, middle-class women. Instead, it looks at "the intersection of the identity categories: race, class, gender, sexual orientation, ethnicity, nationality, age, wellness, etc" (St. Pierre & Pillow, 2000, p. 7). The issue of woman's subjectivity continues to be challenged by poststructuralist feminists who place a greater emphasis on language and discourse that shape the ways women experience oppression (St. Pierre & Willow, 2000). Poststructuralist feminists question the very possibility of finite definitions:

> If "woman" is defined once and for all, then there is no hope of a reconfiguration that might offer different, strategic possibilities for ethical, political, and relational work. What kind of women and what kinds of feminism might we fail to produce if we define "woman" and "feminism" once and for all? (St. Pierre & Willow, 2000, p. 8)

One of the strengths of poststructuralism lies in its ability to continue to "reinvent itself strategically, shifting and mutating given existing political agendas, power relations, and identity strategies" (p. 8). Epistemic privileges and deconstructive practices are central to the critical race theory (CRT) framework. Critical race theories emerged in the 1980s as a reaction to critical legal studies and launched a critical examination of American society and culture in the intersections of race, law, and power. Later these theories included in the context of their investigations the constructs of gender, ethnicity, national identity, and sexual orientation CRT studies which ground themselves in the human and civil rights struggles for justice, and equal opportunity for historically oppressed and disadvantaged groups in the U.S. (Ballard & Cintron, 2010; Bell, 2008; Delgado & Stefanic, 2001; Essed & Goldberg, 2001). Ballard and Cintron (2010) identify three elements of critical race theory: microaggressions, creation of counter-stories, and development of counter-spaces. Microaggression is defined as "a type of subtle abuse aimed at minorities that can be visual, verbal, nonverbal, conscious, or unconscious" (p. 15). The creation of counter-stories is presented as "archives, testimonies, or discussions that marginalized groups use to respond to stories previously espoused by the dominant group" (p. 16). Finally, the development of counter-spaces is seen as a "means of conveying stories of experiences that have not been told, as well as a way to assess and counter dominant stories" (p. 16).

Critical race theory's concern is centered on W. E. B. Du Bois' (1868–1963) account of "double consciousness" as a "complex and constant play between the exclusionary conditions of social structure marked by race and the psychological and cultural strategies employed by the racially excluded and marginalized to accommodate themselves to everyday indignities as well as to resist them" (Essed & Goldberg, 2001, p. 5). Critical racial theories exert a significant influence on the humanities and social science scholarship, especially critical ethnicity studies (Gaspar de Alba, 2003; Noriega, 2000; Saldivar, 1990).

Wedded to the cause of critical theories are the issues of queer studies whose task is to challenge "those U.S. legal and social structures that privilege heterosexuality, patriarchy, white supremacy, and class advantage, with the legal and social liberation of sexual minorities—queers—as its principal focus" (Lugg, 2006, p. 178). The queer legal theory (QLT) emerged in the 1990s in response to some political and legal events, and it "does not expect the researcher to remain 'neutral' on issues of social justice and queer Americans" (Lugg, 2006, p. 177).

Disability studies provide a sharp critique of the social model of disability (Gabel and Peters, 2004). Recent developments in disability studies moved away from the objective-subjective dichotomy while adopting a postmodern position that provides a new space to deconstruct the notion of disability itself. Particularly, Gabel and Peters (2004) employ the postmodern perspective to critique medical and functionalist models of disability which marginalize and pathologize disability. Resistance theory is yet another powerful tool that adds to the deconstructive theory and practice of disability studies "to transgress, disrupt, and confront while also constructing a disability-centered notion of beauty and desire" (Gabel & Peters, 2004, p. 593).

Resistance is inherently political, and the above discussion on its theorizing and practical application provides an indispensable forum for educators to consider their inquiry along the lines of critical theories intersecting socio-economic class, race, ethnicity, gender, ability, or lifestyle issues pertaining to social justice.

### *Epistemological Pluralism on Equal Footing: Non-Western Ways of Knowing*

Our quest to know often leads us to explore uncharted territories populated with different peoples having many and variegated beliefs. These beliefs form a "structure of great complexity, with innumerable changing elements that reflect our continuing experience and thought, our actions and emotions, our learning and forgetting, our inferring and accepting, our revising and rejecting, our speaking and listening" (Audi, 2003, p. 336). An apparent diversity of worldviews is indicative of the fact that we live in the world of "pluralistic epistemologies" (Polkinghorne, 1983). According to Ogilvy (1977), there is "not *one truth* which corresponds to *reality*. Instead, there are *some truths* which hold within communities" (as cited in Polkinghorne, 1983, p. 250). Epistemological pluralism hinges on the notion of context, or community that allows for an "understanding that is greater than the understanding of any one point of view" (Polkinghorne, 1983, p. 251). Epistemological pluralism incites the inquiry that can "reap significant methodological benefits from using multiple procedures for its research designs" (p. 252).

Whereas (for the most part) several preceding centuries were marked by the dominance of some epistemologies and the silencing if not subjugation and ridicule of others, this century (let us hope for the most part) brings to the forefront the power of knowledge unleashed from all four corners of the world on equal footing. The history of an epistemological journey of what can be labeled as "non-Western" traditions carries a record of extraordinary achievements and glory on the one hand, and colonialism and suppression on the other.

It should be noted that the terms "non-Western" and "Western" denote a great deal of ambiguity and confusion. If considered geographically, "non-Western" (as opposed to "Western" or "Western European") applies to most of the world's countries along with their inhabitants. It is estimated, for instance, that there are 196 countries in today's world (Glennon, 1995) (the number varies between 193 and 195 in other sources), out of which, only 44 are officially recognized as "Western European." If taken in political and economic terms, both "Western" and "non-Western" elicit the same amount of ambiguity. "Western" often refers to either Western European, or North American and Western European, or to both, designating several countries in Europe and North America with advanced economic and technological systems ascribed as dominant (perhaps until very recently) within the scope of a global economy. The same countries are often regarded in opposition to "non-Western" because of the history of colonialism. However, the term "Western European" is especially ambiguous due to its re-emergence after WWII, and after the Cold War fought by the U.S. and its allies against the former Soviet-bloc European countries. With the dissolution of the USSR, the political implication of the term lost its meaning, yet it remains popular.

Today's Europe is essentially different from what it was even some 50 or 60 years ago. There are 44 northern, southern, western, and eastern European countries on the world map; out of these 44, only 9 are recognized by the UN as "Western," and out of those 9, probably less than half have been responsible for the history of foreign invasions, slavery, and colonialism. Moreover, many European countries, in their remote and recent historical past, have been fighting for liberty and independence from their neighbors. Ukraine has been separated from Russia since the early 1990s but is now engaged in a brutal war against Russia fighting for its independence anew.

Evidently, the history of European revolutionary ideas and events continues to inspire social and political activism throughout the world. This brief and certainly superficial tour of European history reminds us of some facts that are important to consider when addressing non-Western traditions. And it is from the position of the general context of vast diversity and complexity between and within the world's cultures that we approach non-Western ways of knowing. Both the scope of this book and the space limit of its printed edition allow for the inclusion of some materials but not other materials.

## *Epistemological and Methodological Plurality Across Cultures*

Being selective by no means implies privileging some perspectives over others. On the contrary, the premise of this book posits epistemological and methodological pluralism, which, at its core, recognizes and honors all cultures and their respective ways of knowing. The Eastern world abounds in rich and diverse philosophical thoughts. Chapter 2 outlines briefly Hinduism and Buddhism—the ancient philosophical traditions that originated in India. China is the birthplace of Taoism and Confucianism. Taoism begins with the anthology known as the *Daode Jing* (*Tao-te Ching*) and whose authorship had been ascribed to Laozi (Lao-tzu) who lived in China in ~ 5 BC. At the heart of his message is Tao, translated as "the Way." The Tao of Lao-tzu represents simultaneously the nature of reality, knowledge, and value perceived as a whole. From a Daoist or Taoist perspective, to be knowledgeable means to act in harmony with the Tao, or synchronize with natural rhythm of the universe. Actions that abuse consciousness may rebound and obtain their ecological retribution from persons and societies that have disrupted the equilibrium. Additionally, the Dao or Tao illuminates the principle of reciprocity wherein the outer world reflects the inner conditions and vice versa. Chinese teachers brought Buddhism to Japan. Particularly, Eisai (1141–1215) is considered to be the father of Zen Buddhism in Japan. The monk Dogen (1200–1253) is responsible for spreading Ts'ao-tung or Soto methods and teachings from China to Japan.

In the twelfth and thirteenth centuries, the movement known as the Qabbalah (Kabbalah) or Tradition (originated in Provence and Spain) revived the mystical strand in the Jewish tradition. The Qabbalists explore the techniques of meditation and ecstasy, especially Avraham Abulafia (1240–ca. 1291), who may have been influenced by Sufism or Islamic mysticism. Illuminationist, or Ishraqi, school of Persian philosophy, founded by the Sufi Sheikh al-Suhrawardi (1154–1191) used a linguistic connection between the concept of "Eastern-ness" (*mashriq*) and that of "wisdom" or "light" or "illumination" (*ishraq*). Both words are derived from *sharq*, meaning "the sunrise." Suhrawardi and his followers claimed that Light was the foundation of all existence. Knowledge of the truth is thus achieved through an intuition of Light—an "illumination." Rumi (1207–1273), a Persian Sufi mystic, is the key exponent of Sufism who believed that the ultimate center of human consciousness, our inmost reality, is the "heart" (*dil, qalb*). People's hearts are often "veiled" by innumerable levels of "dross" and "darkness." Transformation occurs when one's heart is completely purified. Love is, therefore, understood as a metaphysical and epistemological principle. Love must be experienced in order to be understood.

Mysticism and esoteric philosophy cross the geographical boundaries between the East and the West and represent an unbroken tradition from the Egyptians, Hebrews, and Greeks, through the Christian West, and continuing to the present. Central to esoteric world traditions is the system of "the One" that cannot be properly expressed in words and that has different interpretations specific to different cultures. The One is the supreme God that emanates in the form of the Intellect or Nous which further emanates in the Soul. It exemplifies the union of human beings with the Infinite. Gnosticism, the teaching of Gnostics, evokes the Sufi knowledge of the heart. Gnostics are said to have lived in AD 300 or AD 400. Gnosis is also known as the knowledge of the heart and its basic precepts are esoteric. "The terms *Gnostic* and *Gnosticism* are derived from the Greek word *gnosis*, which is usually (albeit somewhat misleadingly) translated as 'knowledge.' The knowledge the Gnostic seeks [. . .] is not rational knowledge. The Greek language distinguishes between theoretical knowledge and knowledge gained from direct experience. The latter is gnosis, and a person possessing or aspiring to this knowledge is a Gnostic" (Hoeller, 2002, p. 2). Hoeller (2002) proposes the term "insight" as opposed to knowledge to denote gnosis because it "involves an intuitive process that embraces both self-knowledge and knowledge of ultimate, divine realities" (p. 2). Gnosticism in the first century BC was represented by both Christian and non-Christian schools. Contemporary educational researchers may find it interesting that the hermeneutic tradition in interpretive research has to do, to an extent, with a non-Christian school of Gnosis known as Hermeticism—supposedly the original birthplace of Hermes.

Gnostics should be rightfully credited for their treatment of the feminine principle in the eschatological scheme of world events. *Sophia* is the name that personifies the Divine Feminine in Gnosticism and other esoteric traditions. Literally, "wisdom" in Greek, *sophia* is a female constitutive element of *philosophy* (see Chapter 2). Greek is a gendered language, and perhaps it is not coincidental that the word philosophy conveys the presence of a female principle in a nonetheless almost exclusively male domain. Gendered languages such as Greek or Ukrainian have myriads of words connoting female gender and thus carry empowering messages for women in their respective cultures. In fact, *Sophia* has been revealing herself to different people and under different disguises throughout the history of humankind.

Sophia appears in the Wisdom Books of the Old Testament as Chokmah. Gnostic Philo of Alexandria (ca. 20 BC—ca. AD 50) repeatedly used the concept of Sophia (on a par with Logos, Nous) drawing from the Old Testament. He claimed that God created Sophia in the beginning of creation and then together with Her created the entire universe. Greek philosophers wrestled with the questions of the origins of the world, the role of the divine wisdom-Sophia in the eschatological schemata, and the relationship between Sophia and Logos. Pythagoras, who is traditionally considered the first self-proclaimed "lover of wisdom," recognized Sophia in the Western philosophical tradition. In Plato's *Symposium*, *Diotima* (who might be Sophia personified) appears as the "great priestess of Mantineia" who "dictates to [her teacher, Plato] the ideal, idealized, and [the Platonic] concept of love" (Kristeva, 1987, p. 71). In contrast to the male-dominated structure of the possession-love, Diotima epitomizes the "uniting-love" principle, an "agent of synthesis," and the power of Phallus: "Diotima *is* it; she is that Phallus, even if she doesn't *have* it. She hands it over to the philosopher whose task is to possess it, to conquer it, and to use it to enslave or educate" (Kristeva, 1987, p. 74). Contemporary feminist scholars may find the Gnostic Sophia, if translated into secular imagery, refreshingly empowering.

Mystical world traditions teach us that all living things are one in their inner nature, which can explain compassion:

> Our propensity to identify with one another, to feel with and for one another, which if we were ultimately separate would be either inexplicable or mistaken—and it is compassion that is the foundation of ethics. Our fundamental intuition that the way to treat other people is as we ourselves would wish to be treated is grounded in the metaphysical truth that we and they are the same. (Magee, 1997, p. 453)

Metaphysical beliefs permeate indigenous and aboriginal cultures. Indigenous and aboriginal are often used interchangeably to refer to the people and cultures native to North and South America, Africa, Australia, and Oceania. *Native*, *aboriginal*, and *indigenous* typically identify people inhabiting particular geographical territories from the earliest times or from before the arrival of colonists. In the Americas, for instance, the Toltec culture (~ eighth century) was native to Mexico and preceded the Aztecs in the tenth century. The Incas in Peru have been known since the ~thirteenth century. The Mayan civilization dates back to ~2000 BC. Each of these cultures has left a heritage of sophisticated cosmological systems, myths, rituals, and traces of scientific, technological, and artistic advances. The Toltec were known as "women and men of knowledge" (Ruiz, 2004). They were masters (*naguals*) and students. *Naguals* were forced to conceal the ancestral knowledge-wisdom because of European conquest and misuses of personal power by a few students (Ruiz, 2004). Yet the knowledge was passed through generations of *naguals*. The result of believing in the truth is "goodness, love, happiness" (Ruiz, 2004, p. 19). The Toltec truth, the "story," needs to be "experienced to become legitimate" (Ruiz, 2004, p. 23).

The beliefs of the people residing in the vast areas of the Pacific Ocean represent an array of diversity as well as common patterns. The words *mana* (sacred power associated with gods; holy forces of nature) and *tabu* (or taboo) (that which is forbidden), for instance, are common to most of the Pacific region's inhabitants (Smart, 1998). The Polynesian religion distinguishes between the spiritual (invisible) world and the world of experience (seen), with the two worlds being interconnected. The use of practices such as rituals, magic, witchcraft, wearing masks, and body-painting are common to many cultures in Oceania. Essential to most aboriginals of Australia is the concept of the Dreaming, or Dreaming Time, which can be rendered as yet another way of knowing.

Shamanism originated among the Tunguso-Manchurian people to whom the word *saman* meant "he or she who knows" (Grof, 2006, p. 29). Shamanism is at least 30 to 40 thousand years old. The term also refers to Siberian native healers and it has been widely used for a variety of native healers in different parts of the world who have been popularly known as "medicine men, witch doctors, sorcerers, or wizards" (Grof, 2006, p. 29).

Plurality, depth, and scope of knowledge developed over thousands of years by indigenous peoples throughout the world and are evident in their ways of living. Indigenous knowledges are also diverse in themselves and unique to given cultures, geographies, and societies (Barnhardt & Kawagley, 2005). They have been passed through generations primarily through "storytelling, ceremonies, songs and dances from generation to generation" (Price, 2010, p. 2).

For the most part of their history, the cultures of Africa were viewed by Western colonizers and missionaries as "primitive, backward, and in need of radical reconstruction" (Brown, 2004, p. 4). And most of what has been known through literature about traditional African philosophical thought emerged through Eurocentric characterizations of African cultures (Brown, 2004). African conceptual languages have been replaced with "theoretical idioms from the West" (Appiah, 2004, p. 23). Yet throughout the same history of colonialism, the people of African descent have long engaged in philosophical thought of their own. Traditional African thought was indigenous to sub-Saharan cultures prior to the infusion of Islamic, Judaic, and Christian ideologues (Brown, 2004). Its fundamental feature is

> that there is more to reality and to the realm of experience than that which is readily accessible through empirical inquiry, and that one can acquire an understanding of natural phenomena by appealing to experiences whose characterizations are not empirically confirmable but are nonetheless warrantably assertible. The warrant is rooted in a felt sense that there are spiritual components to nature that influence experiences and perceptions. Underlying this perspective is a commitment to the existence of unobservable entities that can act as causal agents. (p. 159)

Within the realm of traditional African worldview, a person consists of a body made from the "blood of the mother, an individual spirit [*sunsun*] which is the main bearer of one's personality, and the *okra* [from which *sunsun* derives from the father at conception, the kind of a life force sent to a person from Nyame, the high god, and departs the body at death]" (Appiah, 2004, p. 28). In contrast, Western rationalism interprets a person as consisting of a body and a mind (or brain). However, many Europeans and Americans—and Africans—believe that the "departure of the mind from the body is death, and that the mind, released from the body, renamed the "soul," survives somehow, perhaps even somewhere" (Appiah, 2004, pp. 28–29). This seems like a "different theory—*sunsun* and *okra* are dual non-bodily entities, [of] which the mind is one" (Appiah, 2004, p. 29).

The belief in the existence of a spiritual world is not unique to African cultures. Native Americans, for instance, embrace the notion that there are "non-observable" life forms (spirits) that can reside in birds, bears, or streams. The beliefs of many cultures that have been regarded as "inferior" to those of modern Western European views show more commonalties than differences regarding the nature of the universe and human beings. The knowledge of indigenous societies derives from multiple sources, including traditional teachings, empirical observations, and revelations (Castellano, 2008). While traditional indigenous knowledge (a set of absolutes about the nature of reality and being) has been transmitted through generations without questioning, the empirical knowledge is gained through careful observation (e.g., knowledge of ecosystems).

Indigenous "revealed knowledge" is acquired through "dreams, visions, and intuitions that are understood to be spiritual in origin" (Castellano, 2008, p. 24). To understand what the beliefs of African or Native American people are, one needs an investigation that "challenges the ways in which research is conducted *on* Indigenous communities, rather than *with*, or *by* Indigenous communities and researchers" (Langdon, 2009, p. 9). Most aboriginal people who write about aboriginal knowledge have spent a "good deal of their lives interacting with mainstream society and see a need to make explicit those elements of their culture which are at risk if being lost" (Castellano, 2008, p. 31). The knowledge that these cultures can share with us will be a "living fire, rekindled from surviving embers and fueled with the materials of the twenty-first century" (Castellano, 2008, p. 34).

Most Indigenous peoples are currently undergoing "major social upheavals as a result of transformative forces beyond their control"; many of their values, beliefs, and practices are "recognized as being just as valid for today's generations as they were for generations past" (Barnhardt & Kawagley, 2005, p. 9). The process is reciprocal:

> Native people may need to understand Western society, but not at the expense of what they already know and the way they have come to know it. Non-native people, too, need to recognize the coexistence of multiple worldviews and

> knowledge systems, and find ways to understand and relate to the world in its multiple dimensions and varied perspectives. (p. 9)

Indigenous epistemologies continue to transform contemporary realities of Western advanced societies in the fields of medicine, health, law, politics, and education (Dei et al., 2008). The legacy of ancient worldviews, no matter how glorious or painful it might have been, represents a multifarious and at times surprisingly unified picture that finds its mythological expression in a poetic image of the necklace of the Vedic goddess Indra ("Indra's net"). The necklace is made of shining jewels, all interconnected. "It is told that if we take one jewel and look at it, we'll see the reflection of all others, infinite in number. Each of the jewels reflected in one and it reflects all others simultaneously; thus there is an infinite reflecting process occurring" (Robertson, 2009, p. 145). A similar account of a holistic view of the universe is found in the Hwa Yen school of Buddhism.

> The story is told that the Empress Wu, who was unable to penetrate the complexity of Hwa Yen literature, asked Fa Tsang, one the founders of the school, to give her a practical and simple demonstration of the cosmic interrelatedness. Fa Tsang first suspended a glowing candle from the ceiling of a room the entire interior of which was covered with mirrors, to demonstrate the relationship of the One to the many. Then he placed in the center of the room a small crystal and, showing how everything around it was reflected in it, illustrated how in the Ultimate Reality the infinitely small contains the infinitely large and the infinitely large the infinitely small, without obstruction. (Grof, 1985, p. 75)

These ancient Indian and Chinese legends illustrate a holonomic principle of the universe signifying the unity of the whole and its parts. Interestingly, a similar principle was described by German philosopher and mathematician G. W. von Leibniz (1646–1716) in one of his major works, *Monadology* (1714). Likewise, contemporary scientists contemplate the unity principle of the universe. David Bohm (1917–1992), a co-worker of Einstein, who made important contributions to theoretical physics, philosophy, and neuropsychology, believed that "matter and consciousness cannot be explained from, or reduced to each other. They are both abstractions from the implicate order, which is their common ground, and thus represent an inseparable unity" (Grof, 1985, p, 76). Edgar D. Mitchell, the lunar pilot for NASA's Apollo 14 space mission, recalls his experience in space: "I could see the stars, see the separateness of things, but felt an inner connectedness of everything. It was personal. It was wild. It was ecstatic. And it made me ask myself, well, what kind of a brain-mind-body is this that reacts to this vision, this sighting? And it made me realize that our story of ourselves as told by science was probably incomplete, and maybe flawed" (Brown, 2005, p. 56).

### *Ad Infinitum: New Horizons and Possibilities with Artificial Intelligence*

Artificial Intelligence (AI) or Artificial Generative Intelligence (AGI), initially intended as a tool to help amplify knowledge, may have inadvertently become a deconstructive and revolutionary tool, redefining data from how we once knew it and disrupting political, economic, and social structures (Blais & Jungdahl, 2019). Alan Turing is widely believed to have laid the foundation of what became known as artificial intelligence. He was an English mathematician. The Turing Test involved assessing a computer and a human being in separate rooms on the same set of questions and comparing their respective performance. The computer ended up besting the human player, answering more quickly and accurately the same set of questions given to the human player. Through his imitation game, also known as the Turing Test, Turing posited that a computer can be said to possess intelligence if it can mimic human behaviors, including thoughts and actions (St George & Gillis, 2023). Though Turing's prediction that computers would be able to play the imitation game by 2000 has yet to come pass, his work has largely been viewed as the foundation for the development, expansion, and explosion of machine learning and deep learning (Oppy, 2021). While Turing's groundbreaking work laid the foundation in computer science for AI or AGI to emerge, others like Charles Babbage, Howard Aiken, John McCarthy, and scientists who gathered at Dartmouth College for a conference have been widely credited to have tilled the ground for AI exploits to flourish and enable its promises to bear the fruits (Kavanagh, 2019; Mills, 2023). In a nutshell, Artificial Intelligence is embodied by machines (computers and supercomputers) that perform a wide range of tasks with little assistance from human beings, once they have been coded. Essentially, these machines and software tools are programmed to simulate human intelligence; and, once trained through deep learning (DL) and machine learning (ML) through large, complex, and diverse datasets, they become endowed with reasoning and decision-making capabilities that can surpass or supersede human intelligence (Blais & Jungdahl, 2019; Clocksin, 2003). DL is especially fascinating as it is designed like "neural networks" and engineered to mimic how the human brain functions and performs (Mills, 2023, p. 7). Particularly, DL draws upon massive amounts of data from different sources, learns and extricates patterns in these data, and uses them to not only describe but also to predict behaviors and prescribe actions. According to West and Allen (2018), these machines think and behave like human experts in any given field. In many cases, their algorithms perform computations and calculations better and faster than humans can, while automating data analysis and discovery processes accurately and consistently (Gil et al., 2014; Mazzolin, 2020; Minsky, 1966).

Today, AI or AGI has a wide range of applications in various aspects of life and society, including education, computing, aviation, business, supply chain, spy craft, warfare, healthcare, data science, and more (Musib et al., 2017; West & Allen, 2018). The aura of optimism about AI's current impact is so high that its potential applications are touted as limitless (Mazzolin, 2020). As a result, the U.S. government, and governments from around the world for that matter, have taken a keen interest in AGI that is matched probably only by their interest in nuclear armament. In fact, Blais and Jungdahl (2019) review various initiatives that the U.S. government has undertaken to ensure it stays ahead of the curve. These include "enacting a series of policies meant to foster AI-related technologies into the defense and national security sectors" (p. 108). That initiative has manifested in "AI-investment and development . . . and access to federal data" (p. 108) aimed to prepare not just federal workers but all workers across the U.S. economy. Similarly, the U.S. Intelligence Committee (IC) has prioritized the development and deployment of AI-powered supercomputers, automated weapon systems, and unmanned aerial vehicles (UAV) (Blais & Jungdahl, 2019; Musib et al., 2017).

Perhaps, most relevantly for the *Paradigms of Research* project, the burnished optimism about AI's capabilities and its applications in academic disciplines and practices raises many salient questions with far-reaching ramifications for research and higher education Decker (2023), Mills (2023), and Staat (2023) highlight ways in which AI has impacted education and underscore the urgency for educators and scholars to get ahead of the curve. Mills (2023) describes and discusses many ways college campuses have already encountered AI, noting: "Examples include installing bots to answering frequently asked questions on websites, automated machinery in industrial laboratories, and robots welcoming students onto campuses . . ." (p. 1). Additionally, he beckons educators to eschew oscillating and to enthusiastically engage AI and all its promises. Similarly, Decker (2023) provides a blueprint for how educators can leverage AI tools in assignment and assessment designs while engineering curiosity, passion, creativity, and ingenuity in the learning process. For instance, she describes "AI-powered" tools that are currently used to help identify students who need support and students who are prone to suicide ideation. More importantly, Decker points out AI-directed programs such as Khan Academy, Mia Learning, and Pixar in a Box that effectively help teachers personalize learning for different student groups. Finally, Staat (2023) who wrote extensively on the subject led the charge with his editorial work in *Digital Directions*, arguing cogently that AI, as a form of technology, has transformed what was once considered normal and has in fact infiltrated higher education. Hence, the task of educators and higher education professionals is not to tether or hinder AI but to intelligently engage it and curve with it, so to speak, to harness its exploits and potentials.

Perhaps, one of the most consequential intersections of AI and higher education lies in data science, big data, and data analytics. This intersection carries salient implications for the enterprise of knowledge and research in education as a corollary. Scholars and data scientists recognize the saliency of big data, data science, and data analytics, acknowledging its impact on the pursuit, acquisition, and the use of knowledge. Kruse et al. (2016) define big data from the purview of 4 Vs—*volume*, *velocity*, *variety*, and *veracity*, noting: "Big data is commonly defined through the 4 Vs: volume (scale or quantity of data), velocity (speed and analysis of real-time or near-real-time data), variety (different forms of data, often from disparate data sources), and veracity (quality assurance of the data). The first 3 Vs are found in most literature [2, 3], and the fourth V is a goal [4]" (p. 38). As such, big data is being mined and applied in a lot of disciplines and business practices. Accordingly, Cao (2017) notes: "From the disciplinary development perspective, recognition of the significant challenges, opportunities, and values of big data is fundamentally reshaping the traditional data-oriented scientific and engineering fields. It is also reshaping those nontraditional data engineering domains such as social science, business, and management" (pp. 1–2). This presents scholars and researchers an immense opportunity to generate data-informed theories and hypotheses. Particularly, by parsing and molding this AI-powered data, researchers can link theoretical insights to data and triangulate conclusions, which will make relevant impact on educational research and practices, policies, business operations, and decision-making processes in society.

## *Searching the Known and the Not-Yet Known: The Wonder Continues*

Despite our phenomenal excursions and groundbreaking exploits, past and present, into vast epistemological terrains, what can we, as humans, really know about the world around us? The *truths* about it both tempt and elude. The twentieth-century paradigm shifts in "hard" sciences can be looked at through the prism of an ancient Chinese saying: "To be uncertain is uncomfortable, but to be certain is ridiculous" (Boyd, 2012). Albert Einstein's theories of relativity (1905, 1916), quantum mechanics, the discovery of DNA and the ensuing advancements in biology, chemistry, physics, and mathematics have irrecoverably transformed our thinking about the universe and ourselves in terms of certainty of knowledge. Quantum mechanics, more so than other discoveries of the twentieth century, was the "first crack in the wall of the naïve determinism" and produced a domino effect rendering all methods of encryption "obsolete" in quantum computation, which in turn made us wonder how "our grandchildren will manage to keep their secrets" (Rota & Crants, 2000, p. 479). Quantum mechanics raised the questions regarding the prediction of the events at the subatomic level. Matter was no longer conceived as to be comprised of solid atoms; the atom itself was divided into constitutive particles held by different forces. At the subatomic level, particles did not obey to fixed mechanical laws. Quantum mechanics made us give up not only the conventional reality of the particle picture of electrons, but the nature of reality itself—no longer completely predictable, causal, and ordered.

What will the twenty-first century hold? Perhaps it will be as "much an age of philosophy as an age of science," wherein they become equal partners in "our project of understanding the world" (Rota & Crants, 2000, p. 491). In the history of Western and non-Western worlds alike, chaos, creativity, and transformation were understood as forming the fabric of a spontaneous cosmos. The principles of multiplicity, diversity, and seemingly random occurrences as the inheritance of many ancient traditions echo similar principles of contemporary fractal geometry, holographic images, and chaos and complexity theories. The new sciences of chaos and complexity and the study of non-linear dynamic systems have opened venues for Western scientists to consider the pathways toward the interconnected system of a *conscious* universe.

Much like their alchemist counterparts of the "dark ages," contemporary scientists are on the quest to solve the mysteries of the universe. Today we are witnessing the "beginning of a restructuring of our idea of what a scientific theory should be. The old prejudice that all science should be eventually "reduced" to physics was prodded by the simplistic positivism that truculently dominated the philosophy of science in the latter half [of the 20th] century, and that we can now safely relegate to the dustbin of history" (Rota & Crants, 2000, p. 480). With almost 2,500 years of history on its record, contemporary science consists of "extending only incrementally what we can do, or what we can know. But now and then, unpredictably yet inevitably, an event occurs that crystallizes a new insight and reshapes how we perceive things" (Crease, 2003, p. xvi):

> *We choose to examine a phenomenon which is impossible,* absolutely *impossible, to explain in any classical way, and which has in it the heart of quantum mechanics. In reality, it contains the* only *mystery.*
>
> —Richard Feyman (as cited in Crease, 2003, p. 191).

For thousands of years, science and philosophy have shared the "thrill of discovery" and perceived an "intimate connection between the true, the beautiful, and the good, seeing these as 'entangled,' [. . .] inseparably bound up together in a common and deeply lying origin" (Crease, 2003, p. 216). Yet, the world is never fully transparent to us; the world that we want to explore is a "largely unknown entity," and we certainly must "keep our options open" (Feyerabend, 2000, p. 496). As long as we continue the pursuit of knowledge, moving from one location to another and allowing ourselves to be led upward, we can "achieve a more intimate connection with ourselves and the world, and thereby become more human" (Crease, 2003, pp. 216–217).

> *The scientist does not study nature because it is useful; he studies it because he delights in it, and he delights in it because it is beautiful. If nature were not beautiful, it would not be worth knowing, and if nature were not worth knowing, life would not be worth living.*
>
> —Henri Poincaré (as cited in Crease, 2003, p. 217)

Science, philosophy, and spirituality have been important forces in the history of humanity. Each operating within its own "language games," they continue to tread the path toward new insights today as they have been for thousands of years. Whether there is a possibility for convergence of different pathways in pursuit of knowledge remains to be seen as the twenty-first century unfolds. Living in today's world (unless one continues to do so in complete isolation) means dwelling in places within a *globalized* world and, by virtue of a readily available and diverse means of communication and travel, as well as experiencing both virtually and physically its pluralistic milieu. Coincidently, this also means recognizing, on equal footing, diverse worldviews from "quantum-relativistic physics, consciousness research, and neurophysiology" to the "ancient and Oriental spiritual philosophies, shamanism, aboriginal rituals, and healing practices" (Grof, 1985, p. 91). Even if it is against our wishes, a worldview is clearly emerging which may as well be envisaged as global epistemological pluralism.

## *References*

Appiah, A. K. (2004). Akan and Euro-American concepts of the person. In L. M. Brown (Ed.), *African philosophy: New and traditional perspectives* (pp. 21–34). Oxford University Press.

Arendt, H. (1998). *The human condition*. The University of Chicago Press.

Audi, R. (2003). *Epistemology: A contemporary introduction to the theory of knowledge* (2nd ed.). Routledge.

Bachelard, G. (2000). *The dialectic of duration* (M. McAllester Jones, Trans.). Clinamen Press.

Bachelard, G. (2002). *The formation of the scientific mind: A contribution to a psychoanalysis of objective knowledge* (M. McAllester Jones, Trans.). Clinamen Press.

Bachelard, G. (2004). *The poetics of reverie: Childhood, language, and the cosmos* (D. Russell, Trans.). Beacon Press.

Ballard, H., & Cintron, R. (2010). Critical race theory as an analytical tool: African American male success in doctoral education. *Journal of College Teaching and Learning, 7*(10), 11–23.

Barnhardt, R., & Kawagley, A. O. (2005). Indigenous knowledge systems and Alaska native ways of knowing. *Anthropology and Education Quarterly, 36*(1), 8–23.

Baudrillard, J. (1999). Simulacra and simulations: Disneyland. In C. Lemert (Ed.), *Social theory: The multicultural and classical readings* (pp. 481–486). Westview Press.

Bell, D. A. (2008). *Race, racism and American law.* Aspen Publishers.

Blais, J. R., & Jungdahl, A. M. (2019). Artificial intelligence in a human intelligence World. *American Intelligence Journal, 36*(1), 108–113. https://www.jstor.org/stable/27066342

Boyd, T. (2012). The clarity of coincidence. *Quest, 100*(2), 44–45.

Brown, D. J. (2005). *Conversations on the edge of the apocalypse: Contemplating the future with Noam Chomsky, George Carlin, Deepak Chopra, Rupert Sheldrake, and others.* Palgrave.

Brown, L. M. (2004). Understanding and ontology in traditional African thought. In L. M. Brown (Ed.), *African philosophy: New and traditional perspectives* (pp. 158–178). Oxford University Press.

Castellano, M. B. (2008). Indigenous knowledges in global contexts: Multiple readings of our world. In G. J. S. Dei, B. L. Hall, & D. G. Rosenberg (Eds.). *Indigenous knowledges in global contexts: Multiple readings of our world* (pp. 21–36). University of Toronto Press.

Clocksin, W. F. (2003). Artificial intelligence and the future. *Philosophical Transactions: Mathematical, Physical and Engineering Sciences, 361*(1809), 1721–1748. http://www.jstor.org/stable/3559219

Crease, R. P. (2003). *The prism and the pendulum: The ten most beautiful experiments in science.* Random House.

Decker, K. (2023). Artificial intelligence and education. In D. Staat (ed.), *Digital directions: Artificial intelligence pathways for higher education* (pp. 11–25). Rowman & Littlefield.

Dei, G. J. S., Hall, B. L., & Rosenberg, D. G. (Eds.). (2008). *Indigenous knowledges in global contexts: Multiple readings of our world.* University of Toronto Press.

Delgado, R., & Stefanic, J. (2001). *Critical race theory: An introduction.* NYU Press.

Essed, P., & Goldberg, D. T. (Eds.). (2001). *Race critical theories: Text and context.* Wiley-Blackwell.

Feyerabend, P. (2000). Against method. In S. Rosen (Ed.), *The philosopher's handbook* (pp. 493–502). Random House.

Foucault, M. (1967). *Of other spaces.* http://foucault.info/documents/heteroTopia/foucault.heteroTopia.en.html

Gabel, S., & Peters, S. (2004). Presage of a paradigm shift? Beyond the social model of disability toward resistance theories of disability. *Disability and Society, 19*(6), 585–600.

Gaspar de Alba, A. (2003). *Velvet barrios: Popular culture and Chicana/o Sexualities.* Palgrave.

Gil, Y., Greaves, M., Hendler, J., & Hirsh, H. (2014). Amplify scientific discovery with artificial intelligence. *Science, 346*(6206), 171–172. https://www.jstor.org/stable/24917255

Glennon, L. (Ed.). (1995). *Our times: An illustrated history of the 20th century.* Pub Overstock Unlimited.

Grof, S. (1985). *Beyond the brain: Birth, death, and transcendence in psychotherapy.* SUNY Press.

Grof, S. (2006). *The ultimate journey: Consciousness and the mystery of death.* MAPS.

Habermas, J. (1972). *Knowledge and human interests* (J. J. Shapiro, Trans.). Beacon Press.

Haraway, D. (1999). The cyborg manifesto and fractured identities. In C. Lemert (Ed.), *Social theory: The multicultural & classic readings* (pp. 539–543). Westview Press.

Hoeller, S. A. (2002). *Gnosticism: New light on the ancient tradition of inner knowing.* Quest Books.

Johnson, S. (1998). Skills, Socrates and Sophists: Learning from history. *British Journal of Educational Studies, 46*(2), 201–213.

Kavanagh, C. (2019). Artificial intelligence. In *New tech, new threats, and new governance challenges: An opportunity to craft smarter responses?* (pp. 13–23). Carnegie Endowment for International Peace. http://www.jstor.org/stable/resrep20978.5

Kenny, A. (2010). *A new history of Western philosophy.* Oxford University Press.

Kristeva, J. (1987). *Tales of love* (L. S. Roudiez, Trans.). Columbia University Press.

Kruse C., Goswamy R., Raval Y., & Marawi S. (2016). Challenges and opportunities of big data in health care: A systematic review. *JMIR Med Inform*, 4(4), e38. https://medinform.jmir.org/2016/4/e38

Kuehn, M. (2006). Knowledge and belief. In K. Haakonssen (Ed.), *The Cambridge history of eighteen-century philosophy* (Vol. 1, pp. 389–425). Cambridge University Press.

Kuhn, T. (2000). The structure of scientific revolutions. In S. Rosen (Ed.), *The philosopher's handbook: Essential readings from Plato to Kant* (pp. 503–519). Random House.

Langdon, J. (Ed.). (2009). *Indigenous knowledges, development and education.* Sense Publishers.

Lather, P. (2004). Critical inquiry in qualitative research: Feminist and poststructural perspectives: Science "after truth." In K. deMarrais & S. D. Lapan (Eds.), *Foundations for research: Methods of inquiry in education and social sciences* (pp. 203–215). Lawrence Erlbaum.

Lehrer, K., & Paxson, T. D. (1999). Knowledge: Undefeated justified true belief. In L. Pojman (Ed.), *The theory of knowledge: Classic and contemporary readings* (pp. 153–156). Wadsworth Publishing.

Longino, H. E. (2006). Feminist epistemology. In J. Greco & E. Sosa (Eds.), *The Blackwell guide to epistemology* (pp. 327–353). Blackwell.

Lugg, C. A. (2006). On politics and theory: Using an explicitly activist theory to frame educational research. In V. A. Anfara, Jr. & N. T. Mertz (Eds.), *Theoretical frameworks of qualitative research* (pp. 175–188). SAGE.

Magee, B. (1997). *The philosophy of Schopenhauer.* Oxford University Press.

Mazzolin, R., & Centre for International Governance Innovation. (2020). Artificial intelligence and keeping humans "in the loop." In *Modern conflict and artificial intelligence* (pp. 48–54). Centre for International Governance Innovation. http://www.jstor.org/stable/resrep27510.10

Mills, P. (2023). Artificial intelligence background. In D. Staat (ed.), *Digital directions: Artificial intelligence pathways for higher education* (pp. 1–10). Rowman & Littlefield.

Minsky, M. L. (1966). Artificial intelligence. *Scientific American, 215*(3), 246–263. http://www.jstor.org/stable/24931058

Moser, P. K. (2006). Foundationalism. In R. Audi (Ed.), *The Cambridge dictionary of philosophy* (2nd ed., pp. 321–323). Cambridge University Press.

Moser, P. K., Mulder, D. H., & Trout, J. D. (1998). *The theory of knowledge: A thematic introduction.* Oxford University Press.

Musib, M., Wang, F., Tarselli, M. A., Yoho, R., Yu, K.-H., Andrés, R. M., Greenwald, N. F., Pan, X., Lee, C.-H., Zhang, J., Dutton-Regester, K., Johnston, J. W., & Sharafeldin, I. M. (2017). Artificial intelligence in research. *Science, 357*(6346), 28–30. https://www.jstor.org/stable/26399366

Noriega, C. (Ed.). (2000). *The Chicano studies reader: An anthology of Aztlan, 1970–2000.* UCLA Chicano Studies Research Center.

Oppy, G. (n.d.). Turing test. *Stanford Encyclopedia of Philosophy.* https://plato.stanford.edu/entries/turing-test/

Papineau, D. (1996). Philosophy of science. In N. Bunnin & E. P. Tsui-James (Eds.), *Blackwell companion to philosophy* (pp. 290–324). Blackwell Publishing.

Pojman, L. P. (Ed.). (1999). *The theory of knowledge: Classic and contemporary readings* (pp. 153–156). Wadsworth Publishing.

Polkinghorne, D. E. (1983). *Methodology for the human sciences: Systems of inquiry.* SUNY Press.

Polkinghorne, D. E. (2004). *Practice and the human sciences: The case for a judgment-based practice of care.* SUNY Press.

Price, M. W. (2010). Indigenous taxonomy, ethnobotany and sacred names. In P. Boyer (Ed.), *Ancient wisdom, modern science: The integration of native knowledge in math and science at tribally controlled colleges and universities* (pp. 1–13). Salish Kootenai College Press.

Robertson, R. (2009). *Indra's Net: Alchemy and chaos theory as models for transformation.* Quest Books.

Rose, M. A. (1991). *The postmodern and the postindustrial: A critical analysis.* Cambridge University Press.

Rota, G. C., & Crants, J. T. (2000). Introduction: Ten philosophical (and contradictory) predictions. In S. Rosen (Ed.), *The philosopher's handbook: Essential readings from Plato to Kant* (pp. 473–491). Random House.

Ruiz, M. (2004). *A Toltec wisdom book: The voice of knowledge.* Amber-Allen.

Runes, D. D. (Ed.). (1983). *Dictionary of philosophy.* Rowman & Littlefield.

Saldívar, R. (1990). *Chicano narrative: The dialectics of difference.* University of Wisconsin Press.

Scruton, R. (1996). *Modern philosophy: An introduction and survey.* Penguin Books.

Smart, N. (1998). *The world's religions* (2nd ed.). Cambridge University Press.

St. George, B., & Gillis, A. S. (2023, April). *Turing test.* https://www.techtarget.com/searchenterpriseai/definition/Turing-test

St. Pierre, E. A., & Pillow, W. S. (Ed.). (2000). *Working the ruins: Feminist poststructural theory and methods in education.* Routledge.

Staat, D. (2023). *Digital directions: Artificial intelligence pathways for higher education.* Rowman & Littlefield.

West, D., & Allen, J. (2018, April). *How artificial intelligence is transforming the world.* Brookings Institute. https://www.brookings.edu/research/how-artificial-intelligence-is-transforming-the-world/

Westphal, M. (2006). Hermeneutics as epistemology. In J. Greco & E. Sosa (Eds.), *The Blackwell guide to epistemology* (pp. 415–435). Blackwell.

Winkler, K. P. (2006). Perception and ideas, judgment. In K. Haakonssen (Ed.), *The Cambridge history of eighteen-century philosophy* (Vol. 1, pp. 234–285). Cambridge University Press.

# Chapter 3 Paradigms and Educational Research: Weaving the Tapestry

ANTONINA LUKENCHUK AND EILEEN KOLICH

## Paradigmatic Diversity and Educational Research

This chapter lends itself to the nexus of the issues concerning the notion of paradigm, the underpinning and, at times, misconceived assumptions of the nature and various types of educational research, and the value of philosophical inquiry into the underlying principles and constructs of research in human sciences. Our purpose is to establish a chain of interrelated links between epistemological and methodological questions that can lead to a more integrated and broader view of educational research.

One of the points of departure regarding educational research that we took in Chapter 1 was to position it, first and foremost, within the tradition of *human science* research. This tradition has a long history in the West, which is significant to recall because of the great deal of ambiguity surrounding more recent use of the word *science* and its place within the classification of arts and sciences. The word *science* is derived from *scientia* (Latin for knowledge) and can be defined as (1) an "intellectual and practical activity encompassing the systematic study of the structure and behavior of the natural and physical world through observation and experiment," (2) a "particular area of this . . .," (3) a "systematically organized body of knowledge of a particular subject," and (4) a "knowledge of any kind" (Stevenson & Lindberg, 2010, p. 1564). This extended definition of science can be applied to education whose disciplinary boundaries include an intellectual and practical activity aimed at a systematic study of human phenomena. The science of education seeks knowledge and understanding of multitudes of complex issues pervading the realm of human affairs—cultural, social, political, moral, religious, and so forth.

In the West, until about the Industrial Revolution, the above concerns comprised the domain of philosophy, the task of which was to provide a systematic and all-encompassing account of the nature of the universe and human being in physical and metaphysical terms. Educational issues were integrated within the hierarchy of arts and sciences, all of which served overall philosophical goals. Most ancient and modern philosophers did not differentiate their activities as philosophical, scientific, or educational. Socrates, Plato, Aristotle, Confucius, Rumi, to name a few, were all great teachers in their own right. Milesian philosophers (6 BC Ionia, which is present-day Turkey), who became known as the first scientists, taught that life and nonlife, and matter and spirit were all one.

The scientific discoveries and technological advancements following the Industrial Revolution provided an impetus for a separation between and compartmentalization of arts and sciences as well as for a shifting role of philosophy from its royal to a supplementary status serving the purposes of individual disciplines. The eighteenth-century philosopher David Hume attempted the inception of a science of human nature based on observable and measurable moral behavior, which eventually gave rise to behavioral sciences (Polkinghorne, 1983, 2004). The nineteenth-century German historian Droysen marked the distinction between *erklären* (explanation) (as in natural sciences) and *verstehen* (understanding) (as in human sciences), a distinction that presaged methodological debates in educational research. Further, in nineteenth-century Germany, Dilthey coined the word *Geistenwissenschaft*, which cannot be exactly translated into English. It is composed of *vershehen* (German for understanding) and *Wissenschaft* (German for science, learning, or knowledge). The science of understanding, also known as hermeneutics, has thus become a counterpoint to a natural science, the traditional purpose of which was explanation (see Chapters 1 and 2).

At the turn of the nineteenth century, in the West, social sciences emerged as an attempt to study individuals and their behavior within societal groups at the micro- and macrolevels, for example, sociology, anthropology, economics, and political science. Durkheim, Weber, and Marx were the architects of grand social science projects that still continue to provoke the social and political imaginations of contemporary thinkers (Lemert, 1999). August Comte attempted an ambitious positive social science that did not withstand the test of time. By the second half of the twentieth century, all positivistic undertakings in natural and social sciences had failed. The time became ripe for a new vision of science and the methods of scientific inquiry.

Methodological debates surrounding natural and human sciences entailed the revisionist conceptions of knowledge and scientific method from positivistic to post-positivistic (see Chapters 1 and 2). Einstein's relativity theory and quantum mechanics presented major challenges to the positivistic view of science. By the mid-twentieth century, the rejection of positivism by the philosophers of science, and their ensuing consensus that science could no longer produce certain knowledge, signaled radical changes in the understanding of methods applied to the study of human phenomena. Knowledge was conceived as fallible and subject to questioning, rejection, or acceptance as the best explanation available (temporary warrant) by a community of inquirers in a particular field of study.

Accordingly, the new conception of science assumed a critical stance toward scientific progress as an accumulation of and/or addition to the existing body of knowledge. Instead, the acquisition of knowledge represented the process of evolutionary change of paradigms competing for the best explanation of phenomena, accompanied by the process of occasional revolutionary epistemological breaks (paradigm shifts) that could invalidate the previously accepted warrants of knowledge. The tools of traditional scientific method were no longer sufficient to apply to an expanded notion of reason that included "systems logic, hermeneutic logic, pragmatic logic, the understanding and explanation of field theory, organic systems, linguistic statements, and consciousness" (Polkinghorne, 1983, p. 243). Since natural sciences were no longer restricted to the production of indubitable knowledge and, therefore, open to methodological alternatives, human sciences in turn became more receptive to the methods that could provide the most appropriate access to the study of human beings who present the most complex kinds of problems.

Feyerabend's proverbial anything goes (see Chapter 2) propels the idea that it is no longer possible to rely on fixed methods of investigation in any type of research. Methods are "no longer considered correct or right in themselves"; instead, they should be "appropriate ... in relationship to the kind of question being addressed" (Polkinghorne, 1983, p. 273). The above statements underscore our position on knowledge and methods in educational research that can be generally expressed as an epistemological and methodological pluralism. Epistemological pluralism necessarily entails the recognition of diverse beliefs and practices found in today's world cultures and societal groups, and these beliefs and practices should be recognized and legitimized on equal grounds with those that have been [historically] given exclusive privilege, authority, and power, namely with the Western epistemologies (see Chapter 2).

In the previous chapters, we employed a number of metaphors to convey our messages with regard to educational inquiry, knowledge, and the research process. Chapter 1 opens with a spirited discussion of philosophy as a form of inquiry, a pursuit of wisdom or knowledge, which is intrinsic to a human being. Educational inquiry is a pursuit of knowledge writ at large driven by the primordial eros—an unsettling desire that accompanies the level-headed logos. Passionate search for wisdom can be translated into a tapestry of the world's cultural beliefs imbued within their original definitions: *jñāna* in Hinduism, the *Tao* in Chinese philosophy, *ishraq* in Persian tradition, *Sophia* in Gnosticism, and others (see Chapters 1 and 2). Passion is the gateway to things imagined that have inspired the most daring projects in the history of humankind, and philosophers and scientists alike can testify to the passion's triumph over the levelheadedness of reason in their pursuit of knowledge. Nietzsche and Poincaré may have little in common except their shared conviction that life is not worth living if it is not for the pursuit of creating art or discovering nature's wonders.

Alas, there is so much we do not know. There are perhaps as many holes in the spider web of our knowledge of the universe as there are stars in it radiating luring light from above. Like philosophers and scientists, educational researchers venture on passionate journeys to discover what the twenty-first century holds.

So, what are the ways of knowing available for educational researchers to pursue their projects in this day and age? The analysis of numerous philosophical and educational sources pertaining to epistemology and philosophy of science (see Chapters 1 and 2) allowed us to identify six paradigms of educational inquiry encompassing a great variety of beliefs, theories, assumptions, and practices. The number of identified paradigms is contingent on epistemological boundaries and is open to alternatives. The constitutive elements of each paradigm were delineated by taking into consideration existing scholarship on epistemology, philosophy of science, philosophical foundations of research, the accompanying vocabulary, and our own understanding of the conception of paradigm. The six paradigms identified for the purpose of this book are empirical-analytic, pragmatic, interpretive, critical, poststructuralist, and transcendental.

Table 3.1 depicts a typology of these six paradigms and their corresponding conceptual repertoire, epistemologies, methodologies, and selected methods. To fill in each cell of the table, we selected the terminology that is most frequently and widely used in philosophical and educational sources and captures the most important constitutive elements of each delineated paradigm. It is important to mention that the six paradigms are not completely autonomous entities; instead, most of them exhibit conceptual relationships that can be either strong or weak. Figure 3.1 portrays these relationships wherein solid lines demonstrate strong links and broken links, weak links. The description of the paradigms pertaining to Table 3.1 will be accompanied by comments on the paradigmatic relationships in reference to Figure 3.1.

There are numerous definitions of *paradigm* and contemporary educational researchers and scholars disagree on the use of the term. For instance, Yu (2006) prefers *tradition*' to *paradigm* based on his association of the term with Kuhn's definition of *paradigm* (see Introduction and Chapters 1 and 2). Yu claims that Kuhn's definition inevitably leads to an incommensurability thesis. However, if we look closer at Kuhn's argument about competing paradigms of science in the history of Western philosophy of science, it becomes clear that the incommensurability thesis does not apply to competing paradigms across different sciences. It is only within a particular field of study such as physics, where the thesis of incommensurability can be applied—some theories become obsolete in time, others remain credible within limited parameters, yet other theories can become completely overturned.

Our understanding of *paradigm* includes but is not limited to Kuhn's definition. Many educational researchers (e.g., Anfara & Mertz, 2006; Merriam, 2002) use a variety of terms in reference to paradigm: theory, theoretical framework, conceptual framework, model, lenses, a set of ideas, guiding principles, or perspectives. We consider all of these definitions under the umbrella term *conceptual repertoire*. Conceptual repertoire is a figurative expression that means an "endless list of conceptual ingredients," comprising a particular paradigm of research and resembling a list of musical pieces whose endless and different configurations can generate multiple productions. Tapestry of beliefs (see Chapter 1) is another metaphor to convey the same idea. The conceptual repertoire cell consists of ideas, concepts, theories, philosophies, ideologies, traditions, perspectives, and practices (see Table 3.1).

*Paradigm* (from the Greek *para*, beside, and *deigma*, example) is an "example, a model, a worldview, a theory, or a methodology" (Stevenson & Lindberg, 2010, p. 1269). Other dictionary definitions of paradigm include "example, archetype, beau ideal, chart, criterion, ensample, exemplar, ideal, mirror, model, original, pattern, prototype, sample, standard" (Kipfer, 2010, p. 588). Introduction provides a definition of paradigm derived from several dictionaries, resulting in a paradigm pyramid construct (see Figure I.1). For the purpose of this book, we employ a threefold definition of paradigm: (1) a system of inquiry, (2) a model, and (3) a way of knowing.

Polkinghorne (1983) identifies three major paradigmatic possibilities for human science research: deductive-hypothetical, pragmatic, and existential-phenomenological and hermeneutic systems of inquiry. Our use of paradigm as a system of inquiry refers to such overarching historical and philosophical traditions (macro constructs). Based on this definition, five of the six paradigms were identified: empirical-analytic, pragmatic, interpretive, critical, and transcendental (see Table 3.1). Inquiry is a broad term that can designate any research project as an "act of asking for information," posing a "question," and conducting an "official investigation" (Stevenson & Lindberg, 2010, p. 897). We consider this broad meaning of inquiry as integral to our understanding of paradigm as a system of inquiry, which can be subsequently extended to an act of posing research questions within a "set of [beliefs] connected [as] parts forming a complex whole" and following an "organized scheme or method" (Stevenson & Lindberg, 2010, p. 1763).

Our second use of paradigm as a model is based on the assumption of it as a micro construct, such as, for instance, a specific theory that can underpin an individual research project, or a theoretical model that can emerge as a result of conducting an individual research project (e.g., grounded theory). The chapters in Part II of this book demonstrate various microlevel paradigms positioned within the macrolevel overarching systems of inquiry (see Table 3.2). Finally, we conceive of paradigm as a discursive way of knowing that doesn't necessarily fit in within a well-delineated model or system of inquiry. Poststructuralist falls within this definition of paradigm.

The following detailed description of the six paradigms provides insights into the ways we conceptualize each of them individually and in relation to each other. The first row in Table 3.1 shows the interconnections between a paradigm and its constitutive ingredients. The arrow that extends from the cell paradigms onward points to the conception of paradigm as encompassing conceptual repertoire, epistemologies, methodologies, and methods. The arrows that spread from the methodologies cell to the right and to the left point to epistemologies, conceptual repertoire, and methods as constitutive elements of methodology. Thus, the first row in Table 3.1 provides an organizational framework for the description of each paradigm.

*Empirical-analytic paradigm* acquires its label from the long-standing traditions of Western rationalism and empiricism as well as the relevant educational research positions of materialism and behaviorism. Positivism exerted its influence on this paradigm for a relatively short time and was repudiated in the second half of the twentieth century. It is no longer acceptable to equate this paradigm with positivistic research (Yu, 2006); however, some educational researchers continue to do so (e.g., Hesse-Biber & Leavy, 2011; Lather, 2004; Pascale, 2011). Habermas (1972) distinguishes empirical-analytic sciences whose purposes are prediction and control. Polkinghorne (1983) refers to this paradigm as empirical, deductive, or deductive-hypothetical. Creswell (2003) singles out a similar paradigm he identifies as post-positivistic.

| **Paradigms**<br>*as*<br>**Systems of Inquiry**<br>**Models**<br>**Ways of Knowing** | Corresponding<br>**Conceptual Repertoire**<br>ideas, concepts, theories, philosophies, ideologies, traditions, perspectives | Corresponding<br>**Epistemologies**<br>types of knowledge and knowledge claims | Corresponding<br>**Methodologies** | Selected<br>**Methods**<br>within corresponding methodologies |
|---|---|---|---|---|
| **Empirical-analytic** | rationalism, empiricism, materialism, behaviorism, *positivism (minimal and short-lived influence) | probabilistic, fallible, formal, theoretical, approximation to *truth* (small "t") warrant | quantitative<br>can be critical | experimental, quasi-experimental, correlational, survey, causal-comparative, ex post facto |
| **Pragmatic** | pragmatism, empiricism, rationalism, experimentalism, instrumentalism, utilitarianism, materialism | provisional, fallible, best possible explanation, trial-and-error, warrant | quantitative, qualitative, or mixed<br>can be critical | grounded theory, action and practitioner research, case study, various quantitative and qualitative methods |
| **Interpretive** | existentialism, phenomenology, hermeneutics, constructivism, ethnomethodology, symbolic interactionism | understanding (*verstehen*), description, interpretation, meaning-making, contextual | qualitative<br>often coupled with critical | great variety of methods: e.g., case study, [auto]-ethnography, narrative, phenomenology, unobtrusive methods (content, text, discourse analysis), visual, arts-based research |

| | | | | |
|---|---|---|---|---|
| **Critical** | neo-Marxism, critical theory, feminism, critical race and ethnicity theories, queer theory, disability studies, social reconstructionism, social and political activism | emancipation, advocacy, consciousness-raising, social and political transformation, standpoint epistemologies, contextual | predominantly qualitative<br><br>can be quantitative or mixed | various qualitative, quantitative, or mixed methods |
| **Poststructuralist** | antifoundationalism, postmodernism, *simulacra*, chaos and complexity theories, social and political activism | deconstruction of *episteme* as the only true knowledge, epistemological anarchism, discursive, contextual, socially and politically transformative | predominantly qualitative and critical | experimentation with various methods and ways of representation (textual and visual), unobtrusive methods |
| **Transcendental** | foundationalism, Western and non-Western metaphysical systems, world esoteric and spiritual traditions, Gnosticism, most indigenous and aboriginal traditions | ultimate Truth (capital 'T'), finite, intuitive, emotive, spiritually, socially and politically transformative, body-mind-soul unity, revelation | predominantly qualitative<br><br>can be critical | variety of qualitative methods |

*Table 3.1:* Typology of Paradigms as Major Systems of Inquiry, Models, and Ways of Knowing, and Their Corresponding Conceptual Repertoire, Epistemologies, Methodologies, and Selected Methods

*Scientific* also stands for empirical-analytic research paradigm (e.g., Cohen et al., 2008) and its use is appropriate as long as a post-positivistic conception of science is implied. The term that is most frequently used to designate this paradigm is *quantitative* (e.g., McMillan, 2008).

Empirical-analytic research in education yields probabilistic, formal, theoretical, explanatory, and warranted truths/knowledge claims obtained as a result of experiments, analysis of variables, or causal-comparative studies within the theoretical boundaries delineated by each individual project. Although the purpose of empirical studies is to produce foundational knowledge, it can be at best weak foundationalism (see Chapters 1 and 2). Until about the 1970s, empirical-analytic research held an epistemological and methodological privilege over other systems of inquiry in human and social sciences, and it remains highly influential among contemporary educational researchers. Part II features several quantitative research projects described further in this chapter. Empirical-analytic paradigm exhibits several links with other paradigms (see Figure 3.1). In epistemological terms, it is closely linked to pragmatic paradigm, hence a solid line depicting a strong link. Although rare, empirical studies can also be critical in terms of their research purposes. A broken line shows a weak relation between empirical-analytic and critical paradigms (see Figure 3.1).

*Pragmatic paradigm* is important to distinguish because of its unique position on knowledge claims Polkinghorne (1983) defines, via Peirce (see Chapters 1 and 2), as trial-and-error truths that withstand the test of experiment, time, and utility. Pragmatic truth is not a justified belief in a strict epistemological sense, but rather the effectiveness of knowledge demonstrated by the effectiveness of action (Polkinghorne, 1983). Pragmatic truths are warranted assertions that have to be agreed upon and accepted (or rejected) by a community of inquirers. Creswell (2003) singles out pragmatic paradigm as problem-centered and action-oriented and as such it is highly appealing to practitioner and action researchers. Conceptually, pragmatism has the strongest connection with empirical-analytic paradigm and tentative connections with interpretive and critical paradigms (see Figure 3.1). Precisely because of these links, pragmatism is often positioned as an in-between and

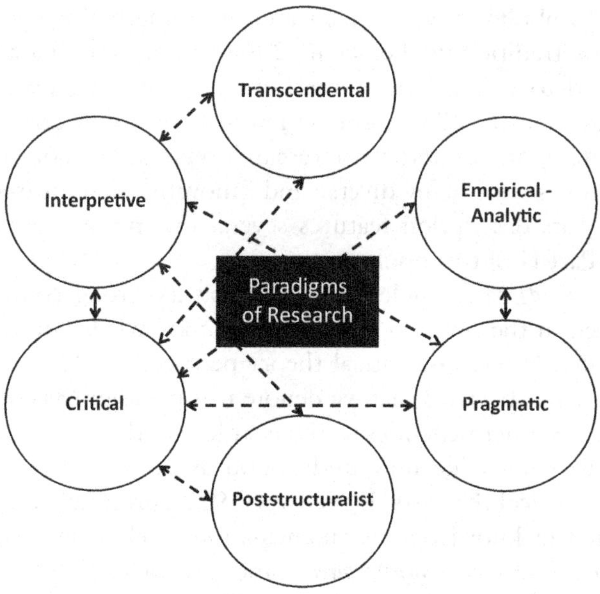


*Figure 3.1:* Conceptual Relationships Between the Paradigms of Research

reconciliatory paradigm (between supposedly pure empirical-analytic and interpretive paradigms) (see Johnson & Onwuegbuzie, 2004). Pragmatism is an overarching paradigm undergirding a variety of qualitative, quantitative, and mixed-methods research projects.

*Interpretive paradigm* has roots in several traditional arts and sciences: anthropology, psychology, sociology, political science, linguistics, and philosophy. Polkinghorne (1983) provides a sophisticated analysis of the origins of this paradigm in the existential-phenomenological and hermeneutic systems of inquiry (see Chapters 1 and 2). Germinating from several nineteenth-century European movements, existential-phenomenology and hermeneutics represented the strongest anti-positivist response (Polkinghorne, 1983) that triggered radical changes in the conception of science, knowledge, scientific method, and appropriate methodologies for the study of human phenomena. *Phenomenological* (or descriptive) and *hermeneutic* (or interpretive) are the historical terms associated with this paradigm. Other terms for it found in research textbooks are *interpretivist*, *qualitative*, or *naturalistic*, which are often used interchangeably. Habermas (1972) distinguishes historical-hermeneutic sciences that aim at knowledge as understanding. *Understanding* (capital *U*) underscores the nature and type of knowledge uniquely attributed to this paradigm. Lather (2004) identifies this paradigm as understanding. Similarly, Creswell (2003) emphasizes understanding as part of constructivist paradigm, which is synonymous with interpretive. Symbolic interactionism and ethnomethodology sprang from the interpretive tradition (Cohen et al., 2008). Interpretive paradigm is most strongly linked to critical, and tentatively to pragmatic, poststructuralist, and transcendental (see "Paradigmatic Diversity and Educational Research" section). Contemporary interpretive research represents a flourishing field of qualitative studies with many diverse and innovative designs (see Table 3.1). Table 3.2 and its description features several interpretive research projects presented in Part II of this book.

*Critical paradigm* is singled out based on its strong conceptual repertoire grounded in the political perspectives on knowledge and research and especially in neo-Marxist or critical theory perspectives. It is by the association with these perspectives that we denote this paradigm as critical. Critical epistemology takes hermeneutics to the next level—the level of emancipation with regard to knowledge now understood as power. One of the leading contemporary critical theorists, Habermas (1972), proposes critical social science grounded in knowledge as emancipation. Following his lead, Lather (2004) employs the term *emancipatory* and Creswell (2003) uses *advocacy/participatory* to identify this paradigm. Lather (2004) reminds educational

| Chapter № | Title | Author | Paradigm | Methodology | |
|---|---|---|---|---|---|
| | | | | **Theoretical Frameworks Perspectives Models** | **Design & Instruments** |
| **Ch 4** | *Narratives of Black Female Elementary School Teachers: Navigating the Normative Discourse of Whiteness* | Thera Tilmon | Interpretive & Critical | Critical Race Theory<br>Black Feminist Theory<br>Intersectionality<br>Transcendental theories | *Qualitative*<br><br>Narrative<br>Counter-narrative<br><br>Interviews<br>Observational & Self-Reflective Notes |
| **Ch 5** | *Sociocultural Perspectives of First Generation Asian Indian Leaders in U.S. Higher Education AnEthnographic Study* | Matthew Woolsey | Interpretive | Sociocultural Lens<br>Bicultural, intercultural, and global perspectives on leadership | *Qualitative*<br><br>Ethnography<br>Biographical narrative<br><br>Interviews<br>Field notes<br>Documents<br>Artifacts |
| **Ch 6** | *Toward the Inclusion of LGBTQ+ Students of Color: A Case Study of Public High Schools in the Midwest* | Joanne Yonan | Interpretive & Critical | Critical Race Theory<br>Intersectionality<br>Queer Theory | *Qualitative*<br><br>Case Study<br><br>Interviews<br>Field Notes<br>Documents<br>Artifacts |
| **Ch 7** | *Navigating Adverse Childhood Experiences for More Effective Learning and Student Well-Being* | Amy Kendryna | Interpretive & Critical | Ecological Model of Human Development<br><br>Social-Ecological Model<br>Ethics of Care<br>Attachment Theory;<br>Social Justice Theory | *Qualitative*<br><br>Case Study<br><br>Interviews<br>Observations<br>Field Notes<br>Documents<br>Artifacts<br>Visual Materials |

| | | | | | |
|---|---|---|---|---|---|
| **Ch 8** | *Is There a Model for Success? A Grounded Theory Approach to Exploring the Facets of Sustainable Professional Employment among the Graduates of Clinical Exercise Physiology Programs* | Regina Schurman | Interpretive & Pragmatic | Model of Sustainable Professional Employment for Clinical Exercise Physiologists | *Qualitative*<br><br>Grounded Theory (Glaser)<br><br>Interviews<br>Documents |
| **Ch 9** | *Critically Engaged Curriculum: A Call for Action to Elementary Public-School Teachers* | Cheryl Jean DeRoo | Interpretive & Critical | Theory of Change<br>Theory of Social Justice | *Qualitative*<br><br>Case Study<br><br>Interviews<br>Observations<br>Documents<br>Artifacts |
| **Ch 10** | *Greek Parents' Perspectives and Experiences regarding their Children's Learning and Social-Emotional Difficulties* | Eirini Adamopoulou | Empirical-Analytic | Ecological Perspective<br>Social-Emotional Learning | *Quantitative*<br><br>Survey Design<br><br>Test of Psychological Adaptation<br>Parent Survey |
| **Ch 11** | *Speech-Language Pathologists' Barriers to Providing Services to the Deaf and Hard of Hearing Children Ages Two to Nine* | Irene S. Garcia-Benavides | Interpretive & Critical | Sociocultural Theory (Vygotsky)<br>Concept of Language Deprivation | *Qualitative*<br><br>Case Study<br><br>Demographic Survey<br>Interviews<br>Observational & Self-Reflective Notes |

| | | | | | |
|---|---|---|---|---|---|
| **Ch 12** | *A Paradigm of Critical Discourse Analysis on Neoliberalism: The Case of Haiti as a Neophyte* | Baudelaire K. Ulysse | Critical (theoretical) | Critical Discourse Analysis<br><br>Ideologies of Neoliberalism | Analysis of semantic macrostructure<br>Analysis of subtle structure<br>Analysis of global and local discourse forms<br>Analysis of specific linguistic realization (hyperbolas)<br>Analysis of content |
| **Ch 13** | *Narratives of Grit by African American Women: Standing Tall Against Racial Microaggressions While Advancing to Community College Senior Leadership Positions* | Toya Michelle Webb | Interpretive & Critical | Critical Race Theory<br>Black Feminist Theory<br>Micro-aggressions | *Qualitative*<br><br>Narrative<br>Counter-Narrative<br><br>Interviews<br>Documents<br>Artifacts<br>Visual Materials |
| **Ch 14** | *Locked Gates and Chain-Link Fences: A Generational Phenomenological Story of Disability* | Sharon Duncan | Interpretive & Critical | Critical Theory<br>Disability Studies<br>Hermeneutics<br>Phenomenology | *Qualitative*<br><br>Phenomenology<br><br>Interviews<br>Documents |

*Table 3.2:* Positioning Part II Chapters within the Paradigms of Research

researchers that the key issue is "how to bring scholarship and advocacy together in order to generate ways of knowing that interrupt power imbalances" (p. 208). Critical paradigm is linked conceptually with all others in terms of its research purposes, and its strongest connection is with the interpretive system of inquiry. Critical inquiry is exceedingly popular among educational researchers, and it inspires an array of research and scholarly projects in feminism, critical race and ethnicity, queer, and disability studies. Table 3.2 and its description in the next section feature several critical inquiry chapters.

The four paradigms that have been described thus far share several important features. First, they encompass major methodologies employed in current educational research (Creswell, 2003, 2012) with various terms ascribed to them. In epistemological terms, all four paradigms designate knowledge claims as provisional, contextual, and contingent. This means that the knowledge/truth that is produced as a result of the research projects conducted within these paradigms is "constructed within [particular] conceptual systems" and is "relative to time and place" (Polkinghorne, 1983, p. 3). Given the characteristics of the knowledge claims of these four paradigms, poststructuralist and transcendental paradigms represent their counterparts, each in their own terms. Between themselves, transcendental and poststructuralist paradigms are epistemological opposites and there is absolutely no connection between them (see Figure 3.1).

*Poststructuralist* can be best described as a discursive way of knowing due to its complete rejection of foundational knowledge. Poststructuralism is an essentially anti-foundationalist project seeking to deconstruct episteme as the only true and privileged knowledge. There is no knowledge as such, according to poststructuralist thinkers; all that we have is text and its endless interpretations—the copy of the copy of the copy, *simulacra*, or *hyperreality* (see Chapters 1 and 2). The poststructuralist way of knowing is conceptually at odds with many structured models of inquiry, yet its representatives ally with emancipatory research agendas proposed by critical researchers. Poststructuralist research does not stand on its own ground—which it resists and rejects—and is typically conducted within interpretive and critical inquiries. Poststructuralist feminist research is especially appealing to educators (e.g., Lather, 2004, 2008; St. Pierre & Pillow, 2000). Poststructuralist thinkers generate innovative ways of conducting research by experimenting with expressive means and genres such as art, literature, cinematography, or digital imaging. Although elusive in terms of its own definition and suspicious of structured approaches to research, poststructuralism is important to singling out creative ways of generating research projects that stir our social imaginations.

Finally, we distinguish *transcendental paradigm* as truly unique among the constellation of contemporary educational research paradigms. It represents a metaphysical alternative to all other paradigms (which are grounded in a materialistic conception of reality) in that it posits the existence of the ultimate reality and Truth (capital letter *T*) and asserts the importance of reason and intuition, or revelation, as the ultimate ways of knowing. What follows from this position is that reality and a human being have at least two dimensions: physical and metaphysical, or body and mind, as in most ancient and classical philosophical traditions. Some similar non-Western traditions identify a threefold conception of the universe and a human being: body, mind (soul), and spirit (see Chapters 1 and 2). Transcendental paradigm deals with the issues of spirituality. *Transcendental* is a conditional term that we use to designate an array of traditions, ranging from Western mysticism to aboriginal and indigenous beliefs. *Transcendental* means "relating to a spiritual or nonphysical realm" (Stevenson & Lindberg, 2010, p. 1838). The word also evokes Transcendentalism, an idealistic philosophical movement begun in New England in the 1830s. Its major representatives, Ralph Waldo Emerson (1803–1882) and Henry David Thoreau (1817–1862), believed in the divine order of nature and humanity and held progressive views on abolitionism, feminism, and communal living. *Transcendental* can be interpreted in both religious and secular terms. In either case, it implies the existence of an internal moral compass according to which a human being establishes her or his relations with others and the surrounding world. Immanuel Kant (1724–1804) calls this compass a "categorical imperative," or a sense of moral obligation. Metaphysical arguments are not easy to discard. Contemporary professional philosophers continue to wrestle with a metaphysical conundrum and its sources: consciousness and freedom (Scruton, 1996). Self-consciousness presents us with a "peculiar idea of unity," which Kant described as a "transcendental unity of apperception" (Scruton, p. 226).

The issues of spirituality are rarely explored by educational researchers, and when they are, the studies focused on these issues are typically conducted in conjuncture with interpretive or critical (or both) types of research. For instance, Dantley (2005) contends that faith grounds contemporary educational leadership when it is inclusive and politically effective. He aligns faith with leadership, specifically with transformational leaders who wrestle with undemocratic practices such as tracking and ability grouping, inequitable funding, and high-stakes testing. According to Dantley, these leaders exercise faith as they "envision schools grounded in democracy and social justice but they labor to bring about what they have created by faith into existence" (p. 11). Tisdell's (2000) study seeks to determine "how spirituality influences the motivations and practices of a multicultural group of women adult educators who are teaching for social change" (p. 67). Tisdell positions her research within the critical and poststructuralist feminist framework, and she discovers that spirituality is elusive as well as all-encompassing and is a force that "gives meaning and coherence to life" (p. 86). And it is this compelling realization that adds an immense value to the participants' efforts to teach for social change.

The examples of research projects presented in Part II do not intersect with either the transcendental or poststructuralist paradigms directly. However, tentative links with the transcendental paradigm, for instance, can be established in the content of Chapters 4 and 14 has an implicit poststructuralist ring to it.

The description and graphical representation of the six paradigms identified for the purposes of this book are yet another conceptual version, among others, of educational research. These paradigms do not exhaust all possibilities, yet we believe that they are sufficiently encompassing in terms of existing educational research alternatives. A different number of paradigms can be potentially identified. Ours is not a matter of concern with the number but, more effectively, with the purpose of this paradigm journey to broaden the conception of educational inquiry and the spectrum of its methodological choices.

### *Toward Methodological Pluralism*

Although the fierce battles between positivistic and post-positivistic camps of philosophers are the remnants of the past, today's researchers continue to debate the issues surrounding appropriate methods of educational inquiry whereby placing positivism in the center of debates. For instance, Howe (2009) posits the existence of a tacit form of positivistic research (new scientific orthodoxy) that presumably is still thriving in educational research. Yu (2006) would question this and similar statements on the grounds of persisting misconceptions and misrepresentations of positivism in educational research (see Chapters 1, 2, and the discussion above).

Current research in hard and soft sciences is engaged in multischematic and multi-paradigmatic inquiries choosing among available and often competing methodological alternatives (Polkinghorne, 1983; Yu, 2006). Epistemological and methodological pluralism, which is the reality of the day, calls into question any assumption of certainty regarding the knowledge of the world and any fixed method designed to unravel all its mysteries. The existing theoretical frameworks and methods in educational research do not represent impervious to criticism or annihilation models but rather alternative and multiple paradigms of research, each of which can represent the best available and most *appropriate* model for individual inquiry, and each of which can be eventually subject to questioning and rejection. Choosing appropriate paradigm(s) for a particular research project is the key to the project's successful planning, that is, selecting appropriate methodologies and that project's subsequent implementation.

Relevant to our discussion on research methodologies is the question of definitions. The terms *methodology* and *methods* are often used synonymously, even though they have very distinct meanings and purposes. Both words have their origins in Latin and their etymology partially was addressed in Chapters 1 and 2. Consulting the etymology of many terms that we use in education is essential to their proper understanding. The roots, prefixes, or endings of these terms often bear important connotations that, if not accounted for, could create controversies and debates around their use (and these occur fairly often among educational researchers and scholars). *Method*, for instance, designates

> particular activities that are used to achieve research results. Methods include various experimental designs, sampling procedures, measuring instruments, and the statistical treatment of data. The word *method* retains the mean of its etymological roots. It is made up of the root words *meta* and *hodos*: *meta* means "from" or "after," and *hodos* "journey." The word *method* is thus a "going-after" or "a pursuit." [I]t is a pursuit of knowledge. (Polkinghorne, 1983, p. 5)

deMarrais and Lapan (2004) define method as specific research techniques used to gather evidence about a phenomenon, and it typically utilizes such research tools as surveys, observations, interviews, and the like. Bogdan and Biklen (2007) define *method* as "consistent with the logic embodied in the methodology" (p. 35).

*Methodology*, on the other hand, reflects an overarching process or plan for researching phenomena. Methodology includes the root word *logos*, which has a rich history beginning with Greek philosophy where it was used to refer to the principle of reason, the source of world order and intelligibility (see above). Methodology is "the examination of the possible plans to be carried out—the journeys to be undertaken—so that an understanding of phenomena can be obtained" (Polkinghorne, 1983, p. 5). Methodology is typically informed by major systems of inquiry, or paradigms, and includes under its umbrella definition specific ideas or theories as part of the conceptual repertoire and corresponding epistemological positions and methods. Epistemological and ontological assumptions ought to be especially carefully crafted since they have a significant impact on how we generate knowledge (Pascale, 2011).

deMarrais and Lapan (2004) reiterate a similar position claiming that our assumptions about what we believe knowledge is "are embedded in methodological discussions, and therefore have consequences for how we design and implement our research studies" (p. 5). For example, ethnographic research can be grounded in a range of epistemological and methodological positions such as symbolic interactionism or critical theory (deMarrais & Lapan), cultural and cognitive anthropology, or feminism (Creswell, 2012). Specific theoretical assumptions about how one defines culture are certainly paramount for ethnographic research (deMarrais & Lapan). Determining which methods to use (e.g., observations, interviews, document analysis, etc.) should first be based on a thorough review of methodologies, which addresses phenomena that can be studied as the method emerges in a related way. Thus, it is imperative that researchers qualify their inquiries by demonstrating how their research is connected to larger theoretical and philosophical dispositions on knowledge that often constitute a system or tradition of inquiry—paradigm (e.g., empirical-analytic, pragmatic, interpretive, critical)—that provides a substantive context for situating and crafting a credible research plan (methodology) that is aligned with appropriate activities and tools for collecting and analyzing data (methods).

Selecting a methodology and accompanying methods can be a daunting task for novice researchers, given the varied and sometimes unique ways in which the overarching research paradigms and methodologies are interpreted by the respective researcher, authors of research methods texts, and articles addressing methodological assumptions. It should be noted that the assumptions of what research is in the field of human and the social sciences has changed significantly over the last several decades. The repudiation of positivism and subsequent changes in the understanding of scientific method, along with the emergence and growing popularity and legitimacy of interpretive methodologies, have changed the nature and scope of educational research.

Although over the years interpretive (qualitative) research has gained proper recognition and place within the constellation of methodologies in social and human sciences, many contemporary educational researchers and scholars continue to debate the nature of the scientific method, which supposedly puts a demarcation line between more scientific quantitative research and its less scientific qualitative counterpart. Moreover, many partisan researchers on both sides of the debate continue to misrepresent positivism by associating it with quantitative research. It is imperative for educational researchers to develop a deeper and clearer perspective on the philosophical underpinnings of quantitative inquiry. We rely primarily on Yu (2006) to demystify positivism in general, especially its misconceived relation to quantitative research. Yu presents a detailed analysis of positivism, its history and its relevance or absence thereof to quantitative methods of analysis:

> While positivism has been universally rejected by philosophers of science over the past fifty years, the current textbooks still either associate quantitative methods with positivist ones or cover quantitative methods within a positivist frame of reference. Despite the fact that newer epistemologies and methodologies, such as post-positivism, critical realism, and critical multiplism, have been discussed in numerous books and articles, the debate regarding the paradigm of quantitative methods seems to be trapped in a time warp. (p. 23)

There are several reasons for the misunderstanding of the relationships between positivism and quantitative research:

> The misunderstanding is due to the association between the one-way reductionism endorsed by certain logical positivist and quantitative methods. In addition, quantitative research includes time-series analysis, repeated measures, and other trend-based inquiries, and thus it is inaccurate to describe quantitative research

> as merely orienting towards outcomes and lacking the process orientation. (Yu, 2006, p. 24)

Further, the perception that quantitative research assumes static reality is attributed to the myth that logical positivists are realists, which is conceptually erroneous. Whereas from a positivistic standpoint reality is equated with experience, quantitative researchers typically posit objective reality as the point of departure for pursuing research. Logical positivism represents conventionalism, relativism, and subjectivism—a position that is essentially antirealist (Yu, 2006). Yu contends that at the ontological, epistemological, and methodological levels, "the Fisherian School, the Neyman/Pearson School, the Bayesian school, the Resampling School, and the Exploratory Data Analysis (EDA) school are fundamentally different, and to some extent are incompatible" (pp. 24–25). This statement clearly supports the epistemological and methodological pluralism position relevant to quantitative *and* qualitative methods as well as the methods *within* each of these categories.

Positivists' major principle of verification represents another dilemma with regard to misconceived relations between positivism and quantitative research. The principle of verification concerns statements of meaning and posits that a statement is meaningless if verification is not possible. Therefore, if statistical methods that are applied cannot yield verifiable results, the effort is useless. In the tradition of quantitative research, there is no evidence that any major quantitative researchers subscribe to this radical epistemology. For example, Cronbach, the famous statistician who introduced Cronbach coefficient Alpha and construct validity, did not restrict his inquiry to only verifiable materials in the logical positivist sense. When Cronbach contemplated the problem of causal inferences in research, he did not employ LISREL or other quantitative causal modeling techniques. Instead, he looked to the more qualitative methods of the ethnographer, historian, and journalist (Yu, 2006). Statistical methods do not provide verification in the logical positivist sense:

> The logic of statistical hypothesis testing is not to verify whether the hypothesis is right; rather, the logic is to find the probability of obtaining the sampled data in the long run given that the null hypothesis is true. However, if we put any theory in the perspective of the "long run," *nothing can be conclusively verified* [our emphasis]. (Yu, p. 29)

In agreement with Yu (2006), we contend that many educational researchers incorrectly attribute causal inferences to logical positivism. Quantitative methods, which include randomized experiments, quasi-experiments, meta-analysis, and structural equation modeling, are not compatible with the anti-cause notion of logical positivism. Yu further argues that it is questionable to attribute positivist reductionism to quantitative research. The history of positivism shows how the originators of many statistical methods—which are still widely used in quantitative research— such as Pearson and Fischer, initially adopted positivistic assumptions predominant at that time. Yet shortly after the overall repudiation of positivism, most if not all scientists abandoned its positions (see Chapters 1 and 2). The point that logical positivism is not—and cannot be—the modern scientific paradigm can hardly be overestimated. Positivistic assumptions of science have become obsolete by default due to the scientific and technological advancements of the recent century, and current methods of going after knowledge are not a matter of certainty but rather a choice that can yield the best explanation or understanding among the existing alternatives.

Various schools in quantitative research utilize different assumptions and could be treated as independent traditions; therefore, methodological pluralism is encouraged by quantitative researchers:

> What is needed is to encourage researchers to keep an open mind to different methodologies by allowing research methods being driven by research questions, while retaining skepticism to examine their philosophical assumptions of various research methodologies instead of unquestioningly accepting popular myths. (Yu, 2006, p. 43)

The perspectives provided by Yu (2006), Polkinghorne (1983), and Ozman and Craver (2008) suggest the need for (1) carefully scrutinized philosophical frameworks, (2) utilizing a syncretic process that incorporates a multi-paradigmatic approach to educational research, and (3) exploring new philosophical directions in an effort to maximize the potential of the researcher's inquiry.

In this chapter, we illustrate how 11 burgeoning researchers coming from various fields of educational study have approached their respective projects using various epistemological and methodological perspectives informed by specific overarching systems of inquiry in an effort to gain a more in-depth understanding of their research and its ramifications (see chapters in Part II). The works of these authors originated from their dissertation research projects that effectively represent inquiries into significant human problems and the attempts to solve them. Table 3.2 exhibits the approach that we take to position the chapters in Part II within the four major paradigms of research: empirical-analytic, pragmatic, interpretive, and critical. In what follows, we provide a brief analysis of these chapters focusing on how specific types of knowledge, theories, and theoretical orientations are linked directly with the steps of the research process.

For instance, Eirini Adamopoulou (Chapter 10) conducted her study within the empirical-analytic paradigm and employed a nonexperimental, descriptive survey design. Eirini's intent was to describe a specific phenomenon: Greek parents' perceptions and experiences about their children's learning and social-emotional challenges in elementary school. Her survey included a large sample of parents who reside in different areas of Greece. In addition to the survey, she used the Test of Psychosocial Adaptation where parents rated their children's social-emotional learning functioning. The study was guided by Bronfenbrenner's ecological systems theory. Using the ecological perspective, she explored the impact of Greek society's limiting factors, constraints and opportunities, and the general environment. The large data sets, the multiple perspectives, and the statistical measures provided a wealth of information that enabled Adamopoulou to gain a depth of knowledge that informs and yet remains fallible and subject to further improvement.

The pragmatic paradigm is the overarching framework shaping Regina Schurman's research in Chapter 8. Schurman selected a grounded theory design for her study because she saw the need for a broad theory or explanation for her particular inquiry. The study reflects qualitative grounded theory and is firmly positioned within the pragmatic tradition. Pragmatism, which reflects Peirce's process of inquiry (abduction, deduction, and reduction), parallels the process Schurman utilized as she wrestled with her research inquiry. The grounded theory design fits her research purposes and questions and is sensitive to the individuals in her setting. Schurman used semi-structured and unstructured interviews with the participants who had graduated from the clinical exercise physiology program. She stayed close to the data in this design by continually analyzing one set of responses that led to an analysis of the next set. Schurman appropriated the Glaserian version of grounded theory that was best aligned with her research purposes to address the employment challenges faced by graduates of clinical exercise physiology programs. Her study resulted in a model of sustainable professional employment that captures the processes that guide graduates to management positions in healthcare systems.

It should be noted that the pragmatic paradigm underpins mixed-methods studies. This paradigm holds a worldview "that focuses on the outcomes of research, that include the actions, situations, and consequences of inquiry" (Creswell, 2012, p. 22). Pragmatism is an exceedingly practical and applied research philosophy (Creswell, 2003). The pragmatic worldview incorporates multiple methods that would best answer the research questions, utilize quantitative, qualitative, or mixed methods for collecting data, address practical applications of ideas, and emphasize the importance of the research problem as the context for conducting the research (see Tables 3.1 and 3.2). In recent years, mixed-methods research has gained relative popularity because its purpose is to reach convergent validity or a stronger warranted assertion. Johnson and Onwuegbuzie (2004), for instance, provide a compelling position regarding the role of mixed-methods research and the need to promote the importance of the pragmatic viewpoint as researchers strive to inform practice with a perspective that reflects inductive and deductive approaches.

Several chapters in Part II present studies conducted within the traditions of interpretive and critical research: ethnography, autoethnography, phenomenology, narrative, case study, and critical discourse analysis (see Table 3.2). For instance, in Chapter 5, Matthew Woolsey selected an ethnographic approach as a framework to shape his exploration of first-generation Asian Indian leaders because it directly addresses his intent to discover how individuals in different cultures and subcultures respond to and make sense of their lived experiences (see Table 3.2). Ethnography is an effective way to understand social reality by directly observing behaviors and interacting with others within the research setting. Woolsey specifically wanted to know which salient features in their backgrounds enabled and nurtured their viability both in India and in the United States especially. He was also interested in identifying the key motivators that influenced Asian Indian expatriate college and university leaders to pursue higher education leadership positions in the United States.

Woolsey actively pursued data to inform his inquiry. He spent hours observing participants, maintaining field notes and reflections, using thick descriptions to establish credibility and capture behavioral nuances, and studying signs in the language (semiotics) that reflect a "stratified hierarchy of meaning structures" (Bogdan & Biklen, 2007, p. 30). He made every effort to become part of the culture in order to gain the trust and the respect of his participants and, moreover, to be able to "understand" what is communicated verbally and silently because he possesses "the insider's view" (Bogdan & Biklen, p. 31) and now has acquired shared meaning.

The critical paradigm has gained special dominance, drawing from the politically transformative events of the Civil Rights and counterculture movements. The political and philosophical ideas and events reflective of this paradigm's epistemological and philosophical underpinnings have given rise to such forms of educational inquiry as feminism, critical race, ethnicity, and queer theories; disability studies; critical discourse and semiotic analyses; and postmodern and poststructuralist inquiries. Critical inquiries are strongly aligned with the interpretive tradition, and this is evidenced in the works of Thera Tilmon (Chapter 4), Joanne Yonan (Chapter 6), Amy Kendryna (Chapter 7), Cheryl Jean DeRoo (Chapter 9), Baudelaire K. Ulysse (Chapter 12), Toya Michelle Webb (Chapter 13) and Sharon Duncan (Chapter 14).

The aforementioned authors have chosen various methodological approaches to explore critical issues within their respective studies. Four of them chose case studies (Chapters 6, 7, 9, & 11) that allow for exploration of real-life contemporary contexts that involve individuals or small groups and organizations bounded by time and place (Creswell & Poth, 2018, p. 96). Case studies typically involve lengthy periods of time spent in particular settings and multiple sources of data collected for the purpose of making a comprehensive case. Thus, Joanne Yonan (Chapter 6) has made a case for advocacy for LGBTQ+ high school students of color in the school district when she has been working for a number of years witnessing the events of discrimination and stereotyping, some of which had resulted in tragic circumstances.

Amy Kendryna (Chapter 7) is a passionate advocate for children with adverse childhood experiences (ACEs). She has dedicated several decades of her life working as an elementary school principal and dealing with numerous cases of ACEs within her school district. Resulting from the years of Amy's leadership and research is the Social-Ecological Model (Figure 7.1) that offers invaluable insight and direction to all those on the path to advocacy for children with ACEs. Cheryl Jean DeRoo shares her path as elementary school leader and passionate advocate for civic engagement through the case study conducted within her school district. Cheryl delves deep into the roots of activism, social justice, and theories of change to understand, reimagine, and promote civic engagement among the teachers, school leaders, and other educational professionals with the purpose of creating lasting and permanent changes in the U.S. school system that can serve the needs of all students toward equity and social justice.

Irene Garcia-Benavides' case study stands out, among others, as one that focuses on professional roles and responsibilities of language and speech pathologists providing services to the deaf and hard of hearing children ages two to five. Unique as it were, Irene's case unfolds a spectrum of issues that arise out of practice of many professionals that serve the needs of these children, as well as the barriers that need to be overcome to provide more effective services. Irene makes a compelling case about the medical vision of the speech-language pathology as being detrimental to proper language acquisition of deaf and hard of hearing children.

Part II features two distinguished examples of critical narrative research by Thera Tilmon (Chapter 4) and Toya Michelle Webb (Chapter 13).

Narrative has gained prominence as tradition and qualitative research methodology since at least the end of the twentieth century (Creswell & Poth, 2018). Narrative has roots in the ancient tradition of storytelling in various cultures, as well as more defined disciplines of literature, history, anthropology, sociology, and socio-linguistics (Creswell & Poth, 2018). Wedded to the narrative tradition is its critical bent of counter-narrative that provides a way for the researchers to present experiences that are contradictory to commonly accepted viewpoints (Goodall, 2010).

Thus, Thera Tilmon ventures on the counter-narrative journey exploring the experiences of elementary school teachers navigating the normative discourses of whiteness when teaching African American students. Toya Michelle Webb (Chapter 13) weaves together powerful narratives of African American women acquiring senior leadership positions in community colleges, while overcoming hidden or overt microaggressions on their path. Toya's personal narrative adds to the valuable insights and unique experiences of the nine participants of her study.

Baudelaire K. Ulysse (Chapter 12) employs critical discourse analysis (CDA) that reflects a number of theories, sampling procedures, and analytic frameworks (Pascale, 2011) to explore his overarching research question: How is the current engine of economic globalization, or the global economy, being propelled by neoliberalism as the dominant discourse? Ulysse is committed to fair-mindedness, freedom of academic practice, and a genuine interest in the human condition, and his passionate commitments drive his thinking and actions. His analysis of the discourse of neoliberalism is informed primarily by the critical theory perspective. Through the use of CDA, and the process inherent within the tool, he has been able to dissect and decipher these texts and resources, determine the underlying messages associated with neoliberalism, and discuss these findings within the context of his research intent. Ulysse's study is a compelling case of the potential of unobtrusive methods of analysis (Hesse-Biber & Leavy, 2011).

Duncan's research (Chapter 14) is done in the intersections of phenomenology and critical inquiry into disability studies (see Table 3.2). Her overall intent is to raise awareness of the lived experiences of individuals with disabilities and the impact these experiences have on their families. As Duncan shares the lived experiences of her participants, she inserts specific connections between the story and the research intent. Her purpose is to identify key themes that ground the phenomenology of disability in specific critical intentionalities as portrayed through the participants' experiences. Duncan reaches her ultimate research purpose as she elevates the level of readers' awareness so that able and disabled can meet at the fence and open the gate.

The above projects, rendered through the context of major theoretical frameworks of educational inquiry, provide ample opportunities for novice researchers to enhance their skills of data analysis, inferring meaning from individual lived experiences, creating theoretical models to improve practice, and emancipating consciousness to fight for social justice, and along the way, to learn to position research projects within appropriate paradigms. Journeying through a variety of research exemplars and paradigms inevitably leads to broadening one's horizons in terms of epistemological and methodological pluralism.

## *Paradigms of Research: Mapping the Final Journey*

British philosopher, mathematician, and educator Bertrand Russell (1872–1970) believed that the value of philosophy can be found in the effects upon those who study it. Many philosophers have attempted to provide definite answers to the fundamental questions concerning the nature of the universe and human being without much success. The value of philosophy, therefore, should be sought in its very uncertainty. Philosophy has its chief value "through the greatness of the objects which it contemplates, and the freedom from narrow and personal aims resulting from this contemplation" (Russell, 1993, p. 4). It has to be studied

> not for the sake of any definite answers to its questions, since no defined answers can, as a rule, be known to be true, but rather for the sake of the questions themselves; because these questions enlarge our conception of what is possible, enrich our intellectual imagination and diminish the dogmatic assurance which closes the mind against speculation; but above all because, through the greatness of the universe which philosophy contemplates, the mind also is rendered great, and becomes capable of that union with the universe which constitutes its highest good. (p. 5)

Collingwood (2005) is critical of the excesses of the modern utilitarian mentality that suppresses emotions and ridicules superstitious beliefs in the irrational. He appeals instead to the intuitive and imaginative powers of our primordial being. Bachelard (2005) echoes in turn by exclaiming that when imagination works, everything works!

Educational researchers pride themselves on implementing the projects that serve practical purposes and solve daily human problems. Yet they also conceive of the value of educational inquiry in posing the questions that enlarge our conception of what is possible and what enriches our intellectual and social imaginations. Imagination is the gateway into the known and the unknown, the mysterious spark that instigates our thinking and desire to pursue daring projects. Imaginative thinking frees us from the constraints of prescriptive rules and standards that dictate how to conduct research projects. Like philosophy, research begins in wonder. Wondering and imagination take precedent over calculation and precision in launching successful and gratifying inquiries, and those of us who have ever experienced this, know *for sure* that it is true. Figure 3.2 has *wonder* as its heart center. Emanating from wonder are research questions, hypotheses, methods, epistemologies, theoretical frameworks—all the ingredients of the research process that are informed by the six paradigms. Figure 3.2 captures the image of the paradigm tapestry as a multi-paradigmatic and holistic representation. Each of the six paradigms envelopes corresponding epistemological assumptions and major research designs. Intersecting the cells of the paradigms are the passages with the inscription "re-search process," which intends to convey the idea that the

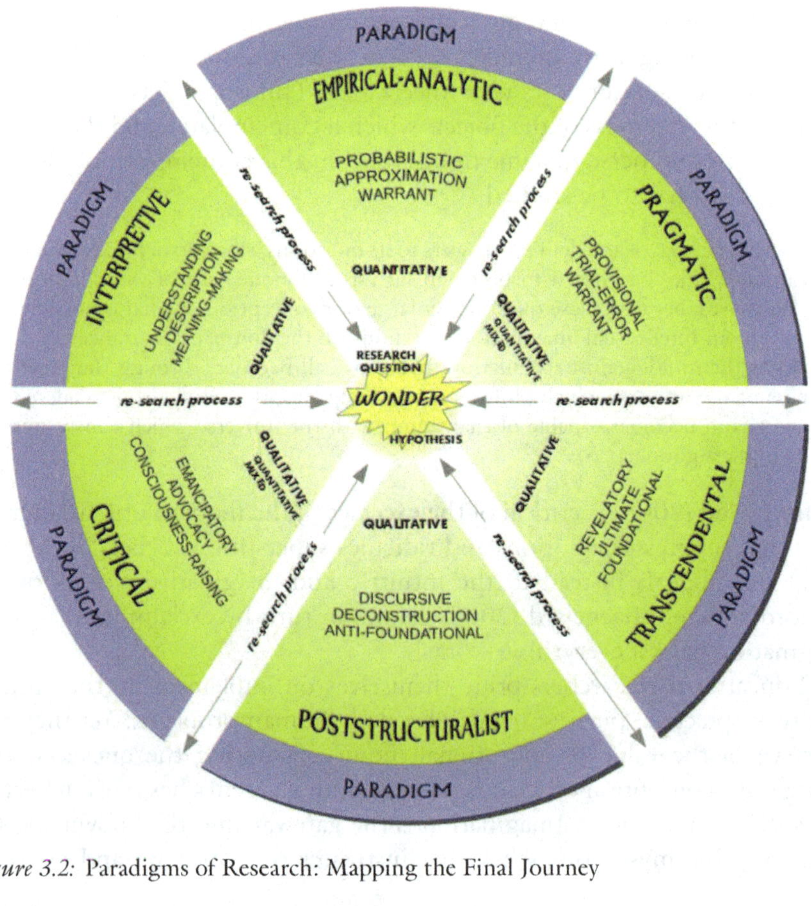


*Figure 3.2:* Paradigms of Research: Mapping the Final Journey

research process is informed from the beginning to end by specific paradigms and that it is circular in nature. Its circular nature is explicated in the word itself: *re*-search, meaning searching all over again. It implies that our knowledge of the world and human phenomena is never complete. The end of any research process, no matter how strongly it can be grounded in foundational knowledge, signifies a new question emerging from the results, and thus the process continues. Open spaces between the paradigms on the outer circle connote the holes in our knowledge and infinite possibilities of its pursuit through multidimensional and diverse paradigmatic research processes. The circle is never complete and the re-search process remains open.

Our paradigm journey ends on the pages of this chapter. It is final, but not complete or finite. We have endeavored this quest out of the desire to broaden our conception of what is possible in educational inquiry and to enlarge our intellectual imagination of it. We are grateful to the readers who joined in along the way. The search for truth begins with wonder at its heart center and continues as we speak.

## References


Anfara, V. A., Jr., & Mertz, N. T. (Eds.). (2006). *Theoretical frameworks of qualitative research*. SAGE Publications.

Bachelard, G. (2005). *On poetic imagination and reverie* (C. Gaudin, Trans.). Spring.

Bogdan, R. C., & Biklen, S. K. (2007). *Qualitative research for education: An introduction to theory and methods* (5th ed.). Pearson.

Cohen, L., Manion, L., & Morrison, K. (2008). *Research methods in education* (6th ed.). Routledge.

Collingwood, R. G. (2005). *The philosophy of enchantment: Studies in folklore, cultural criticism, and anthropology*. Oxford University Press.

Creswell, J. W. (2003). *Research designs: Qualitative, quantitative, and mixed methods approaches* (2nd ed.). SAGE Publications.

Creswell, J. W. (2012). *Educational research: Planning, conducting and evaluating quantitative and qualitative research* (4th ed.). Pearson.

Creswell, J. W., & Poth, C. N. (2018). *Qualitative inquiry research designs: Choosing among five approaches* (4th ed.). SAGE Publications.

Dantley, M. (2005). Faith-based leadership: Ancient rhythms or new management. *International Journal of Qualitative Studies in Education, 18*(1), 3–19.

deMarrais, K., & Lapan, S. D. (Eds.). (2004). *Foundations for research: Methods of inquiry in education and social sciences*. Lawrence Erlbaum.

Goodall, H. L. (2010). *Counter-narrative: How progressive academics can challenge extremists and promote social justice*. Left Coast Press

Habermas, J. (1972). *Knowledge and human interests* (J. J. Shapiro, Trans.). Beacon.

Hesse-Biber, S. N., & Leavy, P. (2011). *The practice of qualitative research* (2nd ed.). SAGE Publications.

Howe, K. R. (2009). Epistemology, methodology, and education sciences: Positivist dogmas, rhetoric, and the education science question. *Educational Researcher, 38*(6), 428–440.

Johnson, R. B., & Onwuegbuzie, A. J. (2004). Mixed methods research: A research paradigm whose time has come. *Educational Researcher, 33*(7), 14–26.

Kipfer, B. A. (Ed.). (2010). *Roget's international thesaurus* (11th ed.). Collins.

Lather, P. (2004). Critical inquiry in qualitative research: Feminist and poststructural perspectives: Science "after truth." In K. deMarrais & S. D. Lapan (Eds.), *Foundations for research: Methods of inquiry in education and social sciences* (pp. 203–215). Lawrence Erlbaum.

Lather, P. (2008). (Post)feminist methodology: Getting lost OR a scientificity we can bear to learn from. *International Review of Qualitative Research, 1*(1), 55–64.

Lemert, C. (1999). *Social theory: Multicultural & classic readings.* Westview.

McMillan, J. H. (2008). *Educational research: Fundamentals for the consumer* (5th ed.). Pearson.

Merriam, S. B. (Ed.). (2002). *Qualitative research in practice: Examples for discussion and analysis.* Jossey-Bass.

Ozmon, H. A., & Craver, S. M. (2008). *Philosophical foundations of education* (8th ed.). Merrill Prentice Hall.

Pascale, C.-M. (2011). *Cartographies of knowledge: Exploring qualitative epistemologies.* SAGE Publications.

Polkinghorne, D. E. (1983). *Methodology for the human sciences: Systems of inquiry.* SUNY Press.

Polkinghorne, D. E. (2004). *Practice and the human sciences: The case for a judgment-based practice of care.* SUNY Press.

Russell, B. (1993). The value of philosophy. In J. Perry & M. Bratman (Eds.), *Introduction to philosophy: Classical and contemporary readings* (pp. 2–5). Oxford University Press.

Scruton, R. (1996). *Modern philosophy: An introduction and survey.* Penguin.

St. Pierre, E. A., & Pillow, W. S. (Eds.). (2000). *Working the ruins: Feminist poststructural theory and methods in education.* Routledge.

Stevenson, A., & Lindberg, C. A. (Eds.). (2010). *New Oxford American dictionary* (3rd ed.). Oxford University Press.

Tisdell, E. J. (2000). Spirituality and emancipatory adult education in women adult educators for social change. *Adult Education Quarterly, 50*(4), 308–335.

Yu, C. H. (2006). *Philosophical foundations of quantitative research methodology.* University Press of America.

# *Part II Paradigms as Educational Research Exemplars*

# *Chapter 4 Narratives of Black Female Elementary School Teachers: Navigating the Normative Discourses of Whiteness*

THERA TILMON

Our ancestors told stories before the written word was developed and long afterward. They used stories to inform, teach, inspire, and motivate. Stories came in many forms, including orature, songs, chants, proverbs, and body language. They provide insights into social phenomena and the human condition. They are important to our history, our future, and our identity. This research stems from my story. A story in which I was often still and silent, in spaces where no one shared my culture or skin color. Spaces in which I was seen but not heard. Spaces in which I struggled to find my place and my sense of being and self. At times, the distance my color afforded me allowed me to size up the group before engaging with it, like testing the water before jumping in, and no one noticed. My color allowed me to be, at times, invisible and ignored. Maybe I enjoyed something about that experience because I continued to find myself in white space. I almost feel comfortable there or it just became familiar. There was also this nameless feeling, which I now know is "cultural alienation." I learned much about the culture and history of the people I shared white space with, but I had a "limited knowledge base of [my own] cultural history" (Shujaa, 2003, p. 182). The difference I felt in white space surpassed my skin color and extended into culture and identity.

I spent much of my life, both in childhood and adulthood, feeling a sense of separateness, pondering my identity, and contemplating how much I would endure, identify, and accept the dominant culture around me (Shujaa, 2003).

I asked myself, subconsciously, how much I would take and how long this would last. In my home as well, I learned to be respectful, invisible, and quiet. I learned not to stick my neck out or ask too many questions. Between the education I experienced at school and the conditioning I experienced at home, I wondered if I would ever find my voice.

With the shortage of Black teachers in America, many Black students like me do not have that cultural and racial connection or understanding in their classrooms. I often consider how my identity development, self-esteem, and overall education would have been different if I had a teacher who looked like me. These thoughts and discussions stir up deep emotion. I find it hard to defend race talk without getting angry and having tears in my eyes. But alas, I am meant to be the expert; it is expected and assumed that I will speak up in White education spaces. As a result, some teachers walk on tiptoes around me, biased in their view of Black women being angry, loud, and confrontational.

As a child, I experienced microaggressions that I did not recognize and, therefore, internalized. Microaggressions are the everyday racist events that occur throughout the lived experiences of many African American people (Doharty, 2018). Microaggressions are subtle, preconscious, or unconscious degradations and putdowns that quietly denigrate people of color (Allen, 2010); (Doharty, 2018). Microaggressions are the passive and commonplace abusive behaviors that marginalize groups, usually groups that are outside the dominant normative group. They can be verbal, physical, non-verbal, inferred, or explicit. These microaggressions contributed to my internal struggle with my Blackness.

In addition, I received confusing messages about how a Black woman should act and feel from my parents, the predominantly White community I grew up in, the media, and many other factors. In my teen years, I felt confused about my Blackness and did not experience that typical "Black experience" depicted on television and in movies. I struggled to understand what it all meant and whether I was truly "Black enough." My parents, who I would now describe as "assimilators," did not help with that clarification. Instead, they transmitted conflicting models. I had no Black teachers to counterbalance the narrative. My friends, mainly White, also had ideas about my Blackness that were based on stereotypes and prejudices. My search for my identity cost me academically as I tried to assimilate as much as possible, only to realize that my skin color could not be changed. In other cases, I rebelled and "tried on" other identities like "justice queen" and "Afro-punk." Most of the time, I conformed and acculturated into Whiteness, creating safe spaces for my White friends and associates that made them feel comfortable, ignoring my needs for comfort and belonging. This process of acculturation allowed me to live and work in White spaces and become "non-threatening and racially innocuous" (Liu et al., 2019, p. 143). This process may have protected my relationships and encounters with White people but damaged my emotional and physical health.

Whiteness is a part of the racialization of humans that defines human beings by their skin color. In the United States, Whiteness takes on another dimension and continues to construct new definitions centered on dominance. Whiteness includes the process of naturalization, which defines White as the norm from which all other races are defined and even ranked. "One of the most powerful and dangerous aspects of whiteness is that many (possibly the majority) of white people have no awareness of whiteness as a construction" (Gillborn, 2009, p. 55). In America, Whiteness transcends racial identity and has evolved into notions of supremacy.

Blackness is the state of belonging to a group defined by the color of their skin, usually a darker shade with components of melanin. In the United States, there is a dominant narrative that places constraints on Blackness, defining, creating, and re-creating Blackness (Acuff, 2018). Blackness is the identity of being Black within a White dominant society. "Racial identity is about shared social status, not shared individual characteristics" (Zuberi & Bonila-Silva, 2008, p. 7). In this study, I wondered about my Blackness and how our shared racial experiences benefit my student's growth. I wondered about whether other Black teachers connect with their students the way that I hope I do. I wondered how they navigate the systems they work under and how they find the balance between the standardization movement rooted in the White narrative and the needs of their students. It is from the lens, that this study was born.

The purpose of this study was to examine the counter-narratives of identity by Black female elementary school teachers within the discourse of Whiteness that remains dominant in the U.S. culture in general and the U.S. public-school system (Lawrence & Tatum, 1999); (Matias & Newlove, 2017). Specifically, I explored the stories of six Black female teachers that illuminate the experiences of success and discrimination, achievement and oppression, and the building of supportive connections with their Black students.

The following overarching research question guided this study: What are the counter-narratives of identity voiced by Black female elementary school teachers within the dominant narrative of Whiteness in U.S. elementary public schools?

Additional secondary questions were:

- How do these teachers navigate the dominant narrative of Whiteness when serving Black students?
- How do these teachers connect with and support their Black students?

## *Methodological Approaches*

My research is centered on telling the stories of Black women. Black women sit in the intersection of Blackness and femaleness, a position that "others" Black women in multiple ways. Othering stems from a dichotomous way of thinking, an either/or process that categorizes people and ideas by their differences. Othering is the social construction of the stranger, the outsider, the other. The others in a society or group can never truly belong. Others stand outside the norms and can threaten the moral and social order of the dominant group. In this way, others define the margins of what is normal; they are the boundaries (Collins, 1991, p. 68).

In this research, I examined not only the stories of Black women as they have experienced racism and sexism, navigated through Whiteness, and realized their own identity, but I also included my counter-narrative. By telling the stories of the experiences of others, I analyzed those experiences in relation to the educational institution. By including my own story, I provided an autobiographical account and reflection through a critical-race lens (Solorzano & Yosso, 2009).

Defining how the "Black experience" contributes to or detracts from the teaching experience, particularly with Black students, required revealing patterns and understanding and interpreting the lived experiences of the teacher-participants. These lived experiences provided a complex web of intersecting identities and experiences that qualitative research addressed in a dynamic process. The analysis of these stories allowed me to understand how all those factors collectively affect participants and students. The research was about exploring the emotional side of the issues in question. These are emotions that are not easily quantified or revealed through quantitative measurements. As a participant researcher, the process of fieldwork or naturally engaging in the process also lent itself to qualitative research. My experiences are a part of the data collection process, combined with the experiences of the participants. Qualitative researchers are interested in "people's subjective interpretations of their experiences, events, and other inquiry domains" (Ravitch & Mittenfelner, 2021, p. 10). My research centered on those experiences, and the stories told by participants were woven with my story.

Identity and intersectionality are also key components in my research and my quest for a deeper understanding of the experiences of Black teachers of Black children. Qualitative research positions the investigations squarely in the participants' lived experiences, bringing this understanding into the light. Qualitative research contributed to the goals of my research to "develop counternarratives to dominant cultural knowledge and normative narratives that circulate in everyday life" (Ravitch & Mittenfelner, 2021, p. 12). The methods I used to tell those counter-stories revolved around critical theories. The power of storytelling was the main data-gathering tool.

## *Theoretical Lens*

This study is positioned within the overarching interpretive and critical paradigms of research. An interpretive paradigm seeks to understand, interpret, describe, or make meaning. It seeks to understand how people engage in meaning-making throughout their daily lives and it draws on the patterns and processes that individuals use to assign meaning (Leavy, 2017). The critical paradigm falls under this category; however, a critical paradigm takes interpretation to the level of "emancipation with knowledge now understood as power" (Lukenchuk, 2013, p. 70). A critical paradigm critiques the power dynamics in society and how that power contributes to the lived experiences of individuals within that society, specifically the interactions between the privileged and the nonprivileged. A critical framework renders that "our lives are mediated by systems of inequity, such as classism, racism, and sexism" (Shields, 2012, p. 4). In addition, the goal is to raise awareness, urge reflection, and lift some of the unheard voices. The intent is to provide and explore multiple perspectives to "identify underrepresented voices and challenge commonly accepted truths" (Shields, 2012, p. 6). A critical lens examines, interrogates, and re-imagines. This qualitative study was informed by critical race theory (CRT), Black Feminist Theories (BFT), Theories of intersectionality (IST), and transcendental theories. (TST).

CRT raises the consciousness of both the researcher and the reader to gain understanding and advocacy for underrepresented members of society. The theory aims to promote social justice and equity through the interpretations of the meaning of Black lives (Creswell & Poth, 2018). Following the branches of CRT, it is important to note that my research is not intended for the "consumption and self-understanding" of the dominant culture. In contrast, using the storytelling methodology, my research gives voice to Black teachers and is, therefore, intended for Black teachers. CRT "questions long-held beliefs in Western methodologies and research that has long disparaged

Black people as a 'problem'" (Leonardo, 2013, p. 63). In that sense, I hope my research is more of a celebration than an indictment. By recording the first-hand narratives of Black teachers, a marginalized group in our society, a different voice can be seen as privileged, and perhaps a new light on the standing and status of these teachers and the lives they touch is revealed and felt by other teachers like them. (Leonardo, 2013, p. 604). Leonardo explains that "subjects live race reality as a relation between their objective and subjective world" (Leonardo, 2013, p. 600). As participants told their stories through narrative inquiry, they did so with their interpretation and perspectives of the world. Through the process of narrative inquiry, stories were revealed. These voices are crucial to our understanding of the Black teacher to Black student dynamic. Critical race theory also examines the social constructs of what knowledge is important, what interests are being served, how power is distributed, and what voices are revealed.

This research followed a Black feminist approach. "Black women bring forth critical perspectives about vulnerability and struggle, resilience and resistance, and love and justice" (Evans-Winters, 2015, p. 129). True to a critical-race approach, my research revolved around the Black feminist theory. This allowed the insights and experiences of Black women to provide the data for the research. A Black feminist approach was the lens from which all the research was being viewed. A lens that "provides a conceptual model for understanding how racism, sexism, and classism intersect to constrain women's bodies and psyches" (Evans-Winter, 2015, p. 133). The experiences, knowledge, and meaning that the participants provided gave voice to Black women to claim and define their realities. According to Evans-Winter (2015), this approach "fosters dialogue for understanding power and privilege" (p. 134) and an understanding of how Black women teachers navigate White supremacy in our school systems and their classrooms.

Part of the Black feminist approach involved the inclusion of my own story as I reflect on my experiences and bring my insights into the research process. Black feminist theory questions the thinking that research should be objective. "Black feminism maintains that research with women and racial/ethnic minorities at the center of the analysis is necessarily subjective, with the intent of promoting social change, self-knowledge and empowerment, or community uplift" (Evans-Winter, 2015, p. 135). Although every Black woman has a different story to tell, they all share "experiences and some form of oppression characterized and related by their class, race, or gender, by their existence as women" (Dillard, 2012, p. 60). With this understanding, my research uncovered many of those experiences and revealed the processes by which Black women navigate through them.

An intersectionality framework includes consideration of multiple influences in an individual's life. Numerous social identities, such as race, ethnicity, gender, and class intersect. "Intersectionality refers to the fluid process inherent in holding two or more social identities that are situated within a historical context" (Jackson et al., 2012, p. 14). The combined experiences provide context for different understandings and meanings for different people. The lived experiences of Black women involve "converging systems of race, class, and gender oppression" (Romm, 2010, p. 220). When investigating the lives and experiences of Black women, it is impossible and impractical to try to separate these converging factors. Black women approach racism and discrimination differently and often according to their class, status, and other factors. This called for an intersectional analysis of the participants' experiences as they worked through "intersecting discrimination" (Romm, 2010). The perspectives gained through participants' stories centered on the multiple social identities that intersect their lives.

The transcendental theories are transformative from a spiritual, metaphysical approach as they seek to explain current symptoms of trauma and subconscious influences. The approach is to link the spiritual influences, unique to a group of people, with advocacy to interpret power imbalances. It is about making space for the mind, body, and spirit in the work. Both the researcher and the participants brought their whole selves to the work, recognizing that the "mind, body, and spirit are intertwined in their functions of maintaining the wellbeing of the individual and community" (Dillard, 2012, p. 81). I conscientiously sought to understand how the spiritual, social, traumatic, and life experiences motivated and influenced the actions of Black women, giving meaning and understanding to the Black experience. Using transcendental theories is about looking beyond the everyday experiences to what lies beneath those experiences. The theory involves explaining what is happening and why it is happening. What are the influences that create that action, emotion, and reaction? A transcendental approach also puts aside any preconceived notions "allowing the true meaning of phenomena to naturally emerge with and within their own identity" (Sheehan, 2014, p. 10). The challenge for me, a participant in the research, was to put aside any notions of reality that I experienced, allowing for new insights and new understandings. An act of reciprocity happened in this research—understanding that "the researcher and the researched are changed in the process of mutual teaching and learning" (Dillard, 2012, p. 81).

### *Narrative Research Design*

Qualitative research design is an ongoing, fluid process. As Ravitch and Mittenfelner (2021) explain, in qualitative research, the "data collection processes are not linear, but rather recursive, iterative, and inductive—with processes that build on and influence each other" (Ravitch & Mittenfelner, 2021, p. 106). Therefore, the design process cannot be dictated or predetermined. Qualitative researchers provide an interpretation of a participant's interpretation of their lived experiences.

#### *Counter-Narrative*

The counter-narrative challenges the dominant discourse and the majoritarian narrative. A majoritarian narrative "privileges Whites, men, the middle and/or upper class, and heterosexuals by naming these social locations as natural or normative points of reference" (Solórzano & Yosso, 2009, p. 28). Instead of simply responding to the common narrative, I used counter-narratives to challenge the notions that Black people's views, preferences, and experiences are not normal or acceptable. The counter-narratives challenged and shifted the White privileged perspective on its head and lifted the voices of historically misrepresented and silenced voices (Milner, 2007). The counter-narrative focused on "disrupting and extending what it means to be normal" (Milner, 2007, p. 389). Instead of maintaining the common narrative about what is normal and whose voices are important, the counter-narrative allowed the participants to name their reality. It made the experiences of the oppressed visible and centered, thus normalizing their experiences and their voices.

My research uncovered and centered the stories of Black women, with an understanding that Black women sit in the intersection of Blackness and femaleness, a position that others Black women in multiple ways. Although I recognize that each person's story is different, telling their stories is important. The counter-narrative is as it implies—the other narrative—or perhaps we could say the narrative of the other. In my research, I examined not only the stories of Black women as they have experienced racism and sexism, navigated through Whiteness, and realized their own identity, but I also included my counter-narrative. By telling the stories of the experiences of others, I was able to analyze those experiences in relation to the education institution. By including my own story, I provided an autobiographical account and reflection through a critical-race lens (Solórzano & Yosso, 2009).

## *Participants*

This study uplifted the voices of Black elementary school teachers. The criterion for participants was that they are elementary public-school teachers who self-identified as Black, African American, or of African Ancestry. These teachers also needed to teach in a school where their classrooms are populated by more than 30% Black students. Additionally, I included participants from various levels of teaching experience from different public elementary schools to gain multiple perspectives and understandings. Six participants accepted the invitation to participate. I began the process of selecting participants using a purposeful and convenient sampling strategy. Purposeful sampling "provides context-rich and detailed accounts of specific populations and locations" (Ravitch & Mittenfelner, 2021, p. 83), which was essential for answering my research questions. The sampling was purposeful because I wanted to deliberately identify the best candidates for my research. The sampling was convenient sampling because it identified participants that I had access. Some were fellow teachers in my school district. This factor is important because my research calls for in-depth, personal interviews. Trusting relationships needed to be established to provide the data required by the research questions. I required time to develop a rapport with participants; therefore, they needed to be accessible. A snowball sampling strategy was employed as I looked to identify new participants from conversations with already identified participants (Leavy, 2017). In my experience, I have noticed that there are few Black teachers in the district compared to White teachers. Black teachers many times form strong bonds with other Black teachers, providing a safe place for solidarity and friendship. Therefore, using a snowball strategy introduced me to Black teachers in the area doing amazing work I was unaware of. One of those teachers agreed to participate in the study.

Once potential participants were identified, I began an informal email correspondence to develop a rapport. Rapport is important in the narrative inquiry process because it is through relationships that the participants will "relate and live through stories that speak of their experience" (Caine et al., 2013, p. 577). These experiences could be painful or traumatic, leaving the participant vulnerable and possibly apprehensive. The more trust we had before the interview, the more in-depth the interview could be and the more valuable the data. Once participants informally agreed to participate in the study, I emailed a formal letter of invitation and a consent form.

### *Sources of Data and Data Collection Strategies*

Narrative interviews are well suited for my research into Black lives and the Black lives of teachers who teach Black students. These interviews provided the bulk of the data for this research and the substance for the interpretative narratives. With the information that was shared, I was able to craft the stories of these teachers' lives as well as my own life experiences in a rich and important tradition that traces back to our ancestors. For many of us, as was revealed in the stories participants told, storytelling proved to be their first language, an ancestral language and methodology passed down from generation to generation and revived often in their daily lives and teaching experiences. This legacy of Black feminism has allowed us to "survive with such spiritedness the assault on our bodies, social institutions, countries, and our humanity" (Edwards, 2018, p. 86). Sharing our stories helped us to share our survival.

The ability to tell our stories is at the heart of narrative inquiry because it "makes visible alternative knowledge often silenced and/or contested" (Grady et al., 2018, p. 153). In many ways, sharing our stories is an act of resistance against the dominant narrative. Dillard (2012) describes it as an act of (re)membering that "is a response to the false divisions created between mind, body, and spirit . . . a response to our ongoing experiences and understanding of difference and identity" (p. 17). The key was to discover and uncover the stories of Black teachers. "Studying persons is to study beings existing in narrative and socially constituted by stories" (Leavy, 2014, p. 197). Stories, however, do not happen in isolation. By combining the stories of the Black teachers in my research, I better understood the connections between experiences, emotions, and instruction. Narrative inquiry also presents reflective, creative, and emancipatory possibilities as well as the production of knowledge (Grady et al., 2018). The goal of the narrative inquiries was to provide multiple experiences outside of my own experience as I sought new understandings. This goal committed me to know other stories to hear and record conditions that may not mirror my own (Dillard, 2010). By asking the correct open-ended questions, rich authentic stories of the lived experiences of the participants were told. I conducted one in-depth interview with each participant that lasted at least 2 hours per participant. I followed up with a couple of short questions via email for a few gaps I found in the research. In all cases, the participants provided a wealth of data and insights. No follow-up interviews were necessary.

The interviews I conducted and the stories I retold required an intensive interview approach. Romm (2010) describes an intensive interview as "a way of generating in-depth talk in relation to experiences/cognitions relevant to discussions around racism" (p. 215). The methodology of this type of interview can be regarded as a mutual effort between the researcher and the participant, much like a conversation as previously referenced. To begin this conversation, I asked the participants to share stories of their lives, from childhood to adulthood; describe how race and gender have affected or have not affected their lives and careers; and reflect on how factors such as spirituality, microaggressions, and racism have impacted their identity development. In the intensive interviews, the participant and the researcher engage "in a mutually humbling experience, where each understands our limitations in speaking for the other" (Dillard, 2012, p. 80). The experiences of the participants revealed troubling, painful, and sometimes repressive experiences. The interviewee's experiences and the retelling of those experiences were also triggering for me, the interviewer. In this sense, we were both vulnerable. We both needed to be introspective, open, and willing to relive those experiences to handle this. As the participants did relive and retell their stories, a wide range of responses happened. For some participants, the retelling promoted healing as they gained mastery of their experience and were unburdened. For others, the retelling process was perhaps triggering. These variables can very well dictate the flow of the interview and the questions asked. This required an active-interview approach rather than a passive approach. The interviews were semi-structured because the research aimed to understand the lives of the participants from their perspectives. The goal was to elicit the story (Kvale & Brinkman, 2009).

### *Memoing and Journaling*

After each interview, I wrote a quick memo that included some observational notes and reflections. Direct observation of the interview video provided further context and understanding of the stories told. In many cases, the stories participants told can be lived in what they say as well as what they do not say (Caine et al., 2013). This process involved observation of body language, facial expressions, and other meaningful cues to generate my understanding. Throughout the research process, I also journaled my thoughts, reflections, and observations. This journal was included in the data as a representation of the personal side of the data collection process. A journal is an "introspective record of the fieldwork" (Spradley, 1979, p. 93) that provided me a tool to consider my biases, feelings, and spiritual connections.

## ***Data Analysis and Interpretation***

Critical qualitative data analysis includes analysis and interpretation in the process of finding meaning. The analysis comes into play as the qualitative researcher summarizes and organizes the data. Interpretation comes into play as the researcher finds or makes meaning. This recursive process blends the two, as the researcher flows back and forth between analysis and interpretation (Leavy, 2017). The process of data analysis begins with the coding process. I began by highlighting the data—after multiple readings, selecting which segments should gain more importance than other segments, and determining which stories, plots, story elements, or characters assist in describing the environment and experiences of the Black teachers. I scanned for and highlighted the nuggets of information that helped me explain how things are and how they got that way, moving beyond descriptions to deeper understanding (Wolcott, 1929). Using a sort of values coding, I coded the text with the drivers, stresses, supports, and influences in the participants' lives based on the interview questions. I asked what the drivers were that motivated the teacher-participants. I looked at what the stresses were that got in the interviewee's way, redirected them, or re-established their purpose. I also looked at what supports helped build the interviewee up, what kept them going, and what protected them in their careers. I looked at what were the influences that contributed to the interviewee's way of thinking, doing, and knowing. I wondered if there was a climactic event that shifted their thinking, their approach, or their choice of where to teach. I highlighted the facts and the transcripts that provided clues to the mystery of Black teachers.

After each interview was highlighted and key story elements were identified, I combined the interviews with observations, memos, and other data to create a more complete narrative based on the participants' experiences (Allaire, 2018). Additional coding on the narratives involved identifying themes and subthemes. In vivo coding "prioritizes and maintains participant's language" which allows "codes to develop organically" (Leavy, 2017, p. 151). In vivo coding added another crucial element of the thematic analysis.

The highlights, themes, and transcripts were then organized by the participant and sorted by the initial emerging themes. This allowed for additional themes to emerge, initial themes to change, and subthemes to be identified. This third phase of coding resulted in a type of "findings display" that was graphic in nature. It made the overlapping ideas as well as the gaps visual. This type of graphic composition could also be useful in highlighting aspects of the study (Wolcott, 1929). Visualizing the data in new ways provided new insights and revealed new themes and subthemes.

The highlights and graphic compositions from interviews were then compared to the highlights from the memos and journal entries to find additional patterns or counter-patterns. I asked myself the main question: What do the stories and facts have in common and where is that one story that takes a different path or against the noticeable grain? I looked for the "broader framework of interpretative and evaluative processes" as a sort of shared interpretation (Romm, 2010, p. 225). The analysis of the data included a process of "looking across data sources" and finding meaning in the complexity of the sources. This looking across data sources began as the first sources of data were gathered and continued throughout the research process. Moving in cycles between storying, re-storying, interpretation, analysis, interpretation, re-storying, and so on. Each part of the process informed the others as data was gathered, interpreted, and analyzed. The analysis involved finding or interpreting the connections between the sources of data in a search for meaning. Leavy (2017) explains that qualitative research analysis includes "the systematic reduction of content, analyzed with special attention to the context in which it was created, to identify themes and extract meaningful interpretations of the data" (Leavy, 2017, p. 146). In narrative research, most of the data are generated from participant interviews. This "text" is investigated to uncover the meanings embedded in the text.

Qualitative analysis can be formative, offering flexibility in the research, such as reflections on the research questions. The analysis can also be summative as the researcher combines multiple theories, perspectives, and stories into new learning or understanding. The goal is to look for "different relationships and frames for data" (Ravitch & Mittenfelner, 2021, p. 244). For example, by interpreting and analyzing each narrative interview as I traveled through the process, I reflected on the environment, the research questions, and the responses of the participants at that moment. To arrive at the meaning, to solve the mystery, involves "surrendering to the data" and allowing the data to reach their optimum depth to find meaning (Wolcott, 1929, p. 28) By going with the flow of data, alternative research questions were identified, and some questions were omitted on the spot as they had already been answered through conversation. Each interpretation of the interviews and the participants' stories were then combined in a more summative way to share perspectives and come to a more holistic understanding.

Interpretation is an ongoing process with qualitative research, particularly with narrative inquiry. Although much of the data gathered in narrative research are descriptive, an interpretative element still exists throughout the inquiry process. As the researcher, I offered an interpretation of the stories related to me and told by me. My observations and memos also lent themselves to an interpretive quality. Despite all efforts to relay the lived experiences of my participants honestly and accurately, everything was presented through my interpretive lens.

### Stories Told to Me

The narrative stories that were shared with me took on an interpretive lens from the participants' points of view before they were transcribed or put to pen. As they expressed their thoughts and narrated their stories, or in other words "re-story," they reflected on and interpreted their own stories. I, as the researcher, in turn, reflected on the stories they told me and reflected on and interpreted the retelling (Clandinin & Connelly, 1989). In the reconstruction of the telling of their stories, the interpretations were refined between me and the participants. These stories also provided themes related to how the participants navigated Whiteness or perceived racism and Blackness.

### My Story Told

My story was also a part of the research, interpretation, and analysis process. My narratives were lived, told, and retold in the research. "Thus, the narratives of participant and researcher become . . . a shared narrative construction and reconstruction through the inquiry" (Clandinin & Connelly, 1989, p. 11). My re-story was an interpretation of my past, present, and future experiences. In the analysis phase, however, I supported those interpretations with triangulation, discussions with critical friends, and other analytic means.

Interpretation also came into play as the data was gathered and analyzed. Interpretation helped to answer the question: "What does it all mean?" Interpretation looked for patterns, links, concepts, and themes. This process included triangulation, which involved multiple data sources (Leavy, 2017). Combining all the data gathered in this triangulation provided a holistic view of the research questions.

### Stories Told, Lives Lived: Introducing the Participants

This research explores the lived experiences and storylines of six Black women teachers in my quest to understand better how Black women teachers navigate through whiteness. Their voices tell the stories of their lives, from childhood to the present, their entrance into teaching, their experience, and their understanding of who they were and who they are today. The stories presented are the counter-narratives this research sought to undercover, answering the overarching research question as well as the secondary questions I sought answers to. I began the work with a biographical sketch of each participant, a chronological birds-eye view of their lives. The stories are then analyzed, revealing themes and subthemes that help answer the research questions.

The participants that were chosen and agreed to participate in this study are all dedicated, hardworking Black female teachers. All but one is currently teaching in schools with a high percentage of Black students. One participant is retired after teaching for more than 30 years in a predominantly Black and Latinx school district. These educators are solid and resilient. They are compassionate, warm, funny, and a joy to interview. These ladies opened their lives and hearts to me in all the interviews. They shared information that surprised me, enlightened me, and inspired me. I found myself in their stories, sharing their joy and trauma. Each participant was given a pseudonym to protect their identity.

## *Discussion of the Findings*

One of the discoveries that revealed itself in the data was the commitment to teaching that the participants displayed. All are devoted and dedicated to the education of Black students and the elevation of Black people in their communities and beyond. Although the participants were at different levels of their identity journey, they share a common thread in terms of responding to the powerful calling to give back and uplift. Each in their own way they provide advocacy and activism. Their stories provide the counter-narrative to how individual lived experiences, such as those of the participants of this study, can challenge and handle othering, form their own notion of Black skin love, and develop their own unique Black identity.

### *Counter-Narrative of Identity*

The common narrative of Black women is based on a set of stereotypes that were developed specifically to dehumanize Black women. The counter-narratives presented in this study reveal the contradiction. Many of their stories included a thread of reverence and honor to the Black women in their lives and Black people in general. Threads of Ancestral greatness appeared throughout their stories and found themselves in different parts of their lives and identities.

The participants recognized the history and legacy of the Diaspora. Many of the participants, for instance, were connected to their ancestry in America. Most of the participants also hold their religions and spiritual practices as sacred and although they may not recognize it, the suppressed and demonized elements of African traditional religions are woven into the Black churches that many of them include in their understanding of themselves as black people, Black women. Many of them spoke about the music they enjoy in Church and about the power of the music. The participants' sentiments about church and spirituality align with the findings of Hamilton-Mason (2009) when they indicated many Black women rely on their faith or spirituality.

### *Safe Haven: Response to Othering*

Each of the participants included elements of their stories that explained how they responded to the process of othering. In all their stories, there was an element of safe haven. A place where they felt valued, human, seen, and heard. Some found this in the same neighborhoods and churches they attended their entire lives and some created communities of their own. These shelters of love and support provide the tools needed to manage the dehumanization process that exists outside their havens. These havens follow the historical pathways from slavery, in which Black women were aware of the larger community, extending beyond their own nuclear family, to an entire community. These teachers bring their entire community with them as they venture out and navigate through their lives and careers. These experiences provide convincing evidence that many Black teachers continue to enter the teaching profession with the intent to uplift the entire community.

### *Black Skin Love Starts with a Strong Foundation*

In all my interviews with participants, there was an overarching sense of Black pride and self-love. For some, that love was always there and for others, it grew over time. The length of the journey to self-Black love was found in the strength of their Black foundation. The participants who had a strong foundation of Blackness struggled less with their identity and found battling racism and stereotypes easier as well. Even the participants that grew up in solid Black communities and experienced poverty still describe a strong connection and love for their Blackness. The women who had those strong Black foundations also seemed to experience less exposure to the stereotype trap. They had less instances of feeling silenced, unable to express their thoughts or stand up to injustice. They had less examples of RBF racial battle fatigue (Acuff, 2018) Although they could site examples of their experiences with the anticipation of discrimination as Canady (2016) explained was a stress-inducing experience, the coping mechanisms they had in place were strong enough to relieve much of that stress. The safe havens that include the workplace also provide fewer microaggressions among the participants. The findings from this study are consistent with what Jones and Day (2018) explain as the socialization of Black girls in Black communities that prepare them better for race-based social and political obstacles, responding to stereotypes, and even assuming family responsibilities.

For the participants of this study who did not grow up in established Black neighborhoods, there was confusion and uncertainty about Blackness. These experiences were very different from the participants who grew up in solid black neighborhoods and felt validated throughout most of their lives. For them, there was an instant sense of pride that never seemed to waver in their lives. There was no question or confusion about their Black identity. Another finding is that the participants who grew up surrounded by Blackness experienced less childhood racial trauma and microaggressions. Their first encounters with explicit racism were well into their teens or adulthood when they were already armed with a shield of Black love to help them move through those experiences. This speaks to the need to maintain Black neighborhoods, retain more Black teachers in those neighborhood schools, and support Black children in Black skin love.

### *The Journey to Strong Identity*

Williams-Washington and Mille (2018) explain that the depth of harm from collective trauma depends on the individuals' sense of identity. The data in this study supports that idea as participants with the strongest sense of Black identity showed fewer symptoms of RES (residual effects of slavery), such as low self-esteem and feelings of inferiority. Some of the participants spent much of their young lives in the pre-encounter stage of racial identity development. As Cross (2016) explained individuals in this state focus on enculturation to remove the label of other. For some the journey was trying to find the right balance between Black and White—just the right amount of assimilation to fit in but still maintain a Black identity. Other participants seemed to skip that stage altogether and spent much of their early years in the encounter stage, where they saw glimpses of racism and inequity but understood their Blackness as significant and important.

All the participants show evidence that they eventually evolved into the immersion/emersion stage where they realized the depth of oppression and racism which led them to the final stage of racial identity—internalization. At this stage, the participants showed that they developed a strong positive self-image, developing Black pride in the recognition of oppression, microaggressions, and racism. It is interesting, however, that all the participants arrived at this place of strength, some taking longer than others. The journey to a strong Black identity in many ways mirrored the journey outlined by Jones and Day (2018). The study showed black women at different phases of the journey from identifying as a woman first, to identifying as a Black person first, to understand that you are simultaneously both. The participants all fell into different identity types. These results validate that Black women are not a monolith and display varying dimensions or levels of Black identity, as identified by Jones and Day (2018) and Cross (1971).

## *Navigating the Dominant Narrative of Whiteness*

Examining how the participants navigated the dominant narrative was also an attempt to see how Black women come to understand and relate to their common experiences of being Black in a society that denigrates and others Black women. This study examined how Black women grapple daily with a conscious and unconscious awareness of their race and gender. Coming from a Black feminist theory, the study places Black women at the center and examines how they cope with the intersectionality of their lived experiences. This navigation includes a survival plan or road map. The road map for many of the participants included a career path that supports collective responsibility, haven communities, spiritual awareness, and special friendships.

### *Survival Plan A: Career Path That Disrupts the Narrative*

White supremacist culture (WSC) focuses on personal success rather than community success. The participants present an alternative, leading more toward an African indigenous culture that focuses on collective responsibility and community cohesion. Almost all the participants started their working lives chasing the WSC dream of money and material success. They all realized, after varying degrees of time, that they couldn't ignore the calling forever. They eventually had to find a way to contribute to the community instead of competing within it. The participants who grew up in strong Black communities spoke fondly of the sense of community and the education that they received in these areas. This is an example of what Collins (1991) wrote when she discussed "cooperative networks" that were created for survival under the harsh realities of slavery and endured long after. It is those enduring networks that the participants all sought in their careers.

### *Survival Plan B: The Safety of Blackness: Validation, not Mitigation*

As WSC has continued to find ways to suppress Black people, the participants all spoke to how they found or created communities to support each other and lift all Black people. They each described how they created a sort of insulated bubble that includes community, church, and family. In some cases that community is the community they grew up in and in some cases, it is the community that they created. But in either case, their community is filled with people like them, either people from the same culture or people with the same mindset. So, one of the ways they navigate whiteness is by returning to the safety of blackness. Fueling themselves with that armor of culture allows them to go out into a WSC culture, experience racism, and microaggression, and know that they have a safe place to land and return to. The safety of Blackness and familiarity also extended to where the participants chose to teach, in Black communities with mostly Black students. The amount of societal pressure, racism, and oppression the participants experienced was lessened because of this cultural safety bubble. Although each participant had that one unforgettable moment when they first experienced racism or saw the glaring discrepancies between what it means to be White in America as opposed to being Black in America, they found healing in the safe Black spaces they created. One of the main things that these communities provide is validation instead of mitigation. In these validating spaces, they are not just tolerated or accepted. Their needs are not ignored or lessened. Instead, they find validation and peace. Reliance on the community as a coping strategy bares out in the research that Davis (2019) encountered. The community provides Black women with the validation they need and a place to be their true authentic selves.

### *Survival Plan C: Spiritual Awareness*

This study provides evidence to support the research that many Black women's survival plan includes a spiritual place or practice that transcends their everyday lives. It could be an organized religion or a universal spirituality. All but one of the participants showed how they find peace within faith in a realm higher than themselves. Four of the participants state the Black Christian Church is one of the safe places that gives them comfort, rejuvenation, and validation. This study revealed how the Black Christian Church serves as more than just a place to worship. There is evidence that these Churches also provide fellowship, friendship, guidance, and support.

### *Survival Plan D: Special Friends*

The majority of the participants spoke about how conversations with other Black women provide them a place to cope, heal, protect their mental health, and build identity. Much of the data collected also shows that these Black women value their friends as protectors of their mental health. They are also selective about who those friends are. Only two of the participants used professional mental health providers when things got especially difficult for them. These relational supports provided the participants with mental health support as well as solace. The data provides the evidence to conclude that Black women tend to "value relational supports rather than mental health services" (Hamilton-Mason et al., 2009, p. 466)—this is in response to the stereotypes and legacy of struggle—we are expected to be strong, so Black women deny the existence of mental health challenges and are reluctant to seek professional help.

## *Connecting and Supporting Black Students*

A major revelation in the research demonstrated how the participants were unified in their love and respect for Black students as well as their commitment to high expectations. They all spoke about how they are tougher on Black students because they know what they will face upon graduation and in the real world. All the participants provided evidence to support the conclusion that Black teachers recognize the advantage of their race and skin color when teaching Black children. They understand how important they are in their role and are committed to their work.

### *Teacher Identity: A Benchmark for Effectiveness*

Much of the connection between Black teachers and Black students begins with the identity development of the teacher. As we know from the research, teachers' identity is wrapped up in how they navigate through various racial and religious communities. The data revealed, as explained above, that the communities that participants navigate through are essential to their identity as Black women. They each, in their own ways, bring those values and beliefs into their school communities (Hodges & Cady, 2012). The depth of these values and beliefs stems from the strength of the teachers' self-worth and how they see themselves as Black women. As Kelchterman (2009) pointed out, teaching is not a neutral endeavor. The data collected in this study supports that concept. Like many Black teachers before them, the participants took on different degrees of racial advocacy challenging the status quo. The participants also saw themselves as uplifters, working to prepare Black students for the future in a WSC world (Lewis, 2008). There is evidence to the conclusion that Black teachers recognize the significance of their place in the educational lives of Black children. Each participant explained how Black children benefit academically, find love and support, and experience validation from them.

## *Teacher Efficacy: The Importance of Blackness*

All the teachers/participants saw value in their Blackness, particularly when teaching Black students. Blackness provides cultural bonds, stronger relationships, and a higher level of commitment to Black students. This study supports the ideas of Farinde (2016), who described how Black teachers can bridge the gap between cultural identity and academic identity with Black children. The participants also recognized that sharing the same cultural/racial identity allowed for a natural bond between students. Authenticity also proved to be an important ingredient as many of the participants explained how being their authentic self-helped to foster stronger relationships, trust, and respect between themselves and their students. This study also revealed how many Black teachers and black students interact. They push these students harder so they're tougher on their black students because they know that the rest that the world at large will be tougher on them. Because of their experiences they understand the value of education and the value of rising above the norm. Sharing a cultural identity and presenting yourself in an honest and authentic way provides children a place where they know they fit in, and they trust you. It is a crucial point in establishing relationships with students.

## *Longevity: Teachers That Stick Around*

One interesting and somewhat surprising detail that came from this study is while many Black teachers come in highly motivated and then quickly get discouraged due to the invasion of WSC, the Black teachers in this study revealed a strong commitment to the profession. Even beyond their love of teaching, they each had a strong tie to the district in which they teach and the children they serve. Even the youngest teacher in the study was committed to staying in the district in which she started teaching, with already 6 years in.

Another surprising trend that came from the study is that the participants did not have countless stories about racism or microaggressions. This indicates that they are either blind to these occurrences or the insulated bubbles they created work so well that they don't have too many incidents. These results are contrary to some of the research conducted by Rinker and Lawler (2018) and Williams-Washington and Mills (2018) among others, that show the depths of long-term racial trauma. Although the symptoms do depend on the level of Racial Identity, current experiences and historical knowledge (Williams-Washington & Mills, 2018). All the participants in this study enjoy the benefit of all those aspects.

## Conclusions

Black women teachers face many obstacles and barriers as they strive to be productive and successful leaders and educators of Black children. Navigating the dominant narrative of Whiteness and WSC while also serving Black students can be a challenging and daunting task. The Black women in this study are showing up every day to do just that—as they prepare to battle their own racist demons and answer their calling to make a difference in the lives of Black children. These women wear invisible armor that is stronger than steel and they carry an invisible shield that protects them and their students from harm. Their armor is their communities, and their shields are their connections. The armor is made of solid, loving, and supportive communities. It is studded with Black church, Black friendships, Black love, and Black power. The shields are made of strong connections—tied to their spiritual selves, tied to their ancestral greatness, and tied to the young lives they teach and inspire.

### *Armor of Community: Black Teachers, Black Students, Black Schools*

One conclusion that is revealed in this study is that Black students thrive when they are in Black schools with Black teachers and Black cultural experiences. The attempt to integrate schools and eliminate Black teachers and culture from the curriculum has harmed our children. The mission was never to leave our communities behind, but rather to have the resources to compete on an even playing field while maintaining the love and support our communities provide our children. The plan was never to assimilate, it was to validate who we are as Black people and ensure that our children feel valued and important. This study revealed a perfect example of how effective Blackness can be to inspire Blackness.

The stories illustrated the strength and power of Black excellence and how much easier it is to reach a high level of Black understanding and Black love when you are surrounded by a community of Blackness. For Black teachers to be effective and for Black children to thrive, we need to create environments in which Black culture is not simply tolerated or even just accepted. Blackness needs to be validated in the same way that Whiteness is validated, every day and in every way. This process becomes easier and almost automatic when children are surrounded by Blackness in their communities.

### *Answering the Call*

One way that Black women can respond to this need is to answer the call to become the educators' Black children need and deserve. That process begins, however, with self-reflection and examination of their individual identity. As Black men and women go about their lives living in their black skin, a certain amount of Black pride and validation must take place first. It is that pride that allows Black teachers to overcome the legacy of slavery, handle generational and societal trauma, and adequately serve Black children. You can't teach what you don't know. So as a Black teacher, you first must know yourself as a Black person, a Black woman. You must answer the call with an authentic, unapologetically Black voice that allows you to bring your full self to the classroom and your full self to the fight for equity and justice. Your students need to see you as the real deal—a fighter for validation, a champion of excellence, and a loyalist that never gives up on them. If you are going to answer the call, you must answer it with passion, enthusiasm and more than anything Black love.

This study followed the lives of six Black female elementary school teachers through a process of narrative research. It examined their identity development, socialization, and career paths. In addition, the data revealed glimpses into the spiritual, social, and traumatic aspects of teaching while Black as well as the intersection of race and gender.

The participants in this study were all examples of dedicated Black teachers that are committed to Black excellence in their students and communities. The data retrieved contradicted many of the stereotypes that dehumanize Black women. The data showed strong spiritual connections, a powerful link to created and evolved communities as power centers or safe havens, and the benefit of a strong foundation of Blackness to protect you from harm. This study also revealed the tool kit for thriving in education as a Black educator. It showed how creating cooperative networks, living, and working in validating spaces, being spiritually aware, and having a close set of Black friendships, work together to strengthen a teacher's sense of self and survival in a white supremacist culture.

At the heart of this study was the connection between Black teachers with a strong sense of self and Black children who are developing their own identity. This is the most significant part of the research as it speaks to the so-called achievement gap and how Black teachers make a difference. It illuminates the idea that Black Teachers matter in the lives of Black children. This study does not compare Black teacher effectiveness with white teacher effectiveness, and it isn't an indictment on white teachers. It is more about the brilliance and celebration of Black teachers. It is a testimony to responding to the call for teaching, giving back to their community, and validating Black lives, including their own.

## *References*

Acuff, J. (2018). Confronting racial battle fatigue and comforting my Blackness as an educator. *Multicultural Perspectives, 20*(3), 174–181. https://doi.org/10.1080/15210960.2018.1467767

Allaire, F. S. (2018). Themes from a narrative analysis of native Hawaiian experiences in science, technology, engineering, and mathematics. *Journal of Ethnographic & Qualitative Research, 12*(3), 173–192.

Allen, Q. (2010). *Racial microaggressions: The schooling experiences of Black middle-class males in Arizona's secondary schools. Journal of African American Males in Education, 1*(2), 125–143, 19.

Caine, V., Estefan, A., & Clandinin, D. J. (2013). A return to methodological commitment: Reflections on narrative inquiry. *Scandinavian Journal of Educational Research, 57*(6), 574–586. https://doi.org/10.1080/00313831.2013.798833

Clandinin, D. J., & Connelly, F. M. (1989). *Narrative and story in practice and research* (p. 25) [Descriptive, evaluative/feasibility].

Collins, P. H. (1991). *Black feminist thought: Knowledge, consciousness, and the politics of empowerment.* Routledge.

Creswell, J. W., & Poth, C. N. (2018). *Qualitative inquiry & research design: Choosing among five approaches* (4th ed.). SAGE.

Cross, W. E. Jr. (1971). *The Negro-to-Black conversion experience: Toward a psychology of Black liberation* (pp. 20, 13–27). Black World.

Cross, W. E. Jr. (2016). *Meaning-making, internalized racism, and African American identity.* SUNY Press.

Davis, S. M. (2019). When sistahs support sistahs: A process of supportive communication about racial microaggressions among Black women. *Communication Monographs, 86*(2), 133–157. https://doi.org/10.1080/03637751.2018.1548769

Dillard, C. (2012). *Learning to (re)member the things we've learned to forget: Endarkened Feminisms, spirituality, & the sacred nature of research and teaching.* Peter Lang.

Doharty, N. (2018). "I FELT DEAD": Applying a racial microaggressions framework to black students' experiences of Black History Month and Black History. *Race Ethnicity and Education, 22*(1), 110–129. https://doi.org/10.1080/13613324.2017.1417253

Edwards, K. T. (2018). Stories of migration: Passing through, crossing over, and decolonial transgressing in Academyland. In *Black Women's Liberatory pedagogies.* Palgrave Macmillan.

Evans-Winters, V. E. (2015). Black feminism in qualitative education research: A Mosaic for interpreting race, class, and gender in education. In V. E. Evans-Winters & B. L. Love (Eds.), *Black feminism in education: Black women speak back, up, and out.* Peter Lang.

Farinde, A. A., Allen, A., & Lewis, C. W. (2016). Retaining Black teachers: An examination of Black female teachers' intentions to remain in K-12 classrooms. *Equity*

*& Excellence in Education*, *49*(1), 115–127. https://doi.org/10.1080/10665684.2015.1120367

Grady, G. O., Clandinin, D. J., & O'Toole, J. (2018). Engaging in educational narrative inquiry: Making visible alternative knowledge. *Irish Educational Studies*, *37*(2), 153–157.

Hamilton-Mason, J., Hall, J. C., & Everett, J. E. (2009). And some of us are braver: Stress and coping among African American women. *Journal of Human Behavior in the Social Environment*, *19*(5), 463–482. https://doi.org/10.1080/10911350902832142

Hodges, T. E., & Cady, J. A. (2012). Negotiating contexts to construct an identity as a mathematics teacher. *The Journal of Educational Research*, *105*(2), 112–122. https://doi.org/10.1080/00220671.2010.529956

Jackson, J. S., Caldwell, C. H., & Sellers, S. L. (Eds.). (2012). *Researching black communities: A methodological guide*. University of Michigan Press.

Jones, M. K., & Day, S. X. (2018). An exploration of Black women's gendered racial identity using a multidimensional and intersectional approach. *Sex Roles*, *79*(1–2), 1–15. https://doi.org/10.1007/s11199-017-0854-8

Kelchtermans, G. (2009). Who I am in how I teach is the message: Self-understanding, vulnerability and reflection. *Teachers and Teaching*, *15*(2), 257–272. https://doi.org/10.1080/13540600902875332

Kvale, S., & Brinkman, S. (2009). *Interviews: Learning the craft of qualitative research interviewing* (2nd ed.). SAGE Publications.

Lawrence, S. M., & Tatum, B. D. (1999). White racial identity and anti-racist education: A catalyst for change. In E. Lee, D. Menkart & M. Okazawa-Rey (Eds.), *Beyond heroes and holidays: A practical guide to K-12 anti-racist, multicultural education and staff development* (p. 12). Network of Educators on the Americas.

Leavy, P. (2017). *Research design: Quantitative, qualitative, mixed methods, arts-based, and community-based participatory research approaches*. The Guilford Press.

Leonardo, Z. (2013). The story of schooling: Critical race theory and the educational racial contract. *Discourse: Studies in the Cultural Politics of Education*, *34*(4), 599–610.

Lewis, E. (2008). Race, power, multipositionality. *Interventions*, *10*(3), 20.

Liu, W. M., Liu, R. Z., Garrison, Y. L., Kim, J. Y. C., Chan, L., Ho, Y. C. S., & Yeung, C. W. (2019). Racial trauma, microaggressions, and becoming racially innocuous: The role of acculturation and White supremacist ideology. *American Psychologist*, *74*(1), 143–155.

Lukenchuk, A. (2013). *Paradigms of research for the 21st century: Perspectives and examples from practice* (Vol. 436). Peter Lang.

Matias, C. E., & Newlove, P. M. (2017). The illusion of freedom: Tyranny, whiteness, and the state of US society. *Equity & Excellence in Education*, *50*(3), 316–330. https://doi.org/10.1080/10665684.2017.1336951

Milner, H. R. (2007). Race, culture, and researcher positionality: Working through dangers seen, unseen, and unforeseen. *Educational Researcher, 36*(7), 388–400. https://doi.org/10.3102/0013189X07309471

Ravitch, S. M., & Mittenfelner, N. (2021). *Qualitative research: Bridging the conceptual, theoretical, and methodological* (2nd ed.). SAGE.

Rinker, J., & Lawler, J. (2018). Trauma as a collective disease and root cause of protracted social conflict. *Peace and Conflict: Journal of Peace Psychology, 24*(2), 150–164. https://doi.org/10.1037/pac0000311

Romm, N. R. A. (2010). *New racism: Revisiting researcher accountabilities.* Springer Science +Business Media.

Sheehan, S. (2014). A conceptual framework for understanding transcendental phenomenology through the lived experiences of biblical leaders. *Journal: Emerging Leadership Journeys, 7,* 11.

Shields, C. M. (2012). Critical advocacy research: An approach whose time has come. In S. R. Steinberg & G. S. Cannella (Eds.), *Critical qualitative research reader* (pp. 2–12). Peter Lang.

Shujaa, M. J. (2003). The widening gap between education and schooling in the post 9/11 era. *The Journal of Negro Education, 72*(2), 179. https://doi.org/10.2307/3211167

Solorzano, D. G., & Yosso, T. J. (2009). Critical race methodology: Counter-storytelling as an analytical framework for educational research. In E. Taylor, D. Gillborn, & G. Ladson-Billings (Eds.), *Foundations of critical race theory in education.* Routledge.

Spradley, J. (1979). *The ethnographic interview.* Holt, Rinehart and Winston.

Williams-Washington, K. N., & Mills, C. P. (2018). African American historical trauma: Creating an inclusive measure. *Journal of Multicultural Counseling and Development, 46*(4), 246–263. https://doi.org/10.1002/jmcd.12113

Wolcott, H. F. (1929). *Transforming qualitative data: Description, analysis, and interpretation.* SAGE Publications.

Zuberi, T., & Bonila-Silva, E. (2008). *White logic, white methods: Racism and methodology.* Rowman & Littlefield.

# Chapter 5 Sociocultural Perspectives of First-Generation Asian Indian Leaders in U.S. Higher Education: An Ethnographic Study

MATTHEW A. WOOLSEY

> What do I think of Western civilization? I think it would be a very good idea. In truth there are as many religions as there are individuals. (Suri, 2011)
>
> —Mohandas Gandhi

I have a nomadic spirit, an indelible curiosity to discover other walks of life unlike my own. Living to learn in another part of the state, country, and world has formed who I am today. Of these influences, none had a more profound impact on my life than the time I spent in India immersing myself in its culture. The people, aromas, food variations, music, religious festivals, chaotic but organized traffic, colors, elephants in the streets, and so much more triggered an indescribable passion within me to learn more. Subsequently, my India persuasion led me to this academic juncture of exploring the individual perspectives of Asian Indians in their interpretive journey that brought them to serve as leaders in what to them was a foreign country—the United States of America. While I have a desire and appetite to discover the ways of life of peoples in lands unlike mine, I wonder whether Asian Indians have the same compulsion with regard to the United States, with, moreover, a drive to become a leader.

* * *

> What you think you become. (Suri, 2011)
>
> —Mohandas Gandhi

## *Background of the Study*

A striking feature of U.S. higher education is the high participation rate of Asian Americans as professionals in that employment sector. As of 2010, Asian American Pacific Islanders made up 7.2% of the total faculty population inclusive of Asian Indians (National Commission on Asian American and Pacific Islander Research in Education, 2010, p. 11). In terms of Asian Indians employed in U.S. higher education, there are more than 5,000 serving as faculty in U.S. post-secondary institutions (U.S. Census Bureau, 2004). With all this effort to attract Asian Indians to U.S. colleges and universities, less than 1% of all institutional presidents are of Indian descent (Yamagata-Noji, 2011). Why is this the case? And, for those Asian Indians who made it to higher education leadership roles, what were the contributing factors? What might the implications of these factors be for other Asian Indians who may aspire to similar positions of leadership?

## *Taking the Leap*

History shows waves of Indian diaspora over time steadily manifesting into sizeable populations across the United States with recent reports of nearly three million Asian Indians in the country (U.S. Census, 2010). Indians who make the conscious decision to fully embrace the American way of life still find some link to their cultural roots (Kakar, 2007). As I reflect on my own experiences working in India as a team leader and trainer, I find it necessary to delve into the cultural nuances of Indian culture if I expect to achieve any level of success. In essence, making this cross-cultural leap requires recognition and effort to learn cultural norms and mores (Hofstede, 2001), incorporate a genuine willingness to learn the unspoken (tacit) culture (Li & Scullion, 2010), and embrace leadership competencies on both local and global dimensions (Cohen, 2007). What does this cross-cultural leap look like for Asian Indians coming to the United States?

### *Research Purposes and Questions*

The study of leadership within the context of U.S. higher education covers the gamut from trait, contingency, and behavioral theories to modern frameworks, including transformational, collaborative, and social constructivism. Particular to Asian Indians in higher education, the bulk of research focuses on the influx of Asian Indian students, and where focus on leaders does occur, studies tend to aggregate all Asians with Caucasian or Other designations (Teranishi et al., 2009). In fact, Museus states, "Asian Americans in the field of higher education ... have been relatively excluded from higher education research and discourse" (Museus & Chang, 2009, p. 95).

The purpose of this study is to acquire an in-depth understanding of a complex world of sociocultural influences and interactions in which Indian expatriates pursue positions of leadership in U.S. higher education. I seek to answer the question: How do Indian expatriates view their highest professional attainments in U.S. higher education from their sociocultural perspectives? In an effort to unpack this main question, I am led to the following questions.

- What are the defining features of the Indian expatriates' backgrounds that sustain their *shakti* (life force) in India and especially in the United States?
- What ultimately motivates them to pursue higher education positions of leadership in the United States?

## *Leadership Inquiry into Asian Indians in U.S. Higher Education*

> A man is but the product of his thoughts. (Suri, 2011)
>
> —Mohandas Gandhi

The stretch of general leadership research, defined as the Transactional age, harkens back to the Industrial Revolution (1830–1978) and focused on deliberate traits, the one-man, hero approach to defining leadership (Stogdill & Coons, 1957). Soon thereafter, the shape of leadership study began to explore the interchange between the leader and follower with the eminent goal for the leader to get the follower to achieve something under the headings of behavioral and contingency theories (Yukl, 2010). The late 1970s and early 1980s ushered in the Transformational leadership age recognizing the value of all working together toward a common goal, which is largely attributed to Burns's seminal book titled *Leadership* (1978). The debate about who plays the true influential role in this configuration continues with further examination. One thing is certain—leadership is no longer a title-honored concept, but rather one based on high moral standards, trust, devotion to followers, the ability for all to lead where social constructs influence self in relation to others, and the circumstances at play (Bass, 1990; Northouse, 2010).

Leadership studies of Asian Indian leaders migrating to the United States shows, from a business perspective, concerted effort required for leaders to make a successful leap. The work of Hofstede (1980, 2011) illustrates five cultural dimensions of difference—power distance, individualism, masculinity, uncertainty, avoidance, and long-term orientation—and Indian and U.S. cultures most notably differ in power distance and long-term orientation. Results from the Global Leadership and Organizational Effectiveness (Chhokar et al., 2008) initiative describe American and Indian leaders as action oriented with similar approaches to work, but they differ in the value Indian leaders put on self-reflection compared to their American counterparts. Studies indicate Indians migrating to the United States experience a shift in values (Budhwar et al., 2008), while other research shows that Western tools for testing may have limitations in accurately measuring leadership style (Dalton & Wilson, 2000).

The U.S. higher education leadership inquiry landscape covers theoretical frameworks from trait to social constructivism (Bensimon et al., 1989; Komives & Woodard, 2003). Recent trends indicate education leaders will need to demonstrate a set of nimble characteristics as technology and global influences pressure the academy. Contemporary research in U.S. higher education is beginning to focus on Asian leaders, though aggregated together with no discrimination between Asian origins (Teranishi et al., 2009).

* * *

> Truth is by nature self-evident. As soon as you remove the cobwebs of ignorance that surround it, it shines clear. (Suri, 2011)
>
> —Mohandas Gandhi

As a frequent visitor to India I became affectionately connected with and inquisitive about the Indian people, culture, and ways of life. I participated in religious activities and built relationships with locals, which led to home invitations. These relationships were based on trust with individuals whom I call my friends; trust is fundamental to relationship building in India. My personal disposition for a culture almost the opposite of my Western roots drives my desire for knowing, understanding, and interpreting the underpinning reasons that drive Asian Indians to lead in a world figuratively and literally opposite from their own.

## *Methodology*

### ***Qualitative Inquiry: Discovering Leadership Phenomenon Meaning***

To examine the leadership phenomenon of a specific group of Asian Indians in U.S. higher education, I employed qualitative methodology, which deals with "multiple realities" and is flexible in nature to address the "shaping influences and value patterns experienced by the researcher" (Lincoln & Guba, 1985, p. 40). While describing the experiences of a group of Asian Indians as they see it, I attempted to create a holistic account and reconstruct the reality of cultural influences on their leadership journey (Creswell, 2009). Through these multiple forms of realities, the result was an emergent framework that renders this phenomenon meaningful and of practical value.

Qualitative research has been identified as a preferred method for leadership studies (Drath, 2001; Uhl-Bien, 2006; Yukl, 1989; Parry, 1998). The Relational Leadership Theory (RLT) approach posits a framework "for the study of leadership as a social influence process through which emergent coordination (e.g., evolving social order) and change (e.g., new approaches, values, attitudes, behaviors, ideologies) are constructed and produced" (Uhl-Bien, p. 668). With this premise, the discovery of context as it pertains to leadership further supports the need to deeply explore perceptions and interpretations through a qualitative approach.

Higher education is a unique, complex culture in which academic leaders fill a critical and influential role (Kezar, 2009; Rhoads & Tierney, 1992). To do this effectively, qualitative epistemology requires me to seek understanding that goes beyond making causal linkages. Lincoln and Guba (1985) state that dialogue between the research participants and me brings to the fore "myriad mutual shapings" where my understanding is reliant on an appreciation of the descriptive structures that emerge from our interactions (p. 152). I challenged myself to persist with genuine curiosity, to dig deeper opening myself to other "forms of order" about Asian Indian leadership in higher education (Shank, 2006, p. 208).

### *Ethnography: Depicting the Journey*

In this study I utilized ethnography as the approach because it examines the human experiences of their journey to leadership as described by the participants. Extensive observation and field notes are required while collecting artifacts and representative cultural materials. Ethnographers are the recorders of life activities for those under study where inquiry is intimate, focusing on life influences like family, friends, socioeconomic structures, and religion (Hesse-Biber & Leavy, 2011).

Ethnography derives from the field of anthropology where researchers went "native" by immersing themselves in the foreign culture, seeking understanding of customs, cultural patterns, norms, beliefs, and behaviors. Since then the concept of *culture* has migrated to the study of *cultures* representing a group sharing common values, beliefs, and life experiences (McMillan, 2008). Flick (2009) emphasizes the criticality of the researcher "going native" to gain an inside perspective of the studied culture while systematizing "the status of the stranger at the same time" (p. 229). The common ground for this study is lived experience as a member of Indian culture and the impact these life experiences made on the selected individuals.

An ethnographic design is somewhat vulnerable given the interpretative and observational methods employed by the researcher. However, in cases where "interpersonal relationships, social structures, creative products, and so on . . . are under examination, quantitative methods simply are not appropriate" (Leedy & Ormrod, 2010, p. 135). Further, the ethnographic design is useful for educational research when it is incumbent on the researcher to collect "multiple sources of information and [spend] considerable time in the field" gathering information when evaluating the credibility of findings purported by the study (Creswell, 2008, p. 493).

***Sociocultural Lens: Elucidating the Experiences***

The process of finding meaning implies a learning process. Wertsch (1985) states that sociocultural perspectives take this a step further where "social contexts and interactions play in the construction of meaning . . . we cannot understand the individual without understanding the social and historical context in which he or she lives" (as cited in Lattuca & Stark, 2009, p. 156). Sense-making, self-interpretation, and language are all influenced by culture where "cognitive processes are . . . cultural processes because they are situated in, and thus created by, relevant interpersonal, social, cultural, institutional, and historical contexts" (Lattuca & Stark, p. 156).

Sociocultural research tends to focus on the interpretation of identity formation after joining a community (Lewis & Moje, 2003, p. 1979). The intent of this project was to examine participant self-reflection and interpretation first from an Indian perspective, and then moving to their adjustment to American culture and their experience in U.S. higher education. By doing this, the discovery not only addressed past experiences but also explored "how they shape identities related to the conflict and tension that is always present in such communities" (Lewis & Moje, p. 1979).

The participants of this study were asked to reconstruct their life stories through a semi-structured interview. Throughout the inquiry, I continued posing these questions to myself: "What happens in the translation of reality into text? What happens in the retranslation of texts into reality or in inferring from texts to realities?" (Flick, 2009, p. 75). While the researcher is dependent on the subject's narrative, the aim is not to discern factual processes. This biographical narrative "becomes a mimetic presentation of experiences, which are constructed in the form of a narrative for this purpose—in the interview" (Flick, p. 81). Instead of mirroring reality, applying mimesis means interpretation happens from not only the subject's narrative but a construction by the researcher and reader as well.

## *Data Collection Strategies*

### ***Interviews***

A major source of data collection for this study came from semi-structured interviews typical of ethnography (McMillan, 2008). Interviews provided me the advantage of asking the respondent to "reconstruct the past, interpret the present, and predict the future" (Lincoln & Guba, 1985, p. 273). The interviewer in a semi-structured approach uses open-ended questions to set the general direction of the dialogue, but the participant controls the discussion, requiring flexibility on the part of the interviewer (Cohen et al., 2008).

I interviewed five Asian Indian expatriate collegiate leaders at the vice-presidential and presidential levels. Given the nature of this study where human interaction between the researcher and participant is necessary, a small sampling for in-depth analysis until reaching saturation is optimal (Creswell & Clark, 2011; McMillan, 2008). Creswell and Clark recommend four to ten participants typical of ethnographic research. The criteria stipulated participants must have:

- Grown up in India at least through their secondary education; and
- Served at the vice president level or higher in U. S. higher education.

A potential candidate list was generated from personal contacts combined with the snowball technique where additional participants were identified. Twelve individuals matched the criteria and seven were invited to participate, five individuals were subsequently interviewed. Interviews ranged from one to two hours each and took place within the participant's office space, except for one who was in-between positions at the time of data collection. Institutions were located in the East Coast and Midwest. Participant composition included a female at the vice president level, a female president, and three males at the president level.

### ***Field Notes***

Field notes, in the form of journaling, "are the data that you gather to make sense of your research setting, and they serve as an aid in writing your research results" (Hesse-Biber & Leavy, 2011, p. 216). My journal entries contain both retrospective and most current memories. While in India, dating back to 2006, I witnessed a myriad of activities and celebrations transforming my perceptions and beliefs about the Indian way of life. I adopted Van Maanen's methodology (1988) called ethnographic impressionism. Van Maanen posits that time away from the field results in a more holistic and complete picture of experiences. My intent was to provide "thick descriptions" incorporating direct quotes, sensory observations such as smells and visuals, along with my feelings and emotions (Hesse-Biber & Leavy, 2011), which contributes to the trustworthiness of this study (Lincoln & Guba, 1985).

#### *Documents and Artifacts*

Ethnographic study lends itself to multiple forms of data, enriching the overall contextual interpretation of the phenomenon in question. Some argue there is not one way for recording field observations. Thus, pictures, documents, and video are considered elements of valid data collection (Hesse-Biber & Leavy, 2011). In addition to my journal entries, documents such as pictures, India Internet resources, a video I recorded featuring a typical drive to work each morning in India, and other leadership resources are contained on my website portal capturing my learning journey through this process.

### *Ethical Considerations of Ethnographic Research*

With qualitative research, trustworthiness (credibility) is what gives the study merit. To be deemed trustworthy, the study must be transparent, have consistency-coherence, and communicability (Rubin & Rubin, 1995). Transparency relates to the manner in which data were collected; consistency references the extent the researcher investigated inconsistent responses, achieving coherence by describing conflicting points of view; and communicability means that the reader is able to contextualize the experiences as described by the subjects (Rubin & Rubin).

Qualitative research assumes multiple realities and it is the researcher's role to translate the interpretation of the subjects being studied (Merriam & Simpson, 1995). Internal validity guided my data analysis. The ultimate goal is to present that reality as accurately as possible by implementing various procedures. One way to ensure research credibility is through triangulating data sources and research techniques. Interviews, documents, and artifacts are meant to triangulate my data sources and to illuminate themes of discovery pertaining to events, facts, and interpretations about key factors and competencies for future Indian natives in pursuit of U.S. higher education leadership. Hesse-Biber and Leavy (2011) recommend looking for emergent themes within the text, then comparing artifacts and field notes to confirm consistency.

I made use of member checking after the interviews were transcribed and themes identified. Member checking is a common practice requiring the researcher to compile interview results and ask participants to confirm their reflections were accurately captured; in my case, one participant made minor revisions to the transcript (Creswell & Clark, 2011). Member checking is the most valuable approach to establishing credibility, and can be done in both formal and informal methods throughout the data collection process (Lincoln & Guba, 1985).

I sought feedback from a colleague, which proves to be an effective way to ensure credibility (Flick, 2009). I engaged a colleague to independently review the anonymous transcripts and that colleague subsequently confirmed my results (McMillan, 2008).

In an effort to maintain a balanced way of my own engagement in the study, of who I am, what I am experiencing, and my subsequent interpretations of the information before me, I maintained reflective dialogue; this approach is often termed *reflexivity* (Flick, 2009; Lincoln & Guba, 1985). Lincoln and Guba recommend the researcher engage in daily journaling, capturing logistical observations, reflecting on self in relation to values and areas for further exploration, and recording ongoing decision-making about methodology. My personal reflections through the written word added to the collection of data for triangulation and illuminated places where I potentially may have been self-imposing my own sociocultural perspective on my participants.

## *Data Analysis: Making the Connections for Understanding*

I began data analysis by transcribing the interviews and coding for themes and categories. I did my first round of descriptive coding manually by hand and then went back to adjust for consistency (Saldana, 2009). All 240 codes called *nodes* were transferred into NVivo9, a qualitative data analysis software tool designed specifically for qualitative research to assist in categorization of content. Digital audio recordings from participant interviews, field notes, and artifacts were subsequently uploaded, resulting in a multidimensional picture for analysis.

Information was categorized as either emic or etic data. The emic and etic data were then assembled into "families of codes" representing "setting and context subjects' definitions of a setting, subjects' perspectives about other people and aspects of a setting, process changes over time, activities, events, and techniques subjects use to accomplish things, and relationships and social structures" (McMillan, 2008, p. 284). The key here was to let the data form the codes, beginning from the specific and moving to the general as multiple layers of analysis were required for robust results (Creswell, 2009). Researcher interpretation required me to go beyond describing the complex themes and digging deeper for understanding.

The data analysis process yielded nine themes specific to this community of practice with seven particular to leadership and two others related to their journey alone and "going to the other side" while linking back to their roots. What follows is the description and representation of the research findings and results from the lives of Dr. Rajan, Dr. Gupta, Dr. Moorthy, Dr. Arora, and Dr. Agarwal.

* * *

> There are times when you have to obey a call which is the highest of all, i.e., the voice of conscience even though such obedience may cost many a bitter tear, and even more, separation from friends, from family, from the state, to which you may belong, from all that you have held as dear as life itself. For this obedience is the law of our being. (Suri, 2011)
>
> —Mohandas Gandhi

## *Exploring the Other Side Alone, Linking Back*

Warren Bennis (2009) states, "Those who travel farther from home learn even more" (p. 84). Exploring "the other side" is a vital aspect with this group of Asian Indians. Filled with an inquisitive spirit, these individuals sought to reach a new land and soared in their new environment. Not only did they literally travel the expanse from East to West, they also embraced the American form of higher education and crossed the chasm from academic to administrative roles. Through each lived experience, the texture of each person's journey became vivid, revealing challenges and triumphs, testing and developing methods for navigation.

A number of participants used the word *alone* when describing elements about themselves whether it was their travels to America, leaving family as a child to attend school, or the work they enjoy as executives here in U.S. higher education. On the surface this makes sense, but in some ways it points to their ability to navigate between groups while preserving their individual identity. To move from where they were in their life required a strategy to permeate any perceived boundaries. A solo-spirit may just be one secret ingredient to their life success.

Hofstede (1980, 2001; Hofstede et al., 2010) describes India as a collectivist society where people help each other and do everything possible to save face. American culture is much more individualistic. Could there be an insight here for Asian Indians who describe themselves as "alone?" Perhaps this descriptor has been part of who they are from birth, which, even though living in a collectivist society as defined by Hofstede (1980, 2001), gave them the skills needed to navigate the Indian ways before moving to the United States. In essence, relocating to the United States provides the perfect entre for them to preserve the alone dimension, but successfully navigate boundaries to get things done. For them, becoming vulnerable, realizing skill strengths and gaps, and approaching the challenge with an eagerness to learn served a transformative platform into a new life construct.

Going to the other side has now mutated into a new career phase as some of the participants are now reconnecting with their India ethnic roots. Dr. Moorthy is forging academic agreements with Indian higher education institutions by which students may transfer to the United States and complete a baccalaureate degree within three years. Dr. Arora is increasing professional ties with Mumbai business leaders. In all cases, each participant makes it a priority to return to India for various reasons but is resolute in the proclamation that he or she is more American than Indian.

### *Immigrant Mentality: Asian Indian Self-Identity*

In the beginning, self-actualization through acculturation and the refining of self-identity coalesced into an immigrant mentality of being American first. This insight bucks research findings asserting first-generation Asian Indians identify as Indian first (Farver, Narang, et al., 2002; Farver, Xu, et al., 2007; Hickey, 2006). Born into a society with predetermined roles and a set of societal expectations, all formed an affinity for collectivism, maintained allocentric components in America "where the self and the family are integral, rather than separate, concepts" (Farver, Narang, et al., 2002, p. 340), but naturally absorbed elements of the individualistic American way of life. This assimilation into American culture netted the best of their Indian roots and positively impacted U.S. higher education leadership execution—leading with care for the home and family.

### *Work Hard: Pull to Serve and the Power of Encouragement*

Working hard and responding to the "pull" gives these leaders the resolve that they are fulfilling their calling by not dwelling on the next strategic career move. This Gandhian approach links tightly back to Indian culture heavily influenced by Hindu constructs where one's role is assigned, all reinforced through ancient Indian teachings of heroism in the Ramayana and Mahabharata epics (Butt, 2004). Steeped in a life with values for doing the right thing, education was a catalyst for each person to elevate their role within society (Bhattacharya & Schoppelrey, 2004). Dr. Moorthy sees this "a calling from God to serve others ... not as much aspirational, but something that sort of tends to pull you." By working hard and doing the right thing, all participants subscribed that the "pull" to the next life challenge presented itself, but all in one way or the other had to be encouraged before pursuing the next career move. This need for encouragement poses an incongruous paradigm since Asian Indians tend not to encourage others (Kakar et al., 2002).

### *Education: Constant Learner*

The genesis for academic achievement in each participant's story was fueled by external stimuli, namely his or her mother, who positioned education as a form of insurance toward a future of prosperity. Dr. Rajan said her "mother made it very clear to my sister and me ... that in order to have insurance of some kind ... and that insurance for us was our education." Wrapped in this motivation to succeed academically, education was a source credited for shaping their self-identity. This identity resulted in a search for truth as they migrated to the United States and becoming scholars in their academic fields. As life experiences synthesized, the "pull" factored into their work ethic, and education served as a catalyst by which each assumed formal administrative posts that led toward executive leadership positions with a drive to make a difference.

### *Credibility: Links to Teaching and Research*

Leading U.S. higher education institutions demands leaders skilled across a portfolio of business-savvy competencies (Bolman & Gallos, 2011; Fullan & Scott, 2009; Waugh, 2003). This community of practice emphasized that while leadership roles can be taxing, maintaining credibility through continued scholarly actions was paramount. Dr. Gupta and Dr. Agarwal profess their admiration for learning and teaching and see these as critical parts of who they are. As president, Dr. Agarwal never really left teaching. Dr. Rajan blocks time on her calendar to meet with her laboratory research team. Dr. Rajan and Dr. Agarwal team-teach at their institutions while Dr. Moorthy remains engaged as a guest lecturer and publishes. The challenge is for leaders to strategically allocate time specific to scholarly activities.

### *Intolerance for Risk Aversion: Principles and Values*

Asian Indian leaders are intolerant of academic leaders who avoid risk as the easy way out to evade potential public institutional scrutiny. Propelled by a spirit of exploration into new worlds, all participants spoke fondly of their formative years in India where they assumed their predestined role and achieved academic success while absorbing fundamental lessons shaping their values. "Entrepreneurial," "rebel," and "competitive" were some of the self-subscribed descriptors about who they are. In many ways, to explore in a highly rigid and structured society such as India is not commonplace since one typically lives within his or her birth role in a given community (caste) (Chhokar et al., 2008). This has changed considerably since the lifting of Licence Raj in 1991 (government laws established in 1947 composed of strict business regulations to control the economy), but for each of them, such exploration was rather novel in the 1960s and 1970s. Dr. Arora referenced Gandhi's essay on the Bhagavad Gita that explained while life may be predestined (dharma), all of us are still active participants and through good actions, actions will bring good. The implication here is that action requires risk taking, a concept strongly promoted by Gandhi's leadership during the liberation movement.

Research indicates people living in cultures with strict prescriptions for life activities and requirements for achieving favor with God, like Christianity in the United States, tend to be risk averse (Miller, 2000). Asian Indians come from a society where religion tends to be more fluid and one's religious journey offers more options about how to achieve a happy life on Earth and after (Bacon, 1999; Falk et al., 2010). Taking risks is more acceptable as long as decisions are moral- and value-laden.

### *Permeate Boundaries: Relational Constructs*

Living in a land interfacing with and engaging in customs and traditions of multiple faiths blurred boundaries for these Asian Indians, allowing for different religions and faiths to manifest together. The Hindi phrase, *Vasudheive Kutumbakam*, means the "whole world is my family." The consideration of the "whole world is my family" influences their perception about the concept of networked relations that extend beyond the immediate, nuclear construct. Dr. Rajan emphasized that "being an Indian you are used to larger groups, larger interactions and networks." Asian Indian executives consider all members of the academic community family—students, staff, faculty, alumni, neighboring community, and the board—no matter role, position, title, or any other designation.

### *Velvet Glove, Steel Hand: Communication with Action*

Communicating with conviction, maintaining a tempered demeanor, fully listening to contrasting points of view, and making bold moves based on core principles is an earmark approach for this community of practice. To circumvent negative perceptions by others about his composed communication style, Dr. Arora said that leaders require a consciousness about the principles at stake as a gauge for implementing a firm communication style. He went on to say, "When people feel the velvet glove they think that you're going to be easy to push around ... But when it comes to the important things, you really have to stick to the principle and not be folding and compromising."

* * *

## *Going Forward*

> Be the change you want to see in the world. (Suri, 2011)
>
> —Mohandas Gandhi

Asian Indians need to encourage others and pull them along. The message for all is to work hard in the moment and do so with a positive mindset. Likewise, Asian Indians need to seek out leadership training for constant refining, which can be done through internal institutional programs or external venues such as educational conferences and organizations. Time and energy must be devoted to sense-making in a world of mixed messages about ethical leadership that will ultimately mitigate any unwarranted compromises.

People know when a person has their interests in mind no matter the given situation (Salovey & Mayer, 1990). Asian Indians have an opportunity to increase influence by collaborating with others, developing relationships, and doing so in overlapping places to incite positive change. Fostering these relationships requires a communication approach that works with Americans who tend to speak loudly and with emotionality (Varma, 2004).

Learning is a foundational dimension and the search for truth can only promote good in all leadership activities. When truth is at the core, Asian Indian leaders have the opportunity to not only discover new paradigms but also make positive differences in the lives around them and build an external network for support and guidance. Being a leader often causes one to compartmentalize and guard certain emotions, requiring time and a place for emotional venting without fear of reprisal to maintain balance.

## *My Journey, "On the Other Side"*

Going to the other side is a metaphorical phrase descriptive of my life journey where the other side stimulated an unquenchable thirst to explore and learn. From my early years, education became a way for me to distinguish myself from the crowd, opening doors for opportunities unbeknown to me at the time. Primary education helped me hone leadership skills in student organizations while I dove into my studies and became skilled in communication and music.

My time at Washington State University (WSU), located on the other side of the state of Washington in relation to my hometown, nurtured this ongoing affinity for education and leadership development. WSU served as a catalyst to my venture in seeing the world, and from there I seized the opportunity to learn and help others, culminating in a career in student affairs. As I forged onward to West Virginia University on the other side of the country, I quickly learned that while part of the same country, a cultural shift came into play because life constructs and perceptions were different from my West Coast mindset. After six years of student affairs work, I made the choice to go to the other side and give the corporate world a chance.

Life on the other side of the planet struck a chord with me because my travels to India exceeded anything required as a work obligation. Education has always been about finding truth—truth as a result of learning about the world and the interpretations other human beings have about truth—and sorting through to create a holistic frame to guide how I live my life. My passion for working with others, my insatiable appetite for learning, and my affinity for cultural interludes have brought me to this intellectual exercise where India, leadership, and education converged.

Along the way, I have featured quotes from one of the most transformational leaders in the modern era, Mohandas Gandhi. Gandhi was heavily influenced by his readings of Hindu, Christian, Buddhist, and Muslim texts, as well as his experiences with racism in South Africa and with the British legal system, and then he developed it into the nonviolent movement after reading Tolstoy, Thoreau, and others. His life, his calling, his "pull" to serve literally changed the livelihood of an entire nation, inspiring people the world over since his walk on Earth to present day. Gandhi's voice had resonance, reaching all factions of Indian society, friend or foe, culminating in action for the greater good. As I continue along this life journey, I hope my voice and actions, big and small, somehow influence the world around me for the better.

## References

Bacon, J. (1999). Constructing collective ethnic identities: The case of second generation Asian Indians. *Qualitative Sociology, 22*(2), 141–160.

Bass, B. M. (1990). *Bass and Stogdill's handbook of leadership: Theory research and managerial application.* Free Press.

Bennis, W. (2009). *On becoming a leader: The leadership classic revised and updated*. Perseus.

Bensimon, E M., & Neumann, A. (1993). *Redesigning collegiate leadership: Teams and teamwork in higher education*. Johns Hopkins University Press.

Bensimon, E. M., Neumann, A., & Birnbaum, R. (1989). *Making sense of administrative leadership: The "L" word in higher education* (ASHE-ERIC Higher Education Report No. 1). George Washington University.

Bhattacharya, G., & Schoppelrey, S. L. (2004). Preimmigration beliefs of life success, postimmigration experiences, and acculturative stress: South Asian immigrants in the United States. *Journal of Immigrant Health*, *6*(2), 83–92.

Bolman, L. G., & Gallos, J. V. (2011). *Reframing academic leadership*. Wiley & Sons.

Budhwar, P. S., Woldu, H., & Ogbonna, W. (2008). A comparative analysis of cultural value orientations of Indians and migrant Indians in the USA. *International Journal of Cross Cultural Management*, *8*(1), 79–105.

Burns, J. M. (1978). *Leadership*. Harper & Row.

Butt, J. (2004). *Visions of service: An introduction to five of the world's great religions, with excerpts from the sacred writings and questions for study and reflection for those engaged in service*. International Partnership for Service-Learning & Leadership.

Chhokar, J. S., Bordbeck, B. C., & House, R. J. (2008). *Culture and leadership across the world: The globe book of in-depth studies of 25 societies*. Psychology.

Cohen, E. (2007). *Leadership without borders: Successful strategies from world-class leaders*. Wiley & Sons.

Cohen, L., Manion, L., & Morrison, K. (2008). *Research methods in education* (6th ed.). Routledge.

Creswell, J. W. (2008). *Educational research: Planning, conducting, and evaluating quantitative and qualitative research* (3rd ed.). Pearson.

Creswell, J. W. (2009). *Research design: Qualitative, quantitative, and mixed methods approaches*. Sage.

Creswell, J. W., & Clark, V. L. P. (2011). *Designing and conducting mixed methods research* (2nd ed.). SAGE.

Dalton, M., & Wilson, M. (2000). The relationship of the five-factor model of personality to job performance for a group of Middle Eastern expatriate managers. *Journal of Cross-Cultural Psychology*, *31*, 258.

Drath, W. (2001). *The deep blue sea: Rethinking the source of leadership*. Jossey-Bass.

Falk, C. F., Dunn, E. W., & Norenzayan, A. (2010). Cultural variation in the importance of expected enjoyment for decision making. *Social Cognition*, *28*(5), 609–629.

Farver, J. M., Narang, S., & Bhadha, B. R. (2002). East meets West: Ethnic identity, acculturation, and conflict in Asian Indian families. *Journal of Family Psychology*, *16*(3), 338–350.

Farver, J. M., Xu, Y., Bhadha, B. R., Narang, S., & Lieber, E. (2007). Ethnic identity, acculturation, parenting beliefs, and adolescent adjustment. *Merrill-Palmer Quarterly*, *53*(2), 184–215.

Flick, U. (2009). *An introduction to qualitative research* (4th ed.). SAGE.

Fullan, M., & Scott, G. (2009). *Turnaround leadership for higher education.* Jossey-Bass.

Hesse-Biber, S. N., & Leavy, P. (2011). *The practice of qualitative research* (2nd ed.). SAGE.

Hickey, M. G. (2006). Asian Indians in Indiana. *Indiana Magazine of History, 102,* 118–140.

Hofstede, G. (1980). *Culture's consequences: International differences in work-related values.* SAGE.

Hofstede, G. (2001). *Cultures' consequences: Comparing values, behaviors, institutions, and organizations across cultures.* SAGE.

Hofstede, G., Hofstede, G. J., & Minkov, M. (2010). *Cultures and organizations: Intercultural cooperation and its importance for survival.* McGraw-Hill.

Kakar, S. (2007). *Indian-ness.* Little India.

Kakar, S., Kakar, S., KetsdeVries, M. F. R., & Vrignaud, P. (2002). Leadership in Indian organizations from a comparative perspective. *International Journal of Cross Cultural Management, 2*(2), 239–250.

Kezar, A. (2009). *Rethinking leadership in a complex, multicultural, and global environment: New concepts and models for higher education.* Stylus.

Komives, S. R., & Woodard, D. Jr. (Eds.). (2003). *Student services: A handbook for the profession* (4th ed.). Jossey-Bass.

Kouzes, J. M., & Posner, B. Z. (1995). *The leadership challenge.* Jossey-Bass.

Lattuca, L. R., & Stark, J. S. (2009). *Shaping the college curriculum: Academic plans in context.* Jossey-Bass.

Leedy, P. D., & Ormrod, J. E. (2010). *Practical research: Planning and design* (9th ed.). Pearson.

Lewis, C., & Moje, E. B. (2003). Sociocultural perspectives meet critical theories: Producing knowledge through multiple frameworks. *International Journal of Learning, 10,* 1979–1995.

Li, W., & Scullion, H. (2010). Developing the local competence of expatriate managers for emerging markets: A knowledge-based approach. *Journal of World Business, 45,* 190–196.

Lincoln, Y. S., & Guba, E. G. (1985). *Naturalistic inquiry.* SAGE.

McMillan, J. H. (2008). *Educational research: Fundamentals for the consumer* (5th ed.). Pearson.

Merriam, S. B., & Simpson, E. L. (1995). *A guide to research for educators and trainers of adults* (2nd ed.). Krieger.

Miller, A. S. (2000). Going to hell in Asia: The relationship between risk and religion in a cross-cultural setting. *Review of Religious Research, 42*(1), 5–18.

Museus, S. D., & Chang, M. J. (2009). Rising to the challenge of conducting research on Asian Americans in higher education. *New Directions for Institutional Research, 142,* 95–105.

National Commission on Asian American and Pacific Islander Research in Education. (2010, December 20). *Reports & publications.* http://www.nyu.edu/projects/care/docs/2010_CARE_Report.pdf

Northouse, P. G. (2010). *Leadership: Theory and practice* (5th ed.). SAGE.

Parry, K. W. (1998). Grounded theory and social process: A new direction for leadership research. *Leadership Quarterly*, *9*(1), 85–105.

Rhoads, R. A., & Tierney, W. G. (1992). *Cultural leadership in higher education.* National Center on Postsecondary Teaching, Learning, and Assessment.

Rubin, H. J., & Rubin, I. S. (1995). *Qualitative interviewing: The art of hearing data.* SAGE.

Saldana, J. (2009). *The coding manual for qualitative researchers.* SAGE.

Salovey, P., & Mayer, J. D. (1990). Emotional intelligence. *Imagination, Cognition and Personality*, *9*(3), 185–211.

Shank, G. D. (2006). *Qualitative research: A personal skills approach* (2nd ed.). Pearson.

Stogdill, R. M., & Coons, A. E. (1957). *Leader behavior: Its description and measurement.* Ohio State University, Bureau of Business Research.

Suri, R. P. (2011). *Inspiring quotes of Mahatma Gandhi* [Kindle version]. Retrieved from Amazon.com

Teranishi, R. T., Behringer, L. B., Grey, E. A., & Parker, T. L. (2009). Critical race theory and research on Asian Americans and Pacific Islanders in higher education. *New Directions for Institutional Research*, *142*, 57–68.

Uhl-Bien, M. (2006). Relational leadership theory: Exploring the social processes of leadership and organizing. *Leadership Quarterly*, *17*, 654–676.

U.S. Census Bureau. (2004). *Fact sheet for Asian Indian alone or in any combination and U.S. 2004 American community survey.* https://www.census.gov/

U.S. Census Bureau. (2010). Retrieved from https://www.census.gov/

Van Maanen, J. (1988). *Tales of the field: On writing ethnography.* University of Chicago Press.

Varma, R. (2004). Asian Americans: Achievements mask challenges. *Asian Journal of Social Science*, *32*(2), 290–307.

Waugh, W. L. (2003). Issues in university governance: More "professional" and less academic. *The ANNALS of the American Academy of Political and Social Science*, *585*(84), 84–96.

Wertsch, J. V. (1985). *Vyotsky and the social formation of mind.* Harvard University Press.

Yamagata-Noji, A. (2011, July 6). *LEAP/APAHE leadership development program in higher education* [Paper presentation]. Annual Leadership Development Program for Higher Education, Kellogg West Conference Center, Pomona, CA, United States.

Yukl, G. (1989). Managerial leadership: A review of theory and research. *Journal of Management*, *15*(2), 251–289.

Yukl, G. (2010). *Leadership in organizations* (7th ed.). Pearson.

# Chapter 6 Toward the Inclusion of LGBTQ+ Students of Color: A Case Study of Public High Schools in the Midwest

JOANN YONAN

> There is no such thing as a single-issue struggle because we do not live single-issue lives.
>
> —Audre Lorde (BlackPast, 2012)

Students crowd around my room; it is the fifth period, and the juniors are having lunch. They are laughing, teasing, and chatting away just like any other high school adolescents. As I open the door, they rush in, load up their music, and start dancing. These students come to my room almost every day because they do not feel comfortable in the school lunchroom. As the music blares, I remind my students, "Keep the noise down." I know that the discipline office will expect them to be in the lunchroom if the noise gets loud. The students hush down quickly because the lunchroom is one place they want to avoid.

The high school lunchroom should be a welcoming place where students can eat and have downtime with their friends. However, for lesbian, gay, bisexual, transgender, questioning+ (intersex, asexual, pansexual, agender, genderqueer, bigender, gender variant, and pangender) students of color, finding inclusion is an elusive event. According to the 2019 GLSEN (Gay, Lesbian, and Straight Education Network) survey, 94% of the students of color who identify as LGBTQ+ (lesbian, gay, bisexual, transgender, questioning+) have experienced bullying at least once, and 60% have repeatedly been harassed, bullied, or experienced name-calling (Zongrone et al., 2020). Statistics for LGBTQ+ students who are White experience similar percentages of bullying, but they do not experience harassment based on their race, nor are they typically blamed for violations against them (Burdge et al., 2014; Kosciw et al., 2018).

For many LGBTQ+ students of color, having to navigate between race, heterosexism, and genderism daily takes a toll on their physical and psychological well-being (Moradi et al., 2009). Repeatedly experiencing microaggressions manifests in 48% of LGBTQ students of color having regular school absences compared to 21% of White LGBTQ+ students. Without considering trauma, missing school lowers a student's grade point average and raises the dropout rate by 5% to 10% (Zongrone et al., 2020). More concerning is the 21% rate of attempted suicide for LGBQ+ non-transgender and, even worse, a 37–40% rate for students who identify as transgender students (Zongrone et al., 2020).

LGBTQ+ students of color represent the most bullied group of students in American high schools (Diliberti et al., 2019; Pew Research Center, 2013). Bullying is a malicious act, and psychologists believe it is an event that can be a lasting memory, creating future isolation and reduction of self to the point where the bullied no longer allow themselves a voice (Espelage & Swearer, 2008; Farrington & Baldry, 2010; Ryan, 2010; Ryan et al., 2010). Adolescence is the time when self-esteem, sense of identity, and voice are constructed. That is why having a supportive and inclusive environment is crucial for LGBTQ+ students of color (Kosciw et al., 2020). The World Health Organization (WHO, 2017) states that an individual's environment influences the changes taking place during adolescence and those changes will affect that person for a lifetime. For LGBTQ+ students of color, this is specifically important because so many students report severe anxiety and depression at an alarmingly high rate (Platt, 2020). For these students, the high school environment is often the framework for creating emotional instability and a future life of low self-esteem and confidence, two qualities necessary for success in adulthood.

All high school students feel insecure and vulnerable at some time during their adolescence; however, LBGTQ+ students are the most vulnerable demographic that struggles to survive these formative years. Kosciw et al. (2020) identify this segment of American high school students as representing the highest percentage of bullying and attempted suicides. Moreover, even less is known about the experiences of LGBTQ+ students in the context of race because these students face more than one disenfranchisement (Toomey et al., 2017). LGBTQ+ students of color encounter more marginalizing experiences associated with sexual and gender identities along with race and ethnic background, exposing them to heightened institutional and interpersonal racism, heterosexism, and transphobia. Even worse, they are exposed to violence and sexual abuse at a time when they are extremely fragile and searching for their place in the world (Kosciw et al., 2018).

Looking at these severe statistics, one must wonder what public schools are doing to address our LGBTQ+ population. According to Kosciw et al. (2018), a GSA (Gay-Straight Alliance) creating anti-bullying policies and allowing for safe spaces keeps students safer in school, but is this enough? Cleary (2018) identifies the importance of educators creating an environment of inclusion: "Educators often suspect that the social world of adolescents is beyond their reach and out of their control, but that's not really so; teachers have leverage because they set the tone for their schools that indirectly shape their students' future" (p. 1).

The research of Robinson and Espelage (2011) suggests that educators are the most influential in making students feel included by finding correlations between educators and the messages received from adults, peers, and themselves. According to Robinson and Espelage (2011), teachers are the key message shapers who build student inclusion. The GSLEN surveys present statistics for the last seven years that show that establishing a gay-straight organization in school provides opportunities for education and advocacy that reduces harassment and bullying by students' non-LGBTQ+ counterparts (Kosciw et al., 2020). Further, Latinx lesbian and homosexual students experience a 20% reduction in harassment while African Americans experience a 12% reduction; however, for bisexual students of color, this result is much less, with a 7% reduction in cases. For the transgender community of color, GSA produced little change in harassment, bullying, and discriminatory discipline, indicating that this sector of LGBTQ+ is not participating or it has no impact on this demographic of students.

LGBTQ+ students of color are falling behind their peers academically. They have lower GPAs (grade point averages) and are twice as likely not to attend school regularly (Kosciw et al., 2020). Further, this sector of students often experiences poverty, homelessness, depression, and lack of proper medical care (Gates, 2017; Goldstein, 2016). Ten years into the future, LGBTQ+ adults of color will be the majority, representing an estimated 60% of the LGBTQ+ population or 10 million people. (American Psychological Association [APA], 2019). As a result, our education institutions must address this fragile sector of America, or 10 million US adults could continue to struggle with the same issues they experienced as adolescents. (APA, 2019). That is why it is imperative for educators to address LGBTQ+ issues for students of color so they can build a bridge of equity for all students.

Building classroom communities for LGBTQ+ students of color improves attendance, academic grades, and graduation rates (Marx & Kettrey, 2016). This is particularly true for students with multiply marginalizing experiences, such as, students of color who have alternative sexual identities. Several studies (e.g., Kosciw et al., 2020; Kosciw et al., 2018; Marx & Kettrey, 2016) claim schools that show support for LGBTQ+ students through active LGBTQ+ organizations, and support an anti-bullying policy see a greater retention of students who graduate and go on to attend college. In addition, students who report feeling included have fewer incidents of bullying and reports of suicidal thoughts (Kosciw et al., 2018; Marx & Kettrey, 2016). According to Parent et al. (2013), changes in the school environment through SAGA (Straight and Gay Alliance) groups and anti-bullying policies mainly address LGBTQ+ White, middle-class students. It appears from the Zongrone et al. (2020) and the African American Trevor Report (Price-Feeney, 2020) that classroom curriculum and norms provide more inclusive support. The question becomes, how can norms, policy, and curriculum create inclusion and belonging for LGBTQ+ students who experience multiple societal marginalization within society?

### *Positionality Statement*

I embarked on this journey of researching the experiences of LGBTQ+ high school students of color after taking a class in epistemology and discovering the concept of Intersectionality. Intersectionality provided answers to the confusion I have felt for much of my life about why I felt unaccepted. Having an immigrant background, being ADD, and being a female in STEM does not always fit with the status quo. Crenshaw's (2017) theory of intersectionality explains that societies have multiple points of oppression that exist in American society. Intersectionality relates to everyone who experiences discrimination and exclusion, and being a teacher, I realized that extended societal oppression, particularly seen in marginalized individuals, is trauma.

As a high school teacher, I always reflect upon my students' social, emotional, and mental well-being, particularly those who are being pushed out by the system. Kosciw (2020) surveyed the LGBTQ+ student population, resulting in LGBTQ+ students of color reporting the highest levels of ostracization by other students and faculty. Russel and Horn (2017) reviewed juvenile prison demographics and found that LGBTQ+ students of color are experiencing the school-to-prison pipeline at a much higher rate than other demographics of students. Thinking back over the years of teaching LGBTQ+ students of color, I am heartbroken imagining their struggles weighing on their future success. At the first read, I questioned Russel and Horns' findings, and then I discovered that Kosciw et al. (2020) also collected data showing that LGBTQ+ students of color experience regular school discipline, disparaging grades, lengthy periods of isolation and do not finish high school.

The purpose of this qualitative case study was to explore the teacher practices intended to offset oppressive behavior and build classroom inclusion for LGBTQ+ urban high school students of color. The underlying narratives need to be heard, and the K-12 public system needs to know of the practices that pioneering teachers have implemented to offset the oppression these students experience. The following research questions guided this study:

1. What are the issues that LGBTQ+ students of color experience when attempting to find inclusion within an urban high school context?
2. What teacher practices in the classroom can remove barriers to inclusion for LGBTQ+ students of color?
3. How can the addition of LGBTQ+ students of color into the curriculum play a role, if any, in building inclusion for these students?

Throughout this chapter, I utilized the following terminology and definitions to provide a shared common understanding:

- *Asexual*: A person who does not experience sexual attraction, but may experience other forms of attraction (e.g., intellectual, emotional) (Human Rights Campaign, 2018).
- *Bisexual*: This term originally meant attraction to both males and females. However, since the 1990s, according to the LGBT network, bisexuality is currently defined as a person who likes all types of sexual identities and the term is no longer restricted to the ideal of just male and female (LGBT Network, 2021).
- *Binary*: The societal categorization of people as male or female only (Human Rights Campaign, 2018).
- *Gender Non-conforming*: A term created in 1991 by Lisa Diamond, Susan Bonner, and Janna Dickenson describing how one's self-concept deviates from societal norms of masculine or feminine (Merriam-Webster, n.d.).
- *Queer*: An umbrella term that was a derogatory term during the 1940s and 1950s meant to describe a sexual orientation, gender identity, or gender expression that does not conform to dominant societal norms. The LGBT community now uses it as a neutral or positive term to mean people who have sexual orientations the exist in and out of the sexual binary (Human Rights Campaign, 2018).

- *Questioning*: A person who is in the process of understanding and exploring what their sexual orientation and/or gender identity and gender expression might be (Human Rights Campaign, 2018).
- *Transgender*: A person whose gender identity and/or expression are not aligned with the gender they were assigned at birth. "Transgender," in the late 1990s, became an umbrella term under the LGBTQ community to encompass many identities related to gender nonconformity (Human Rights Campaign, 2018).
- *Cis-gender:* A person whose gender identity and expression are aligned with the gender they were assigned at birth and is a term created by German sexologist Volkmar Sigusch in 1998 (McIntyre, 2021).
- *Heteronormative*: A person who identifies as their sex at birth and is emotionally and/or physically attracted to members of the opposite gender. This term was coined by Warner (1999) in *The Trouble with Normal*, a book that discusses what societies expect, demand, and allow when they consider relations between men and women to be the only normal sexual orientations.
- *Intersex*: An umbrella term used to describe a variety of conditions in which a person is born with reproductive and/or sexual anatomy that does not seem to fit the medical definitions of female or male (Planned Parenthood, 2021).

## *Theoretical Lens and Research Design*

This exploratory study examined how high school students experience school from two intersecting points of oppression and how teacher practices addressed race and preferred identity to build inclusion for these students. Critical race theory (CRT), intersectionality, and queer theory shaped this study's purpose and research questions. CRT allows for a critique of societal and political norms. Queer theory disputes sexuality and gender expression occurring at birth; instead, it views sexual identity as fluid and changing throughout one's life (Wiggin & Watson, 2016). Queer theory refutes the assignment of gender and sexuality as standardizing humanness for the purpose of politicizing sexuality through the defining of alternative identities as divisive and disruptive to respectability (Plummer, 2004). Policing behavior benefits those who view society as harming those who want to embrace their identity. Queer theory embraces one's right to sexual ambiguity, stating that binary norms have no physiological or emotional position other than to control personal expression resulting in psychological and emotional trauma (Browne & Nash, 2014).

According to Walton and Cohen (2007), belongingness uncertainty depletes the energy children need to succeed in school. According to the theory of Intersectionality, identification with a certain group can set you up for lack of social bonds or equitable support and assistance because you do not conform to societal norms (Crenshaw, 2013). Walton and Cohen (2007) state that American LGBTQ youth are emotionally taxed and, therefore, lack the energy necessary for motivation and achievement in school. Within the framework of intersectionality, LGBTQ+ people of color have fewer ties, which thwarts their intellectual influence and voice. According to Cho et al. (2013), elements of power are embedded in language, disciplinary action, economics, and other signs. Intersectionality addresses those whose oppressive elements of power. According to GLSEN, identities considered subversive by Butler, such as body dysmorphia, receive the least amount of support from school staff, the highest level of harassment from fellow students, and increased disciplinary action in comparison to the cis-gendered identities of their counterparts.

Critical race theory and the framework of intersectionality disrupt the system that perpetuates race discrimination in America. CRT's five tenets uproot the American white social narrative of "meritocracy" that one can achieve by merits alone. CRT addresses the second-class citizenship of color that permeates our institutional system, such as inequitable education and justice for people of color. CRT is an ongoing ever, ever-evolving retort that challenges the status quo by questioning who is benefiting from America's social construct of color. CRT recognizes society's judgment of others based on skin color versus merits alone and the necessity of unseating the historical narratives to achieve equity for all.

Viewing education through the lens of CRT, intersectionality, and queer theory provide explanations for the achievement gap, the school-to-prison pipeline, and the dropout rate for students of color. Statistics show that transgender students of color are the most disciplined and the highest demographic in prison. Both theories support the necessity of hearing the counter story and the recognition that neither race, which is a social construct, nor sexual preference, which is an identity and not a subversive behavior, needs to be controlled. This qualitative study looks into the classrooms of teachers who alter the social narrative and the techniques they employ to achieve this change.

## *Case Study*

A qualitative case study was used to provide an in-depth evaluation of teachers' praxis at one Midwestern urban high school known for building inclusion for their LGBTQ+ students of color. This study is considered exploratory because of the limited available data and the focus on finding practical solutions. Qualitative research studies individuals in their natural settings and attempts to make sense of or interpret phenomena in relationship to the meanings (Denzin & Lincoln, 2008). In this study, I explored how teachers within their natural school settings and their typical daily engagements influenced the student social environment. Therefore, marginalized students are given a place within the classroom. By utilizing the qualitative research approach, I looked below the surface and focused on what, how, and why questions related to the lived experiences of those involved in this study (Stake, 2010). Particularly, this research landed itself on the premises of an exploratory, intrinsic, and descriptive study (Creswell & Poth, 2018) as the most suitable design to explore the ways in which teachers build inclusion for LGBTQ+ students of color.

The site for this study was a Midwestern urban public high school. The participants were teachers with experience working with students of color who are LGBTQ+. The high school was selected because it was convenient and easy to access, making interview scheduling less burdensome. The participants were found by emailing all the teachers at one high school, explaining my research study, and asking if they would like to participate. From the teachers who responded, participants were sent a letter of consent if they had been teaching for more than ten years of service and if they had taught and are currently teaching LGBTQ+ students of color. I recruited a total of eight participants.

I employed several sources of data for this study: semi-structured interviews, field notes, documents, and artifacts. The utilization of multiple sources ensures data triangulation. Triangulation is the collection of data from at least three different sources to give greater breadth to the data and add validity to the study's accuracy (Saldaña & Omasta, 2018). The application of triangulation, or multiple data sources, can enhance the validation of the study findings. The purpose of the interviews was to evoke rich and thick descriptions of an observed episode, linkage, or explanation (Saldaña & Omasta, 2018). According to Saldaña & Omasta (2018), the researcher can use several methods from a predetermined list of questions and suggested topics for discussion or allow the interview to evolve based on the questions and responses of the participants. All the interviews were audio-recorded, transcribed, and sent to participants for accuracy verification.

For further verification, I kept a spiral notebook of self-reflective notes that I used during the interviews, and I wrote in the margins of the transcribed interviews to remember some of the side information and observations to mark down. These notes were used to build the rich and in-depth information I needed to remember about each interviewee. I also collected documents to show visual representation of the resources used by participants. The resources were examples of lessons and activities participants used to address and discuss racism and sexual identity in the classroom.

### *Data Analysis*

Qualitative data analysis covers many approaches and methods to provide consistency and accountability of findings. This is why Creswell and Poth (2018) recommend following a process to provide a chain of evidence in case-study analysis that creates credibility for the results. The first step in my process was transcribing, cataloging, and sorting the data into different ways to identify patterns and points of intersection. My second step was using the interview questions to determine potential category themes. My third step was separating the data by person and by question. My fourth step was cutting the data into individual quotes and separating these by hand. Finally, I ran a word analysis to evaluate word choice to ensure I had separated the quotes and information into the correct themes. Studying the data and finding a general sense of the information, even writing down observations, or recording general thoughts. This coding method assisted me in summarizing, synthesizing, linking, and interpreting the data.

## ***Validation Criteria and Ethical Considerations***

Validity of qualitative research is often expressed through trustworthiness, authenticity, and credibility. Credibility refers to the truth of the findings, and dependability is the capacity for the findings to be repeated within the same context. In contrast, transferability demonstrates that the results can be successfully applied to other contexts (Creswell & Poth, 2018). Member checks were used to enhance the construct validity of the research findings (Yin, 2009). In this study, member checks examined their downloaded data, and then when their responses were separated into categories, I sent them to the participants again for approval. Confirmability, which is part of authenticity, shows that the responders shape the findings from the study and are not influenced by the researcher's bias, motivation, or interest (Creswell & Poth, 2018). This was performed through reflexivity and triangulation.

Reflexivity is a safeguard against potential researcher biases (Creswell and Creswell, 2018). Reflexivity is the awareness of the influence that researcher bias has on the topic and the participants who are being studied. Researchers should engage in active self-reflection and analysis of one's own preconceived ideas, assumptions, or biased thoughts precisely because researchers can exert unintentional influence on people or the topic being studied (Yin, 2018). To become aware of my biases, I have kept a spiral notebook of self-reflections focused on exploring my assumptions, emotional reactions, and cultural positions throughout the research process. Triangulation of data also helps in mitigating any researcher bias. For this reason, I used different sources of data such as interviews, written lessons, my journal of personal notes of thoughts, quotes of what I heard, feelings, and my personal metacognition of events, as well as personal and member checks to see if different sources provide similar results.

## *Discussion of the Findings*

Listening to the stories of the eight participants allowed for a deeper understanding of praxis teacher utilize to build space for marginalized students. The teachers dialogue brought home the struggles to belong and the extra effort to succeed that students of color with non-hetronormative sexual identities need to be successful in urban public schools. Extensive analysis of interviews and additional sources of data has resulted in identification of three main themes: (a) "LGBTQ+ Students of Color: Confronting the Issues"; (b) "LGBTQ+ Students of Color: Building Inclusion Beyond Curriculum"; and (c) "Advocating for My LGBTQ+ Students of Color."

The first main theme was the common issues all participants witnessed while teaching LGBTQ+ students of color. The second is the praxis of each participant, which included altering the class environment and incorporating the LGBTQ+ narratives into the curriculum. Finally, all the participants felt that students of color need strong advocates from their teachers to set the tone of inclusion so all students build empathy and compassion for their fellow classmates. Throughout the interviews, participants in this study shared their educational best practices and methods to foster the inclusion and integration of LGBTQ+ students of color into their classroom communities.

### *Confronting the Issues*

The participants admitted barriers that LGBTQ+ students of color experience in their school, which refer to being misidentified, insensitive remarks, teachers referring to them by their deadname, not being out to their family, being blamed because of the color of their skin, and not allowing them to use the bathroom of their choice. Every participant shared their strategy for change and agreed to start with three things. First, they acknowledged the importance of learning students' preferred names and pronouns. Some participants struggled with the guilt of misidentifying students; however, they felt strongly that teachers influence student change. Second, standing up to misidentification and insensitive remarks is paramount. Every participant stressed the importance of students being known by their preferred identity and having the support of at least one teacher to overcome derogatory comments or references to a student's former name. Further, knowing who is "out" to their parents is also important because teachers mentioned having outed students in the past. Third, the participants expressed the need to create classroom norms around how to show respect and speak to each other with respect.

All participants voiced methods of deliberate classroom interactions that build space for LGBTQ+ students of color. The participants emphasized that this requires correctly identifying students while recognizing ethnicity and culture. For instance, Betty, one of the participants, emphasized that having dark skin affects how people treat her. She feels that having pictures and quotes for all races, types of families, and sexualities lets students know she is open-minded and accepting. All participants support a classroom environment that fosters respectful, empathetic, unstructured conversations to create a safe space. Other participants felt that creating inclusive conversations happens when teachers deliberately build questions into the curriculum while maintaining normed boundaries based on respect.

The participants of this study pointed to several examples that illustrate the isolation of LGBTQ+ students of color. For instance, the participants witnessed staff members avoiding preferred names and pronouns, and a few even struggled to allow preferred bathrooms. Others could provide examples of staff members avoiding the LGBTQ+ issue because student family members were unaccepting. One participant even spoke about the uncertainty of how to approach students about their status when class members are uninviting. One participant spoke of teachers avoiding name changes because their parents did not accept their children using alternative names. Another participant discussed how the hue of one's skin color determines if LGBTQ+ students are accepted or ridiculed. The study participants mentioned that points of oppression are individual, and teachers should never assume or stereotype experiences; teachers must work to make their classroom a safe space where everyone is respected. All the participants stated that having different methods and practices to build inclusive classrooms for LGBTQ+ students of color is important because there is no perfect method. Every teacher in this study took time and reflection to find strategies that worked with the students they had at that moment to build environments of respect so that all voices could be heard.

Regarding the first research question, the findings of this study confirm that LGBTQ+ students of color experience a series of issues when navigating the school system, and the feeling of isolation is at the top of the list. The participants reported witnessing the isolation of LGBTQ+ students of color in their school. For example, observing staff members denying students access to the bathroom of their choice. Further, faculty failing to correct students who showed verbal disrespect through name-calling and shaming students based on their sexual identity and color. This confirms what Kosciw et al. (2020) found that gay high school students of color report the highest amount of isolation from students and teachers.

The other most commonly mentioned issue by the participants was that their LGBTQ+ students of color experience overt disrespect through derogatory comments, jokes, and insults that marginalize and isolate them from their classmates, which confirms what Dinkins and Englert (2015) found in their study. Another important component links the issues of isolation and disrespect that often get placed on the LGBTQ+ student for instigating the behaviors, especially if you're a student of color. Dinkins and Englert (2015) say that teachers often find themselves in uncharted territory when it comes to school policies and resources provided for teachers to resolve the unfair treatment of LGBTQ+ students of color in their schools. However, Dinkins and Englert (2015) state that teachers are the best resource for making a profound difference in how others see and treat LGBTQ+ students.

### *Beyond the Curriculum*

Most participants felt that they must build multiple voices and perspectives into daily instruction, therefore exposing students to stories that counter the societal message. Not all participants agreed on how this happens in the classroom. One teacher supported it happening organically and indirectly through reading, writing, and class discussion, while the other two participants supported teaching the information directly. Further, participants in the language arts suggested using character development to bring out voices and articles on discrimination to create awareness and empathy for the struggles experienced by LGBTQ+ people of color. All participants agreed that the classroom curriculum should build-in humanity by including various identities, races, and cultures.

Another practice recommended by the participants was embedding LGBTQ+ and race-related issues in the curriculum. This practice confirms Blackburn's (2015) statement that students must compare their unique perspectives to those of "othered voices" through the curriculum to understand how societal values impact LGBTQ+ students of color. A participant, named Lisa emphasized this in her unit on synthesizing texts. Her unit, structured to counter discrimination around race and sexual identity, helping students to be better informed in discussing these issues. Kumashiro (2019) states that schools should challenge the myths and interpretations students experience outside school by including "othered" voices embedded into their disciplines. One participant mentioned using LGBTQ+ authors where students can compare content and context to recognize different voices and perspectives.

The participants differed in how they embedded the intersection of race and sexual identity into the curriculum based on developmental level. Some participants worked with older high school students and recommended that students discover the counter story through articles, books, and short stories written in the voice of an LGBTQ+ person of color. In contrast, others felt that some students need direct lessons around LGBTQ+ issues. One participant, a gay cis-gender science teacher, felt that students need to understand how genetic inheritance and preferred identity differ. All the participants felt that the LGBTQ+ community should be interjected into the curriculum around prior background and knowledge of the students in the room.

Beyond curriculum changes, participants stated that students need open and honest discussions between teachers and students. All the participants expressed that teachers need to develop open-ended questions that build conversations around race and the LGBTQ+ community. The participants felt that teacher-student communication is vital in creating critical open-ended questions and points of empathy and understanding with their peers. Participants who teach science said that including experiences that open their world makes them realize that life is not a monolithic event. Several participants maintained that honest questions about the gay community should be addressed immediately because that is where responses have the most impact. For example, in the story of Gordo, students had to discover the character from the context of the book. Teachers in this study emphasized that pressing students with critical questions to reveal the main character's identity created deeper and more thoughtful discussions.

Teachers who work with students stated that students talk together better when student-to-student discussions happen daily. She believes that discussions model how students should talk to each other, primarily how to embrace everyone's differences positively and empathetically. One participant insisted that it is the student-to-student discussions that make the difference. This participant believes that personalized voices build insight into individual and alternative perspectives that allow space for acceptance for LGBTQ+ students of color. All participants agreed that student-to-student discussion is the best method for building community inclusion. Every participant stated that unstructured peer conversations are better when students regularly discuss issues among themselves. At this level of interaction, students can safely and openly talk to each other. Adding in texts provides additional information about LGBTQ+ perspectives and creates more information for students to look through to find similarities with their peers.

Every participant in this study agreed that classrooms, where discussions around color and sexual identity happen teach students to be inclusive. Furthermore, they felt that organic and deliberate discussions are more impactful, as one participant stated, "Wonderings are understood best when addressed as they arise." Still, every participant shared the need for deliberate ideas to be inserted into the discussion. Overall, classrooms need practices and methods that build space for LGBTQ+ students of color by using proper pronouns, norming a classroom around respect, advocating for LGBTQ+ students of color, encouraging daily discussions among students, and incorporating gay voices and subjects of race through articles, readings, or teacher-led discussions.

Going beyond the curriculum, LGBTQ+ students of color often face challenges when navigating a high school system that may not be friendly or inclusionary. The findings of this study uncovered several issues ranging from teachers' hesitancy to use the students' preferred names and pronouns to the hidden prejudices on the part of their peers or the instances of overt disrespect through derogatory comments, jokes, and insults that marginalize and isolate them from their classmates. Most of the participants felt that having student-to-student daily discussions is important for building positive classroom rapport with their classmates.

This study supports Blackburn (2015), who demonstrated that LGBTQ+ students of color need their identities seen and recognized by their teachers and classmates for inclusion. The participants in this study stated that they altered their teaching methods by recognizing and building in situations where students felt empathy and compassion for students of color who are different because they have struggled with their LGBTQ+ identity. The teachers who participated in this study also created opportunities for student-to-student unstructured discussions where alternative voices could be heard; therefore, they are showing value and importance for marginalized students' voices so they would be heard.

One of the main findings of this study demonstrates the participants' struggle to build inclusion of LGBTQ+ students of color in their classroom settings and beyond. This finding confirms what Lee and Smith (2023) identify as the struggle to build inclusion in public schools when the classroom does not make room for alternative voices. The participants of this study felt that teachers need to daily build a place for students who have marginalized identities. The participants all felt that this comes from the consistent use of proper pronouns and preferred names. One of the inclusive practices that all participants created was an environment of respect through daily class discussions. In these discussions, the students practice sharing, with their tablemates or elbow partners, opinions about a class topic, a current event, or a puzzling situation. The participants mentioned that students need to know proper boundaries in classroom discussions by stating that students must be honest and truthful about their opinions, they must take turns sharing and listening, and when they disagree they place the disagreement on opinion but not the person. Stulberg's (2017) study on respecting and hearing alternative voices claimed that pushback must happen for LGBTQ+ students of color to gain the self-esteem and confidence to realize their authentic selves. The participants of this study stated that they practiced daily intra-student dialogue to deliberately teach students to interact in a respectful, inclusive classroom community.

Blackburn (2015) found that LGBTQ+ students of color need their identities seen and recognized by their teachers to feel part of the classroom. Every student wants recognition and support. That is why the participants stated that instructors confidently and regularly use a student's proper identity. Most participants stated that they do this immediately to ensure they determine student identities from a student survey or other methods. Then participants stated how important it is to correctly identify students properly within the first week. Teachers who misidentify students silently permit others to misidentify them (Kosciw, 2020; Delgado & Stefanic, 2012). The participants stated that students appreciate it when teachers work hard to properly name and identify students.

Next, participants believe in creating an environment of respect by teaching students how to correctly address their classmates and to practice daily class discussions, whereby students practice sharing with their tablemates or elbow partners. How the participants chose to do this differed, but the norms they stated that having in place was important to ensure respect remains consistent. Furthermore, the participants mentioned that students need to know proper boundaries in classroom discussions, stating that students must be honest and truthful about their opinions and that students must take turns sharing and listening so every student is heard. The participants confirmed that norming student-to-student discussion was where students build empathy for each other because they listened and reflected on what others said versus just debating, which contributes to Stulberg's (2017) study on respecting and hearing alternative voices as respectful pushback must happen in order for LGBTQ+ students of color to gain the self-esteem and confidence to stand up for their authentic selves. The participants of this study stated that they practiced daily intra-student dialogue with their students to deliberately teach how to interact in a respectful, inclusive classroom community.

The participants singled out several such practices regarding curricular practices. Classroom dialogue was the number-one method used to build inclusion for queer students of color, echoing the findings of Wiggin and Watson (2016), who found that teachers empower the voices of marginalized students with dialogue. Students cannot effectively build inclusion without knowing how to have respectful, structured dialogue. One of the participants in this study said that deliberate classroom conversations break down cliques and eliminate gossip, bringing the classroom into a more cohesive unit. All the participants felt that student-to-student conversations should be practiced daily so that every student feels heard and included.

Yet another method recommended by the participants was embedding LGBTQ+ and race-related issues into the curriculum. According to Blackburn (2015), students need to compare their unique perspectives to those of "othered voices" through the curriculum to truly understand how societal values impact marginalized people. The participants also emphasized that some direct instruction should be included in lessons and units so students are better informed about what it means to be LGBTQ+. Finally, the participants mentioned that putting students into the content and context enhances learning about the different voices and perspectives in the context of LGBTQ+ students of color.

### *Advocating for LGBTQ+ Students of Color*

The importance of teachers' advocacy for these students can hardly be overestimated. Sewell (2019) says LGBTQ+ students of color suffer severe isolation in high schools because teachers do not consistently stand up for them. Gay students of color often choose their race over their sexual identity, particularly if they do not feel supported by the school (Sewell, 2019). Advocacy can be a daily practice in peer-to-peer discussions in which teachers deliberately include opportunities for honest, respectful discussions about marginalized students' experiences. Although the participants of this study limited their advocacy to classroom practices, they all agreed it is imperative to take advocacy beyond the school environment to the outside world that often mutes the voices of marginalized groups.

Participants deemed as particularly important is to stand up for any witnessed injustice. Students who are misidentified, insulted, or rejected in the classroom based on their race or sexual identity must be corrected immediately. The participants felt this must happen consistently and immediately to be effective. The findings of this study confirm that all involved believed that supportive teachers understand the importance of standing up for students' preferred pronouns and names (Sewell, 2019). Instructors must confidently take pride in correcting any person, staff, admin, or student, who mislabels any person within their school community (Sewell, 2019). Educators play a crucial role in building positive self-esteem and confidence in a student's identity, which is extremely important for LGBTQ+ students of color who typically are suffering.

The participants admitted that many staff members felt conflicted when using preferred names and pronouns because they did not want to draw attention to students with alternative identities, especially in the case of transgender students. However, all participants felt that many of their LGBTQ+ students of color were lonely and isolated at their school because their identity was not authentically known. The participants stressed that their best practices arose because they wanted their students to choose their authentic identity and to create an inclusive curriculum and environment where all members of the classroom address every student with respect for their identity. Every participant in this study mentioned how some teachers struggle to adopt the practice, which echoes what Delgado and Stefanic (2012) mentioned about the fear of pushing up against societal values or accepted "norms" are oppressive causing many people to remain silent. The participants were adamant about the importance of advocating for LGBTQ+ students of color.

The participants stated that high school students grow socially by discovering new ways to see the world other than their own perspective. Ashcroft (2012) found there is no better place than safe classrooms for vastly different students to exchange ideas, ask questions, and hear how "othered" students live and think about life, which is what the findings of this study confirm. Teacher-facilitated dialogue builds acceptance of every student by giving them space for a voice through the telling of their story. These statements are supported by the findings of Blackburn's (2015) study that confirmed the importance of fostering daily student-to-student conversations. In Brian's words, "Having real conversations between students about sexual orientation and/or color will change the environment from institutional to community because now everyone is learning to understand each other's perspective." All the participants supported student-to-student conversations as the place where real discussion and understanding occur.

The participants of this study asserted that building in marginalized voices takes practice and intentionality on the part of the teacher. Most participants agreed on how important daily discussion is to open students' minds to different lived experiences. One participant even stated that LGBTQ+ students of color have lived experiences that most high school students do not understand. As students explore other experiences outside their own, they build a base to honestly and authentically connect to the experiences of LGBTQ+ students of color, which may cause them to be less judgmental (Collins, 2019). Many participants shared how everyone's life is so unique that they may not see that LGBTQ+ students of color suffer from many points of oppression. That is why all participants felt that regular student-to-student conversations unmask and expose moments of oppression so that they are seen and discussed.

This study underscores the importance of always standing up for your students. Every participant in this study felt that we need to be real about our students lives and to reflect on how the societal messages can be crippling to students who are not fitting into the cookie cutter method of thinking. Just as the theories of this study require a call to action, the participants felt that instructors need to be the leaders in the classroom by standing up for every child's chosen identity, adding in stories and messages that are not often heard, and allowing space for students themselves to share their realities so that everyone sees the multidimensional aspect of humans and how they live.

This study gave space to instructors who work to underscore the importance of advocacy for LGBTQ+ students of color by teachers and leaders. The teachers who were the participants expressed their dedication to advocating for all their students, particularly LGBTQ+ students of color, recognizing not just the importance but, more so, the urgency of the cause. They all agreed on the need to deliberately put certain practices and methods into place to create space for LGBTQ+ students of color. The participants' expression of advocacy supports Crenshaw's (2002) call for educators to be creative in overcoming the system. Similarly, Lee (2023) appeals to teachers as activists who create space for empathy and community so that all students can be seen and heard.

## *Conclusions*

All in all, the findings of this study confirm that students need honest conversations about LGBTQ+ and race to create inclusive discourse, which supports the conclusions of several studies by Ashcroft (2012), Blackburn (2015), and Sewell (2019), who stated that students who stand in the instruction of marginalized voices have a greater appreciation and richer understanding of how society misrepresents their humanity. The participants of this study expressed that students must stand in the context of many perspectives and lives through daily student-to-student conversations supported by practiced norms of respect. Kumashiro states in his 2019 study that schools must challenge the myths and interpretations students experience outside school through the inclusion of "othered" voices embedded into the curriculum. Clearly, and as the findings of this study confirm, students need to hear and ask hard questions about race and sexual orientation because the LGBTQ+ story has many perspectives, and everyone's story is unique. Finally, the participants of this study asserted that embedding the content of alternative lifestyles into the school curriculum humanizes LGBTQ+ communities and builds empathy for those historically marginalized by the system.

## *Recommendations for Educational Professionals*

First and foremost, all educational professionals should be more aware of the vulnerability of LGBTQ+ students of color. The issue of sexual identity remains highly debatable in U.S. politics, mass media, and the broader public. It is a sensitive issue, especially when educating K-12 students. LGBTQ+ students of color have the highest rate of homelessness, suicidal ideation, and depression among high school students. Policymakers need to be more determined to reinforce legislation requiring schools to create policies that allow students to use their bathroom of choice and require teachers and staff to recognize students' preferred names and pronouns. I believe if the school does not support these students, then it sets up the most vulnerable students for a life of drug addiction, poverty, and possible imprisonment (Kosciw, 2020).

School leaders and teachers should advocate more fiercely for a curriculum that includes different cultural, ethnic, and sexual identities. School principals should make professional development sessions that focus on sexual identity mandatory. School leaders should instruct teachers to regularly call out students who misidentify or demean another student because of their identity. There should be a disciplinary school policy for students who do not want to address other humans respectfully and with kindness and respect. I believe if school leaders make space for their LGBTQ+ students of color, then it might create healthier students who understand other types of students better.

Teachers should make more effort to create an inclusive curriculum that does not leave out LGBTQ+ students of color. Teachers need to be deliberate about what students learn and what topics are discussed. Teachers must create space for students to respectfully and truthfully discuss the issues that LGBTQ+ students of color face. Best practices can include having regular classroom discussions among students as peers who learn from and about each other, including their sexual identities. Students should learn about the experiences of people who are different from them, particularly about the histories of people historically discriminated against in the United States.

Pre-service educational programs in higher education should emphasize the importance of identity for the LGBTQ+ community. Pre-service teacher educators should be better prepared to teach students who represent diverse cultural, racial, ethnic, gender, sexual orientation, or immigrant groups who have made enormous contributions to the United States. Since the LGBTQ+ community of color remains a minority group within the dominant discourse of heterosexuality, providing more space for the voices representing this group in teacher education curricula can make classrooms more inclusive. Finally, the more diverse and authentic voices are included in the professional and personal discourses, the more humane they become.

## References

American Psychological Association. (2019). *Lesbian, gay, bisexual, and transgender persons & socioeconomic status.* https://www.apa.org/pi/ses/resources/publications/lgbt

Ashcroft, C. (2012). Literacy and sexuality: What's the connection? *Journal of Adolescent & Adult Literacy, 52*(7), 636–686. https://doi.org/10.1598/JAAL.52.7.9

Blackburn, M. V. (2015). *Interrupting hate: Homophobia in schools and what literacy can do about it.* Teachers College Press.

BlackPast, B. (1982/2012, August 12). *Audi Lorde, "Learning from the 60's."* BlackPast.org. https://www.blackpast.org/african-american-history/1982-audre-lorde-learning-60s/

Browne, K., & Nash, C. J. (2014). Resisting LGBT rights where "we have won": Canada and Great Britain. *Journal of Human Rights, 13*, 322–336. https://doi.org/10.1080/14754835.2014.923754

Burdge, H., Licona, A. C., & Hyemingway, Z. T. (2014). LGBTQ youth of color: Discipline disparities, school push-out, and the school-to-prison pipeline. *Gay-Straight Alliance Network and Crossroads Collaborative.* http://doi.org/10.13140/2.1.1362.6568

Cho, S., Crenshaw, K. W., & McCall, K. (2013). Toward a field of intersectionality studies: Theory, applications, and praxis. *Signs, 33*(4), 785–810.

Cleary, J. (2018, October). The number one factor in student success? Relationships with teachers. *Learning Science International.* https://www.learningsciences.com/blog/number-1-factor/

Collins, P. A. (2019). *Intersectionality: As a critical social theory.* Duke University Press.

Crenshaw, K. W. (2017). *On intersectionality: Essential writings.* The New Press.

Creswell, J. W., & Poth, C. N. (2018). *Qualitative inquiry & research design: Choosing among five approaches* (4th ed.). SAGE Publication.

Delgado, R., & Stefancic, J. (2012). *Critical race theory: An introduction* (2nd ed.). New York University Press.

Denzin, N. K., & Lincoln, Y. S. (2008). The discipline and practice of qualitative research. In *Strategies of qualitative inquiry* (3rd ed., pp. 1–43). Sage Journal.

Diliberti, M., Jackson, M., Correa, S., & Padgett, Z. (2019, July). *Crime, violence, discipline, and safety in U.S. public schools: Findings from the school survey on crime and safety: 2017–18* (NCES 2019-061). U.S. Department of Education. National Center for Education Statistics.

Dinkins, E., & Englert, P. (2015). LGBTQ literature in middle school classrooms: Possibilities for challenging heteronormative environments. *Sex Education, 15*(4), 392–405.

Espelage, D. L., & Swearer, S. A. (2008). Addressing research gaps in the intersection between homophobia and bullying. *School Psychology Review, 37*(2), 155–159.

Farrington, D., & Baldry A. (2010). Individual risk factors for school bullying. *Journal of Aggression, Conflict and Peace Research, 2*(1), 4–16. https://doi.org/10.5042/jacpr.2010.0001

Gates, G. J. (2017). LGBT data collection amid social and demographic shifts of the US LGBT community. *American Journal of Public Health, 107*(8), 1220–1222. https://ajph.aphapublications.org/doi/full/10.2105/AJPH.2017.303927

Goldstein, T. (2016). Border crossing in the classroom through performed ethnography. *Perspectives on Urban Education, 13*(1), 4–19. https://files.eric.ed.gov/fulltext/EJ1103885.pdf

Human Rights Campaign. (2018). *Glossary of terms.* https://www.hrc.org/resources/glossary-of-terms

Kosciw, J. G., Clark, C. M., Truong, N. L., & Zongrone, A. D. (2020). *The 2019 National School Climate Survey: The experiences of lesbian, gay, bisexual, and transgender youth in our nation's schools.* GLSEN. https://eric.ed.gov/fulltest/ED535177.pdf

Kosciw, J. G., Greytak, E. A., Zongrone, A. D., Clark, C. M., & Truong, N. L. (2018). *The 2017 School Climate Survey: The experiences of lesbian, gay, bisexual, and transgender youth in our nation's schools.* GLSEN.

Kumashiro, K. K. (2000). Toward a theory of anti-oppressive education. *Review of Educational Research,* 70(1), 25–53.

LGBT Network. (2021). https://lgbtnetwork.org/content/2017-impact-statement

Lee, A. F., & Smith, G. D. (2023). Where is the love, y'all? Punk pedagogy in high school choir. *Research in Education.* https://doi.org/10.1177/00345237231152605

Marx, R. A., & Kettrey, H. (2016). Gay-straight alliances are associated with lower levels of school-based victimization of LGBTQ+ youth; A systemic review and meta-analysis. *Journal of Youth and Adolescence, 45*(7), 1269–1282. https://doi.org/10.1007/s10964-016-0501-7

McIntyre, J. (2021). *Explainer: What does it mean to be "cisgender"?* The Conversation. https://theconversation.com/explainer-what-does-it-mean-to-be-cisgender-103159

Merriam-Webster. (n.d.). Gender non-conforming. In *Merriam-Webster.com dictionary.* Retrieved June 1, 2021, from https://merriam-webster.com/dictionary/gender%20nonconforming

Moradi, B., Mohr, J. J., Worthington, R. L., & Fassinger, R. E. (2009). Counseling psychology research on sexual (orientation) minority issues: Conceptual and methodological challenges and opportunities. *Journal of Counseling Psychology, 56*(1), 5–22. (EJ827086). ERIC. https://eric.ed.gov/?id=EJ827068

Parent, M. C., DeBlaere, C., & Moradi, B. (2013). Approaches to research in intersectionality: Perspectives on gender, LGBT, and racial/ethnic identities. *Sex Roles, 68,* 639–645.

PEW Research Center. (2013, June 13). A survey of LGBT Americans. *Social and Demographic Trends.* https://www.pewsocialtrends.org/2013/06/13/a-survey-of-lgbt-americans

Planned Parenthood. (2021). *What's intersex?* https://www.plannedparenthood.org/learn/gender-identity/sex-gender-identity/whats-intersex

Platt, L. C. (2020). The presenting concerns of transgender and gender nonconforming clients at university counseling centers. *The Counseling Psychologist, 48*(3), 407–431. https://doi.org/10.1177/0011000019898680

Plummer, K. (2004). Queers, bodies and postmodern sexualities: A note on revisiting the "sexual" in symbolic interactionism. *Qualitative Sociology, 26*(4), 515–530.

Price-Feeney, N., Green, A. E., & Dorison, S. (2020, October 6). *All Black lives matter: Mental health of black LGBTQ youth.* The Trevor Project. https://thetrevorproject.org/2020/10/06/all-black-lives-matter-mental-health-of-black-lgbtq-youth/

Robinson, J. P., & Espelage, D. L. (2011). Inequities in educational and psychological outcomes between LGBTQ and straight students in middle and high school. *Educational Researcher, 40,* 315–330.

Russell, S. T., & Horn, S. S. (2017). Sexual orientation, gender identity, and school: Learning from the past, envisioning the future. In S. T. Russell & S. S. Horn (Eds.), *Sexual orientation, gender identity, and schooling: The nexus of research, practice, and policy* (pp. 377–389). Oxford University Press.

Ryan, C. (2010). Engaging families to support lesbian, gay, bisexual, and transgender youth: The family acceptance project. *The Prevention Researcher, 17*(4), 11–13.

Ryan, C., Russell, S. T., Huebner, D., Diaz, R., & Sanchez, J. (2010). Family acceptance in adolescence and the health of LGBT young adults. *Journal of Child and Adolescent Psychiatric Nursing, 23*(4), 205–213. https://doi.org/10.1111/j.1744-6171.2010.00246.x

Saldaña, J., & Omasta, M. (2018). *Qualitative research: Analyzing life.* SAGE Publications.

Sewell, J. P. (2019). Being black, male, gay and gifted. *Journal of African American Males in Education, 10*(1), 39–57.

Stake, R. E. (2010). *Qualitative research: Studying how things work.* Guilford Press.

Stulberg, L. M. (2017). *LGBTQ social movements*. Polity Press.

Toomey, R. B., Huynh, V. H., Jones, S. K., Lee, S., & Revels-Macalinao, M. (2017). Sexual minority youth of color: A content analysis and critical review of the literature. *Journal of Gay & Lesbian Mental Health*, *21*(1), 3–31. https://doi.org/10.1080/19359705.2016.1217499

Walton, G. M., & Cohen, G. L. (2007). A question of belonging: Race, social fit, and achievement. *Journal of Personality and Social Psychology*, *92*(1), 82–96. https://doi.org/10.1037/0022-3514.92.1.82

Warner, M. (1999). *The trouble with normal: Sex, politics, and the ethics of queer life*. Free Press.

Wiggan, G., & Watson, M. J. (2016). Teaching the whole child: The importance of culturally responsiveness, community engagement, and character development in high achieving African American students. *Urban Review*, *48*, 766–798.

World Health Organization. (2017). *FAQ on health and sexual diversity; An introduction to key concepts*. https://www.who.int/

Yin, R. K. (2018). *Case study research and applications: Design and methods*. SAGE.

Zongrone, A. D., Truong, N. L., & Kosciw, J. G. (2020). *Erasure and resilience: The experiences of LGBTQ students of color*. GLSEN.

# Chapter 7 Navigating Adverse Childhood Experiences for More Effective Learning and Well-Being

Amy Kendryna

## The Reality of Adverse Childhood Experiences

This is a not-so-uncommon true story. Paul arrived at school in a taxi cab. It is late fall and the wind is cold on his bare arms. He didn't eat breakfast and no one said goodbye to him before he left for school. He is wearing the same shirt he wore for the last five days, and probably the same pants, and no socks. As he enters the school Mrs. S warmly says hello and Paul nods to her and goes into the commons for breakfast. He takes his breakfast and the cafeteria lady gives him another breakfast for a snack later that day. Another student makes fun of his shoes and he shrugs it off as the offending student leaves with a teacher. Another teacher asks how he is doing and he says OK. But his face shows he is not OK, he is unhappy and worn out.

He has a lot to be unhappy about, as he has endured many tragedies in his young life. His dad died from gun violence in Chicago and his mom is a drug addict and cannot care for him. She is trying to stay clean so she can have him back in her life, but it is a long, hard road. Paul is 11 years old, and in elementary school; his big six-foot frame hangs over the table as he eats the donut holes and cheese stick. Later that day the class had a local police officer come in to teach Drug and Alcohol Resistance Education (DARE). Paul looks around the room to see who is watching him, as he reaches for the DARE officer's gun, not to grab it, just to get attention from his classmates. He makes a "watch me" face while stretching his arm out and the officer backs up and Paul touches the gun. That evening several students tell their parents what happened and one parent calls the police and files a complaint. The DARE officer called me, the principal, and told me that he didn't even see the student touch the gun. Another police officer was assigned to investigate.

While Paul is waiting in the office he is telling me how much he wants to go back to living with his Aunt. Her house was the fifth DCFS and foster care placement in the last two years. His aunt took him in and then decided it was too difficult to take care of another person in her household. He had only been living with her for five months. She placed him back in the Department of Children and Family Services (DCFS) system. DCFS placed him in a homeless shelter until another foster parent could be found. The homeless shelter is 18 miles away and that is why Paul takes a taxi to school.

### *Adverse Childhood Experiences: Background*

The Adverse Childhood Experiences (ACE) study was developed by two family physicians Anda and Felitti (2004), who first coined the term ACEs. They initially operated a weight loss clinic, where they discovered that many of their patients were using obesity to ensure against unwanted sexual advances. Almost all the non-responders to the weight reduction program Anda and Felitti (2004) assert had a history of sexual abuse. These significant findings led to the development of the ACE study.

Trauma, the researchers emphasize, can include any event that harms the body, self, or spirit and can regard a one-time or continual event. Trauma covers a broad range of hurtful experiences, including physical, sexual, mental, or emotional, and usually regards a combination. Anda and Felitti (2004) identify various common and less common kinds of trauma as ACEs.

The study's findings were profound, showing significant correlations between the number of traumatic childhood experiences and the amount of physical and mental distress experienced as adults (Anda et al., 2004).

Adverse childhood experiences (ACEs) are potentially traumatic events that occur in childhood (0–17 years) that can have negative, lasting effects on health and well-being as children and into adulthood. These experiences range from physical, emotional, or sexual abuse. Also included are aspects of the child's environment that can undermine their sense of safety, stability, and bonding such as growing up in a household with substance misuse, mental health problems, or instability due to parental separation or incarceration of a parent, sibling, or other members of the household (CDC, 2020).

Numerous studies indicate toxic stress and trauma lead to a decrease in the volume of the brain's hippocampus, corpus callosum, cerebellum, and prefrontal cortex. Decreased volume in these areas of the brain impact learning, memory, and executive functioning (Child Welfare Information Gateway, 2018). Trauma is also associated with major psychological disorders such as reactive attachment disorder, disinhibited social engagement disorder, post-traumatic stress disorder, acute stress disorder, adjustment disorders, and intermittent explosive disorder. In the classroom setting, the cognitive and psychological effects of trauma exposure are paired with difficulties in academic and social functioning. Goodman, Miller, and West-Olatunji (2011) determined students with histories of traumatic stress when compared to those without these histories, scored lower on standardized tests and were three times more likely to have an Individualized Education Program (IEP). Cicchetti (2010) found deficits in academic achievement were also prevalent for students with histories of maltreatment. In addition to academic underachievement, children with trauma histories display a wide range of externalizing and internalizing behaviors including irritability, aggression, withdrawal, difficulty with authority, and hyperarousal (National Child Traumatic Stress Network, 2017). These behaviors present themselves as early as preschool and have the potential to continue into adulthood (Shonkoff & Garner, 2012).

Child abuse and neglect are common. At least 1 in 7 children have experienced child abuse and/or neglect in the past year, and this is likely an underestimate. In 2018, nearly 1,770 children died of abuse and neglect in the United States. Children living in poverty experience more abuse and neglect. Rates of child abuse and neglect are five times higher for children in families with low socioeconomic status compared to children in families with higher socioeconomic status.

Children who are abused and neglected may suffer immediate physical injuries such as cuts, bruises, or broken bones, as well as emotional and psychological problems, such as impaired social-emotional skills or anxiety. Chronic abuse may result in toxic stress, which can change brain development and increase the risk of problems like post-traumatic stress disorder and learning, attention, and memory difficulties. ACEs are common across all populations.

The ACE study directed both professional and public attention to the impact of ten family-related adverse events occurring in childhood. Since then, the psychological harm caused by a wide variety of events and circumstances, including disasters, social violence, racism, and poverty, has received increasing attention (Carter & Blanch, 2019). Without proper interventions, the trajectory of life satisfaction for children with multiple ACEs is indeed very flat.

## The Impact of Societal Woes

Students need to feel safe and have supportive relationships for social, emotional, and academic learning to occur. Students experiencing trauma, such as a public health crisis, weather disasters, or other disturbing events, may have been exposed to unpredictable schedules, inconsistent supervision, or food insecurity (CDC, 2020). These students desperately need school to be safe, predictable, and positive, especially if they have been displaced or are without utilities or basic comforts.

Childhood trauma often involves a negative reaction, called traumatic stress, following an overwhelming, upsetting, or frightening experience—called a traumatic event—that challenges a child's ability to cope. Many students suffer adverse childhood effects and in turn have difficulty accessing academic learning. According to Sachs, Murphey, and Moore (2013), approximately 1 in 10 students in the state of Illinois, have more than two ACEs. For some students the trauma event may be temporary (e.g., death of a pet), while for others the trauma event may be more long-term. Children with a strong support system can overcome trauma, but many students do not have strong support systems and struggle to regulate their emotions. Many teachers do not have the training for trauma-informed care and those who do may not see that their verbal and non-verbal interactions affect the students' learning. According to Craig (2016), "Trauma has the unfortunate effect of leaving children in the past, unable to move forward" (p. 32). The type of relationship and interactions the teacher has with a student who suffers from multiple ACEs, can hinder the child's learning, and worse, further traumatize the child. Children with adverse childhood experiences suffer on multiple levels, with a lack of social belonging being one of them. Many children become susceptible to loneliness, social anxiety, and clinical depression in the absence of belonging. Children who suffer multiple Adverse Childhood Experiences (ACEs) need specialized services and support to navigate and access school, learning, and life, successfully.

## *Problem Statement*

It is important to continue to study ACEs and their impact on the students' academic performance and well-being. This research focused on beliefs, understanding, and actions of classroom teachers regarding students with ACEs because the classroom teacher is the gatekeeper to social-emotional supports and mental health services.

## *Research Purposes*

This qualitative case study explored ways in which elementary public- school teachers identify their students with adverse childhood experiences and create a classroom learning environment conducive to the well-being of those students. As a result, the student would have a better chance to succeed in the areas of social-emotional and academic growth. While educators cannot change the fact that a child may suffer ACEs, they can provide a classroom environment that is trauma-informed and conducive to learning.

## *Theoretical Lens*

Several theoretical perspectives helped shape this study's purposes, research questions, and the strategies for data analysis: Ecological Model of Human Development, Social-Ecological Model, Ethics of Care, Attachment Theory, and Social Justice Theory. The concepts of Adverse Childhood Experiences and Social-Emotional Learning were examined through the lens of these theoretical perspectives, all of which comprise an original integrated model displayed in Figure 7.1.

Through the middle of the diagram is the Ecological Model of Human Development and the Multi-Modal Social-Ecological Model. They mirror each other in that the broad categories are similar: self to individual; micro and meso to social environment; exto to systems-level and macro and chrono are not a part of the Multi-Modal Social-Ecological Model but are factors when examining Adverse Childhood Experiences (ACEs) and Social-Emotional

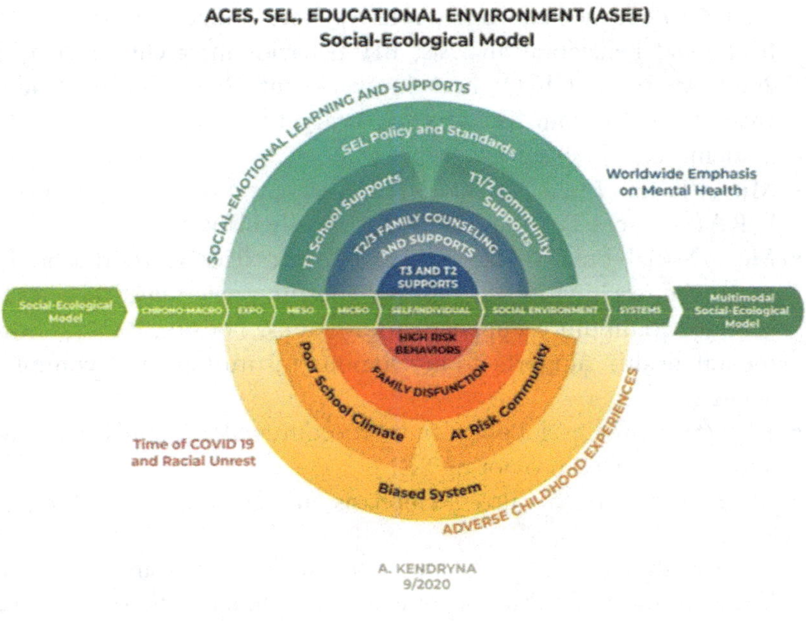


*Figure 7.1:* ACES, SEL, Educational Environment (ASEE) Social-Ecological Model

Learning (SEL). ACEs are delineated in the bottom half of the figure and SEL in the top of the figure.

Moving from the middle of the model outward through the lens of ACEs, the bottom half of the model includes:

- Self/Individual High-Risk Behaviors: cutting, attempted suicide, drug abuse, alcohol abuse, self-inflicted injuries.
- Micro/Social Environment-Family Dysfunction: violence, battered adults, battered children, adult drug and alcohol abuse, incarceration, neglect, criminal activity, poverty.
- Meso/Social Environment-Poor School Climate and Et-Risk Community: high needs schools, bullying, low academics, high staff turnover, lack of resources, violence, high crime rate, low employment opportunities, little to no access to health care, and food, inadequate housing.
- Exto/Systems-Level Policy and Procedures-inherent bias and systemic racism.
- Macro and Chrono-COVID 19, racial unrest, politically divided country.

Moving from the middle of the figure upward through the lens of Social-Emotional Learning:

- Self/Individual-Tier 3 interventions: hospitalization for psychiatric treatment, social work services-private and/or in school, FBA-functional behavioral analysis, BIP-behavior intervention plan, Tier 2 interventions: CICO-check in check out, SAIG-Social, Academic Instructional Groups: small groups targeting social-emotional skills, academics, and behaviors.
- Micro/Social Environment-Tier 3 interventions: family counseling, WRAP services Tier 2 interventions: family plans.
- Meso/Social Environment-School Climate: Tier 1: good school climate, the teaching of SEL lessons, morning meetings, monthly SEL survey; Community Supports: food banks, housing-PADS, shelters, mental health supports from religious institutions and community agencies.
- Exto/Systems-Level Policy and Procedures-SEL Standards, Federal and State policies promoting SEL.
- Macro and Chrono-Current emphasis on mental health services.

Ethics of care, attachment theory, and social justice theory are embedded in parts of this figure. For Ethics of Care and Attachment Theory: Micro and Meso/Social Environment-home, school, places of worship, clubs, groups, activities are all places where relationships are formed. Adult caregivers in those places can form positive attachments with children and contribute to positive relationships and build social-emotional skills. Those relationships can be just the opposite and create more trauma or adverse childhood experiences for the children in their care.

Nel Noddings' (2015) work, which takes ethics of care and applies it to the field of education, informed this study as teachers needed to care for and take care of students with ACEs. The social-emotional well-being of students needs to be monitored before any emphasis on academics can occur. If a teacher attends to the needs of the student, the student will be able to depend on the teacher. Some students may come to school not knowing how to attach to others because of traumatic events or abuse. It takes an informed teacher to notice this deficiency and choose to resolve it at least within the student-teacher relationship.

For social justice theory: Exto/Systems-Level (policy and procedures) and Macro and Chrono (societal values and time in history) are the levels where social justice theory is prevalent. While the outer levels of the diagram have less influence on the child than the levels closest to the child, the outer levels can still have an impact. People in positions of power and influence can determine if they are going to eradicate institutional bias and systemic racism or contribute to it. One of the tenets of trauma-informed care is to help create a happier, healthier, and more ethical society (Figley, 2012). This tenant is directly linked to social justice theory. While this study does not address larger societal issues like equitable monetary resources, access to health services, fresh food, and safe areas to live for all, there would be fewer stressors and children with a smaller number of ACEs. However, teachers can be advocates for children in their care, making sure the children who need it are provided with resources and kept safe while in the care of educators.

## *Case-Study Design*

A case study was the most suitable design for this study's research purposes. Yin (2018) offers this twofold definition of a case study as a research method that (a) "investigates a contemporary phenomenon (the "case") in-depth" and (b) "within its real-world context, especially when the boundaries between phenomenon and context may not be clearly evident" (p. 15). This study was conducted in a real-world context of a classroom, seven out of eight observations were in a physical classroom and one was in a virtual classroom. It aimed at investigating the belief systems of teachers regarding how they view and interact with students with ACEs in great depth.

According to Stake (1995), "The first criterion should be to maximize what we can learn. Given our purposes, which cases are likely to lead us to understandings, to assertions, perhaps even to modifying generalizations?" (p. 4). Thus, this case study fitted within an instrumental type. The close examination of teachers' belief systems about students with ACEs deepened an understanding of how to educate the students more effectively.

### *Site and Participants*

This study was conducted in a Midwestern suburban public elementary school. I have been the Principal of this school for the last ten years. Over the past five years, we have seen an increase in the number of children with multiple ACEs and increasing poverty in our community. The percentage of students who receive free or reduced lunch has gone from 13% to 37% within those ten years. All of the townhomes behind the school are now Section Eight housing. That transition started seven years ago. Three years ago, all of the teachers started teaching Second Steps, a tier-one, social-emotional learning program. This program is aimed at helping all students build social-emotional skills. While the participants saw the benefit of (this) SEL program with some of their students, many of the students with ACEs still react atypically in common situations and cannot regulate their emotions, resulting in students running out of classrooms, refusing to do classwork, crying, hitting others, and throwing items across the classroom. Even more seriously, the participants have seen an increase in students on anxiety medication and students who threaten to commit suicide at younger and younger ages in the last few years.

The participants of this study included five general education elementary teachers in grades kindergarten through fourth grade. I chose participants using purposeful sampling, with maximal variation and convenience (Creswell, 2012, p. 208). Saldana and Omasta (2018) agree that explicit intentionality and convenience of choosing the site and participants validate purposeful and convenience sampling strategies in qualitative research. The participants represented teachers with similar schedules or availability, and the most varied grade levels.

### *Sources of Data and Methods of Data Collection*

Case-study research involves various methods of data collection. According to Yin (2018) for a qualitative case study, "there are six sources of evidence: documentation, archival records, interviews, direct observations, participant observation, and physical artifacts" (p. 114). For this case study, I conducted semi-structured interviews with five teachers; I made two observations of teacher-student interactions during class time and I recorded field notes. I collected artifacts and visuals that pertained to the teachers' understanding of ACEs and SEL. Multiple sources of data ensured triangulation, validated the findings and gave greater breadth or depth to the data (Saldana & Omasta, 2018).

### *Observations*

At the beginning of this study, I conducted two observations of the participating teachers. Participant observation requires observing, listening, and using one's senses to take in and record the rich details as people interact with each other and their environment (Stake, 1995). The qualitative case-study researcher, during the observation, needs to concentrate on what constitutes a tally-what is key to the research-but also look for other factors that may be influencing the result (Stake, 1995, p. 62). The field notes included a record of any statement that highlighted the student-teacher relationship. The emphasis during the early stages of the observations was discovery (Bloomberg & Volpe, 2019). Observations allowed me to take detailed first-hand accounts of the specific phenomenon being studied.

### *Semi-Structured Interviews*

Interviews are most commonly used in case studies and they played a key role in the data collection for this study. "Case study interviews resemble guided conversations rather than structured queries" (Yin, 2018, p. 118). Semi-structured interviews follow a line of inquiry that is aligned to one's case study but also allows for an open, non-threatening line of questioning that may help the researcher get deeper, richer data. Interviews can get to the *how* and *why* that is the focus of the research (Yin, 2018, p. 118). Interview guide (Appendix A) was used to stay on the topic of the inquiry but I was also able to add deeper questions from some of the participants, which resulted in richer data than I anticipated. The interview guide was developed to ascertain what the teacher knows about ACEs, how they affect student learning, what the teacher does to mitigate the harmful effects of ACEs, and advocate for the students.

### *Documents, Artifacts, and Visual Materials*

The focus of this study was on the teacher. I took pictures of the teachers' classrooms hoping for an indication of the climate of the classroom. Stake (1995) contends that most studies find the need for some type of documentation.

Gathering "data by studying documents follows the same line of thinking as observing or interviewing" (Stake, 1995, p. 68). I took pictures of parts of the school to show the influence of the school community on SEL.

### *Strategies for Data Analysis*

Analyzing case-study evidence includes organizing and displaying data in different ways, looking for patterns, insights, and concepts, developing an analytic strategy, considering analytic techniques, and addressing contradictory explanations and interpretations (Yin, 2018). Qualitative data analysis typically consists of several cycles of coding (Saldaña & Omasta, 2018). Saldaña and Omasta (2018) describe one of the four types of coding methods as In Vivo for coding qualitative data. IN Vivo coding only considers the responses from the interviewee, not the questions from the interviewer. To start the coding process, I began with a close reading of the transcript and open coding. I coded the data to determine the themes within the interviews and the observations. The interviews were coded by "aggregating the text into small categories of information" (Creswell & Poth, 2018, p. 190). Throughout the analysis, I looked for specific phrases that refer directly to ACEs, SEL, trauma, cues to the teacher-student relationship, and teacher as an advocate.

After determining the major themes and subthemes from multiple sources of data, I placed the themes in a graphic organizer to see if any other themes emerged. I reread the transcripts to see if there are any other emerging themes. Coding allows the researcher to summarize, interpret, synthesize, and extend alternative interpretations. The interviews and observations were put into a program called Dedoose, that made it easier for me to look for themes. Yin (2018) suggests that the researcher look back at the original questions and look at the evidence that addresses the original questions. Yin goes on to suggest that the researcher continue that process until all research questions have been examined. The themes that occur more frequently, across all of the data collected, should be given more weight in the analysis. Ultimately, I have created a model for ACEs, SEL, and the learning environment (ASEE), (Figure 7.1) to analyze the data.

### *Validation Criteria*

I employed several criteria for validation of data analysis: reflexivity, triangulation, member checks, authenticity, and rich and thick descriptions. Reflexivity offered me the way to turn the problem of subjectivity in research into an opportunity (Finlay, 1998). The reflexive process can unfold new understandings.

Personal and methodological reflexivity should be included as an element of research and that without it the validity of the research could be undermined. Reflexivity is a safeguard against potential researcher biases therefore requires that the researcher stay conscious of biases, values, and experiences brought to the study. Reflexivity is an awareness of the influence that the researcher has on the participants and the topic. I have kept a journal of my reflections, thoughts, emotions, and assumptions throughout this research process.

A major strength of case-study data collection is "the opportunity to use many different sources of evidence. Case studies using multiple sources of evidence were rated more highly, in terms of their overall quality" (Yin, 2018, p. 126). One reason triangulation of data is important in case studies is to help the researcher get an in-depth look at a phenomenon in a real-world setting. In this case study, I used multiple data sources to obtain a more holistic understanding of the data and reasonable explanations of the phenomenon being studied.

Member checks are taking the data back to the participants and asking them to review the data collected to assure accuracy. "Member checks-taking data and tentative interpretations back to the people from whom they were derived and asking them if the results are plausible" (Merriam, 1998, p. 204). I used member checks when I sent the transcripts of the interviews to the participants for verification of accuracy. Using member checks helps the process to be transparent and credible. Additionally, rich and thick descriptions provide insights into the lived experiences. They help to create a picture in the reader's mind, to see the situation as clearly and as deeply as possible. "Generating a 'thick' description means the researcher needs to capture the details, emotions, and voice of the participant" (Creswell & Poth, 2018, p. 245). The authenticity and quality of educational research can be judged by the procedures used to address reliability, validity, and triangulation (Scott, 2007). Authenticity evokes a sense of what is real, real to the participant.

## *Discussion of the Findings*

The circumstances under which persons are born can play an enormous role in who these persons can become as adults. There may always be an exception to the rule: a student who was once homeless can go to Harvard or a rich white man can end up in jail. But exceptions are just that, exceptions, and not the norm. Unfortunately, the norm for adverse childhood experiences (ACEs) is that nearly 18% of the population of children ages zero to 18, in the United States, has suffered two or more ACEs (Center for Youth Wellness, 2019). Suffering ACEs can derail a child's chance at accessing education.

Children who have suffered ACEs require additional support in and outside of the school setting. Brain science (Navalta et al., 2018) shows that, in the absence of protective factors, toxic stress damages children's developing brains. Toxic stress can arise in response to living for months or years with a screaming alcoholic father, a severely depressed and neglectful mother, or a parent who copes with life's frustrations by beating a child. While ACEs have been linked to poor health outcomes in adulthood, researchers are beginning to understand the mechanisms leading to disease and early death due to toxic stress and multiple exposures to trauma. Left unaddressed, toxic stress affects the fundamental biological functioning of the body and, in many children, healthy brain development.

Research indicates that "roughly 1 of 5 children have diagnosable mental health disorders but that roughly 70% do not receive indicated services" (Cook et al., 2015, pp. 166–167). The mental health issues surface in a variety of ways, such as, for instance, self-harming, aggressive behavior, criminal behavior, and low academic scores. These issues have important implications for children's health and well-being, including the need for increased attention toward the early detection and treatment of children affected by trauma. Prevention is the goal first and foremost, however it is illogical to believe that one or more school programs, whether behavioral or Social-Emotional Learning (SEL), can provide students with mental health issues or multiple ACEs the type of support they need. Social work and wraparound services provide the solution in cases where only 1–2% of students suffer from ACEs. In a school of 400, student wraparounds are possible for 4 to 8 families, however research shows that 9% of students have suffered three or more ACEs and that 13%–20% of those students have mental health issues. These families need this intensive type of service, but schools and most communities lack the resources to provide wraparound services for 35–80 families. I refer to these statistics because that is exactly what the participants of this study face. My study also revealed that if the participants and other teachers do not provide Tier Two services for students who need them, and they refer all of those students to the social worker, the students will not receive services at all because one social worker does not have the capacity for providing services to all students who need Tier Two and Tier Three supports.

Teachers can begin with a solid foundation of Tier One instruction in SEL, but monetary and personnel support are needed to develop a model of Tier Two support for students who struggle with trauma and mental health. In the history of American education, this is the first generation to recognize the ravages of child abuse and neglect and begin to act in response and this is also the first generation to begin to heal ourselves physically and psychologically from the harmful effects of ACEs. Through trial and error as well as research like that of Felitti et al. (1998), educators can constructively apply our new knowledge and skills to help all of our children. Let us consider the societal implications—if all children could have well developed social and emotional skills, then as adults they would be able to thoughtfully solve problems in nonviolent ways. The most important influence in a school setting is the person closest to the child: the teacher.

## *Adverse Childhood Experiences*

Teachers, especially at the elementary level, are the adults who spend the most time with the school age child. Students with ACEs need more support than a good climate, even more than a Tier 1 intervention for SEL. The resources available make it impossible for social workers to meet with and conduct groups with 20% of the school population (CASEL, 2018). Teachers and other school staff should find ways to provide students with much-needed services. Though school social workers and counselors are often viewed as the primary providers of mental health services in schools. The participants of this study identify some ACEs as hypervigilance. To reiterate some of the participants' responses, the students didn't trust any adults and had an exaggerated startle response when someone came near.

Franklin et al. (2012) highlight the role that teachers currently play in delivering mental health services to children in schools. Though teachers typically co-deliver these services, according to Franklin, nearly 1 in 5 school-based mental health interventions are led solely by teachers. These data account only for the formalized delivery of interventions, like Tier One programming, in the schools and do not address the informal mental health support teachers provide on a daily basis (Franklin et al., 2012).

## *Social-Emotional Learning: We Need a Tier 2 Band Aid*

I considered several theoretical models that address ACEs and I have developed my own, integrated ASEE model that puts an individual child in the center. The spheres of influence on the well-being of a child gradually decrease in their intensity during the process of that child's growth and development. Worth noting is the second sphere of influence, from the middle, that represents the family and the school. As stated above, school personnel and especially the classroom teacher have significant influence on a child.

Students with social-emotional skills have the ability to perceive emotions about themselves and others, understand them and regulate them. This in turn can promote intellectual growth (Solovey & Mayer, 1990). When teachers teach each student the five SEL skills, this can affect the climate of the classroom and school in a positive way. It is best if students are able to generalize the skills into all areas of their life, even outside of school. While most SEL programs have three tiers of suggested support, no SEL program specifically targets students with ACEs, but my ASEE model makes that direct connection for educators and other professionals.

The findings of this study revealed that the participants believed that it is part of their role as a teacher to help students address their social-emotional issues that prohibit them from learning. The participants admitted that they do not have a systematic way to identify students with ACEs, they learn by what they seek from previous teachers and from the children themselves. The participants stated that they did not have the training necessary to address the Tier Two and Tier Three supports needed. It was unclear if they believed that providing Tier Two and Tier Three supports was a part of their responsibility as a classroom teacher. The participants did not know how to advocate for students beyond their classroom, nor did some of them think it was beneficial. They felt the same way about policy, either disinterested or ineffectual.

Importantly, the results of this study echo the very precepts of the ethics of care (Noddings, 2015). The participants of this study are highly devoted to their craft and primarily to the children they teach. Put differently, they do care *for* their students a great deal. They understand the ACEs of their students and do their best to make sure these students find their school as a warm and welcoming environment. They have a deeper understanding and commitment to the well-being of their students, including students with ACEs. Such attitudes on the part of the participants of this study speak volumes to support the Attachment Theory (Bowlby, 1982). The closer the teacher is to the student, understanding the student, and knowing them deeply, the more the teacher is inclined to care *for* the child and provide supports.

## *Mental Health and Well-Being*

Mental health and well-being of children are indicators of future success, oftentimes more than academic adeptness. The study data confirm that the students with ACEs are more likely than not, to be the bully, or the victim, and the student with emotional and social maladaptations (CDC, 2020). The 2020 CDC report, "Preventing Adverse Childhood Experiences (ACEs): Leveraging the Best Available Evidence," indicates that about 61% of adults surveyed across 25 states reported that they had experienced at least one type of ACE, and nearly 1 in 6 reported they had experienced four or more types of ACEs. While educators cannot change the fact a child may suffer ACEs, they can recognize students with ACEs, provide a conducive climate, and Tier One and Tier Two supports, *if* the teacher is knowledgeable in these areas, which is what this study confirms.

With nearly half of all children experiencing at least one adverse childhood event ("Child and Adolescent Health Measurement Initiative," 2013b), teachers' approach to trauma in the classroom is critical. The findings of this study support the fact that a better understanding of teachers' knowledge and confidence in supporting students exposed to traumatic events can be instrumental in enhancing these students' well-being. Existing research suggests that teachers often feel unprepared to address the needs of this group of students (Alisic, 2012). This may or may not be true to all teachers; however, what this study affirms is the teachers' unwavering dedication to get to know their students with ACEs more and to provide them with the best services they can, even if they may not be fully aware of a variety of resources available to them.

The participants of this study all agreed that students come first, their needs, their access to education and most importantly their social-emotional needs. The students need to be ready to learn before learning can take place. A child who comes into school late, didn't eat breakfast because there was no food in the house, and is upset because her mother's boyfriend was yelling at her, is not ready to learn. The first place the child goes to is the classroom. If the teacher in that room does not recognize that the student is upset and is not aware of the ACEs the child has or has had, that child will not be able to access the learning needed to be successful for that day and in the future.

The participants could give examples of ACEs and could name a few students they knew who had ACEs. They identified the students' ACEs through talking to former teachers and sometimes from the parents or students themselves. As a matter of fact, there is no formal process for identifying students with ACEs. Once the teacher knows the student has ACEs the teacher waits for the student to act up, shut down, or run away before taking any action to address the ACEs.

All participants agreed that having a good classroom and school environment was vitally important for all students, especially those with ACEs. Teachers could name many things that make a good classroom and school climate: greeting students by name, knowing the students' likes and dislikes, singing and dancing as students come into school each day, attending to students' basic needs, and student choice. The participants of this study emphasized that classroom community building can promote school and civic engagement, which can result in improved academic outcomes

(Rimm-Kaufman et al., 2014). Knowing a student's culture and celebrating that culture can help all students feel good about themselves and their heritage. If teachers connect students' cultural assets and use them to teach academic skills and concepts, then the student starts with their funds of knowledge and can better understand the new material. This may provide access to resources for educational rigor for all students. Also, knowing the norms of a culture can stop actions that people of that culture may find offensive and for students with Aces, may be a trigger.

The participants of this study showed an immense knowledge about social-emotional learning and its paramount importance in the teaching-learning processes. All of the participants have morning meetings where students learn social-emotional skills and get to know each other. Some participants spoke about CICO, a Tier Two support for students who need someone to check in with another adult before class and at the end of the day. If students had greater needs the teachers said they would contact the social worker. Yet the participants did not make the connection between the levels of ACEs to the levels of SEL supports. In this regard, I questioned the reasons behind the lack of the connection between their extensive professional development, on the one hand, and their lack of awareness of SEL support resources, on the other.

### *Recommendations for Educational Professionals and Researchers*

Considering the results of this study, several recommendations are worth noting. First and foremost, there needs to be a mandated systematic way of identifying students and families with ACEs. This could be completed by measuring students' social-emotional skills, habits, and mindsets, which, in turn, may be assessed through student self-reporting on surveys, teacher observations, or performance assessments. Whichever method of assessment is employed it needs to clearly identify whether children have or do not have ACEs.

While there exist surveys that assess the general climate of the school, a more specific survey needs to be developed and conducted to find out if the climate of the school helps or retraumatizes the students with ACEs. It is paramount for school teams to meet regularly to discuss the results of the survey and data that include attendance, discipline and special education referrals. School teams may want to reimagine the school day in order to include SEL in each part of the day based on the data from the survey on the students' needs, the survey that should be taken every week. Clearly, the students with high needs would need more time in terms of SEL supports. Tier two systems that have the capacity for large groups of students need to be funded and implemented. After-school and before school programs that have SEL supports and mentoring should also be a priority in order to connect youth to other caring adults.

For educators to be able to make informed decisions further research is needed to determine if teachers have the capacity to provide Tier Two supports within the structures of the school day to large groups of students needing Tier Two supports. Also, further research is needed to find out why teachers with extensive professional development in ACEs and SEL do not make the connection between the two.

Finally, various types of research can be employed to investigate the aforementioned issues further: a longitudinal study conducted in the same school district that would include all elementary schools; a mixed-methods research that could present a more comprehensive view of the state of affairs in the same school; a multi-site qualitative case study within several school districts that reflect broader diversity of demographics; or a comparative quasi-experimental research conducted in two schools with drastically different demographics. Regardless of methods employed, what ultimately matters is a concerted effort on the part of all stakeholders to engender the change that will alleviate the suffering of children with ACEs.

## *A Too-Common Ending*

The police tell the principal that they have to arrest Paul, even though she has explained that he was only kidding, trying to get much-needed attention. The police officer takes Paul into the gym and handcuffs him. The principal starts crying and tells the police officers to take the handcuffs off. Paul tries to reassure the principal that it is OK. She screams that it is not OK and the police officer takes him to the squad car just outside the gym doors.

I tell this true story because this boy is one of many children who suffer multiple Adverse Childhood Experiences (ACEs). He is in need of specialized services and support to navigate school, learning, and life successfully. Nearly 35 million U.S. children have experienced one or more types of childhood trauma and are in schools.

I wonder how Paul's experience changed if he moved in with his aunt, who had a stable job, enough money to feed her family, free of alcoholism and who was able to express love and care to him? I suspect, very different. But what if the home experience was the same and his school experience was different? What if Paul's kindergarten teacher saw how the ACEs affected Paul and connected his family and him with critical support at an early age? What if Paul came into breakfast and met with a small circle of students and a counselor who spoke to them about what they were feeling that morning? If Paul went to class where a teacher warmly greeted him, knew about his circumstances and got to know him on a personal level? If classmates regularly gave kudos to each other? If Paul had access to a social worker whenever he was feeling overwhelmed? If all people treated Paul like the beautiful young man he is, and schools provided the support he and his family needed, then maybe he wouldn't have had the need to get attention by touching an officer's gun.

I have been an educator and administrator for the last 30 years. I have taught in public, private and military schools in several states across this country and in Puerto Rico. I have taught in schools where the parents of the children are multi-millionaires residing in the north shore of Chicago, Illinois, and in schools where the families live in houses with dirt floors, in the hills of northwest Pennsylvania. Many of the families in each situation have a common thread of trauma. Some families have support systems to help guide each member through the trauma on to mentally healthy lives, and others are not so lucky. I personally suffered several Adverse Childhood Experiences. While my family never went without food, shelter and clothing, a member of my family was alcoholic and my dad traveled a lot for his job. My younger brother, by 13 months, had juvenile diabetes and was in the hospital at least three times a year, since first grade. He passed away at the age of 27. There was constant stress in our house and a lack of supervision. On occasion there was corporal punishment, but no one called DCFS; this was a new agency in the 1960s.

School was my sanctuary and several adult relationships in elementary school helped me to see more possibilities for my life, beyond my current circumstances. Somewhere deep inside I knew I had to be a teacher, so I could help the students like me. As a teacher I saw many students who suffered from Adverse Childhood Experiences (ACEs). These troubled and often marginalized groups of students have atypical reactions to problems and disappointments. As an administrator, for the last 16 years, I have seen the number of students with ACEs climb and the severity of the ACEs go up.

Spanning my thirty-year career in education, I have always been deeply concerned about two groups of students: the externalizers known as the high flyers-students who have consistent behavioral issues, and the internalizers, the quiet students who appear unhappy, but are not behaviorally or academically on the school staff's radar. In getting to know these students personally, I find that many of them have experienced several adverse experiences (ACEs): divorce, loss of parent job, death of a family member, physical, sexual or verbal abuse, foster care, homelessness, and others. The more trauma, or higher the intensity, the child has experienced, the more likely the effects of the trauma will manifest itself either externally or internally. In my experience Tier One universal social-emotional intervention programs are not enough. Tier One instruction occurs with a whole class, teachers can introduce social-emotional skills to students using programs like Second Steps, and help emotionally stable students grow in those skills. It is not designed to and it does not help traumatized students to recognize their lack of skills nor provide needed intensive instruction. Teachers aware of a gap between student need and teacher ability are in a position to seek opportunities to improve their understanding of trauma and its influence on children's emotional, behavioral, and academic functioning. Much more work in the area of ACEs and SEL needs to be done.

## References

Alisic, E. (2012). Teachers' perspectives on providing support to children after trauma: A qualitative study. *School Psychology Quarterly*, *27*(1), 51–59. https://doi.org/10.1037/a0028590

Anda, R., & Felitti, V. (2004). Childhood abuse, household dysfunction, and indicators of impaired adult worker performance. *The Permanente Journal*, *8*(1). https://doi.org/10.7812/tpp/03-089

Bloomberg, L., & Volpe, M. (2019). *Completing your qualitative dissertation*. SAGE.

Bowlby, J. (1975). Attachment theory, separation anxiety, and mourning. In S. Arieti (Ed.), *American Handbook of Psychiatry* (Vol. 6, pp. 290–308). Basic Books.

Carter, P., & Blanch, A. (2019). A trauma lens for systems change. *Stanford Social Innovation Review*, Summer 2019, 49–54.

CASEL Collaborative for Academic, Social, and Emotional Learning. (2018). *What is SEL?* http://www.casel.org/what-is-sel/

Centers for Disease Control and Prevention. (2020). *Preventing adverse childhood experiences (ACEs): Leveraging the best available evidence*. https://www.cdc.gov/index.html

Center for Youth Wellness. (2019). *ACEs and toxic stress science*. https://centerforyouthwellness.org/the-science/

Child and Adolescent Health Measurement Initiative. (2018). *National Survey of Children's Health (NSCH) data query*. www.childhealthdata.org

Cicchetti, D. (2010). Resilience under conditions of extreme stress: A multilevel perspective. *World Psychiatry*, *9*(3), 145–154. https://doi.org/10.1002/j.2051-5545.2010.tb00297.x

Cook, C. R., Frye, M., Slemrod, T., Lyon, A. R., Renshaw, T. L., & Zhang, Y. (2015). An integrated approach to universal prevention: Independent and combined effects of PBIS and SEL on youths' mental health. *School Psychology Quarterly*, *30*(2), 166–183.

Creswell, J. (2012). *Research designs: Qualitative, quantitative, and mixed methods approach* (4th ed.). SAGE.

Creswell, J. W., & Poth, C. N. (2018). *Qualitative inquiry & research design: Choosing among five approaches* (4th ed.). SAGE Publications.

Felitti, V. J., Anda, R. F., Nordenberg, D., Williamson, D. F., Spitz, A. M., Edwards, V., Marks, J. S. (1998). Relationship of childhood abuse and household dysfunction to many of the leading causes of death in adults. *American Journal of Preventive Medicine, 14*(4), 245–258. https://doi.org/10.1016/s0749-3797(98)00017-8

Figley, C. (2012). *Encyclopedia of trauma: An interdisciplinary guide.* https://doi.org/10.4135/9781452218595

Finlay, L. (1998). Reflexivity: An essential component for all research? *British Journal of Occupational Therapy, 61*(10), 453–456. https://doi.org/10.1177/030802269806101005

Franklin T. B., Saab, B. J., & Mansuy, I. M. (2012). Neural mechanisms of stress resilience and vulnerability. *Neuron, 75*(5), 747–761. https://doi.org/10.1016/j.neuron.2012.08.016. PMID: 22958817.

Goodman, R. D., Miller, M. D., & West-Olatunji, C. A. (2012). Traumatic stress, socioeconomic status, and academic achievement among primary school students. *Psychological Trauma: Theory, Research, Practice, and Policy, 4*(3), 252–259.

Merriam, S, B. (1998). *Qualitative research and case study applications in education.* Jossey-Bass.

National Child Traumatic Stress Network, Schools Committee. (2017). *Creating, supporting, and sustaining trauma-informed schools: A system framework.*

Navalta, C., McGee, L., & Underwood, J. (2018). Adverse childhood experiences, brain development, and mental health: A call for neurocounseling. *Journal of Mental Health Counseling, 40*(3), 266–278. https://doi.org/10.17744/mehc.40.3.07

Noddings, N. (2015). *Philosophy of education.* Routledge. ProQuest Ebook Central. http://ebookcentral.proquest.com/lib/nlu/detail.action?docID=5352127. 10.1037/0003-066x.63.9.852

Rimm-Kaufman, S., Larsen, R., Curby, T., Baroody, A., Merritt, E., Abry, T., & Wanless, S. (2014). Efficacy of the responsive classroom approach: Results from a three-year, longitudinal randomized control trial. *American Educational Research Journal.* https://doi.org/10.3102/0002831214523821

Sacks, V., Murphey, D., & Moore, K. (2014). Adverse childhood experiences national and state-level prevalence. *Child Trends.* https://doi.org/10.13140/2.1.1193.8087

Saldaña, J., & Omasta, M. (2018). *Qualitative research: Analyzing life.* SAGE.

Scott, D. (2007). Resolving the quantitative-qualitative dilemma: A critical realist approach. *International Journal of Research and Method in Education, 30*(1), 3–17.

Shonkoff, J., & Garner, A. (2012). Committee on psychosocial aspects of child and family health committee on early childhood, adoption, and dependent care and section on developmental and behavioral pediatrics. The lifelong effects of early childhood adversity and toxic stress. *Pediatrics, 129*(1), e232–e246.

Salovey, P., & Mayer, J. D. (1990). Emotional intelligence. *Imagination, Cognition and Personality*, *9*(3), 185–211. https://doi.org/10.2190/DUGG-P24E-52WK-6CDG

Stake, R. (1995). *The art of case study research.* SAGE.

Yin, R. K. (2018). *Case study research and applications: Design and methods* (6th ed.). SAGE.

# Chapter 8 Is There a Model for Success? Exploring Sustainable Professional Employment among Clinical Exercise Physiology Program's Graduates

Regina Schurman

When I say that I am a clinical exercise physiologist, people usually think I am either a personal trainer or a physical therapist. While there is some overlap between the skill sets of clinical exercise physiologists, personal trainers, and physical therapists, there are important differences that set clinical exercise physiologists apart. Personal trainers and clinical exercise physiologists assess various indices of physical capability of their clients and develop exercise programs to improve deficiencies; however, only clinical exercise physiologists possess the training necessary to work with individuals who have a variety of chronic health conditions. Physical therapists work with a broad range of conditions that limit mobility (American Physical Therapy Association [APTA], n.d.) but usually do not work with a patient until an event has occurred whereas clinical exercise physiologists utilize exercise as a means of chronic disease prevention (CEPA, n.d.; Potteiger, 2011).

Unlike other healthcare professions such as nursing or physical therapy, clinical exercise physiology is relatively new. The work of Levine, Lown, and Hellerstein, who used exercise in the rehabilitation of cardiac patients, led to the establishment of cardiac rehabilitation programs in hospitals in the 1970s (Potteiger, 2011). Despite several decades of practice, it was not until 2010 that the Bureau of Labor Statistics finally created a separate Standard

Occupation Code (SOC) for exercise physiologists (U.S. Department of Labor, 2010). Between the confusion over what clinical exercise physiologists do and the delay in receiving government recognition, it is no wonder that the general public does not understand the scope of practice for clinical exercise physiologists.

Why would someone go into the field of clinical exercise physiology given all the challenges that the profession is facing? Clinical exercise physiology has its origins in anatomy, physiology, and medicine and thus appeals to students who want to better understand both the human body's response to exercise as well as the power of exercise to improve health (Potteiger, 2011). The practice of clinical exercise physiology is broader than that of personal trainers who typically only work with healthy individuals. While physical therapists are typically limited to treating a specific body part, clinical exercise physiologists look at the whole person as they work to manage chronic disease and promote lifestyle habits that enhance health.

The students who enter our master's clinical exercise physiology program at Benedictine University usually have the goal of obtaining full-time employment in the field after graduation. Most of them seek employment in cardiac rehabilitation or cardiac diagnostics departments at hospitals. Several of the adjunct faculty who teach in our program have full-time positions as managers of these types of departments at local hospitals. These individuals serve as exemplars when prospective students inquire about their prospects for finding employment post-graduation. How these individuals attained their career success despite competition from other professions as well as the lack of licensure for clinical exercise physiologists is unclear.

It is apparent that more than a master's degree is needed to be successful in the competitive job market in the field of clinical exercise physiology. Graduates face many challenges in securing positions due to the economy, healthcare reform, and a lack of license for their profession. However, in spite of these challenges, some students are able to secure professional employment with opportunities for future advancement. There seem to be other factors involved that allow these students to succeed in an adverse job market.

This study was needed since the profession of clinical exercise physiology does not have a clear career path like physical therapy or nursing. Marketing materials for clinical exercise physiology graduate programs state that exercise physiologists can be found in leadership roles in cardiac rehabilitation programs, fitness centers, and agencies. However, it is left up to the students to determine the best way to secure their desired career post-graduation.

The flash of insight that focused me on the substantive area of this study was the realization that there were several clinical exercise physiologists in the Chicago area who held management positions in hospitals. This was interesting because clinical exercise physiologists are not licensed, except in the state of Louisiana. However, this lack of licensure had not held back these individuals from achieving positions as managers in cardiac rehabilitation and cardiac diagnostic departments. The departments these clinical exercise physiologists manage have a mix of healthcare professions, including nurses, respiratory therapists, echocardiography technicians, and other licensed professionals. This insight led me on a process of abduction to form a hypothesis of how this was possible and to conduct a research study in a manner that generated a substantive theory to explain my observations.

The purpose of this study was twofold: (1) to describe the clinical exercise physiology profession from the perspective of its practitioners and the graduates of clinical exercise physiology programs and (2) to develop a model of sustainable professional employment that exhibits the processes that allow graduates from clinical exercise physiology programs to attain management positions in a healthcare system dominated by licensed professionals.

This study was guided by the following questions:

- What are the graduates' perceptions on sustainable professional employment within the clinical exercise physiology profession and the path to its highest attainment?
- What are the perspectives of clinical exercise physiology professionals on sustainable professional employment and what is the career path toward their highest professional attainment?
- What is the model that exhibits the processes that allow clinical exercise physiologists to obtain sustainable professional employment and to attain management positions in a healthcare system dominated by licensed professionals?

## *Theoretical Positioning of the Study*

Pragmatism provided the foundation of this study in terms of methodological and epistemological assumptions. Pragmatism was selected because this study seeks to provide "practical solutions to practical problems" (Ozmon & Craver, 2003, p. 138). Clinical exercise physiology students seek guidance on how to best prepare themselves to attain sustainable professional employment in today's competitive job market. Identifying the factors that contribute to securing employment in the field and thus creating a model of sustainable professional development is one of the solutions offered by this study. Wedded to my pragmatic goals is the choice of a qualitative grounded theory that is rooted in the philosophical tradition of pragmatism. Qualitative methodology would allow the experiences of clinical exercise physiology practitioners to be captured and provide the opportunity to probe more deeply into themes that may be revealed during interviews.

Grounded theory method originated with Glaser and Strauss's 1965 publication of their research in *Awareness of Dying*. At the time of the development of grounded theory method, qualitative methods were viewed as inferior to quantitative ones (Glaser & Strauss, 1967). Therefore, Glaser and Strauss wanted to prove that there were forms of qualitative research that could have as much rigor as quantitative research (Bryant, 2009). In the publication of the grounded theory method their philosophical worldview was never explicitly defined, which perplexed many, including Bryant, since Strauss had a pragmatist background being from the Chicago School of Sociology.

The two founders of grounded theory method parted ways when Strauss published *Basics of Qualitative Research* with Corbin in 1990, a book which Glaser rebutted in his book *Emergence vs. Forcing: Basics of Grounded Theory Analysis* in 1992. Despite this split, the use of the method grew in popularity. In the 1990s, those using the method realized that the issues of the role of the researcher, induction, and prior knowledge needed to be addressed, and thus many argued that grounded theory method was based on interpretivism or constructivism (Bryant, 2009). However, using constructivism does not solve the criticisms of grounded theory method since constructivism has as its basis that knowledge depends on the participants' meanings rather than on an objective view of reality (Bryant; Creswell & Clark, 2011; Mills et al., 2006). A researcher's view of truth and reality can influence him or her to justify study outcomes based on the belief that knowledge was provisional and dependent on the participant's perspectives (Bryant). However, researchers are part of the research process and their humanness will influence the construction of knowledge (Mills et al., 2006).

Positioning grounded theory method in the framework of pragmatism resolves this lack of a solid epistemological footing (Bryant, 2009). Despite a lack of an explicit reference to American pragmatism in the writings of Glaser and Strauss, Strauss did stress that it was a key part in his intellectual formation because he was exposed to the writings of Dewey and James when a student in the 1930s (Bryant). Strauss referred to the influence of pragmatism on his work as "a red thread running through my work" (Bryant, para. 51). Bryant's reconsideration of grounded theory method in the worldview of pragmatism leads to a more cohesive method that can be defended and that turns "the red thread into a lifeline" (para. 58). When taking the pragmatist view that any theories or concepts developed should be judged by their "usefulness rather than their truthfulness," the features of grounded theory become more understandable in terms of generating substantive theory (Bryant, para. 61).

In selecting a method to perform the inquiry for this study, it was important that I choose one based on the scientific method in order to generate the substantive theory for my model. What Glaser and Strauss (1967) mean by substantive theory is that it was developed for a particular "area of sociological inquiry, such as patient care, race relations, professional education," as opposed to a conceptual area of sociological inquiry, such as "stigma, deviant behavior, formal organization" (p. 32). Glaser and Strauss (1967) label these theories as "middle-range" because they "fall between the 'minor working hypothesis' of everyday life and 'all-inclusive' grand theories" (pp. 32–33).

Clinical exercise physiology is a scientific field; therefore, the primary audience for this study is those accustomed to reading research articles that use solid quantitative research. This audience typically values hard numbers higher than the softer qualitative research often used in social sciences. Some of the problems associated with the use of qualitative data include producing a study full of "undisciplined speculation laced with interesting anecdotes" (Mullen, 1996, p. 63). By utilizing a method guided by pragmatism, it was possible to generate substantive theories and a model that can be judged by its practicality in helping subjects resolve their main concern (Bryant, 2009). This aligns with Dewey's view of knowledge as instrumental, which allows theories to best be considered as tools (Bryant). The theoretical model generated by this study is a tool for future practitioners in the field to guide them onto a path to sustainable professional employment.

Grounded theory method consists of the typical stages of analysis employed in traditional scientific inquiry. However, the process of inquiry begins with abduction, or that "flash of insight" (Bryant & Charmez, 2007). Founder of pragmatism C. S. Peirce (1839–1914) believed that abduction was the only type of inference that would allow the creation of new knowledge since both induction and deduction were rooted in the development of existing knowledge. Peirce "always saw abduction as a form of reasoning that develops from surprise or sudden flashes of insight" (Bryant, 2009, para. 93).

Glaser and Strauss were considered radical by positioning grounded theory method as an open-minded, inductive model. In the ensuing years, this has led to criticism of the method when researchers do not explicitly position the method in an appropriate worldview. Utilizing pragmatism as the philosophical worldview for this study, in conjunction with grounded theory method for data collection and analysis, yielded a model that is robust and truly grounded in the data (Merriam & Simpson, 1995).

## *Grounded Theory Method*

Grounded theory method is intended to develop new theories, but what "a theory" means is ambiguous (Bryant, 2009). Theories span the range of those based on conjecture to those that have been extensively tested and challenged and yet still hold up (Bryant). By adopting an instrumental view of theories, it can be shown the ways a particular theory holds up in practice (Bryant). Theories developed with the grounded theory method are tied to the context in which the research is based, thus becoming substantive (Bryant). Glaser and Strauss (1967) explain that "generating a theory from data means that most hypotheses and concepts not only come from the data, but are systematically worked out in relation to the data during the course of the research" (p. 6).

A test of a theory or model generated with qualitative methodology is whether the findings will be applicable beyond the specific research subjects and setting (Bogdan & Biklen, 2007). I expect my model to hold up and be reproducible since it is grounded in the data due to the use of the scientific method as described by Peirce and Dewey. The relationship between theory and practice in a worldview of pragmatism lies in the utility of the theory in practice (Bryant, 2009). If the theory that is generated makes a difference in people's understanding and actions, then it is substantive (Bryant). The ultimate goal of this study was to make a difference in the career outcomes of the graduates of clinical exercise physiology programs.

## *Data Collection and Analysis Techniques*

Grounded theory is unique because analysis of the data is done concurrently with data collection. The primary data for analysis were gathered through semi-structured and unstructured interviews with the participants—graduates from clinical exercise physiology programs practicing in the field. The codes that emerged from each interview were compared with previous interviews in order to guide the collection of additional data as well as to identify when enough data had been gathered (Merriam & Simpson, 1995). The goal of the data collection process was to gather sufficient information in order to identify common themes and generate a model of sustainable professional employment. I felt this method best revealed the factors that were involved in my study's participants achieving career success.

Qualitative semi-structured and unstructured interviews provided my main source of data because I wanted to understand my participants' unique journeys to their career success. An open-ended question asking the participants to describe their experiences from the time they started college to their current position began each interview. Questions were added to the later interviews to provide insight on themes that were revealed earlier in data collection, which is consistent with constant comparative analysis. Grounded theory method mandates that the researcher remain open to what is being said in order to observe and determine the main concern of the interviewees and how they were able to resolve it (Glaser & Holton, 2004).

A total of 21 interviews were conducted. Seventeen interviews were conducted with veterans in the field and four interviews were conducted with recent graduates of Benedictine University's program who aspired to higher positions within the healthcare system. By the time of the last few interviews, I felt I had gathered enough data since very little new information was revealed. This is consistent with Glaserian grounded theory method in that it proscribes interviews be conducted until saturation of the categories is achieved (Glaser, 1992, 1998).

Grounded theory method begins with Glaser's concept of *theoretical sensitivity*, which is essential to being able to generate concepts from data and turn them into theory. Glaser writes extensively on emergence, meaning concepts emerge from the data that in turn lead to the development of theories from the concepts that are identified. Development of grounded theory is based on taking the data collected and turning it into concepts referred to as *codes*. Theoretical coding begins with examining the data collected and grouping incidents into substantive categories. Substantive categories refer to particular aspects of the area being studied. These substantive categories are then examined to see how they might relate to each other in order to begin to develop the hypotheses that will eventually be turned into theory. Theoretical codes can be thought of as giving the big picture or a new perspective of what is occurring (Glaser & Holton, 2004, para. 47).

During open coding, the data are looked over carefully or line-by-line in order to determine what substantive codes can be found. Open coding can be thought of as the step where the story is broken apart so that the descriptive material can be reorganized into concepts (Mullen, 1996). The constant comparative method is one of the two foundational concepts of grounded theory, the other being theoretical sampling, which drives the development of the theory that emerges from the data. This is often referred to as a method to "tease out the similarities and differences in order to refine concepts" (Bryant & Charmez, 2007, p. 607).

Because grounded theory involves the simultaneous collection and coding of data, certain categories will become saturated earlier and this will help prevent the researcher from collecting redundant data (Holton, 2010).

Saturation refers to the point at which "no new conceptual properties or dimensions are emerging" (p. 27) and, therefore, no additional data need to be obtained for that category since one more indicator or incident will not expand on the theory being developed. Glaser describes the core variable as the category that emerges and can explain most of the variation surrounding the main concern of the study. The core variable serves the function of linking together as many other categories as possible. It is what provides "grab" for the formal theory that is being developed (Glaser & Holton, 2004, para. 54).

Memo writing is important in capturing the analyst's thoughts, hunches, and impressions about the data as they are coding or just after an interview. Memos provide a way to help bring out the emerging theory. These memos are not detailed notes; rather, they are theoretical descriptions. Upon reaching the point of theoretical saturation, the analyst takes the memos and sorts them. This is how the data that have been broken apart during all the coding processes can be put together to form a cohesive theory. Because there are no preconceived notions with classic grounded theory, this allows for a richer and more robust theory. The relevant literature is brought into the theory during this process. Parsimony is the key here—what is the simplest explanation of the resolution of the core concern expressed by the participants (Glaser & Holton, 2004, para. 66–70)?

The next step is sorting the memos in order to explain the most variation in the data with the least number of concepts. According to Glaser and Holton (2004), this will result in a theory that will be able to explain how the subjects are able to resolve "their main concern with concepts that fit, work, have relevance and are saturated" (para. 71–74). This goes back to the pragmatist view that theories should be viewed as tools and they should be judged by how well they help people resolve their main concerns (Bryant, 2009, para. 103).

I concur with Bryant that when grounded theory is based on a worldview of pragmatism, the theories and concepts generated are evaluated based on how applicable they are to certain situations (Bryant, 2009). Being able to generate a model out of my research that can be used to help counsel students to sustainable professional employment in the clinical exercise physiology profession reflects the pragmatic orientation of this study.

## *Turning Words into Theory*

Classic grounded theory utilizes the participant's own words to derive the theory, therefore, generating an inductive, substantive theory. The process of analysis began with line-by-line coding that entailed examining the words of the participants and assigning codes to concepts conveyed. No predefined list of codes was used so as to avoid preconceiving what would be found in the data (Glaser, 1992). This first pass of coding the interview transcripts yielded numerous codes, many of them repetitious. These codes were compared and those that were very similar in terms of the concept they were trying to describe were combined. Then the categories were examined for their relationships with each other and how accurately they represented the participants' concerns. Codes were also examined to determine their best fit within the categories that were identified. This was an iterative process, and numerous additional passes of the data were made until it was felt that the categories derived accurately described the participants' observations.

It was during this interactive process that a core category appeared to emerge that represented the main concern of the study participants. Other categories also emerged that supported this core category. Eventually this process yielded 11 main categories as follows: *academic preparation*, *competitive job market*, *professional development*, *career satisfaction*, *professional identity*, *credentials*, *compensation*, *licensure*, *scope of practice*, *boundaries of expertise*, and *recognition of the expertise of clinical exercise physiologists*. The relationships among these categories were examined in order to produce a model that explains the key factors involved in the attainment of sustainable professional employment in the clinical exercise physiology field.

The development of the model of sustainable professional employment for clinical exercise physiologists has been central to my research purposes. The model reflects the processes involved in the journeys of successful clinical exercise physiologists, starting with their academic careers and culminating in an understanding of their current level of career satisfaction. In addition to deriving the factors that influenced their success, the challenges encountered in the practice of clinical exercise physiology were examined and are represented in the model.

The model created as a result of this study is pragmatic in the sense that it is a tool that can be used by others to address the concerns faced in practicing the profession of clinical exercise physiology (Bryant, 2009, para. 103). These categories form two main components of the model: (1) *the path to employment in cardiac rehabilitation and diagnostics environment*, and (2) *recognition of the expertise of clinical exercise physiologists*.

## The Path to Employment

The bottom portion of the model shown in Figure 8.1 describes the process of becoming a successful practitioner in the field. The information derived from the interviews spanned many years. No matter the length of their

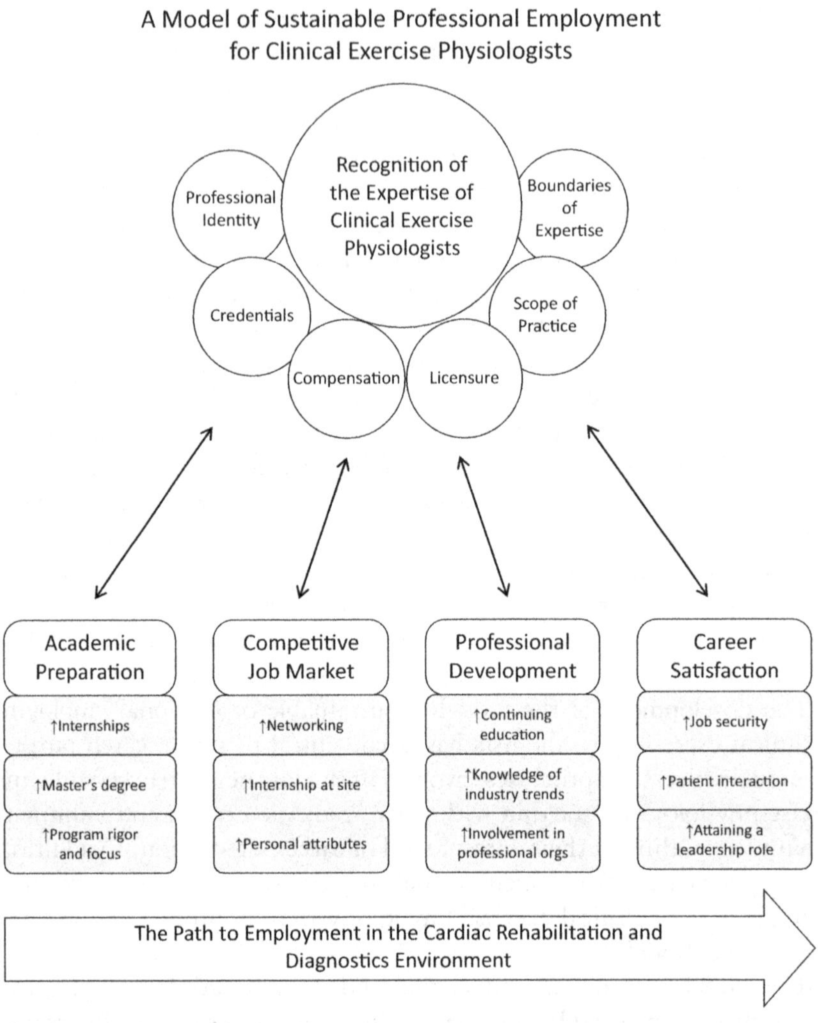


*Figure 8.1:* Model of Sustainable Professional Employment for Clinical Exercise Physiologists

journeys, all participants went through a process of transformation in order to become the successful practitioners they are today. No two participant's journeys were the same; however, there were many commonalities among them. All of the participants' journeys, *the path to employment in the cardiac rehabilitation and diagnostics environment*, consisted of four main categories: (1) *academic preparation*, (2) *competitive job market*, (3) *professional development*, and (4) *career satisfaction*.

## *Academic Preparation*

In the Chicago area, a master's degree is usually required to secure a position in cardiac rehabilitation and diagnostics departments. Key components of academic preparation are clinical internships as well as the program of study's rigor. Nearly all of the study's participants felt that their internships were a critical component of their academic preparation (Ives & Knudson, 2007). The participants agreed that internships are a form of anticipatory socialization that allows a student to try on a career (Callanan & Benzing, 2004). It was through clinical internships that several of the participants discovered how much they loved the field of cardiac rehabilitation.

Hennemann and Liefner (2010) stress that an important component of an academic program is the development of competence. The goal of my participants when they have student interns is to have them as competent as regular staff by the end of their internship. *Academic preparation* is linked with the *competitive job market* through the networks that students begin to develop when they perform their internships. Many of the participants attained their first positions in the field through their internships.

## *Competitive Job Market*

The next step in the path is entering the job market. The cardiac rehabilitation and diagnostics environment is very competitive in the Chicago area; thus, enhancing one's employability is key. Employability encompasses the "skills, understandings, and personal attributes" (Atlay, 2010, p. 19) that improve the chances that graduates will obtain employment in the occupation of their choice. Internships serve as a means for students to demonstrate their employability to potential employers.

My participants constantly emphasized the importance of networking, not only to enter the field but also their ability to advance within the field. Networking is a critical component in securing employment in addition to internships since both provide a means for students to demonstrate their competencies to potential employers (Sherman & Dyess, 2010). Henley's (1999) comment that "what you know counts, but who you know counts, too" was reflected in the number of instances where practitioners in this study obtained positions before they were even advertised.

## *Professional Development*

Attainment of a position in the field is not the final step; those who hope to advance need to continue to invest in professional development. It is important to keep up with the changes in healthcare in terms of treatments, patient demographics, and insurance reimbursements that have a direct impact on participants' departments and, in turn, their job security. Continuing education is a means of lifelong learning and a way to develop professionalism (Garman et al., 2006). This study's participants utilized different approaches toward continuing education. Educational opportunities offered through professional societies are a common way that practitioners stay current in the field. *Professional development* is linked with the *competitive job market* primarily through the networks participants built through service in professional organizations.

### Career Satisfaction

The culmination of *the path to employment in cardiac rehabilitation and diagnostics environment* is achieving satisfaction with your career choice. The vast majority of this study's participants had engaged in internships in the area in which they are currently employed. The awareness of the work environment produced by internships contributed to students making a commitment to the profession (Callanan & Benzing, 2004; Cranmer, 2006). Career success and fulfillment are a "function of the individual optimizing the 'fit' between their personal characteristics and their work environment" (Callahan & Benzing, p. 82). This was reflected in the passion that the successful practitioners exhibited when they spoke of their work with patients, which is also consistent with the findings of Ng and Feldman (2010) regarding the factors that contribute positively to a sense of well-being.

### It Is a Profession! Recognition of the Expertise of Clinical Exercise Physiologists

A key concept in the development of grounded theory is that the researcher is to determine the main concern of the interviewee and how the person was able to resolve it (Glaser & Holton, 2004). This study's participants shared much information about their journeys, but the one key concern that kept emerging was the difficulty of having their expertise recognized by other healthcare practitioners. This main concern, or core category, is positioned in the center of the top section of the model presented in Figure 8.1. Surrounding the core category are the categories, or factors, that influence it. These supporting categories include *professional identity*, *credentials*, *compensation*, *licensure*, *scope of practice*, and *boundaries of expertise*. The model represented in Figure 8.1 also portrays the interrelationships between these categories and those that comprise *the path to employment in the cardiac rehabilitation and diagnostics environment.*

## Professional Identity

Even though Brown (2000) argues that exercise physiology is not a profession, this study's participants felt that it *was* a profession. As part of the push for licensure to further establish exercise physiology as a profession, academic programs in clinical exercise physiology are being encouraged to attain accreditation. As part of accreditation, academic programs must demonstrate that their curriculum will ensure their graduates will possess a defined set of knowledge, skills, and abilities. Without this standardization it is hard for others to know what expertise a clinical exercise physiologist should possess. This results in a lack of a clear professional identity that works against attaining the *recognition of the expertise of clinical exercise physiologists* among those in the healthcare community.

In addition, clinical exercise physiologists are not united behind a single professional organization unlike other professions such as physical therapy. Only some of this study's participants were members either of the American Association of Cardiovascular and Pulmonary Rehabilitation (AACVPR) or the Illinois Society for Cardiopulmonary Health and Rehabilitation (ISCHR). However, these organizations do not represent those practitioners who work outside of cardiac rehabilitation. The lack of a single organization that actually represents all of clinical exercise physiologists hinders the attainment of the *recognition of the expertise of clinical exercise physiologists.*

## Credentials

One way to address the current lack of a standardized curriculum is for practitioners to take certification examinations to prove that they do have the knowledge, skills, and abilities required of those who desire to work in the cardiac rehabilitation and diagnostics environment. Despite Keteyian's (1999) findings that certification examinations help address concerns from other healthcare professions regarding the academic preparation of exercise physiologists, this study's participants felt that examinations were of limited value because they only tested book knowledge. In addition, there was much confusion over what the differences were between the Exercise Specialist (ES), Clinical Exercise Specialist (CES), and Registered Clinical Exercise Physiologist (RCEP) certifications offered by the American College of Sports Medicine (ACSM).

### *Compensation*

This study's participants are frustrated because they are paid less than nurses even though they have a higher level of education; they do not feel that their compensation reflects their expertise (Davis et al., 2001). Although Davis and colleagues and Ives and Knudson (2007) suggest that the employment of exercise physiologists might be favored over other licensed professionals such as nurses because of the salary differences, this was not consistent with what this study's participants reported. Due to the limits on scope of practice, nurses were still needed and, in fact, it was the versatility of nurses that made utilizing them preferable in cardiac rehabilitation and diagnostics departments despite their higher wages. Some of this study's participants suggested that licensure would increase the utilization of exercise physiologists.

### *Licensure*

The lack of licensure for clinical exercise physiologists poses several problems. Of biggest concern to this study's participants is the lack of professional equality they feel when compared with other healthcare professionals. On a microlevel, they reported excellent working relationships with the other professions in their department, but on a macrolevel, there were concerns about the discrepancy in pay as well as limitations on what they could do as part of their jobs.

Related to *licensure* is *professional identity*. As a profession, we have not done a good job defining who we are and what we do since there are so many different career paths that clinical exercise physiologists can pursue. Berry and Verrill (2012) argue that "achieving licensure will finally enable the CEP to be viewed in the same light and with the same respect as other licensed health care professionals who work in the rehabilitation fields" (p. 37). Foster and Porcari (2012) outline the great difficulty involved in convincing legislators to support licensure due to the lack of evidence showing that large numbers of the general public are being harmed by the activities of unqualified practitioners. The points made by Foster and Porcari echo what this study's participants have mentioned—that we in the profession are not coming together to present a unified front in terms of minimal educational standards as well as working together with larger organizations, such as the physical therapists, to better define how our profession can work effectively with other professions in delivering patient care.

## *Scope of Practice*

This category is related to *licensure* as part of the process of creating a practice act for a profession that defines those activities practitioners are permitted to engage in and what is prohibited. This study's participants repeatedly related how they were not able to perform certain activities, such as giving medications to a patient or taking orders from a doctor, due to the restrictions of the Nurse Practice Act. Several expressed frustration over how these restrictions limited their ability to service their patients. *Scope of practice* affects compensation because exercise physiologists are not able to function independently in cardiac rehabilitation. For smaller cardiac rehabilitation outreach sites, this often means that a registered nurse will be utilized since they are more versatile, thus keeping staffing to a minimum. Several of this study's participants suggested an expansion of scope of practice for clinical exercise physiologists could result in need for fewer nurses. This, in turn, could have a positive impact on *competitive job market.*

## *Boundaries of Expertise*

Nancarrow and Borthwick (2005) found that professional boundaries are dynamic due to staffing shortages caused by changes in healthcare policies. Many of this study's participants reported a high degree of role sharing between exercise physiologists and nurses. The ability of clinical exercise physiologists to perform a wide variety of roles in the cardiac rehabilitation and diagnostics environment demonstrates their broad expertise. *Scope of practice* is related to *boundaries of expertise* since the scope of practice helps to define what should be expected of each profession. Regarding the scope of practice for exercise physiologists, ACSM mentions the use of exercise as a means of therapy for clinical situations such as those found in cardiac rehabilitation and diagnostics environments (Verrill & Keteyian, 2010). This study's participants felt that exercise prescription was best left to clinical exercise physiologists. Several participants believed patients were not being served well when cardiac rehabilitation programs only utilized registered nurses. They felt the lack of training for nurses in exercise prescription was a disservice to the patient.

## *Recognition of the Expertise of Clinical Exercise Physiologists*

The main concern of this study's participants was earning recognition of their unique expertise from the other healthcare professionals. Many of this study's participants felt that they were being held back because they are not licensed professionals like nurses or physical therapists. As was previously discussed, there are several facets to this perception of a lack of recognition of expertise. A strong *professional identity*, such as that possessed by other professions, can help practitioners earn respect because it clarifies the role that the practitioner serves on the healthcare team. However, as was previously discussed, clinical exercise physiology practitioners are not unified behind one organization.

An acknowledgment of a practitioner's expertise is often demonstrated when they are paid in accordance with their *credentials*. However, the reality that a nurse with only an associate's degree has a higher starting salary than a clinical exercise physiologist with a master's degree makes some question their career choice. Other practitioners in this study take a more philosophical view—that it is more important to do something you are passionate about rather than earn a higher salary but not enjoy your work.

*Licensure*, despite being touted as a means to gain credibility and recognition, does not appear to be anywhere close to becoming a reality in the majority of states. Furthermore, this study's participants were mixed in their feelings regarding the benefit they would actually derive, and they questioned whether it would cause an additional burden, not only in terms of limits on the activities they could perform but also the expense practitioners would have to assume in attaining and maintaining a license.

Practitioners often feel that their unique expertise is not recognized due to the limitations imposed on their *scope of practice* by the Nurse Practice Act. This goes along with establishing *boundaries of expertise*. Clinical exercise physiologists have a significant investment in acquiring expertise in exercise prescription and the body's responses to the stress of exercise. They desire to utilize their expertise to provide better outcomes for their patients. While some of this study's participants feel that their expertise is recognized and sought out by other professions, it was not a sentiment that was shared by all.

The model of sustainable professional employment for clinical exercise physiologists generated by this study reflects the processes by which this study's participants have achieved their career success in addition to presenting their main concern of achieving recognition of the expertise of clinical exercise physiologists. This model shown in Figure 8.1 has been developed out of the analyses of the interviews that were conducted and has been further substantiated by relevant literature in the field. Arrows are used to represent how *the path to employment in the cardiac rehabilitation and diagnostics environment* interacts with *recognition of the expertise of clinical exercise physiologists.*

This model represents a pragmatic and inspiring tool to be used by practitioners in the field as well as those who hope to pursue new levels of career attainment. The inclusion of the perspectives of recent graduates into the creation of this model helps to strengthen its applicability to those students who seek to enter the field.

The original idea for this study started with a flash of insight when I observed so many exemplars in the field that had inexplicably overcome the challenges of the profession of clinical exercise physiology and attained career success. The use of grounded theory method revealed much about the preparation and practice of clinical exercise physiologists employed in the cardiac rehabilitation and diagnostics environment. I gained insight into the importance of clinical internships and the development of professional networks in attaining employment. I was dismayed to discover how widespread the lack of name recognition is for clinical exercise physiologists, even in a healthcare setting. Clinical exercise physiologists make significant contributions in cardiac rehabilitation due to their extensive master's level academic preparation that is the equivalent of nurses, dieticians, and physical therapists. Clinical exercise physiologists often work side-by-side with these professions, yet lack the recognition of expertise that licensure conveys. I was saddened to learn they are treated as the odd duck in the clinical environment because they do not exist independently despite being highly skilled (Foster & Porcari, 2012). Much work remains to unite our profession and elevate its standing in the healthcare setting.

## References

American Physical Therapy Association. (n.d.). Who are physical therapists? http://www.apta.org/AboutPTs/

Atlay, M. (2010). *Introducing CRe8—The curriculum review 2008*. https://www.beds.ac.uk/

Berry, R., & Verrill, D. (2012). POINT: Licensure for clinical exercise physiologists—An argument in favor of this proposal. *Journal of Clinical Exercise Physiology, 1*(1), 35–38.

Bogdan, R. C., & Biklen, S. K. (2007). *Qualitative research for education: An introduction to theory and method*. Pearson.

Brown, S. P. (2000). Profession or discipline: The role of exercise physiology in allied health. *Clinical Exercise Physiology, 2*(1), 52.

Bryant, A. (2009). Grounded theory and pragmatism: The curious case of Anselm Strauss. *Forum: Qualitative Social Research, 10*(3). http://www.qualitative-research.net/index.php/fqs/article/view/1358

Bryant, A., & Charmaz, K. (Eds.). (2007). *The Sage handbook of grounded theory*. SAGE.

Callanan, G., & Benzing, C. (2004). Assessing the role of internships in the career-oriented employment of graduating college students. *Education & Training*, *46*(2), 82–89.

Clinical Exercise Physiology Association. (n.d.). *Consumer information: Clinical exercise physiology*. https://www.acsm-cepa.org/

Cranmer, S. (2006). Enhancing graduate employability: Best intentions and mixed outcomes. *Studies in Higher Education*, *31*(2), 169–184.

Creswell, J. W., & Clark, V. L. (2011). *Designing and conducting mixed methods research* (2nd ed.). SAGE.

Davis, S., Jankovitz, K., & Cooper, J. (2001). California cardiac rehabilitation practitioners and their staff preparation preferences. *Clinical Exercise Physiology*, *3*(2), 94.

Foster, C., & Porcari, J. P. (2012). COUNTERPOINT: Licensure for clinical exercise physiologists—A desirable goal with an elusive outcome. *Journal of Clinical Exercise Physiology*, *1*(1), 38–40.

Garman, A. N., Evans, R., Krause, M., & Anfossi, J. (2006). Professionalism. *Journal of Healthcare Management*, *51*(4), 219–222.

Glaser, B. G. (1992). *Emergence vs. forcing: Basics of grounded theory analysis.* Sociology.

Glaser, B. G. (1998). *Doing grounded theory: Issues and discussions.* Sociology.

Glaser, B. G., & Holton, J. (2004). Remodeling grounded theory. *Forum Qualitative Social Research*, *5*(2). http://www.qualitative-research.net/index.php/fqs/article/view/607

Glaser, B. G., & Strauss, A. L. (1965). *Awareness of dying.* Aldine de Gruyter.

Glaser, B. G., & Strauss, A. L. (1967). *The discovery of grounded theory: Strategies for qualitative research.* Aldine de Gruyter.

Henley, R. J. (1999). Enhancing what you know through who you know. *Healthcare Financial Management)*, *53*(12).

Hennemann, S., & Liefner, I. (2010). Employability of German geography graduates: The mismatch between knowledge acquired and competences required. *Journal of Geography in Higher Education*, *34*(2), 215–230.

Holton, J. A. (2010). The coding process and its challenges. *Grounded Theory Review*, *9*(1), 21–40.

Ives, J. C., & Knudson, D. (2007). Professional practice in exercise science. *Sports Medicine*, *37*(2), 103–115.

Keteyian, S. J. (1999). Trained in a discipline and practicing as a professional. Who we are, revisited. *Clinical Exercise Physiology*, *1*(2), 55.

Merriam, S. B., & Simpson, E. L. (1995). *A guide to research for educators and trainers of adults.* Krieger.

Mills, J., Bonner, A., & Francis, K. (2006). The development of constructivist grounded theory. *International Journal of Qualitative Methods*, *5*(1), 1–10.

Mullen, P. D. (1996). Cutting back: Life after a heart attack. In B. G. Glaser (Ed.), *Gerund grounded theory: The basic social process dissertation* (pp. 60–72). Sociology.

Nancarrow, S., & Borthwick, A. M. (2005). Dynamic professional boundaries in the healthcare workforce. *Sociology of Health & Illness*, *27*(7), 897–919.

Ng, T., & Feldman, D. (2010). Human capital and objective indicators of career success: The mediating effects of cognitive ability and conscientiousness. *Journal of Occupational & Organizational Psychology, 83*(1), 207–235.

Ozmon, H. A., & Craver, S. M. (2003). *Philosophical foundations of education.* Merrill Prentice Hall.

Potteiger, J. A. (2011). *ACSM's introduction to exercise science.* Lippincott Williams & Wilkins.

Sherman, R. O., & Dyess, S. (2010). New graduate transition into practice during turbulent economic times. *Journal of Nursing Education, 49*(7), 367–368.

U.S. Department of Labor, Bureau of Labor Statistics. (2010). *Standard occupational classification: 29–1128 exercise physiologists.* https://www.bls.gov/

Verrill, D. E., & Keteyian, S. J. (2010). Evolution of the clinical exercise physiologist. In J. Myers & D. C. Nieman (Eds.), *ACSM's resources for clinical exercise physiology: Musculoskeletal, neuromuscular, neoplastic, immunologic, and hematologic conditions* (pp. 280–287). Lippincott Williams & Wilkins.

# Chapter 9 Civically Engaged Curriculum: A Call for Action to Elementary Public-School Teachers

Cheryl Jean DeRoo

We develop our positionalities early and often based upon our life experiences. The early school years of my childhood were spent in a stereotypical White, suburban neighborhood where mothers were nearly always at home ready to care for kids, clean, cook, and provide all of the daily necessities. The vast majority, if not all of the families on our block were White, and the school we attended matched the neighborhood. If there were other diverse ethnic groups, I cannot recall. Recent experiences have helped me to understand that my lack of knowledge was a convenient benefit of my White privilege.

As my dad's business grew, my parents also had outgrown the neighborhood and were ready to move to a larger home. We were not included in the search, but were pleased with our new living space. We moved to what was probably considered a higher-income neighborhood just outside of a small city. It had a community pool, tennis courts, and plenty of activity. We did not know it at the time, but our lives as school children would look much different. My older sister and I attended a middle school right in the heart of the downtown area of the city. The diversity in the student body took me by surprise. The mix of Black, White, and Hispanic students was new to me, and early on, I was quite uncomfortable. I recall the first day feeling overdressed and out of place, unsure of how or if I would ever fit in. My experiences would prove my initial reactions wrong. Though during this time period there were often visual and social racial divides in our school, it was also a time filled with opportunities for me to personally thrive. Those years did not bring us to have conversations about race, ethnicity, or inclusion; however, I grew in my relationships with all students while developing an interest in other races and cultures. In some people, the seed grows; in others, it does not. I believe this move had a profound impact on the person I would grow up to be.

As an elementary school principal, a majority of my time is spent inside classrooms observing teacher practices and student learning. Often these observations are done in a formal manner, while many times, I am informally assessing overall teacher practices. At times, it brought back memories of my own teaching career, while at other times, I was struck by the new, more interesting, and innovative practices that teachers had developed over the years. However, even the untrained eye would notice that most of the days are spent in the world of literacy and mathematics, with little time for social studies and science. Over the years, I saw social studies lessons here or there; however, they were primarily readings shared with the students, often in the form of a chapter from a 20-year-old textbook followed by a list of questions for students to answer. That brought back memories. Memories from my days in school when I was bored out of my mind reading words from a three-inch-thick social studies text that lacked interest to me and words ran together in a meaningless way. There has to be a better way! Where, I have often wondered, are the experiences? How can we find the time to make social studies curriculum more meaningful to students and create a connection to their personal lives?

It did not occur to me that becoming a school building leader would have me learn more about power and equity than I would about how children learn to read. That is exactly what happened over the past 15 years as an elementary school principal. It first struck me while opening our school doors for the first time during a local election. We only had a single precinct, but I was thrilled for the students to be able to have a chance to witness a real election. To my surprise, the polls were empty; very few voters came out to cast a ballot. I was certain that in the next presidential election year, we would see a much different story. Our first African American presidential candidate, Barak Obama, was running for office, while on the opposing side, a female, Sarah Palin, was attempting to fill the vice-presidential seat with John McCain as the presidential nominee. The students had been talking about the election and they were excited. Students were excited to share their voting choices, typically repeating the verbiage from the conversations heard at home. The election ended, and the curriculum moved on. Four more years of focus on textbooks, dry readings, and a lack of rigor. Yet increased testing practices, pressure from district leaders, and outdated materials continued to delay the change that I was hoping for—a curriculum based on real-life experiences, action, and problem-solving that would engage and inspire our students. This long-carried frustration and unfulfilled hope compelled me to embark on this study in the hope of contributing to civic research and student engagement.

## *Statement of the Problem*

Today, across the media, Americans see civil unrest, distrust in government, and the nation divided among political lines. It is difficult to see any positive outcomes of continual conflict. Despite the current challenges in the United States, this conflict may be providing motivation for people to share their voices. Early voting results show record numbers of voters going to the polls. In a National Public Radio (NPR) interview, University of Florida professor Michael McDonald summarizes his voter-tracking information: "We continue to pile on votes at a record pace. We've already passed any raw number of early votes in any prior election in U.S. history" (Sprunt, 2020, para. 4). In addition, according to the Center for Information and Research on Civic Learning and Engagement (CIRCLE) (2020), youth activism and civic engagement are increasing.

While the increase in civic participation is a reason to hope for advocates of social studies education, the barriers created have continued to marginalize social studies curriculum, particularly in the early grades. These barriers can be based on federal and state mandates and testing but they also come from pressure at the district and school administrative levels (Pace, 2011). Pace (2011) points to previous research that affirms this is particularly the case with schools serving low-income populations: "Narrowing of curriculum occurs disproportionately in low-performing schools with large minority populations, thereby contributing to educational inequity in the name of narrowing the achievement gap" (p. 33).

For decades, academic scholars have recommended an integrated approach to the curriculum, particularly at the elementary school level: "More recently, content integration has received renewed interest in the Common Core State Standards (CCSS) and is a key component to CCSS" (Huck, 2019, p. 3). Integration, however, poses additional challenges for classroom teachers. Heafner (2018) explored perspectives of both teachers and an administrator on the move to an integrated ELA and social studies integrated curriculum model and found several challenges. Teachers, in Heafner's study, reported ambiguity and confusion due to limited training. Teachers also reported that a wide variety of hands-on materials were available yet there was little time to plan or work with grade-level teams, causing a lack of enthusiasm and frustration. Additionally, the administrator suspected a lack of teacher expertise in social studies itself as a concern for implementation (Heafner, 2018).

It is important then to determine how it is that teachers develop the professional agency to design and implement civically engaged curriculum. Despite the challenges that we face, with teacher training and preparation, I believe that civic engagement can—and should—begin in elementary school.

## *Research Purpose and Questions*

The purpose of this case study was (a) to investigate ways in which elementary teachers develop their positionality with regard to civically engaged education and design and implement civically engaged curriculum, and (b) to examine the conditions under which these teachers can develop agency to advocate for action-oriented civic education. The following questions guided the study:

1. How do elementary teachers develop positionality with regard to civically engaged education?
2. How do they design and implement civically engaged curriculum within the constraints of federal, state, and district mandates?
3. What prevents them, if anything, from implementing civically engaged curriculum?
4. How can these teachers motivate their students to understand the importance of civic responsibility and engagement in civic learning?
5. What are the conditions under which these teachers can develop agency to advocate for action-oriented civic education?

## *Methodological Approach: Theoretical Lens*

The theory of change and social justice theory are the perspectives that informed this study's research purposes, questions, and the entire research process. Teachers themselves design their day-to-day complex instruction based upon the criteria provided by their districts, states, and the federal guidelines. However, teachers report that they need far more planning time than they are afforded by their school districts (Merritt, 2016). Additionally, through collaboration, teachers can share their voices. "One of the major messages from Visible Learning is the power of teachers learning from and talking to each other about planning" (Hattie, 2012, p. 60). Thus, in this study, the use of teacher voice and collaboration lend themselves well to both the theory of change and to social justice theory.

## *The Theory of Change*

The theory of change has long been associated with school reform and the times political and economic climate (Goodson, 2014). Progressive change models reflect the need to include educator voice within the change process in order to provide change that can represent all the people the school serves. Educators' areas of expertise serve as the primary voice within the change process, although that voice must represent the people they serve. In the United States, White teachers continue to represent the majority, while their students represent those of color. According to the statistics of the Institute of Education Sciences (IES) (2020), the majority of teachers were White in schools where a majority of students were Hispanic (54%), Black (54%), Asian (60%), or American Indian/Alaska Native (61%). These data show that in schools where a large percentage of teachers were White, the majority of their students were not White. Thus, it is paramount to acknowledge these teacher voices in a collaborative way.

Additionally, Hargreaves (1996) encourages researchers to acknowledge teacher voices without silencing the voices of students and parents: "Though silenced in research and in policy, teachers' voices often prevail inordinately within their own institutions, to the exclusion of students' and parents' ones" (p. 14). Through this research, I listened to the voice of the teacher, focusing on each person's life history and their current positionality in an effort to discover ways in which they motivated and engaged their students in action-oriented civic education.

## *Social Justice Theory*

Social justice theory (SJT) primarily concerns itself with providing equitable and fair opportunities for all within society (Rawls, 1971). Within education, SJT finds common ground with the change model; its focus is the needs and interests of the students and the community in which they teach. "Educational content and processes are connected to social justice theories and practices by deliberate and explicit interventions tailored to specific students, communities, and society in contexts" (Bogotch, 2002, p. 3). Teachers need to address barriers that students may come across as they embark on new curriculum. Villegas (2007) reminds educators that although schools have made progress in the work of social justice, there needs to be continued effort to focus on inequities, making learning an active process that brings in former life experiences, helping students to build bridges to prior knowledge, and constructing understanding. These were the practices that I listened for and looked for throughout my data collection and analysis. For students, lessons embedded in social justice concepts allow for critical thinking and problem-solving for change.

Freire (1968/2000) promotes liberating action of the oppressed so that they may transform and recognize their current reality to bring about transformative change. Freire (1968/2000) suggests that "to achieve this goal, the oppressed must confront reality critically, simultaneously objectifying and acting upon that reality" (p. 52). Furthermore, Freire supports teachers acting as advocates in this liberation by eliminating the banking model of education that focuses on the teacher as the expert, and moving toward a model where problem-solving and transformation can occur.

Liberation is a praxis: the action and reflection of men and women upon their world in order to transform it. Those truly committed to liberation must reject the banking concept in its entirety, adopting instead a concept of women and men as conscious beings, and consciousness intent upon the world. They must abandon the educational goal of deposit making and replace it with the posing of the problems of human beings in their relations with the world (Freire, 1968/2000, p. 79).

Social justice theorists and change theorists continue to advocate for this transformative learning as critical elements for educational models. According to Brown (2004),

> Employing a critical, transformative pedagogy requires professors to be active facilitators and co-learners who go beyond simply meeting the expressed needs of the learner. Through a wide array of roles, methods, and techniques, they need to take on the responsibility for growth by questioning the learner's expectations and beliefs. Transformative learning is a process of critical self-reflection that can be stimulated by people, events, or changes in context that challenge the learner's basic assumptions of the world. (p. 87)

The use of change theory and social justice theory as the theoretical bases for my study provided me with a framework to connect previous research to this study.

## *Research Design: Case Study*

Qualitative methods offer effective ways to design a study of teacher positionality, agency, and action-based civic curriculum. I employed a case-study approach to gain an in-depth understanding of the conditions that emerge across a variety of individual cases. According to Stake (1995), "qualitative case study was developed to study the experience of real cases operating in real situations" (p. 3). Yin (2018) further defines case-study research as "an empirical inquiry that investigates a contemporary phenomenon (the 'case') in depth and within its real-world context, especially when the boundaries between phenomenon and context may not clearly evident" (p. 15). A case-study approach allowed for a deeper insight into the real-life experiences of the teachers participating in my study and the curriculum they create.

Stake (1995) recognizes that holism is a special characteristic of all qualitative research, defining it as contextually well developed, bounded, resistant of reductionism and elementalism, and noncomparative. Stake (1995) additionally identifies that qualitative studies, and thus this case study, are empirical, interpretive, and empathetic. The design of this study focused on these aspects through observations, interactions, and interpretations, yet although intentional, the structure was responsive to the experiences as they occurred.

Stake (1995) further differentiates between instrumental and intrinsic case study. An instrumental case study is "a research question, a puzzlement, a need for general understanding, and a feel that we may get insight into the question by studying a particular case" (Stake, 1995, p. 3). Conversely, intrinsic case study is one in which the researcher is studying the case to fill a particular need: "We are interested in it, not because by studying it we learn about other cases or about some general problem, but because we need to learn about that particular case" (Stake, 1995, p. 3). This case study was instrumental in that its intent was to gain insight into questions of teacher positionality, agency, and their effects on the design of action-oriented civic curriculum.

## *Research Site and Participants*

The site for this study was a public elementary school in a large suburban school district located approximately 30 miles outside of a major metropolitan city in the Midwest. The school was a diverse school with approximately 57% of the students coming from low-income households. Additionally, the students attending the school came from a variety of ethnic and cultural backgrounds with 51% of the students identifying as Hispanic, 28% White, 11% Asian, 6% Black, and 3% or less identifying as one of a variety of other races. The 33 different languages spoken in the homes of its families also indicated the diversity of the school. While the student body was diverse, the teaching staff was less so. The school had 23 classroom teachers, 16 of which identified as White and seven as Hispanic. At the time of this study, the school site was also the place where I was one of the administrators. The site was selected based on its convenience for me and its ease of access to the participants. Additionally, due to the fact that school remained online during the COVID-19 pandemic, this setting needed to be accessible both on site and in the virtual setting.

The main participants in this study and on the site were classroom teachers. Participants were sought out using purposive sampling. Saldaña and Omasta (2018) explain that most qualitative research employs purposive sampling, in which participants are deliberately selected because they are most likely to provide insight into the phenomenon being investigated due to their position, experience, and/or identity markers (e.g., demographics, such as gender, race/ethnicity, health status) (p. 96). The participants were selected based upon their willingness to volunteer for the study after being provided its information and its purpose. This method was based on a convenience sampling because all of the participants were from the school in which I served. Additionally, because teaching teams often have strong knowledge of one another's practices, I asked teachers to recommend those who they think may be good examples for the study. This network sampling allowed me to identify further participants for the study.

## *Data Sources and Methods of Data Collection*

### *Interviews*

Interviews have the advantage of allowing the researcher to gain specific knowledge of the participants' experiences, values, attitudes, and beliefs about topics that relate to the particular study (Saldaña & Omasta, 2018). As Merriam (1998) explains, "the main purpose of an interview is to obtain a special kind of information" (p. 71). Patton (1990) further clarifies that the researcher is seeking information that is "in and on someone else's mind" (p. 278). I conducted the teacher interviews using a semi-structured approach, leaving me with the ability to modify my questions throughout the interview and create a more conversational tone. The semi-structured approach allows the researcher to adjust the line of questioning throughout the interview based on the participant's response.

The interview allowed me to hear a teacher's voice, understand their historical background, and note any potential biases that the interviewee may have. The interview also allowed me to gather data regarding the participants' understanding of the curriculum, resources, and the participants' perceptions of student engagement within their lessons. The interviews consisted of primarily open-ended questions to lead us into a conversation.

It was important for me, as an administrator in the building, to be aware that I held a power that could affect the responses of my participants. According to Saldaña and Omasta (2018), "researchers should be aware that interpersonal dynamics will likely affect any type of interview; we encourage researchers to make efforts to create as equitable a relationship as possible" (p. 90). In this case, it was vital that I set a conversational tone in the interview and then held the interview in a space that was free of distractions. Additionally, as a researcher, making eye contact, paraphrasing, and adjusting my questions was important in order to build trust with the participant.

### *Observations*

Observations comprise additional sources of data gathered from real-world situations and events. I conducted multiple-observations, focusing on the engagement of the civic curriculum design. As an administrator who frequently acts as an informal observer and classroom participant, I joined the classroom as a participant-observer in order to assume a more natural researcher role. This active role allowed me, as the researcher, first-hand experiences of the work of the participants in the study. Throughout the observation, I recorded field notes, including timestamps, in a journal and purposefully scheduled time after an observation to review and type up the notes to ensure clarity. As with the interviews, procedures limited the number of in-person observations; therefore, some observations were done virtually.

### *Documents and Artifacts*

Throughout the research period, I gathered several documents and artifacts in an effort to gather additional evidence. I analyzed curriculum documents, classroom work samples, and photos collected from students doing the work. To further add to my analysis, I focused my data collection on the teacher's lesson design, whole classroom work products, and the teacher's perceptions of the students' thinking, rather than on the actual student work production.

## ***Data Analysis and Interpretation***

When reviewing data using a qualitative approach, as a researcher, I analyzed the data with a critical eye. The interviews were recorded, transcribed, and coded along with the field notes, documents, and artifacts. I then analyzed the data to look for themes.

I began condensing the data by coding both the narrative data (observations, field notes, and transcriptions) and the visual data (photos, journals, lesson plans, etc.). Because there were multiple sources of data, I asked the teacher-participants to take photos of engaging and doing projects, taking precautions to conceal all identities. These photos were used as documentation of the curricular work and as part of the conversations with teachers to help them to recall lessons and past student engagement. The photos remained unpublished and were used with parental consent. I chose photos at random, which ensured neutrality on my part as well as that of the classroom teacher.

Coding the data is a vital part of qualitative research. These data needed to be coded multiple times so as to narrow down the themes and to find patterns within the data. While looking for patterns, I purposefully noted the routines, rituals, roles, and relationships that appeared throughout, labeling them as I moved through the data. I used the participants' own words to ensure that their voice was heard throughout the research; therefore, one method of coding that I used was in vivo coding. According to Saldaña and Omasta (2018), when referring to in vivo coding, "this coding method utilizes the participant's own language as a symbol system for qualitative data analysis" (p. 121). Process coding, a means to analyze coding, was useful as I analyzed the participants' design and implementation of civically engaged curriculum. A third type of coding that I used to identify teacher positionality, motivation, and agency was that of values coding. It is particularly important, as Saldaña and Omasta (2018) remind researchers, that the researcher use multiple sources of data to corroborate the findings.

### *Validation Criteria and Ethical Considerations*

To ensure valid research, I employed several tactics throughout the research process. Creswell and Poth (2018) summarize the many views and understandings of validation to say, "we consider 'validation' in qualitative research to be an attempt to assess the accuracy" (p. 259) of the findings, as best described by the researcher, the participants, and the readers (or reviewers). Lincoln and Guba (1986) apply rigor as a parallel to trustworthiness, both serving as criteria to establish credibility within the inquiry process. They propose the use of a variety of techniques, such as prolonged engagement with the phenomenon, triangulation, member checks, and thick descriptions to build upon the inquiry's credibility.

The use of interviews, multiple-observations, and the collection of various documents and artifacts provided me with a variety of ways and views in which to engage with my topic of research to gain a holistic understanding. Triangulation further ensured an accurate interpretation of the vast amount of collected data. Creswell and Poth (2018) advise that "typically, this process involves corroborating evidence from different sources to shed light on a theme or perspective" (p. 260). The multiple data sources utilized in this study allowed for effective triangulation.

Member checks provide an additional validation strategy for qualitative research. Stake (1995) describes the process as "the actor is requested to examine rough drafts of writing where the actions or words of the actor are featured, sometimes when first written up but usually when no further data will be collected from him or her" (p. 115). The member checks in this study were conducted at the end of each interview. Case-study research also requires thick and rich description as a means of validation. This helps the reader to visualize the environment and transfer learning to other settings. Merriam (1998) describes rich, thick description as "providing enough description so that readers will be able to determine how closely their situations match the research situation, and hence, whether findings can be transferred" (p. 211). The vivid imagery allowed me as the researcher to interpret the data within my field notes and provide me with clear, articulate data.

Throughout the research process, reflexivity is a key component of increasing validity with qualitative research. Saldaña and Omasta (2018) describe reflexivity as looking inward at the data. I worked to remain reflexive, taking note of how my personal biases may affect the outcome of the data. I served in a supervisory role in the district and had a preconceived notion that action-oriented civic education is a strong strategy that needs to be considered. These things remained at the forefront of my mind while reflecting on the data in order to minimize my personal biases.

Additional ethical considerations must be considered when collecting qualitative research data, including gaining permission to conduct the study from the school district that served as a research site. Stake (1995) cautions: "School districts usually have permission procedures that should be followed" (pp. 57–58). Additionally, to ensure that my research followed legal and ethical guidelines, I complied with the requirements of the Institutional Review Board (IRB) at National Louis University. Furthermore, I shared with all potential participants prior to beginning, the details of the study as well as what I hoped to learn. Once the details were shared, as per legal and ethical guidelines, I obtained consent from all participants in my research study using the informed consent document and made it clear that they could withdraw consent at any time. This process allowed for the protection of the privacy and confidentially of all subjects.

Yin (2018) maintains that "the study of 'a contemporary phenomenon within its real-world context' obligates you to important ethical practices akin to those followed in medical research" (p. 88).

Finally, confidentiality, which is closely tied to consent, was of utmost importance throughout the research process. According to Saldaña and Omasta (2018), "researchers should always clearly inform participants what (if any) measures will be taken to ensure their anonymity and the confidentiality of the information they share" (p. 193). Throughout this study, the school district and its study participants were identified with pseudonyms for the express purpose of protecting their identities.

### *Discussion of the Findings*

Creating civic leaders among our children requires twenty-first-century students to engage in their learning. Levine and Kawashima-Ginsberg (2015) remind educators that such learning goes beyond developing rote skills. It requires skills in critical thinking, problem-solving, collaboration, communication, self-directed learning, and the development of an academic mindset (Levine & Kawashima-Ginsberg, 2015). As a young child, most of my school day was spent on memorizing content predetermined and controlled by the powers that be, likely from the perspective of the White male because they were the primary policymakers. Schools were in the business of disseminating information into the minds of children. It was only through personal experiences that I received a clear understanding of what it meant to be culturally responsive. Perhaps it was by accident, or perhaps it was the mindset of our family culture that brought me to take an interest in the diversity of the American people. Unfortunately, the instruction within my schools did not create or support this belief.

Schools originated with the mindset of the Common School Movement operating under the pretense of unity for all; however, in actuality, they began as exclusive institutions filled with segregation and one-sided political values (Boyte, 2003; Warren, 2001). Throughout the decades and through multiple school reform efforts, the government took on more control, implementing standards, testing, and other accountability measures. Despite the work of educators and researchers across the country who advocated for critical thinking, problem-solving, effective communication, self-directed learning, and the development of an academic mindset, these efforts did little to protect and create equality for all children, with each state determining its own curricular purpose (Kawashima-Ginsberg, 2015).

Today, the reality of this inequity has come out of hiding. Technology and cell phones make it easy to document real-world problems and concerns within communities. The burden to equalize education has been laid primarily in the hands of teachers as they work tirelessly to ensure that each child has access to a high-quality education (Darling-Hammond, 2019). This study reveals the strains on teachers and the uncertainty of creating a social-justice-oriented civic education model for elementary students, given the constraints that teachers face. What follows is the discussion of the findings of this study and the ways they contribute to existing research and scholarship on civically engaged curriculum and a variety of issue pertaining to it.

## *Reimagining Civically Minded Elementary Education*

Learning takes place when students connect new knowledge with prior knowledge in an active, meaningful, real-world context. Dewey (1916/2011) reminds us that education must be a vehicle to create social change, and it can do so when combining social interest and relationships. Social reconstructionists, such as Schiro (2013), agree that students make meaning as a result of interaction and contact with experiences, people, and the environment. Thus, children become contributing members of society and become vehicles for potential change.

This study highlights the voice of teachers regarding creating a meaningful curriculum that connects students to the real world. The teacher-participants in this study brought unique experiences to their classrooms and, at the same time, shared some similarities in what brought them to determine the primary values they held explicitly in regard to teaching civics.

The key findings of this study can be summarized in several main statements. First, the participants affirmed that past relationships and early life experiences were critical to developing their own civic mindset. Each participant told stories of important role models who impacted how they came to develop their own values and thus better understand their role as teachers. Campbell (2012) explains, "such values are at least in part expressions of one's personal experiences and background" (p. 189). These experiences impacted teachers' positionalities, which gave them the agency to seek out social justice experiences for their students. Second, while the participants spoke of feeling the need to prioritize civic education, they also voiced the lack of professional training in social studies education. Participants pointed out that only one social studies course was required in their teacher training. Additionally, once they were hired as a school teacher, they received little training in social studies education and no training in civic instruction. Their primary means of understanding came from collaborating with colleagues.

Observations in classrooms revealed a direct correlation between social justice concepts and civic education. Although participants did not narrate where they received their knowledge in social justice, several did point to their dual-language training as a means of support for bi-cultural experiences. This brought me to notice my third point, that is, that teachers implemented social justice ideals as a way to create civic-minded individuals.

Third, the teacher-participants designed lessons to include real-life problems; however, they fell short on creating a curriculum that included action-based experiences. The participants indicated that the lack of action-based experiences primarily stemmed from a feeling that providing these kinds of experiences was just too difficult to manage due to barriers within the educational system. Educators "have often moved from being proactive and constructive, to reactive and compliant" (Goodson, 2014, p. 771). The teachers in this research study found it easier to be compliant with policies rather than to push and plan for field-based experiences.

### *Unraveling Positionality*

Participants in this study recalled stories of their youth and early adulthood where they were exposed to people and ideas that differed from their own. Through church groups, their parents' career choices, and the reality of their community experiences, each could point to specific examples where they developed a passion for helping others. While teachers bring their personal stories, they must recognize that their accounts may be vastly different from those of their students. Thus, a teacher's positionality then is of utmost importance. Borrero et al. (2018) assert that "particular positionalities, such as those that allow critique of power dynamics in schools, may work to improve the educational outcomes of culturally diverse students as opposed to those positionalities that endorse dominant deficit beliefs about those students" (p. 458).

Ladson-Billings (1995) encourages teachers to get to know their students, their families, the cultures, languages, and the values that they bring. Each participant's classrooms were filled with students from diverse cultural and economic backgrounds, with the majority of them from low-income households. The Carnegie Corporation of New York and Circle (2003) highlight the disparity of political and civic knowledge in immigrant and low-income families: "Race and family income can predict political and civic knowledge, and family income, education, and gender can predict voting patterns" (p. 19). With regard to this study, classroom observations and participant interviews routinely pointed to relationships and inclusive curriculum as key to student understanding of civics.

### *Lessons in Schooling*

Similar to the participants' home experience, each of them pointed to specific incidents in school that had an impact on their civic development. Interestingly enough, most experiences appeared to have unintentional consequences, creating strong civic-mindedness in each of them. It is surprising that the teacher who had the earliest experiences with action-based civic education, Kevin, was the only one who cited that they grew up in a high-poverty area. Researchers in the United States find a disparity of civic teaching among the neediest of schools (NCSS, 2013). However, Kevin's experiences growing up in Mexico supported the need for real-world connections that were meaningful to students. In Kevin's experience, the community and the school were very much integrated, supporting one another. The teacher gave no textbook or skill-builder civics lessons; instead, the civic mindset came from the families and shared responsibilities to maintain and support the school. Upon moving to the United States as a pre-teen, Kevin almost immediately was thrust into the idea of assimilation and a banking model of education. His home language was discarded in lieu of learning English as quickly as possible. Schooling looked and sounded completely different from the early experiences in Mexico. Banks (2017) recalls that schools contribute to failed citizenship when they teach through an assimilation approach to civic education by requiring minoritized students to deny their home culture and language. Kevin's experiences in Mexico and transitioning to the United States only solidified his need to create a civic experience for his students.

The other participants recalled relationships with specific teachers as key to their commitment to civic education. Each of them cited exposure to ideas, cultures, and beliefs that were different from their own as a key area of deep learning. Levine and Kawashima-Ginsberg (2015) advocate for a focus on "deep learning," which goes beyond content to skills building in critical thinking and problem-solving, collaboration, effective communication, self-directed learning, and the development of an academic mindset. For many students, these experiences will not naturally be present in their everyday experiences. Therefore, schools must create ways to embed multiple perspectives and views into daily instruction. The participants in this study pointed to the use of various texts and other media to recognize biases and different viewpoints in their classrooms. They also recognized student discourse to engage students in conversations about the social issues of today. Weinstein (2004) emphasizes that students must be taught to listen to multiple perspectives through cognitive conflict and the teaching of controversy and worldviews within the school curriculum. Stuteville and Johnson (2015) define this type of curriculum as cultural pluralism, where students learn about the values of other cultures in order to make their own decisions regarding whether they will accept or reject societal and political beliefs. This, Weinstein (2004) offers, is an important skill for students as they prepare for a political life in the adult world. While it may not be entirely possible to identify the impact of the participants' intentional use of inclusive pedagogy, the previous research points to the likelihood that the students in the participants' classrooms will be prepared for a civically active life.

### *Social Justice as the Key Element of Curricular Change*

Throughout this study, elements of social justice were consistently featured in the daily instruction in each classroom. Practices such as debating ideas, reading about characters from various backgrounds, role-playing, hearing multiple perspectives, collaboration, and discussing today's controversy were essential to each teacher-participant. This finding speaks to what Banks (2017) refers to as an imperative for citizenship education. Banks advocates for a civics curriculum that reflects students' diverse backgrounds and incorporates essential aspects of their ethnic and community cultures.

Schools with low-income families also suffer when students are not exposed to problem-solving. Carnegie Corporation of New York and CIRCLE (2003) note the lack of overall civic knowledge, particularly in low-income families where discussions around politics are not common. The school participating in this study had a low-income population of 58% and was representative of many other schools across the state and the nation. Villegas (2017) asserts that teachers need to be prepared to teach for social justice in order to educate students in the knowledge and skills they will need to be successful in their adult lives. The participants in the study regularly spoke of deliberative practices to ensure that students shared their own voices and opinions, and ideas related to civic education topics. Without creating inclusive pedagogy, students are at a disadvantage and thus may be less engaged in their learning. As Danielson (2013) suggests, teachers need to plan appropriate learning activities to avoid gaps or misconceptions.

Professional development in social justice and civic education also were topics discussed throughout this study. As participants pointed to their own professional development, all of them agreed that the lack of training, from college through career-based professional development, left them uncertain and ill-prepared to develop lessons that included meaningful, active, civic engagement. The same sentiment is found in Levine and Kawashima-Ginsberg (2015), who claim that controversial issues boost students' knowledge and interest and are especially valuable for children from homes where there is not much political discussion. Teachers need the training to support students to engage in these discussions while facilitating the conversations.

When asked how they came to this understanding of civic education, teachers cited the standards laid out in the curriculum documents provided by the school district. This, in turn, corresponds to what Stuteville and Johnson (2015) note in their study when they claim that most of the standards across the United States were primarily written from a legalist position, a claim based on the presentation of factual material about law, structures of government, and how government works.

Upon reviewing each of the participants' grade level's curriculum documents, which are provided by the school district, each contained requirements of connecting the past to the present to ensure student understanding. All teacher-participants affirmed the value of connecting significant concepts and ideas of the past to current realities. Teachers planned ways for students to better understand the past and present by looking at topics from multiple perspectives. Teachers often compared and contrasted past events with current events to help students to think critically. Techniques such as role play, comparing and contrasting, and deliberation and debate were used to help students fully understand concepts. The active and deliberative lessons, which I observed and were also spoken of by the participants, provided a means for students to engage in meaningful, real-life connections with today's social and political patterns.

What seems to be missing from the lessons of the participating teachers in this study was an action-based pedagogy. This supports the work of Kawashima-Ginsberg (2015) who suggest that most teachers do not regularly use pedagogical techniques designed to build civic participation skills. Further, a similar conclusion can be made based on what Ladson-Billings (1992) stresses as the importance of teaching using culturally relevant pedagogy (CRP). In this regard, CRP requires academic success for all students while also developing cultural competence and critical consciousness skills. According to Ladson-Billings (1995), this can be done when students must engage in personally meaningful curriculum beyond the standards. Therefore, college teacher preparation programs and school district training must provide opportunities for the development of teachers' skills in action-based civic education, even for our youngest learners.

### *Creating Lasting and Permanent Change*

Experts on change theory agree that the collective teachers' voice must be a part of long-term systems change to create change. Goodson (2014) asserts that teacher voice must not be ignored, while Hargreaves (1996) suggests that the voice must come from multiple teachers' stories and perspectives. The teacher-participants in this study cited the teacher voice as an important key to strong curricular practices. The participants of this study explained that the current curriculum lacked multiple teacher's perspectives, which required teachers to seek out one another as support for creating a meaningful curriculum for their students. Furthermore, the participants in this study added to their lack of resources limited training for social studies and no training for action-based civics. The participants recalled only a single college course; each focused on general methods of teaching social studies such as backwards design, which is consistent with what Fullan (2006) argues about the missing components in professional development regarding understanding what teachers actually do within the classroom to improve instruction. The participants in this study also mentioned that district professional development focused on the materials and standards rather than teaching practices for social studies education.

This study's participants also cited policy and interfering with action-based curriculum as problematic because the logistics for planning action-based curriculum was too complex to make it worthwhile. These teachers felt overwhelmed by the procedures required to have students leave the school building for any period of time, citing that all of the jumping through hoops was too difficult. This finding points to the ways in which teachers need to be encouraged in their endeavors to create a positive change.

### *Developing Teacher Agency: The Barriers Teachers Face*

Mark et al. (2019) point to the work of researchers across the field to show that teacher agency can often be limited by mandates and accountability measures. Each participating teacher pointed to barriers in the educational system as reasons why they lacked the agency to take steps to ensure students take action. These barriers include the reality of the current pandemic, fear of parents' pushback, the lack of materials, an overabundance of standardized testing, lack of time, strict and overwhelming policies and guidelines, and minimal training. These findings echo what Biesta and Tedder (2007) explain as agency, which is not something that people have, but rather something that people do. The participants in this study appeared to have the agency to implement social justice practices into their lessons; however, they lacked the agency to engage students in action.

Parent pushback became a common fear for a few of the teacher-participants. With parents literally "in the room" with students during instruction, conversations were often taken out of context and became one-sided. The teachers reported that students did not always feel free to share their own ideas. When a student did share, a parent in the room with the student did not always appreciate the discussions that were taking place, arguing that these discussions were a way for teachers to push their own political agendas on their students. This was a risk that teachers often took because they espoused inclusive practices such as multi-perspective teaching, racial injustice, biases, and discussions around current events. The participant-teachers at times lacked the agency to promote some of these student conversations despite the risk to student learning. Pantić and Florian (2015) directly associate inclusive teacher pedagogy with teacher agency. They recognize that promoting inclusive practices and social justice implies the need to challenge and transform current structures and requires a willingness to take a risk to improve students' learning.

The study participants also cited time and procedures and policies as barriers to creating actual action-based lessons. Participants pointed to the district's short school day of only five instructional hours as a challenge to leaving school for any length of time. Furthermore, the transportation policy documents reviewed for this study show that going out of the school building for any reason would require a plethora of red tape. Teachers must obtain parent permission and charge expensive and unmanageable fees for the use of buses.

Additionally, chaperone guidelines, such as requiring background checks for volunteer supervisors and providing a male chaperone on each trip, caused additional stress for teachers. The teacher-participants in this study found that planning was less cumbersome when they were able to use video resources and readings to simulate field experiences. In this regard, Dewey's (1897) advice that students should take a hands-on approach by exploring their own interests within the community seems to withstand the test of time. Further, Schiro (2013) promotes democratic citizenship by acknowledging the work of social reconstructionists who maintain that students must take action through involvement with social issues directly within their environment in which the issue occurs. The Carnegie Corporation of New York and Circle (2003) emphasize students' engagement to live what they learn. Teachers cannot be held responsible when charged with engaging curricular practices without the support and resources needed.

The results of this study distinctly articulate the need for permanent and lasting change in the way elementary teachers engage students in action-based, real-life civic opportunities. However, as teachers and leaders, we must understand that without a restructuring of the school day and explicit teacher training, civics education curriculum will continue to be minimalized at the elementary school level. I believe that by continually leaving civic education behind, we are also leaving behind the leaders of tomorrow.

## *In Conclusion*

The findings of this study surface some insights into the work that needs to be done at the public elementary school level to create sustainable action-based civic education. It is imperative to include civic education at the elementary school level, throughout the curriculum, not as an add-on but rather an integrated curriculum component. Furthermore, as my study verifies, civic education curriculum must include social justice and culturally relevant practices in order to engage all students and prepare them for future adulthood and citizenship.

Teachers cannot be expected to do this important work without support and training. Therefore, teachers need to receive training that focuses on applying civic education to the community in which their students live. Professional development needs to be carefully designed so that it meets the teachers where they are in regard to their own civic development. Needs of teachers may range from support with lesson design and development to planning and implementing field-based experiences for their students. It is vital that this training is not simply a "one and done" workshop, but rather training that is based upon a long-term training and implementation plan.

Teachers in the classroom live the work of student learning each and every day. However, as this study's teacher-participants pointed out, they are the experts in their field, but their voices are often limited, or worse yet, excluded from district change initiatives. To achieve transformative change, teachers' voices must be heard and taken into account, as a collective, in the curriculum writing process to ensure that all perspectives are included in the process.

Finally, mandated and unfunded educational policies must be discontinued. All educators and educational leaders must take action themselves to encourage policymakers, school board members, legislators, and advocacy groups to develop policies that encourage and adequately fund action-based, community-based civic education for elementary school children and their teachers.

I cannot remember a time when I did not want to be a teacher. As a very young child, I remember playing school, helping my teacher aunt, and dreaming of the day when I would stand at the head of the class, imparting knowledge to little ones. When I signed on to be a part of the business of education, I had no idea where the journey would take me. With experience comes wisdom. The complexity of teaching taught me that each child has their own wisdom to bring to the table. With that knowledge, the ultimate responsibility we have as educators is to allow that child to develop into a problem-solving, critical thinking, independent, and active citizen.

Over the 30 plus years that I have served in education, I have seen initiatives and practices come and go. Policies created by the dominant members of society do not consider the vast array of cultures and experiences that our students come to school with. Testing and accountability practices change with each administration, yet these practices and supporting policies continue to ignore the voices of teachers and minority groups. I have seen the responsibilities of educators increase tenfold with little benefit accruing to the students who should remain at the center of what we do. However, more than ever in this 2020–2021 school year, as we all witness a divided nation, it is clear that our students must be given the tools to create a future where all people matter. It is long-overdue time to rise up and use our voices, as educators and Americans, to fight for what is best for our kids.

All children have the right to live in a nation where they can participate and lead a responsible, engaged, active civic life, a nation in which all voices are heard through the policies that are made. Each person should learn to have concern for the future world while honoring the current space in which they live. As an educator, I believe that we have the opportunity and the responsibility to provide the space for teaching these democratic skills. As Justice Sandra Day O'Connor asserted: "The practice of democracy is not passed down through the gene pool. It must be taught and learned anew by each generation of citizens" (as cited in Levine & Kawashima-Ginsberg, 2017, p. 19). Rather than crossing their fingers and hoping for the best for the future, teachers must provide the space for students to develop the skills they need to create a world in which each of us can hold an equal voice.

Children learn both academic and social norms from an early age. The teacher-participants in this study shared stories about how their beliefs were formed from early childhood experiences. Unfortunately for all of us, social studies education, particularly inclusive and civics education, is often left to the high school and college years. The teacher-participants showed a strong interest in creating curriculum through the lens of social justice; however, they often felt paralyzed by the barriers presented and the lack of "how-to" knowledge regarding curriculum design.

This study provides teacher educators and curriculum leaders with ways to support new and seasoned teachers to develop and prioritize civically engaged curriculum for young learners so that each child will grow up to become active and engaged adult citizens. We must prioritize our children's future by ensuring that they have the skills, interest, and better yet, a growing commitment to lead our great nation equitably.

## *References*

Banks, J. A. (2017). Failed citizenship and transformative education. *Educational Researcher*, *46*(7), 366–377. https://journals.sagepub.com

Biesta, G., & Tedder, M. (2007). Agency and learning in the lifecourse: Towards an ecological perspective. *Studies in the Education of Adults*, *39*(2), 132–149.

Bogotch, I. E. (2002, March 1). Educational leadership and social justice: Practice into theory. *Journal of School Leadership*, *12*(2), 138–156. https://doi.org/10.1177/105268460201200203

Borrero, N., Ziauddin, A., & Ahn, A. (2018). Teaching for change: New teachers' experiences with and visions for culturally relevant pedagogy. *Critical Questions in Education*, *9*(1), 22–39. (EJ1172314). https://files.eric.ed.gov/fulltext/EJ1172314.pdf

Boyte, H. C. (2003). Civic education and the new American patriotism post-9/11. *Cambridge Journal of Education*, *33*(1), 85–100.

Brown, K. M. (2004). Leadership for social justice and equity: Weaving a transformative framework and pedagogy. *Educational Administration Quarterly*, *40*(1), 77–108. https://doi.org/10.1177/0013161x03259147

Campbell, E. (2012, March 23). Agency in curriculum contexts. *Curriculum Inquiry*, *42*(2), 183–190. https://doi.org/10.1111/j.1467-873x.2012.00593.x

Carnegie Corporation of New York & CIRCLE. (2003). *The civic mission of schools* [Report]. https://circle.tufts.edu/sites/default/files/2020-01/civic_mission_schools_2003.pdf

Center for Information and Research on Civic Learning and Engagement (CIRCLE). (2020). *2020 election*. https://circle.tufts.edu/

Creswell, J. W., & Poth, C. N. (2018). *Qualitative inquiry and research design: Choosing among five approaches* (4th ed.). SAGE.

Danielson, C. (2013). *The framework for teaching evaluation instrument*. The Danielson Group. https://www.danielsongroup.org

Darling-Hammond, L. (2019). *Investing for student success: Lessons from state school finance reforms* [Brief]. The Learning Policy Institute. https://learningpolicyinstitute.org/product/investing-student-success-school-finance-reforms-brief

Dewey, J. (1897). *My pedagogic creed* (No. 25). E. L. Kellogg & Company. https://books.google.com/books?hl=en&lr=&id=EgwVAAAAIAAJ&oi=fnd&pg=PP5&dq=Dewey+My+pedagogic+Creed&ots=MKl8ePIFmF&sig=CaYRgRQBHNh0Nk_Pwix1HimrSgo#v=onepage&q=Dewey%20My%20pedagogic%20Creed&f=false

Dewey, J. (2011). *Democracy and education: An introduction to the philosophy of education*. The Free Press. (Original work published 1916)

Freire, P. (2000). *Pedagogy of the oppressed* (M. B. Ramos, Trans.). Bloomsbury Academic. (Original work published 1968)

Fullan, M. (2006). *Change theory: A force for school improvement* (Seminar Series Paper No. 157). Centre for Strategic Education.

Goodson, I. F. (2014). Context, curriculum and professional knowledge. *History of Education*, *43*(6), 768–776. https://doi.org/10.1080/0046760X.2014.943813

Hargreaves, A. (1996). Revisiting voice. *Educational Researcher*, *25*(1), 12–19.

Hattie, J. (2012). *Visible learning for teachers: Maximizing impact on learning*. Routledge. https://doi.org/10.1080/02667363.2012.693677

Heafner, T. L. (2018). Elementary ela/social studies integration: Challenges and limitations. *The Social Studies*, *109*(1), 1–12. https://doi.org/10.1080/00377996.2017.1399248

Huck, A. (2019). Elementary social studies content integration in CCLS: An analysis of content integration. *The Social Studies*, *110*(1), 1–16. https://doi.org/10.1080/00377996.2018.1524359

Institute of Education Sciences. (2020, September). *Race and ethnicity of public school teachers and their students* (NCES 2020-103). National Center of Educational Statistics at IES. https://nces.ed.gov/pubs2020/2020103.pdf

Kawashima-Ginsberg, K. (2014, March). *Harry, Hermione, Ron and Neville—Portraits of American teenagers' extracurricular involvement, and implications for educational interventions* (CIRCLE working paper No. 80). Center for Information and Research on Civic Learning and Engagement (CIRCLE). https://circle.tufts.edu/

Ladson-Billings, G. (1992). Culturally relevant teaching: The key to making multicultural education work. In C. A. Grant (Ed.), *Research and multicultural education: From the margins to the mainstream* (pp. 106–121). Falmer Press.

Ladson-Billings, G. (1995). But that's just good teaching! The case for culturally relevant pedagogy. *Theory into practice*, *34*(3), 159–165. https://doi.org/10.1080/00405849509543675

Levine, P., & Kawashima-Ginsberg, K. (2015). *Civic education and deeper learning: Deeper learning research series* [Report]. Jobs for the Future. (ED559676). ERIC.

Levine, P., & Kawashima-Ginsberg, K. (2017, September 21). *The republic is (still) at risk—and civics is part of the solution* [Brief]. Tufts University.

Lincoln Y. S., & Guba, E. G. (1986, June). But is it rigorous? Trustworthiness and authenticity in naturalistic evaluation. *New Directions for Program Evaluation*, *30*, 73–84. https://doi.org/10.1080/19439342.2017.1306577

Mark, S., Id-Deen, L., & Thomas, S. (2019). Getting to the root of the matter: Preservice teachers' experiences and positionalities with learning to teach in culturally diverse contexts. *Cultural Studies of Science Education*, *13*, 453–483.

Merriam, S. (1998). *Qualitative research and case study applications in education: Revised and expanded from case study research in education* (2nd ed.). Jossey-Bass. (ED415771). ERIC. https://eric.ed.gov/?id=ED415771

Merritt, E. G. (2016). Time for teacher learning, planning critical for school reform. *Phi Delta Kappan*, *98*(4), 31–36. https://kappanonline.org/time-teacher-learning-planning-critical-school-reform/

National Council for the Social Studies. (2013). *College, career, and civic life (C3) framework for social studies state standards: Guidance for enhancing the rigor of K–12 civics, economics, geography, and history.* https://www.socialstudies.org/sites/default/files/c3/c3-framework-for-social-studies-rev0617.pdf

Pace, J. L. (2011, Winter). The complex and unequal impact of high stakes accountability on untested social studies. *Theory & Research in Social Education, 39*(1), 32–60. (EJ920268). ERIC. https://eric.ed.gov/?id=EJ920268

Pantić, N., & Florian, L. (2015). Developing teachers as agents of inclusion and social justice. *Education Inquiry, 6*(3), Article 27311, 333–351. (EJ1209656). ERIC. https://eric.ed.gov/?id=EJ1209656

Patton, M. Q. (1990). *Qualitative evaluation and research methods* (2nd ed.). SAGE. https://doi.org/10.1002/nur.4770140111

Rawls, J. (1971). *A theory of justice.* Harvard University Press. https://doi.org/10.2307/j.ctvjf9z6v

Saldaña, J., & Omasta, M. (2018). *Qualitative research: Analyzing life.* SAGE. https://doi.org/10.1177/1090198118795018

Schiro, M. S. (2013, August 29). *Curriculum theory: Conflicting visions and enduring concerns.* SAGE Publications. (ED500227). ERIC. https://eric.ed.gov/?id=ED500227

Sprunt, B. (2020, November 1). *93 million and counting: Americans are shattering early voting records.* NPR. https://www.npr.org/2020/10/26/927803214/62-million-and-counting-americans-are-breaking-early-voting-records

Stake, R. E. (1995). *The art of case study research.* SAGE.

Stuteville, R., & Johnson, H. I. (2015, Summer). Citizenship education in the United States: Perspective reflected in state education standards. *Administrative Issues Journal: Connecting Education, Practice, and Research, 6*(1), 99–117 (EJ1104347). ERIC.

Villegas, A. M. (2007). Dispositions in teacher education: A look at social justice. *Journal of Teacher Education, 58*(5), 370–380.

Warren, D. (2001, Fall). Original intents: Public schools as civic education. *Theory into Practice, 27*(4), 243–249. https://doi.org/10.1080/00405848809543360

Weinstein, J. R. (2004). Neutrality, pluralism, and education: Civic education as learning about the other. *Studies in Philosophy and Education, 23*(4), 235–263.

Yin, R. K. (2018). *Case study research and applications: Design and methods* (6th ed.). SAGE.

# Chapter 10 Greek Parents' Perceptions and Experiences Regarding Their Children's Learning and Social-Emotional Difficulties

Eirini Adamopoulou

## *Introduction*

A major issue confronting the mental health service system for children and adolescents worldwide is the role of the family. Children, for the most part, cannot access services on their own; parents must provide permission, transportation, knowledge of available sources, and financial resources for a child to receive care (Farmer et al., 1997). Cultural and ethnic differences are associated with differences in parents' beliefs about children's problems, the pathways that lead youngsters into mental health care, the kinds of referral problems identified by parents when they do seek help, and the kinds of interventions for those problems preferred by parents (McMiller & Weisz, 1996). Therefore, efforts to advance mental health services for children and adolescents in a particular country should include an examination of parents' distinct cultural differences and perceptions regarding their children's mental health.

Greece is one of the countries with the smallest changes in the family system and one of the most traditional countries in the European Union (EU). This is evident by the numbers of marriages, divorces, single-parent families, families with three generations, and interactions with relatives compared to other European countries (Georgas et al., 2004). Studies of the functional elements of the Greek family indicated that the family functions expand to a larger kinship network of extended family members and close relatives (grandparents, uncles, in-laws, aunts, and cousins) with very frequent visits and telephone contacts (Georgas, 1997, 1999a, 1999b; Georgas et al., 2004). At the same time, the family institution continues to be the most important kinship group for Greeks (Georgas et al., 2004; Giotsa, 1999; Sutton, 2001). The Greek nuclear family and the traditional extended family have strong expectations for social uplifting and enhancement of family prestige through the academic success of their children (Georgas, 1988; Kataki, 1998; Madianos, 1989). Even though Greek parents seem to be very involved in anything that has to do with their children's schooling, there is limited research on their perceptions and experiences regarding their children's learning and social-emotional difficulties.

At the same time, there has been a general reluctance among Greek parents to acknowledge their children's psychological problems and seek professional help due to prejudice and lack of adequate information (Bouhoutsos & Roe, 1984; Tsiantis, 1993b). Tsiantis (1993c) notes that referrals for mental health services were usually made around serious incidents as children were brought to the mental health providers after they had experienced severe health or social-emotional episodes. Additionally, Greek parents of students with disabilities often denied the need for special education services because they did not want their child in a special school or class (Kassotakis et al., 1996; Vardis, 1994). One reason for this rejection might be that Greek society viewed special schools with prejudice because of their history, as students with severe disabilities were secluded and marginalized in special schools in the recent past (Zoniou-Sideri, 2000). Nevertheless, the number of special classes in mainstream schools has dramatically increased in the past two decades due to the special attention that has been given in the development of special education (Kassotakis et al., 1996; Nikodemos, 1994). Despite the recent educational laws concerning special education services and psychological services in Greek schools, the vast majority of the student population with special educational needs attends regular schools and programs, and could benefit from special education services (Hatzichristou, 1998; Kassotakis et al.; Nikodemos; Υπουργείο Εθνικής Παιδείας και Θρησκευμάτων, 2008). Koliadis (1994) notes that even though there has been an emphasis on learning difficulties in recent years in Greece, teachers and parents frequently viewed the weak student in reading and spelling, who might have also failed in other academic subjects, as a "bad and lazy student." Thus, it is imperative to explore how parents are evaluating their children's academic and social-emotional functioning in contemporary Greece. Additionally, it is important to explore the significance that Greek parents attribute to their children's problematic behavior in relation to the interventions they adopt to support their children's needs.

Furthermore, the particular geographical composition of Greece has favored the creation of distinct residential, demographic, and cultural features. There is an inequality in the available mental health services and school special education services because of the geographic remoteness, overcentralization of services, and lack of efficient coordination and personnel (Bouhoutsos & Roe, 1984; Dellassoudas, 1994; Gari & Sofianidou, 2000; Hatzichristou et al., 2007; Mazi et al., 2004; Tsiantis, 1993a, 1993b, 1993c; Vardis, 1994). Hence, not all Greek families have access to the same level of state resources and services. The availability of community-based resources can impact how Greek parents identify and what type of services they prefer to address their children's learning and social-emotional difficulties.

### *Purpose of the Study and Research Questions*

The purpose of this study was to explore the perceptions and experiences of Greek parents whose children experience learning and social-emotional difficulties. Seven research questions were addressed by this study. The research questions were as follows:

1. What are the parents' perceptions of their children's learning and social-emotional difficulties?
2. What children's behaviors are the parents most concerned about?
3. What do the parents perceive as the causes of their children's learning and social-emotional difficulties?
4. Who do the parents consider as responsible for solving their children's learning and social-emotional difficulties?
5. What is the perceived burden that the parents experience due to their children's learning and social-emotional difficulties?
6. What are the parents' actions to support their children's learning and social-emotional difficulties?
7. What are the parents' views and experiences with the available community services to support their children's needs?

## ***Research Methodology***

### *Conceptual Framework*

This study design was guided by an ecologic understanding of parents' perceptions and experiences, suggesting that a myriad of factors at the child, family, and environmental levels simultaneously impact Greek parents' understanding of their children's problems and what they do to try to solve them.

As Bronfenbrenner (1979, 1989) points out, influences on children's behavior and development extend from the immediate family to schools, friendship networks, relatives, neighborhoods, communities, and geographical locations. These influences need to be conceptualized in terms of both individuals and the nested set of ecosystems within which they develop and function. Following an ecological perspective, this study examined Greek society's limiting factors and resources, constraints and opportunities, and the general environment, which can promote or undermine students' well-being and academic competence in regular Greek schools.

Specifically, this study assumed that Greek parents' decision to seek and utilize help for their children was based on their perceptions of the nature of their children's problems, the causes, and responsibility for solving their children's learning and social-emotional difficulties, as well as the cultural norms of Greek society. Even though one can imagine a plethora of possible causes inducing children's learning and social-emotional difficulties, this study included four causes: child, family, school, and sociocultural factors. Using an ecological perspective, an attempt was made to explore factors not only deriving from the child him- or herself, but also factors deriving from his or her immediate environment such as the family, his or her wider environment formed by teachers, educational system, neighborhood, and even possible immigration from another country. In addition, the proposed responsible persons for solving children's difficulties were the child, family members, school professionals, and specialists. These persons emerge from the child's immediate environment to broader dimensions of his or her surroundings.

An additional important variable is the perceived burden that Greek parents might experience due to the child's learning and social-emotional difficulties. The parental perceived burden was measured in three aspects: personal experience, relationships with family members and friends, and the family's finances and everyday activities. This study also examined the parents' actions to support their children's learning and social-emotional difficulties beginning with their personal efforts and extending to the supporting sociocultural environment in terms of the informal sources (e.g., family) and formal sources (e.g., community services) available for receiving help.

## *Research Design*

Traditional educational and psychological research has commonly followed one of the two research paradigms: empirical-analytic versus interpretive. This study used primarily a quantitative method, which is derived from empirical-analytic research paradigm. Although in this conception, knowledge comes from systematic testing of hypotheses through experimentation (or quasi-experimentation), this study was primarily exploratory and was not derived from systematic testing of hypotheses. Measurement (including psychological testing) provides an objective, interpretation-free record of empirical regularities (Maxim, 1999).

In quantitative research, inquiry begins with a specific plan, a set of detailed questions and/or hypotheses. Researchers seek facts and causes of human behavior and want to know a lot about a few variables so differences can be identified. They collect data that are primarily numerical, resulting from surveys, tests, experiments, and so on (Maxim, 1999). Most quantitative approaches manipulate variables and control the research setting. Quantitative research allows the researcher to generalize research findings, and provides precise, quantitative, and numerical data. In addition, the research results are relatively independent of the researcher, and it is useful for studying large numbers of people (Johnson & Onwuegbuzie, 2004).

This study used a descriptive survey design that involves the collection of data from the population of interest on a particular problem or issue (Ravid, 2005). Specifically, this is a nonexperimental quantitative research that used questionnaires with categorical and quantitative variables. This method was selected because it is a means to describe systematically, factually, and accurately the characteristics of an existing phenomenon or to document its characteristics (Belli, 2008; Maxim, 1999). In this study the phenomenon included Greek parents' perceptions and experiences regarding their children's learning and social-emotional difficulties in elementary schools. As there has been limited research in this field of inquiry, I selected a quantitative methodological approach to summarize large amounts of data and reach conclusions and generalizations based on numerical descriptions (Roberts, 2004). Studying a larger sample of parents provided an opportunity to explore trends from a diverse population from different areas of Greece. The quantitative methodology and, specifically, the completion of surveys, also addressed the issues related to the time constraints of conducting research in another country. Specifically, I was able to travel only for a two-week period during January 2009 to Greece to collect the data, which were later analyzed through the SPSS version 16.0 for Windows in order to derive the numerical findings. Thus, there were time economics gained in this approach during the collection of the data and the use of accepted statistical analysis methods. Another advantage of this method is that it offered the possibility of collecting data anonymously.

However, quantitative research cannot capture the meanings people attach to the activities and events in their world as qualitative research can

(Roberts, 2004). To offset this limitation, I included narrative data (open-ended questions and open responses) in the quantitative study. I collected the quantitative data using a Likert scale on two structured questionnaires about parents' perceptions and experiences regarding their children's learning and social-emotional difficulties. The qualitative data included two open-ended questions and open responses on the same questionnaire completed by the same number of participants (parents) who completed the quantitative items. The quantitative data and their analysis enabled further exploration of the research questions. The embedded qualitative responses enhanced our understanding of Greek parents' perceptions and experiences regarding their children's learning and social-emotional difficulties. Thus, using the qualitative methods complementary to quantitative method I was able to validate and expand on the quantitative findings of the survey (Creswell & Plano Clark, 2007).

For the purposes of this research, the parents completed the Test of Psychosocial Adaptation of Preschool and Elementary Children (Test of Psychosocial Adaptation), where they evaluated their children's learning and social-emotional functioning, and the Parent Survey, which explored their perceptions and experiences regarding their children's learning and social-emotional difficulties. The Test of Psychosocial Adaptation of Preschool and Elementary Children is a rating scale that was developed recently in Greece to identify the skills or deficits in the social and emotional domains, and the personal, interpersonal, and school adaptation of a child (Hatzichristou et al., 2008). The Parent Survey was created based on the themes identified by the literature review. A pilot study was conducted to explore the use of the Test of Psychosocial Adaptation with Greek parents, to ensure and develop the questions of the Parent Survey, and examine the procedures of the study.

## *Procedure*

With the permission of the Greek Ministry of Education and Religious Affairs, 30 primary schools were asked to participate in the study from five different areas of Greece. Primary schools in Greece covers 6 years of elementary education between the ages of 6 to 12 (Georgas, 1988; Hatzichristou et al., 2007; Vlachos, 2004). Nineteen primary schools from four different areas of Greece agreed to participate in the study resulting in a 61.29% permission rate. These areas represent different population densities and cultural and socioeconomic diversity. Parents were asked to complete the Test of Psychosocial Adaptation and the Parent Survey and return it to the school. The questionnaires were self-administered by parents.

Of the 1,000 questionnaires that were distributed to parents through their children's schools, 298 were returned, which resulted in a 29.8% response rate. The majority of the questionnaires (*N* = 209; 70.1%) were gathered from 15 schools in the capital city region of Athens. The schools in the area of Athens belong predominately to the northeast suburban school district (63.7%). Eight-nine questionnaires (29.9%) were returned from three rural areas: one school from a city in the northeast part of Greece, one school from a small town in the south of Greece, and two schools from an island in southeast Greece.

## *Participants*

The sample of this study consisted of 298 parents of elementary students aged 6 to 11 years old. The majority of parents were female (*N* = 235; 78.6%) and in 25 cases both parents completed the questionnaires. The majority of the participants' ages ranged from 30–39 years (*N* = 129; 43.1%) to 40–49 years (*N* = 144; 48.2%). In terms of education, 134 mothers (44.9%) completed lyceum/college or technical school and 122 mothers (40.9%) held an undergraduate/graduate degree. Forty-eight percent of the fathers graduated from lyceum/college or technical school (*N* = 143) and 95 held a undergraduate/graduate degree (31.9%). Compared with the monthly minimum wage in Greece, the majority of the participants had a middle- to upper-class monthly income (Eurostat, 2009). With regard to housing, the majority of participants owned their house or apartment.

## *Model for Data Collection and Analysis*

This study included two phases of data analysis. In the first phase of the data analysis, the responses of 298 Greek parents of elementary school students, aged 6 to 11 years, on the Test of Psychosocial Adaptation and on the first part of the Parent Survey were analyzed. Data from these two measures assessed children's learning and social-emotional difficulties and Greek parents' concerns and accessed services.

In the second phase of the analysis, 105 of the 298 Greek parents' responses on the second part of the Parent Survey were examined. The sample of the 105 parents was selected because their ratings on the Test of Psychosocial Adaptation identified their children with significant behaviors at least 1 *SD* below or above the mean. In this part of the Parent Survey, parents reported (1) the causes and responsibility for solving their children's difficulties; (2) parental perceived burden; and (3) actions, as well as (4) the use, likelihood to use, and barriers in accessing community services regarding their children's learning and social-emotional difficulties.

## *Discussion of Research Findings and Results*

Prevalence and Types of Children's Learning and Social-Emotional Difficulties Based on parents' ratings on the Test of Psychosocial Adaptation, 35.2% of Greek elementary students aged 6 to 11 years experienced significant learning and social-emotional difficulties. Greek parents rated higher those behaviors that are more obvious and noticeable, especially in interpersonal relationships and groups on the Test of Psychosocial Adaptation. By contrast, parents had the tendency to rate the internalized behaviors of their children as significant when they were accompanied by externalized behaviors. Consequently, results from the Test of Psychosocial Adaptation suggest that Greek parents gave importance to children's social aspect of behavior and underreported introvert behavior.

### *Greek Parents' Concerns and Accessed Services*

Almost one-third of Greek parents from the total sample of participants reported having concerns over their children's behavior and only 13.1% responded in the Parent Survey that they have accessed services. Even though parents reported mostly concerns over their children's social-emotional difficulties (e.g., anxiety, socialization, anger, and low self-esteem), the majority of their accessed services included support for their children's learning difficulties (e.g., dyslexia). From the parents who accessed services, only a small number reported a variety of other types of services for their children (e.g., occupation and play-based therapy).

### *Child's Responsibility*

About a half of the parents appeared to consider their children's character as an important cause of their children's learning and social-emotional difficulties. This finding suggests that when parents attribute responsibility to their children for their problematic behavior, they consider these difficulties as part of their temperament, an innate characteristic. This was also reflected in parents' responses regarding who is responsible for solving their children's difficulties in these areas, where almost 60% of the parents attributed responsibility to their children for improving their behavior. This indicates that some parents regard children as responsible both for causing their learning and social-emotional difficulties and for solving these problems. In conclusion, when Greek parents believed that children's character caused their behavior, they held children accountable for changing and ameliorating their learning and social-emotional difficulties.

## *Parents' Role*

More than half of the parents did not believe they were mainly responsible for children's learning and social-emotional difficulties. The role of parents was more important in parents' opinions about who is responsible for solving or improving their children's problems. Around 80% of parents indicated that both parents should have the responsibility for solving or improving their children's behavior. Furthermore, in accordance with their perceptions about the responsibility for solving children's learning and social-emotional difficulties, parents indicated a greater preference for the use of personal actions and positive incentives to support their children over other interventions. Parents also did not ask the recommendations or support of their extended family for their children's challenges. The level of personal burden Greek parents experience due to their children's learning and social-emotional difficulties might also explain their preference for personal actions to support their children's needs. Specifically, almost half of the parents indicated a significant general level of family impact, especially on their personal competence as parents, as a results of their children's learning and social-emotional difficulties. Hence, the high level of these parents' personal and family burden can influence their actions and type of intervention implemented—in this case their preference for personal efforts.

## *Educational System*

Another important finding is that more parents ($n$ = 40%) attributed responsibility of their children's learning and social-emotional difficulties to the current structure of the Greek educational system than to the teachers' methods ($n$ = 26.7%). One other interesting aspect was that even though 60% of parents indicated teachers or school personnel as responsible for improving their children's behavior, only one-third of Greek parents reported that they had consulted a teacher or other school personnel to support their children's needs.

## *Mass Media*

It is notable that half of the participants indicated that television, movies, and video games were significant causes of their children's learning and social-emotional difficulties. For some parents these ratings might be an indication of their concerns about their children's overexposure to these programmings. This finding also underlines the important role of parents in limiting the amount of exposure their children have to television, movies, and video games to improve their children's behavioral challenges.

### *Sociocultural Factors*

Greek parents did not attribute their children's learning and social-emotional difficulties to sociocultural and environmental factors such as low family income, type of neighborhood, speaking a second language, or recent immigration from another country. It should be noted that the majority of parents had children who were born in Greece (98%) and had not experienced immigration and second language acquisition challenges. In terms of the neighborhood, the majority of participants came from the northeastern suburban area of Athens, which includes mainly middle- and upper-class families who owned their house or apartment. Thus, the majority of the parents in this study appeared not to consider the socioeconomic conditions in which they live to have a negative impact on their children's behavior or the reverse.

### *Community Services*

Overall, a very small number of Greek parents indicated that they had accessed community services to support their children's learning and social-emotional needs (responses ranged from 1% to 5%). Of these community services, private clinicians appeared to be the preferred service for parents ($n$ = 13.3%). At the same time, parents reported an increased likelihood to use community services. Private clinicians were again the service with the highest future utilization based on parents' reports ($n$ = 21.9%). It is significant that almost one-third of the parents reported that the lack of knowledge about the services, the time it takes to initiate services and long waiting lists, and the lack of specialists were barriers in the access of community services. These numerous barriers can limit children's access to community mental health care.

## Conclusions

The results of this study are subject to the limitations of any self-report survey. Despite the limitations, this study provided useful information as there is little evidence and research in this domain. These research findings can provide professionals with information regarding the help Greek parents prefer when conducting assessment and implementing interventions. Finally, this information can contribute to a model of mental health delivery system that includes parents and provides culturally sensitive and effective services to Greek children.

## *References*

Belli, G. (2008). Nonexperimental quantitative research. In *Lapan*. http://media.wiley.com/product_data/excerpt/95/04701810/0470181095-1.pdf

Bouhoutsos, J. C., & Roe, K. V. (1984). Mental health services and the emerging role of psychology in Greece. *American Psychologist, 39*, 57–61.

Bronfenbrenner, U. (1979). *The ecology of human development: Experiments by nature and design*. Harvard University Press.

Bronfenbrenner, U. (1989). Ecological systems theory. In R. Vasta (Ed.), *Annals of child development* (Vol. 6, pp. 187–251). JAI.

Creswell, J. W., & Plano Clark, V. L. (2007). *Designing and conducting mixed methods research*. SAGE.

Dellassoudas, L. G. (1994). Ειδική επαγγελματική κατάρτιση: Προτάσεις για την αναβαθμισή της [Special professional development: Recommendations for its advancement]. In M. Kaila, N. Polemikos, & G. Filippou (Eds.), *Ατομα με ειδικές ανάγκες* (Vol. 1, pp. 206–221). Ελληνικά Γράμματα.

Eurostat. (2009). *Population and social conditions: Minimum wages in January 2009*. Eurostat, Beate CZECH.

Farmer, E. M. Z., Burns, B. J., Angold, A., & Costello, E. J. (1997). Impact of children's mental health problems on families: Relationships with service use. *Journal of Emotional and Behavioral Disorders, 5*, 230–238.

Gari, A., & Sofianidou, E. (2000). Δομή και λειτουργία φορέων διάγνωσης και αντιμετώπισης διαταραχών παιδικής και εφηβικής ηλικίας. Παρουσιάση, σχολιασμός, και σύνθεση προτάσεων ομάδων εργασίας [Structure and function of providers of diagnosis and care of child and adolescent disorders: Presentation, comment, and synthesis of recommendations from working teams]. In A. Kalantzi-Azizi & I. Besevegis (Eds.), *Θέματα επιμόρφωσεις ευαισθητοποίησης στελεχών ψυχικής υγείας παιδιών και εφήβων* (pp. 105–112). Ελληνικά Γράμματα.

Georgas, J. (1988). An ecological and social cross-cultural model: The case of Greece. In J. W. Berry, S. H. Irvine, & E. B. Hunt (Eds.), *Indigenous cognition: Functioning in cultural context* (pp. 105–123). Martinus Nijhoff.

Georgas, J. (1997). Ψυχολογικές και οικολογικές διαστασείς στη δομή και τη λειτουργία της οικογένειας [Psychological and ecological dimensions in the structure and function of family]. In J. Tsiantis (Ed.), *Βασική Παιδοψυχιατρική. Εφηβεία* (Vol. 2, pp. 101–143). Εκδόσεις Καστανιώτη.

Georgas, J. (1999a). Ecological theory in social psychology. *Psychology, 6*(2), 111–123.

Georgas, J. (1999b). Family in cross-cultural psychology. In J. Adamopoulos & Y. Kashima (Eds.), *Social psychology and cultural context* (pp. 163–175). Sage.

Georgas, J., Gari, A., & Mylonas, K. (2004). Σχέσεις με συγγενείς στην ελληνική οικογένεια [Relationships with relatives in the Greek family]. In L. M. Mousourou & M. Etratigaki (Eds.), *Ζητήματα οικογενειακής πολιτικής: Θεωρητικές αναφορές και εμπειρικές διερευνήσεις* (pp. 189–225). Gutenberg.

Giotsa, A. (1999). Ο προσωπικός χώρος και η γειτονιά: Διαπολιτιστική έρευνα σε γειτονιές της Γενεύης, της Αθήνας και της Κεφαλλονιάς [Personal space and neighborhood: Cross-cultural research in neighborhoods of Geneva, Athens and Kefallonias]. *Psychology, 6*(2), 124–136.

Hatzichristou, C. (1998). Alternative school psychological services: Development of a data-based model in the Greek schools. *School Psychology Review, 27*(2), 246–259.

Hatzichristou, C., Polychroni, F., Besevegis, G., & Mylonas, K. (2008). *Εργαλείο Ψυχοκοινωνικής Προσαρμογής Παιδιών Προσχολικής και Σχολικής Ηλικίας* [*Test of psychosocial adaptation of preschool and elementary children*]. Υπουργείο Εθνικής Παιδείας και Θρησκευμάτων-ΕΠΕΑΕΚ.

Hatzichristou, C., Polychroni, F., & Georgouleas, G. (2007). School psychology in Greece. In S. R. Jimerson, T. D. Oakland, & P. T. Farrell (Eds.), *The handbook of international school psychology* (pp. 135–145). Sage.

Johnson, R. B., & Onwuegbuzie, A. J. (2004). Mixed method research: A research paradigm whose time has come. *Educational Researcher, 33*(7), 14–26.

Kassotakis, M., Papapetrou, S., & Fakiolas, N. (1996). Φραγμοί στην εκπαίδευση και την επαγγελματική αποκατάσταση των ατόμων με ειδικές ανάγκες [Barriers in the education and professional development of people with special needs]. *Διαστάσεις του κοινωνικού αποκλεισμού στην Ελλάδα: Κύρια θέματα και προσδιορισμός προτεραιοτήτων πολιτικής* (Vol. 1, pp. 449–473). Εθνικό Κέντρο Κοινωνικών Ερευνών.

Kataki, C. (1998). *Οι τρεις ταυτότητες της ελληνικής οικογένειας* [*The three identities of the Greek family*] (8th ed.). Ελληνικά Γράμματα.

Koliadis, M. (1994). Οργανωτικά-διοικητικά σχήματα και ψυχοπαιδαγωγικά μοντέλα αντιμετώπισης των μαθησιακών δυσκολιών στο χώρο του σχολείου [Structural-administrative schemas and psycho-pedagogic models for the intervention of learning difficulties at school]. In M. Kaila, N. Polemikos, & G. Filippou (Eds.), *Ατομα με ειδικές ανάγκες* (Vol. 1, pp. 290–301). Ελληνικά Γράμματα.

Madianos, M. J. (1989). *Κοινωνία και ψυχική υγεία* [*Society and mental health*]. Εκδόσεις Καστανιώτη.

Maxim, P. S. (1999). *Quantitative research methods in the social sciences.* Oxford University Press.

Mazi, M. S., Nenopoulou, S., & Everatt, J. (2004). Dyslexia in Greece. In I. Smythe, J. Everatt, & R. Salter (Eds.), *International book of dyslexia: A guide to practice and resources* (pp. 103–108). John Wiley & Sons.

McMiller, W. P., & Weisz, J. R. (1996). Help-seeking preceding mental health clinic intake among African-American, Latino, and Caucasian youth. *Journal of the American Academy of Child & Adolescent Psychiatry, 35*, 1086–1094.

Nikodemos, S. (1994). Αγωγή και εκπαίδευση των παιδιών με ειδικές ανάγκες στην Ελλάδα: Γενικές διαπιστώσεις, σύγχρονες τάσεις-προοπτικές [Education of children with special needs in Greece: General findings, contemporary tendencies-expectations]. In M. Kaila, N. Polemikos, & G. Filippou (Eds.), *Ατομα με ειδικές ανάγκες* (Vol. 2, pp. 623–631). Ελληνικά Γράμματα.

Ravid, R. (2005). *Practical statistics for educators* (3rd ed.). University Press of America.

Roberts, C. M. (2004). *The dissertation journey: A practical and comprehensive guide to planning, writing, and defending your dissertation.* SAGE.

Sutton, S. B. (2001). Greece. In M. Ember & C. R. Ember (Eds.), *Countries and their cultures* (Vol. 2, pp. 887–899). Macmillan Reference.

Tsiantis, J. (1993a). Η εκπαίδευση για την ψυχική υγεία του παιδιού [Education for the mental health of the child]. In *Ψυχική υγεία του παιδιού και της οικογένειας* (pp. 229–241) Εκδόσεις Καστανιώτη.

Tsiantis, J. (1993b). Προτάσεις για την παιδοψυχιατρική περίθαλψη στην Ελλάδα [Recommendations for child psychiatric care in Greece]. In *Ψυχική υγεία του παιδιού και της οικογένειας* (pp. 242–271). Εκδόσεις Καστανιώτη.

Tsiantis, J. (1993c). Ψυχοθεραπεία στο γενικό παιδιατρικό νοσοκομείο [Psychotherapy in the general children's hospital]. In *Ψυχική υγεία του παιδιού και της οικογένειας* (pp. 242–271). Εκδόσεις Καστανιώτη.

Vardis, P. (1994). Η ενσωμάτωση των παιδιών με ειδικές αναγκές: Περιεχόμενο και φιλοσοφία ενσωμάτωσης [Integration of children with special needs: Content and philosophy of integration]. In M. Kaila, N. Polemikos, & G. Filippou (Eds.), *Ατομα με ειδικές ανάγκες* (Vol. 2, pp. 740–751). Ελληνικά Γράμματα.

Vlachos, A. (2004). *Οδηγός του ελληνικού εκπαιδευτικού συστήματος* [*Guide of the Greek educational system*]. Βιβλιοσυνεργατική ΑΕΠΕΕ.

Zoniou-Sideri, A. (2000). Η εξέλιξη της ειδικής εκπαίδευσης: Από το ειδικό στο γενικό σχολείο [The evolution of special education: From special to general school]. In A. Zoniou-Sideri (Ed.), *Ατομα με ειδικές ανάγκες και η ενταξή τους* (pp. 22–38). Ελληνικά Γράμματα.

Υπουργείο Εθνικής Παιδείας και Θρησκευμάτων. (2008). Ειδική αγωγή και εκπαίδευση ατόμων με αναπηρία ή με ειδικές εκπαιδευτικές ανάγκες [Special education of individuals with disabilities or special educational needs]. *Εφημερίς της Κυβερνήσεως της Ελληνικής Δημοκρατίας, 199*(1), 3499–3520.

# Chapter 11 Speech-Language Pathologists' Barriers to Providing Services to the Deaf and Hard of Hearing Children Ages Two to Nine

IRENE GARCÍA-BENAVIDES

Once parents find out that their children present with a hearing loss, they are surrounded by professionals who focus on this child being out of "normal" parameters. The first professionals with whom they relate speak about concepts as: loss, deficiencies, abnormalities, disability. Parents receive only one side of the views related to hearing loss: the medical vision. Parents start getting in contact with otolaryngologists, audiologists, and speech-language pathologists. The first information received come from these professionals. However, parents are not exposed to a social perspective of deafness from any professionals during the process of finding out their child presents with hearing problems. This is the case for parents who present with normal hearing, which is around 90% of the parents of children with hearing loss.

The level of acceptance toward the use of spoken language (English), sign language (ASL), or a combination of both, seems to be determined by the setting where therapy services are provided. The services at hospitals, home health agencies, and clinics tend to provide services through spoken language as the first choice. Early childhood intervention professionals as well as school professionals seem to be more open to the use of ASL along with spoken language. On the one hand, professionals who work at hospitals, home health agencies, and clinics usually have a medical vision; on the other hand, professionals who work in early intervention, and schools usually have a sociocultural vision when providing services for deaf and hard of hearing children.

The purpose of this qualitative study was to investigate ways in which SLPs approach their practice of providing services to the deaf and hard of hearing children ages two to nine and the barriers they can encounter along the path. This study sought to uncover the knowledge, perceptions, and experiences of SLPs related to the cultural and linguistic processes of the Deaf culture when assessing and treating deaf and hard of hearing children between two and nine years of age in different occupational settings. The primary research question that guided this study was, "What are SLPs' knowledge and experiences related to the culture and linguistic processes of the deaf culture when assessing and treating deaf and hard of hearing children ages two to nine?" Additional research questions:

- What are the linguistic barriers, if any, that SLPs encounter when assessing and treating the language skills of the deaf and hard of hearing children ages two to nine?
- How do SLPs' knowledge and experiences of the culture and linguistic process of the Deaf culture inform Speech and Language therapy practices for the deaf and hard of hearing children ages two to nine?

## *Theoretical Lens*

This study was informed by two theories. First, the sociocultural theory created by Lev Vygotsky (Alkhudiry, 2022). Second, the concept of language deprivation, created by Neil Glickman (Hall et al., 2017). I chose these two frameworks as the focus revolve around the importance of being part of a linguistic community in order to develop language and cognitive skills. The sociocultural theory highlights the importance of a collaborative environment that includes people, objects, and events in order to learn and develop (Javadi & Tahmasbi, 2020). For Vygotsky it was important to determine the ultimate societal goals of education (Linask, 2019). For this purpose, Vygotsky created "The Big Triad," of positive differentiation, creative adaptation, and dynamic development (Skyer, 2020).

Positive differentiation is the need for education to have social goals. Creative adaptation is the need to teach deaf students to use models that are comprehensible along with cultural tools. In this conception, the challenge is for the Deaf educators to reject the concept of deficit by focusing on the many capabilities Deaf children possess. Dynamic development designates the capacity that Deaf children have to develop as any typical-hearing child, but to foster this development, it is necessary to develop the children's mode of knowledge, communication, and language. It is crucial to identify that the brain can develop language through signed or oral modalities. For Vygotsky, being Deaf was not the cause of disability. The social environment was the one that caused disabilities (Skyer, 2020). Vygotsky believed that higher mental functions as attention, memory, formation of concepts, and problem-solving depended highly in language (Ehrich & O'Donovan, 2019; Linask, 2019). A person who is deprived of language experiences the absence of having an own voice. This results in separation from social experiences, which causes exclusion. This idea changed Vygotsky's opinion regarding sign language throughout his professional career.

Additionally, this study was informed by the concept of language deprivation. Hall et al. (2017) defined language deprivation as the result of a "chronic lack of full access to a natural language during the critical period of language acquisition" (p. 762) around five years old. The National Association of the Deaf (NAD) has a position statement regarding the consequences of language deprivation and its effects on early cognitive and language development and education of deaf and hard of hearing children (NAD, 2014). Hall et al. (2017) included the disruption in the area of language development as a factor of social nature that affects the epidemiology of mental illness. NAD (2014) identified language deprivation as a factor that affect the educational and employment development among deaf people lifespan regardless of the good intentions of government, schools, and professionals.

Listening and spoken language specialists, propose refraining any visual cues and exposure to sign language for deaf children, which seems to be a high-risk idea that expose children to not having a strong foundation neither in signed or spoken language (Gulati, 2014; Glickman et al., 2020; Hetch, 2020; Szarkowski, 2018). Language dysfluency designates the stronger language a person possesses as not fluent (Hall et al., 2017). Language deprivation results in a non-fluent primary language. Not knowing the rules and structures of the strong language makes a person dysfluent in his/her own language, which affects all aspects of life (Hall et al., 2017). The lack of native abilities in any language (signed or spoken) is a disadvantage that expose deaf children to "cognitive, socio-emotional, and behavior challenges" (Glickman et al., 2020; Hall et al., 2017).

The most noticeable difference between signed and oral languages is the modality: manual versus spoken (Baker et al., 2016). Hearing parents would teach hearing children sign language in an effort to increase language skills; however, hearing parents would not allow deaf children to use signs in order to learn how to communicate (Hall et al., 2017). Parents are not advised of how language acquisition in oral and sign language follow a common trajectory. Sandler and Lillo-Martin (2006) brought awareness of commonalities between spoken and signed languages by the concept of "separating the code from the mode." Deaf children are denied the possibility of having sign language as a strong language, as well as the possibility to be bilingual by learning the language of the community (Wilkinson & Morford, 2020).

There is an equivalent implicit sequence for acquiring oral and signed language (Hall, 2017) as cognition is the mode to acquire a language (code). However, language acquisition appears to differ around the age of three years (Cupples et al., 2018) when children take the most advantage of language role models available. Given more than 90% of deaf and hard of hearing children are born into a hearing family (Baker et al., 2016), there is a lack of signed language role models, which produces language deprivation demonstrated in late and incompetent first language acquisition (Henner et al., 2019; Sehyr et al., 2018). The number of sign language users is expected to decrease as powerful hearing devices are used in order to switch from signed to oral languages; however, not all recipients of state-of-the-art hearing technology end up mastering an oral language, which has caused language deprivation as a consequence (Hall et al., 2019). For this reason, it is important to develop a strong first language (Sanzo, 2022) in order to be able to acquire spoken language.

## *Case-Study Research Design*

Qualitative case study was chosen as best suitable methodological approach to explore the experiences of SLPs in "natural settings" and as a "bounded system" (Creswell & Poth, 2018). Stake (1995) claimed that case-study research is not a methodology but a choice of what to be studied. Subsequently, my choice was to get an insight into the knowledge and experiences related to the culture and linguistic processes of the Deaf culture when assessing and treating deaf and hard of hearing children ages two to nine. The case as a bounded system for this study represents several parameters, namely, the participants' experiences within the space of their various professional practices and within the timeframe, to date, of their experiences, as well as the issues that constitute the focus of this study. This study represents a single instrumental case study as "having a research question, a puzzlement, a need for general understanding, and feel that may get insight into the question by studying a particular case" (Stake, 1995, as cited in Creswell & Poth, 2018, p. 98).

## *Participants*

The participants for this study included 12 SLPs from five different working settings: early intervention, home health, schools, outpatient clinics, and hospitals. The participants provide services for deaf and hard of hearing children between two and nine years old. Participants have different level of experience mostly (average of 8 years) treating the deaf and hard of hearing children. All participants hold a minimum of a master's degree in communication sciences and disorders. All participants treat deaf and hard of hearing children ages two to nine and provide services through different types of settings. Early intervention professionals provide services for children from birth to three years old. School professionals provide therapy services starting around four years of age. Professionals working on home health, outpatient clinics, and hospitals provide services for deaf and hard of hearing children from birth up to 21 years old. All these professionals work with ages considered in this study.

## *Data Collection*

This study utilized a demographic survey, semi-structured interview, as well as observational and self-reflective notes as sources of data.

### ***Demographic Survey***

The online survey obtained basic information regarding demographics as well as awareness of ASL and Deaf culture. The survey was the first instrument to collect data. The survey was made of questions that focus into obtaining the following information: demographics, years of education, bilingual status, types of certifications, and basic information related to deaf and hard of hearing concepts.

### ***Interviews***

Interviews typically provide main data for qualitative research (Creswell & Poth, 2018; Saldaña & Omasta, 2018; Taylor, 2005). I used semi-structured interviews as a tool to describe and analyze the experiences of SLPs on their professional path working with deaf and hard of hearing children ages two to nine throughout the different settings where these children receive services. The interviews were conducted virtually through the platform *Zoom.* Interviews were video recorded for authentication of data. Interviews were transcribed verbatim and sent to the participants for verification of accuracy. I analyzed the participants' knowledge and experiences regarding the value of knowledge of ASL and Deaf culture as tools to improve services for this population. The inclusion of the experiences of the participants provided a better picture of issues considered as barriers to the provision of services.

***Observational and Self-reflective Notes***

Arms Almengor (2018) stated there is a process of "learning to do it" (p. 21) that takes place during the practitioner's experience in order to generate knowledge and theories. Self-reflection creates a more mature attitude among individuals (Park et al., 2022). Reflective journals and reflective writing are tools to be used to increase the ability of weighing the experiences. During this study I used a journal in order to keep records of thoughts and lessons learn from the study. This written information provided a better insight of data analysis.

## *Data Analysis*

Data analysis is the process by which researchers address the issue of representing the data (Creswell & Poth, 2018). Data collection determines the quality of research (Polit, 2017). This skill is crucial to manage and reflecting on data (Saldaña & Omasta, 2018). I started the analysis by processing the data through the transcription of interviews. I identified similar words and groups of words and sentences. I labeled the information using codes (Graneheim & Lundman, 2004). I coded the information using the three analytical approaches: the template analysis, the story analysis, and the metaphor analysis (Cassell & Bishop, 2019). The template analysis is referred to the use of the whole data set to make possible to compare all responses on a given issue. The story analysis highlights the emotional aspects of the phenomenon without asking directly. The metaphor analysis allows different interpretations of the same phenomenon to be identified. It was important for this study to identify themes; however, it is also important to analyze the emotional aspects related to the acceptance or rejection toward the use of ASL and knowing the Deaf culture to provide the best services to the Deaf and hard of hearing population. I set aside the information using data regarding language and cultural barriers as well as lack of awareness of the culture of the Deaf community. Categories and subcategories that made evident what were the language(s) used to assess and treat speech and language needs as well as the existence (or not) of culturally and linguistically informed practices. This information highlighted the importance or lack thereof of ASL and Deaf culture to provide speech and language services.

As a result of data analysis, I identified the following main themes: (a) "The Scope of Practice," (b) "Barriers Regarding Culturally and Linguistically

Informed Practices," and (c) "Awareness of Similarities and Differences in Language Acquisition and Structures in English and ASL." The Scope of Practice theme includes the following subthemes: context of service, assessments used and rationale, and language use and rationale. The Barriers Regarding Culturally and Linguistically Informed Practices theme includes the following subthemes: Language deprivation, ASL proficiency, and lack of knowledge and training related to the deaf and hard of hearing communities. The Awareness of Similarities and Differences in Language Acquisition and Structures in English and ASL theme includes the following subthemes: similarities in language acquisition, language similarities and differences, language similarities and differences and main differences between English and ASL. It should be noted that the language differences include: word to sign correspondence, importance of fingerspelling, iconicity of signs, role of space in ASL, phonology of ASL: handshape, placement, and palm orientation.

The participants of this study provided important information through their knowledge and experience regarding linguistic and cultural informed practices as well as barriers encountered when treating deaf and hard of hearing children ages two to nine. Participants have described the deaf and hard of hearing population under their care by informing of their scope of practice, the processes to evaluate and provide services for deaf and hard of hearing children while taking this population's unique cultural and linguistic characteristics, as well as their family environment. Participants also described coursework during their preparation as students and how this knowledge and experiences have contributed to influence their current professional practice. Participants have also provided information regarding the language(s) used to provide services and how linguistic and cultural barriers have determined the way in which their practice take place at this time.

With regard to the primary research question of this study, the participants expressed their full agreement regarding that the parents seek services from speech-language pathologist, mainly to help their children to produce spoken language. Having spoken language as the ultimate goal for the majority of the parents of deaf and hard of hearing children ages two to nine, SLP's knowledge and experience are important for critical aspects as deciding what language to use in therapy, and how to avoid language deprivation. Most participants highlight the fact that upon hearing loss identification, parents are exclusively presented with the medical perspective of hearing loss. After referrals to otolaryngology and audiology, speech pathologist are the professionals who educate parents regarding communication options and school placement. However, speech pathologists are not educated regarding Deaf culture and/or ASL. Participants report this situation as challenging.

As far as linguistic barriers that SLPs encountered when assessing and treating the language of the deaf and hard of hearing children, the participants of this study indicated that their context of service greatly influence the language in which therapy takes place. The use of ASL for therapy has greatly been reduced to spaces as school, while the use of listening and spoken language is more prestigious and is mainly offered at hospitals or clinics. Moreover, there are clinics that specialize in providing services through listening and spoken language. Parents prefer the use of spoken language over ASL, and even if the progress is limited. Generally, it takes around a year for parents to attempt the use of ASL to increase language and communication skills. Most of the participants of this study were not aware of the existence of assessments that have ASL as the language in which testing tools are standardized in order to assess vocabulary, phonology, morphosyntax, and narrative skills.

Regarding cultural barriers, several of the participants expressed that parents seeking services for their children who are deaf and hard of hearing, are not aware of the existence of a Deaf culture. For these parents, being deaf means only having a diagnosis. What is even more surprising is that a lot of participants of this study have expressed not having been around people who are deaf or hard of hearing prior to treating this population. The participants' knowledge of deaf and hard of hearing people comes only from books that express a medical but not a cultural vision of deafness. During the participants' professional preparation years, SLPs generally do not have a chance to "listen" to Deaf perspective regarding speech and language therapy services.

Finally, there are several components that inform speech and language therapy practices for the deaf and hard of hearing children. The participants of this study singled out several of such components as the scope of practice, the barriers to provide culturally and linguistically informed practices, and awareness of similarities and differences in language acquisition and structures in English, and ASL. Surprisingly, some participants stood out in their responses to expose the point of view of those who received speech and language therapy services during their childhood. This perspective contribute to our professional knowledge and experience and must leave an impression regarding the way speech and language therapy should be viewed and performed.

## *Discussion of the Findings*

The responses and experiences of each participant have been useful to provide context, information, and data regarding the questions of the of the study and understand the reasoning behind their professional practice with deaf and hard of hearing children ages two to nine. The participants have been implementing therapy throughout the years in order to serve this population. In order to better understand these experiences their responses were analyzed under the lens of two theories: the sociocultural theory and the concept of language deprivation. The sociocultural theory recognizes the importance of a linguistic community in order to develop language skills. The concept of language deprivation highlights the fact that a language cannot be acquired without having full access to it and a community where to learn this language from. For this reason, the Deaf community does not consider itself as a handicapped, but as users of another language (Gannon, 2012; Shaw & Delaporte, 2015).

With regard to the speech-language pathologists' knowledge and experiences related to the culture and linguistic processes of the Deaf culture when assessing and treating deaf and hard of hearing children ages two to nine, the participants reported working with all types and levels of hearing loss at five different working setting. Hearing loss included conductive, sensorineural, and mixed types. Degrees of hearing loss fluctuated from mild to profound, as well as unilateral or bilateral. The caseload included children being furnished with hearing aids and/or cochlear implants. These professionals serve children having in mind parents' goals. It should be mentioned that the parent goal for all the participants of the study always includes to make children talk (Glickman & Hall, 2019; Glickman et al., 2020; Hall et al., 2017).

Participants working on early intervention made clear to parents that language exposure is not the same as language access (Hall & De Anda, 2021). For this reason, participants encourage the use of sign language at home and in the community, as a way to learn spoken language (Anderson et al., 2016; Glickman & Hall, 2019; Gulati, 2014). Professionals from home health focused on using listening and spoken language as the main mode of communication, with the close supervision of a listening and spoken language specialist. Therapy services in the home prioritize articulation skills while language skills are targeted at the school environment, as ASL is recognized for educational activities exclusively (Rosen, 2022).

Participants in the hospital setting would strongly support the medical vision of using listening and spoken language to target language development. It should be highlighted that in a recent survey (Ozelie et al., 2022) the use of American Sign Language and interpreters was considered the second most unreasonable accommodation among students in the clinical settings. After all, hospitals have otolaryngologists, audiologists, and speech pathologist "in house" while those who are certified as "Auditory Verbal Therapists" are considered the most knowledgeable professionals to work with deaf and hard of hearing children, regardless of how widely results vary from one child to another (Hecht, 2020; Kelley & McCann, 2021). Once listening and spoken language skills hit plateau, the use of ASL is required. Then, patient is referred out to a speech-language pathologist who is fluent in ASL, even though only 618 SLPs in the nation self-identify as fluent (ASHA, 2021) in ASL.

## *Culturally and Linguistically Informed Practices*

Being culturally informed for SLPs deals with being in contact with the Deaf culture, its language, and its values (Padden & Humphries, 2005). For participants who use ASL in therapy, children are viewed as future members of the Deaf community. It means to pay attention to the experiences Deaf adults have had while they were enrolled in therapy as children. Also being able to use sign language while being around Deaf people while "voice off" is enforced. For participants who are part of the Deaf culture, it is hard to imagine serving Deaf people without being able to communicate with most of the members of the community, which means using ASL (Padden & Humphries, 2005).

For SLPs, being linguistically informed means to self-educate regarding language concepts, and also to be able to educate parents regarding this issue (Murphy, 2018). Self-educating regarding language means to seek opportunities to learn about language development in general as well as general language milestones and language development in ASL. It also means to be aware of how typical and atypical ASL development looks as well as spoken language. SLPs need to know that there are language assessments that have been created for ASL-users having ASL as the language for testing with standardized measures. There are tests that will allow SLPs document children's progress throughout the provision of therapy services.

It is important to inform families about the concepts of language access, language immersion, and effortless language acquisition. Families need to be aware of the dangers of language deprivation, which should be avoided at all costs (Glickman & Hall, 2019; Gullati, 2014). It is necessary to highlight the fact that children can be bilingual. That children can learn to use ASL as well as spoken language (Rowley et al., 2022).

## *Professional Preparedness*

The participants of this study give a different level of importance to the classes taken during their professional preparation years. For professionals working with listening and spoken language, Audiology seems to be the most important class. Along with Audiology, classes such as Acoustics, hearing technology, and those that focus on the audiological management of patients. This makes evident that for participants working on listening and spoken language, the most important aspects of the profession are viewed under medical model perspective, which echoes with what Martin (1997) mentioned in their study.

For ASL-user participants, audiological information (audiometry) appear to be less important than it is for those who focus on listening and spoken language, as clients start therapy after years of language deprivation. The focus for these professionals is on language milestones through the use of the most accessible language: ASL. Therefore, spoken language is not targeted. "Language over speech," seems to be the motto of these participants. This is also related to the fact that ASL classes are part of professional coursework only as an elective class, if offered. Never as a core class, especially in programs with a specific auditory therapy track where some basic classes of ASL are offered, but as electives.

## *Assessment and Treatment Practices*

Most of the participants reported feeling prepared to use tests to assess children's language skills. However, bilingual English-ASL professionals reported not feeling prepared secondary to ASL not being their first language. These participants reported evaluations would be better if provided by an ASL native user, which demonstrates language and cultural awareness. Participants who use English or another spoken language to provide evaluations considered themselves as prepared. A few participants consider themselves capable of providing testing secondary to having an SLP license, but being aware of the many aspects their professional preparation might be missing. This also demonstrates being humble (Moroz et al., 2017) when assessing deaf and hard of hearing children for therapy services.

Tests utilized to assess deaf and hard of hearing children are mostly adapted from tests created for normal-hearing children. Some of the tests were standardized with a sample of deaf and hard of hearing children. Listening and spoken language participants reported not adapting tests created for typical-hearing children when testing the language skills of deaf and hard of hearing children. Listening and spoken language participants would not adapt tests created for normal-hearing children to test the language skills of deaf and hard of hearing children. Very few participants were aware of the existence of evaluations created to assess ASL skills being these tests standardized for the deaf and hard of hearing population throughout different ages as noted by Quinto-Pozos et al. (2017).

### *Therapy Language*

Most participants do not evaluate or provide therapy through ASL. Participants who promote the use of spoken language, might be able to use a few gestures or consider valid the use of these at a very basic level. However, participants who consider themselves as bilingual English-ASL provide therapy through ASL, especially for children who have experienced language deprivation. Spoken language is a goal if children get benefits from this approach. Participants who provide speech and language therapy through the use of spoken language, reported to review children's progress every six months. Once a child does not present with progress through spoken language, then participants start referring children to therapy using sign language or another approach that includes visual cues. This means, the professional should refer children out as this is out of their scope of practice; however, often times participants will continue to provide listening and spoken language upon parent request, even when the child receives little to not benefit, as therapy should revolve around parent goals, which means spoken language (Hecht, 2020).

There is an extended conception that assumes that learning ASL would impede learning spoken language (Baker et al., 2016; Shaw & Delaporte, 2015). This idea assumes that the visual cortex "conquers" the auditory cortex, making impossible to learn spoken language at the same time ASL is learned. This contradicts the idea that the brain should be "wired" with language regardless of its modality as the same areas are used in the brain for language regardless of it being spoken or signed (Banaszkiewicz et al., 2021; Blanco-Elorrieta et al., 2018; Cheng et al., 2020; Newman et al., 2015). Another well extended myth is related to learning ASL can happen at any age. These participants appear to ignore the effects of language deprivation as well as the difficulties faced when presenting a non-fluid first language as indicated by ~~Hill~~ Hall et al. (2019).

It appears some participants are not aware of how similar language acquisition by sight and hearing is (Sandler & Lillo-Martin, 2006). However, there is a condition that should be fulfilled: access to language. Being exposed to listening and spoken language at an early age, and using powerful hearing aids, are not enough to consider listening and spoken language as accessible (Hall & De Anda, 2021). Young children are not able to express if they are having access to all the sounds in the speech range. Not all hearing devices work in an efficient manner or are well calibrated; however, language acquisition through ASL is always effective. And even if not effective, it does not produce any harm, as exclusively auditory language exposure does (Hall, 2017).

### *Language Commonalities and Differences*

Regarding the main differences between ASL and English, it was evident that participants were aware of sign language being its own language with its own rules. An aspect that participants were aware is the fact that English is a linear language, while ASL is a three-dimensional language that can express many concepts at the same time due to its visuo-manual nature (Bradley et al., 2022). Monolingual participants were aware of many, but not all of the aspects presented on the questions of the interview. The lack of correspondence between ASL signs and English words is a well-known concept by all of the participants of the study. The role of fingerspelling is understood by monolingual participants only as a way to loan words from spoken language to ASL, just like any spoken language loans? words from another. However, the role of fingerspelling goes beyond naming (Miller et al., 2021). Some participants are confused regarding fingerspelling as a way to put "in writing" words produced with English grammar. Fingerspelling has been considered as leading to more literacy success as signs that include fingerspelling (Miller et al., 2021) also improve reading and orthographic skills.

Awareness of language commonalities and differences is a first step to understand that therapy can take place in more than one language, in order to provide children with an accessible language (Hall & De Anda, 2021). Access to a language allow kids to understand the world around and to express their thoughts and feelings through their own. The use of the most accessible language for deaf and hard of hearing children is ASL and it should be included as the language in which therapy is provided.

### *Relevance of the Findings to Theoretical Framework*

Throughout the study it was evident that most of the barriers speech-language pathologists face to provide services for deaf and hard of hearing children are due to the lack of culturally and linguistic informed practices, as well as limited awareness of similarities and differences in language acquisitions and structures in English and ASL. One of these barriers include memory as the concept formation that highly depends on language, which is what Vygotsky claims in his studies (Ehrich & O'Donovan, 2019). The hallmark of Vygotsky's theory is the importance of sociocultural contexts in which education takes place and, by extension, language acquisition occurs. This study confirms that children need to have language access through a community of sign language user, as a visual modality is the most accessible and effortless way to acquire a language. It is important for Deaf and hard of hearing children to acquire a strong first language (signed) in order to learn listening and spoken language. In other words, the importance of being part of a linguist community in order to develop language and cognitive skills can be hardly overestimated.

The findings of this study support what Glickman and Hall (2019) called "language deprivation" that negatively impacts the lives of deaf and hard of hearing individuals throughout their lives. While language exposure through hearing is considered the norm, language exposure through visual input is still left outside of the equation for deaf and hard of hearing children (Glickman & Hall, 2019; Glickman et al., 2020). The participants of this study confirmed just that when referring to their professional practice. Regardless of the modality (signed or oral) language acquisition at an early age should be the norm. Speech-language pathologists need to educate themselves and parents regarding the importance of an accessible language in order to develop listening and spoken language.

## *Conclusions and Implications for Practice*

The findings of this study have several implications for the way in which speech and language therapy services are provided for the deaf and hard of hearing children ages two to nine. One of the most important aspects of this study is making evident how the medical vision of the speech-language pathology profession continues to inform speech-language pathology practices (Cripps et al., 2016; Hernández & Hadley, 2020) from assessment to therapy without taking into consideration aspects as language acquisition, commonalities between spoken and signed languages, and the possibility to develop bilingual skills without neglecting the most naturally accessible language. The purpose should be to avoid language deprivation (Gullati, 2014) and to increase communication skills (Hecht, 2020).

Experiences from the deaf and hard of hearing community should also be taken into consideration. The use of ASL has been taken out of the clinical environments and has been only placed on the educational needs (Rosen, 2022), but there are certainly needs regarding disorders in users of sign language (Quinto-Pozos et al., 2017). Speech-language pathologists should be in charge of identifying how typical or non-typical sign language acquisition is taking place (Visser et al., 2017), the order in which sentences take place (Hall et al., 2017), word retrieval regarding categories (Marshall et al., 2018), and/or issues related to literacy (Cammarata-Scalisi et al., 2020; Muncy et al., 2019). Communication is one of the core values of our professional association. All these aspects should be mentioned to parents who seek services for their deaf and hard of hearing children. Therefore, educating parents regarding communication above listening and spoken language turns crucial in order to provide language input for deaf children in order to eliminate language deprivation.

As a speech-language pathologist providing therapy services through ASL, it is my hope that more SLPs will educate themselves and parents regarding the multiple benefits of learning this language. It does not only fulfill the human right of communication, but it also opens doors to have more SLPs who are native users of ASL. This is, I believe, the only manner in which speech-language pathologists can pave the way of ASL to be considered as part of the languages offered for speech and language therapy. Native language users providing services should be the norm in the speech and language therapy field.

By knowing SLPs' struggles as professionals, many barriers can be destroyed in order to provide the best professional services. This study connects with research regarding professional preparedness and is intended to be a contribution to assess strengths and weaknesses in the areas of culturally and linguistically responsive practices. Throughout our professional preparation, speech-language pathologists are conditioned to have a medical vision of hearing loss. I encourage my colleagues to develop a sociocultural vision and to look beyond the diagnosis. When parents seek guidance, let us not be the "permanent grief" individual who perpetuates social, emotional, and cognitive delays. A person with a hearing loss is not a broken person; however, a person without access to one, is. Let us promote the most accessible language available: sign language. Only strong skills in sign language can build strong spoken language skills. Let us not deny the possibility of having strong and meaningful relationships and lives to those who need their language rights to be respected. Let us stop promoting the use of signs among hearing children due to its multiple benefits, while we deny this possibility to those who need it the most. Hearing technology is a great tool that helps our children to find more than one way to communicate. We have the biggest gift of all in our hands: language.

## References

Alkhudiry, R. (2022). The contribution of Vygotsky's sociocultural theory in mediating L2 knowledge co-construction. *Theory and Practice in Language Studies, 12*(10), 2117. https://doi.org/10.17507/tpls.1210.19

Arms Almengor, R. (2018). Reflective practice and mediator learning: A current review. *Conflict Resolution Quarterly, 36*(1), 21–38.

American-Speech-Language-Hearing Association. (2021). *2021 demographic profile of ASHA members providing multilingual services.* https://www.asha.org/siteassets/surveys/demographic-profile-bilingual-spanish-service-members.pdf

Anderson, M., Wolf Craig, K., Hall, W., & Ziedonis, D. (2016). A pilot study of Deaf trauma survivors' experiences: Early traumas unique to being Deaf in a hearing world. *Journal of Child & Adolescent Trauma*, *9*(4), 353–358. https://doi.org/10.1007/s40653-016-0111-2

Baker, A., Van den Bogaerde, B., Pfau, R., & Shermer, T. (2016). *The linguistics of sign languages: An introduction.* John Benjamins.

Banaszkiewicz, A., Bola, Ł., Matuszewski, J., Szczepanik, M., Kossowski, B., Mostowski, P., Rutkowski, P., Śliwińska, M., Jednoróg, K., Emmorey, K., & Marchewka, A. (2021). The role of superior parietal lobule in lexical processing of sign language: Insights of sign language: Insights from fMRI and TMS. *Cortex*, *135*, 240–254. https://doi.org/10.1016/j.cortex.2020.10.025

Blanco-Elorrieta, E., Kastner, I., & Emmorey, K. (2018). Shared neural correlates for building phrases in signed and spoken language. *Scientific Reports*, *8*(1), 5492. https://doi.org/10.1038/s41598-018-23915-0

Bradley, C., Malaia, E. A., Siskind, J. M., & Wilbur, R. B. (2022). Visual form of ASL verb signs predicts non-signer judgment of transitivity. *PLoS ONE*, *18*(2), 1–25. https://doi.org/10.1371/journal.pone.0262098

Cammarata-Scalisi, F., Willoughby, C. E., Cardenas Tadich, A., Labrador, N., Herrera, A., & Callea, M. (2020). Clinical, etiopathogenic, and therapeutic aspects of KID syndrome. *Dermatologic Therapy*, *33*(4), e13507. https://doi.org/10.1111/dth.13507

Cassell, C., & Bishop, V. (2019). Qualitative data analysis: Exploring themes, metaphors and stories. *European Management Review*, *16*(1), 195–207. https://doi.org/10.1111/emre.12176

Cheng, Q., Silvano, E., & Bedny, M. (2020). Sensitive periods in cortical specialization for language: Insights from studies with Deaf and blind individuals. *Current Opinion in Behavioral Sciences*, *36*, 169–176. https://doi.org/10.1016/j.cobeha.2020.10.011

Creswell, J. W., & Poth, C. (2018). *Qualitative inquiry and research design: Choosing among five approaches* (4th ed.). SAGE.

Cripps, J., Cooper, S., Supalla, S., & Evitts, P. (2016). Meeting the needs of signers in the field of speech and language pathology. *Communication Disorders*, *37*(2), 108–116. http://ezproxy.acu.edu:2059/login.aspx?direct=true&AuthType=sso&db=eric&AN=EJ1084726&site=eds-live&scope=site&custid=s8479690

Cupples, L., Ching, T. Y. C., Leigh, G., Martin, L., Gunnourie, M., Button, L., Marnane, V., Hou, S., Zhang, V., Flynn, C., & Van Buynder, P. (2018). Language development in deaf or hard-of-hearing children with additional disabilities: Type matters! *Journal of Intellectual Disability Research: JIDR*, *62*(6), 532–543. https://doi.org/10.1111/jir.12493

Ehrich, J., & O'Donovan, R. (2019). Morality, language use, and ontogenesis: Vygotsky and Shotter revisited. *Linguistics Journal*, *13*(1), 197–207. https://www.researchgate.net/profile/John-Ehrich/publication/335676200_Morality_Language_Use_and_Ontogenesis_Vygotsky_and_Shotter_Revisited/links/5d733cf34585151ee4a3e049/Morality-Language-Use-and-Ontogenesis-Vygotsky-and-Shotter-Revisited.pdf#page=197

Gannon, J. (2012). *Deaf heritage: A narrative history of Deaf America.* Gallaudet University Press.

Glickman, N., & Hall, W. (2019). *Language deprivation and Deaf mental health.* Rutledge.

Glickman, N. S., Crump, C., & Hamerdinger, S. (2020). Language deprivation is a game changer for the clinical specialty of deaf mental health. *Journal of the American Deafness & Rehabilitation Association (JADARA)*, *54*(1), 54–89. https://nsuworks.nova.edu/jadara/vol54/iss1/4

Graneheim, U. H., & Lundman, B. (2004). Qualitative content analysis in nursing research: Concepts, procedures and measures to achieve trustworthiness. *Nurse Education Today*, *24*(2), 105–112. https://doi.org/10.1016/j.nedt.2003.10.001

Gullati, S. (2014). *Language deprivation syndrome.* ASL Lecture Series. https://www.youtube.com/watch?v=8yy_K6VtHJw, Brown University.

Hall, M. L., & De Anda, S. (2021). Measuring "Language Access Profiles" in Deaf and hard-of-hearing children with the DHH Language Exposure Assessment Tool. *Journal of Speech, Language, and Hearing Research*, *64*(1), 134–158. https://doi.org/10.1044/2020_JSLHR-20-00439

Hall, M. L., Hall, W. C., & Caselli, N. K. (2019). Deaf children need language, not (just) speech. *First Language*, *39*(4), 367–395. https://doi.org/10.1177/0142723719834102

Hall, W. C. (2017). What you don't know can hurt you: The risk of language deprivation by impairing sign language development in deaf children. *Maternal & Child Health Journal*, *21*(5), 961–965. https://doi.org/10.1007/s10995-017-2287-y

Hall, W. C., Levin, L. L., & Anderson, M. L. (2017). Language deprivation syndrome: A possible neurodevelopmental disorder with sociocultural origins. *Social Psychiatry and Psychiatric Epidemiology*, *52*(6), 761–776. https://doi.org/10.1007/s00127-017-1351-7

Hecht, J. L. (2020). Responsibility in the current epidemic of language deprivation (1990–Present). *Maternal & Child Health Journal*, *24*(11), 1319–1322. https://doi.org/10.1007/s10995-020-02989-1

Henner, J., Novogrodsky, R., Caldwell-Harris, C., & Hoffmeister, R. (2019). The development of American Sign Language-based analogical reasoning in signing Deaf children. *Journal of Speech, Language & Hearing Research*, *62*(1), 93–105. https://doi.org/10.1044/2018_JSLHR-L-18-0062

Hernandez, P. A., & Hadley, A. J. (2020). Exploring relationships between curriculum and cultural competency in pre-service speech-language pathology students.

*Journal of Cultural Diversity*, *27*(1), 3–13. https://search.ebscohost.com/login.aspx?direct=true&profile=ehost&scope=site&authtype=crawler&jrnl=2169415X&AN=142291601&h=ahuduJTQt%2F5a%2FHJq7Mf3r8gj9TB52TpPrXu9FnF3Lk%2BowqPQxxsrP4kaU%2F7vZZlwgCuec9KokjWNstffUK3zdA%3D%3D&crl=c

Javadi, Y., & Tahmasbi, M. (2020). Application of sociocultural identity theory to education in EFL textbooks development. *Theory & Practice in Language Studies*, *10*(5), 536–541. https://doi.org/10.17507/tpls.1005.07

Kelley, L. E., & McCann, J. P. (2021). Language intervention isn't just spoken: Assessment and treatment of a deaf signing child with specific language impairment. *Language, Speech & Hearing Services in Schools*, *52*(4), 978–992. https://doi.org/10.1044/2021_LSHSS-21-00038

Linask, L. (2019). Vygotsky's natural history of signs. *Sign Systems Studies*, *47*(1–2), 257–304. https://doi.org/10.12697/sss.2019.47.1-2.10

Marshall, C. R., Jones, A., Fastelli, A., Atkinson, J., Botting, N., & Morgan, G. (2018). Semantic fluency in deaf children who use spoken and signed language in comparison with hearing peers. *International Journal of Language & Communication Disorders*, *53*(1), 157–170. https://doi.org/10.1111/1460-6984.12333

Martin, F. N. (1997). *Introduction to audiology. A review manual.* Allyn and Bacon.

Miller, P., Banado-Aviran, E., & Hetzroni, O. E. (2021). Developing reading skills in prelingually deaf preschool children: Fingerspelling as a strategy to promote orthographic learning. *Journal of Deaf Studies & Deaf Education*, *26*(3), 363–380. https://doi.org/10.1093/deafed/enab004

Moroz, A., Flanagan, S., & Zaretsky, P. (2017). *Medical aspects of disability for the rehabilitation professionals* (5th ed.). Springer Publishing Company.

Muncy, M., Yoho, S., & McClain, M. B. (2019). Confidence of school-based speech-language pathologists in assessing students with hearing loss and other co-occurring disabilities. *Language, Speech, and Hearing Services in Schools*, *50*(2), 224–236. https://doi.org/10.1044/2018_LSHSS-18-0091

Murphy, D., Rena, L., Clare, C., Caulfield, M., & de Paor, G. (2018). Communication as a human right: Citizenship, politics, and the role of the speech-language pathologist. *International Journal of Speech-Language Pathology*, *20*(1), 16–20.

National Association of the Deaf. (2014). https://www.nad.org/about-us/position-statements/position-statement-on-early-cognitive-and-language-development-and-education-of-deaf-and-hard-of-hearing-children/

Newman, A., Supalla, T., Fernandez, N., Newport, E., & Bavalier, D. (2015). Neural systems supporting linguistic structure, linguistic experience, and symbolic communication in sign language and gesture. *Proceedings of the National Academy of Science of the United States of America*, *112*(37), 11684–11689. https://doi.org/10.1073/pnas.1510527112

Ozelie, R., Bock, J., Gervais, S., Schneider, L., & Silhavy, C. (2022). Is It Reasonable? Reasonable and unreasonable Accommodations for occupational therapy students in clinical settings. *Open Journal of Occupational Therapy (OJOT)*, *10*(2), 1–11. https://doi.org/10.15453/2168-6408.1913

Padden, C., & Humphries, T. (2005). *Inside Deaf culture.* Harvard University Press.

Park, K. H., Kam, B. S., Yune, S. J., Lee, S. Y., & Im, S. J. (2022). Changes in self-reflective thinking level in writing and educational needs of medical students: A longitudinal study. *PLoS ONE*, *17*(1), 1–11. https://doi.org/10.1371/journal.pone.0262250

Polit, D. F. (2017). Data collection methods. In J. Fitzpatrick (Ed.), *Encyclopedia of nursing research* (4th ed.). Springer.

Quinto-Pozos, D., Singleton, J. L., & Hauser, P. C. (2017). A case of specific language impairment in a deaf signer of American Sign Language. *The Journal of Deaf Studies and Deaf Education*, *22*(2), 204–218. https://doi.org/10.1093/deafed/enw074

Rosen, R. S. (2022). Foreign language ideology and American Sign Language in US public education. *International Journal of the Sociology of Language*, *2022*(275), 159–185. https://doi.org/10.1515/ijsl-2021-0001

Rowley, K., Snoddon, K., & O'Neill, R. (2022). Supporting families and young deaf children with a bimodal bilingual approach. *International Journal of Birth & Parent Education*, *9*(3), 15–20. https://www.research.ed.ac.uk/en/publications/supporting-families-and-young-deaf-children-with-a-bimodal-biling

Saldaña, J., & Omasta, M. (2018). *Qualitative research. Analyzing life.* Sage.

Sandler, W., & Lillo-Martin, D. (2006). *Sign language and linguistic universals.* Cambridge University Press.

Sanzo, K. (2022). Benefits of visual language: How acquisition of signed language complements spoken language development. *Perspectives of the ASHA Special Interest Groups*, *7*(2), 418–425. https://doi.org/10.1044/2021_PERSP-21-00124

Sehyr, Z. S., Geizen, M., & Emmorey, K. (2018). Comparing semantic fluency in American Sign Language and English. *Journal of Deaf Studies & Deaf Education*, *23*(4), 399–407. https://doi.org/10.1093/deafed/eny013

Shaw, E., & Delaporte, Y. (2015). *A historical and etymological dictionary of American Sign Language: The origin and evolution of more than 500 Signs.* Gallaudet University Press.

Skyer, M. E. (2020). The bright triad and five propositions: Toward a Vygotskian framework for Deaf pedagogy and research. *American Annals of the Deaf*, *164*(5), 577–591. https://doi.org/10.1353/aad.2020.0004

Stake, R. E. (1995). *The art of case study research.* Sage.

Szarkowski, A. (2018). *Language development in children with cochlear implants: Possibilities and challenges.* Taylor and Francis. https://doi.org/10.4324/9781315166728

Taylor, M. C. (2005). Interviewing. In *Qualitative research in health care* (pp. 39–55). McGraw-Hill.

Visser, J. C., Rommelse, N. N., Lappenschaar, M., Servatius-Oosterling, I. J., Greven, C. U., & Buitelaar, J. K. (2017). Variation in the early trajectories of autism symptoms is related to the development of language, cognition, and behavior problems. *Journal of the American Academy of Child & Adolescent Psychiatry*, *56*(8), 659–668. https://doi.org/10.1016/j.jaac.2017.05.022

Wilkinson, E., & Morford, J. P. (2020). How bilingualism contributes to healthy development in deaf children: A public health perspective. *Maternal & Child Health Journal*, *24*(11), 1330–1338. https://doi.org/10.1007/s10995-020-02976-6

# Chapter 12 A Paradigm of Critical Discourse Analysis on Neoliberalism: The Case of Haiti as a Neophyte

BAUDELAIRE K. ULYSSE

Mining answers for research questions as well as calibrating one's findings necessitate efficient tools. In this context, tools refer to methods. As such, methods putatively enable the researcher to delve into a subject matter and advance consciously and cautiously along both charted and uncharted paths to cull relevant and sound answers. Charted paths represent extant scholarly works on a particular subject, while uncharted paths represent possibilities of latent theories, perspectives, and new interpretations of established assumptions that lie beneath extant data. However, the search for an efficient method is daunting because there is a multitude of methods available to the researcher.

## *Critical Discourse Analysis as a Method or Tool for Research*

Researchers from a wide array of disciplines have deployed Critical Discourse Analysis (CDA) as a tool in research (McCloskey, 2008), and this trend is even more rampant in educational inquiries (Rogers, 2011). McCloskey (2008) uses discourse analysis as a tool to conduct research in the field of nursing and has found that the structure of this field inheres policies and practices which reflect the components of discourses. By the same token, Rogers (2011) does not simply use discourse analysis in her research, but also teaches discourse analysis. In fact, her work draws upon quantitative data from her own students' understanding as well as effective use of critical discourse analysis. Her data analysis provides insights into the arduous process of students grappling with the tool of critical discourse analysis and effectively using it in their own research. Their deep understanding and effective use of critical discourse analysis yielded multilayered interpretations of how discourse operates within social spheres of human societies. Overall, Rogers' research adds credence to the credibility and validity of discourse analysis as an effective research tool.

## *Assumptions of Critical Discourse Analysis*

Like a theoretical lens, CDA has a few assumptions. It maintains that language is a social phenomenon (Fairclough, 2001). This means that individual human beings, institutions, and social structures have values and meanings that are expressed through language in systematic ways. Thus, according to Fairclough, language has played a vital role in what people do and say, and why and how. This also plays out in the behaviors of multinational corporations, including the goods and services they decide to offer. Further, Fairclough notes that language plays a significant role in providing goods and services offered in the marketplace, particularly the strategic interactions that take place between staff and customers, in printed documents and signs, as well as the messaging and promotion for said products and services. This use of language means that the struggle to impose or resist the new order is in large part a struggle for or against a new language. Hence, any critique of documents such as policies, academic publications, and press releases related to discourse practices becomes imperative before one can successfully delineate as well as assess the discourse of neoliberalism (Fairclough, 2001).

Perhaps more pertinent for the current study is CDA's interest in the nexus between language and power (Fairclough, 2001; Gee, 2005). According to Gee (2005), this relationship between language and power manifests itself pervasively in that "language-in-use is everywhere and always political" (p. 1). In this relationship, language emits and solidifies power, and in turn power reinforces language, which nurtures it to both coexist and self-perpetrate in an extremely dominant way. By the same token, Fairclough (2001) offers helpful insights on the relationship between language and power. He coins the notion of "power behind discourse" and outlines three "aspects" of how power plays out in a discourse—*standard language*, *effect of power*, and *power and access to discourse.*

In all three aspects, discourse is engendered and maintained by the interest of powerholders. In this type of discourse, "the whole social order of discourse is put together and held together as a hidden effect of power" (Fairclough, 2001, p. 46). All three aspects, as discussed by Fairclough, feature explicitly or implicitly a positive correlation of power and domination.

Particularly, the third aspect—*power and access to discourse*—is especially salient because it touches on the issues of inequity and inequality, which are evident in the discourse on neoliberalism and economic globalization.

According to Fairclough (2001), power and access to discourse play right into how the value of *free speech* is implemented in social practice. He argues that the notion of free speech is in fact a myth because there is "a plethora of constraints on access to various sorts of speech and writing" (p. 52). Essentially, these constraints determine what group gets access to cultural capital in each society.

Inequity and inequality represent major concerns in contemporary debates, and the present study maintains that they are inextricably connected to the causality of the power dynamics in the neoliberal discourse. Consequently, the following analysis will focus on delineating and deconstructing these issues, while presenting an alternate vision that is consistent with social justice principles such as freedom, equality, and equity in all democratic contexts.

Gee (2005) credits Fairclough, Wodak, and Meyer, among others, with the use of CDA within the discourse analysis tradition, and he suggests they all share the fundamentals of discourse analysis, albeit they differ in tools of inquiry and linguistic tradition (pp. 116–117). However, all iterations of CDA take a keen interest in language-in-use and its effects on social, political, and economic structures. As such, they examine how language is used on discourses to enact activities and identities (little-d). A combination of the little-d discourse (language-in-use) and non-language "stuff" to enact specific identities and activities yields big-D discourse (p. 7).

Non-language stuff is understood by Gee (2005) as ways of living in the world—acting, feeling, believing, and valuing. Thus, he notes: "All life for all of us is just a patchwork of thoughts, words, objects, events, actions, and interactions in discourses" (p. 7). According to Gee, language has meanings only in and through social practice. People use language when they make things significant, engage in certain activities, build relationships, and argue for or against perspectives.

Also important is that contemporary approaches of discourse analysis assume a *reflexive* component of the relationship between language and context. Accordingly, Gee (2005) posits that "[r]eflexive here means that, at one and the same time, an utterance influences what we take the context to be and context conversely influences what we take the utterance to mean" (Gee, 2005, p. 57). Similarly, Fairclough (1995, 2001, 2008) links Gee's framework of discourse to critical theory. Thus, Fairclough (1995) describes discourse analysis as both analytical and critical. As such, CDA serves as "a resource for people who are struggling against the domination and oppression in its linguistic forms" (p. 1). Central to Fairclough's discussion of CDA are the notions of *text*, *discourse practice*, and *sociocultural practice.* Hence Fairclough expands the boundaries of discourse analysis from linguistic analysis to textual analysis, which includes language, written text, and social institutions. Accordingly, texts for Fairclough could be the content of linguistic texture and structure in written documents where value-driven ideologies are embedded.

Also, texts are viewed as *social spaces* wherein identities of individuals in a particular society are being formed. These individuals, or peoples in general, are being formed precisely in social spaces through certain processes, which Fairclough (1995) alludes to as "cognition and representations of the world and social interaction." Additionally, he argues that "[d]iscourses include representations of how things are and have been, as well as imaginaries—representations of how things might or could or should be" (Fairclough, 2008, p. 207). Thus, these elements, *cognition*, *representation*, and *social interaction* are integral parts of discourses, and they should be factored into any CDA research design. In Gee (2005), these elements would be considered as little-d discourses that contribute to the big-D discourse.

Based on this understanding of discourse as text, Fairclough (1995) argues that the successful analysis of any text or discourse must meticulously and critically analyze one or more of its key elements:

> Such analysis requires attention to textual form, structure and organizations at all levels; phonological, grammatical, and lexical (vocabulary) and higher levels of textual organization in terms of exchange systems (the distribution of speaking turns), structure of argumentation, and generic (activity type) structures. (p. 7)

Fairclough (1995) does not relegate the primary preoccupation of CDA with language. Instead, he views language or linguistic patterns as a broader structure, encompassing written texts and spoken texts (speech or other delivery systems) along with the vital components necessary for proper functioning. Fairclough's schema, which stresses text, discourse practice, and sociocultural practice as key components of discourse, expands the scope of discourse, thus providing a wider range of texts as targets for deeper analysis.

By the same token, Reisigl and Wodak (2009) underscore "text" as an embodiment of power and domination, and thus represent spaces for social struggle. Accordingly, they note:

> [T]exts are often sites of struggle in that they manifest traces of differing ideological fights for domination and hegemony. Thus, we focus on the ways in

> which linguistic forms are used in various expressions and manipulations of power. Power is discursively exerted not only by grammatical forms, but also by a person's control of the social occasions by means of the genre of a text, by the regulation of access to certain public spheres. (p. 89)

In the preceding statement, Reisigl and Wodak espouse and aptly argue for a broader view of text, which is like that of Fairclough (1995). Hence, this broader view of language or text as an embodiment of domination and oppression serves as a suitable framework not only to understand and interpret phenomena associated with global neoliberalism, but also to critique and deconstruct neoliberalism's hegemonic and oppressive agenda.

## *Research Methodology and Methods*

When methodology is discussed as part of a research project, methods become part of the process. As such, methods are used to mine data or data sources in search of evidence and insights are also requisites. This study subsumes the presuppositions of CDA. One of those presuppositions is that discourse uses texts (both spoken and written) to control as well as enact practices (linguistic, social, cultural, institutional, and political) in societies. This enables one group to dominate, control, and or oppress another group (Fairclough, 1995, 2001, 2008; Wodak & Meyer, 2009). Another presupposition is that discourse ironically is "resisted in text and talk in the social and political context" (van Dijk, 1993). Accordingly, in this critical analysis of the discourse of neoliberalism in the global economy context, texts from various sources and disciplines are considered. For instance, the analysis will scrutinize published materials for and against the neoliberal discourse, institutions such as government, schools or educational systems, primarily those in Haiti and the United States, with special attention given to how they support and embody the neoliberal discourse, and materials written about intergovernmental institutions such as the International Monetary Fund (IMF), World Bank (WB), World Trade Organization (WTO), and United Nations Educational, Scientific and Cultural Organization (UNESCO). Additionally, the analysis draws on data from various strata, while concentrating on key aspects such as those proposed by van Dijk (1993): analysis of semantic macrostructure, topics for macrostructure, analysis of local meanings, analysis of subtle structure, analysis of global and local discourse forms, analysis of specific linguistic realization (hyperbolas), and analysis of content. Those aspects are not exhaustive; neither do they lend themselves to a reductive choice of all or none. Rather, they comprise a list of options from which the researcher may select elements to examine based on their topic, research questions, or purposes.

### *Analyzing the Discourse*

To successfully analyze aspects of the neoliberal discourse, this chapter draws from an array of books, journal articles, and respected newspapers that extensively address globalization's history and its current juncture—social, political, educational, and economic—through the prism of neoliberal ideologies. Essentially, the data sources referred to above are delineated, analyzed, compared, contrasted, expounded on, and synthesized to unveil and critique the nature of the discourse or discourses as well as its inherent injustice.

Drawing on Gee's vernacular (2005), particularly his differentiation between big-D discourses and little-d discourses, the analysis of neoliberalism pays close attention to the subtleties and complexities of how power and politics are embedded in "languages" in local settings as embodied in written content. Thus, initiatives such as educational reforms, school textbooks, enactment of trade agreements, and privatization of public assets could be said to represent little-d discourses that take place in local settings while contributing and shaping, both subtly and explicitly, the big-D discourse within the macrocosm of neoliberalism and economic globalization.

### *Neoliberalism as Discourse: A Politico-Economic Ideology*

Neoliberalism, as an ideology, has wielded tremendous influence, both pull and push on human societies across the world (Davies & Bensel, 2007). The influence of neoliberalism is not confined to just one aspect of these societies—its presence is ubiquitous and global. It reaches and impacts many aspects that profoundly affect the material conditions of social, economic, and political structures. One of the consequential shifts in the material conditions of societies engendered by neoliberalism is the transition from a social welfare state to a neoliberal market-driven state, which has served as an apparatus for individual and entrepreneurial interests (Nafstad et al., 2007). Along with this market-based or economic emphasis in neoliberalism, there is a strong push to strengthen nation-states and their law-and-order system (Wacquant, 2010). Neoliberalism may benefit from weak nation-states where lawmakers are easily swayed by personal gains and where capital can be acquired and moved from shore to shore, but it does not fare well in chaos or anarchy where respect for property rights is not enforced. According to Wacquant (2010), law enforcement, the judicial system, and large prison complexes are favored by neoliberalism because these systems "enable political elites to reassert the authority of the state and shore up the deficit of legitimacy officials suffer when they abandon the mission of social and economic protection established during the Fordist-Keynesian era" (p. 198). Other shifts caused by neoliberalism are manifest in social policies enacted in certain societies around the world. For instance, developing countries have embraced privatization as a core market practice. As a result, government-run services, and programs such as telecommunications, electricity, and water plants are now being sold to and run by private enterprises. The most convincing reasoning behind the transfer of these services to private entities is the lack of efficiency and profits. Laden by bureaucracy, corruption, and overhead cost, governments are said to lack the resources and tools to continue offering these services in a sustainable and profitable manner. The solution, according to proponents of neoliberalism, is the private sector where investors are more inclined. Plus, services can be more consistent, and pricing can be driven by supply and demand, and not by necessity of making up shortfalls in governments' budget and coffers. Prime examples of countries that have experimented with these neoliberal or market-based policies are the United Kingdom, Poland, Haiti, Brazil, and Chile. These various shifts engendered by neoliberalism have led many to conclude that the neoliberal agenda has been very effective on a global scale.

Jilberto and Mommen (1993) have correctly noted that "neo-liberalism as political and economic ideology has been one of the most successful elements of the reconstruction of capitalist hegemony over the global system" (p. 3). Similarly, Apple (1999), Hill (1998), and Miraftab (2004) have each painted neoliberalism as a powerful ideological tool that is drastically transforming the fiber of many societies around the world. Miraftab (2004) examines the role neoliberalism plays in the governance of different states around the world, and paints a rather stunning picture of how neoliberalism relates to politics and economies in developing countries:

> Neo-liberal policies and structural adjustment programs have deeply slashed governments' budget for public expenditure and have redefined the state's responsibilities for public services. For example, in developing states in the 1950s–1970s the primary agenda for national economic growth was to provide basic services and infra-structure. But that role has now been shifted to private firms, both local and international, in a market-led strategy for providing basic public services and infrastructure. (p. 240)

While Miraftab's depiction reflects realities as well as actualities in the developing world, neoliberalism's growing influence is by no means confined to that segment. After all, neoliberalism has long achieved a certain pinnacle regarding global dominance, making it undeniably a full-fledged ideological discourse. As Miraftab (2004) points out, neoliberalism has attained such global dominance precisely by strategically creating alliance, albeit coercively at times, with what one might call client governments around the world.

### *Neoliberalism in Education: Standards, Tests, Accountability, Market, and Profits*

If there is doubt about neoliberalism being a discourse or about neoliberalism's global reach, Apple (1999) provides a scathing portrayal of neoliberalism which is sure to dispel such doubt. His work, entitled *Freire, Neoliberalism, and Education*, traces the connection between American conservative ideologies and neoliberalism. This work represents by far one of the most courageous assessments of, and thus a verdict against, neoliberalism in terms of the subtle way in which neoliberalism controls policies related to U.S. economy and education. According to Apple (1999; 2004), one of the major neoliberal hallmarks in education is the No Child Left Behind (NCLB) federal law. The aim of NCLB is to increase "economic productivity" by "improving education," and among its strategies are "increased accountability, high-stakes tests, standards, choice, and centralized regulation of schools" and the reduction of inputs from "teachers and communities" (Lipman, 2008, p. 46). On the surface, the aim of the law appears reasonable, but, as Hursh (2007) notes, "it is not enough to examine a particular policy' stated purpose" (p. 494). In fact, a closer look at NCLB reveals a broader but discursive "...policy texts that are political, cultural, economic as much as they are educational treatises ..." (Olssen et al., 2004, p. 2), which diminish the autonomy and agency of students and teachers. Consequently, schools become like private enterprises with a "single-minded pursuit of profit and showing significantly less regard for the need to limit social costs or for redistribution based on nonmarket criteria" (Tabb, 2002, p. 29). Similarly, the Common Core States Standards (CCSS) initiative, which was enacted nearly a decade after its predecessor, NCLB, promised to usher in a new era in student's preparedness for college and career turned out to be ironically a repackaging of the same neoliberal educational policies, although CCSS gives back some flexibility and agency to teachers and school administrators to augment and implement the curriculum (Applebee, 2013).

Arguably, the most pernicious manifestation of neoliberalism in education is the privatization of school along with its high-stakes tests accountability (Dee et al., 2013). Patterned after market-based principles, it prioritizes the preparation of "workers for jobs in a global economy where capitalism can move jobs wherever it wishes—that is, countries where profits trump working conditions and salaries" (Weiner, 2012, p. 36). Most countries, especially in the third world, where neoliberalism has been implemented have tried to replicate NCLB in their educational systems. Particularly, Haiti's educational system has been molded to reflect similar standards.

## *Neoliberalism: Economic Policies and Political Interests of the Dominant West*

Davies and Bensel (2007) discuss the shift to or the emergence of global neoliberalism. They trace the development of neoliberalism back to the economic policies of Great Britain and the United States. Davies and Bensel also show how neoliberalism started spreading across the world through the concerted effort of neoliberal stakeholders such as France, Great Britain, and the United States. Essentially, they postulate that the spread of neoliberalism has been facilitated by the consent of nation-states' official governments in countries across the world. When these governments grant consent, neoliberalism becomes endowed with unlimited political and economic leverage to influence or undermine existing laws as well as enact new ones which favor the unfettered operation of multinational corporations and other interest groups. This relationship or arrangement between governments of nation-states and global interest groups begets as well as controls the framework within which the neoliberal discourse is promulgated, implemented, and sustained.

Operative within this discourse are various philosophies or notions. These terms, which have surfaced in earlier discussions in no respective order, are *capitalism*, *hegemony*, *neoliberalism*, *colonialism*, and *imperialism*. The assumptions of the study posit that the discourse, which embodies neoliberalism and economic globalization, subsumes most, if not all, of the concepts highlighted above.

## *Neoliberalism as a Global Expansion of Capitalism*

Capitalism is by no means a new phenomenon. It is an economic system or philosophy that has been implemented in many economies around the world, particularly in Western economies such as Great Britain and the United States of America (Frieden, 2006). It is not confined to a restrictive definition, but most economists concur that capitalism refers to and embodies values such as free market and free choice. Because of its putative element of freedom, capitalism is thought by many to be ideal and most compatible with human societies (Bernstein, 2005).

Placing this philosophy in the context of a local economy, it becomes characterized by five distinct features: private property and freedom of choice, self-interest, markets and prices, competition, and limited government intervention (Friedman, 2002; 2007). Thus, the global economy is essentially capitalism driving economies of both the developing and the developed countries into an integrated whole. This entails a "closer integration of the [economies of] countries of the world through the increased flow of goods and services" (Stiglitz, 2003, p. 4).

## *Neoliberalism as Political and Economic Hegemony*

Hegemony, being understood as the dominant discourse (Apple, 2004) or the concurrent enforcement mechanism of a particular ideology by those in control, represents an ideology of domination by others. It is a fascinating phenomenon in that it can be implemented through either coercion (Clayton, 1998) or in a subtle persuasion medium such as spoken languages, educational systems, curricular approaches, and publications. From the vantage point of colonialism and imperialism, the cultures and educational systems of previously colonized countries are steeped in the legacies of their colonizers (Ginsburg & Clayton, 2006), thereby perpetuating and enforcing hegemony.

The type of hegemony discussed and illustrated above reflects a subtle domination, however strategic and intentional. Although this type of hegemony should not be equated with empire, it is often the result of imperial legacies perpetuated through education, cultural, and linguistic devices. However, hegemony also inheres an aggressive dimension that is particularly manifest in economic implementation of neoliberalism and its political ramifications in the global context. Agnew (2005) thinks this kind of hegemony is U.S.-infused and argues that the U.S. usually enlists the help of other countries in propagating and advancing it. Thus, he defines it as "the enrollment of others in the exercise of your power by convincing, cajoling, and coercing them that they should do what you want" (p. 1). According to Agnew, this characterizes the relationship between the U.S. and the rest of the world, particularly in the context of globalization. In fact, he views globalization, without qualification, as a "hegemonic project intimately connected to the geopolitical calculus of U.S. government" (p. 2), thereby dismissing neoliberalism, or "liberalization" as he labels it. The present analysis does not equate globalization with liberalization or neoliberalism because there are various factors contributing to the globalizing process. However, the current engine of economic globalization, or the global economy, is being propelled by neoliberalism as the dominant discourse. Hence, contrary to Agnew's position, the hegemony of neoliberalism in economic globalization cannot be viewed simply through the American prism. In its analysis, this study has assessed that economic globalization stems from a broader coalition among the most powerful and elite economies of the world, including the U.S. Ultimately, this coalition is committed not only to incubate and implement neoliberalism, but also to propagate it in other countries, particularly countries in the developing world.

## *Ideologies of the Neoliberal Discourse*

Having become the preferred economic philosophy in the context of a global economy, capitalism has given rise to a capitalist expansion known as neoliberalism. Neoliberalism represents a hegemonic discourse in the context of globalization (Giroux, 2004; Harvey, 2007), and is manifest particularly in economies, government, and education globally (Giroux, 2004).

## *Privatization*

Megginson (2005) defines privatization as a "deliberate sale by a government of state-owned enterprises (SOEs) or assets to private economic agents" (p. 3). As such, privatization favors private enterprise and private ownership over public or government enterprises. Like deregulation, privatization is another neoliberal ideology that advocates for less publicly run or government-sponsored services. Further, it maintains that private ownership and enterprises ultimately foster entrepreneurship, individual responsibility, competitions on the market, and better services and more competitive pricing for consumers.

Since its introduction, privatization has rapidly become the *darling* of all economic reforms in developed economies and is a major component of neoliberalism as a dominant discourse. Megginson (2005) notes that Chile and Germany experimented with privatization in the 1970s, but he suggests those two countries harvested nominal results from the implementation of privatization. According to Megginson, Great Britain has been particularly singled out as an exemplar that successfully implemented privatization in the early 1980s. Further, other countries such as "France, Austria, Belgium, Canada, Chile, Denmark, Holland, Italy, Jamaica, Japan, Malaysia, Singapore, Spain, Sweden, and the United States all executed significant privatization through public share offerings during the mid-1980s" (p. 17).

As those countries embarked on the journey to implement privatization, there was an aura of heightened optimism that privatization would make their governments more efficient, raise financial capital for their gross domestic product (GDP), and ultimately boost their economies. To date, other countries have launched similar privatization projects. Accordingly, Megginson (2005) estimates that "the cumulative value" of all privatization undertakings "now has surpassed 1.5 trillion dollars" (p. 21). Apparently, there is very much to be had when governments privatize.

### *Haiti: The Case of a Neoliberal Neophyte*

It is no wonder that privatization is being pushed in many developing countries around the world. Haiti is one among many developing countries where privatization as a neoliberal economic reform is currently being implemented. Neoliberals have been courting Haiti on such reforms for a long time. The 1994 return of Aristide, the then-exiled and now former president of Haiti, served as the turning point in this pursuit since Aristide supposedly agreed to a deal that guaranteed his return in exchange for the implementation of neoliberal reforms. However, Aristide had been reluctant to follow through on such reforms because they were not popular among the Haitian masses that rely heavily on public services (Girard, 2005). As it turned out, Aristide's reluctance did not earn him favor with powerful neoliberal interest groups, which arguably became the ground for a second ouster that sent him into exile in Africa.

Since Aristide's second exile, which occurred in 2004, and with the advent of the re-election of Mr. Rene Préval for a second nonconsecutive term as president in 2006, much funding had been disbursed to Haiti through World Bank and International Monetary Fund, purportedly from neoliberal interest groups whose precondition was implementation of the neoliberal agenda (Girard, 2005). Privatization is one focus of this agenda and is typically sold to developing countries as a catalyst for economic development. Harvey (2007) explains how neoliberalism ties privatization to economic advancement:

> Neoliberals are particularly assiduous in seeking the privatization of assets. The absence of clear private property rights—as in many developing countries—is seen as one of the most institutional barriers to economic development and the improvement of human welfare ... Sectors formerly run or regulated by the state must be turned over to the private sphere and be deregulated (free from any state interference). (p. 65)

Economic reforms of this nature pervade many countries, both developed and developing, around the globe. Haiti a country that has been oscillating at the juncture of economic development in the context of neoliberal economic discourse. As a direct result of neoliberal economic reforms in Haiti, a few institutions or services previously run by the Haitian government have been privatized. For instance, Haiti's flourmill and cement factory, which were formerly run by the Haitian government, have been privatized. In 2010, the former Haitian president, Rene Préval, announced that the privatization plan for Téléco, the Haitian national telephone company, was being finalized (Sprague, 2009).

Although the then-president claimed privatization to be in the best interest of the Haitian economy, many Haitians, especially those intimately affected by it, are not particularly thrilled with privatization or other reforms. The fire of neoliberal reforms in Haiti is currently being fanned, and it will likely remain sparked and aflame for a long time because the cash-strapped Haitian government has apparently bought into the neoliberal ideologies, and neoliberals have leveraged that to great effect in exerting influence in the political process in Haiti. Evidence of such influence is seen in the exclusion of the most popular political party in Haiti in the April 2009 senatorial elections. With no constitutional or legal ground, the Haitian national electoral council banned politicians of that party from participating in the elections (Reuters, 2009; Sprague, 2009). Critics of this decision suggested that politicians from this popular party were likely to get elected but unlikely to support the neoliberal agenda. Hence, to clear the way for unfettered and undeterred neoliberal reforms in Haiti, neoliberals purportedly colluded with the election officials to orchestrate a political hacking, resulting into the conundrum in Haiti (Gupta, 2010).

Subsequently, the neoliberal project of liberating the Haitian market promised several milestones, and both local and international businesspeople were invited to learn about how to make money in Haiti (Loewenstein, 2017). Neoliberal initiatives were accelerated after the devastating 2010 earthquake. A key component of these initiatives was the construction of industrial parks to attract foreign manufacturers. Accordingly, Iqbal (2021) notes: "In 2011, the US-controlled Organization of American States (OAS) collaborated with the Haitian elite to install Michael Martelly as the president. Martelly was a neo-colonial stooge, responsible for eviscerating an already weak Haiti through his "Open for Business" policy. The opening of a South Korean manufacturing plant in Caracol, an area in northeast Haiti unaffected by the earthquake, displaced hundreds of Haitian farmers, confiscating arable land" (para. 24). Along with the park, a nearby port was planned as well. The logic of these projects was to attract foreign companies by the prospect of cheap labors, but neither the park nor the port had enough funding to bring them to fruition. While a project of this magnitude may be considered a milestone for the neoliberal project in Haiti, many have seen it as a failure for several reasons. First, the location was formerly farmland where food was grown locally for the people living in that region. Farmers were forced out to make room for the industrial park. The most probably part of this quandary is that farmers were sold on the prospect of getting jobs. Accordingly, Kushner (2019) observes: "While the port stalled, the industrial park underdelivered. When Bill and Hillary Clinton flew to northern Haiti to inaugurate the $300m Caracol park in 2012, the overall project had created just 1,500 of the 65,000 jobs that were promised. In fact, many Haitians may have lost their livelihoods because of Caracol: in the end, 366 families were evicted from their land to make way for the project, according to a report by the NGO ActionAid" (para. 32). Unfortunately, as Loewenstein (2017) points out, these jobs pay low wages, making farmers reliant on the capitalist production instead of producing their own food. Once these farmers get paid, they end up having to use their earning to buy on the marketplace foods that have been imported from the United States and other countries. In the final analysis, the real winners of these transactions are foreign companies that benefit from cheap labors and Western consumers who get to buy lower-priced products manufactured in that context. Meanwhile, Haitian are denied the opportunity to achieve food security and economic development from within (Ramachandran & Walz, 2015).

The evidence on neoliberalism in Haiti shows that privatization or private enterprise rarely delivers on what it purports to do, especially as it pertains to economic development in third-world countries. Giroux (2004) perceptively notes that neoliberalism "pushes for the privatization of all non-commodified public spheres and the upward distribution of wealth. [I]t supports policies that increasingly militarize facets of public space in order to secure the privileges and benefits of the corporate elite and ultra-rich" (p. xxiv). Despite the fact that privatization serves the interests of only a select few, its proponents continue to sell it as a catalyst for widespread economic development in poor countries.

## *Neoliberalism as "Free" Market*

From a policy standpoint, regulations represent rules or interventions by the government intended to contain the market's reach and protect investors from erratic turns (Reback, 2009). Presupposed in the government's regulatory interventions in the market mechanism is a clairvoyance that "the market system may not function ideally in monopolistic or oligopolistic industries" (Baumol & Blinder, 1986, p. 272). For instance, regulation restricts what prices firms and corporations can charge and, in many situations, how products and services are distributed to the markets. Also, regulations may enact and enforce antitrust policies to deter monopolistic business practices (Reback, 2009). These aspects of regulation, among many others, are intended to create competition and fair business habits among firms and to protect consumers and investors who do business transactions on the market (Baumol & Blinder, 1986; Reback, 2009).

In stark contrast to regulation, *de*regulation seeks to minimize government's interventions since government interventions are usually perceived as interference that inhibits the market and that prevents it from naturally stimulating competition in pricing and the production of better products. Further, much like liberalism, this deregulation element of neoliberal ideology holds and professes an unwavering trust in the market, touting the market as sovereign and capable of independently running itself smoothly, equitably, and fairly (Friedman, 2002; Oatley, 2008). Highlighting neoliberalism's influence on economies for the last 20 years and the emphasis on free market, Oatley (2008) notes:

> Neoliberalism is highly skeptical of the state's ability to allocate resources efficiently and places great faith in the market's ability to do so. And in contrast to structuralism's advocacy of protectionism and state intervention is neoliberalism's advocacy of the withdrawal of the state from the economy, the reduction (ideally, elimination) of trade barriers, and reliance on the market to generate industries that produce for the world market. (p. 139)

Further, proponents of neoliberalism argue that deregulation reduces prices on products, improves services, renders the market more competitive and accessible, and makes entry of new businesses feasible and profitable (Baumol & Blinder, 1986). However, it should be noted that these advantages of deregulation do not represent the norms of market's behaviors or across industries. By contrast, opponents of deregulation have argued that regulation initiated by government toward the market fittingly represents the sole, albeit imperfect, restraining force against the excesses of the market (Reback, 2009). In fact, critics have viscerally and adamantly contested neoliberalism's trust in the market, noting that the market lacks the moral or logical autonomy to operate in a socially just fashion (Stiglitz, 2003).

Regarding the issue of moral fiber of the market, Giroux (2004) aptly observes: "Within the discourse of neoliberalism, democracy becomes synonymous with free markets while issues of equality, social justice, and freedom are stripped of any substantive meaning and used to disparage those who suffer systemic deprivation and chronic punishment" (p. xviii). These points made by Giroux adeptly capture some of the issues revolving around the supremacy awarded to the market mechanism.

### *Philosophical Foundations of Neoliberalism: Freedom and Discontents*

Milton Friedman was perhaps the most astute and prominent advocate for the supremacy of the market. In fact, Friedman (1990) co-authored *Free to Choose* with his wife Rose Friedman. Friedman and Friedman (1990) attributed the success of American capitalist economy to the notion of free market, particularly the philosophy that advocates and demands that the market be freed from political influence. Grounded in the arguments originally advanced in Adam Smith's *The Wealth of Nations* (1776), Friedman and Friedman postulated that in almost all cases where the U.S. government has intervened with the goal of protecting the public good and the interests of its citizens, it has managed to produce just the opposite. To corroborate their thesis, they extensively examined services such as education, social institutions, social security, employment, and fiscal matters where the government has frequently yet unsuccessfully intervened.

Having espoused the ideal of free market, they suggested that it is through the "voluntary exchange" among self-interested individuals that an economy develops, grows, and sustains itself. According to them, this voluntary exchange is dictated and facilitated by the pricing structure inherent in the market system and not by some externally commanding force such as the government. As far as the government is concerned, Friedman and Friedman argue that its role must be confined to the protection of its citizens and the administration of justice. This, according to them, will secure the parameters of a free society wherein its people are free from "outside coercion" and free to engage in transactions that are mutually beneficial for all parties involved. Overall, their view can be summed up as such: "Economic freedom is an essential requisite to the political freedom. By enabling people to cooperate with one another without coercion or central direction, it reduces the area over which political power is exercised" (Friedman & Friedman, 1990, pp. 2–3). Hence, Friedman and Friedman effectively linked the *Declaration of Independence* to the economic principle of free market, and they supposed that the parties operating in the market equally enjoy the same freedom.

However, recent conditions and events on the market have challenged the notion of the market as a free mechanism. For instance, the Great Recession between 2007 and 2012 was largely blamed on the malfeasances, speculations, and manipulations by greedy and self-interested players. By the same token, the near failure of several financial institutions was attributed to the lack of deregulation. This is one of the reasons why Harvey (2007) sharply disagrees with the free-market philosophy advanced by Friedman and Friedman.

The crux of Harvey's disagreement is that political freedom does not necessarily translate into freedom for everyone making transactions in the market, and that the neoliberal application at its core undermines both personal and political freedom. Similarly, Chua (2003) argues that the neoliberal ideology destabilizes democracy globally. Giroux (2004) notes that "[n]eoliberalism devitalizes democracy" (p. 69); Stiglitz (2003; 2010) describes how neoliberalism extorts developing countries and brings the global economy to the brink of sinking.

Freedom is assumed for everyone in Milton Friedman's view, and it represents a major premise in his argument for capitalism or its most current form in neoliberalism. However, Friedman has oversold the notion of freedom as understood and practiced in capitalism and neoliberalism, which Harvey demonstrates correctly by portraying the market as an unlevel playing field where equals play fairly. In fact, the evidence shows that the market is a field where unequal people, by virtue or the extent of their power to affect the outcome of transactions, engage in unfair and underhanded play. Ultimately, some players, including nations, get super-rich, while other players lose and remain at the bottom of the totem pole (Frieden, 2006; Stiglitz, 2003; 2010). This process is sanctioned and enjoined by neoliberalism itself, which makes economic freedom virtually impossible to be enjoyed on an equal basis. Therefore, the ethos of freedom in neoliberalism seems more symbolic than material; hence its paradoxical nature is warranted. As such, it is used to create an illusion of democracy and choice to lure weaker players. In fact, the structure, the principles, and the practices of the neoliberal market embed this lack of evenhandedness in transactions, resulting in social inequality, and economic and educational inequities within the hegemonic, oppressive, and exploitative discourse (Giroux, 2004). Further, Stiglitz (2010) suggests that Friedman, along with his followers, is partly responsible for the asphyxiation of freedom and the failure of neoliberalism.

## Conclusion

Using the assumptions and tools of CDA, the preceding discussions depict neoliberalism as a discourse, embodying ideologies that parlay political and economic freedom for all but purvey only the interests of the few. Further, they draw on arguments and documents by various scholars to demonstrate how neoliberalism operate, including its implement and reinforcement in political, economic, and social domains. Specifically, they examine how neoliberal ideologies infiltrate, both overtly and covertly, politics, education, and the market through linguistic equivocation, the use of coercion, and consent.

Overall, neoliberalism, despite its promises of political freedom and economic advancement, remains the embodiment of discursive practices and ideologies that predetermine and control, both consciously and subconsciously, the thoughts and behaviors of people from various societies across the globe.

## *References*

Agnew, J. (2005). *Hegemony: The new shape of global power.* Temple University Press.

Apple, M. (1999). Freire, neo-liberalism and education. *Discourse: Studies in the Cultural Politics of Education*, *20*(1), 5.

Apple, M. (2004). Creating difference: Neo-liberalism, neo-conservatism and the politics of educational reform. *Educational Policy*, *18*(1), 12–44.

Applebee, A. N. (2013). Common Core State Standards: The promise and the peril in a national palimpsest. *The English Journal*, *103*(1), 25–33. http://www.jstor.org/stable/24484057

Baumol, W., & Blinder, A. (1986). *Economics: Principles and policy.* Harcourt Brace Jovanovich, Publishers.

Bernstein, A. (2005). *The capitalist manifesto.* University Press of America.

Chua, A. (2003). *World on fire: How exporting free market democracy breeds ethnic hatred and global instability.* Doubleday.

Clayton, T. (1998, November). Beyond mystification: Reconnecting world-system theory for comparative education. *Comparative Education Review*, *42*(4), 479.

Davies, B., & Bensel, P. (2007). Neoliberalism and education. *International Journal of Qualitative Studies in Education (QSE)*, *20*(3), 247–259.

Dee, T. S., Jacob, B., & Schwartz, N. L. (2013). The effects of NCLB on school resources and practices. *Educational Evaluation and Policy Analysis*, *35*(2), 252–279. http://www.jstor.org/stable/43773431

Fairclough, N. (1995). *Critical discourse analysis: The critical study of language.* Longman.

Fairclough, N. (2001). *Language and power.* Longman.

Fairclough, N. (2008). *Analyzing discourse: Textual analysis for social research.* Routledge.

Frieden, J. (2006). *Global capitalism: Its fall and rise in the twentieth century.* W. W. Norton.

Friedman, M. (2002). *Capitalism and freedom.* The University of Chicago Press.

Friedman, M. (2007). *Milton Friedman on economics: Selected papers.* The University of Chicago Press.

Friedman, M., & Friedman, R. (1990). *Free to choose: A personal statement.* Harcourt Books.

Gee, J. (2005). *An introduction to discourse analysis: Theory and method.* Routledge.

Ginsburg, M., & Clayton, T. (2006). Imperialism and education. In D. Levinson, P. Cookson, & A. Sadovnik (Eds.), *Education and sociology* (pp. 387–392). Rutledge Falmer.

Girard, P. (2005). *Paradise lost: Haiti's tumultuous journey from pearl of the Caribbean to third world hotspot.* Palgrave Macmillan.

Giroux, H. (2004). *The terror of neoliberalism.* Paradigm Publishers.

Gupta, A. (2010, February). The U.S. in Haiti: Neoliberalism at the barrel of a gun. *The Indypendent.* http://www.indypendent.org/2010/02/18/us-in-haiti/

Harvey, D. (2007). *A brief history of neoliberalism.* Oxford University Press.

Hill, D. (1998). Neo-liberalism and hegemony revisited. *Educational Philosophy & Theory, 30*(1), 69.

Jilberto, A., & Mommen, A. (1993). The political economy of global neo-liberalism. *International Journal of Political Economy, 23*(1), 3–12.

Kushner, J. (2019, October). Haiti and the failed promise of US Aid. *The Guardian.* https://pulitzercenter.org/stories/haiti-and-failed-promise-us-aid

Lipman, P. (2008). Chapter 2: Education policy, race, and neoliberal urbanism. *Counterpoints, 316,* 45–66. http://www.jstor.org/stable/42979838

Loewenstein, A. (2017, September). Haiti: The neoliberal model imposed on the country is failing its citizens. *The Guardian.* https://www.theguardian.com/commentisfree/2014/feb/05/haiti-the-neoliberal-model-imposed-on-the-country-is-failing-its-citizens

McCloskey, R. (2008). A guide to discourse analysis. *Nurse Researcher, 16*(1), 24–43.

Megginson, W. (2005). *The financial economics of privatization.* Oxford University Press.

Miraftab, F. (2004). Making neo-liberal governance: The disempowering work of empowerment. *International Planning Studies, 9*(4), 239–259.

Nafstad, H., Blakar, R. M., Carlquist, E., Phelps, J. M., & Rand-Hendriksen, K. (2007). Ideology and power: The influence of current neo-liberalism in society. *Journal of Community & Applied Social Psychology, 17*(4), 313–327.

Oatley, T. (2008). *International political economy.* Pearson/Longman.

Olssen, M., Codd, J., & O'Neill, A.-M. (2004). *Education policy: Globalization, citizenship, and democracy.* SAGE.

Ramachandran, V., & Walz, J. (2015). Haiti: Where has all the money gone? *Journal of Haitian Studies, 21*(1), 26–65. http://www.jstor.org/stable/24573148

Reback, G. (2009). *Free the market: Why only government can keep the marketplace competitive.* Portfolio.

Reisigl, M., & Wodak, R. (2009). The discourse-historical approach (DHA). In R. Wodak & M. Meyer (Eds.), *Methods of critical discourse analysis* (pp. 87–121). SAGE Publications.

Reuters. (2009, November 26). Haiti bars ex-President's party from elections for parliament. *New York Times.* http://www.nytimes.com/2009/11/26/world/americas/26haiti.html?_r=1

Rogers, R. (2011). Becoming discourse analysts: Constructing meanings and identities. *Critical Inquiry in Language Studies, 8*(1), 72–104.

Smith, A. (1776). *The wealth of nations.* W. Strahan and T. Cadell.

Sprague, J. (2009, April). Haiti: Fanmi Lavalas banned; voter apprehension widespread. *Interpress Service News.*

Stiglitz, J. (2003). *Globalization and its discontents.* W. W. Norton.

Stiglitz, J. (2010). *Free fall: America, free markets, and the sinking of the world economy.* W. W. Norton.

Tabb, W. (2002). *Unequal partners: A primer on globalization.* The New Press.

Van Dijk, T. (1993). Critical discourse analysis. *Discourse & Society, 4*(2), 352–371.

Wacquant, L. (2010). Crafting the neoliberal state: Workfare, prisonfare, and social insecurity. *Sociological Forum, 25*(2), 197–220. http://www.jstor.org/stable/40783391

Weiner, L. (2012). Privatizing public education: The neoliberal model. *Race, Poverty & the Environment, 19*(1), 35–37. http://www.jstor.org/stable/41762537

Wodak, R., & Meyer, M. (2009). Critical discourse analysis: History, agenda, theory, and methodology. In R. Wodak & M. Meyer (Eds.), *Methods of critical discourse analysis* (pp. 1–33). SAGE Publications.

# Chapter 13 Narratives of Grit by African American Women: Standing Tall Against Racial Microaggressions While Advancing to Community College Senior Leadership Positions

Toya Michelle Webb

Being the first in my family to graduate from high school led to a never-ending journey to pursue higher education and a higher calling to one day help those who come from backgrounds analogous to mine. I have been faced with numerous life events that seemed unrelenting and impossible to overcome. By the time I turned 21, my second child was born. Married, with two small children, a high school diploma, and a passion for learning, it was my time to go to college. I was nervous. No one in my immediate family had ever taken this step. I was afraid, but I did it anyway. As I walked through the doors of my community college in Upstate New York, only miles from the Fort Drum military base where my husband was stationed, I felt an overwhelming sense of anxiety.

My thoughts almost became paralyzing. But I had come too far and endured too much to cave in to fear. Besides, my two toddlers were counting on me. I knew it would be hard. I also knew it would be worth it. I chose to silence those inner voices and I walked bravely into the admissions office to begin a new journey that would ultimately change the course of my life. Fast forward 20 years later. After earning an associate degree, a bachelor's degree in journalism and sociology, a master's degree in integrated marketing communications and working as a journalist and public relations professional, I found myself back in the community college setting. This time, instead of as a student, I was an employee eager to help improve lives and further the community college mission. As I worked my way into the ivory tower, I was never blinded by my race or gender. Neither was anyone else.

## *Understanding Microaggressions*

Microaggressions is a term from the 1970s that is credited to Chester Pierce (1927–2016), a Black psychiatrist and tenured professor at Harvard Medical School. As an expert on the topic of microaggressions and an author of numerous books and articles, Pierce declared that in today's day and age people of color are more likely to be prone to racism that is subtler than the days of the pre-civil rights era when racism was more blatant and overt (Bridges, 2019). However, Cole (2016) argues that contemporary racism is multifaceted. The same is true of racial microaggressions, defined as brief and everyday slights, insults, indignities, and denigrating messages that are sent to people of color (usually) by well-intentioned White people who are unaware of the hidden messages being communicated (Sue, 2010). "In their totality, racial microaggressions are inescapable and are cumulative expressions of racist views, dysconscious ideologies, and institutionalized practices toward people of color" (Corbin et al., 2018, p. 630). Research has shown that the impact of racial microaggressions is emotional (Holder et al., 2015), physiological, and financial. In fact, Gates (2014) explains that microaggressions in the workplace can diminish and stigmatize employees, contributing to a \$450 billion to \$550 billion per year loss in U.S. workforce productivity.

Zamani (2003) argues that inequities and injustices in the United States against African Americans as a group have led to the oppression of Black women (p. 3), making their double outsider status even more detrimental. Holder et al. (2015) assert that exposure to the daily assault of racial microaggressions has significant mental health consequences such as anxiety, paranoia, depression, sleep difficulties, lack of confidence, worthlessness, intrusive cognitions, helplessness, and loss of drive (p. 165). Microaggressions have become the norm and even though they can be intentional or unintentional, they communicate hostile, insulting messages that negatively impact people of color, as noted by Davis (2018), Sue et al. (2007), and Wang, Castro, and Cunningham (2014).

## *The Impact of Microaggressions*

Bridges (2019) describes incidents of microaggressions to be verbal (spoken comments) or non-verbal (behavior), interpersonal (individuals who inflict microaggressions on others), or institutional (organization-level arrangements that communicate negative or hostile messages to people of color). To further explicate, Sue et al. (2007) describe three forms of microaggressions:

1. *Microinvalidation.* It is "characterized by communications that exclude, negate, or nullify the psychological thoughts, feelings, or experiential reality of a person of color" (p. 274). This includes telling a Black person that he or she sounds "articulate" or asking a person of Asian descent "where are you really from?" The hidden messages in these examples are the insinuations that Black people do not normally speak well and that Asians are foreigners.
2. *Microassault.* It is an "explicit racial derogation characterized primarily by a verbal or nonverbal attack meant to hurt the intended victim through name-calling, avoidant behavior, or purposeful discriminatory actions" (p. 274). These "old-fashioned" acts of racism may include racial epithets, swastika displays, or refusing to serve Blacks in a restaurant.
3. *Microinsult.* It is characterized by "communications that convey rudeness and insensitivity and demean a person's racial heritage or identity" (p. 274). Bridges (2019) suggests an example of a microinsult is when President Donald J. Trump referred to Mexican immigrants as rapists, drug dealers, and criminals during his 2016 presidential campaign (pp. 214–216).

Additional examples of microaggressions, according to Sue et al. (2007), include "color blindness," the concept of refusing to acknowledge a person's race by stating "I don't see color" or "there is one race, the human race" (p. 282). Edwards (2017) argues:

> By refusing to acknowledge color or privilege, European Americans can reduce guilt while experiencing antagonistic attitudes toward members of racial and ethnic minority groups by blaming them for the continued discussion of race. These challenges, contrary to the expressed beliefs of those who endorse Color-Blind Racial Attitudes (CoBRAs), make resolution of prejudice in our society more difficult. (p. 12)

Moreover, "Second-class citizen" microaggressions transpire when a White person is given preferential treatment as a consumer over a person of color

(Sue et al., 2007, p. 276). The microaggression in this case, according to Sue et al. (2007), is carried out when a Black person is passed over by a taxi driver who instead picks up a White passenger with the assumption that Whites are less dangerous. Another example is when a person of color is mistaken as a service worker or "the help." The underlying message is that Blacks are servants and do not hold high-status positions.

The aforementioned stereotypes, coupled with microaggressions, may add another layer of complexity for the Black woman, thus making it more of a constant struggle for them to succeed in the workplace. While Terry (2013) studied Black women in senior leadership positions in a technical college in North Carolina and confirmed the growing need to further explore the impact of stereotypes, the study did not explore microaggressions (daily slights based on race) against Black women in higher education and the impact thereof. My study sought to understand the repercussions of microaggressions and how Black women successfully navigate these occurrences, in addition to the responsibilities she must handle as a leader. To be successful, it is without question that these women must possess grit.

## *Statement of the Problem*

Even from the days of slavery, a Black woman's full worth has never been fully appreciated (DuMonthier et al., 2017). From the cotton fields to breastfeeding and caring for the children of their White slave masters, the Black woman is no stranger to hard work. Yet, she remains denigrated and disregarded (Burkley. 2010). Even if she tried, she cannot separate her race from her gender. Dualism, the reality of being Black and a woman can feel like a curse (Mosley-Anderson, 2001).

The mass media broadcast of Black women in reality shows can sometimes perpetuate the stereotypes such as the ones that portray Black women as welfare queens, angry, promiscuous, and aggressive (Collins, 2000). The stigma from these stereotypes also carries into the workplace, creating yet another obstacle for Black women to overcome (Corbin et al., 2018; Dickens & Chavez, 2017; Durr &Wingfield, 2011; Jones et al., 2016; Mason, 2016). Stereotypes then become the basis for microaggressions, daily verbal or non-verbal insults based on race, leading to "racial battle fatigue," a term used to describe the stress associated with microaggressions that rear their heads as mental, emotional, and physical strain (Acuff, 2018, p. 175). This can lead to isolation and marginalization of Black women in the workplace. For clarification, the terms African American and Black are used interchangeably throughout this study.

When examining the topic of African American women administrators in higher education, most studies focus on their leadership styles, obstacles to career advancement, their need for mentors, and their experiences with overt racism (Byrd, 2016; Corbin et al., 2018; Hall et al., 2011; Mason, 2016). However, there remains an information gap in the body of research focusing specifically on African American women and their experiences with dealing with microaggressions as senior leaders in community colleges and what motivates them to persist.

## *Research Purposes and Questions*

The purpose of this qualitative study was to explore narratives of grit through the lenses of African American women serving as senior leaders in Illinois community colleges and to share their personal stories of fortitude and perseverance. This study provided a deeper understanding of the challenges that African American women face in positions of leadership at Illinois community colleges and insights into their determination to succeed. The central question guiding this narrative study was: *What are the pathways of African American women to their senior leadership positions in Illinois community colleges?* Additional guiding questions were:

- What are the various contexts of these women's lives that have been shaping their individual identities as African American women and leaders?
- How have their life and work experiences been affected by racial microaggressions?

## *Theoretical and Methodological Approaches to the Study*

One of the dominant research paradigms applied in educational research is the critical paradigm, which suggests that we live in a power-laden society. Lukenchuk (2013) further explains that critical paradigm is grounded in political perspectives on knowledge and research and on neo-Marxist or critical theory perspectives. It is a popular focus among educational researchers and inspires an array of research and scholarly projects focused on feminism, critical race and ethnicity, queer, and disability studies. "The critical paradigm situates its research in social justice issues and seeks to address the political, social, and economic issues, which lead to social oppression, conflict, struggle, and power structures at whatever levels these might occur" (Kivunja & Kuyini, 2017, p. 35). This study drew upon several critical perspectives, including Critical race theory and Black feminist theory, which this study examines in detail.

Creswell (2012) describes qualitative research as an inquiry approach useful for exploring and understanding a central phenomenon. To learn about the phenomenon, the researcher asks participants broad, general questions, collects the detailed views of each participant in the form of words or images, then analyzes the information to create themes. From these data, the researcher interprets the meaning of the information, drawing on personal reflections and past research. This process typically results in a structured report that is flexible and displays the researcher's biases and thoughts (Creswell, 2012, p. 626).

This study employed a qualitative research design by incorporating the following six steps as identified by Creswell (2012): (a) identifying a research process, (b) reviewing the literature, (c) specifying a purpose for research, (d) collecting data, (e) and analyzing and interpreting data. Hesse-Biber and Leavy (2011) define qualitative research as a holistic approach that explicitly integrates epistemology, methodology, and method in order to develop unique approaches to the study of the social world (p. 5).

Hesse-Biber and Leavy (2011) use a metaphor to describe qualitative research as a dance routine, as compared to the linear, step-like characteristic of quantitative research. For example, this qualitative study began with an inductive approach; it started with "specific data out of which more general ideas or theories" later emerged (Hesse-Biber & Leavy, 2011, p. 13). The authors further explain that in qualitative research, questions tend to be exploratory and descriptive in order to: (a) describe social phenomena and their meanings to relevant actors (the *what* questions), and (b) understand and explain social patterns and processes (the *how* questions). The *what* questions in this study focused on individuals (African American women) in social settings (Illinois community colleges), looking for meanings that exist in, emerge from, and are consequential for those settings (Gubrium & Holstein, 1997 as cited in Hesse-Biber & Leavy, 2011, p. 14).

In particular, qualitative researchers attempt to interpret the social meaning people attribute to their experiences, circumstances, and situations. Hesse-Biber and Leavy (2011) further add that, for qualitative researchers, at the heart of their work is the meaning they extract from their data (p. 4). As such, the purpose of this qualitative study was to explore narratives of grit through the lenses of African American women serving as senior leaders in Illinois community colleges and to share their personal stories of oppression and perseverance. This study provided a deeper understanding of the challenges that African American women face in positions of leadership and gained insights into their determination to succeed.

## *Critical Race Theory*

This qualitative study was informed by critical race theory (CRT), an umbrella term for diverse research developed in a multidisciplinary and interdisciplinary context. CRT accepts that racism is insidious and normalized (Hesse-Biber & Leavy, 2011, p. 24). Atwood and López (2014) assert that CRT also counters the traditional methodologies by providing a framework that addresses and ameliorates issues of oppression, poverty, or deprivation of people of color, adding that CRT "challenges dominant stock stories that construct realities in order to legitimize the power of the dominant group" (p. 1144). This study benefited from CRT precisely because it featured African American women whose lives were directly impacted by microaggressions and racism, resulting in marginalization, isolation, invisibility, discrimination, and unfair treatment (Corbin et al., 2018; Graham, 2015; Holder et al., 2015; Howard-Hamilton, 2003; Patitu & Hinton, 2003).

## *Black Feminist Theory*

Black feminist theory was utilized in this study as a theoretical lens that focuses specifically on African American women and their lived experiences. While Black feminist thought can be difficult to encapsulate, Collins (2000) explicates the following:

> Black Feminist Thought must both be tied to Black women's lived experiences and aim to better those experiences in some fashion. When such thought is sufficiently grounded in Black feminist practice, it reflects this dialogical relationship. Black Feminist Thought encompasses general knowledge that helps U.S. Black women survive in, cope with, and resist our differential treatment. (p. 31)

Howard-Hamilton (2003) affirms that using Black feminist thought and critical race as theoretical frameworks offer "promise for understanding the intersecting identities of African American women" and can explain ways in which their needs can be effectively addressed (p. 21). Additionally, there are three key themes that encompass Black feminist thought:

- First, it is shaped and produced by the experiences Black women have encountered in their lives.
- Second, although the stories and experiences of each woman are unique, there are intersections of experiences between and among Black women.
- Third, although commonalities do exist among Black women, the diversity of class, religion, age, and sexual orientation of Black women

as a group are multiple contexts from which their experiences can be revealed and understood. (Howard-Hamilton, 2003, p. 21)

Using CRT and interpretive paradigms, in addition to Black feminist theory, provided a rich foundation for exploring the goals of this study. African American women leaders in Illinois community colleges face a variety of challenges that can be examined in depth and detailed precisely through their lived experiences. Qualitative critical research allows the reader to visualize and better connect to participants' stories through a narrative inquiry and counter-storytelling approach.

While the percentage of Black women holding leadership positions in the Illinois community college system is both dismal and concerning, this study delved deeper into the lived experiences of these women and shared how they navigate the challenges related to their double insider status. Additionally, while some studies describe in broad terms incidents of microaggressions, this study further explored the three forms of microaggressions and dissected the hidden messages and racist ideologies through a storytelling approach. This study explored the challenges, including microaggressions, that these community college leaders face using storytelling and counter-storytelling as a way to delve deeper into their lived experiences and to learn more about their formative years using critical race theory and Black feminist theory as theoretical underpinnings.

## *Narrative Inquiry Research Design*

Wertz et al. (2011) reveal that narrative research aims to explore and conceptualize human experience as it is represented in textual form. Grounded in hermeneutics (interpretive paradigm), phenomenology, ethnography, and literary analysis, narrative research eschews methodological orthodoxy in favor of doing what is necessary to capture the lived experiences of people in terms of their own meaning-making and to theorize about it in insightful ways (p. 225).

Kohler Riessman and Speedy as noted in Clandinin (2006) argue that since the late 1960s "the idea of narrative has penetrated almost every discipline and school," emphasizing that it is "no longer the sole province of literary scholarship, narrative study is now cross-disciplinary, not fitting within the boundaries of any single scholarly field" (p. 45). Clandinin and Connelly (2000), who are experts on narrative inquiry, define the narrative process as a "collaboration between researcher and participants, over time, in a place or series of places, and in social interaction with milieus" (p. 20). The authors further add that the "inquirer enters this matrix in the midst and progresses in the same spirit, concluding the inquiry still in the midst of living and telling, reliving and retelling, the stories of the experiences that made up people's lives, both individual and social" (p. 20). Wertz et al. (2011) explain that a unique aspect of narrative research is that "it endeavors to explore the whole account rather than fragmenting it into discursive units or thematic categories. It is not the parts that are significant in human life, but how the parts are integrated to create a whole—which is meaning" (p. 226).

Narrative, and counter-narrative by extension, was the best suited methodological approach to this study, which sought to understand the lived experiences of African American women from their childhood experiences to the challenges they face as leaders in Illinois community colleges.

### *Counter-Storytelling*

Solórzano and Yosso (2002) define counter-storytelling as a method of telling the stories of those people whose experiences are not often told (e.g., those on the margins of society). Counter-storying is a tool for exposing, analyzing, and challenging the majoritarian stories of racial privilege. Furthermore, counter-stories can shatter complacency, challenge the dominant discourse on race, and further the struggle for racial reform (p. 32).

Much like the stories that come alive in this study, Merriweather Hunn, Guy, and Manglitz (2006) assert that narrative and counter-stories take time to tell, to unpack, and to address, especially when they contain components that make them emotionally liable and invite resistance and denial. Honoring the voices of those who are telling their stories allows the time and respect for experience to be communicated and discussed, thus emphasizing the importance of what is being said (p. 115). Merriweather Hunn et al. (2006) describe three genres of counter-stories that are typically used by CRT scholars. The first is "personal stories"; these include the experiences of persons of color and detail how they have dealt with race discrimination and other unfair treatment. The second is "other people's stories or narratives"; these comprise of stories that other people tell that have a "larger than life" quality. They are usually powerful and relatable to those who have similar experiences or stories to tell. The third genre of counter-stories is "composite stories," which is an accumulation of individual stories (p. 245). This study utilized "personal stories" through narrative inquiry to illustrate the participants' struggles and underscore the need for change.

Ikemoto (1997, as cited in Solorzano & Yosso, 2002) asserts that responding to the majoritarian stories should not be the sole purpose or outcome of counter-stories: "By responding only to the standard story, we let it dominate the discourse" (p. 136), adding that there are numerous stories of people of color whose counter-stories remain unheard and that storytelling and counter-storytelling can help strengthen traditions of social, political, and cultural survival and resistance. Finally, part of the rationale for employing counter-stories is based on the premise maintained by Solorzano and Yosso (2002) that counter-stories serve at least four functions:

1. They can build community among those at the margins of society by putting a human and familiar face to educational theory and practice.
2. They can challenge the perceived wisdom of those at society's center by providing a context to understand and transform established belief systems.
3. They can open new windows into the reality of those at the margins of society by showing possibilities beyond the ones they live and demonstrate that they are not alone in their position.
4. They can teach others that by combining elements from both the story and the current reality, one can construct another world that is richer than either the story or the reality alone. (p. 36)

Moreover, Atwood and López (2014) add:

> Counter-stories highlight what conventional analytic methods, traditional social science theories, and post-positivist research methods often miss: an understanding that the world is not racially neutral but is always already rife with racism . . . counter-stories do not aim to provide a truer understanding of truth, but rather, to complicate our understanding of "truth" as such. In fact, as a theoretical and political movement, CRT does not seek permission or approval from the larger research community. (p. 1145)

CRT counter-stories seek to counter the master narrative through the voices of those who have been marginalized and whose lived experiences have been negatively portrayed. As such, narrative inquiry and counter-storytelling were both suitable for this study considering the marginalization and stereotyping of African American women driven by the master narrative has been the dominating discourse since the days of slavery. This study aimed to help change that narrative and reshape how Black women are perceived and treated in today's society and within the confines of academia.

Additionally, this study was born out of a paucity of research that currently exists on the obstacles that Black women encounter as leaders in higher education, especially challenges related to grit and the everyday occurrences of racial microaggressions. While Duckworth et al. (2007) and other researchers such as Arouty (2015), Boatmun (2016), Bogin (2017), Chang (2014), and Patron (2012) have all studied grit, the focus was mainly in relation to student success and was usually conducted through quantitative studies.

Furthermore, a limitation of Kearns's (2015) study on grit in superintendents was that a quantitative instrument could not adequately measure and address "what" contributed to the grittiness demonstrated by participants. With insights gleaned from Kearns's (2015) study, I employed qualitative methods to explore the formative years of participants that allowed me to delve deeper into their stories as well as the "why" in addition to the "what" behind their motivation to persist as leaders in higher education.

## *Participants*

According to Leavy (2014), sampling approaches in qualitative research may be convenient, theoretical, or purposive. Sampling is "the strategic, referred, random, and/or serendipitous selection of participants" (Saldaña, 2011, p. 33). For this study, through purposive sampling based on specific characteristics determined by the goals of the study, I recruited a group of nine homogenous participants out of which all nine consented. Hesse-Biber and Leavy (2011) assert that homogenous groups, members with similar traits or characteristics, "are appropriate when the researcher wants to gain in-depth understanding about how members of a particular group experience or think about a given issue" (p. 179), adding that because qualitative researchers are after meaning, they look at a "process" or the "meanings" participants attribute to their given social situations (p. 4).

During the research phase of this study, I visited the websites of all 48 community colleges in Illinois and discovered that there were only four African American women at the presidential helm; including one who resigned, narrowing the pool of African American women presidents down to only three, thus making the sample size too small to be suitably considered for this study. Additionally, because this study aimed to re-story the lived experiences of African American women who were still advancing to senior leadership positions, college presidents, who had already reached the highest office in academia, did not meet these criteria for this study.

Participants were selected based on the following criteria: Women who (a) identify as Black or African American; (b) work as senior administrators, defined as an associate dean, dean, executive director, chief, or vice president, working in an Illinois community college and still advancing in their careers; and (c) currently reside in close proximity to a large metropolitan city in the Midwest. Nine women agreed to participate in this study.

## *Sources of Data and Data Collection Strategies*

In qualitative research, it is important for the researcher to obtain useful data from an array of sources in order to adequately address the research questions. As such, there were several sources of data that were appropriate for this study: face-to-face interviews, journals and memos, artifacts, and visual materials.

## *Interviews*

Hesse-Biber and Leavy (2011) maintain that an in-depth interview is a commonly used method of data collection in qualitative research because it "relies on individuals as the point of departure for the research process and assumes that individuals have unique and important knowledge about the social world that is ascertainable and can be shared through verbal communication" (p. 94). Kim (2016) further explains that the purpose of interviews in narrative inquiry is to allow stories to be told of those who might have been marginalized or alienated from the mainstream and whose valuable insights and reflections would not otherwise come to light (p. 166). Over 10-weeks, I conducted nine individual face-to-face audio-recorded interviews with Black women leaders from five different community colleges in Illinois.

## *Documents, Artifacts, and Visual Materials*

Qualitative researchers interpret meaning from the data gathered in many forms. This includes documents such as letters, e-mails, journals, files, and other artifacts that participants are willing to share to help tell their story. I used a journal to record my reflections, thoughts, and observations along the way. As noted in Hesse-Biber and Leavy (2011), researchers should describe the research participants in sufficient detail to allow readers to get a clear picture of the salient characteristics. In essence, the descriptive picture drawn of each participant should come alive. Saldaña and Omasta (2018) contend that artifacts have stories of their own, adding that they speak of origins, histories, moments, how they were collected, created, inherited, and/or purchased. "Since artifacts can't speak for themselves, researchers need to infer their history or use them as conversation pieces with participants to learn more about the relationship between objects and humans" (Saldaña & Omasta, 2018, p. 74).

### *Data Analysis*

Individual, face-to-face interviews were the main source of data analysis for this study. Janesick (1998) likens qualitative researchers to choreographers who must find and design a sequence of steps to tell an effective story. This study benefited from building on John Dewey's (1859–1952) theory of experience by utilizing the closely related Deweyan theory outlined by narrative researchers Clandinin and Connelly's (2000) three-dimensional narrative inquiry space—*interaction* (personal and social), *continuity* (past, present, and future) and *situation* (place). Clandinin and Connelly (2000) explain that "interaction" involves a notion that encompasses a four-directions inquiry (Inward, Outward, Backward, and Forward):

- *Inward* (feelings, hopes, aesthetic reactions, and moral dispositions)
- *Outward* (existential conditions such as the environment)
- *Backward* and *Forward* (temporality—past, present, and future) (p. 50).

By employing Clandinin and Connelly's (2000) three-dimensional space approach as well as the three research questions that guided this study, I was able to garner rich data that led to a rigorous coding process.

At the end of this process, the following four major themes emerged: (a) *Challenges with Being Black and a Woman*, (b) *Deconstructing Microaggressions*, (c) *More Than Perseverance: Grit Redefined*, and (d) *Untold Stories: On the Quest to Change*.

### *Challenges with Being Black and a Woman*

#### *Undervalued*

For the participants in this study, being undervalued was a common thread in their experiences. This ranged from being thwarted from promotions to being underestimated to not being recognized for the contributions they made to their institutions. Instead of being respected leaders, many of them were treated as if they were of lower rank and authority.

#### *Disregarded*

Imagine being in a room full of executives and sharing an idea that will benefit the institution only to be ignored until a White colleague joins the discussion and who later, gets all the credit. This was a typical work day for most of the participants in this study, who often felt that they had no voice, little influence, and were overlooked by their peers.

*Defiled by Stereotypes*

Stereotypes are still negative forces that impede the success of Black women in the workplace. One of the stereotypes that was cited by all nine participants was the angry Black woman trope. Despite having a noble characteristic of strength, the participants also noted that, if a Black woman is perceived as *too* strong, she may be considered threatening or intimidating. In addition to being perceived as aggressive, other stereotypes described by the participants varied from being viewed as lazy to being labeled a "bitch."

## *Deconstructing Microaggressions Standing Tall: Conquering Microaggressions*

One of the most significant insights that this study contributes to the body of research is the examination of microaggressions and the realization of their pervasiveness in the workplace. While there remains a paucity of research on the topic of microaggressions, specifically in regard to African American women leaders in higher education, solutions on how to address and avert microaggressions in the workplace are also in dearth supply.

While many of the participants in this study agreed that one must maintain a high degree of professionalism when confronted with microaggressions, they all contended that microaggressions in the workplace must not be ignored. From training to confronting the issue head on, each participant offered suggestions on how to respond to microaggressions in the workplace, adding that ignoring them can eat away at productivity and further inflict unjust pain on people of color.

## *More Than Perseverance: Grit Redefined*

In addition to the challenges that participants faced being Black and a woman, along with the pervasiveness of racial microaggressions in the workplace, this study found the concept of grit to be more than just a commitment toward long-term goals. Grit, for the participants in this study, was about how they each interpreted and responded to hardships, believed in their own strength, and sustained an unshakeable faith.

In recent years, researchers have become increasingly interested in the topic of grit; yet, their focus usually pertained to quantitative studies and grit was declared as a trait that only doggedly determined warriors possess. Therefore, as a result of this study, I offer an amended definition of grit. As demonstrated by the participants in this study, grit was shown to be a combination of faith, failure, and fortitude. Despite the general perception of ironclad grit, this study revealed that gritty individuals do grow weary, do get discouraged, and they do fail; however, they do not accept failure as final.

Furthermore, the most common definition of grit is described by Duckworth et al. (2007) as passion and perseverance, or sustained effort over a period of time to reach long-term goals. For the purposes of this study, grit was defined as firmness of mind or spirit, unyielding courage in the face of hardship or danger. From the challenges participants faced to how they overcame them, grit was a dominant theme illustrated throughout this study. It also is another factor that ties to the second research question about the contexts that have been shaping their lives. While many and various factors can be taken into consideration when analyzing the successful careers of the nine participants, including their upbringing, education, character, values, and especially their faith and religion, it was evident that grit was vital to their survival.

## *Untold Stories: On the Quest to Change*

As I ended each interview, I realized that the participants' stories of bravery, success, and courage were not the stories that are typically broadcast in the media. Rarely are there televised stories of Black women, like the participants, who are recognized as educated scholars, system disruptors, and advocates for social justice. These women flourish in places and spaces where they are not welcomed. They persist in the workplace in the midst of intolerable pressure and pain. They stand tall against microaggressions and their stories should not be hidden. They represent the untold and often unseen characteristics of Black women as resilient, beautiful, and survivors, descriptors that if used in the media and in everyday life, could help combat stereotypes and change the narrative.

## *Summary of the Findings*

Essentially, the purpose of this qualitative study was to explore narratives of grit through the lenses of African American women serving as senior leaders in Illinois community colleges and to share their personal stories of fortitude and perseverance. This study was designed to provide a deeper understanding of the challenges that African American women face in positions of leadership in Illinois community colleges and insights into their determination to succeed. Through several cycles of coding and rigorous data analysis, this study used narrative inquiry to re-story the lives of nine participants who discussed their everyday struggles and the realities that have hindered them in the workplace. This study emerged from gaps identified in the body of research and recommendations for future studies made by several researchers and revealed the need for additional studies that focus on the storytelling of Black women working in higher education.

Through narrative inquiry, I aimed to uncover each participant's story, how she developed her sense of identity on the path to leadership, and the obstacles she encountered along the way. As such, this study contributes to lessening an insufficient existing body of literature that denotes a growing interest in exploring those challenges, including the pervasiveness of racial microaggressions, grit, and additional research on Black women in leadership. Moreover, it is important to note that the concept of grit became a major component of this study. Through in-depth data analysis shaped by the participants' stories, this study explored the notion of grit and redefined its characteristics, expanding it from a commonly understood focus on perseverance and endurance to reach long-term goals to a more holistic embodiment that encompasses faith and personal fortitude developed in the formative years.

Overall, data from this study provide convincing evidence demonstrating a harsh reality, confirming that being Black and a woman comes with a double layer of hardship. Each participant in this study detailed various obstacles she encountered due to her race and gender, making it difficult for her to advance or be recognized for her work. Each participant mentioned that being Black and a woman placed her under a microscope that unfairly scrutinized her work and her emotions, leaving her exhausted and oftentimes discouraged. Participants in this study also reported being alienated, denied opportunities for promotion, and being unfairly judged when they showed emotion or expressed an opinion that differed from their White colleagues.

Many participants asserted that their discriminatory and inequitable treatment was related to long-held beliefs and stereotypes about Black women. Throughout this study, the participants shared examples on how they were unfairly treated in comparison to their White colleagues. From being ignored to passed over for opportunities that they were more than qualified for, the data provide convincing evidence demonstrating that Black women are treated differently in a number of ways. For example, when it came to performing on the job, the participants' work was under greater scrutiny and they were expected to carry out their duties with little to no support from their supervisors as compared to their White colleagues. When it came to being considered for promotion, the standard was lowered for their White colleagues who were able to seamlessly advance to higher positions even though they were not the most qualified.

Another insight from this study reveals an inability for Black women to express themselves in meetings, or openly disagree with ideas without being condemned. For example, when my participants countered ideas or expressed themselves in a professional manner, they were perceived as aggressive and even disrespectful, while they noted that White men are seen as powerful when they disagree. These findings portend that if Black women continue to be criticized when they speak up, it will remain nearly impossible for them to successfully challenge inequitable systems and change the status quo. This study also found that even though the nine participants were considered to be leaders at their institutions, at times, the obstacles they faced and a lack of support and resources rendered them powerless.

This study also revealed that the participants in this study, unlike their White colleagues, were often overlooked and not given credit for ideas or noticed for their contributions, even though most of them arrived to work early and stayed late into the night in order to fulfill their duties. An important revelation that surfaced about the motives behind their work ethics, was, despite how they were perceived by their colleagues, my study participants did not work to be praised or to be in the limelight; instead, they worked in higher education because they wanted to make a difference and believed they played a crucial role in transforming the lives of others through the power of education.

The challenges of being Black and a woman are clearly different from a woman of any other race as well as that of a man, including a Black man. However, like most Black women, the participants in this study seemed to project a high level of confidence and a strong sense of self developed early on and fostered by their parents and grandparents. The prevalence of racial microaggressions is another factor among the many challenges that my participants encountered in the workplace. The challenge with microaggressions is that they can be so subtle that the victim may not understand what is happening in that moment. Furthermore, if not addressed, microaggressions can turn into "micro-traumas" and result in "death by a thousand cuts" (Dastagir, 2018, "Death by Cuts," para. 1). Therefore, to combat microaggressions, participants in this study provided suggestions on how to address them when they occur in the workplace. Additionally, the participants called on college presidents and chief human resource officers to lead the charge by offering cultural competence training and taking a stand against all forms of racism, including microaggressions.

The general picture that emerged from data analysis conducted as part of this study reveals that even though the participants concurred that microaggressions should be addressed as soon as they happen, depending on the situation, they were wary that it might be perceived as confrontation and may perpetuate stereotypes of the Angry Black Woman trope. Therefore, the need for institutions to provide education and ongoing professional development is deemed a critical factor in creating an environment conducive to crucial conversations, with the ultimate goal of improving race relations in the workplace. Furthermore, many of the participants stated that institutions must also be willing to see the impact that inaction and silence can have on employees, their greatest resources, in addition to perpetuating a racially hostile work environment.

Additionally, institutions must be culturally responsive, not through lip service or words carefully crafted in their Strategic Plans, but they must be committed to the cause. This will require courageous leaders and fearless change agents. As such, the findings of this study reveal the need for the president of the institution, the president's executive team, and the board of trustees to join forces and leverage this as a means to invest in employees, students, and the overall mission of the institution.

Overall, it appears that institutions struggle with understanding the long-term effects of microaggressions, and uncertainty remains on how to handle these everyday occurrences in the workplace. This lack of knowledge and awareness of the pervasiveness of microaggressions continues to create a conundrum for Black women who desire to stand up for themselves, but must avoid perpetuating stereotypes that can become self-destructive and counterproductive to what they would hope to accomplish.

Additionally, a clear and consistent finding throughout this study was the need to challenge systems that hinder Black women. However, in order for change to occur, there must be fearless change agents leading the cause, and change takes time, years, decades, and even centuries. Many of my study participants would argue that Martin Luther King Jr.'s dream is still a vision yet to be fully realized and that dismantling systems, where racism thrives, is not an easy feat.

"Stronger together" is not just a saying, but a reality from which people from all races can benefit. In fact, the participants in this study contend that nothing will change if people are not willing to challenge systemic and institutional racism, which is primarily responsible for many of the challenges Black women encounter in today's society. Equally important, this study reveals a need for institutions of higher education to take the lead by providing education and ongoing professional development for students and employees.

To put it differently, the participants in this study assert that institutions are well suited to be leaders in this area and must be committed beyond mere words. They portend, that if more people become educated and more light is shed on these pervasive societal issues, positive change would likely infiltrate classrooms, workspaces, and society as a whole in an effort to counter the dominant narrative on how Black women are treated, regarded, and perceived, while simultaneously dismantling stereotypes.

Moreover, when it comes to how Black women are sometimes perceived in relation to their roles and responsibilities, participants in this study recounted times when their qualifications and experience were questioned. This common phenomenon is based on stereotypes that classify Black women as intellectually inferior, even though, according to NCES (2019) and Roberts et al. (2018), Black women are one of the most educated demographics in the United States. The overall composition of my sample population also contradicts this stereotype with eight of the nine participants having earned at least a master's degree, five of them holding terminal degrees, and three of them pursuing their doctorates at the time of this study. Still, it is concerning that with a post-graduate education and years of experience in their respective fields, many of my participants were still undervalued and treated as if they were "unqualified."

Furthermore, it is apparent that stereotypes continue to create an extra invisible barrier for Black women, an impediment that has existed since their childhoods. For instance, during their interviews, participants in this study referenced a coach or another influential figure in their formative years who made them feel inferior during a time when they were still constructing their sense of identity. Their experiences confirm what Thomas et al. (2011) posit, that Black girls tend to experience oppression in their youth and have negative expectations placed on them from a variety of sources, including the media and teachers. By the same token, participants in my study identified the mainstream media, reality TV shows, and the dominant culture as perpetuating negative stereotypes that drive a false narrative.

Finally, in recent years, researchers have become increasingly interested in the topic of grit, yet the focus has mainly centered on quantitative studies related to student success. Researchers have also conceptualized grit as a trait that only doggedly determined warriors possess. However, data from my study show that grit is more than just endurance and the ability to achieve long-term goals.

For the participants in this study, grit was shown to be a combination of faith, failure, and fortitude. Grit is not only the ability to achieve goals, but it encompasses the disposition one possesses when working toward achieving those long-term goals. Specifically, as it relates to the women featured in this study, grit was found to be a four-letter word for faith. Participants referenced

Christ as their cornerstone and faith as their source of hope developed from childhood experiences and shaped through various trials and tribulations.

This study validates previous studies by Byrd (2016), Counts (2012), and Graham (2015) that conclude that Black women's reliance on faith or spirituality is a way to cope and sustain them during times of adversity. Likewise, Stevenson (2012) found that Black women coped with hardships through prayer and support systems. A surprising revelation that emerged from this study recognized that gritty people, as demonstrated by the participants in this study, do indeed fail, but they do not accept failure as final. Participants shared stories of how they bounced back from disappointments and failed opportunities and they credited their faith in Christ, who sustained them. However, faith was only part of their ability to persevere; it was not only their belief in their Savior, but also in themselves that fueled their motivation to persevere.

Noting the scarcity of African American women encompassing less than 5% of administrative positions in the Illinois community college system, Graham (2015) sought to identify the obstacles these women faced and the coping methods they employed to help them persist. Graham's recommendation to increase the sample population was also an impetus for this study; as a result, my study more than doubled the sample size of Graham's study increasing the number of participants from four to nine.

Insights gained from this study can be leveraged by institutions to help retain African American women in positions of leadership as well as to support African American women who aspire to higher levels of leadership. Findings from this study can also be utilized by human resources professionals to dismantle racist hiring practices, reshape institutional policies, address microaggressions, and create administrative procedures that mandate ongoing professional development with a deliberate focus on diversity, equity, and inclusion. Last, this study calls for African American women working in community colleges and those who work alongside African American women in community colleges to step up and serve as mentors and allies in a unified effort to overthrow decades-old racist ideologies and systems.

The findings of this study provide valuable insights into the unique challenges encountered by nine African American women serving as senior leaders in Illinois community colleges. Their narratives of hardship and grit provide first-hand knowledge of the struggles these participants have endured and continue to face. In addition to filling a gap in the body of research, especially as it relates to grit and racial microaggressions, this study provides thorough recommendations and advice on how institutions can improve the work environment in order to attract and retain African American women. I strongly believe that through qualitative analysis that resulted in four major themes and four subthemes, this study provides substantial evidence and in-depth information that can be leveraged to effect change.

Disturbingly, this study confirmed that the duality of race and gender for Black women, along with the pervasiveness of microaggressions and stereotypes still overshadow their success. Yet, the nine women in this study fought back and refused to be silenced; they remained hopeful, resolute, and firm in their faith as they encountered various obstacles and unexpected hurdles along the way.

## *References*

Acuff, J. (2018). Confronting racial battle fatigue and comforting my Blackness as an educator. *Multicultural Perspectives*, *20*(3), 174–181.

Arouty, D. (2015). *Does character matter? The role of grit and resilience in predicting academic success* (Publication No. 3734789) [Doctoral dissertation]. ProQuest Dissertations and Theses Global.

Atwood, E., & López, G. R. (2014). Let's be critically honest: Towards a messier counterstory in critical race theory. *International Journal of Qualitative Studies in Education*, *27*(9), 1134–1154.

Boatmun, T. (2016). *Hope, grit, and academically successful non-traditional students at a regional, rural university: A narrative inquiry* (Publication No. 10038708) [Doctoral dissertation]. ProQuest Dissertations and Theses Global.

Bogin, L. (2017). *A portrait of college success: Grit, theories of intelligence, and cumulative life adversity* (Publication No. 10689593) [Doctoral dissertation]. ProQuest Dissertations and Theses Global.

Bridges, K. M. (2019). *Critical race theory: A primer.* Foundation Press.

Burkley, M. (2010). Are Black women invisible? *Psychology Today.* Retrieved from https://www.psychologytoday.com/us/blog/the-social-thinker/201012/are-black-women-invisible

Byrd, T. (2016). *Experiences of intersectionality: A phenomenological exploration of how black American women leaders respond to stigmatization in the workplace* (Publication No. 10196490) [Doctoral dissertation]. ProQuest Dissertations and Theses Global.

Chang, W. (2014). *Grit and academic performance: Is being grittier better?* (Publication No. 3681407) [Doctoral dissertation]. ProQuest Dissertations and Theses Global.

Clandinin, J. D. (2006, December), Narrative inquiry: A methodology for studying lived experience. *Research Studies in Music Education*, *27*(1), 44–55.

Clandinin, J. D., & Connelly, M. F. (2000). *Narrative inquiry: Experience and story in qualitative research.* Jossey-Bass.

Cole, M. (2016). *Racism: A critical analysis.* Pluto Press.

Collins, P. H. (2000). *Black feminist thought.* Routledge.

Corbin, N. A., Smith, W. A., & Garcia, J. R. (2018). Trapped between justified anger and being the strong Black woman: Black college women coping with racial battle fatigue at historically and predominantly White institutions. *International Journal of Qualitative Studies in Education*, *31*(7), 626–643.

Counts, S. A. (2012). *Invisible woman? Narratives of black women leaders in southeastern two-year colleges* (Publication No. 3525892) [Doctoral dissertation]. ProQuest Dissertations and Theses Global.

Creswell, J. W. (2012). *Educational research: Planning, conducting, and evaluating quantitative and qualitative research* (4th ed.). Pearson.

Dastagir, A. E. (2018, February 28). Microaggressions don't just "hurt your feelings." *USA Today*. Retrieved from https://www.usatoday.com/story/news/2018/02/28/what-microaggressions-small-slights-serious-consequences/362754002/

Davis, S. M. (2018): When sistahs support sistahs: A process of supportive communication about racial microaggressions among Black women. *Communication Monographs*, *86*(2), 133–157. https://doi.org/10.1080/03637751.2018.1548769

Dickens, D. D., & Chavez, E. L. (2017). Navigating the workplace: The costs and benefits of shifting identities at work among early career U.S. Black women. *Sex Roles*, *78*(11–12), 760–774. https://doi-org.libweb.ben.edu/10.1007/s11199-017-0844-x

Duckworth, A. L., Peterson, C., Matthews, M. D., & Kelly, D. R. (2007). Grit: Perseverance and passion for long-term goals. *Journal of Personality and Social Psychology*, *92*(6), 1087–1101.

DuMonthier, A., Childers, C., & Milli, J. (2017, June 26). *The status of Black women in the United States*. Institute for Women's Policy Research.

Durr, M., & Wingfield, A. M. (2011). Keep your "N" in check: African American women and the interactive effects of etiquette and emotional labor. *Critical Sociology*, *37*(5), 557–571.

Edwards, J. F. (2017, Summer) Color-blind racial attitudes: Microaggressions in the context of racism and White privilege. *Administrative Issues Journal: Connecting Education, Practice, and Research*, *7*(1), 5–18.

Gates, J. F. (2014, August 31). *Microaggression: The new workplace bigotry*. HuffPost. https://www.huffpost.com/entry/microaggression-the-new-w_b_5544663

Graham, M. (2015). *African American women administrators at community colleges of Illinois: An investigation of obstacles and persistence* (Publication No. 3739510) [Doctoral dissertation]. ProQuest Dissertations and Theses Global.

Hall, J. C., Everett, J. E., & Hamilton-Mason, J. (2011). Black women talk about workplace stress and how they cope. *Journal of Black Studies*, *43*(2), 207–226.

Hesse-Biber, S. N., & Leavy, P. (2011). *The practice of qualitative research* (2nd ed.). SAGE Publications.

Holder, A., Jackson, M. A., & Ponterotto, J. G. (2015). Racial microaggression experiences and coping strategies of Black women in corporate leadership. *Qualitative Psychology*, *2*(2), 164–180.

Howard-Hamilton, M. F. (2003). Theoretical frameworks for African American women. *New Directions for Student Services, 2003*(104), 19–27. https://doi-org.libweb.ben.edu/10.1002/ss.104

Illinois Community College Board. (2019). *Illinois community college system facts.* https://www.iccb.org/wp-content/pdfs/reports/ICCS_African_American_Report_2018.pdf

Jones, K. P., Peddie, C. I., Gilrane, V. L., King, E. B., & Gray, A. L. (2016). Not so subtle: A meta-analytic investigation of the correlates of subtle and overt discrimination. *Journal of Management, 42*(6), 1588–1613.

Kearns, J. (2015). *The examination of grit in California superintendents* (Publication No. 3738522) [Doctoral dissertation]. ProQuest Dissertations and Theses Global.

Kim, J. (2016). *Understanding narrative inquiry: The crafting and analysis of stories as research.* SAGE Publications.

Kivunja, C., & Kuyini, A. B. (2017). Understanding and applying research paradigms in educational contexts. *International Journal of Higher Education,* 6(5), 26–41.

Leavy, P. (Ed.). (2014). *Oxford handbook of qualitative research.* Oxford University Press. https://ebookcentral.proquest.com

Lukenchuk, A. (Ed.). (2013). *Paradigms of research for the 21st century: Perspectives and examples from practice.* Peter Lang

Mason, P. A. (2016). *The lived experiences of African American female superintendents* [Doctoral dissertation]. https://etd.ohiolink.edu/!etd.send_file?/accession=ohiou1450790580&disposition=inline

Merriweather Hunn, L. R., Guy, T. C., & Mangliitz, E. (2006, May 18–21). Who can speak for whom?: Using counterstorytelling to challenge racial hegemony. In M. Hagan & E. Goff (Eds.), *The many faces of adult education: Proceedings of the 47th Annual Adult Education Research Conference,* (pp. 244–250). University of Minnesota.

Mosley-Anderson, J. M. (2001). *Their perceptions of how others perceive them: Black women administrators internalize others perceptions of them as leaders* (Publication No. 3023265) [Doctoral dissertation]. ProQuest Dissertations and Theses Global.

National Center for Education Statistics. (2019). *Fast facts: Degrees conferred by race and sex.* U.S. Department of Education. https://nces.ed.gov/fastfacts/display.asp?id=72

Patitu, C. L. & Hinton, K. G. (2003). The experiences of African American women faculty and administrators in higher education: Has anything changed? *New Directions for Student Services, 2003*(104), 79–93.

Patron, I. M. (2012). *Exploring the experiences of successful first-generation community college students in Florida: A qualitative study* (Publication No. 3512970) [Doctoral dissertation]. ProQuest Dissertations and Theses Global.

Roberts, L. M., Mayo, A. J., Ely, R. J., & Thomas, S. A. (2018, MarchApril). Beating the odds. *Harvard Business Review.* Retrieved from https://hbr.org/2018/03/beating-the-odds

Saldaña, J. (2011). *Fundamentals of qualitative research: Understanding qualitative research.* Oxford University Press. https://ebookcentral.proquest.com

Saldaña, J., & Omasta, M. (2018). *Qualitative research: Analyzing life.* SAGE Publication.

Solórzano, D. G., & Yosso, T. J. (2002). Critical race methodology: Counter-storytelling as an analytical framework for education research. *Qualitative Inquiry, 8*(1), 23–44.

Stevenson, T. N. (2012). *Racial battle fatigue, role strain, and African-American faculty at public community colleges* (Publication No. 3530464) [Doctoral dissertation]. ProQuest Dissertations and Theses Global.

Sue, D. W. (2010, October 5). Racial microaggressions in everyday life: Is subtle bias harmless? *Psychology Today.* https://www.psychologytoday.com/us/blog/microaggressions-in-everyday-life/201010/racial-microaggressions-in-everyday-life

Sue, D. W., Capodilupo, C. M., Torino, G. C., Bucceri, J. M., Holder, A. M., Nadal, K. L., & Esquilin, M. (2007, May-June). Racial microaggressions in everyday life: Implications for clinical practice. *American Psychologist, 62*(4), 271–286.

Terry, D. (2013). *At the Intersection of race and gender: A narrative analysis of the career experiences of Black women senior leaders in community and technical college* (Publication No. 3575666) [Doctoral dissertation]. ProQuest Dissertations and Theses Global.

Thomas, A. J., Hacker, J. D., & Hoxha, D. (2011). Gendered racial identity of Black young women. *Sex Roles, 64*(7–8), 530–542.

Wang, K. T., Castro, A. J., & Cunningham, Y. L. (2014). Are perfectionism, individualism, and racial colorblindness associated with less cultural sensitivity? Exploring diversity awareness in White prospective teachers. *Journal of Diversity in Higher Education, 7,* 211–225.

Wertz, F. J., Charmaz, K., McMullen, L. M., Josselson, R., Anderson, R., & McSpadden, E. (2011). *Five ways of doing qualitative analysis: Phenomenological psychology, grounded theory, discourse analysis, narrative research, and intuitive inquiry.* Guilford Press.

Zamani, E. M. (2003). African American women in higher education. *New Directions for Student Services, 2003*(104), 5–18. https://doi-org.libweb.ben.edu/10.1002/ss.103

# Chapter 14 Locked Gates and Chain-link Fences: A Generational Phenomenological Story of Disability

SHARON DUNCAN

## *Roots Planted: A Story*

Once upon a not-so-distant time and in a not-so-distant land lived three little girls. Their lives revolved around playing Barbies, games of "ghost beware" at dusk, sewing lessons, riding the bus to Ford City, buying penny candy at the pet shop, and square-scooped sherbet cones at Prince Castle. At times their lives seemed to them idealistic and somewhat fairytale; as they were growing up in a middle-class suburban neighborhood in the 1960s, with stay-at-home moms and dads who arrived home at five for family dinner. The girls were connected by proximity, living in houses separated only by cyclone fences and a grassy alley. They lived so close you could call out, "Yo, Laura," or "Yo, Sharon," or "Yo, Debbie" till someone would answer the door. They shared the same Catholic faith, attended the same parish school, and were all about the same age. They shared dreams and made up fairytale stories while lying on blankets under Sharon's big backyard tree, sipping Kool-Aid from shiny metal tumblers, while munching on sugar wafer cookies. "So what do you want to be when you grow up?" "Where do you think we will live?" "Think we'll still be friends when we're old and married?"

Three girls, three friends for life ... and they lived happily ever after?

In order to understand the present, one has to look into the past. I (Sharon) am the collector of the group. I am compelled to collect the stories, to uncover the lived experiences that were interwoven in the fabric of our lives ... the common threads that bound us together then and continue to link us in the present.

The nine-year-old me runs through the kitchen, pulls open the pantry door and grabs an eight pack of empty Pepsi bottles from the floor. I have a shiny quarter in my pocket just waiting to be spent. With the 16 cents I would get from the bottles, I would be able to get a lot of penny candy. "Mom, I'm going," I yelled. "Where are you going young lady?" my grandmother Mere inquires. "Just up town with Laura and Debbie." "Be careful." "Don't worry Mere." I run by my Aunt Jackie washing dishes at the sink. I grab her apron string pretending to untie it and she slaps my hand. "Oh, Sharon, what a kidder." "See ya!" I run out the screen door and it slams behind me. I hear Mere yelling in the distance, but I'm off ... across the porch ... down the steps ... crisscrossing my fenced backyard, running through the back gate, which is hanging slightly open. I give it an extra shove to open it all the way and I head across the alley to Laura's yard. "Yo, Laura." She comes to the door with a brown bag in her hand holding two empty quart bottles from beer. (She will get five cents each for those.) "Ready? Let's go get Debbie." We travel down the driveway toward Central Avenue to go next door to Debbie's. We approach the fenced-in yard. A locked double gate extending across the driveway stops us in our tracks. Laura takes her free hand and opens the latch while I take my free hand and pull up the pole. In we go. We are sure to lock the gate again or face the wrath of Mrs. E., Debbie's mom. The gate must remain locked at all times. "Yo, Debbie," we call out on her back stoop. "Hi guys! I can go, but I have groceries to buy for my mom at Freshline." She goes back in the house and comes back out with her mom's old brown wallet and a list in one hand, and her little brother Chuckie's small chubby hand tightly clenched in the other. "I gotta bring Chuck; my mom gave me money so we can get sherbet cones from Prince Castle on the way back." We walk down the drive. Laura and I open the gate and Deb pulls Chuck through. We lock it behind us. Looking both ways, we cross Central Avenue. Mere's "be careful" rings in my brain. Laura and I take the lead. "Come on Chuck, walk faster," Deb says. As we make our way from our neighborhood and the safety of the locked gates and cyclone fences into the vast world ... we called: UPTOWN.

> Fenced yards, protecting Chuckie, shopping for groceries, locked gates, teasing Aunt Jackie, being corrected by Mere; the roots of our childhood; the common strings that joined our lives.

As I embarked on my research, I returned to the past: to the relationships, the values, the truths, that connected our experiences. I was compelled to provide a visual to represent the people and the relationships, which represent the roots of this inquiry. I was determined to seek a fluid representation for the connected history. Visually, I was drawn to a root structure and all the little threads that come from and connect to the root. The cyclone fence (like the one that surrounded my backyard and Debbie's whole yard) with its supporting bar and all the angular connections, kept coming to my mind. I visualized the fences and the gates, keeping us in, locking us out, but still allowing us to see out to the other side. The fence provided safety but was imprisoning at the same time. We could lift the lock, pull up the pole, and get out from time to time, but we were compelled to go back into safety.

One can see the correlations with the structure of a chain-link fence and rhizome in the view point of Kurokawa (2001) in an essay covering Deleuzio-Guallaria's architectural theory: "A rhizome is an interlocking web. It is a conjunction of dynamic relations producing bulbs here and there, interweaving with great complexity, reaching outward in its continuing growth" (p. 1031).

## *Linkages Through Disability Studies*

It is critical for a disability study to investigate various ontological and epistemological assumptions underpinning the field and the lived experience of disability. My purpose was to examine the whole of the experience. As a field, disability studies challenge the stereotypes historically associated with disabilities yet does not restrict one to have a singular epistemological understanding of disability (Barnes et al., 2002). Disability studies developed as a field in response to a problem, seeking clarification about the place and meaning of disability in society (Albrecht et al., 2001).

Disability studies embrace an eclectic approach with the ultimate goal of emancipation and self-fulfillment in all areas of life for individuals with disabilities. Disability studies do not emphasize barriers but, instead, they focus on possibilities. Relevant to a disability study is resistance theory that "maintains the social model's focus on the politics of disablement and adds to it recognition of the complexities of resistance" (Gabel, 2005, p. 8). Resistance theory proposes to look at the entire experience of disability. Looking at the totality of the experience is imperative when uncovering meaning, the body and medical support cannot be totally disregarded. Elements of disabled identity are the voice that cannot be heard in a typical way, the brain that works in a particular fashion, or ambulation with a wheelchair.

The rhizome and the fence metaphorically represent the resistance scenario, as they are juxtaposed in "a push me-pull me" connectiveness; the fence with the shutting out but providing protection, and the rhizome, open to all the possibilities that occur in the lived experience of disability. A theory of resistance embraces disability in all its complexity and entirety. My perspective of disability is grounded in disability studies and rooted in resistance theory.

## *Looking Back, Going Forward--Phenomenologically*

Phenomenology allows the researcher to explore the symbolism, the words, and experiences that give meaning to living. Phenomenologists are challenged to describe the lived experience in a manner that portrays person-world intimacy. The *lifeworld* (one of the key notions in phenomenology) includes all the everyday goings-on in life. My lifeworld, as well as my family's and friends' over three generations, and the interconnections to disability were the subject of our story-making. Viewing the lifeworld offers the opportunity to explore the intricacies that hold people and their world together, and view the physical, aesthetic, spatial, and emotional aspects of human life.

This research was a return to my roots, it served as an opportunity to dig into the soil and let it run through my fingers. I delved into the memories, the thoughts, and the lived experiences. Phenomenology served as the "till" for my research. Founded by Edmund Husserl (1859–1938), phenomenology is considered to be one of the most important philosophical movements of the twentieth century (Morse & Richards, 2007). Phenomenology is the study of human experience (Moustakas, 1994; Van Manen, 1990; Seamon, 2000); it serves as a means to give "a rigorous description of human life as it is lived, and reflected upon, in all of its first person concreteness, urgency, and ambiguity" (Pollio et al., 1997, p. 5).

Phenomenological inquiry allowed me to explore endless possibilities of the rhizome and to uncover its multiple meanings. Phenomenological "root strands" of an event are more clearly understood when we bring ourselves "wholly to the transparency of the imaginary, to think about it without the support of any ground, in short, withdraw to the bottom of nothingness. Only then could we know what moments positively make up the being of experience" (Pollio et al., 1997, p. 111).

I sought to "bring into the nearness that which tends to be obscure, that which tends to evade the intelligibility of our natural attitude of everyday life" (Van Manen, 1990, p. 57). It is with a fresh sense of wonder that I immersed myself in research to reveal a story (Merleau-Ponty, 1962). Phenomenology is about revealing, uncovering, exposing, and connecting. The rhizome as an image of thought serves as a model of an open-ended interactive system. There are roots in place, grounded in friendship, family, proximity, history, and disability. The rhizome is fluid and has the ability to grow and change, tiny threads will emerge from the root, linking to other threads, which will grow and flourish over time. Rhizomes are about possibilities, whereas the fence served as a protective boundary, protecting us from the dangers that lurked just outside.

> "Go home Sharon ... bye, ... we already started" ("but I have all my Barbie Stuff"), "take your Barbies and just go" ... (My lip starts to quiver and tears

come to my eyes), "You're a big crybaby! You act retarded, just like your mongoloid Aunt Jackie and we don't want to play with you!"

Girls from the neighborhood were sitting at the picnic table playing Barbies. I had rushed and gathered my stuff when I saw them out there. The twin girls that lived just on the other side of the fence, right behind my house, yelled at me in unison, adding to the insults in a tag team fashion. I was upset, and I really wanted to play Barbies that day. At first I was mad that they told me to leave, but then my eight-year-old self realized that they called my Aunt Jackie retarded. "No, Jackie's not retarded, Debbie's brother Chuck is retarded, and I heard him called mongoloid, too." Those words described Chuckie, not my Aunt Jackie. Jackie could talk. Jackie took care of me. I ran away, dragging my Barbie cases, and finally I threw them on the ground (I heard the girls laughing at me in the background). I ran faster through the yard and into the house. By now, I was crying loudly in my typical dramatic fashion.

Throwing open the back screen door, I yelled into the house, "M-o-o-o-om, the twins said Jackie is retarded." My grandmother gave me a dirty look (my voice was bellowing through the house). My mom ushered me into the bedroom and told me to "ssh" (now I'm thinking Jackie must have been in hearing distance as the first floor of our house was not large). Between my sobs, my mom tried to speak. She closed the door and said, "I should have told you, but I couldn't." She explained Jackie was "slow." She did not say retarded, she did not say mongoloid. I was told to stop crying and to not say anything to Jackie or in front of my grandmother (Jackie's mother).

Over time, I came to realize both Jackie and Chuck were born with Down syndrome. In the late 1960s, Down syndrome was often called "mongoloid." So Chuck and Aunt Jackie actually were the same, as far as a disability category anyway. They were my roots.

I go back to the past and return home. I was situated in a particular circumstance of disability. I lived in a home where disability and "retardness" (as it was referred to then), was somewhere else, not in our house. Although my Aunt Jackie had a disability due to an intellectual disability, my grandmother refused to call or label her disabled. The norm when my aunt was born in the late 1930s was for children who were declared retarded or mongoloid to be put away. Children like those were sent to institutions. My maternal grandparents, but most especially my grandmother (Mere), defied the norm and made Jackie fit. She taught Jackie to walk, talk, count, read, close her mouth (drooling was not an option) and was determined that she reached those milestones in typical developmental stages.

Although as a child, I never thought of Jackie as different, I always knew Chuckie, my friend Debbie's brother, was "different." He could not read; he needed help with everyday tasks and went to a "special" school. I thought the experience of disability was beyond my fenced yard. It was over there; in Debbie's fenced-in house on the next block. However, as I grew older and more aware of the stares and heard the names, the reality began to hit home. My mom explained to me at ten years old, after my grandmother passed away (at 53 years old), that Jackie and Chuckie both had Down syndrome (much nicer sounding than mongoloid). Laura, Debbie, and I continued to be friends, from high school into young adulthood until today. Our lives were still connected like the links in the fence. Our friendship was a stronghold, and we could always return back to our girlhood memories and the stories of our shared experiences.

> *Friendship, history, labels, families and the impact of disability from the past to the present, and into the future; the links that continue to connect our lives.*

There is a profound story here; a story that crosses generations and stereotypes. This story is "our social construction of what happened" (Ferguson et al., 1992, p. 5). A broad theme of phenomenology is intentionality a "basic structure of human existence that captures the fact that human beings are fundamentally related to the contexts in which they live" (Pollio et al., 1997, p. 7). Home and in-home experiences have been addressed by many phenomenologists. Day (1996) studied "at-homeness," signifying a timeless quality, positive attunement to the present moment, the relatedness to a lived interplay between safety and familiarity. Home offers an attunement into oneself in relationship to others; home relates to healing and personal well-being. Home for us was more than houses on Central or Parkside Avenue. Home was an emotional place where we felt protected and loved. Home is the sense of no matter what occurs around me, I have a place where I am safe emotionally, physically and psychologically. Home is where a person can truly be free, just to be.

Phenomenological incentive to go "back to the things themselves" (Husserl, 1970) prompted me to return again and again, through reflection, to the interviews with family members and with the individuals with disabilities.

## *Reflections on Perceptions*

The eight-year-old me had no thoughtful concept of disability. Rarely were people with disabilities in the public eye in the early 1960s. I never thought of my Aunt Jackie as disabled. The word people used to describe people with intellectual disabilities at the time was "retarded," but even that term was rarely said out loud in my personal experience. Sometimes I noticed Jackie did and said silly or inappropriate things. Yet, for some reason Jackie did not do those "not so adult-like things" around my grandparents or other adults. She seemed to have two distinct personas, the one who acted like an adult and the other who was my own personal silly friend.

I had this internal nagging tension about when to listen to Jackie or not, or why Jackie did things at times that most adults did not do in public. There was also an unspoken rule in my household not to ask about Jackie, especially around my grandmother. Chuckie, my girlfriend's brother with Down syndrome, was never discussed either. Chuck was the only person I knew as a young child with a disability. Jackie, who often said out loud what she was thinking, did talk about Chuck and very sympathetically called him "poor 'tarded Chuck." I share these vignettes about life as I knew it then, because as an adult, I have come to realize that my childhood experiences with Jackie served as a catalyst in forming my own theory about disability. The nagging questions of the little girl, who was to be seen and not heard, are ever present in this adult, as I engage in thoughtful introspection. My view of disability is rooted in my past experiences as a little girl hanging out with Jackie and Chuck. My past cannot be disregarded or set aside but serves as a connective root strand now watered by a disability studies perspective.

Jackie, Chuck, Jonathon, and Jamee made and are making their own histories. Society, cultural factors, family situations, and their particular place in time had much to do with the formation of their personal histories.

## *Rhizomes and Stories*

By virtue of her year of birth in 1991 and her place in this connective rhizome, Jamee has reaped the benefits of the rich soil that has been watered by the experiences of those who have come before her in time. Once upon a time there were three young girls living in the 1960s who were linked by proximity, friendship and disability. These three girls—Laura, Debbie, and Sharon (me)—are connected intricately with Jamee through the offshoots of the rhizomic experiences that have connected our lives through the generations. Jamee is the great-granddaughter of Dorothy, the courageous mother of Jackie who was determined to defy the social constructs of disability imposed on her in the late 1930s.

Stubborn will power and steadfast determination flow through the blood of Dorothy's granddaughter Colleen, the mother of Jamee, as she advocates for choices for her daughter. Colleen (my sister) never knew our grandmother Dorothy (Mere), she was only two years old when she passed away, but when

I look at Colleen, I see my grandmother's sense of control, strong will, and dominance. It is almost as if Colleen had some predisposition to be Dorothy in another time to raise a child with a disability.

Colleen walked up town with Laura, Debbie, Chuck, and I as a young child. Colleen played in Chuck's yard and shared swing time with him. Growing up as Jackie's niece, and sharing personal space with Jackie for more than 20 years, gave Colleen an understanding of living with and loving a person with an intellectual disability. Laura gave birth to a child with a disability (Jonathon) four years previous to Jamee. Laura has been very helpful to Colleen, providing her with the names of orthopedic specialists and programs to support Jamee. Three girls, three families connected through the generations and still growing, continuing the rhizomic connections established between the fences of our youth.

## *Connections and Revelations*

A connective strand that united the families was a fear of the unknown. Typically, when a new baby comes into the world, the family is filled with anticipation and dreams for the future. The birth of a child is a joyful experience. These families had little time to bask in the happiness of a new life. Instead they embarked on emotional quests searching for answers. Initially, the parents sought answers so they could understand their role as parents. They wanted to find the means to assist their children. All of the families in this research went through emotional struggles with the professionals. The parents in this story were all subjected to "category bound activities" (Sacks, 1972).

Parents of children with disabilities are looked at in a particular manner. The parents were told by medical professionals they could not handle their child, or nothing was wrong in Jamee's case. The professionals put the parents in categories. Colleen, Dorothy, and Mrs. E. (Chuck's mom) were dismissed as young mothers. Laura was thought of as being too assertive. Social constructs of which the families had no control caused additional anxiety to these families who were already under much pressure. Upon realizing that the professionals did not have all the answers, after time, the parents discovered that they had the answers all along. All of the parents found the strength from within themselves to do whatever was necessary for their children.

Externally the families went about their lives, yet within the spatiality of their homes their experiences were complex. Without any training, my grandmother took on the roles of therapist and teacher. She discovered that neckties and belts were useful in supporting Jackie as she learned to walk, and match sticks could be used as manipulatives as Jackie learned to count. Chuck's parents discovered that elastic bands could be used to stretch Chuck's limbs. Jonathon, born with agenesis of the corpus callosum, was sent home from the hospital to die. Laura and her husband Steve decided their son was going to live and found programs to support his growth. Colleen and Bob kept bringing Jamee to doctors to treat her medical difficulties and sought help from anyone and everyone. All the parents took action, but fear remained under the surface.

### *Fears*

Fear connected the families, but it was manifested differently in their lived experiences. Historically, parents or siblings of children with disabilities often wondered what they did to deserve this fate, or if they did something wrong for this to occur in their family. My grandmother is representative of this as she was trying to place the blame on someone for Jackie's "condition." Much of this blame had to do with the time in history. People did not understand the medical reasons for Down syndrome. I cannot fathom the deep anxiety a mother would feel upon realizing their beloved child was viewed by society as subhuman, a burden, or a product of sinfulness (Castles, 2004). Parents who gave birth to children with obvious disabilities in this era were often fearful of people trying to come and put their child in an institution. Due to this particular time in history, as a member of the silent generation (Strauss & Howe, 1992), my grandmother did not discuss her feelings regarding Jackie's disability. She repressed her fears and had emotional breakdowns.

With the progress of medical science over the decades and having a clearer understanding of the etiology of their children's disabilities, the other parents did not have the same type of fears as my grandmother. Yet fear was a connective element experienced by all the families in this research. Chuck's parents are not preparing financially or psychologically for Chuck's future. Laura still checks on Jonathon when he sleeps too long. Colleen worries if caregivers in Jamee's future will care for her medical needs and provide her with choices. Jenna, Jamee's sister, cried as she discussed her worries about Jamee's physical fragility. Jonathon fears being alone and is purposely working on overcoming his shyness. The fear was ever present, but it was accompanied by resilience and resistance.

### *Resistance*

The rhizomic strand of resistance was evident as the stories were told. This was demonstrated by my grandparents refusing to call Jackie anything but Jackie and demanding that she attend the local Catholic school with her sister.

Chuck's parents (Mr. and Mrs. E.) moved to the suburbs to find a school for Chuck, and continued to fight the school district for funding because their son was happy at his private school. Chuck resisted societal expectations when he is the "man in charge" on his work crew. Laura confronted the doctor when he did not think baby Jonathon should have prostheses because of his fragile state. She continued to resist the expectations of doctors and other professionals throughout his childhood. Demonstrating resistance, Jonathon enrolled in anatomy and physiology classes against the advice of his counselors and received *A*s in the classes. Colleen demonstrates resistance by living in the moment; she does not dwell on the past, but moves forward, providing Jamee with choices in her daily life. Jamee, through making choices and navigating her environment with the support of her communication device and power wheelchair, is resisting the social constructs assigned to individuals with significant intellectual and physical disabilities. The families in this story had unique perspectives and situations, yet self-fulfillment for their own child was a personal goal in each circumstance.

### *Mother to Mother*

A common strand, linking story to story, generation to generation, is the inner strength of the mothers. The mothers are resilient and strong, taking on doctors, teachers, and anyone who denied their children opportunities. These women played the dominant role while the husbands played supportive roles (Herbert & Carpenter, 1994). The women were grounded in actualization and hope; negativity was not an option. Each of the women was fenced-in by the constraints of the times in which they lived. Historicality served as a fence for which they had no control.

### *Historicality*

Jackie was born in the era of when disability was regarded as sinful, deviant, or a societal burden (Kevles, 1995). In the 1930s, institutionalization was recommended for most people with disabilities. My grandparents did not give in to the societal expectations of the time. As Jackie's parents, they negotiated their lived experience through rebelling. By putting their daughter "out there" in the local catholic school, the community, family gatherings and social situations, they were quietly, but forcefully, rebelling. Particularly revealing was the fact that my grandmother put Jackie out into the world full of pride, but internally she was fighting her own emotional difficulties. The literature (Blancher & Baker, 2007) does indicate that many parents with children with disabilities have internal and emotional struggles. Unfortunately, my grandparents' personal and emotional struggles support the studies that indicate that parents could exhibit depression or emotional shock.

The 1930s and 1940s was a difficult era to live openly with a child of disabilities and my grandparents were victims of the societal fences of their times. The fact that Jackie lived in this time, yet portrayed a level of self-confidence and did not see herself as disabled, had much to do with the fences they collectively built to protect their daughter.

Chuck was born in the time of parent involvement (Schwartzenberg, 2005). Down syndrome now had a biological explanation, so once he was diagnosed his parents at least had a name and a reason for his particular disability. While the Mr. and Mrs. E. did not define Chuck by a label, they needed to have a diagnosis to understand why Chuck was not developing like his sister Debbie. While medical science had come far, there were still many misconceptions about Down syndrome. At the time of Chuck's birth, Down syndrome was still being referred to as "mongoloid" (Trent, 1994). The Es were told Chuck would not live long and were also told to think about placing their son in an institution. The Es resisted the advice offered to them and began to make plans for their son. They sought a new life in the suburbs because they had heard there were schools nearby "for children like Chuck." Chuck had a special school to attend, and during his school years, laws were written to mandate education for children with disabilities. They, like many parents in the 1960s, joined with other parents to support their child with a disability.

White, middle-class parent advocacy groups were able to help society make the shift from disability being thought of as undesirable, sinful, or lower class (Trent, 1994). The Es were representative of their particular time in history, their son was not hidden away and they were creating programs for his support. As a grass root organization, Chuck's school was representative of the time (Kliewer, 1998; Winzer, 1993). My grandparents could be considered cutting edge in their accessing an inclusive education for Jackie in the 1940s, the Es' situation is representative of the historicality of disability in the mid-1960s.

Jonathon and Jamee went to school in the era of inclusion (Friend, 2008). They were the products of school systems in the infancy stages of such practices. The school districts in both Jonathon's and Jamee's early educational experiences were working through the kinks in their own school settings. Their education was full of fences and rhizomic possibilities, isolation and inclusion involved in an intricate dance with everyone trying to learn the new steps. Initially, both families desired an inclusive school experience for their children. Jamee's parents, while philosophically embracing inclusion for all people with disabilities, had to act in the best interests of their daughter and transfer Jamee to a more secluded school setting. For two years Jamee's parents worked with the school district to bring about changes in the inclusion program. During this time Jamee was actually regressing. The community school was experiencing constant personnel and philosophical changes and lacked the training and understanding to support students with significant disabilities. Colleen and Bob could no longer risk their daughter's personal growth in order to bring about change in the school. There are circumstances when parents have to make difficult decisions to support their child that may not necessarily reflect their philosophical stance.

Another example of a philosophical conundrum was when Jonathon entered high school and Laura and Steve felt it was in his best interests to be in a more secluded freshman program. Laura had fought for the least restrictive learning environment for Jonathon throughout his elementary years and yet supported his placement in the freshman learning center program. Jonathon himself faces a struggle with his own personal philosophy as he accesses support in college. Jonathon told me he does not embrace the label of "disabled," yet he must have a disability label to navigate in the university setting. He also recalled that his high school counselor seemed angry when he insisted on enrolling in a higher level physiology and anatomy class. Mercer (1973) describes this construct and states, "People with disabilities are rewarded for behavior that conforms to the social expectations associated with the disability role and are punished for behavior that departs from the expectations" (p. 73). Jonathon had his own personal expectations, which did not coincide with the counselors desire to keep Jonathon within a particular construction.

Jonathon and Jamee did benefit, however, from a society that had grown in awareness both philosophically and technologically. They both had the benefit of technology to assist them in accessing their education, which was not available for Jackie and Chuck. Their parents also reaped the benefits derived from a historical era that was beginning to be more open about disability. Laws had been implemented to not only educate but also to include children with disabilities in school. Parents of children with disabilities in contemporary times have the ability to engage in mediation and voice their concerns. Laura and Colleen were not products of the silent generation, and as such they were able to voice their concerns in a more open forum than my grandmother and Mrs. E.

## *Exposure*

A theme that represents the stories of the families and the corporality and temporality of their situations is: "They were there." They put themselves and their children out in the community to face whatever life had to offer. Simultaneously, the parents were there to protect their children from whatever society put in their way. They exposed them to opportunity, but put up fences whenever necessary. To these families, life was and is something to partake and opportunities are not only for the strong, but for everyone. Laura and Colleen stressed over and over, "It is what it is." In fact, all of the parents used those words to describe their lives of raising their children. The rhizomic strand that served as a connection in the shared stories is acceptance. The parents sought answers for the purpose of helping their children, and they focused on the possibilities, not the disabilities. Laura said she "wasn't going to have a pity party." Colleen said she never said, "Why me?" Mr. and Mrs. E. told people, "Don't feel sorry for us, Chuck is a gift, not a burden."

## *Roots*

The neighborhood of our youth served as the soil for our rooted experience. Representing the existentials of spatiality and relationality, it served as the place where the families became connected. Disability was not thought of as something abnormal, it was life. It was our life. The neighborhood was surrounded by busy streets; danger right outside Laura's and Debbie's front doors, but there was the grassy alley that protected us, separated us, and connected us. We could cross the alley and be together. As children, we had an idealistic view of life. We knew if we yelled loud enough, someone's mother would come and save us, we knew our Dads would come home at the same time for dinner every night, and most important we knew we had each other. In our lived space, Jackie would entertain us, we would take our siblings uptown or to the park; life was simple. The "fence" was difficult to break through. In many ways the fence kept us naive and unaware of the big world outside. Children were seen and not heard. We did not question why Jackie could not drive, or why Chuck and Debbie always had to play in their yard. We were so blinded by simplicity that we did not even realize that Chuck and Jackie looked alike, until someone pointed that out to us in a cruel way. We held Chuck's hand both figuratively and literally and walked him home.

### *It's Just Life*

Perhaps because as children we were steeped in this particular lived experience, Laura and Colleen, upon giving birth to children with disabilities, understood the experience as life. They went about the business of mothering their children. It was not different for them, it was life. Colleen tagged along with Laura, Debbie, and I when she was a toddler. The strands of the rhizome connected Colleen back to Laura as an adult. Jamee continues to receive physical therapy from the therapists recommended by Laura more than 15 years ago. The rhizomic threads still continue to connect the families generationally, mother to mother.

### *Gardening*

I am the gardener, keeping the roots fed, watering the soil, making sure the root strands stay strong. I could never surmise that I truly understand their lived experiences, but I know my life is intricately linked to theirs; passing on information, being there to listen, or just being present. We are linked because we were there. We share our beginnings; we know where we came from, surrounded by strong women, caring men, and air filled with the aroma of protection.

Jackie, Chuck, Jonathon, and Jamee have taken all of us linked to their lives, places we never thought we would go. They have forced us to look outside ourselves, to be empathetic involved people. While others may see disability as wrong, it is normal for us.

### *Jackie's Life*

Compared to the majority of the individuals born with disabilities in the late 1930s, Jackie led an accomplished life. Most important, Jackie did not think she was disabled, just "short." Disability to Jackie was "poor 'tarded" Chuck across the alley, or the people in wheelchairs at her club—it definitely was not her. Disability was not her identity. Shakespeare and Watson (2002) remind me that "to assume that disability will always be the key to [their] identity is to recapitulate the error made by those from the medical model perspective who define people by their impairment" (p. 22). Disability did not define Jackie.

### *Jonathon's Perceptions*

Jonathon refuses to call himself disabled. Yet he is well aware of his blindness, his brain agenesis, along with a myriad of medical issues. He is supposed to have an intellectual disability, but he has a different type of intelligence and he has determined how to negotiate school and life using his intelligence.

Rapley (2004) suggests that it is not necessary to theorize or retheorize intellectual disability: "Maybe we should just refuse to do so" (p. 206). Jonathon is an example of just such refusal. He has constructed a fence blocking out disability. The fence has served him well, leading to possibility as he now exemplifies a college graduate with a medical research degree.

### *Chuck's World*

Chuck is not able to voice his feeling about disability. Based on immersing myself in the world of Chuck, he appears content with his life. He has activities he enjoys, work which has given him a level of self-assurance, his girlfriend Lee, and parents who are very dedicated to his well-being. Chuck does not appear to mind living in a protective environment. His needs are simple and watching his TV programs and being a part of a day program brings him a certain level of comfort and joy.

### *Happy Jamee*

Jamee is a happy young woman. Her difficulties with mobility and communication do not appear to affect her spirit. She has never known life as anything different. Jamee has definite interests and is able to express them in her individual manner. Utilizing an augmented communication device for her school work, she can access her education on her level. Routine is clearly important to Jamee and her family recognizes and honors this need. Within her structured world there are choices. Her quick smile and pleasant personality denotes a young woman who is content. Her contagious laughter resonates with pure joy.

### *Connected Individuals*

Through watering the rhizome with independence and fertilizing it with love, these individuals identified themselves as Jackie, Chuck, Jonathon, and Jamee, not as intellectually disabled, retarded, or a person with Down syndrome. To be called "retarded is to have one's moral worth and human value called into question" (Bogdan & Taylor, 1982, p. 14). Jackie was referred to as Jackie, Chuck is just Chuck, Jonathon is "what he is," and Jamee is Jamee. They are one of us.

## ***Uncovering Meaning***

The purpose of this research was to uncover the meaning of the lived experiences of four individuals with intellectual disabilities and their families over three generations. While this journey took me to places I never imagined, I believe I uncovered the meaning of their lived experiences by sharing their stories. Van Manen (1990) asks, "Can phenomenology, if we concern ourselves deeply with it, do something with us?" (p. 47). This process was revealing for me and yes it did something to me. I am not the same person I was when this root was planted. I have evolved and find myself in a new place.

In this new place I am further convinced that a theory of disability must be malleable. There must be a meeting at the fence. Individuals with disabilities must bring the dominant culture into their "yards" and the gates to the world must be universally designed so everyone can have access. The gate keepers must be the individuals with disabilities themselves, not members of the dominating social institutions. For change to evolve there must be negotiation. Resistance theory allows Jonathon, for instance, to push against the stereotype, yet to negotiate a system of support. I especially found Jonathon's idea about disability refreshing—and truthful. He has his own theory about disability. He said, "When you call someone 'blah, blah, blah' then you expect them to act 'blah, blah, blah' and you think they need 'blah, blah, blah.'" He refuses to be defined. Jonathon has never read a book about disability theory or models of disability, yet in those words, he is describing the medical model of disability that ascribes certain attributes to people with disabilities. He is also rejecting such notions. Jonathon has come to this philosophical viewpoint through his lived experience. His voice is a voice of resistance. A theory of disability based on resistance can bring society into to Jonathon's way of knowing and understanding.

The stories must be written, lives must intersect; able and disabled can meet at the fence and open the gates. Rich stories written within a phenomenological perspective can allow people who have not been heard to have a voice. Stories can bring about social reform and understanding.

Three childhood friends, four families, four individuals with disabilities connected by proximity, understanding, and love. Together, we wrote a story.

*Once upon a time lived three little girls, their lives were connected by friends, family, and disability.*

## References

Albrecht, G., Seelman, K., & Bury, M. (2001). Introduction. *Handbook for disability studies.* (pp. 1–10). SAGE.

Barnes, C., Oliver, M., & Barton, L. (2002). *Disability studies today.* Polity.

Blancher, J., & Baker, B. (2007). Positive impact on intellectual disability on families. *American Journal of Mental Retardation, 106*, 173–188.

Bogdan, R., & Taylor, S. (1982). *Inside out: The social meaning of mental retardation.* University of Toronto Press.

Castles, K. (2004). Nice average Americans. In S. Noll & J. Trent (Eds.), *Mental retardation in America* (pp. 351–370). New York University Press.

Day, M. (1996). *Home in the postmodern world: An existential phenomenological study* [Paper presentation]. International Human Science Research Conference, Halifax, VA, United States.

Ferguson, P., Ferguson, D., & Taylor, S. (1992). *Interpreting disability: A qualitative reader.* Teachers College Press.

Friend, M. (2008). *Special education, contemporary perspectives for school professionals.* Pearson.

Gabel, S. (2005). *Disability studies in education: Readings in theory and method.* Peter Lang.

Herbert, E., & Carpenter, B. (1994). The secondary partners: Professional perspectives and a father's reflections. *Children and Society, 8*(1), 31–41.

Husserl, E. (1970). *The crisis of European sciences and transcendental phenomenology.* Northwestern University Press.

Kevles, D. (1995). *In the name of eugenics: Genetics and the uses of human heredity.* Harvard University Press.

Kliewer, C. (1998). *Schooling children with Down syndrome.* Teachers College Press.

Kurokowa, K. (2001). Towards a rhizome world or chaosmas. In G. Gensoko, G. Deleuze, & F. Guattari (Eds.), *Critical assessments of leading philosophers* (pp. 1027–1034). Routledge.

Mercer, J. (1973). *Labeling the mentally retarded.* University of California Press.

Merleau-Ponty, M. (1962). *Phenomenology of perception.* Routledge & Kegan Paul.

Morse, J., & Richards, L. (2007). *Users guide to qualatative methods* (2nd ed.). SAGE.

Moustakas, C. (1994). *Phenomenological research methods.* SAGE.

Pollio, H., Henley, T., & Thompson, C. (1997). *The phenomenology of everyday life.* Cambridge University Press.

Rapley, M. (2004). *The social construction of intellectual disability.* Cambridge University Press.

Sacks, H. (1972). On analyzing the stories of children. In J. Gumper & D. Hynes (Eds.), *Directions in sociolinguistics: The ethnography of communication* (pp. 329–345). Holt, Rinehart & Winston.

Schwartzenberg, S. (2005). *Becoming citizens: Family life and the politics of disability.* University of Washington Press.

Seamon, D. (2000). A way of seeing people and place: Phenomenology in environment behavior research. In S. Wapner, J. Kemick, T. Yamamoto, & H. Minami (Eds.), *Theoretical perspectives in environment-behavior research* (pp. 157–178). Plenum.

Shakespeare, T., & Watson, N. (2002). The social model of disability: An outdated ideology? *Research in Social Science and Disability, 2*, 9–28.

Strauss, W., & Howe, N. (1992). *Generations: The story of America's future 1584–2069.* Morrow.

Trent, J. (1994). *Inventing the feeble mind: A history of mental retardation in the United States.* University of California Press.

Van Manen, M. (1990). *Researching lived experience.* State University of New York Press.

Winzer, M. (1993). *The history of special education from isolation to integration.* Gallaudet University Press.

# Postscript

Antonina Lukenchuk

## *Once upon a Time, the Message of Love Was Born*

> What is truth is real.
> What is not truth is not real.
> It's an illusion, but it looks real.
> Love is real.
> It's the supreme expression of life.
>
> —*A Toltec Wisdom Book* (Ruiz, 2004, p. xiv)

Before the curtain falls on work of this book, I would like to reflect on aspects of it which I deem are particularly meaningful in terms of its conception and advancement. Rather selfishly, I must admit, I have received absolute satisfaction from being able to engage in this work. Coincidentally, throughout the process of composing this manuscript, *my ego* had a chance to be transformed into *a sense of self with a new level of understanding*. The process has enabled me to dialogue with myself, to come to terms with my intellectual discontents and emotional frailties, and to evoke *my redemptive self* (McAdams, 2012). I have traveled a full *re*-search circle only to realize all over again that at the end of this journey, my *inquisitive self* has emerged with a renewed *sense of wonder*.

Wonder is natural to human beings and it sparks a desire within to pursue unimaginable projects. We may never know many details of how our ancestors went about their lives, but the vestiges of their existence reflect different stories of heroes, warriors, craftsmen, magicians, and builders. The coded messages of our ancestral tales tell us that ancient people also contemplated existential questions: *Where do we come from? What are we? Where are we going?* They were, in brief, philosophers and their pursuit of knowledge had been essentially through the exchange of ideas (Kenny, 1997).

The beginnings of philosophy, which are as ancient as humankind, can be rightfully considered the beginnings of research. Like philosophy, research begins in wonder and attempts to answer multitudes of questions and to solve myriads of problems pertaining to the human realm and its near and far surroundings. Like philosophers, researchers have at their disposal many and varied intellectual and methodological tools to employ in their quest to know. Extraordinary opportunities are open, especially for twenty-first-century researchers who can choose from among many and alternative paradigms of knowledge to pursue projects focusing on specific issues and amplifying our understanding of them contingent upon conceptual and methodological boundaries. Competing paradigms of knowledge do not necessarily imply privileging some of them over others. Instead, existing paradigms compete for the best available explanation or understanding, taking into account new vistas in the future that can challenge them.

Epistemological pluralism is the fact of the day even though some may not agree with or accept it. Contemporary researchers and scholars seek new ways of understanding themselves and their realities within and beyond the boundaries of their geographical locations. Modern marvels of communication and travel afford them the possibility of crossing the borders of the world's continents and countries much faster and to go farther than their predecessors could in the remote past. It is no surprise that the exchange of ideas and learning experiences among different people transpires at an unprecedented rate in this day and age. The accounts of most Westerners' journeys to other parts of the world are no longer accounts of conquest, colonization, enslavement, or prejudice. In the twenty-first century, most Westerners undertake pilgrimages to learn from the global world and, as a consequence, have an opportunity to rethink their personal identities, stories, and histories.

Imagine a white American woman, a professional psychologist, venturing on a spiritual quest around Mount Kailash, one of the three sacred mountains in Tibet. Mount Kailash is a spiritual center to the religions of Hinduism, Buddhism, Bön (a syncretic religion in Tibet), and Jainism. The sacred ritual of prostrations around Mt. Kailash is said to have been attempted by only a few representatives of these religions, and certainly not by many foreigners. What drew Tracy Allyson to this sacred pilgrimage was the spiritual passion which she considers integral to her practice as a professional psychologist. Without any special training or preparation, except for her prior travel to and knowledge of Tibet's cultural and spiritual traditions, Allyson performed prostrations around Mt. Kailash at an elevation of 14,500 feet, with the highest point of the path located at an altitude of 18, 500 feet. "I did not know," writes Allyson (2008), "if my body would hold up. There was nothing to encourage myself, nothing to gauge progress, and really, this is as it should have been. There is no progress, no goal. There is the experience and there is surrender to the invitation to attempt this" (p. 91).

Circumambulating Mt. Kailash is called *khora*. It took Allyson 28 days to finish the prostrations:

> Doing khora was an invitation that came to me in prayer. I felt that my role was to show up and do the best I could each moment. Khora is surrender in the not-knowing. The Void filled me. It wrapped itself around me. It was inside and outside of me. It was infinite, it was everything. I let the Void hold me because I just did not know; I could not assess or control my experience; I could only show up or not show up. There is an enormous freedom when we let go of the illusion of knowing. After all, life is enacting itself along some pattern, some dance, but that dance is not for me or you. It is for itself, it is dancing itself. (Allyson, 2008, p. 91)

To Allyson, doing khora turned into the most difficult and most meaningful experience of her life. She returned "home" "more mature, more open, less knowing, more conscious, more loving, more humble, and more confident" (Allyson, 2008, p. 91).

The twenty-first-century paradigms of knowledge offer educational researchers endless possibilities to advance rigorous inquiry that can illuminate economic, social, political, psychological, or spiritual dimensions of the human realm and their power to transform the lives of individuals and communities. For many people who hold spiritual beliefs dear to their hearts and minds and who practice various forms of spirituality, an engagement in social and political arenas constitutes an integral part of their day-to-day existence. Many of them consider the various aspects of their lives as manifestations of the whole, or wholeness of the experience. Spirituality can be conceived as life force, wholeness, or interconnectedness (Tisdell, 2000). Spirituality and social justice efforts can be integrated into empowering ways of life and doing research. Researchers may find themselves inspired by "new insights from different paradigms and [...] spiritual traditions" (Tisdell, 2000, p. 84).

Russell (2009) shares his experience of participating, with a group of Hispanic Roman Catholics, in an annual, hundred-mile pilgrimage to a shrine of healing dirt in New Mexico. To him, this journey becomes a discourse on social compassion. Driven by the desire to know, this "middle-aged, Anglo professor from Brooklyn" with a "recalcitrant agnostic spirit" trod the path that challenged his "niche in academe" and offered him a "model of compassion to sustain social concern" (p. 583). Prior to taking this journey, Russell researched, spoke, and wrote about pilgrimage. Yet he admits that it was *walking* the pilgrimage that had shifted the conception of it from description to performance, from telling to showing: "Walking is integral, a connecting thread of movement as coherent as a thread of thought. In pilgrimage, walking becomes a medium for understanding spiritual participation in the world" (Russell, 2009, p. 584).

The *performance* of pilgrimage is a "way of knowing," a way of learning to walk—learning through singing, healing, sacrifice, mistakes, humility, vulnerability, and learning step by step. It is also learning to return.

> My lessons in pilgrimage began with unlearning. I had been ignorant of my cultural resistance to the rich symbolism and embodied practice of Roman Catholicism. My old, familiar *habitus* was shaped by a Protestant, middle-class aesthetic more comfortable with a priest in a white lab coat than a black cassock. Religious sacrifice seemed superstitious to me [...]. My Anglo culture's ignorance and my middle class discretion about the messiness of [these] issues seemed Victorian in its avoidance of physical and emotional contact. The pilgrim community of compassion was a startling alternative to the stoic despair of my secular world. (Russell, 2009, p. 591)

Russell's return "home" illuminates the most significant lesson that he has learned throughout the journey and along the path: that the practices of pilgrimage "teach compassion for others"; that the routes themselves represent "the moral and ethical strength of [the] experience"; and that "the paradigm of walking to a holy place is a paradigm of access to power, [which is] compassion, the only healing power we truly possess" (Russell, 2009, pp. 600–601).

The possibilities of choosing among many alternative paradigms entail responsibilities of educational researchers to master their craft beyond the technical knowledge of *how* and to develop creative approaches to research and the innovative ways of its representation. Our capacity to wonder enables us to choose the paradigms that resonate with our artistic sensibilities and the *new ways to see* (Leavy, 2009; Stanczak, 2007). Visual research methods, such as photography, film, digital images, and website designs, represent shifting relationships between the production of a written text and new digital possibilities (Stanczak, 2007). Arts are known for being "emotionally and politically evocative, captivating, aesthetically powerful, and moving" (Leavy, 2009, p. 12). The practice of arts-based research is "one about fusion, affinity, resonance, and above all *holistic approaches to research*" (Leavy, 2009, p. 253). Image conveys meaning. Visual and arts-based research practices are about "composing, weaving, and orchestrating—creating tapestries of meanings" (Leavy, 2009, 254):

*Finally, my heart understands it: I hear a song,*
***I see a flower,***
***Behold, they will not wither!*** **(Unknown Aztec philosopher-poet)**

Truly, we live in a remarkable time when the sky becomes the only limit to pursuing inquiries of our own liking. Scientific, spiritual, socioeconomic, political, pragmatic, or arts-based paradigms of research as multiple and alternative ways of knowing call forth our imaginative powers *to know*, *to understand*, *to test*, *to emancipate*, *to deconstruct*, or *to reveal* the truth.

Reflecting on this journey granted me the opportunity to reenact the story of my personal quest for knowledge. I was accompanied on this journey by a few dedicated pilgrims with whom I had the privilege to share the path. Many roads lead to the truth and each of us chooses our own road. What can bind us together in the long run is *the paradigm of walking*—an act of communion that evokes the redemptive and healing power of compassion. We learn to love as we walk together.

***

*Love cannot be contained within our speaking*
*or listening; Love is an ocean whose depth cannot*
*be plumbed.*
*Would you try to count the drops of the sea?*
*Before that Ocean, the seven seas are nothing.*
*Love cannot be found in erudition and science,*
*books and pages. Whatever is discussed by people—that is not*
*the way of lovers.*
*Whatever you have said or heard is the shell:*
*The kernel of Love is a mystery that cannot be divulged.*

—Rumi

## References


Allyson, T. (2008). One woman's journey around Mount Kalish. *Quest*, *96*(3), 87–91.

McAdams, D. P. (2012). Exploring psychological themes through life-narrative accounts. In J. A. Holstein & J. F. Gubrium (Eds.), *Varieties of narrative analysis* (pp. 15–32). SAGE Publications.

Kenny, A. (Ed.). (1997). *The Oxford illustrated history of Western philosophy*. Oxford University Press.

Leavy, P. (2009). *Method meets art: Arts-based research practice*. Guilford Press.

Ruiz, M. (2004). *A Toltec wisdom book: The voice of knowledge*. Amber-Allen Publishing.

Russell, L. (2009). Learning to walk. *International Review of Qualitative Research*, *1*(4), 583–602.

Stanczak, G. C. (Ed.). (2007). *Visual research methods: Image, society, and representation.* SAGE Publications.

Tisdell, E. J. (2000). Spirituality and emancipatory adult education in women adult educators for social change. *Adult Education Quarterly*, *50*(4), 308–335.

# Notes on Contributors

## Editor

ANTONINA LUKENCHUK is Professor of Educational Foundations and Research at the School of Advanced Professional Programs, National College of Education, National Louis University, Chicago, IL, where she teaches graduate courses in educational foundations and research. She holds advanced degrees in English and General Linguistics from Chernivtsi University, Ukraine. She also holds a doctorate degree in Adult Education from Northern Illinois University, IL. Antonina's scholarly interests are in philosophy of education, epistemology, higher education, and international education. Some of Antonina's recent publications include: Against all odds: Reflections on violence and civility through personal narratives of Ukrainian students (2021) *Journal of Ethnographic & Qualitative Research*, *15*(4), 284–299; *Outliving Your Dissertation: A Guide for Students and Faculty* (Peter Lang, 2017).

## Contributors

EIRINI ADAMOPOULOU holds a doctorate in Educational Psychology/Human Learning and Development from National Louis University. She is currently the project coordinator of the RaRE Project at the National Centre for Social Research (EKKE), Greece. She has worked as a school psychologist at public schools in US and Greece, as well as in non-formal education programs for the psychosocial support of refugee and immigrant families and children. She has taught educational and school psychology courses in the National and Kapodistrian University of Athens, Aristotle University of Thessaloniki and University of Crete, Greece. She has written articles and contributions in scientific journals and books and has participated in international workshops and conferences. Her main teaching and research interests are the promotion of well-being and resilience in educational settings, development of multi-level prevention and intervention programs in the school community and building trauma-informed schools.

CHERYL DEROO holds a doctorate degree in Education with a Major in Curriculum, Advocacy, and Policy from National Louis University, Chicago, IL. She is currently an Independent Consultant and Principal Mentor for the Illinois Principals Association. She holds a strong belief in the value of Action-Based Civic Education as a means for children to grow into problem-solving, critical thinking, independent, and active citizens. Her research and scholarly interest are in developing educators, both administrative and class-rooms teachers, to hear the voice of their students, families, and communities to create a future where today's children are an integral part of a more equitable nation.

SHARON DUNCAN holds a doctorate degree in Disability and Equity Studies at National Louis University, Chicago, IL. Sharon's research interests include literacy for students with significant intellectual disabilities, models of disability, neurodiversity and family stories. She has worked in Puerto Plata in the Dominican Republic providing training for special educators and caregivers. Sharon is passionate about advocating and supporting individuals with disabilities as the founder and director of the Abide in Me charitable organization, which provides assistance to individuals with disabilities for leading engaged lives. Sharon volunteers as an advocate and as a former Professor of Special Education in the Graduate School of Education at Purdue Calumet University in Hammond, IN, she continues to support her students and teachers. Dr. Duncan is the author of *Roots and Fences: A Generational Story of Friends, Family, and Disability.*

IRENE GARCÍA-BENAVIDES holds a doctorate degree in Educational Leadership from Abilene Christian University, TX. She is currently a Senior Bilingual Speech-Language Pathologist at Texas Children's Hospital. Irene advocates for the use of American Sign Language for the provision of Speech-Language Pathology services. Irene is also passionate about languages and the many commonalities among them. Her research interests include, but are not limited to, investigations of the barriers that speech-language pathologists face in order to provide services for the deaf and hard of hearing children.

amy kendryna holds a doctoral degree in Curriculum, Advocacy, and Policy from National Louis University, Chicago, IL. She is currently a semi-retired elementary school principal who serves, on an as needed basis, as a school administrator for the Elgin U-46 School District. She also works for the Illinois Principals Association as a mentor to first year school administrators across Illinois. Amy is passionate about equity in public education and her dissertation includes the views of classroom teachers about students with Adverse Childhood Experiences (ACEs).

EILEEN M. KOLICH holds a doctorate in curriculum and instruction from the Pennsylvania State University. She is emerita Professor of Education in the College of Education and Health Sciences at Benedictine University in Lisle, IL. Eileen co-founded the doctoral program in Higher Education and Organizational Change (HEOC). She taught a number of HEOC courses, including qualitative research methods, and supervised doctoral dissertations. Her research interests focus on the scholarship of teaching and learning as it relates to instructor collaboration in the development of curriculum for qualitative research courses in HEOC.

REGINA SCHURMAN holds her doctorate in Higher Education and Organizational Change from Benedictine University, Lisle, IL. She is currently the Director of Pre-Health Professions at Benedictine University. Regina's passion lies in the area of preparing her students to be well-prepared applicants for professional school. Previously she was the Administrative Program Director of the Master of Science in Clinical Exercise Physiology program. Her doctoral research was focused on developing a model of the factors that make practitioners successful in the field of clinical exercise physiology. Many of these factors overlap with the preparation of pre-health students and are being used to counsel students as they prepare for admission to professional programs.

THERA TILMON holds a doctorate degree in Education, curriculum, and Advocacy from National Louis University, Chicago, IL. She is currently the Assistant Professor of Early Childhood and Elementary Literacy at National Louis University. As an instructor, Dr. Tilmon focuses on preparing prospective teachers for the challenging entry into the teaching profession. Her qualitative study centers on the narrative stories of Black female elementary teachers and the strategies these teachers use to navigate Whiteness in our society and schools. Her dissertation incorporates inspiring storytelling with sound scholarly research.

BAUDELAIRE K. ULYSSE holds a Doctorate in Curriculum and Social Inquiry from National Louis University, Chicago, IL. Additionally, he is finishing his Master of Science in artificial intelligence/machine learning. He has taught various master and doctoral courses at National Louis University, including action research, curriculum theory, and social justice perspectives on class, gender, and race. Currently, he teaches moral philosophies at Elgin Community College, IL, where he has also served on various committees and led impactful, advocacy-driven institutional initiatives. He has published numerous works on moral philosophies (Eastern and Western), environmental ethics, business ethics, research ethics, racial identities and politics, gender and sexual ethics, school reform and policies, qualitative research methodologies, and artificial intelligence/facial recognition. *Racialized Consciousness: Mapping the Genealogy of Racial Identity and Manifestations in Socio-Political Discourses* (2018), and *In Search of Moral Equilibrium and Wisdom: Assessing and Applying Ancient, Medieval, and Modern Moral Philosophies to Controversial Issues* (2021) are his two most recent books. *The Curvature of Feminist Activism in the #MeToo Movement* is forthcoming (under review by Peter Lang). Also, he founded a consulting, marketing, and training firm, OrganoSys Corp., that provides, among others, support for startups and dissertation services for doctoral students.

TOYA WEBB holds a doctorate in Higher Education and Organizational Change from Benedictine University, Lisle, IL. She is currently the Chief of Staff and Vice President of Strategy at Waubonsee Community College, Sugar Grove, IL. Previously she served in various leadership capacities, ultimately advancing to the role of Chief Marketing, Communications, and Government Relations Officer at Elgin Community College, IL, where she is currently an adjunct faculty member. As a certified professional life coach and the CEO of Dr. Webb Inspires LLC, Toya is a sought-after speaker and a staunch advocate of Diversity, Equity, Inclusion and Belonging. A dynamic trailblazer and visionary leader, her career has been marked by her ability to successfully lead organizations through strategic and innovative change management initiatives. Toya is also a passionate narrative researcher whose in-depth qualitative study centered on the experiences of Black women leaders in higher education and the harmful impact of racial microaggressions. Her dissertation incorporates profound storytelling with sound scholarly research.

MATTHEW WOOLSEY holds a doctorate in Higher Education and Organizational Change from Benedictine University, Lisle, IL. He is the recipient of the Edward R. Murrow Award for Excellence in Broadcasting from Washington State University. Dr. Woolsey's expertise spans communication, leadership, team development (including cross-cultural teams), and strategic visioning for human capital in domestic and international markets. His expertise and learning programs have received recognition by the Association of Professional Communication Consultants, Consulting.Com Magazine, and Experience.com. His research interests include Asian Indian leaders in America's higher education institutions with future projects targeting leadership competencies specific to this community of practice. Dr. Woolsey is a certified professional coach (ICF credentialed) and an executive leadership consultant and trainer.

JOANNE YONAN holds a doctorate in Education with a major in Curriculum, Advocacy and Policy from National Louis University, Chicago, Illinois. She has an in-depth background in Life Sciences with degrees from Purdue, Cornell, and the University of Arkansas. Currently, she is working with Dual enrollment students at Chicago City Colleges in science instruction, mentoring first-generation college students to successfully bridge from their high school diploma to their first year of college. Joanne Yonan is dedicated to altruism, and she is a part-time farmer and master gardener who consistently works in native restoration to reduce future flooding and produces organic vegetables and fruits for those in need.

COUNTERPOINTS

## Studies in Criticality

*Series Editor*
*Shirley R. Steinberg*

Counterpoints publishes the most compelling and imaginative books being written in Education and Cultural Studies today. Grounded on the theoretical advances in critical theory, feminism, and postcolonialism in the last two decades of the twentieth century, Counterpoints engages the meaning of these innovations in various forms of educational expression. Committed to the proposition that theoretical literature should be accessible to a variety of audiences, the series insists that its authors avoid esoteric and jargonistic languages that transform educational scholarship into an elite discourse for the initiated. Scholarly work matters only to the degree it affects consciousness and practice at multiple sites. The editorial policy of *Counterpoints* is based on these principles and the ability of scholars to break new ground, to open new conversations, to go where educators have never gone before.

For additional information about this series or for the submission of manuscripts, please contact:

Shirley R. Steinberg, Series Editor
msgramsci@gmail.com

To order other books in this series, please contact our Customer Service Department:

peterlang@presswarehouse.com (within the U.S.)
orders@peterlang.com (outside the U.S.)

Or browse online by series:

www.peterlang.com

Made in the USA
Monee, IL
08 April 2025

15389239R00208